REAL WORLD
BRYCE 2

SUSAN A. KITCHENS

PEACHPIT PRESS
BERKELEY, CALIFORNIA

LIGHTSPEED PUBLISHING
GLEN ELLEN, CALIFORNIA

REAL WORLD BRYCE 2
Susan A. Kitchens

Peachpit Press
2414 Sixth Street
Berkeley, CA 94710
510/548-4393
800-283-9444
510/548-5991 (fax)

Find us on the World Wide Web at:
http://www.peachpit.com

Peachpit Press is a division of Addison Wesley Longman

Project Editor: Victor Gavenda
Editor: Scott Calamar, LightSpeed Publishing
Cover design: Mimi Heft and Susan A. Kitchens
Cover illustration: Susan A. Kitchens
Interior design: Mimi Heft
Production: Tina Quarequio

ISBN 0-201-69419-0

9 8 7 6 5 4 3 2

Printed and bound in the United States of America

DEDICATION

For my grandfather, Bruce O. Buckland, and my parents Bill and Joan Kitchens. Grandpa, thanks for bringing my folks into the digital age. Mom, Dad, now that Grandpa's given you that infernal computer, you just might be able to understand this book!

ACKNOWLEDGMENTS

A tremendous shout of thanks is in order for all those whose contributions have found their way into these pages and the CD-ROM.

Thanks to those responsible for Bryce's existence—Eric Wenger, Kai Krause, and John Wilczak, without whom the software (and this book) would not have seen the light of day. Phil Clevenger, Sree Kotay and Brian Wagner provided invaluable assistance, answering my many questions about the software's workings. In addition, Julie Sigwart, Leslie Miley, Jim Tierney, Rob Sonner, and Scott Krinsky provided assistance and answers intermittently throughout the course of the project.

In addition to those at MetaTools, I was aided significantly by members of the worldwide Bryce community. Brycers who post messages in the AOL Bryce forum and members of the kpt-list shared their comments, questions, tips and frustrations with both the Mac and Windows versions of Bryce, providing valuable guidance. Dennis Berkla of DIGarts, Chris Casady, Gary Deal, Bill Ellsworth, Rodney L'Ongnion, Robert Mann, Andrew Pennick, Glenn Riegel, and Brian Strauss shared specific techniques, and Scott Tucker shared a bit about the relationship between Bryce and photography.

I'm especially grateful for all the assistance I received with all matters concerning Windows and Bryce. Thanks to my team of "book beta readers" who each eagerly tore through a couple of chapters of the Macintosh manuscript and told me how the Windows version differed. They are: Bill Bauer, Jeff Borenstein, Cheryl Boswell, Rich Cordy, Jinny Davis, Laura Falkner, Victor Gavenda, Lynn Harriet, Garry Hodge, Steve Lawnick, Jonathan Lawrence, Chris Minshall, Michael Murdock, Joe Prager, Jeffrey Wall. When it came to orchestrating the manuscript portions to send to each reader, I was assisted by the ever-capable Lee Kurtz, who handled the matter with her splendid mix of attention to detail laced with her ready wit. In addition, participants in the AOL Bryce forum and members of the kpt-list were extremely helpful in answering my Windows newbie questions.

Thanks to the many contributors of Bryce images contained in these pages and in the CD-ROM's gallery. The creative vision and eagerness to discover new ways to realize that vision is both a tribute and an inspiration. You are the ones for whom I wrote this book.

I had assistance in constructing illustrations by Chris Casady, Gary Hatfield, Michael Murdock and Greg Santelices.

The book was technically reviewed by Michael Murdock, who double-checked the manuscript against Bryce for accuracy, and methodically worked through each of the book's tutorials, offering suggestions and shedding light on portions needing clarification. Further, he advised and aided me in keeping my computers running smoothly throughout the course of the project. There might have been the occasional writer's block, but never a fatal problem with a master directory block due to Michael's ever-resourceful assistance.

Thanks to those individuals and companies who contributed software and data for the CD-ROM: Jan Nickman, Rob Sonner, Rodney L'Ongnion, for the Planetary Traveler movie trailer; Linda Ewing, for the Gem & Mineral tutorial; Ken Badertscher, for DEMview; Peter Lee, for Peter's Player; Brian Strauss, for the QTVR tutorial; Mark L. Hessenflow, creator of Waves World, for Waves World; Cha-Rie Tang and Bruce Hubbard, Direct Imagination, for the Grammar of Ornament; Richard Enriquez, MetaTools, for MetaPhotos; Pjer Zanchi, Onyx Computing for the Onyx Tree Professional demo and samples; Marilyn Harroun and Shawn Hammon, Viewpoint DataLabs International, for 3D DXF models; Dan Farr, Zygote Media Group, for 3D DXF models.

There are those whose expertise was called upon for the first edition; they deserve renewed thanks for their contribution: Mike McDowell, who advised me on geology matters; Ken Badertscher for information about Digital Elevation Models; Rodney L'Ongnion and Victor vonSalza for information on stop-motion animation; Ben Weiss for the math behind rendering; and, of course, Eric Wenger, for the Deep Texture Editor (no small thing, that!).

Many thanks to Peachpit Press—Ted Nace, who got the ball rolling, and Nancy Aldrich-Ruenzel and Victor Gavenda, who worked with me mid-course to steer this Mac book into cross-platform territory and who saw the project through to its completion. Thanks to Peachpit's Design Queen, Mimi Heft, whose book design and behind-the-scenes work on numerous production matters shaped the final appearance of these pages. They were partnered in the process by the able folks at LightSpeed Publishing—Joel Fugazzotto, who managed the project and production and is the proud owner of yet another big hard disk to store all the images for this book, and Scott Calamar, the Grand Vizier of the Order-of-those-who-hate-many-words-hypenated-together, who edited this book with humor and patience (um, don't even try to make me remove those hyphens, Scott!).

All the color illustrations created for this second edition of the book were separated using some form of Live Picture. The images for the sky chapter were separated in Live Picture and the remainder were separated using the Live PictureXT extension for Quark. This book was printed using direct-to-plate technology. Thanks to Bruce Fraser, author of *Real World Photoshop 4*, and to Peachpit's Production Manager, Cary Norsworthy, for allowing me to piggyback a few pages on a print test in order to try out the Live Picture XT extension for Quark (look ma, no CMYK tiffs!). Thanks to Sydney Stein, Mark Sangster, Holly Fisher and Jo Dee Thelen at Live Picture, Inc., for software and assistance in using it.

In the I-couldn't-have-done-it-without-you category, thanks go to Southern California Edison, for selling me an unceasing flow of electrons, the source of all those ones and zeroes that underlie this book from beginning to end, as well as the air-conditioning to keep my brain cool when Monrovia was far too hot. Let it be known that when nine western states went down, I was still up and writing! Thanks to the Prio Corporation, who supplied eye-friendly computer glasses that allowed my eyes to focus on the monitor for untold hours without undue eyestrain. To Bean Town in Monrovia I extend thanks for keeping me plied with delicious high-octane caffeine. And to Basil restaurant in Arcadia and Café Mundial in Monrovia, for providing me with a place to have have milestone dinner celebrations, especially when the going got tough.

Many thanks to Brian and Caryl Strauss, whose basement studio was transformed into a writer's retreat when I was in their part of the world teaching a seminar while simultaneously juggling a deadline.

Finally, thanks to friends and family whose unflagging support and encouragement sustained me throughout the book.

Susan Aimée Kitchens
susan@auntialias.com • http://www.auntialias.com/

Text Credits

CONTENTS AT A GLANCE

TABLE OF CONTENTS

FOREWORD

What, *another one?*

These are the cries one can hear echoing all through the canyons of Bryceland. Bouncing off the mirrored balls and the silver pyramids that every early Brycer inevitably has to get out of his or her system. It seems the big question is no longer the meaning of life and whether it's "42" but if the hidden deep editor will ever get redone.

Luckily for some, notably the author of this book (who needs something to explain of course), as well as numerous Trance/Dance/Freelance graphic artists that need to charge by the pixelpound for their Brycework, we have been lenient so far and kept certain items cryptic and weird.

Just enough so there can be a cottage industry of books converting weird into word. Just for you, Susan.

Sure we *could* have fixed it all and made it really easy but no, you had to write another book and *pleaded* with me every day to keep the software obtuse and confusing.

Well, revisionist history aside, it *is* all still a bit confusing in there and thank dog for Her Explanatory Highness Susan to set it all straight.

Without going into explanatoids, we really did not have much of a chance to truly forge ahead with Bryce just as we would have liked at the time we were developing it. Bryce 2 (for the Mac) came out seriously limping in what can only be described as a huge clash between the forces of good and evil (insert little tiny mugshots of your choice here, ahem…) and if you look in the dictionary under "C" for "Choiceless" you will find a photo of me looking bewilderbeested.

We did not have much choice. Quarterly timing is ruthless. Then the larger choiceless choice had to be made: do we make the Mac version animate or do we take the entire thing apart completely and then put Humpty Dumpty back together again on the PC platform. Guess which choice we had to make…duhhh!

Anyhow, where we are currently with Bryce 2 is on one hand a compromise, but, on the other hand, it still puts out images like nothing else out there. Wanna argue that? Hmm…? Wanna?

Seriously, we still are seeing new images done in Bryce that we ourselves can hardly believe. There is *so* much in there that ran away from the creators that we can barely see the horizon of all the potential worlds implied therein.

And that's where this book comes in (crescendo fanfares fading in!) because if you dig deeper you find out that all the really *really* cool Bryce images were indeed done not by accidental poking around and random permutations, but with fore-thought and know-how. When you see the "Planetary Traveler" scenes or the MetaTools Bryce Calendar pictures by Robert Bailey and Jackson Ting you have to realize that it was not the random mutation pearls that got them there.

All professionals seem to have that dividing line between them and the dilettante amateurs: using a plumb line to get a wall straight is the mason's first step and the Sunday home builder's "ah, I can skip that" mistake.

Maybe one of the curses of Bryce is that it's so deceivingly easy to get "pretty good" results right off the bat and get to the 60% mark of what truly could be achieved beyond the valley of the ultrabryceness. But from there to 100% will take *experience* and *knowledge* and there is no shortcut to that—wait cut that—short of…reading a good book like this!

I said as much in the incarnation of this tome's older sibling, but this time I am serious. OK that's it, young person, you better read this or ELSE! As long as you have your legs under MY software table you will READ what we put on your plate! And you will LIKE it!

What's not to like?

Susan sprinkles her deepest technical treatise with lighthearted daisies of quotelets from famous philosphers, say, Winnie the Pooh and such, and then really brings it home with details and details on the details.

You probably have read forewords of mine. Or maybe just four words of mine. And usually the angle is exactly this—if you only find *one* idea or hint or tip or trick, the book already is worth its weight in M&Ms, right?

Well, since this is her second book, I will up that ante a little: if you only find *two* tricks already it would be worth *half* its weight in Remy Martin Napoleon, the serious Bryce coders' cognac of choice. Unless you have Louis XXIII handy, which however is a cool grand a bottle. Once, at the Four Seasons in NYC, we almost got the bottle (cut Baccarat crystal) since the last sip usually gets it, and we… .

But I digress. Slightly.

See, if you get *one* tip out of it, including the fact that they have Remy Martin Louis XXIII there, you are definitely way ahead. Never mind that you could buy three of these books for the same price as one glass—eeek.

Which, neatly, leads us back to the topic: You can do killer glass in Bryce. And Susan is here to save your journey and will tell you how.

She has truly sacrificed herself to make your lives easier and surely you better appreciate that or she could get very cross! It does sometimes take one person to do such a selfless act ("I will find Asia by sailing the wrong way! I will!!!") and everyone can enjoy the fruits of this altruism. Lest you young 'uns and hipsters think this stands for some alt-dot-ruism newsgroup, altruism is an often over-looked method of doing unto others as you might ultimately not mind being done unto yourself. Her efforts here may be on one hand a commercial venture, (she is not a charity organization,) but she has taken the route of true sacrifice and selfless torture to get there. In other words, that newfangled scam of actually giving you tons of value for your money...I hear that can still work!

Kai Krause
Co-Founder and Chief Science and Design Officer, MetaTools, Inc.

CHAPTER ONE

Introduction

When you get the thing dead right and know it's dead right, there's no excitement like it.
It's marvelous. It makes you feel like God on the Seventh Day—for a bit, anyhow.

DOROTHY L. SAYERS, *GAUDY NIGHT*

THE HISTORY OF BRYCE

Bryce is the brainchild of Eric Wenger, a talented artist, musician, and programmer from France. The son of a geologist, Eric grew up with a sensitivity to Earth's form and environs. That kind of sensitivity was combined with an artist's careful, observing eye. I saw a landscape triptych of the American southwest desert painted by Eric; those paintings captured the essence of the area's sweeping basins interspersed with rocky plateaus. To put down all those details on canvas requires that one *see* them. The exacting scrutiny required in the art of drawing and painting led to the creation of software that makes such realistic images.

Eric wrote D3 (what would eventually become Bryce) on the side, while working at other tasks. (Notable among those was the creation of the software application ArtMixer.) It was a personal pursuit, a digital form of grinding his own pigments and mixing them with binder to make paint so that landscape pictures could be painted onscreen. Instead of cadmium, cobalt, and oxide of chromium, Eric worked with new discoveries of fractal geometry for generating rugged mountainous terrains. Adapting the sound synthesizer model to visual noise, he developed an intricate means of putting realistic surfaces on those rugged terrains. He built an entire world in which to place those surfaces and other objects, with lightsource and the atmospheric effects of clouds, haze, and fog. He culminated the process by using a ray-tracing renderer as the binder to adhere mathematical "pigment" to the computer monitor's "canvas."

Although Eric was by no means a "Sunday painter," this was nevertheless a private pursuit. He wrote the software for himself—the result of, and for the sake of, his artistic, observing eye.

Eric showed his software to his friend Pierre Bretagnolle, who, in turn, brought it to the attention of Andreas Pfeiffer, the editor of France's largest Macintosh magazine, *SVM Mac*. Pfeiffer was instrumental in introducing Eric and his landscape application to John Wilczak and Kai Krause of MetaTools (then HSC Software). From that introduction grew the partnership that brought Eric's personal creation into a form for the general public.

Kai had a vision and an observer's eye no less exacting than Eric's. He, however, concentrated on a different area—creating user interfaces that put a friendly face on top of powerful features, without bogging down the user in the complex details. Kai had, through his Kai's Power Tools, pioneered precedent-setting new standards for user interfaces that provide tons of functionality while hiding the underlying mathematical complexity. So, continuing in this vein, he worked with Eric to make Bryce an application that is easy to use. As a result of the shell he created for Bryce, a beginner could get a quick start from the preset combination palettes and, in only a matter of minutes, be on the way to creating a new Brycean world.

Kai made the interface three-dimensional so that a user can instinctively reach for this control or that knob to perform this technique or that manipulation. Palettes divide the flow of work according to logical sequence. The user can go to different palettes to create objects, to edit them, to design the atmospheric environment, and to render the scene, all the while navigating in the scene using the Camera controls.

Yet, the 1.0 version of the software was not the culmination of the dynamic creative process by Eric and Kai (aided by Phil Clevenger and others at MetaTools). More was yet to come. Even as they shipped version 1.0, they knew that they wanted to add in light sources and the ability to import three-dimensional models created by other applications. They wanted to continue working to enhance the interface design to make the Bryce technology even easier to use. But it was time to call a halt to the development process, draw a line in the sand, and say, "This is it. Let's introduce it to the public. Let's put Bryce out there." Thus version 1 of Bryce was released.

Bryce 2

Since that time, the developers acted on their wish to improve the software. Bryce 2.1 has seen the addition of a rich plethora of new features. Eric's continued work has focused on the addition of primitive forms, new atmospheric features, separate light sources, the ability to generate random polyhedron rocks, importing 3D models created outside of Bryce, boolean operations, additional terrain processing algorithms, and a far more powerful way to combine textures for more intricate and realistic surface materials. While Eric pursued the deeper algorithmic matters, Kai and Phil set to work on redesigning the user interface, using Bryce itself to create its own interface. Sree Kotay implemented the interface changes, adding many of his own touches in the anti-aliased wireframes with depth cueing, more efficient render processes, Solo mode, and his crowning contribution—the newly revamped Terrain Editor. They stuffed new features into every nook and cranny of Bryce, making the software much more powerful while fulfilling their collective vision to make software that was easy and fun to use. They continued the Bryce tradition of software with "soul."

After bringing out version 2.1 on the Macintosh, the application was ported to the Windows platform. In doing so, the software code has been completely re-written into the MetaTools proprietary graphic code library, Axiom. This sets the stage for further cross-platform development. From here, Bryce will move forward into animation, complete with many other new features and functions.

Although the underlying software code differs from Macintosh to Windows, MetaTools has aimed to have an identical feature set between the platforms. Of course, things being what they are, there is some divergence from one version to the other. (You'll find out more about that in these pages.)

The other hidden part of this equation is computing power. Although Bryce is easy to use, this doesn't mean the technology behind it is trivial stuff. The mathematics that underlie it are staggering. So staggering, in fact, that the program would not run on computers that only a few years ago were state of the art. Today, with the faster Power Macintosh (and the 040 Macintosh) and with the Pentium (and 486) on the PC side, the means to create one's own worlds is available to a wide population.

WHY "BRYCE"?

Why is this software called Bryce? In the southern part of Utah, there is a national park called Bryce Canyon (see Figure C1–1 in the color section). The park is a place of fantastic geological columnar formations, called hoodoos, that were created by millennia of erosion. The formations look like fanciful images, and many are named for the myths and legends and images that are evoked by their shapes.

Bryce Canyon is not really a canyon; it is a rim, with a drop-off into a deep valley. The high elevation (over 8,000 feet) and high level of precipitation result in snow and freezing temperatures for more than half the year. Because of the daily cycle of freeze and thaw, water works its way into the rock formations and expands as it freezes in the rock crevasses. In the daytime, with each thaw, the water runs off, taking with it a tiny bit of rock. This process produces the crevasses and formations of the hoodoos. The play of light on these formations in the early morning and late afternoon creates dramatic vistas. You can hike down from the rim to walk among the tall hoodoos deep into a wonderland filled with discovery that stirs the imagination.

Wandering into a natural place of mystery—this is Bryce the place. Bryce the software, which enables you to create your own fantastic creations, is named for that park. It is software that allows you to make your own landscapes—personal visions of mystery and wonder.

AN EMOTIONAL EXPERIENCE

Those visions of mystery and wonder are integral to the experience of working in Bryce. One time when I had the opportunity to work side-by-side with Eric, we talked about the software and its success. He asked me why I thought it is so popular. I answered without hesitation, "It's the emotional experience that comes from working with it." And there is an excitement to working in Bryce. Bryce is addicting. From the first click on the Create Terrain icon on the Create Palette, to watching the erosion process unfold in front of you in the Terrain Editor, to adjusting the clouds and haze to be just so, to the satisfaction at getting the surface appearance just right, to solving a problem or discovering a new way to go about a particular task, to being mesmerized while watching each successive render pass as more and more detail emerges—there is something inherently satisfying about the creative process of working in Bryce.

WHAT THIS BOOK COVERS

This book covers Bryce 2.1, on both the Macintosh and Windows 95/Windows NT platforms. (Version 2.1 is free upgrade for all registered users of version 2.0 on both platforms. If you haven't yet upgraded, do so *now!*) The book is the product of my own keen observer's eye as I've sought to answer the questions, "What does it do?" and "What can I do with it?" I observe Bryce's behavior and tell you what it does. This book—a revision of my earlier *The KPT Bryce Book*—has been completely rewritten to document software that has undergone extensive modification and enhancements.

While I apply my behaviorist eye to the software, I am assuming a couple of things. I assume you know how to use your computer's operating system. If you don't, please refer to the documentation that came with your computer.

I also assume that you have at least looked through the *Bryce 2 Explorer's Guide* (the manual) and have at least done the "Whirlwind Tour" at the beginning. Although there is sufficient overlap with the manual to get you oriented, this book takes up where the manual leaves off. If you're new to Bryce, you'll get background on some key concepts, but this book will push you onto the "Bryce Power User" track. There are plenty of tutorials and guided explorations where key Brycean concepts are introduced. Follow along with the book in one hand, and your computer's mouse in the other.

Bryce takes you into a complex world—not as complex as our own, but complex nonetheless. In Bryce, everything is related to everything else. When writing about it, there's a risk of oversimplifying while looking at the big picture, or getting mired in the detail while exploring all the possibilities. I take an approach that cruises between these two risks, providing a look at the big picture while examining plenty of detail. Because everything is related to everything else, however, there are some cross-references that take you back and forth to other chapters.

Here's a basic rundown of what you'll find in each chapter. The first section unlocks the pieces and parts of the software itself:

- *Chapter 2—Hardware Considerations*. Here I attend to an initial bit of housekeeping. I discuss the details of hardware requirements, and tell you what you can do with your hardware to make Bryce run smoothly on your machine.

- *Chapter 3—Camera and Scene*. In this chapter, I delve into the concept of camera and scene, discussing ray tracing, and, since we're talking about cameras, explain how to use the Camera controls.

- *Chapter 4—Brycean Objects.* In this chapter I take a look at each of the object types in Bryce, and just about all the options for selecting objects and groups of objects in order to work with them, and how to navigate into and out of Solo mode.

- *Chapter 5—Streamline Your Brycing.* Here I present a global perspective of the work process in Bryce, all the while sounding the refrain, "Make it efficient." That is, set up your work so as to reduce unnecessary render time. I also discuss general Bryce behavior that's consistent throughout the software.

- *Chapter 6—Editing and the Internal Bryce Grid.* In this chapter, I introduce you to the unseen grid structure of Bryce, and discuss the controls on the Edit Palette, where you can edit single objects, multiple objects, and replicate your one object into multiple objects. Here's where you'll find everything you need to know in order to manipulate your objects within Bryce Space.

- *Chapter 7—Booleans and Multiple Object Construction.* This chapter explores the techniques for working with multiple objects to create models, exploring more of the Bryce multi-replicate options, and taking an in-depth look at boolean functions and merging two scene files together.

- *Chapter 8—Terrains, Symmetrical Lattices, and the Terrain Editor.* This chapter explores the Terrain Editor, Bryce's separate "room" for working with grayscale-to-height image processing. The grayscale-to-height image defines the look of Bryce mountainous forms, used by both terrains and symmetrical lattices.

- *Chapter 9—Material World.* Here, in the deepest chapter of the bunch, I delve into all those things that define the surface of your objects in Bryce's Materials Composer. I also reveal the secrets of the Deep Texture Editor—the heart of Bryce that MetaTools has included in the software, but does not document.

- *Chapter 10—Brycean Skies.* In this chapter, I discuss all that goes into creating your Bryce environment, exploring in detail the options that make up the shape and color of your Brycean sky.

- *Chapter 11—Bryce EnLightenment.* This chapter delves into all things concerning lights, from the pseudo-lights of glowing objects that do not cast light nor shadow, to the separate light objects that cast special light into your Bryce world.

- *Chapter 12—Render unto Bryce.* Here I give some background on how rendering works, tips for rendering, and some ideas for using the alternative render options.

The remaining chapters go beyond the mere recounting of features and tutorial exercises to discuss ways to integrate Bryce's components to achieve certain effects.

- *Chapter 13—Bryce and Other Software.* From the pre-processing done elsewhere—especially in 3D modeling applications that are subsequently imported into Bryce—to post-processing applications that work with the rendered results of Bryce scenery, this chapter discusses how Bryce and other software work together.

- *Chapter 14—Superlative Nature Imagery.* In this chapter, I examine scenes and draw conclusions about the best ways to make scenery that imitates nature. In addition, I walk you through the thoughts and steps that went into creating "Lighthouse at Twilight," the default scene for Bryce 2.1.

- *Chapter 15—Brycing Out of This World.* In this chapter, I cover outer space scenes and a few other assorted odds and ends.

- *Chapter 16—Printing Bryce Images.* This chapter introduces you to all the concepts involved with getting your images from monitor screen onto paper.

- *Chapter 17—Professional Images and Real Bryce Projects.* This is the eye-candy chapter, a printed sampling of some of the work being done in Bryce all over the world. There is also a discussion of how Bryce can be used for animation and other types of projects.

There are a lot of illustrations in this book, to aid you in your Bryce exploration. The images that are in color have a C preceding their figure numbers. You saw that already in Figure C1–1. When you see the C, look in the color section for the figure.

And finally, the CD. Tucked into the back cover of this tome is a little plastic disc. Take it out and look at what's on it; there's so much more to be seen. Many of the scenes used in this book's illustrations are included on the CD so that you can go in and poke around yourself. I've included a folder that corresponds with each chapter where scenes related to that chapter reside. Most of the scene files I direct you to along the way will be found in that particular chapter's folder.

In addition to the tutorial and related scenes for you to work with and explore, there is also a host of goodies on the CD-ROM. You'll find step by step slide shows and image samples for different processes. The "What's Wrong With This Picture?" chapter from the previous edition of this book, diagnosing the most common problems creating Bryce scenes, has moved to the CD-ROM (it is mostly visual). There is sample software, resources and tips, QTVR animations, and animated movies. Finally, there is a gallery of images from more than 80 contributing artists from all over the world—quite a body of work to admire and be inspired by! If you don't have a CD-ROM drive, then beg, borrow… well, see if you can get your hands on something that will enable you to take a look at the CD's contents.

If you are a Windows user, the CD-ROM has everything you need to get through the tutorials, as well as access to the gallery of images done by Brycers all the world over. There is a publisher's coupon in the book that offers a more robust Windows CD-ROM, with reference scene files converted to the Windows format.

A Cross-Platform Book

This book covers both the Macintosh and Windows versions of Bryce 2.1. When describing key commands and procedures, I will provide first the Mac key command and then the Windows key command. Both platforms use a key called "Control," and each platform uses the "Control" key differently. In order to avoid confusion between the two, the respective keys will be described as they appear on the respective keyboards: The Macintosh Control key will be spelled out, whereas the Windows Ctrl key will be abbreviated, as shown. Where there are simple key combinations, I will use the Macintosh shortcut for the Command key: ⌘, as in ⌘-S. Where there are lengthier keyboard combinations, they will be shown in this fashion: ⌘-Option-E (Macintosh) or Ctrl+Alt+E (Windows).

When discussing the keyboard, I also distinguish the Return key from the Enter key. The Return key is on the regular portion of the keyboard, next to the Shift key and the \ key. The Enter key is on the numeric keypad. The Macintosh marks them as such, but the Windows keyboard does not (both are marked Enter). In Bryce, the two keys have unique functions, so I use the two names to distinguish between them.

For the benefit of Macintosh Bryce 2.1 users who've used the 1.0.1 version of Bryce, I provide occasional comparisons to Bryce 1. Those using the Windows version of Bryce may ignore those sections.

A FINAL WORD...

As a final word, please be an observer. Let what you are doing in Bryce aid your observation of the world out there and let the world out there aid your observation of what you're doing in Bryce.

And let this book hang out and be your companion while you work. I trust you will find my observations and explanations to be of value.

Most important, please play. You probably are reading this book because you're already having fun with the software. I certainly have had fun with Bryce while writing this book. I recorded my observations in a spirit of the playfulness that is a part of the software, and, indeed, a part of the creative process in general. So have fun with the software and take joy in your own creations!

CHAPTER TWO

Hardware Considerations

Resistor, transistor, condensers in pairs,
Battery, platter, record me some airs;
Squeaker and squawker and woofer times pi,
And Baby shall have his own private Hi-Fi.

FREDERICK WINSOR, *THE SPACE CHILD'S MOTHER GOOSE*

IN THIS CHAPTER...

- The hardware to fit the software: what your computer needs to run Bryce

What do you need in the way of hardware to run Bryce? This brief chapter takes a look at the basic setup, and then touches on some optional hardware and software.

HARDWARE REQUIREMENTS

To run Bryce, you need a suitable Macintosh or Intel-based computer, enough RAM, and color video output.

Macintosh

Bryce runs on the PowerPC-based Macintosh, Performa or MacOS clone families of computers and the 68040 Macintosh family of computers. (The 68040 has a math co-processor and can run Bryce. The 68040LC does not have a math co-processor; Bryce will not run on it.) If you want to do more than dabble around in Bryce, I'd stick to the Power Macintosh machines. Otherwise version 2 of Bryce is too slow, even running on a Quadra-level Macintosh. In fact, I'll bluntly state that this book has a definite Power Macintosh bias, as the 68k Mac that I own (a IIcx, with a 68030 processor, not a 68040) will not run Bryce. To those of you who have 68k machines, you knew when you purchased your computer that it is basically a solid state thing that runs well for years but at the same time is quickly obsolete, right? Here's more proof.

Windows

Bryce 2 for Windows runs on Intel 486- and Pentium-based computers. Pentium is preferred, since the processor speeds are faster and the Pentium chip has better means of handling floating-point mathematical calculations (the all-important part to rendering Bryce images). There's no substitute for fast processing speeds. For those who have Windows NT running on dual-processor machines, Bryce does not take full advantage of the hardware and system in order to thread the instructions to both processors; Bryce will run on one processor leaving the other free for other tasks. I'll not address the multitude of specific hardware configurations for Intel-based machines; that mystic art is better left to those who know what they're talking about, and lies well beyond the scope of this book. I'll stick to the basics: 486 or Pentium. Got it?

RAM

What Bryce is undertaking—ray-tracing—is not trivial. Not only does it require some hefty processing power, but Bryce wants RAM. Lots of it. Aside from the amount of RAM it takes to launch the application with its splendid user interface resources, there are two factors that determine how much RAM a scene needs: the amount and complexity of objects and the final render size.

A good amount of RAM is required in order to render a scene. You can create default size scenes on a machine that has 12 MB RAM. However, for smooth operation of Bryce or for rendering large images, you need more. Bryce holds all information for the scene in RAM at one time. If your scene has a lot of terrains and if some or all of those have resolutions larger than the default of 128 pixels (256, 512, 1024), then more RAM is required.

The image resolution size of a scene is also affected by the amount of RAM allocated to Bryce. The larger the render size, and therefore the greater number of ray-traced computations involved, the more RAM required. A 640 × 480 scene requires more RAM than a 320 × 240 scene.

If your scene is too large for the amount of RAM available, Bryce will display an alert telling you that there is not enough memory to complete the operation. If this happens when you attempt to render a larger size and you don't have more RAM to give to Bryce, you can do a special render to disk, bypassing the need to keep all the image resolution inside of dynamic memory. See Chapter 12, "Render Unto Bryce," for more information about this.

If you're the paranoid type, you might be convinced that Bryce 2 was released to the world as part of a conspiracy by RAM manufacturers to get you to buy more of their product. If you're the more level-headed type, simply be aware that Bryce 2 is an application that will take as much RAM as you can supply it—and more.

If your machine has limited RAM, you can use any of the RAM extender utilities, such as RAM Doubler for the Macintosh (by Connectix) or MagnaRAM for Windows (by Quarterdeck). RAM extenders will not increase the physical amount of your RAM, but will allow you to assign an amount equivalent to the full RAM allotment to more than one application, including your system software. The absolute minimum physical RAM configuration I'd recommend for Bryce is 12MB. To this bad news I offer the following cheerful news: RAM prices have been dropping, so the physical RAM upgrade won't set you back as much.

24-Bit Color—It Looks Better That Way; It Really Does!

The Bryce interface is full color, which makes sense, as there's a full-color environment in Bryce. Optimally, your video display will have full 24-bit color. On the Mac, it's referred to as millions of colors; in Windows, it's referred to as True Color. In Bryce, you are making adjustments to atmospheric conditions and multiple lighting colors, so the more color information you have, the better.

Many of the newer Mac models come with only 16-bit color (thousands of colors), and some older ones have only 8-bit (256 colors). Windows video display is dependent on the type of video disply card that you have installed. If your system has only 8-bit or 16-bit, rest assured that Bryce internally operates at full 24-bit color, although you may not see all the colors on your screen. If you render an image on a machine that has a 16-bit display and then transfer the image to a computer that has a 24-bit display, you'll see all the colors.

The current Macintosh models can accept Video RAM (VRAM) upgrades for increased color resolution. VRAM is usually the least expensive means of achieving higher video output.

You can also buy video accelerator cards to get millions of colors on your Macintosh or True Color on your PC. Either way, enhanced video is money well spent. Not all video cards work equally well with Bryce; your mileage may vary.

OPTIONAL HARDWARE AND SOFTWARE

In addition to the normal computer equipment that is necessary to use with Bryce, there is optional hardware and software that can be very useful. This section discusses some of the most handy additions: digitizing tablets, software accelerators and hardware accelerators.

Digitizing Tablets

If you are using a digitizing tablet, such as a Wacom tablet, you'll find that Bryce is sometimes difficult to work with. Some of the controls respond to continued pressure in a dizzying fashion; Bryce responds to a tablet's "mouse down" signal differently than it does with a mouse. It confuses a mouse press with a mouse drag, sending you into potential tailspins when you keep the stylus pressed to the tablet. You can fix most of the strange pen-induced behavior by making sure that the preferences for your tablet are set to "relative." The relative setting makes your table act like a mouse, where you can pick up the pen and place it down again on a different area of the tablet, and the cursor on your monitor stays in the same place. In the Terrain Editor, where you can use painting tools, the tablet lets you paint with eye/hand coordination. Bryce does not, however, support pressure sensitivity, so you cannot call upon the digitizing tablet's ability to interpret the pressure signal to make a stroke wider or more opaque.

Software Accelerators

Software accelerators are add-on utilities that optimize your computer's performance in some way.

LibMotoSh is a freeware shared library that accelerates mathematical calculation for MacOS PowerPC computers. Since Bryce uses a lot of math, it's a good thing to have. Do not install the software in your extensions folder, however. System-wide acceleration sometimes results in system crashes while using other software. Install LibMotoSh in the same folder with the application; that way Bryce will be accelerated. You can download LibMotoSh from Motorola's website at http://www.mot.com/SPS/PowerPC/library/fact_sheet/libmoto.html.

Speed Doubler (by Connectix) is an optimization utility to enhance speed on your Macintosh. It accelerates certain Finder and disk access operations, putting a bit of zing into your computer. It will not, however, cause an increase in the processor performance for rendering.

Hardware: To Accelerate or Not to Accelerate

Since Bryce is a 3D application, and since there are third party accelerator cards that are made specifically to speed up computer performance for 3D, is it a good idea to get an accelerator to speed up Bryce? No. In order to take advantage of the speed increases offered by an accelerator, the Bryce software needs to be modified to recognize that extra card sitting in that slot on the computer's motherboard and to send certain (or all) instructions to it so that the accelerator card can do its blazingly fast thing. Bryce is not modified in that way; it works with the computer's main processor.

Any accelerator cards or clock chips that speed up the overall performance of your computer's processor will enhance Bryce performance. These Bryce-friendly hardware accelerators come in five different flavors.

- *Cache card (Macintosh).* A cache card works alongside the CPU to store recently-used instructions, reducing the time needed to retrieve those instructions from the computer's RAM and therefore speeding up processing time.

- *Processor upgrade card (Macintosh).* A processor upgrade card enables you to change to a higher-performing central processor without completely replacing your computer motherboard. The last of the 68k Macs were advertised as being

"Power PC Ready" so that you could purchase a Power PC upgrade card to move up to the next level. Nowadays Apple and the MacOS clone vendors offer certain computers with the CPU on a daughterboard, so that you can swap out this year's CPU with next year's CPU for an increase in performance.

- *Clock chip accelerator (Macintosh).* These handy little gizmos attach to the chip that controls the CPU's speed, accelerating it to a higher level. Using these might void your manufacturer's warranty, but then again, you're probably using this to speed up an older computer whose warranty has already expired. I've used one of those to make a Power Mac 6100/60 run at a higher (though not blindly fast by today's standards) 80 MHz speed.

- *Intel OverDrive Processor.* This family of processor chips is offered by Intel for both the 486 and Pentium line of processors. All of the Overdrive Processors increase the clock chip speed, to make the processor work faster. Although the Pentium OverDrive for the 486 includes the Pentium-based enhanced capability to do floating-point calculations, the remainder of the 486 motherboard operates at a slower speed. If you decide to try this solution, check with your system manufacturer or Intel for specific system compatibility.

- *CPU upgrade (Pentium).* Some Pentium 3-volt motherboards (75 MHz and higher) are able to support a higher-level CPU. You can purchase a boxed Pentium processor and replace your current CPU with a faster one. Check with your computer manufacturer or Intel to find out if you can get a CPU lift without buying a completely new computer.

CHAPTER THREE

Camera and Scene

"Remarkable view," announced the Humbug, bouncing from the car as if he were responsible for the whole thing.

"Isn't it beautiful?" gasped Milo.

"Oh, I don't know," answered a strange voice. "It's all in the way you look at things."

…Milo turned around and found himself staring at two very neatly polished brown shoes, for standing directly in front of him …was another boy just about his age, whose feet were easily three feet off the ground.

…"How do you manage to stand up there?" asked Milo, for this was the subject which most interested him.

…"Well, in my family everyone is born in the air, with his head at exactly the height it's going to be when he's an adult, and then we all grow toward the ground. When we're fully grown up, or, as you can see, grown down, our feet finally touch…. You certainly must be very old to have reached the ground already."

"Oh no," said Milo seriously. "In my family we all start on the ground and grow up and we never know how far until we actually get there."

"What a silly system." The boy laughed. "Then your head keeps changing its height and you always see things in a different way? Why, when you're fifteen things won't look at all the way they did when you were ten, and at twenty everything will change again."

NORTON JUSTER, *THE PHANTOM TOLLBOOTH*

IN THIS CHAPTER…

- The concepts of three-dimensional space, the virtual world, and the two-dimensional camera

- The Camera controls on Bryce's Control Palette

- How to better work with the Bryce camera

In Bryce, you make scenes and then take pictures of them with your Render "camera." Working in Bryce is analogous to making pictures of our own three-dimensional world. The world itself is three-dimensional, and the camera captures a two-dimensional representation of one place and time of that world. Similarly, when you're working in Bryce, you are balancing between manipulating the three-dimensional world and moving your camera around to make a two-dimensional snapshot of a particular place and time.

YOUR WORLD AND WELCOME TO IT

Your Bryce world, and all objects in it, have width, height, and depth. In addition, the camera, though it records an image of the three-dimensional world on a two-dimensional plane (a picture that has width and height, but not depth), has a three-dimensional orientation within the World Space.

Each of the three dimensions is referred to as an axis: Width is the x axis, height is the y axis, and depth is the z axis. Each object has an independent existence in the larger space within Bryce. Therefore you can manipulate each, placing it anywhere in the width, height, and depth of the virtual world. (More on the particulars of Brycean objects is found in Chapter 4, Objects, and placing them in Chapter 6, Edit.)

Brycean objects exist in Space. Aside from Bryce's World Space establishing distance between objects, the World Space itself is manipulated to give a particular environment to your scene. Using the atmospheric controls, you can make it outer space or a home world or an alien world. These settings are manipulated in the Sky & Fog Palette, where you can adjust the lighting, atmospherics, and moisture (including clouds, haze, and fog).

These factors can make for an extremely complex world with an infinite number of possible combinations. It *is* your world. Create it with reckless abandon and then make as many computer snapshots of it as you please!

BRYCEAN KODAK MOMENTS

Remember your world in pictures. Bryce creates PICT (Macintosh) or BMP (Windows) images of the wireframe scenes by rendering them. The particular process involved is called 3D ray tracing.

"Take a Picture"—How 3D Ray Tracing Works

To best help you understand how ray tracing works, I'll follow our real world/ virtual world model and take a moment to discuss how the eye and the camera register visual information.

How the Eye Sees and How a Camera Sees

In the real world, light emanates from a source (sun, moon, electric lights) and bounces off of Earth's surfaces. Depending on the color of those surfaces, different rays of light are absorbed and what is not absorbed bounces. Those bounced light rays that reach the eye are focused through the eye's lens onto the retina. The light information is then transmitted to nerve impulses that travel through the optic nerve to the visual portion of the cerebral cortex of the brain.

The camera "sees" in the same way (see Figure 3–1). Light from the external world passes through the camera's lens and then exposes film. The film is processed, and prints or slides are created that show the image. The film or transparency and printed photographic paper are all two-dimensional surfaces. (Okay, okay, all have just a touch of thickness, making them three-dimensional. But a millimeter's thickness notwithstanding, they are "flat" surfaces.) The process of seeing with a camera involves a dimension shift from a three-dimensional world to a two-dimensional image.

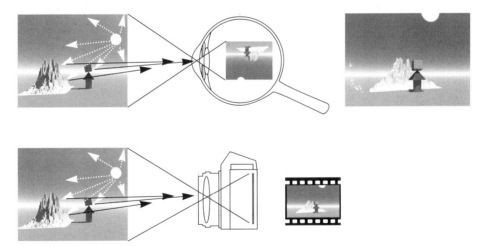

Figure 3–1 The eye and the camera both register visual information. Light emanates from a source, bounces off objects, and is registered on the eye's retina or a camera's film.

How Bryce "Sees"

In the real world, there are real objects, real atmosphere, and real light sources. When seeing with your eyes, you are continuously registering moments in time. When making photographs, you capture a particular moment in time.

In a corresponding way, Bryce has a virtual world with virtual objects and virtual illumination. Bryce renders a two-dimensional image to capture a moment in its virtual space and time. How does Bryce do this? By ray tracing. When Bryce renders, it shoots virtual rays into the world to determine the colors of the image. It's not a process of photochemically registering *what is already there,* where the results are seen instantaneously (with the eyes) or with a reasonable delay (film processing). Rather, Bryce's virtual world requires mathematical calculations to follow those rays as they bounce through the world and to record the color of the ray's final destination. Therefore, instead of talking about an entire image, or what can be seen on a piece of film, I'll narrow it down to seeing pixel by pixel.

For each pixel in the scene, Bryce shoots out a virtual ray into the image. Where does it go? For one particular pixel, the ray's path may take it to one side of a terrain. Ah! This particular portion of the terrain has a basic texture color of sienna brown. But the ambient light is a light naples yellow, so the sienna brown is altered based on the ambient light. Further, the surface is very matte, so it doesn't create any direct reflections but rather reflects the light in a diffuse manner. Also, the sun is close to the horizon and is a reddish color. So the color of that portion of terrain is reddened by the sun's color.

Now, for a different pixel in the same scene, the ray bounces out into the world to find the ultimate color and light source, so the color may be different where the terrain is in shadow. But the scene also has a few reflective spheres. A ray of light that shoots out toward one of the spheres bounces off the sphere into the world surrounding it. Reflective surfaces increase the ray's journey time. Or, in the case of multiple reflective objects nearby, the ray may bounce from this sphere here to that other sphere, to the terrain way over there. All atmospheric conditions complicate the situation, adding more variables into the calculation that answers the question, "What color will this pixel ultimately become?" If there are transparent objects, then there are further diversions of that ray. And what if the transparent object bends the light as it passes through the object? The ray will go off into a slightly different direction as it seeks out its final color resting place.

As Bryce ray traces, it uses a progressive method. Bryce will go through six passes (with the faster Accelerated Raytesting method it won't *seem* like six) as it renders. The first pass takes the image in chunks of 1024 pixels (32 × 32) and shoots one ray into the scene for each chunk to determine that pixel's color (see Figure 3–2). When it completes that pass, it divides those pixels in half, shooting one ray out for each 256 pixels (16 × 16 pixels). During the second pass, it performs four more calculations than during the previous pass. Each successive pass makes four times the number of

a
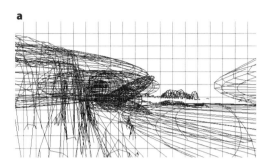

b
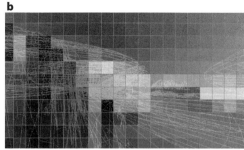

Figure 3–2 a) The wireframe view with a grid comprised of 32 × 32 pixels (the first rendering pass) superimposed. For each square, Bryce shoots a ray into the scene to determine the final color. b) The result after the first rendering pass. (Wireframe view is barely visible for reference.)

calculations as the previous pass, resulting in a more detailed image. Finally, at the sixth pass, each ray shot out into the scene calculates the color for one pixel.

Bryce makes that ray-traced calculation for every pixel in the scene. It follows the light to its source to determine what color it is. For a scene that's 640 × 480 pixels, 307,200 rays go out into the world, bouncing here and there to determine the final color for each pixel! (And we haven't even talked about what happens at the anti-aliasing pass, where several rays are shot out to determine the color of one pixel!) That's a *lot* of calculations! When you first started using Bryce, perhaps you thought all this mumbo jumbo about math co-processors for Bryce wasn't really that necessary. Do you think differently now?

A Flexible Approach

So, you have a virtual three-dimensional world that is rendered into a two-dimensional image. This gives you flexibility as you approach world making and rendering.

- *You Can Change Your Mind.* The progressive render process allows you to experiment and then change your mind. After a couple of rendering passes, you can determine if you like what you see so far, and then decide whether to let the render progress further. You don't have to wait until the entire image is rendered single pixel by single pixel (whew!). You can stop after a bit and alter the entire scene. Or you can hone in on one section by drawing a marquee around the critical section and then letting that render out more fully. Or you can scrap the scene altogether and take a different approach to get your Brycean Kodak moment.

- *You Can Have Multiple Views of One Scene.* You don't have to necessarily have a one scene document/one view for your scene. All the information is there for that world. You can save several different views of it, and it will all be in one file. (More on this later in the chapter.)

- *You Can Select Different Times of Day.* You can save a series of skies for your scene (time of day and so on) in the Skies presets or the Skies Memory Dots in order to keep track of your different times of day for any particular scene. (See the Sky chapter, Chapter 10, for more particulars for this.)

(However, if you will be rendering your scenes using the drag-and-drop feature, you will need to create individual scene documents for each view of the scene. Create your series of scenes and then drag the scene document icons onto the Bryce application icon, turn off your monitor, and leave the office or go to bed. Bryce renders each one in turn so that when you come back, you'll have one or more scenes completely rendered.)

Obviously, you can spend a good deal of time perfecting one world. Then once it's in satisfactory condition, take rendered pictures of it to your heart's content! Look at it from the south in the morning and then saunter over for an east view in time for Brycean noon. Spend Bryce's late afternoon focused on one detail area and then at sunset take a panoramic view to the northwest. Don't forget to slip out at night to take it all in once more under Bryce's perpetual full moon. It's all the same world, shown at different times of day focusing on different sections.

Bryce's Document Structure

Bryce makes worlds and then takes rendered pictures of them. Bryce's entire file structure is based on these two processes: working in the three-dimensional world and then taking a two-dimensional snapshot of that world. In doing these two processes, Bryce creates two documents, one for each mode of operation. The three-dimensional world information—including objects, terrains, materials, sky and camera settings for the scene—are saved in a scene document. The rendered scene is saved in an image document (PICT for Macintosh, BMP for Windows). Figure 3–3 depicts Finder (Macintosh) or Explorer (Windows) icons for both documents. On Windows, the file extensions are .BRC and .BMP for the scene file and rendered result, respectively. Windows automatically assigns those extensions to your Bryce files. On the Macintosh side, the PICT rendered image file receives a suffix of .P, which Bryce automatically assigns when you save a scene.

A PICT document format has four channels (or 32 bits). The first three—red, green, and blue—contain the image itself. The fourth contains the information about the render's progress. Figure 3–4 shows the fourth channel of an image

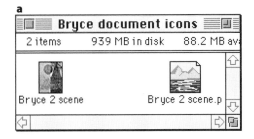

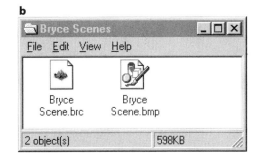

Figure 3–3 The icons for scene document and image document: a) Macintosh; b) Windows.

being rendered. The information is recorded in the very dark tones of gray, so for this image, the overall balance was adjusted for you to see the distinctions of colors. Sky becomes gray, and objects become dark tones that aren't quite black. Finally, with anti-aliasing in the final pass, (see Figure 3–4b) the pixels are white where anti-aliasing has taken place.

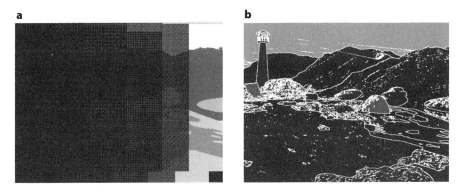

Figure 3–4 A comparison of fourth channels for comparing the render's progress (Macintosh only): a) Image showing six passes, with color balance adjusted so you can see the detail; b) after anti-aliasing.

In Windows, Bryce's image document is a BMP (bitmap), which has only three channels—R, G, and B (red, green, and blue). There is no fourth channel to store information about the render's progress. So where is that information stored? In the Bryce scene file itself. (This is but one of the reasons that Bryce 2.1 scene files cannot be traded back and forth between Macs and PCs. Bryce Windows can open up a Macintosh 2.0 or 2.1 scene file, but you cannot open up a Bryce Windows scene file on a Mac.) The difference between storing render progress information in the scene file (Windows) and in the image file (Macintosh) has implications for Windows batch rendering. For more information, see the batch render section in Chapter 12, "Render Unto Bryce."

VIEW AND CAMERA CONTROLS

When you're working on your scene, there are two basic ways you can look at it. Look at your scene through the camera. Or, look at the scene through one of six views along each dimension—God's eye views. The View and Camera controls on the Master Palette are divided into these two areas. The Camera controls are for positioning Bryce's virtual camera in Bryce's World Space, and to adjust the focal length of the lens. The View controls enable you to select from top/bottom, left/right, and front/back views to look at your scene.

As with any real-world camera, you must consider certain factors when positioning Bryce's camera. Where is the camera in the scene? Is the camera upright? Is it rotated this way or that? Then there's the matter of the kind of lens that's on the camera. How much of the surrounding world enters the lens? A long telephoto lens shows only what's ahead; a wide angle lens shows more of the range.

In addition, both ways of viewing your scene have another element in common—the two-dimensional plane onto which the image falls. This flat plane is analogous to film. The Pan and Zoom tools adjust the placement of the image on that plane. Those settings are located on the right interface strip.

Figure 3–5 shows the Master Palette and a cutaway of the narrow palette on the right, with each of the camera and view controls labeled.

Next, I'll take a more detailed look at each of the View and Camera controls.

The View Control

The Select Views control (also referred to as the View Diorama control in Bryce 1) allows you to look at your Bryce scene from seven different directions. Available views are current view (the camera's perspective), top, right, front, left, back, and bottom.

Clicking or dragging the Select Views control changes the preview on the Master Palette. Release the mouse button, and your view of the scene changes to match the control view. If you wanted, say, to put your scene in top view, drag the Select Views control until you see the top view preview, release the mouse, and your main scene changes to top view.

Alternatively you can navigate to other views via the View pop-up menu, where you can select—with no possibility of ambiguity—the different views.

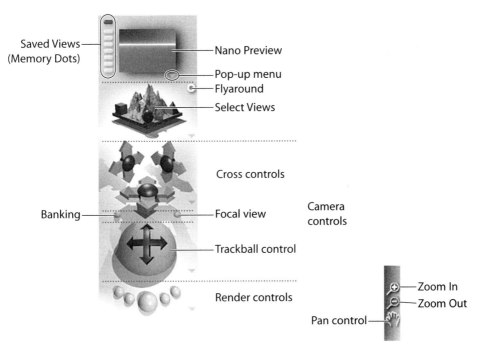

Saved Views
(Memory Dots)

Nano Preview

Pop-up menu

Flyaround

Select Views

Cross controls

Banking

Focal view

Camera
controls

Trackball control

Render controls

Zoom In

Zoom Out

Pan control

Figure 3–5 The View, Camera, and Pan & Zoom controls.

TIP: Here is a speed tip for when you're in another view and you want to go back to camera view: You can drag all the way to the left to go there directly. This tip is helpful if your machine is slow or if the scene is so complex that Bryce pauses before drawing the wireframe view of the scene.

TIP: Now, here is a major speed tip. The absolute best way to navigate quickly is to use the number keys to shift between views. Starting with 1 as the camera view, the numbers correspond to the positions in the Views menu list. Use either the numbers at the top of your keyboard or, on extended keyboards, the numeric keypad.

Camera view	*1*
Top view	*2*
Left (side) view	*3*
Front view	*4*
Saved views	*5–9*

Since this is a holdover from the old version of Bryce, where there were only front, side and top views, the keypad numbering has not changed. Therefore there is no quick way to get to back, other side, and bottom. If this book is biased toward certain orthogonal views, know that it's because the keypad shortcut has made its way into certain working habits, making it harder to get to the orthogonal views that have no numerical equivalents.

Orthogonal Views

When you are looking at your scene in any view other than the camera view, you are looking at the scene in an orthogonal view. What does orthogonal mean? Orthogonal is *not* some fancy term for a hybrid of agony and orthodonture. Orthogonal means that the view is perpendicular; you're looking at the scene from a perfect right angle. When you're in any view other than main view, you won't be looking at your scene in perspective. Should you want to align objects precisely, you'll be able to do so without guesswork.

The Windows version of Bryce does not have true orthogonal perspective-less alternative views. You are, in fact, looking at your view *in perspective* from a far off distance. The side, front, and top views are set up in such a way that the camera is way, way, way removed from the scene, in hopes of getting a nearly-orthogonal view.

In all versions of Bryce, no matter what type of perspective or lack thereof for the side, front, and top or bottom views, the renders from those views are in perspective.

When you are in an orthogonal view, the Camera controls are grayed out. In Bryce's case, this grayed-out Macintosh-ism is literal, as all the color is drained out of the Camera controls, and they show only in grayscale. Should you want to move closer to your object or set the view directly overhead some other part of the scene, zoom in or out and pan to navigate this way and that. (More on panning and zooming later in the chapter.)

There is a way to bust out of a perfect orthogonal view, however. If you want the old way back, where you look at your scene in true perspective (top, bottom, front, back, left or right):

1. Set your view to one of the orthogonal views.

2. Invoke the momentary Nano editor display. Press both the space bar and Option key (Macintosh) or Alt key (Windows) while your mouse is within the active scene area. Then when you press and drag the mouse in the area, you'll be making adjustments.

3. Adjust your view to your heart's content. All the standard manipulations apply.

4. When you release your mouse, you will find your scene has snapped into temporary side/front/top perspective view.

What breaks the magic? Selecting Reset Views from the Views pop-up menu returns the views to their original orthogonal state. You can also return the view to its default state by selecting the Edit Camera dialog box and changing the angle back to its standard. In orthogonal views, two axes are set to 0°, and the other one is set to either 90° or –90°. (More about the Edit Camera dialog box follows later in the chapter.)

View Pop-up Menus

Bryce's Views pop-up menu, located just off of the View Diorama, has several view options on it. (See Figure 3–6.) Besides the orthogonal views and the camera view, there is another option: Reset Views. This option takes you back to the default Bryce camera position and puts you at the default Zoom setting of 100%.

Figure 3–6 The View control and pop-up menu.

The Nano Preview

The Nano Preview at the top of the Master Palette was inherited from Bryce 1's Sky & Fog Palette. Besides its migration over to the Master Palette, it gained a lot of flexibility and new features. It displays a preview in three different states: the Sky Only (same as before), the Full Scene, or the Wireframe (both are new).

When you are looking at the Nano Preview in either the Full Scene or the Wireframe View, you can choose to look at the preview from any of the view options— independent of the main view. Use the pop-up menu to choose a different view or a different mode. (See Figure 3–7.) Not only can you view any of these in the same view as you are seeing in the main work window, but you can make the preview's view *different* from the one you have in the main window. This is a very powerful feature: When placing the camera, for instance, you can be in top view in the main window, dragging the camera to different places, and after each incremental adjustment, let the preview render to give you immediate feedback to see if your camera is "there" yet.

Figure 3–7 The Nano Preview and pop-up menu.

There are three ways to make the Nano Preview render, one automatic and two manual. In the pop-up menu, you can select auto-update. That will cause the Nano Preview to render after each incremental adjustment is made to your scene. Of the two manual ways to control the Preview render, one involves a mouse click and the other is a menu item/keyboard shortcut. Click directly inside the render window to force the Nano Preview to update. The second menu/keyboard option is accessed from the File menu: Nano Render Update, or Control-R (Macintosh), or Ctrl+Alt+Shift+R (Windows). Either of those will make the Nano Preview render only when you want it to.

I recommend switching on the auto-update *only* when you are doing some concentrated work on object or camera placement or anything that requires constant feedback. Then, when that stage is complete, switch off the Nano Preview and ask for render updates periodically only when you need them.

The same technique works for precise object alignment; you can be in side view in the main window, adjusting the elevation of your object (a body of water, for instance) and pause after each movement to see how it looks as it renders in the preview window.

Why would you want to look at a render in the Nano Preview? First, render time is quicker. You get a literal thumbnail of your scene. Second, it can be more streamlined. You don't have to make a change, switch to render mode, update render, go back to wireframe mode, make another change, switch to render mode, update to see how it went, ad awkwardum. Rather, you can work in the main scene window and see the results of each move, or change immediately in the Nano Preview.

Nano Preview is not particularly helpful when your scene is set up in an aspect ratio that differs widely from the basic horizontal ratio shown in the Nano Preview render area. (The Nano Preview area is fixed at 80×60 pixels or a 4:3 ratio.)

Nano Preview WalkThrough

In this sample walkthrough, I'll lead you through some guided steps to work with the Nano Preview. You'll learn how to take advantage of the small render and quick render time while working in the main scene window.

1. Open up the Scene NANO PREVIEW SCENE BEGIN from the CD-ROM (see Figure 3–8a).

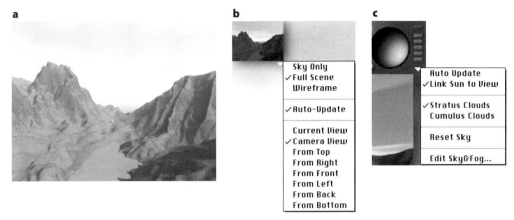

Figure 3–8 Getting set for Nano Preview: a) Open the scene; b) settings for Nano pop-up menu; c) settings for Sky Options pop-up menu.

2. Make sure that your Bryce application settings are as follows: In the Nano pop-up menu, make sure that the following options are checked: Full Scene, Auto-Update , and Camera View (See Figure 3–8b). The scene should update in the Nano Preview window. In the Sky Palette, make sure that Auto-Update is *un*checked (See Figure 3–8c).

3. Change the view to top view (see Figure 3–9a) See the set of tori? Position the camera so that you can see into the center of the torus rings. Drag the camera to the left. Figure 3–9b shows the camera after it has moved left, with the corresponding Nano Preview.

4. It's getting there, but it is not completely centered in the rings yet. To do that, the camera needs to be moved vertically. To better see what is going on with vertical camera placement, switch to view from the right (tap the 3 key). Figure 3–9c is the same scene as part b, as seen from side view.

5. Now you can see where the camera is in relation to the tori. Just a lil' move up and you're there! Figure 3–9d shows the result.

Since this is the camera chapter, I focused on the Nano Preview for camera movements. But don't be limited by that. This is an excellent way to work in orthogonal views of your scene while editing objects, too.

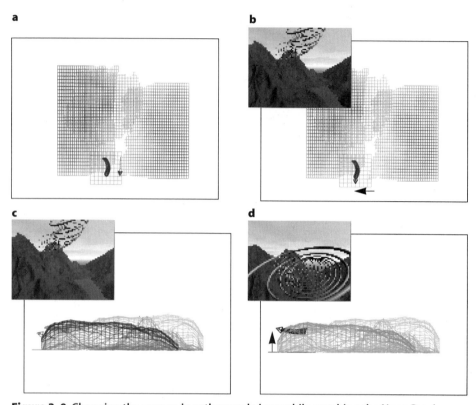

Figure 3-9 Changing the camera in orthogonal views while watching the Nano Preview window: a) Begin in top view; b) after moving the camera left; c) same results in side view; d) after moving the camera up.

Cross Controls

The Cross controls move the camera's position from within Bryce. Since the camera is placed in the width, height, and depth of the Bryce environment, the camera position is referred to in x, y, and z terms. However, these axes are not fixed in Bryce's World Space, where the x axis is east-west, the z axis is north-south, and the y axis is altitude. Rather, the x, y, and z axes are fixed to the camera's own reference point. Therefore x will always be right-left, y will be up and down, and z will be forward and backward. Those directions will not change, no matter which way you face in the Bryce world. Figure 3-10 shows how the camera movements occur independently of the Bryce world orientation. The first panel of the illustration shows the starting place for camera movement. In the second panel, the camera has moved along the x axis to its own right; the new camera placement has no bearing on the Bryce world x (east-west) axis.

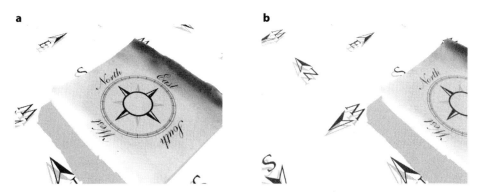

Figure 3-10 a) Placement before camera is moved to the right along its *x* axis; b) after moving along the camera's *x* axis.

Three crosses make up the Cross controls. Each cross corresponds to more than one axis. Each cross moves the camera along two axes. As Figure 3–11 shows, each axis is represented twice in the entire set of Cross controls. Each Cross control will move the camera along a plane, whether the movement is limited to the horizontal plane (the X-Z Cross) or to the vertical plane (the Y-Z Cross and the X-Y Cross).

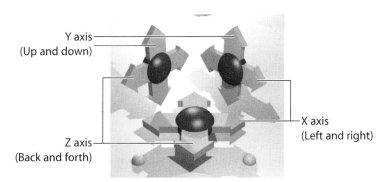

Figure 3–11 Each of the three Cross controls shares an axis with another of the Cross controls.

The image in Figure 3–12 show the camera and the respective planes of motion that are brought about by each of the Cross controls. The two vertical planes represent the range of camera movement using the two upright Cross controls, and the horizontal plane represents the range of motion using the flat Cross controls.

Bryce handily tells you which axis you're moving your camera along. When you place the cursor over the particular arrow on the cross, the pointer changes to one of the axis indicators.

You can constrain all of the camera movements. The Cross controls will change to show you when they are constraining camera movement in one direction. You can also use the modifier keys on the Macintosh to constrain in one direction: Control key for the *x*-axis, Option key for the *y*-axis, and Command key for the *z*-axis.

Figure 3–12 The virtual camera with three planes emanating from it; the planes match the range of motion provided by each of the Cross controls.

Keyboard Navigation

Tired of dragging from the Cross controls this way and that to move the camera? There are some arrow key combinations that imitate the movement of the Trackball and Cross controls.

Command (Macintosh) or Ctrl (Windows) plus the arrow keys moves the camera in trackball fashion. Here are the combinations. The up and down arrow is the same as dragging up and down on the Trackball control (*y* axis). The foreground rotates around World Center in the same direction as the arrow; up arrow moves the foreground up, and consequently, moves your perspective down; down arrow moves the foreground down, moving your perspective up. The left and right arrow keys, used in conjunction with the Command (Macintosh) or Ctrl (Windows) key, are the same as dragging left and right on the Trackball control (*x* axis). The foreground rotates to the right with the right arrow, and to the left with the left arrow.

The same arrow keys are used to imitate the Cross control for camera movement, this time using the Control (Macintosh) or Ctrl+Alt (Windows) keys. Control or Ctrl+Alt with the right and left arrow keys moves the camera left and right along the *x* axis. Control or Ctrl+Alt and the up and down arrow keys moves the camera forward and backward along the *z* axis. What about the *y* axis? In Windows, there's no key equivalent to get movement along the *y* axis. On the Macintosh, Control-Option down arrow moves the ground down (and the view up), but Control-Option up arrow, even though it momentarily displays the watch cursor—as do the other camera arrow keys—results in no change whatsoever. For some odd reason, the Control-Option plus left and right arrow keys move the camera as well—along the *z* axis (which used the up and down arrow keys before). Go figure.

Note: Option (Macintosh) or Alt (Windows) key with the arrows moves selected objects within the scene. See the Edit chapter, Chapter 6 for more information.

Camera Controls Pop up Menu

There are four additional options available in the Camera controls pop-up menu (see Figure 3–13). The Camera control changes the position of the camera in relation to the ground level of the scene, or to objects that are in the scene. The Center commands (Center Scene, Center Selection) change the rotation, swinging the camera around so that it points to a particular place. With the

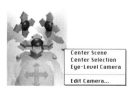

Figure 3–13 Camera controls pop-up menu.

exception of the last option, these menu items can be selected only when you are in normal Bryce viewing mode. They do not work in orthogonal views.

Center Scene. This option points the camera at the center point of your scene. How can you tell what *is* the center point of the scene? If you were to select all your objects so that they had a common bounding box, the camera would be pointing at the center of that bounding box. Although your objects aren't all selected, Bryce knows where that center point is, and points the camera there. Figure 3–14 is a series of screen shots, in both main and top view of the default camera perspective (before) and center scene (after). The top view is also shown with all objects selected so that you can see the center point of the bounding box. Note how the "after" camera position points directly to the center of the common bounding box. Use this command to bring your scene back into view, if you somehow managed to navigate your camera so that the scene is out of view. (In the sample shown here, the scene is probably a bit more extreme than normal; most scenes are not so widely dispersed.)

Center Selection. This changes the rotation of the camera, not its position, so that the selected object is smack dab in the middle of your scene window. The same principle as center scene applies; Bryce points to the center of the bounding box. Rather than take the imaginary bounding box for the entire scene, Bryce uses the actual center of the bounding box for the selected object or objects. Use this to point the camera smack dab on a particular object.

Eye Level Camera. Unlike the two Center controls, this doesn't operate on camera rotation, but on offset. It lowers the camera to about "eye level," which, in the camera numerical readout, puts it at 5 Bryce units above the ground, or nearly a grid unit (for more about Bryce units, see the Edit chapter, Chapter 6). Of course,

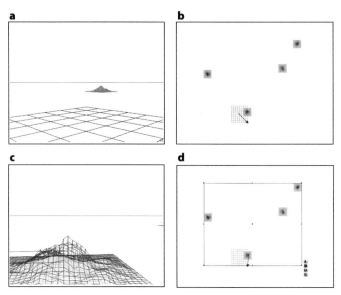

Figure 3–14 Centering the scene: a) Before, in default view;
b) before shown in top view; c) after centering scene, main view;
d) after centering scene (with all objects selected to show
bounding box's center), top view.

if your camera is placed lower than ground level, it raises the camera to just above ground level. Camera rotation is not changed.

Edit Camera. This takes you to the Camera dialog box, which can also be accessed by double-clicking the Cross or the Trackball controls. The Camera dialog box allows you to change the numerical values for the camera position. This menu item is the only means to access the Camera dialog box when you are in orthogonal views. When accessed while in one of the orthogonal views, the numbers you see will differ greatly from the numbers in the Camera dialog box in camera view. I'll discuss the Camera control dialog box a bit later, after going through the rest of the Camera controls.

The Trackball Control

The Trackball control changes the camera position in relation to the entire world. Movement is not restricted to horizontal or vertical, but is an integrated rotation around a central point. Choose the mode that the Trackball will rotate around from the Trackball pop-up menu. (See Figure 3–15.) The camera will rotate around Bryce's

Figure 3–15 The Trackball pop-up menu.

World Center, around a selected object, and around its own center, as though it were atop a tripod.

When you set the Trackball to Trackball mode, it works like this: Suppose your Bryce world is inside a globe (see Figure 3–16a). When you rotate the camera, its distance from the globe's center stays the same, even though it moves up or down, or left or right to change position (see Figure 3–16b).

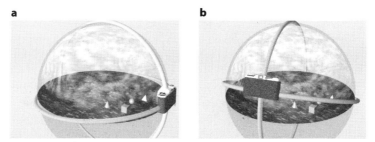

Figure 3–16 The Trackball control, in default mode: a) Before rotation; b) after rotation.

Since the camera moves relative to World Center, then the position of individual objects in Bryce Space will affect apparent camera movements. If you are, for example, trying to rotate the camera around a particular object and you happen to have your object placed way off center, your rotation actions will not be pleasing; the world will seem to rotate on an ellipse.

This is where the second option comes in handy—Center to Selection. In this case, rather than rotating around World Center, the camera's rotation is adjusted so that it treats the selected objects as the temporary World Center. So camera adjustments can be made away from World Center without throwing you way off. However, there are a couple of conditions that need to be met for Center to Selection to act as expected. You need to have an object that is selected. If there is no selected object, this mode acts identically to the Trackball mode, rotating around World Center. When you do have an object selected, your camera needs to be pointing directly at it. If not, you'll be rotating around the point halfway between the selected object and where the camera is pointing. The Center Selection menu item under the Camera Crosses menu will rotate your camera so that it points directly at your selected object. Figure 3–17 depicts Bryce's camera rotating around the selected object—the one with the wireframe showing. There will be times when you can easily live with the ambiguity of the not-quite on center in order to make your camera adjustments. But if you were trying to rotate

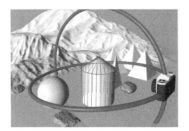 

Figure 3-17 The Trackball in Center to Selection mode.

around, say, that cube over there, and it wasn't quite working, your camera probably wasn't pointing directly at the object.

When you have multiple objects selected, Bryce draws a common bounding box around the objects. When that selection is centered, then you can see the camera rotating around the center control point of the bounding box.

Finally, there is a third option for the Trackball. Selecting Tripod from the Trackball pop-up menu will set the rotation center to be the camera itself, as if it were sitting on a tripod. The entire scene rotates around the camera, while the camera stays stationary. See Figure 3-18.

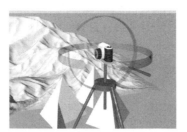 

Figure 3-18 The Trackball Tripod rotates the world around the camera location.

In each of these cases, you can use the constrain keys in conjunction with the Trackball for precise movements. To rotate around the *x*-axis (horizontally), hold down the Control (Macintosh) or Alt (Windows) key. This is a very helpful constraining motion to keep the camera from wobbling. To pan up or down from one spot, press the Option (Macintosh) or Ctrl+Alt (Windows) key to constrain movement along the *y*-axis.

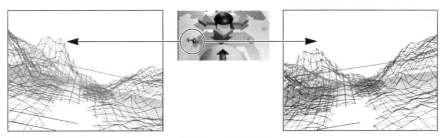

Figure 3–19 Banking tilts the world along the horizon line.

Banking

There is now a functional tilt control for the camera. Adjust it by dragging the Banking control, located to the above left of the trackball. Whatever direction you drag toward, that side of the scene will be raised. So if you drag to the right, the right side of the horizon will get higher than the left. See Figure 3–19. With the addition of this control, you now have full three-dimensional rotation in the Main Palette Camera controls.

Field of View—
A Camera with Different-Sized "Lenses"

The Field of View control is analogous to switching lenses on a camera. A wide-angle lens takes in more area than a telephoto lens. For the numerical measurements, though, don't think of Field of View as the equivalent of camera lens focal length. Bryce uses degrees, not millimeters. (The numerical degree measurements are in the Camera dialog box, accessed by double-clicking the Cross or Trackball controls.) The degree number corresponds to the angle that you see. With the largest, 180°, you'll see half the world before you. On the small end, 1° is a tightly focused, narrow view.

Drag to the right to increase the Field of View setting or to widen your perspective. The scene seems to move farther away, but actually, the scene "decreases," since the camera is letting in more image area to the left and right of the scene. Drag left to decrease the Field of View setting. You get "closer" to the image, and the perspective decreases. Move the camera back on the *z* axis, and you have just created a long-lens telephoto perspective. Figure 3–20 shows a scene at different Field of View settings.

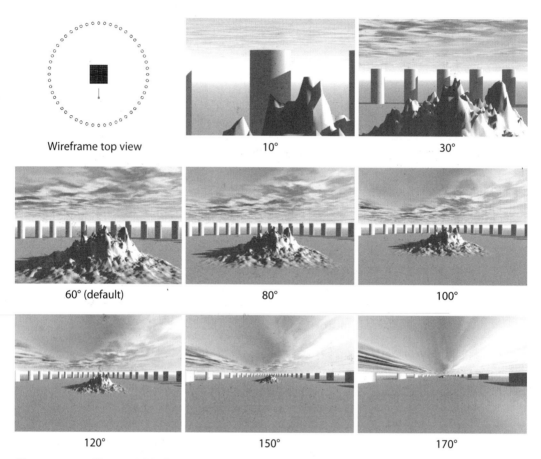

Figure 3–20 Different Field of View settings for a Bryce scene.

Pan and Zoom on the Second Dimension

Earlier in the chapter I mentioned that there is an element common to both the View and the Camera controls—the two-dimensional plane. The Pan and Zoom controls allow you to alter the two-dimensional plane on which the Bryce scene is projected. Say what? Weren't we talking about a three-dimensional scene here? Then why all of a sudden am I talking about a two-dimensional plane? If you're asking these questions, keep reading.

Think of the two-dimensional plane as the place where the "film" is, recording the image projected from the scene. Your camera can be oriented in Bryce Space in any position and facing any direction. Wherever the "film" is, the 2D plane extends outwards on all sides. The "film" of that camera is measured in pixels.

(The size of the "film" is set in the Document Setup dialog box where you choose your scene's resolution.) It is the active "photosensitive" area of the 2D plane that captures light. I refer to this photosensitive area of the plane as the "active image area." The plane can be slid up or down, left or right, to make any portion the active area. You can also zoom in or out from that spot. The Pan and Zoom tools in the lower right-hand corner of the Bryce user interface allow you to do that.

Panning

To scroll along the plane, use the Hand tool. Or press the space bar while dragging the mouse. This infinite plane extends out in all directions (in Figure 3–21, it is represented as finite, if only to indicate its presence). The camera position itself does not change, but the plane may be slid over to determine a new active image area. Think for a moment of the finite infinite plane and ask, "Is the active image area in the upper left-hand corner? The lower right-hand corner? How about along the bottom edge in the center?"

a

b

Figure 3–21 a) A virtual Bryce scene on a virtual monitor with a virtual infinite plane (here it is finite so you can tell it is there). b) After scrolling up and to the left, the active image area changes.

There are differences between moving a camera up and moving the 2D plane up to "frame" the image just so. In the scene in Figure 3–22a, the horizon line is right smack dab in the middle. There's too much sky and not enough of the foreground terrain. If you drag up on either of the Upright Crosses to move the camera, you'll change the relationship between objects (Figure 3–22b). Instead, scroll up with the Hand tool to maintain the relationship between objects (Figure 3–22c). The camera angle does not change.

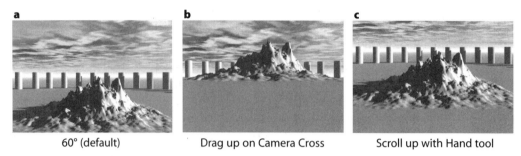

| 60° (default) | Drag up on Camera Cross | Scroll up with Hand tool |

Figure 3–22 The difference between moving the camera and scrolling the 2D plane: a) Original image; b) dragging up on the Upright Cross; c) scrolling up with the Hand tool.

If you want to reset the Pan back to the default position, press the Option (Macintosh) or Alt (Windows) key and click the hand Pan tool. You'll snap back to the default state.

Zooming

There are several ways to zoom to change the magnification of your image.

- *Magnifier tools.* Clicking the Zoom In magnifier tool—the one with the plus (+)—zooms you into the image. This action is not the same as moving the camera closer to the image. Instead, you are focusing on a smaller area and making that area fill the entire active camera view.

- *Keyboard modifier clicks.* Command-space bar (Macintosh) or Ctrl+space bar (Windows) with a click zooms you in, and Option-⌘-space bar (Macintosh) or Ctrl+Alt+space bar (Windows) zooms you out. The location of your cursor when you click affects the way that you zoom. This is not a pure zoom; it is a zoom and pan. While zooming in, it generally works this way: the location of the cursor before the click will tend to move toward the center in the resulting preview (it won't become the exact center, though). If you click with the magnifier above the horizon line, you'll see more area above the horizon line; the horizon line—and all objects on the ground—moves down. Click below the horizon line and you see more area below the horizon (the horizon line moves up). Until you get this idea of both zoom and pan, this method seems quite erratic (even *after* you get the idea it will seem erratic, too). Zooming out using Option-Command-space bar or Ctrl+Alt+space bar does not behave as erratically as zooming in. It's just a straight move out.

- *Key commands.* On the main keyboard, plus (with the Shift key pressed) zooms you in, minus zooms you out. It's simpler on the keypad for extended keyboards, just tap the plus or the minus key without worrying about the Shift key for plus. This is my zoom of choice. (Beware tapping the equal key alone; equal will change your selection back to unity shape. See Chapter 6 for more on unity.) On the Macintosh, you can also use the Command keys with the main keyboard's plus or minus keys; Command-plus (or Command-=) and Command-minus. Windows has no key equivalent.

To revert the scene back to the default 100% magnification, hold down the Option (Macintosh) or Alt (Windows) key and click either of the Zoom tools.

Zoom to Selection

The Zoom to Selection option is another way to define a view. It's the Bryce version of the tricky modifier key combination used while marqueeing an area. "Hey, I'd like to do a close-up on that," you say. Suppose you have a finished render and there is one area of the image that interests you.

- *Wireframe mode.* (Macintosh only.) Press the Command key and space bar. The cursor changes to a Magnifying tool. Drag the tool around the area you want to focus on. Release the mouse and that area fills the screen.

- *Render mode.* When you have the rendered image showing, make sure that you are have Plop Render switched on (accessed from the Display options to the right). Drag a marquee around the image area you want. Then select Zoom to Selection from the pop-up menu (see Figure 3–23a). That area then fills the window (see Figure 3–23b). Render again (see Figure 3–23c) and select File > Save As... to save your detail image as a separate scene.

You can create several snapshots of the same scene in this way. Consider it your "Postcards from the Bryce Edge."

a

b

c

Figure 3–23 Bryce close-ups in Render mode: a) Marquee an area and choose Zoom to Selection; b) the marqueed area fills the screen; c) the rendered image.

Zoombiguity

There's a problem with the word "zoom." In camera terms, you can alter the focal length of a zoom lens on the fly. It's a smoother way of changing lenses, say, from 50 mm to 80 mm to 200 mm. You zoom in and out, all the while being positioned in one place. Standing in one place, zoom from 60 mm to 130 mm. This will bring you closer to your subject. This is analogous to the action in the Field of View control.

However, I'm talking about using zoom in the Macintosh sense. In other Macintosh applications, you change the view of the document by zooming. You can look at something in actual size, you can magnify it, or you can reduce it so that the entire page fits in the document window. This is a two-dimensional zoom process.

When Bryce uses the Zoom In and Zoom Out controls and the Zoom to Selection option in the Plop Render's pop-up menu, it is acting like the more classic Macintosh (or graphical-user-interface) zoom-to-magnify. It is a two-dimensional zoom. The fact that you're in a three-dimensional application that uses something called a camera may make zoom confusing.

When you click the Zoom In or Zoom Out magnifying tools in the lower right hand corner, you are selectively choosing smaller or larger areas of the "scene" to project onto the 2D Projection plane. You're magnifying that particular area when you zoom in and you're reducing it when you zoom out.

Zooming in Orthogonal Views

You can do the same thing in orthogonal views to bring you closer or take you further from your subject. There is a different twist to zooming in orthogonal views. If you have an object selected, the panning will change so that your selected objects are centered in your scene.

In my opinion, zooming works best in orthogonal views. It is a 2D magnification process. Orthogonal views do not have true perspective to them, so zooming works splendidly for enlarging or reducing objects as needed. In the main current view, zooming can result in perspective distortion—this is true especially when you zoom out; you are asking Bryce to put more and more of the entire 2D plane into your little area. The perspective is more extreme the farther away from the center of the image you go.

Camera Dialog Box

To get a little more control over the camera position, double click either the Crosses or the Trackball to open the Camera dialog box. See Figure 3–24. You can also access the Camera dialog box by selecting Edit Camera... from the Camera Crosses pop-up menu. This dialog box allows you to use numerical settings to alter the camera's angle and position, as well as to change where you are on the flat 2D Projection plane from where you view Bryce. Each item in this dialog box is labeled according to its corresponding controls on the Master Palette. The Camera controls are in the left part of the box and the 2D Projection controls are on the right.

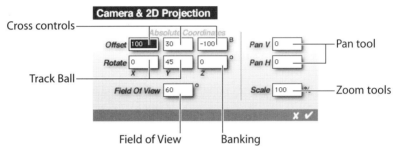

Figure 3–24 The Camera controls dialog box, labeled to match the items on the Control Palette.

Camera: Offset

The Offset part of the Camera dialog box is for changing the camera's location. To change these settings, use the Cross controls, since you are moving the actual camera location.

The offset concerns the position of the camera in Bryce Space. "Offset" means the camera's offset from World Center.

You can use arrow keys to modify the numbers in the dialog box; see the Edit chapter (Chapter 6) under 3D Transformations where I discuss this in detail.

Camera: Rotate

The Rotate part of the Camera dialog box describes the camera's orientation in space. The orientation is indicated in degree increments. Whereas Bryce 1's treatment of these numbers added an extra decimal place for precision (so that 360 degrees was expressed as 3600), Bryce 2 has returned to a normal mode of recording degrees—360 degrees is 360 degrees. If there are increments in between, they come after a decimal point. If you'd gotten used to that with Bryce 1, lay down your weary load. If this is your first encounter with this dialog box, rest easy. You don't need an advanced degree to figure out what Bryce considers a degree or a partial degree.

The Trackball changes the settings of the camera angle. However, the Trackball only changes the x and y value. The z value is changed by the Banking control to make the camera do a roll.

Field of View

The Field of View part of the dialog box is the number that controls the camera's focal length. The default is 60°. If you need to, you can reset the Field of View here. (You can also Option-click the Field of View control on the main Control Palette.)

Scale

Scale% refers to the zoom factor. Here are the numbers for the Zoom In (+) or Zoom Out (–) controls. Think of it as the enlargement or reduction of the scene on the active viewing rectangle. The default is 100%. Zoom up or down.

The zoom works in factors of 1.5. So from 100%, it multiplies that figure by one and a half to get 150. It then multiplies that figure by one and a half to get 225 and so on up to the maximum. On the Zoom Out side, the zoom takes 100 and divides that by 1.5 to get 66, then 44, and so on down to the minimum.

If you don't like those particular numbers and want to see something in between, say, at 135% or 89%, all you need to do is type your own numbers in the Scale% portion of the dialog box.

When you change scene sizes in the Document Setup dialog box, Bryce adjusts the scale accordingly.

To reset the numbers back to the default of 100%, enter that number for the Scale %. (You can also Option-click the zoom tools to reset to default.)

Pan V and Pan H

Pan V and Pan H each have a numerical value—v is for vertical and h is for horizontal. These numbers measure the amount that the 2D projection (film) plane is offset from World Center. Bryce 2 now has set the default center image to have values of 0,0. When you pan to the right, so that you are looking on the left part of the image, the horizontal value will be a positive number. Panning to the left results in a negative number.

When you change scene sizes, Bryce gives its best guess, putting the old scene in the new active image area. Both the Pan and the Scale% are adjusted. You may need to tweak either setting after changing sizes.

HOW-TO: CAMERA PLACEMENT THAT'S JUST SO

Now that I've talked about the theory of the Camera controls, I offer some additional working information for setting up your camera positions. You don't always need to adjust your camera by using the controls on the Master Palette. You can also directly manipulate it while working in the orthogonal views of your scene.

The Little Blue Box

When looking at your scene in one of the orthogonal views, the camera is represented on the screen as a blue box with a line extending from it. There is also a wireframe pyramid hood that indicates the camera direction. The pyramid stays in wireframe view, and changes to reflect any adjustments made in wireframe depth cueing (For more information on depth cueing, see the wireframe section of Chapter 4, Objects.). The camera itself is the box and line. The box and line can be directly manipulated to change the camera position. On the Macintosh, when you drag the box, the camera momentarily turns red to indicate that it is selected, and as soon as you release the mouse it switches back to blue. Immediately after changing the camera, the pyramid hood snaps into position to reflect the new position. (These two behaviors do not occur in Windows, though you can change the camera's position by directly dragging it.) There are two basic ways to change the camera. It can be moved directly by dragging the box. Drag the box to move the entire camera (see Figure 3–25).

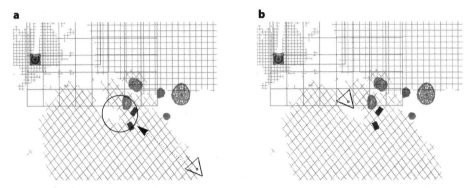

Figure 3–25 Repositioning the camera by dragging the blue box (top view): a) Before (showing where the camera is headed); and b) after.

On the Macintosh, you can precisely aim the camera by moving the tip in the direction you want to point your camera. To aim the camera at a particular object, drag the tip until it touches the object (see Figure 3–26a). When you release the mouse button, the camera retracts to its original size, but is aimed directly at the

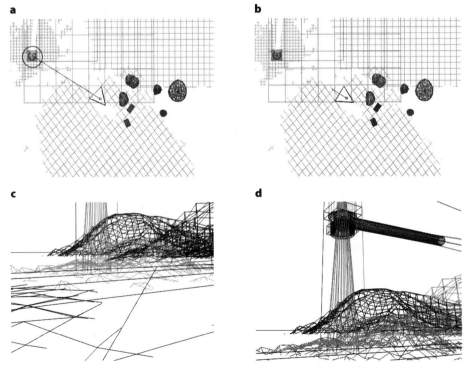

Figure 3–26 Changing the camera view: a) Dragging the tip of the camera to the object (top view); b) after releasing the camera (top view); c) the lighthouse in the precise center of the scene (main view); d) after adjusting the camera up using the Trackball set to tripod.

object (Figure 3–26b). When you go back to main view, the object will be placed in the center of your view (Figure 3–26c). (Since, in this case, the object is tall, changing the trackball setting to tripod and dragging down on the Trackball control aims the camera up, so that the top part of the lighthouse can be seen. See Figure 3–26d.) The Windows version of Bryce does not support this method of aiming the camera. (To precisely aim your camera at an object under Windows, switch back to camera view. Select the object on which you want to focus the camera. Then use the Center Selection command under the Camera pop-up menu. It will rotate the camera around to directly face the object.)

Changes made to the camera wireframe are not undoable in the same way that using the Camera controls are, however. Of course, in Bryce 1, none of the camera movements were undoable using Command-Z or Ctrl+Z. Bryce 2 allows you to undo movements made with the main controls (the Crosses and the Trackball) but you cannot undo direct manipulations of the camera in orthogonal views.

When you do a test render in orthogonal views, you can still see the camera on top of the rendered image. Some beta testers back in Bryce 1's early days thought this was a software bug. Not so! It's a very powerful feature. It enables you to precisely place the camera in your scene. Say you have a terrain that has deep ravines. You need to get the placement just right or else the camera will be hidden inside the ground. Not a great view. If you use the Cross controls to navigate yourself to that ravine, you will probably put your computer in danger of ruin (or worse!) from your frustrated outburst after many tries to place your camera just so. Don't sweat it. There's an easier way.

Render the scene a little from an orthogonal view (top view works well for this). When you click to stop the render, the camera should reappear. (If it doesn't, then toggle to wireframe view and back with the Escape—Esc—key. The camera should reappear.) Now you can place your camera while you look at the accurately rendered scene. Figure 3–27 shows an example of how this works. The terrain has lots of dips and peaks, thereby making it hard for you to navigate deep within the narrow places using the Camera controls on the Control Palette.

Figure 3–27 A scene with ravines that might be difficult to navigate through with the Camera controls.

This idea has been extended in Bryce 2 with the ability to see both the wireframe and rendered view simultaneously. Not only can you move the camera while viewing the rendered scene as a reference, but you can move any of the objects while looking at the render. The Display Mode select tool in the lower right hand corner of the interface switches between wireframe, render, and wireframe-plus-render modes.

Precise Camera Placement from Top View

Figure 3–28 shows the terrain from Figure 3–27 in top view. There's quite a bit of dramatic viewing, if only you can get your camera in there. However, placing the camera when you're in the wireframe view of the same terrain is problematical. Depending on the amount of depth cueing and other factors (how close you are zoomed to the entire terrain), you may or may not be able to tell from the wireframe information alone where to put the camera. In this case, depth cueing on the terrain made it fairly obvious (see Figure 3–28a). If that won't work, then render the scene in top view (Figure 3–28b). After a few render passes, the situation will become obvious. You will see where to place the camera. There might be times when seeing the wireframe is also helpful; Figure 3–28c shows both the top view render and the wireframe, as well as the camera.

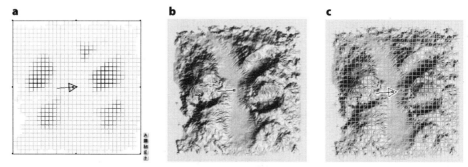

Figure 3–28 Camera placement in top view: a) With wireframe depth cueing; b) rendered; c) showing both wireframe and render.

Here are a few general Bryce tips to help you while you do this:

- In the Sky & Fog options menu, make sure that Link Sun to View is unchecked. Otherwise you'll get something generally very dark, as overhead sun is actually shining from your horizon.

- Placing the sun not exactly overhead will show the heights and depths of the terrain by casting slight shadows where the canyon is deep.

- You can work faster if your terrain doesn't have a three-dimensional texture applied to it. The default gray plastic texture you get when Bryce first opens is ideal for this kind of treatment. (Or, render with the Textures on/off button depressed.)

Flyaround View

For an overall wireframe preview of your scene, and for choosing possible new camera angles, the Flyaround takes you on an aerial tour of your scene. Click the little white donut to the right of the Views Diorama. Or, alternatively, select Objects > Flyaround or type Command-Y (Macintosh) or Ctrl+Y (Windows). (Though the menu calls it "Flyaround" and the readout at the bottom of the Control palette on the Macintosh calls it "Aerial Preview" they both refer to the same thing. I'll use both terms here in my description.)

The scene rotates around World Center, while you are looking off from the distance in a type of "God's eye" view. You can see the current camera location; it is indicated by the blue pyramid. (Now the reason for the wireframe nature of the camera pyramid becomes obvious—you can see it in Flyaround view!) If you have set your wireframe preview to have depth cueing, then you'll be able to tell which objects are farther away and which ones are closer while the scene rotates. (For more information on wireframe and depth cueing, see Chapter 4, Objects). Figure 3–29 shows a stuttered "time lapse" of the Flyaround mode as the world rotates on its center before you.

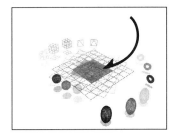

Figure 3–29 The scene in Flyaround mode.

Note: Although this Flyaround is a wireframe animation, this does not mean that you can animate the motion you are seeing—yet. That is yet to come in the next revision of Bryce.

There is more to this Aerial Preview feature than stealing a rare moment to float ethereally above the wireframe as it rotates below, all the while admiring your handiwork (though there are times when that's a fine enough reason to click the donut and watch your scene for a bit). The Flyaround provides a fluid way to explore the scene from different vantage points and so to choose a new camera view. There are two steps to the process. In the first stage, explore the view. The second step is to go there and let that become the new camera view. Since the end of the process is much simpler than the beginning, I'll take a moment here and talk about the conclusion before stepping back and discussing the lengthier matters of exploration.

When you get to something that is pleasing enough to declare "my new camera view," hit the Return key. The Return key completes the process. If the Flyaround were to be likened to the statement "Wherever you go, there you are," then the first step of exploration is "wherever you go." The Return key takes you to the new spot, which has now become the current view. The Return key takes you to the conclusion: "there you are."

Of course, you don't have to change your camera view at all; once you click the mouse, you exit Flyaround mode and go back to where you were before. So the click of the mouse key is "Wherever you went, there you aren't."

That was the conclusion. Now, onto the exploration process. The process always takes longer than the conclusion, and there is always more than one option for getting there. This is yet another case where Bryce Imitates Life. During Flyaround mode, you can use different modifiers along with mouse movements to control the view.

Wherever You Go—Exploration

All the range of movements in the Flyaround mode mirror those of the Trackball (in Trackball mode) and the z portion of either the YZ or the XZ Camera Crosses. You will always be facing World Center in Flyaround, but you can move around it smartly.

Moving the mouse up and down (not dragging, when the mouse button is pressed, but simply moving the mouse to change the pointer position) will adjust the height of your perspective. The first few times you do this, you're no doubt putting too wide a range of motion, with the result that your aerial Flyaround is bobbing and heaving wildly, threatening to give you motion-sickness. Ouch! Don't pull out the dramamine, just make sure to keep the mouse movements small and subtle when in Flyaround mode.

There is a method to the movement madness: whatever direction the mouse moves in, it takes the nearer foreground with it. Or, to put it in terms of the x, y and z axes, the world's rotation on the x axis is controlled by your mouse movement. It's as if the world has been pierced by a huge skewer that runs parallel to the monitor, and the ground tilts up or down depending on the mouse movement. So when the mouse moves up, the closer ground (between the axis "skewer" and you) moves up closer to you. It will level out, as the ground gets very close to your perspective. Keep moving up and the ground will rotate above your perspective, and you'll be looking up at the ground from below. Conversely, when the mouse moves down, that near ground moves down, placing your perspective high in the air, until you're looking straight down at the ground. Keep moving the mouse down and you'll eventually turn the world upside down as if you're in the air with the ground plane above you, or, to put it another way, you've moved over onto the other side of the world's *x* axis, suspended upside down. The left column in Figure 3–30 represents the results of moving the mouse up and down while in Flyaround mode.

Moving the mouse left to right does nothing (except for random vertical movements, as it's nigh unto impossible to move the mouse horizontally without introducing *some* vertical movement). The range of mouse movement to rotate the entire scene on the *x* axis is limited by the size of your monitor. The larger your monitor, the greater the number of full rotations you can do as you move the mouse up or down.

Now add a modifier key. Press the Command (Macintosh) or Ctrl (Windows) key and move the mouse up and down. Moving the mouse up and down will move you in and out of your scene, as you are closer to or further from World Center. Moving the mouse down brings the scene closer to you, while moving the mouse up pushes it back into the distance. This is movement on the *z* axis. The *z* axis here is always oriented between your vantage point and World Center. In Flyaround mode, you don't rotate the world on the *z* axis, you only move yourself closer or farther from World Center along the *z* axis. Once you press the Command or Ctrl key and move the mouse, you'll suspend all of the *x* axis rotation I described earlier. You'll stay at the same angle where you were just prior to pressing the Command or Ctrl key. The middle column in Figure 3–30 shows the results of moving the mouse up and down while the Command or Ctrl key is pressed in Flyaround mode.

Here, too, the limit of motion is determined by the distance between your mouse cursor and the monitor's edge. You may run out of mouse room before you've moved as far into your scene as you want to. (Picking up the mouse and setting it down again does nothing to give you additional room to move. Once you've hit the edge of the monitor, you're stuck there.) To get around this minor edge-of-monitor problem, release the Command or Ctrl key to go back into basic up and down motion, move the mouse up until you do a complete 360° flip of the scene to the same angle, with the mouse's cursor closer to the top of the monitor, then press the Command or Ctrl key and resume moving the mouse down so the scene continues toward you. True Command/Ctrl key gymnastics, that!

Finally, there is one more modifier key— the space bar. Pressing the space bar will pause the aerial rotation around the Brycean *y* axis. On the Macintosh, you need to keep the space bar pressed continuously to pause the rotation, whereas in Windows, a simple tap will pause the rotation. Tap again to resume rotation.

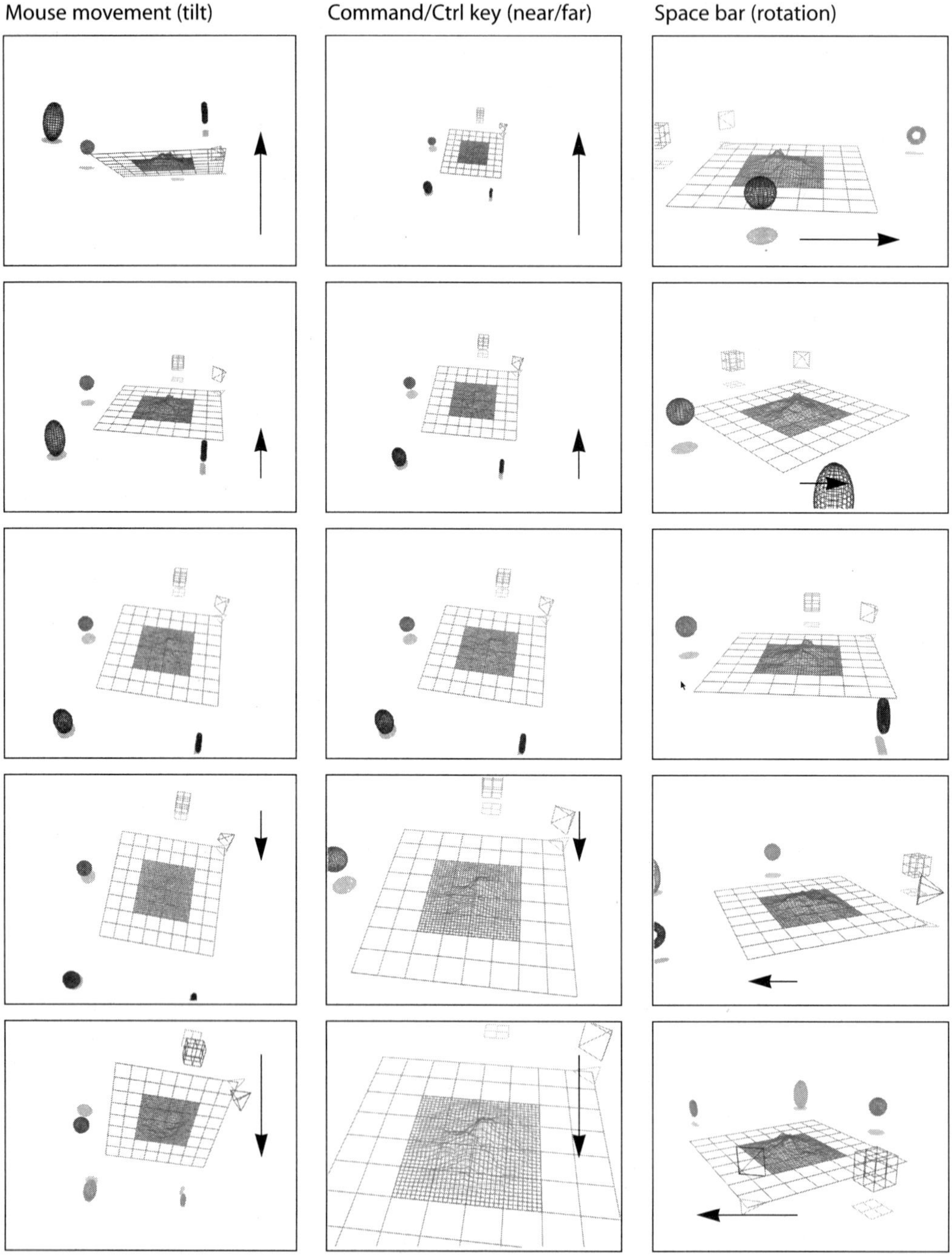

Mouse movement (tilt)   Command/Ctrl key (near/far)   Space bar (rotation)

Figure 3–30 Flyaround mode and mouse movements. Left column: mouse motion; Center column: mouse motion with Command/Ctrl key pressed; Right column: mouse motion with space bar pressed.

When it's paused, you can move the mouse left and right to control the rotation of the scene. You'll have none of this auto pilot stuff when you're pressing the space bar; you can still move the mouse up and down to adjust the "tilt" of the land, and press the Command or Ctrl key as well to move in and out of your scene. The right column in Figure 3–30 represents the change in rotation that occurs when dragging the mouse left to right with the space bar pressed in the Flyaround mode.

Although I compared the Flyaround mode to using the Trackball control, there is one difference. When the space bar is pressed, mouse movement is opposite that of the horizontal mouse movement when using the Trackball control. The Trackball rotates the world in the direction of the drag, whereas the Flyaround space bar/mouse movement rotates the world in the opposite direction. Go figure.

There You Are—The Conclusion

Finally, remember the Return (or Enter) key. All this mouse movement with the modifier keys amounts to diddley unless you press the Return key at the end to pop your camera position into this new place. For your peace of mind, don't just lightly tap the Return key, especially on the Macintosh. Press it down for a second or so. Bryce seems to take half a moment to register that the Return key has been pressed, and if for some reason it doesn't, then your carefully navigated new view will drift on by. (In Windows, the Enter key is quite responsive to the simple tap.) Here's my conjecture for this behavior: Once you're in Flyaround mode, Bryce tells the computer processor to "move the picture" and all the computer's resources are bent on moving the scene and displaying the image in a fluid manner. Your light tap on the Return key mayn't be long enough for the computer's processor to register that there's a change of state. Keeping the Return key pressed for a few "ticks" leaves no room for doubt.

Of course, you don't have to have the space bar pressed when you do hit the Return key to end this flyaround session. Press the Return key while the scene is still rotating. (I knew I had you pegged for the roulette gambler type!)

Before talking about some of the practical ways of working in Flyaround mode, here's a summary review of the process and a table that lists the movements you can make in Flyaround mode:

Flyaround is a combination of x, y, and z movement around the World Center. It begins with the world rotating on its vertical axis, much as our own Earth rotates. (This is the y axis.) You can manually control that by pressing the space bar and adjusting the rotation yourself. Then, with the addition of mouse movement up and down, you are adding the x axis, tilting the foreground toward you or away from you. The Command or Ctrl key mouse movement moves you on the z (or distance) axis closer to or farther away from the center of the world. (The z axis extends from World Center to wherever your camera is located.)

Modifier Key	Mouse Action	Result
	Mouse click	Exit Flyaround view
	Move mouse up/down	Changes "tilt"
Command or Ctrl key	Move mouse up/down	Closer and farther
Space bar		Stops Flyaround rotation
Space bar	Mouse left/right	Manual rotation
Return key		Changes camera view to current flyaround view

A Bit of Practice

All right. So now you know which is which. Use all three controls! Trade 'em with your friends (ahem, well…)! Once you've gotten the hang of the digital gymnastics (here digital means literal finger-digits), you can use them in combination to navigate your camera to the place you want.

The directions for this little exercise are quite simple; they're more as a guide to show you where to develop fluency and some eye-hand coordination skills. You'll probably have enough going on tangling your Command key (or Ctrl key), space bar key and Return key fingers and mouse up and down movements without having to crane your neck to peer at these pages for the next bit of instructions. What you need to do here is easier *done* than *said*! Think of this as practicing scales on the piano or another instrument; what you're doing right now is not really all that beautiful, but you'll develop skills for beautiful things down the road.

1. Create a scene file with a terrain at its center and various objects surrounding it. Or, open up the scene file entitled FLY AROUND ME! in the folder for Chapter 3 on the CD-ROM. Click the donut or type ⌘-Y (Macintosh) or Ctrl+Y (Windows). Welcome to the spinning world!

2. Move the mouse up and down. Find an angle that you like.

3. Press the Command key (Macintosh) or Ctrl key (Windows) and move the mouse up and down.

4. Try alternating between Command or Ctrl key pressed and unpressed. When you get up close to the terrain with the Command/Ctrl key pressed, let go of the Command/Ctrl key and readjust the angle. Press the Command/Ctrl key again and move closer or farther. Release the Command or Ctrl key.

    (If you need to move still closer, remember to release the Command or Ctrl key, move the mouse up to completely flip the world back around to place again, then press the Command/Ctrl key again and continue the move-mouse-down to move-World-Center closer. Snazzy, eh?)

This next step introduces the space bar.

5. Press the space bar. (If you're on a Mac, keep it pressed. If you're on Windows, tap the space bar once to stop the rotation.) Move the mouse left and right. Now move the mouse up and down.

6. While the space bar is still down (Mac) or while the rotation is still stopped (Windows), press the Command or Ctrl key, and move the mouse down to move closer to World Center.

7. With both space bar and Command (or Ctrl) key pressed, move the mouse left and right. Try moving the mouse in diagonal movements.

8. With the space bar still pressed (or the rotation stopped), press the Return key.

Saving Camera Views

The way cool thing about the camera is that you are not limited to one particular view. The freedom to explore a scene from different perspectives leads to the question, "which one should I pick?". Bryce allows you to store the options so that you can go back and forth between those contenders for *the* perspective on the scene. The Memory Dots in Bryce 2 significantly differ from the method used by Bryce 1 to store camera view settings. This section will focus on Bryce 2's controls, but will also mention some procedures you should do to the saved camera views from your old Bryce 1 scene files before opening that scene file in Bryce 2.

Memory Dots

Bryce 2 enables you to save up to seven camera settings simultaneously (besides the default setting) in the Memory Dots section, to the left of the Nano Preview window. The settings are saved with your scene file, so they'll be there when you open up the scene again. When you create a new scene, it inherits the Memory

Dots from the previous saved scene. Though you automatically transfer settings to new scene files, you can't transfer them from one saved Bryce scene file to another one that has already been saved. ⌘-N or Ctrl+N (new scene) transfers settings; ⌘-O or Ctrl+O (open scene) does not. If you want to transfer a camera setting from one saved scene file to another, open up the Camera controls dialog box for the scene whose camera setting you want, jot down all the numbers, open the transfer-to scene and enter those numbers into the Camera dialog box for that scene.

How the Dots Work

The Memory Dots take on three different appearances depending on the state of the dot. When there are no camera views saved, the dot is light gray, matching the background. Green means that something is saved. The white spot on green means that "this saved view is currently active;" the camera is using that view dot at the moment. The camera Memory Dots can all be white, all green, or a mix of the two, but you'll never find more than one memory dot that is green with the white spot. (See Figure 3–31.) This is true even if you click all the dots from the same camera view. Only one will show the green-with-white-spot dot. The top one, set apart slightly from the rest, is "hard-wired;" it is the default view.

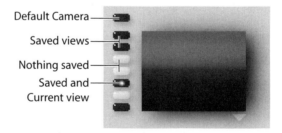

Default Camera
Saved views
Nothing saved
Saved and
Current view

Figure 3–31 The camera Memory Dots.

The first click on a gray dot will save that particular camera view. Once clicked, the dot turns green-with-a-white-spot. Suppose you want to alter that particular view? Once you move the camera's position (or adjust the 2D plane), the dot loses its white spot. Anytime after the dot is green, a simple click will switch the camera's position to the setting stored there. At that point, the green dot again becomes the green-with-white-spot dot. To clear the camera setting, press the Option (Macintosh) or Alt (Windows) key when clicking the green spot. That turns the dot back to the neutral gray. Remember the Option-click (or Alt-click).

After clicking once to create the setting, it's far too easy to do one last little (inevitable) tweak and say, "*now* it's right," click the green dot again, and—oops!—pop back to the previous position. Don't follow the inevitable tweak with an inevitable sigh or growl, remember to Option-click or Alt-click to reset the setting. You can then click again to set the new improved tweaked camera view in the camera Memory Dots.

Incidentally, Option-(or-Alt)-click-to-reset is a new MetaTools interface standard, implemented here in Bryce 2. Get used to it; you'll be seeing more of it elsewhere, and you won't go wrong to invoke it to clear out a setting back to the default or neutral state.

What, No Names?

If you've used Bryce 1 and saved camera settings, you've probably wondered where the names of saved camera views went to in Bryce 2. I join you there. Unlike BoPeep's sheep, I don't think that they'll come back on their own. Instead of 16 possible named views, you have a total of seven numbered views.

This loss of more than half the capacity, coupled with the inability to name camera views, is one "feature" of Bryce 2 that I hate. It's very odd… the developers placed high priority—and a bit of fanfare—on Bryce 2's new ability to give names to presets for materials, objects, and skies, complete with additional descriptions to help jog your memory. You can do this and your names will be displayed in way cool anti-aliased type, to boot. Yet for camera positions, the ability to refer to them by name was taken away. Those who are building one scene for which there are many camera views will have to count on their toes and fingers to remember which one is which. I miss the old way, and look forward to something reappearing again in the next evolution of Bryce, so I can save many camera settings and call each one by name.

What becomes of the saved settings from Bryce 1 scenes when they are opened up in Bryce 2? (If you haven't used Bryce 1 or you're on the Windows platform, ignore the rest of this section!) Bryce 2 does import settings from Bryce 1 scenes. However, since Bryce 1 scenes can hold 16 settings and Bryce 2 scenes hold seven, you'll probably have to pare down camera views before you bring an older scene into Bryce 2. The Bryce 1 camera numbering in the Camera controls dialog box was changed substantially for Bryce 2. You can't copy numbering from one version to the other.

Note: When you open up a Bryce 1 scene in Bryce 2, you won't see a green-with-white-spot dot for any of the options until you click one of the dots. In Bryce 2 you already clicked a dot to set it in the first place, so the first Memory Dot that you set will display the green-with-white-spot dot.

This section is to prepare Bryce 1 scenes for work in Bryce 2. Open up your scene in Bryce 1. On the Master Palette, access the Views pop-up menu. How many saved views are there? If there are more than seven, you won't get all of them when you open the scene in Bryce 2. Very likely, you don't want the ones that are there at the top. Figure 3–32a shows the Bryce 1 saved views for a particular scene. Image b shows the Bryce 2 equivalent for that same scene, with lines drawn between them to show what "made it in" and what was left behind. The Bryce 1 list has the nearly ubiquitous compass directions at the top, followed by views 1 and 2. They are crowding out the valuable saved views. You probably won't need the top options, so go ahead and delete them so that you can focus on the remainder, your own special favorites.

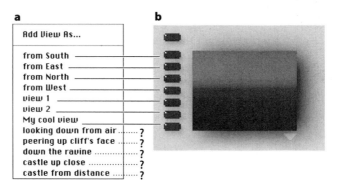

Figure 3–32 Transferring saved views from Bryce 1 to Bryce 2: a) Bryce 1's list of saved views; b) Bryce 2's Memory Dots with all slots filled.

Compare the lists in Figure 3–33a through c. Part a has all the unnecessary views at the top. Those are the ones to get rid of. To delete views, press the Option key when accessing the menu. Part b shows what the menu looks like when you do so: all the options are listed as "Delete view such 'n such." Part c shows the result of deleting the west view. The bottom item on the list jumped to fill the vacated place.

So by the time you've finished purging the fluff from the top of the camera views list, your views will be mixed up in a different order. If you need to have them be in a certain order when you open them up in Bryce 2, you'll have to endure a few twists and turns.

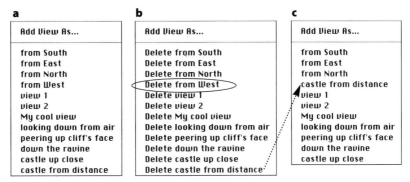

Figure 3-33 Comparison of Views pop-up menus from Bryce 1: a) The list at the beginning; b) when getting ready to delete a view; c) the result of "Delete from West."

Whatever you delete will be not replaced by the next item in the list, but by the bottom item in the list. So you can duplicate items you want to the bottom of the list. First, go to the view you want to duplicate. It's your current view. You can save it again. Do so by selecting the Add view as… option in the menu. When you delete something at the top of the list, that newly-created item will pop to the top. You can do an add-delete, add-delete routine until you have set the top seven options to have the views that you want in the order that you want.

If you need to keep more than seven views, save two versions of the scene, with different views removed (as a shortcut, you can open up a new scene in Bryce 1 and the saved camera view list will be carried over)

Think Like a Photographer!

A final note. Think like a photographer! You are both creating a world and then making a picture of it, so when you set up your camera position you will be doing the same things that all photographers do when they make pictures: composing the shot.

If you are a photographer, or you've taken any photography classes, you'll recall that the discussion on composition relates to what you're doing in Bryce. Here are a few compositional pointers.

Vary the Horizon Line

Bryce's default position for the horizon line is smack dab in the middle. It cuts your image right in half. It's more interesting and pleasing to place the horizon lower or higher than exact center. Try the upper third or lower third as an alternative. The top row of Figure 3–34 shows different horizon lines. Compare the image divided in half (on the left) with the asymmetrical division of other two. See how boring the half and half is? The others are more pleasing and balanced. In both asymmetrical cases, one side is dominant and the other is secondary. As a result, your eye is led to look at one side or the other.

Feature a Dominant Element

Your image will have some elements that are dominant and others that are secondary. If all are dominant or all are secondary, the image will not be as interesting.

Look at your image. Are there lines or elements that lead your eye toward the one dominant element?

The middle row of Figure 3–34 shows various placements of a single terrain in an image. The left image is the standard Bryce default: center terrain on a centered horizon. Boring. The others in that row are more interesting. In the center image, the terrain is not centered. Combine that with a high horizon, and there is a focus on the terrain in the lower left, with a dominant diagonal line, all of which is balanced by the open space to the right. The right image takes things further. A gradual series of diagonals levels out as the terrain becomes more distant.

The images in the bottom row show more complex compositions. The left image has flowing s-shaped lines. Your eye is led from the front to the back. The center image has a contrast between vertical lines on the left and horizontal lines on the right. The right image has foreground elements, which frame the distant terrain.

If all this composition stuff is new to you, try this. On a blank piece of paper, use a pencil to draw a series of rectangular boxes, similar to those shown in the figure. They don't have to be big. Make them about the size of large postage stamps. Then fill them in with different strokes. Round, angular, squiggly, whatever. Make a few strokes in one, then go on to the next. Don't consciously try to make landscape thumbnails. (If you are making landscape thumbnails, fine; don't fight it.) Just play and go for interesting shapes. When you have a half a dozen to a dozen, stop and look back over them. Are there any that you prefer? Why? When you can think of why, even if it's not necessarily a left-brain verbalized understanding, you're on your way to developing a sense of what makes a good composition.

Another composition idea: Look at some published material that has landscape or nature photography, such as *National Geographic, Arizona Highways,* and *Audubon,*

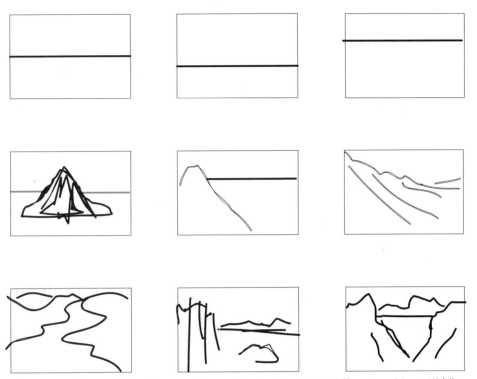

Figure 3–34 Composition elements. Top row: The horizon line in different positions; Middle row: dominant element in different positions; Bottom row: more complex compositions.

coffee table books, and Sierra Club calendars. Analyze the images that you find appealing. What is it about this or that one that makes it nice?

If you're interested in more on the composition and design of your world, there is an excellent book on design: *Design Basics*, by David A Lauer and Stephen Pentak (Harcourt Brace College Publishers). It explains the basics of design, using many examples.

So, as you are composing your picture, keep in mind the following:

• Include some kind of dominant line in the image.

• Sticking with the horizontal format isn't necessary. For a more dynamic, striking, image, try vertical.

• Add lines in the image. For example, diagonal and serpentine shapes draw your eye into and through the image.

• Place something close for interest and something far away for scale.

Other things you can do as a "photographer" of your Bryce image:

• Adjust the camera position. What was dull seen from one perspective becomes downright visually engaging when seen from another. Photographers do it all the time.

• Change the focal length of the lens. Use the Field of View control to adjust the angle of the lens. Skies are wonderful when you open the angle of vision way up wide.

• Adjust the time of day. Photographers are notorious for going to places at certain times of day, looking for the most dramatic light. The best time of day is just after sunrise and just before sunset. Midday lighting tends to be harsh. When working in Bryce, though, you don't need to go out at sunrise in order to capture the delicate light of dawn. All you need to do is adjust the light in your Bryce scene.

All of this thinking about taking photographic concepts into Bryce is reciprocal. The "Photography and Bryce" sidebar by Scott Tucker provides a perspective of an experienced Brycer who finds new depth in his photography after using Bryce for a year and a half.

A Photo Bonus Sidebar
Photography and Bryce

BY SCOTT TUCKER

In photography we are always trying to convey the wonderful landscape we saw and bring it back to the viewer as best we can, just the way we saw it. The challenge comes from representing that 3D world we saw (reality) on a two-dimensional piece of photographic paper or slide. Bryce has made me so aware of the spatial relationships of things and the result is much more depth in my photographs. Technically, I always knew what to do (stop down the lens and use a tripod) but until I gained this heightened spatial awareness (via Bryce), I just wasn't always *really* thinking about the 3D-ness of what I was shooting. Building 3D worlds in Bryce showed me how objects work together in space—in there I move around objects specifically thinking that my final goal is a two-dimensional representation of these objects in the main view. All this spatial-ness has carried forward to my photography. Now, when I shoot a picture I am automatically aware that I need to convey that sense of depth to the viewer. Now I really see that foreground rock and how it can be used to show that zone in space. Now I really see that middle ground and out to the horizon. Moving objects around in Bryce has taught me how to positively convey a 3D world on a 2D plane.

The best news is this: in Bryce we are always photographing our worlds. I have spent hundreds, probably thousands of hours in Bryce walking around with that little blue camera and taking photographs. I could never do as much work on my photography as I have in Bryce this past year and a half. Bryce lets me take those field trips at night when the Brycean sun still shines undaunted! Don't get me wrong, Bryce is not a substitute for fresh air, a good hike, and some work on the photographic skills. Bryce is a proving ground, it is a holo-deck for photography—for the art of photography. When I do venture forth into the real world the photos are so much better, because of all the virtual hours I have logged in Bryce.

CHAPTER FOUR

Brycean Objects

Milo… glanced curiously at the strange circular room, whose sixteen tiny arched windows corresponded exactly to the sixteen points of the compass. Around the entire circumference were numbers from zero to three hundred and sixty, marking the degrees of the circle, and on the floor, walls, tables, chairs, desks, cabinets, and ceiling were labels showing their heights, widths, depths, and distances to and from each other.

NORTON JUSTER, *THE PHANTOM TOLLBOOTH*

IN THIS CHAPTER...

- Bryce objects
- All about the object's Object attributes
- Bryce's internal matrix
- Object wireframes
- Selecting Bryce objects
- Solo mode

Bryce objects are the building blocks for your scenes. This chapter will take a look at each object type, noting *what* the objects are, and examining the object matrix and object attributes. Since all objects are displayed in wireframe view, this chapter will examine the controls for wireframe display. Finally, this chapter examines the different options available to select an object or set of objects, including the Solo mode. When it comes to the palettes of Bryce, this chapter concerns itself with the

Create Palette, the Wireframe Palette (lower half of Display/Wireframe Palette on the right), and the Selection Palette.

WHICH OBJECTS

All objects in Bryce, with a couple of exceptions, are created from the Create Palette (see Figure 4–1). This section will break them down into their logical groupings.

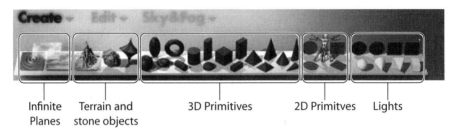

Infinite Planes   Terrain and stone objects   3D Primitives   2D Primitves   Lights

Figure 4–1 Create Palette.

Infinite Planes Three

There are three types of infinite planes. While in wireframe view they seem to be limited in size, they actually stretch out infinitely in all four (flat) directions. Figure 4–2 is a scene made from three infinite planes (the ground plane at a tilt). The wireframes for each plane are showing.

Figure 4–2 The three infinite planes create a scene, with wireframes showing.

Terrain/Stone Objects

Whereas in Bryce 1 there was but one terrain type—the terrain— Bryce 2 has added two more: the symmetrical lattice, a modified terrain form; and the stone, a free-standing polyhedron. See Figure 4–3.

- *Terrain.* The terrain object is the basis of Bryce' mountains, and other "injection mold" shapes that have nothing whatsoever to do with mountains. When terrains are created, their shape is randomly generated with fractal noise for rugged, rocky shapes.

Figure 4–3 The terrain and stone objects: terrain, symmetrical lattice, and stone.

This is the old, the familiar, the tried and true staple to Bryce scene making.

- *Symmetrical Lattice.* Cousin to the terrain object, the symmetrical lattice is the equivalent of two identical mirror-shaped terrains placed back-to-back. Like the terrain, each symmetrical lattice is created with a unique random shape, and is based upon editable grayscale-to-height information that can be changed in the Terrain Editor.

- *Stone.* This is a polyhedron object, created inside of Bryce. Like the terrain and the symmetrical lattice, each new stone is a randomly generated shape. No two are exactly alike—unless duplicated, of course.

3D Primitives

Bryce primitives are simple geometric shapes—the literal building blocks of Brycean worlds. Most of the 3D Primitives—with the exception of the torus—come with two variations, a stretched and a squashed version. They also may be rotated from their original native position.

- *Sphere.* It's round! It's a geometrical object that is equidistant from one point. It's a sphere. In Figure 4–4a, the bull's eye disk shows how the object's shape radiates from the center.

- *Torus.* This primitive is new to Bryce 2. It, too, is round, like a tire's inner tube or donut. Geometrically, it's a circle with another circle extending from it. The first circle defines how big the object is, and the second defines how fat the tube-part is. See Figure 4–4b

- *Cylinder.* Here's another roundish object. Flat on top and bottom with round sides, the cylinder has a straight vertical spine, and its round barrel side edge is determined by an equidistant measure from that spine. See Figure 4–4c. The cylinder is the variation-hog of the Bryce Create Palette, having the most variations (four). Perhaps it stole one of those spots from the torus, which has but one?

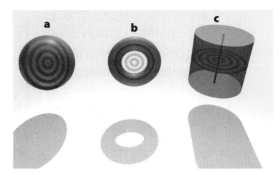

Figure 4–4 The "round" objects of Bryce: a) Sphere, b) torus and c) cylinder.

- *Cube*. The basic square building block, the cube is a six-sided square. You can't get more basic than this. See Figure 4–5a.

- *Pyramid*. This is a five-sided polygon, with a square bottom and triangular faces as the object converges to a point at the top. See Figure 4–5b.

- *Cone*. The cone is also a converging shape. It starts out with a circular base, with a smooth, continuous face that focuses at the top. See Figure 4–5c.

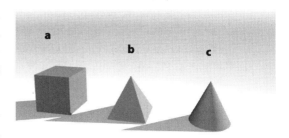

Figure 4–5 Square objects and cone.

2D Primitives

2D Primitives are flat geometrical shapes, they don't take well to booleanizing. Figure 4–6 shows a sample of each type of object.

- *2D Circle/Disk*. It's round, it's flat, it's a disk.

- *2D Square*. The square is, well, square: flat with four sides.

- *2D Pict Object*. This is a specialized square. It opens up directly to the Picture library,

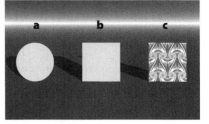

Figure 4–6 2D Primitives: a) Circle; b) square; c) pict object.

where you assign the picture for the object, and then it emerges into the scene, scaled to the aspect ratio of the picture.

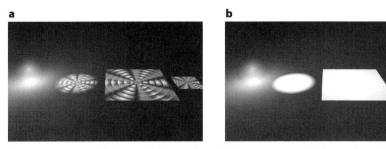

Figure 4–7 Bryce lights: radial, round spotlight, square spotlight, and parallel spotlight. a) Casting light through a Pict Gel; b) unadorned.

Lights

Bryce now has light sources other than the primary sun. These are shaped like four primitives. Each casts light in a different manner. Figure 4–7 depicts each type of light, casting light alone (default) and creating light patterns using a Pict Gel. I'll discuss more about lights in depth in Chapter 11, "Bryce EnLightenment".

- *Radial.* Radial light. A sphere light bulb (or, more accurately, orb).

- *Round Spotlight.* A cone that projects a circle of light in one direction.

- *Square Spotlight.* A pyramid that casts a square-shaped light in one direction.

- *Parallel Spotlight.* A square that projects light without any spread.

Special Case "Objects"

There are two other types of objects. You won't find them in the Create Palette, but they are treated as separate object types by Bryce in selection controls.

- *File > Import Object…* Import 3D objects created in other modeling applications. Bryce refers to them as polyhedrons. They don't enter the scene by the Create Palette, but by the File menu. The types of file formats Bryce imports are DXF

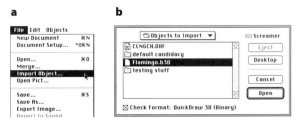

Figure 4–8 Import objects: a) Command from the File menu ; b) resulting dialog box for selecting 3D models.

and 3DMF (Quick Draw 3D, Apple's 3D Format). (See Figure 4–8.) More file formats will be added to the list as import plug-ins are developed.

- *Groups.* Here is another not-an-object that is treated like an object. A group is a set of objects, that, when grouped, acts like one object (see Chapter 6, "Editing and the Bryce Internal Grid," for more about groups). When it comes to selecting a category of object, though, groups are treated like a distinct object type. Figure 4–9 shows a grouped set of tori along with the other special case objects.

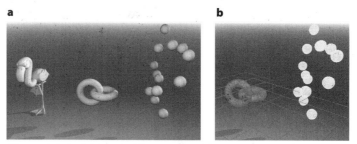

Figure 4–9 Special case objects: a) 3D object import, a grouped set of tori, a family of spheres; b) wireframe view showing family coloring for spheres.

- *Object Families.* Though not its own object type, there are times when Bryce Object Families are treated as an object category all their own. This is a good thing, as you may have different types of objects (say, a sphere, cylinder, and cube) and you want to work with that collection as its own category or family. Object Families will do that. There are a total of 25 possible families. Each has its own color and can be assigned its own name, as well. (This is the Bryce 2 Equivalent of the KPT Bryce 1's "Wireframe Color.") Figure 4–9b shows the unique coloring (depicted as grayscale values) of the wireframe family for sphere family members.

When objects are newly created in Bryce they get the charcoal gray "Default Family" designation. Change them to another color using the Object Family dialog box (called a plop-up by the program's creators; see the section on plop-up dialog boxes in Chapter 5, "Streamline Your Brycing" for more info). The way to the Object Family plop-up is through the small square color icon that shows when you select a Brycean object.

This is the closest that Bryce gets to creating object hierarchies, and the closest to any sort of a list of the objects in a scene.

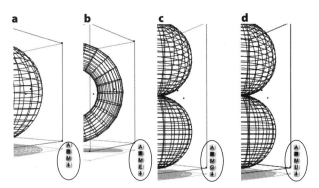

Figure 4–10 Modification icons for selected Bryce objects: a) Single object selected; b) object editable with E; c) two objects selected with G group option; d) grouped objects with U for ungrouping.

OBJECT CONTROLS

As you've probably figured out by now, there is a set of controls associated with any selected object or set of selected objects. They show up in the wireframe view. There are up to seven different quick modifications that can be accessed by the icon controls that are next to the wireframe object. The modification icons show up when the object is selected (Figure 4–10). Here is a quick list of them. Different ones show up at different times, depending on the conditions present. Most of them are doorways to dialog boxes, but some of them are not.

• *Object Attributes.* The A icon. This leads to the plop-up dialog box that determines where the object is positioned in Bryce Space.

• *Object Color.* This color swatch matches the object's wireframe color. It is the doorway to the Families plop-up dialog box, where the object can be assigned to any of the 25 families, the family name edited, and the wireframe color edited.

• *Edit Object.* For certain objects (terrain, stone, symmetrical lattice, torus, light objects, imported 3D polyhedron objects), clicking the E icon will take you into a place where you can perform some Edit function that is particular to that object. For instance, in the Terrain/Object Editor, you can smooth the polygons, adjust the torus' center, or adjust the lights.

• *Edit Materials.* The M icon takes you to the Materials Composer.

The next set of modification options do not take you into a separate room or dialog box.

- *Ground/Land Object*. The up or down arrow will land the object.

- *Group Object*. When more than one object is selected, there is the option to group them together by clicking the box labeled G.

- *Ungroup Object*. Any grouped object will display the U button to ungroup.

  If you have selected several objects, including a group and other objects, you'll see both the option to group all of them and to ungroup the group. (There is your maximum of seven possible modifier icons. If you find more than that, let me know!)

OBJECT ATTRIBUTES

This is a discussion of the Object Options plop up dialog box. When you access the dialog box, you see some Bryce-styled checkboxes and numerical entries. There are two sets of attributes in the checkbox items. The left column concerns itself with boolean matters. The right column is a combination of wireframe display and locking. Figure 4–11 shows the Object Attributes dialog box.

Figure 4–11 Object Attributes dialog box.

Boolean attributes. The left column of attributes has three items that determine whether a special combination of objects takes place. When two or more objects overlap, boolean attributes can create an altogether different resuting shape. The default is Positive on the Macintosh, and neutral on Windows (no item checked in left column). No substantive change occurs when objects are in the default state. When the two objects overlap, it appears as though they occupy the same space. When Negative is checked, the object's shape will be subtracted out of another object which it overlaps. When Intersect is checked, all you will see is the area that is common to both objects. In Windows, when Positive is checked, you won't be able to see any seam between the two objects. The objects must be grouped together in order to have a boolean effect. (See Chapter 7, "Booleans and Multiple Object Construction," for more about booleans.)

Locked objects. When your wireframe appears as locked, then the wireframe is gray. You cannot select it by directly clicking the object, but you can select it by using other select controls (see later in this chapter for more on selecting objects). Even though you can select the object, you cannot edit it in any way. The only purpose for selecting it is to change it back to unlocked using the

Object Attributes plop-up dialog box. Figure 4–12 shows a locked object. The wireframe color is gray, even though it's still considered to be a part of a distinct family.

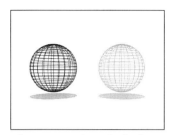

You can group a locked object. But it does not move when you move the group. You can also make changes to it in the Object Attributes dialog box. If you make it negative and then group it with another object, the locked object will be part of a

Figure 4–12 An unlocked and locked sphere.

boolean group. Similarly, any numerical changes that are made in the Object Attributes dialog box will change the object. Consider locking in this way: you won't be able to make accidental changes to the object through an inadvertent drag here or a wayward click there. Doing so in the Object Attributes dialog box will change the object, since, once you've entered there, Bryce assumes that you probably know what you're doing. You can duplicate a locked object, but the newly duplicated object remains locked.

Other things that you can do with locked objects: change wireframe color, boolean, change size through the Object Attributes dialog box, and group. A locked object responds to selecting by family, select all, select by type, tabbing through, and arrow selecting (for more on selecting, see the Selecting section later in this chapter).

Show as box. This will take the wireframe and display it as a box. The keyboard equivalent for this is ⌘-B (Macintosh) or Ctrl+B (Windows). To change back to the normal wireframe view, type ⌘-L (Macintosh) or Ctrl+L (Windows); show as lattice. When you are working with complex scenes where the task of displaying all those wireframes weighs Bryce down and consequently makes it run as fast as molasses, displaying

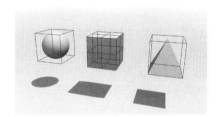

Figure 4–13 Wireframes shown as boxes compared with the normal cube wireframe.

wireframes as boxes will speed things up. See Chapter 5, "Streamline Your Brycing," for a bit more on this. Figure 4–13 displays three objects rendered with wireframes showing; the cube object in the middle has lines on the center of each of its six planes, distinguishing it from the plain-sidedness of the show-as-box object wireframes.

Numerical attributes. Bryce objects have three sets of characteristics, all measured on the *x, y,* and *z* axes.

• *Size.* Each object has its own size, or width, height and depth dimensions.

• *Position.* Each object occupies its own position in the three-dimensional space. Think of this as location. How far is it offset from World Center (the center of Bryce's world)?

• *Orientation.* Each is oriented in the three-dimensional space. It can be rotated on any of the three axes: *x, y,* and *z* .

They are the size of the object, the offset from World Center and the object's rotation. The units for both offset and size are in Bryce's special binary numbering. The default size of objects is 20.48 Bryce units. The default offset depends on a Preferences setting. The Bryce default is to create the object in view. The other choice is to create the object at World Center. Then the object rests upon the ground, but its center is aligned with World Center. (This is true for the default-sized objects, the stretched and squashed ones act a bit differently.) The numerical setting for resting on the ground is half of the size of the object's height. So, for an object whose default size is 20.48, the offset for *y* (altitude) will be half of that, or 10.24. When objects are created in view, then the offset depends on the camera height and other things. The object will be created so that its center visually lines up with the horizon line (see Figure 4–14). For stretched and squashed objects, the vertical offset is 20.48. Since stretched objects are twice as tall as normal objects, stretched objects are created so that they rest on the ground. Squashed objects are generally one-half to one-quarter height, so they float in the air above the ground, but not so high that they are at horizon level. Figure 4–14b and c shows how this works with both representative stretched and squashed objects, and a basic cube wireframe for comparison.

a
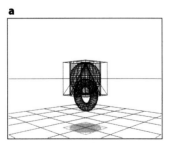

b
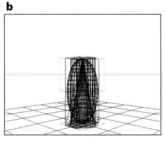

c
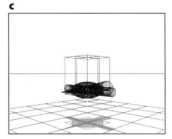

Figure 4–14 Default sizes of different types of primitives: a) Basic standard objects; b) stretched objects; c) squashed objects.

For more particulars on the binary numerical units for Bryce, see Chapter 6, "Editing and the Bryce Internal Grid."

Object Position. How far away is the object from World Center? This is called offset, since it measures how far an object is offset from World Center. For an object to be at World Center, it is positioned at 0, 0, 0. The object itself is measured from its own center. So, for an object to be resting on World Center but be grounded on the ground, it will be at 0 x and 0 z, but on the y axis, it will be half of the number of the height. For newly created objects that haven't been resized, that amount will be 10.24, as it is half of 20.48, the default dimension for primitives. Figure 4–15a shows this, with an object created, appearing above World Center, and when the preferences are set for creating at World Center (Figure 4–15b). In Figure 4–15c, the object is shown as it is created, resting on the ground at World Center.

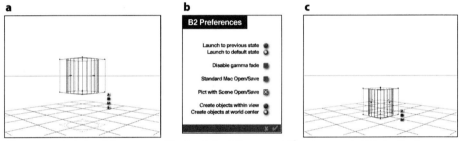

Figure 4–15 a) An object created in the default "create within view mode;" b) the Preferences dialog box; c) the object created at World Center.

MATRIX

As mentioned, all the numerical settings in the Object Attributes dialog box comprise the object's *matrix*. These three sets of attributes are the object's size, (height, width, depth), orientation in space (rotation) and a location, or offset. Besides the Object Attributes dialog box, the object matrix can be adjusted in the Edit controls by using the Three R's controls— Resize, Rotate, and Reposition. The 3D Transformation dialog box, accessed through the Edit Palette, also adjusts the object's attributes. (See Chapter 6, "Editing and the Internal Bryce Grid," for more information on 3D transformations.) You can also copy and paste only the matrix information for an object by using the Copy Matrix and Paste Matrix commands under the Edit menu.

How Bryce Thinks in Its Own Internal Matrix

As you start working in your scene, click the various create object icons and the object wireframes appear. You adjust them and then go on from there. How does Bryce keep track of all objects? It has an internal database of them. As each object is created, it is added to the master list, with all the different attributes following along. The object matrix is a part of the database.

Here's a hypothetical example of a scene. Follow along if you'd like to.

1.   Create a new scene (⌘-N on the Macintosh, Ctrl+N on Windows). There is a ground infinite plane there already. Click Create Torus. Press the right arrow key three times to move the torus along the *x* axis.

2.   Create Stone. Press the down arrow key three times to move the stone forward along the *z* axis. Click the down arrow to land it on the ground. See Figure 4–16a for the scene at this point.

3.   Create Pyramid. Press the left arrow key five times.

4.   Create a terrain. See Figure 4–16b.

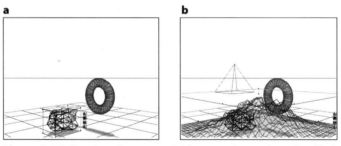

Figure 4-16 Creating the scene: a) After creating and moving the torus and stone; b) after creating pyramid and terrain.

So how does Bryce refer to the objects? There is a database with entries for all the attributes. If Bryce were a spreadsheet application, listing the object attributes in different cells, then Figure 4–17 shows what the scene would look like. First, each object type is listed in the order it was created. Then the attributes that comprise the object matrix are listed for each object. Finally, additional elements, such as material setting, whether the object is locked or is part of a boolean operation, are included.

How would you like it if *this* were your Bryce scene? Yuck. Yes, I agree. I prefer looking at the wireframe view of the scene to see which is which. Even better, I

Order	Object Type	Offset X	Offset Y	Offset Z	Rotate X	Rotate Y	Rotate Z	Size X	Size Y	Size Z
1	Infinite Plane	20.48	0.01	-20.48	0°	0°	0°	163.84	20.48	163.84
2	Torus	35.84	20.48	-20.48	-90°	0°	0°	20.48	20.48	20.48
3	Stone	20.48	7.78	-35.84	0°	0°	0°	23.8726	15.5934	29.5384
4	Pyramid	-5.12	30.72	-20.48	0°	0°	0°	81.92	20.48	81.92
5	Terrain	20.48	10.24	-20.48	0°	0°	0°	81.92	20.48	81.92
6										
7										
8										
9										
10										

Figure 4-17 Bryce scene as a spreadsheet.

like looking at the final render. Phooey on all this internal database stuff, right? Well, yes, for the most part. There will be a couple of times when it's important to be aware of the database and the *creation order* when you're dealing with sets of Bryce objects. The important thing to note here is that there are times when the creation order matters. There will be times when there might be adjustments to more than one object, the "eldest" object will take precedence. This will explain some seeming quirks in editing the materials for several objects. When you select several objects having different surface materials, and then you access the Materials Composer, the material you'll edit will be the one belonging to the eldest of the objects. (By clicking the OK check mark to leave the Materials Composer, you'll assign the eldest object's material to all the selected objects.)

Practical Matrix Uses

If you haven't been a matrix copier and paster before now, you will be. Once you've started using the Copy Matrix and Paste Matrix commands, there's no going back. So then, what are some of the practical uses for copying and pasting an object's matrix?

Updating different versions of the same scene. Say you are working on a scene. You have made some adjustments to that scene and saved it with a different name. Your scenes are related, however, and what you've done to the one you want to do to the others. After making one edit to an object, copy the matrix, save the scene, then open up the other scene and select the object and paste the matrix. It pops right into place.

Special Case Alignment. You have an object that you want to align with another object. You want the new one to take on the exact placement of the older one (or close enough). Instead of using the alignment tools (explained more in Chapter 6, "Editing and the Bryce Internal Grid"), copy and paste the matrix.

Generating a new object to take an old object's place. Say you want to replace a certain object with a newly created object, and you want the newly created object to be sized and positioned right where the old one was. Select the old object. Copy matrix. Delete the object. Create a new object. Paste matrix. Voila! So easy! So convenient! How did we ever get along without it? (Of course, you may have to copy and paste the old object's material, too... in that case, don't delete the old one just yet.)

A close corrollary to copying and pasting the matrix is to use the Object Conversion tool on the Edit Palette, described briefly in the next section, with more elaboration in Chapter 6, "Editing and the Internal Bryce Grid."

68K to PPC and Pyramid Objects (Macintosh only)

There's a little leftover thing from Bryce 1 that yet lives on in Bryce 2.1. Pyramids created in scenes on 68K Macs will render weirdly when the scene files are later transferred to and rendered in Bryce running on a Power Mac. Rather than a pyramid, the result is a scary multi-colored thing that stretches way out in one direction. Eeeew. Happily, though the problem still exists, the solution is far simpler. Select the pyramid. In the Edit Palette under the object transform, select pyramid. You are changing the pyramid to a pyramid. Ta-Daaa! A Power Mac pyramid, good as new!

WIREFRAME OBJECT

As you work with your Bryce objects, you will be working in Bryce's wireframe view. As part of this consideration of all Brycean objects, this next section examines the workings of wireframes. To the right of the Bryce user interface, there is the Display/Wireframe Palette. The lower grouping of controls affects the appearance of wireframes. (See Figure 4–18.) These controls aid you in the care and feeding of your Bryce wireframe objects.

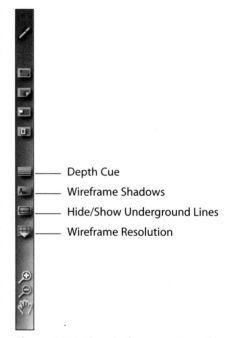

—— Depth Cue
—— Wireframe Shadows
—— Hide/Show Underground Lines
—— Wireframe Resolution

Figure 4–18 The wireframe portion of the palette on the right of the Bryce scene window.

Adjustments That Can Be Made to Wireframe Views

Bryce's adjustments enable you to change how the wireframe is displayed on your screen. Compared to a render, which takes a while to complete, a wireframe view is an instantaneous rendition of the objects in your scene. However, "instantaneous" is a relative term. Depending on the number of objects, the amount of detail to the wireframe, and the speed of your particular computer, Bryce will take *some* amount of time to display the object. The lower the amount of detail, the more "instant" the display. The higher the wireframe detail, the more laggard the display.

There are three settings you can adjust to see the objects. Those are accessed from the bottom of the wireframe section.

They are motion, static, and selected. In all three cases, the higher the number, the more detail you'll see; hence the longer it takes for Bryce to draw the scene on the screen. This is why the motion wireframe numbers are lower than the static and selected ones; Bryce has to display them while you are dragging the terrain from point A to point B—showing every step in between.

- *Motion.* This is the type of wireframe displayed when you are moving objects, camera, or are in Flyaround view.

- *Static.* This is what you see when camera and objects are at rest.

- *Selected.* This is what you see when you have one or more objects selected (while at rest).

The Selected setting, new in Bryce 2, lets you look at certain wireframes in higher detail than the rest. After all, it stands to reason that you want to know about the object you've selected. Say, for example, you are moving a terrain. If you set the static wireframe setting to some high obscene number (such as 64), it'll take Bryce a while to show your scene. Each time you make a change, you'll have to wait for the wireframe to update in a manner that will be painfully reminiscent of the days of very slow computers. So you can split the difference and make all your wireframes coarser than coarse when they're at rest, and throw all the computing effort into displaying the selected object. That way you can get a feel for more of the object's detail while working with it. Figure 4–19a shows the minimum setting for an object, 16, whereas b shows the maximum, 64.

So what setting do you give to each of these three settings? Find a happy medium between the amount of detail you need to see and the amount of speed you can

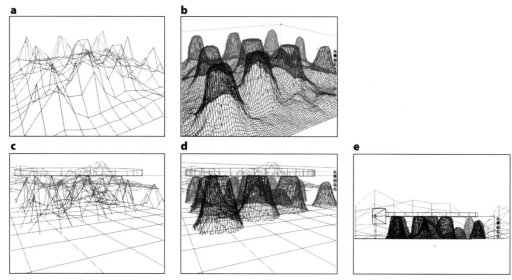

Figure 4–19 Wireframes at different resolutions: a) Static terrain at 16; b) selected terrain at 64; c) confusing jumble of objects at static setting of 16; d) greater clarity with selected objects at higher setting; e) side view for alignment.

live with. Your happy medium will probably be in the motion numbers; you are given plenty of options for those. Set the numbers lower for general working purposes. If you need higher detail in order to check something, set the selected object to be higher. You probably won't want to keep to the extremes I chose for Figures 4–19c and d, where the same settings are shown again but with additional objects in the scene. See how jumbled all the wireframes are when they are at low resolution? Even though the selected one is at higher resolution, providing more clarity to the scene as you work, you may find it best to set the selected setting lower than this one (64). Or you may want to momentarily set it to the maximum for a few brief adjustments and then bring it back down to a lower setting for normal work. You can imagine how this might work in Figure 4–19e, where a side view of the selected terrain makes for ease in precise alignment.

Show/Hide Underground

The next control up the Wireframe menu is the Hide/Show Underground control. You can show and hide underground lines by clicking the little toggle switch. When you hide underground lines, any wireframe that falls below Bryce's ground level disappears from view. In addition, Bryce displays the blue horizon line. When underground lines are shown, then all wireframe portions are shown and the blue horizon line goes away. When underground lines are hidden, all objects

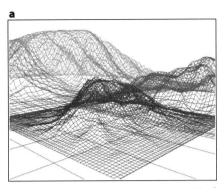 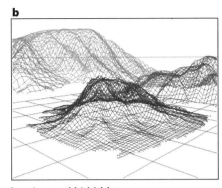

Figure 4–20 Underground lines: a) Wireframes showing and b) hidden.

change when they encounter—and drop below—the ground plane level. The horizon line shows, since it is the representation of the ground plane way, way off in the infinite distance. When you show underground lines, it's the same thing as banishing the ground plane and its influence, complete with the horizon line in the distance. Figure 4–20 compares the same scene with wireframes showing (a) and hidden (b).

Depending on the kind of scene you're working on, you'll find that either showing underground lines or hiding them is the preferable state. Hide underground lines any time you are positioning objects in relation to the ground. Like wireframe shadows (see the next section), this is a way to see characteristics of your scene in relation to the ground, without resorting to a full-blown render.

When is it good to show them? Show underground lines when you're adjusting terrains or other objects below the surface, especially in the case of island water, or other placement where an object is partially "submerged" below the ground. Also, showing underground lines is preferable when you do not have a ground plane in your scene.

Shadows

When the wireframe shadow is invoked, each object casts a small shadow onto the ground plane level of the Bryce Universe. The shadow is cast on the ground plane as if from a light source directly overhead. It's a cue to tell the location of the wireframe. The shadow is cast whether or not you have "hide underground lines" selected, or whether or not there is a ground plane present. The object's shadow takes on the muted color of the wireframe itself. Selected objects cast a pale red shadow, default objects cast a pale gray shadow, and objects of other families will cast pale shadows of their family wireframe color.

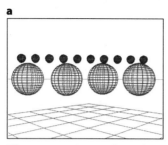
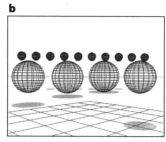

Figure 4–21 Four spheres in wireframe: a) Without wireframe shadows; b) with wireframe shadows.

Why use wireframe shadows? They show depth and relative location and, consequently, relative size. The size of the wireframe by itself doesn't necessarily mean anything, as you can see in Figure 4–21a. But when the shadow falls on the ground plane going "up" toward the back, then you know that the wireframe is farther away than some other object (see Figure 4–21b). The horizon line is at eye level in the distance. It represents the ground level. The lower the shadow appears on the ground, the closer it is to the camera. The higher the shadow appears, the farther away it is. The wireframe shadows, then, provide a clue of the object's location, and, from that, the relative scale of the object.

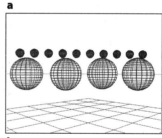
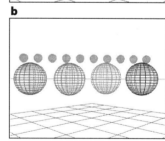
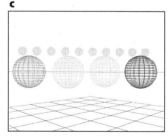

Figure 4–22 Depth cueing in three ranges: a) Minimum, b) default, c) maximum.

Depth Cue

Depth cue is another means of seeing distance—in fact, it's a purer form than wireframe shadows. Since, as you look at your scene, you see only wireframes, you can't tell right off whether one object is in front of the other. All you see are those little wireframes. Nothing more. Bryce helps you to figure out which object is closer and which is further away by rendering the wireframes in depth cueing. In order to see depth, you need to have your monitor set to 24-bit color. (The System's Monitors control panel says that you're displaying millions of colors; this is also the only way that you can see anti-aliased wireframes.) Dragging up on the control will decrease the depth effect, so that all wireframes appear to be bolder with no differentiation between near and far. Dragging down increases the effect of depth, so that you can more easily distinguish whether an object is near or far. Figure 4–22 shows three ranges of wireframe depth cueing states, ranging from no cueing, default, and maximum cueing. As you can see by Figure 4–22c, when maximum cueing is activated, even near objects appear faded. Depth cueing works in all views. Try it out looking at a terrain from top view, as well. See Figure 4–23.

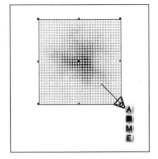

Figure 4–23 Depth cueing of a terrain from top view.

Bryce's default state is to have a medium amount of depth cueing. To change that one control to its default state, Option-click the control, and it will revert back to its default state.

Wireframe Colors—Object Families

Aside from all the wireframe adjustments that can be made using the Wireframe controls on the palette to the right of the scene window, you can also change the wireframe color of an object. This is good for keeping objects in logical grouping types. First I'll talk about the wireframe color and creating different families of objects, and then discuss some of the particulars of object groups and wireframe color. Consider this a section that addresses wireframes, paying particular attention to the "special object types" of object families and groups.

Organizing Objects by Family/Wireframe Color

Without using the Group command to make assorted objects into a group, you can roughly categorize different sets of objects by assigning them different colors. There are a couple of good reasons for doing this. First, when you have several different objects that all share the same material attribute, make them all the same wireframe color. In this way, if you change the material setting, you can change them all very easily. By selecting by family prior to making the adjustment, none of the objects with that particular material setting will be left out. Second, when you are constructing a very complex conglomerate object with many individual parts, assigning different objects of the conglomerate to be members of different families helps in the construction process. Besides having a number of related objects share a common color, they can also have a name of their own.

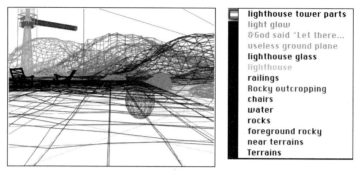

lighthouse tower parts
light glow
&God said "Let there...
useless ground plane
lighthouse glass
lighthouse
railings
Rocky outcropping
chairs
water
rocks
foreground rocky
near terrains
Terrains

Figure 4–24 Lighthouse wireframe view.

Figure 4–24 shows the wireframe view of a lighthouse scene, with the Family pop-up menu showing so that you can see all the names. Notice how the groupings are either logical or are grouped with objects that have the same material setting (lighthouse railing, rocks, imported chairs, near terrains with textures, far terrains without, etc.). For more on how the lighthouse scene was created, see the latter part of Chapter 14, "Superlative Nature Imagery."

Color and Grouped Objects

This section is not a discussion of "why to group things that are the same color." It's more a set of warnings about the way object color behaves with grouped objects.

The default wireframe color is charcoal; when you freshly launch Bryce and create an object, the wireframe color will be charcoal, and the object will belong to the Default Family. After you have created a couple of objects, you may decide that you want to change the object's family color. Thereafter, when you create a new object, its wireframe color will be the Default Family color.

However, when you group a set of objects, the group's bounding box wireframe color will inherit the most recently adjusted family color, whether the most recent adjustment was creating a new object (default color) or some other family's color.

Try this:

1. Create a new scene. Create a sphere. Change its family and color to another color, say the lime green of Family 19.

2. Then create a cone. It emerges into Bryce at the default color. Drag it to another location in the scene.

3. Create a cube. Change its color to a different color, say the navy blue of Family 22.

4. Drag a marquee around all three objects to select them, and group by clicking the G icon. Click in the background area to deselect the group. See how the group takes on the navy blue color of the cube?

Now, start all over again to see the other way this works. Drag the group to one side.

5. Create a cone. Let it stay the default color. Move it to one side by dragging it.

6. Create a cylinder. Change its color/family to another color, say the lime green of Family 19.

7. Create a torus. Now drag a marquee around all three objects to select and group them. Click in the background to deselect the group. See how the group takes on the default wireframe color?

Now, the group was assigned the wireframe color that was last used, whether an object just received a new wireframe color, or whether a new object was created in Bryce with the default color. In both of these cases, the wireframe color differs from some of the objects that are part of the group. What if you want to change the group color? If you change the wireframe color of the group, then the group and all its members will take on the new color/family you assigned to it. If you want the group to belong to a certain family without all the members belonging to the family, then ungroup, change an individual wireframe color, and regroup. The group will be the color of that wireframe.

Try it.

8. Select the group by clicking it. Change the wireframe color of the group to a different color, say, the hot pink of Family 3. Deselect the group. See how the group and all its members are changed to hot pink?

9. Move the pink group aside and click the first group you worked with to select it. Ungroup the group by clicking the U icon.

10. Select the sphere. (Its color is lime green.) Now change its color to a new color, say the orange of Family 20. In fact, change the Family 20 name to something blasé and obvious, such as "group." Clicking the Family 20 name in the Families dialog box brings up a text insertion point where you can type the new name. Select the three objects and group. The group now takes on the "group" family color—orange.

NATURAL SELECTION

Of course, once you have created an object and are viewing it ever-so-nicely in wireframe mode, you may like to do something to it. Move it. Change its size. Give it a surface property. Rotate it. In order to make any adjustments to an object, you must first select it. There are several ways to select Bryce wireframe objects. You've already seen how to select an object by clicking it or dragging a marquee around it. When you have a scene with several (or dozens!) objects in it, it's helpful to know all of the different ways by which you can select and deselect the different objects in your scene. Here are your selection choices:

- Click the object directly.

- Drag the marquee over the center(s) of one or more objects to select it (or them). (This is a change from the way that Bryce 1 works; formerly you could drag over any portion of the wireframe to select it; now you must drag over its center to select it.)

- Use the Tab key to cycle through different objects in a scene.

The bottom of the user interface is the home of the selection controls. There are four different sets of controls:

- Select by object type using object selection icons.

- Select by family (wireframe color).

- Select using the Selection Arrows.

- The pop-up menu also gives you the option of selecting the inverse of what you currently have selected, selecting all, selecting polyhedrons (imported 3D objects), or changing the manner in which the Selection Arrows work.

Figure 4–25 shows the Selection Palette with each option identified.

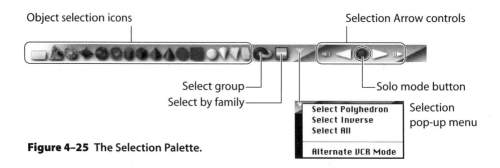

Figure 4–25 The Selection Palette.

Object Selection Icons

The object selection icons are fairly easy to figure out. Click the sphere selection icon and all spheres will be selected. Click the terrain and all terrains will be selected. The interlocked tori represents a group. The object selection icons can be used in conjunction with the Shift key, too. More on that in a bit when I discuss the Tab and Shift keys.

Selection by Family

Once you have given one or more of your objects different family/wireframe colors (or you have created stones, infinite plane water, or infinite plane sky, which all emerge into the scene with a different wireframe color), you can select objects according to the family by choosing from the Family pop-up menu.

VCR Mode and Arrows

The other large area on the Selection Palette are the Arrow or VCR controls. They are called "VCR" for their resemblance to the arrows on Video Cassette Recorder machines (plus, incidentally, a host of other audio visual equipment). Bryce's Arrow controls have nothing to do with a VCR, however. But you need to be aware of this titling convention because there's an item in the miscellaneous selection pop-up menu that changes the arrows. It's called "Alternate VCR Mode." Aside from that, I shall call them the Arrow controls or Selection Arrows.

There are two sets of arrows for cycling through objects in your scene, and two directions to cycle in. They are Previous Object, Previous Object Type, Next Object Type, and Next Object. The larger set cycles through object types: infinite plane, terrain, cylinder, sphere, etc. Once you have hit upon the type of object you want, then the smaller arrows will cycle through all of the objects of that type: first sphere, second sphere, third sphere, etc.

If you are watching your scene while you click the Arrow controls (and you probably are), you might be confused by the order in which Bryce selects objects, especially if you don't have many objects in your scene, or many object types. As an alternative, to understand what is transpiring as Bryce cycles through object types, click the Next Object Type repeatedly while watching the object selection icons on the Selection Palette.

To aid you in this process, open up the file on the CD (More Info For Each Chapter> Chapter 4> Selecting > OBJECTS TO SELECT.) The scene document has many different object types. When it is open, click the Next Object Type Selection Arrow.

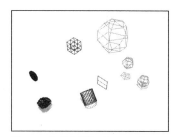

Notice that the scene has several object types in it: a symmetrical lattice, a torus, a pict object (square), a cylinder, a cube, and three radial lights. (See Figure 4–26.) When you open the scene to wireframe view, there is no object selected.

Figure 4–26 Wireframe view of the scene entitled OBJECTS TO SELECT.

Walkthrough

1. Click the large right arrow on the Selection Palette, and keep clicking it. Watch the Select by Object icons. Notice that as the type is selected, that particular type highlights. Bryce selects objects according to the order of the objects on the bottom panel.

    In this scene file, the first object selected is the symmetrical lattice. Then the torus, then the cylinder, and so on, throughout the list.

2. Keep clicking. You're not through yet. Notice that the first time through, after going through all the objects, the Family icon lights up and a set of objects is selected. There are two family groups here, the lights and everything else. When you keep selecting, Bryce alternates between then. First, click until the Light family is selected, then click again through all the object types, and this next time, the Default Family is selected. (For more on selecting and families, see "Bryce Family Values" later in this chapter.)

3. When you get to one of the lights, click the smaller arrow to select individual objects from that object type. So Bryce has an agenda here; select this type object, and then, once you're on the particular object, you can cycle through all the other individual objects of that type.

Alt VCR Mode; Select by Creation Order

In the Selection Options pop-up menu, there is an item called "Alternate VCR Mode." This switches the Selection Arrows into a different mode, where the objects are selected in a different order—the order in which the objects were created. The Alternate VCR Mode is the same as the way that the Selection Arrows operated in Bryce 1. The right arrow cycles you forward from one object to the next, and the left one cycles you backwards. In the outer set, the arrows cycle you through the different object families. (Incidentally, the Tab key works in the same way as the Alternate VCR mode Next Object arrow.)

Keypad/Keyboard Entities

There are three types of keyboard keys that are concerned with the selection process. The first type (Tab key/Enter key) cycles through all objects in a manner similar to the arrow keys. The second, the Shift key, acts as a toggle and a way to select or deselect multiple objects. The third, using the key command equivalents to pop-up menu commands, allows you to select all or to select inverse.

Tab/Enter Key

The Tab key (or, on the keypad, the Enter key), cycles through all your objects. If no object is selected, it starts with the first object created, then cycles through in the order in which objects were created. If an object is selected, it starts with that object and moves through the objects in the order of their creation. The Tab key acts like the alternate VCR mode of the Selection Arrows. In order to cycle backwards through the objects, press the Option key while tabbing through the objects. (This cycle backwards shortcut has no key equivalent in Windows.)

Shift Key and Selections/Deselections

Get more control of selecting by using the Shift key. Use it to select more than one object or as a toggle to deselect/select an object. This is most intuitive in the direct "click-object-to-select-it" process.

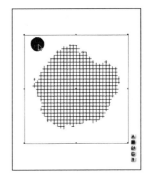

Sometimes when clicking an object, you'll inadvertently select two objects. In the image in Figure 4–27, this happens easily in top view when a portion of the terrain is "hidden underground." You may not be able to see it, but it's still there, and it will be selected when you click it. So if both objects are selected but you want to select only one, hold down the Shift key and click on the terrain (or whatever you don't want selected) to deselect it.

Figure 4–27
Inadvertantly selecting two objects when one has underground lines hidden.

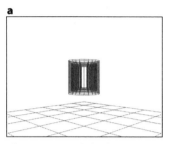 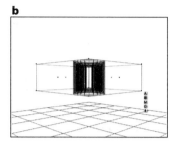

Figure 4–28 Shift-clicking to select all objects located under the mouse's pointer.

Sometimes you will have several objects that are perfectly aligned with the camera. That is, there are several objects, but it looks as if there is only one. In this case, clicking on the visible object usually selects the first object and not all the other objects behind. If you want to select all the objects, hold down the Shift key and click. Bryce will select everything under the cursor. Figure 4–28a shows a set of cylinder wireframes that are positioned one behind the other, aligned with the camera's perspective. When holding down the Shift key and clicking, they are all selected (Figure 4–28b).

You could easily find yourself in a situation where you have several terrains and other objects, all of which overlap one another as you view them from the camera's perspective. With that complex a scene, if you click something directly, you'll select a whole host of objects. It's at that point that you should consider the other options for selecting.

Shift Key and the Select Control Icons

You can use the Shift key in conjunction with the selection icons. Select all spheres by clicking the Sphere Selection icon, and then add to that by pressing the Shift key and selecting the cones as well. You can also use the Shift key and the selection icons to deselect certain objects. Bear in mind, however, that the Shift key works as a toggle, so if you have one of your three spheres selected and hold down the Shift key while clicking the Sphere Selection icon, you'll select the others and deselect the one that was selected.

Say, for example, you have two terrains and a sphere selected and you want to deselect the sphere. Hold down the Shift key and then click on the Sphere Selection icon. Voila!

Now, let's say that you have all of those objects selected and you want to add the pyramid to your selection. Hold down the Shift key and click the pyramid. The pyramid will be added to your selection.

In fact, using the Shift key in *all* cases adds to or deletes from a selection, depending on your starting place.

Shift Key and the Families Pop-up Menu

If you want to select all of the objects which belong to the Default Family, simply use the Families pop-up menu. Then, if you want to add an object(s) from another family, hold down the Shift key while selecting that family.

Bryce's Family Values

Fine, well, and good. With so many different object types, this selection stuff looks like a piece of cake. But when you're clicking on the Arrow control to get a certain object—when you have a limited number of objects or object types—say one or two—Bryce's behavior seems mighty confusing. It just selects the one, the group, and then the other, then the group. Repeated arrow-selecting never gets around to selecting each object. What's going on? Is Bryce "stuck?"

When cycling through the objets using the Selection Arrows, Bryce treats a Family as if it were a particular object. But Bryce is trying to play fair, knowing that there is most probably more than one family in the scene. In celebration of family diversity, and all the different colors that families can come in, Bryce seeks to give equal opportunity to all. So each time Bryce completes a selection cycle, when it comes back to the "family" type, it selects a *different* family.

If you're wondering what the heck Bryce is doing while selecting objects, then try this walkthrough, and I'll explain it as I go.

Family Values Walkthrough

1. Open up the file HOUSE OF CAPULET from the CD-ROM under the selection chapter. (Or, start a new document, and delete the ground. Create an object, duplicate it a bunch of times, and move those objects around so that they can be individually discerned.)

2. Click the Next Object Type control (large right arrow) a few times. You will toggle back and forth from the one torus to the Default Family. (See Figure 4–29.)

a

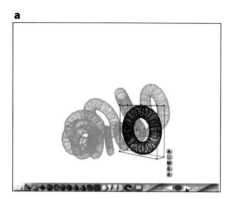

b

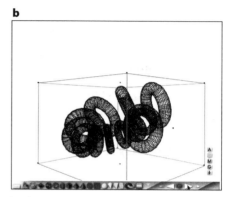

Figure 4–29 House of Capulets' two states of selection when using the Selection Arrows.

3.   When one torus is selected, click the smaller arrows to cycle through the different individual tori.

Montagues and Capulets

It can get more complicated with additional families. In fact, it usually does. Consider the Montagues and the Capulets.

1.   Open up the scene MONTAGUES AND CAPULETS. There are two different families, named for those two ill-fated families of Verona. The Montague family is the charcoal-gray, the cylinders. The Capulets, lavender, are the tori. See Figure 4–30.

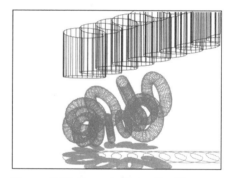

2.   Click the large arrow. Notice that the order of selection object goes something like this: torus, cylinder, family, torus, cylinder, other family, torus, cylinder, (first) family, torus, cylinder, other family, ad infinitum.

Figure 4-30 Two wireframe families, Montagues, Capulets.

3.   Stop and take a side tour. When a torus is selected, click the smaller arrow to cycle through the different tori.

4.   After you've grown bored with that, click the large arrow to select the next type of object, a cylinder. Then click the smaller arrow to cycle through all the cylinders.

5. You'll quickly tire of that, no doubt. So click the large arrow to select a family. Now click the small arrow to cycle back and forth between the two families. If there were still other families, you'd be cycling through each one. Ah, but in this case, we've got the love-hate relationship between those two, the Capulets and the Montagues.

Solo Mode

Bryce has an alternative for viewing wireframe objects. Select one or a few, and look at those only in Bryce's Solo mode. Activate the Solo mode by clicking the round button between the Selection Arrows on the bottom selection palette. (See Figure 4–31.) Then only those objects that were

Figure 4–31 The Solo mode button on the Selection Palette.

selected will appear, and everything else will disappear temporarily—giving you a reprieve from wireframe clutter, and giving your computer a bit of a reprieve; it doesn't have to draw those objects on screen. To get back to regular mode, simply click the red button again. It goes back to its normal green state, and you see everything in your scene again.

Now that you have a general idea about the way Solo mode works, here is a list of likely reasons you'd want to use it.

Uses for Solo Mode

• Clutter reduction—Look at only those objects that you want to see without being distracted by other objects.

• Select objects that would otherwise be difficult to select.

• Select an object within a boolean or group.

• Narrow down selection further.

• Render only certain objects—the same reasons as already given, but instead of selecting and working with only a group, render only the few and the proud and the solo.

Groups and solo mode

Groups and Solo mode together behaves a bit differently in each version of Bryce. On the Macintosh, groups will be "ungrouped" for the duration of time you're in

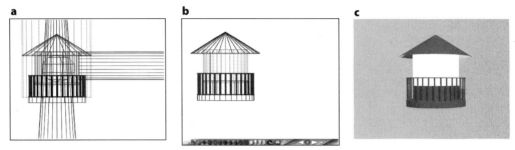

Figure 4–32 Boolean object in Solo mode: a) Regular mode; b) some objects in Solo mode with no group lines; c) but it still renders as a boolean.

Solo mode, so that you may freely select and move objects around inside of groups. They do not, however, lose their grouped status. Once you exit Solo mode, they'll go back to being their regular grouped selves. While in Solo mode, you can do all the normal things to objects that you could do before: select, move, resize, rotate, align, duplicate, edit materials. However, you cannot delete objects that are part of a group.

If there is a boolean group, it will still render as a boolean. In Figure 4–32b, where a portion of the lighthouse is in Solo mode, the wireframe doesn't show the groups for the booleaned cones, nor the booleaned cylinders. Yet the object renders with boolean features intact (see Figure 4–32c).

In Windows, the group behaves the same in Solo mode as it does in the regular wireframe view. The bounding box for the group is there the whole time, and you cannot directly click an individual object that's part of a group to select only it. Select individual members of a group by clicking the Next Object Type Selection Arrow.

If you create a *new* group inside of Solo mode, it will act like a normal group, complete with wireframe bounding box, and all the normal grouped behaviors (a group acts like one object). Do that either by creating new objects and grouping them, or by selecting existing objects and grouping them. However, if the existing objects belonged to a group already, then there are consequences—which are different, depending on which version of Bryce you're using. If you're using the Mac version of Bryce, you won't be able to create a new group from members of a previous group. They'll refuse to be grouped. An alert box will tell you that you cannot group objects that are already in groups. Under Windows, you will successfully be able to create a second group from a new object and a member of a previous group. You won't see the G icon when the objects are selected, but you will be able to use the Ctrl+G command to group them. The object that is common to both groups will respond to edits made to either group. You'd best stay away from that kind of a double-grouping arrangement.

Once Inside of Solo Mode

Once you're inside of Solo mode, you'll have your subset of all Bryce objects in your scene. It's almost like declaring those objects that you brought into Solo mode as your temporary universe of fewer objects. Bryce's Selection tools work in Solo mode as well. They'll operate only on those objects that you brought with you. So if you have an overall scene with a dozen spheres and two cylinders, and you brought the cylinders and one sphere into Solo mode, then when you select by object type (sphere), the one sphere will be selected. Bryce temporarily forgets about the objects that aren't in Solo mode. Use the other Selection tools to your heart's content to work with the objects you brought into Solo mode with you. You can select all, you can select by object type, you can select by wireframe family, and you'll select your objects as you see fit.

Selection of the Fittest

Of course, the easiest thing to do is to select something and then go to Solo mode. Work with the objects there, and then go back to normal mode.

But you can also use Solo mode as a temporary state to further narrow down your selection. This technique is based on the original Solo mode cardinal rule: only selected objects will show in Solo mode. If you're already in Solo mode, you can select a subset of objects, pop back out to normal mode, and quickly pop back into Solo mode. You'll only bring the selected objects back with you. Depending on the number of objects in Solo mode, you can directly select everything you want to remain selected, or select those objects you want to get rid of, followed by a Select Inverse command.

Figure 4–33 is an example of the Solo mode winnowing process using the Select Inverse command. First the column elements in Figure 4–33a were brought into Solo mode. The objects comprising the column base needed to temporarily disappear. So they were selected, and then, from the pop-up menu on the Selection Palette, Select Inverse (also ⌘-Shift-A or Ctrl+Shift+A) was chosen. See Figure 4–33b. A quick click on the Solo button exited Solo mode, then an immediate click reactivated it again, having successfully gotten rid of the unwanted column base. (See Figure 4–33c.)

Similarly, you can use Solo mode to cut down clutter while you make changes to your selection, exit Solo mode and add another object to the selection, enter Solo mode again and make further changes. To add objects to Solo mode, select all the objects before leaving Solo mode. Leave Solo mode. Shift-click the next object to select it. Go back to Solo mode for further refinements, if necessary.

Here's another example of the way to use Solo mode to successfully deselect some objects. Figure 4–34 shows the top view of a set of tori. From top view, it's a mess. The object here is to place a set of radial lights inside the tunnel created by the booleans. From top view, it's hard to know how to click in order to select the objects. Selecting by object yields all three of them (see Figure 4–34b). Using Shift-click to deselect will result in a never ending "deselect this while selecting, that, that, and the other one." The smart way to do it is to take those objects to Solo mode (see Figure 4–34c and d) deselect the ones you don't want, and then emerge from Solo mode with the one object selected. Figure 4–34e shows the result of the process.

Popping into Solo mode is good for grabbing an object from a group, if you're Brycing on a Mac. While you can select by type and select an object within a group, if you have many of those object primitive types in your scene, you'll also select those, too, causing a painstaking deselect-in-order-to-select process. Solo mode is much better. Once you have selected the object, you can freely manipulate it.

a

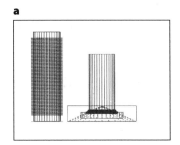

b

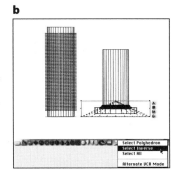

c

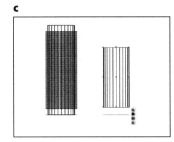

Figure 4–33 Column construction and the solo deselect process: a) Side view of two columns; b) in Solo mode, deselecting base of column on right; c) after exiting and re-entering Solo mode: the pared down wireframes.

Rendering in Solo Mode

When you render in Solo mode, you will render only those objects that you see in that mode.

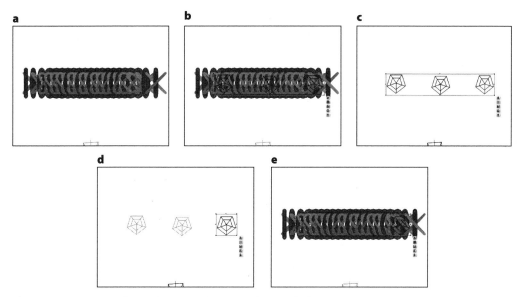

Figure 4–34 Using Solo mode to deselect with cluttered objects: a) Many objects; b) all radial lights selected by object type; c) in Solo mode; d) deselect; e) back to standard wireframe view with the one light selected.

BRYCE EASTER EGG OBJECTS

Finally, as a little bonus for you Mac Brycers, I'll reveal the location of a secret set of objects in Bryce. What's this? A secret set? Well, yes.... click a hidden spot on the Create Palette, and they show up. If you click the space just above the cylinder object, you'll get a pop-up menu. There are five different objects on that pop-up menu. Figure 4–35 shows both the spot where you click (indicated by the little star burst) and the pop-up menu.

There are the sphere set, the disk set, the gnrl polyhedron, the spike and the gauss. Figure 4–36 shows the object wireframes and rendered objects.

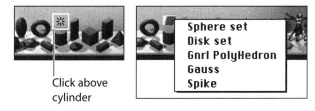

Figure 4–35 Finding the secret objects: a) Where to click; b) the pop-up menu that appears.

Let me make some observations about these objects. They are probably left over from the development stage of Bryce. As such, they are not documented, supported, or, for that matter, reliable. I'd like to say right off the bat, stay away from the gnrl polyhedron (I think that gnrl is an abbreviated form of General—or maybe it's short for gnarly). Nothing renders, and after creating one of those, I've had objects created subsequently show up as nothings. That's why it isn't shown in Figure 4–36.

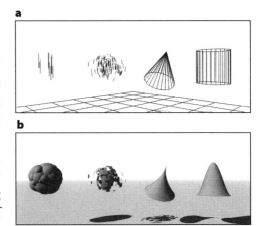

Figure 4–36 The secret objects, in wireframe and rendered form: sphere set, disk set, spike, and gauss.

The remainder of the objects can be broken down into two types. The sphere and disk sets are each clusters of one type of object, and the other two are variations on the cone, with curvature. The spike is tapered in as moves from base to point, and the gauss follows a bell curve shape.

Notice that the wireframes for the spike and the gauss do not differ from that of the cone and the cylinder. Though by looking at the wireframe you can't tell one

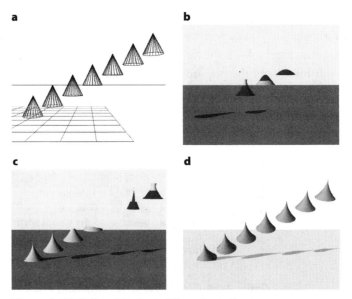

Figure 4–37 Spike objects at different rotations.

apart from the other, Bryce knows a gauss from a cylinder. When both wireframes are in a scene and you click the select cylinder icon, the gauss will remain unselected. The same holds true for a spike versus a cone.

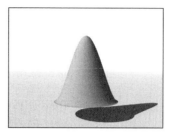

How do you tell them apart, then? Here's where the family settings come in handy. Give that object a wireframe color all its own and then give it a name that you can remember—spike!

Figure 4–38 The gauss object close up, with tiny transparent line where object "intersects" horizon.

Earlier I mentioned that the objects are not reliable. Of the objects that are worth experimenting with, the one that is least reliable is the spike. Depending on spike's rotation and location relative to the horizon line, portions of the object will not render, or may render in darker coloring. Here, for your behind-the-scenes pleasure (or frustration) is an example of a case of ray-traced rendering gone awry. But, since these objects aren't really here, and not advertised as such, you can't complain too much. Figure 4–37 shows some different elevation and rotation examples of the spike

The gauss seems to be a far more solid Bryce citizen. The only problem I can detect is that there are render artifacts when the gauss intersects with Bryce's horizon. Check out Figure 4–38, especially where the gauss object's level intersects the horizon behind. It's faint, but there's a hint of transparency.

The sphere set is a wonder—think of those clouds; this is a find, ladies and gentlemen! If you have the patience for the increase in render time, the sphere set is the source for skies with realism that will make your friends and family (and art directors and clients) gasp in amazement. However, normal "this object doesn't really exist" disclaimers apply. Don't expect to call up MetaTools and get technical support if all of a sudden the sphere set decides to up and re-write your hard drive (however, since you are reading this in a printed book, it is a good indication that it doesn't really do that; after all, I have hard drives that made it through this process).

Finally, there is the disk set. It groups a set of disks together, radiating out from a center axis.

Figure 4–39 The sphere set is random; each one is slightly different.

The wireframes for both sphere sets and disk sets show just the center axis of each single sphere or disk. You can tell the two apart from the way that they differ from one another, but sometimes selecting the object is not the simplest thing. Also, both sets produce random arrays of objects, so that each one differs slightly from another one. Figure 4–39 shows how each sphere set is slightly different. The only way to make them identical is to duplicate an individual sphere or disk set.

> **TIP:** *The wireframes, with their simple lines, show up fine in main view. But if you look at the objects from top or other views, they may not (this is especially true of the sphere set, which can easily disappear). In order to see the objects from the different views in Bryce, make the wireframe show as box (⌘-B). The box can be seen from any angle, so the object won't "disappear" on you in certain views.*

The disk set might have some interesting uses, too, as it is shaped in a way that lends itself well to foliage making.

CHAPTER FIVE

Streamline Your Brycing

"Well," said Rabbit,... "We'd better get on, I suppose. Which way shall we try?"

"How would it be," said Pooh slowly, "if, as soon as we're out of sight of this Pit, we try to find it again?"

"What's the good of that?" said Rabbit.

"Well," said Pooh, "we keep looking for Home and not finding it, so I thought that if we looked for this Pit, we'd be sure not to find it, which would be a Good Thing, because then we might find something that we weren't looking for, which might be just what we were looking for, really."

"I don't see much sense in that," said Rabbit.

"No," said Pooh humbly, "there isn't. But there was going to be when I began it. It's just that something happened to it on the way."

A. A. MILNE, *THE HOUSE AT POOH CORNER*

IN THIS CHAPTER...

- Setting up your Mac or PC for efficient Brycing

- The most efficient order to set up scenes

- Effective rendering and batch rendering

- Using Bryce's Display Palette controls for efficiency

- Other general things about Bryce that are good to know in the interests of speed and efficiency

- Working with Bryce's Preset Libraries

- Working with Bryce's palettes

- Preferences setup

In this chapter, I tell you how to optimize your Bryce working method and answer the question, "Given the time it takes to render scenes, what is the most efficient way to work in Bryce?" Different activities in Bryce cost more in processing time. It's best when working in Bryce to postpone for as long as possible introducing the effects that cost the most. There are many steps needed to create a scene; ensure you are getting the most out of the early stages. Then when you do test renders to ensure your image is going as planned, you won't have to wait for unnecessary things to render.

When Bryce 1.0 first came out on the Mac, it worked on 68K machines that were slower than today's (equivalent to the PC 386 and 486), and render time was an all-time premium. The important thing to bear in mind was that renders would be time consuming, so it was of utmost importance to keep the most for last. Nowadays, Macs are faster. From 68K to the Power Macintosh 601 chip to the 604 chip, the render that took overnight now takes a lunch hour, or even a coffee break. Bryce has seen speed improvements due to faster machines and render engine optimization.

Meanwhile, the same processor speed improvements that have taken place on the Mac have been echoed on the PC side, with the Pentium microprocessor. Bryce 2 has entered the Windows world on a comparable level of computing speed. The speed enhancements have allowed for room to build additional features into the software. Bryce 2 sees the inclusion of things such as advanced display options, independent lightsources, booleans, imported objects, and more complex materials—all of which would have brought the already slow 68K version of Bryce to a complete crawl (in fact, for Quadra level Macs and 486 PCs, it does just that!). So, whether you have a computer that is simply slower, or you want to take advantage of all the new power-hungry goodies that are a part of Bryce 2, you'll be better off if you think in terms of efficient working in Bryce.

The basic idea is to work smart so that the real time-consuming stuff—rendering—is not bogged down in all the fine detail until the very end of the process.

OPTIMAL SETTINGS

If you want to work efficiently in Bryce, you'll need all of your computer's processing power available for all those calculations Bryce needs to make. There are some settings you can make both to your computer and within the software to make Bryce run at its peak. I'll explore them both here.

Your Computer

Make your computer system run efficiently. To do this, free it up from any unnecessary activities that it has to perform. First, make sure that you don't have extensions or programs loading at startup that you don't need. Those blinking eyeballs may be cute, but those and other toys take RAM and CPU cycles away from where you want them dedicated: a bare-bones system, and Bryce.

Macintosh

Now that your system is running lean and mean when it starts up, do the most important thing: Turn off the calculate folder sizes option in the Views control panel. Do it *now*! Yes, right now! (You'll thank me later!) Calculate folder sizes is handy when you're trying to find out where the heck all that disk space went when you have to clear off a hundred megs. But it is not practical for everyday working on the computer, since the system wrests every spare cycle to calculate how much stuff is in each folder.

This next matter is not as cut-and-dry as the previous one, but having your computer set for File Sharing slows down the computer. If you have but one computer, go to the control panels and turn that damn thing off! If you do have a network, then it's not so simple. You'd be best off if you do stealth networking—get by with the minimum amount of shared networking that you can. You can access other computers over a network without enabling File Sharing on your own computer, though when another server goes down, it takes yours with it.

Windows

If you're using Windows, here are some basic things to make your computer run more efficiently. Don't include anything in the Startup Group unless it's absolutely vital. Once your computer has started up, make sure that you have adequate swap space on your hard drive. To keep things running smoothly, run ScanDisk and Defrag often enough to keep your hard disk in healthy shape. Also, anytime you experience a crash (from any Windows software or applications) that forces you to restart the computer, always run ScanDisk.

Bryce

Now that you've set up the computer for efficiency, turn your attention to making Bryce efficient. Here, your strategy is the same: Make sure that you give as much time to your CPU as you can for Brycing. What are the things that might take away unnecessary processing time? Most important is the Nano Preview's Auto-Update setting, especially on a Mac, where the Nano Preview's render is fast, but not instantaneous. Having that switched on all the time is akin to having your Views control panel set to calculate folder sizes: Bryce becomes unreasonably lethargic. If you're used to the brisk pace of Bryce running without it, then when it's on, you'll notice how Bryce gets the blahs. The Auto-Update option is a wonderful thing to have on *when you want it on* but I'd recommend that you save those times for when you're working with it directly.

Having the Sky & Fog Options set to Auto-Update is a different thing; it is a matter of personal taste mixed with the speed of your computer. If you are manipulating objects or camera perspective, you won't encounter any updating. The Sky & Fog Auto-Update is not as obtrusive as the Nano Preview. When working with the sky, you may want it on or off. If you want to see a move-by-move update of what you're doing in the Sky & Fog Palette, but your computer is a slow one, this may be a time when you want to set the Nano Preview to Sky Only and turn Auto-Update *on*. When the Nano Preview and the Sky & Fog Options are *both* set to Auto-Update, the priority goes first to the Nano Preview and then to the scene in general. Make your adjustments accordingly.

In the next sections I'll discuss some more strategies for efficient Bryce working, but this one is a general catch-all time saver.

SETTING UP YOUR SCENE

The first part of efficient working in Bryce is to set up your scene and your working conditions in the program.

Start Small

When setting up your scene, keep in mind that you're working in a three-dimensional world that you will eventually render to a two-dimensional image (Macintosh: PICT; Windows: BMP). When choosing your file resolution, don't think along the lines of, "Well, my final resolution has to be 1500 × 800 pixels," and then create a scene with that render size. You have an entire three-dimensional world there inside your scene, no matter the render size. So take liberties! Take *small* liberties. Start out small by using Bryce's default setting or one of the settings listed in the Document Setup dialog box, or the Render pop up menu. (See Figure 5–1.)

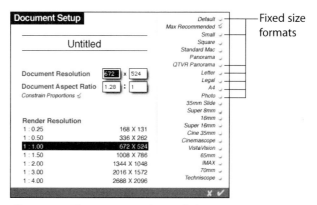

Figure 5–1 The Document Setup dialog box, with fixed sizes indicated.

When you're first building your scene, it's a good idea to make sure that the scene size is not larger than your monitor size, and that you start out with your scene and render at a 1:1 ratio. When your scene is smaller than your monitor, you'll have all your objects on the monitor, present and accounted for (it's a pain to find items that are located "off" your monitor, and Bryce doesn't allow for a quick zoom out to take a look at the scene in a smaller view, as it does in Render mode). When you are building and rendering at a 1:1 ratio, then there's no guesswork to translate to the object location here and where it renders over there. Save those fancy ratios and large scene and render sizes for later, after you've completed the scene building process.

The Document Setup dialog box, with a few exceptions, enables you to accomplish these two efficient scene setups easily. Most of the size ratios that are listed on the right of the dialog box will not go higher than the maximum allowed by your computer. In Figure 5–1, the exceptions are noted as Fixed size formats. No matter what size your monitor is, those options have fixed dimensions. The left side of the dialog box, containing Document Resolution and Render Resolution, allows you to set the scene-to-render sizes at different multiples.

There are actually two different ratios at work here. First, there is the proportion ratio that you see in the Document Resolution portion. The default is 4:3. There are four horizontal units to three vertical units.

Second, the Render Resolution has a list of ratios, beginning with 1:0.25 and ending with 1:4.00. These are the ratios between scene size and render size. The default is

1:1. It makes for the simplest and most painless way to work. To render at double the size of the scene, select 1:2.00. To render at half size, select 1: 0.50.

If you need to create your scene at half the size that's currently indicated, enter the numbers from that ratio listing into the Document Resolution above; the numbers below with all the scene:render ratios will adjust themselves accordingly, and you'll be set at 1:1. (This is especially helpful if you have a smaller monitor.)

If you know ahead of time that the scene you're working on will eventually become extremely wide or extremely tall, you may not want to go to the Document Setup dialog box just yet. If your scene will have many objects, and you need to peer at it a lot from top view, hold off a bit. An extreme aspect ratio will make things more difficult to see when you're looking at top view. A little bit later, when you have most of your objects placed, go ahead and narrow the dimensions.

When you change an image from a basic size ratio to one that is extreme, you may have to change the camera angle some. Bryce gives the newly resized scene its best guess for camera angle and so on, but invariably, you'll have to adjust a little bit to get things just so.

Placing Objects in Your Scene: Eric's Mountain Eroded Image

Now that you've optimized your settings for the overall way Bryce works, and you have your scene size established, it's time to focus on ways to optimize the scene creation process. In this section, I'll take a look at a scene created by Eric Wenger, Mountain Eroded, using it as an example of the things to do during the early part of the creation process, and the things to do later.

This scene began with the creation of a distant high mountain range, and a foreground range that was shaded by hills. Early on, Eric established the sun's direction.

First, he created the mountains with four terrains. Two terrains are the large mountains in the distance, then there is a lower set of hills which is eventually to be shaded by a cloud, and then there is a hilly area in the foreground. (See Figure 5–2.)

Because the cloud-shade is a part of the overall composition, creating the shade was the next step. For that, a cylinder was placed above and assigned a cloudy material setting. Here is one case where materials are established earlier in the scene, as the shadow is needed to establish the basic look of the scene. Notice,

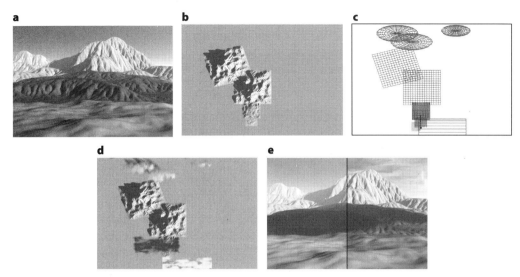

Figure 5–2 Mountain Eroded series: a) The terrains in front view; b) part a shown in top view; c) top view in wireframe for added clouds; d) top view with clouds rendered; cylinder cloud casts shadow on mid-ground terrain; e) after cylinder cloud placement (with and without rest of sky and clouds).

though, how it was the last element to be established for the composition. Figure 5–2 shows the top view render with and without the clouds in place.

At this point, the other clouds were added to the scene and placed, since they, too comprise the overall part of the composition of Bryce objects. The final scene before render is fairly complete; there is a mood well established, long before the terrains have been given custom materials settings.

From this creation order process, we can draw some conclusions about efficient working in Bryce. I'll discuss them next.

Creation and Composition Always Come before Material Goods

The single most important thing you can do to save time while working in Bryce is to refrain from assigning any material settings to your objects until the end of your scene creation process. When you first launch Bryce, all objects take on a generic smooth gray surface. For your initial setup, this is fine. Work first on the overall shape of your world and what goes where before you begin tinkering with the intricacies of materials for each object. And if you have a scene with any complexity at all (more than one object), you *will* have to do a bit of tinkering.

In Mountain Eroded, Eric first created the terrain mountain shapes. Fairly early on, he established the camera angle on his scene. (Depending on your working style, you may want to go with this or not. Sometimes it's fun to create a scene and then later discover other ways of looking at it. Take your pick.)

If you need to provide contrast between one object and another while setting up the scene, change one object's color. In the Materials Composer, assign it a different Diffuse color. You'll be able to distinguish the new object from the others, but you haven't traversed into time-consuming render territory.

There are two different strategies for cutting down on the render time. The first is the one taken here in this Mountain Eroded example. Don't assign any material settings, other than perhaps a change in the diffuse color to distinguish one object from another. When you need clouds to be a part of your composition, you'll be able to see them okay.

The second strategy, using the Textures On/Off render button, reduces any materials settings to naught. (The color comes from the diffuse color setting and the sun's color.) This will take any materials settings and reduce them to a plain vanilla plastic, and the object's color will be determined by any colors set in the color swatch controls. The sky will be a flat color, determined by whatever is the "No Atmosphere" color (see Chapter 10, "Brycean Skies," for more information). This is a good thing to come back to if you find that you need to go back to an earlier stage of work in Bryce after assigning materials to your object.

But there are times when you do *not* want to use this. In the Mountain Eroded image, where the spheres were made into clouds for the sake of composition, consider how unsuccessful a Texture Off render would be as all the clouds return to their native spheres, and the opaque cylinder above casts a threatening shadow indeed (see Figure 5–3). Yuck.

Figure 5–3 Mountain Eroded in Texture Off; efficient but unsuccessful.

(The old Bryce 1 solution to temporarily take away textures, which involved changing the texture setting back to None in the Materials Composer, won't work cleanly in Bryce 2. Once Bryce "forgets" the texture that has been assigned to any of the surface properties of the object, it won't remember it the same way it did in version 1. If you "forget" all but one property, you can retrieve the others, but it's not the simple solution it was in Bryce 1.)

Now Blue Sky It

When you are focusing on your sky settings, you'll need to make sure that the Texture On/Off is set to On, and it's a good idea to have the Fast Preview mode shut off as well, since it tends to render the skies inaccurately.

Here are ideas for making skies render quickly. Generally, they'll render more quickly than terrains with lots of bump or other details anyhow.

- Use the Nano Preview to get a feel for your sky. Set it to either show Sky Only or Full Scene. Set it to Auto-Update if you would like to take precedence over everything else when you are working. (When you're done with that portion of work on your scene, switch it off again!)

- Drag a marquee around a partial strip of the image. Set the Sky options menu to Auto-Update (and switch *off* Auto-Update in the Nano Preview mode). This is the only place Bryce will render, thereby giving you faster rendered responses to your atmospheric choices.

Now experiment with abandon to get just the right sky setting. Each time you make a change, your Nano Preview or the strip of image renders again, showing you in a few brief passes what the sky will be like.

Congratulations! You've accomplished much so far in setting up your scene. How much longer would these renders take if you'd included the sluggish parts? Now that you've got everything else out of the way, it's time to bring on that time-consuming stuff!

The Costly Things in BryceLife

What is the time-consuming stuff? The surface attributes of objects, primarily three-dimensional, texture-based materials, cause the rendering process to take longer. Even so, some parts that make up the material setting are costlier than others. What are the "costly" parts of the materials? Reflectivity, transparency, bump gain, and high-contrast detail. This list describes those, as well as other parts of Bryce that make for expensive render times.

Reflectivity. As the ray is traced to find the color for that pixel, the material bounces the ray from here to there to some other place in order to get the final color. Higher physics notwithstanding, the shortest distance between two places is a straight line. By adding reflection, you introduce bouncing rays, and the render time increases.

Transparency. Bryce needs to calculate how much of the ray stays with the object and how much goes through the object to whatever lies beyond. Transparency is a variation on the not-so-short distance between two places, since part of the ray travels beyond the normal stopping place.

Bump gain. Each individual bump needs to be calculated, and because there's a change in the surface, the new element—height—is added to the width and depth equations. Also, the introduction of indentation in the surface structure results in tiny shadows and light shifts, thereby giving Bryce more to do when it comes time to anti-alias the image. A bumpy, mottled surface takes longer to render than a smooth surface does.

High-contrast detail. When there is a lot of color contrast in a close space, a lot of calculation will take place, especially during the anti-aliasing pass of the render cycle. Bryce will look to the surrounding 8 pixels to determine the final color of the one in the center. If there's high color contrast in those pixels, then Bryce needs to look more "carefully" in order to determine the final color.

Lighting costs. For every light source in your scene, Bryce has to calculate its effect on each object, down to every pixel. The more lights you have in your scene, the more complex is every calculation in the render process, and the lengthier the render time.

Imported DXF objects. DXF objects, when imported into Bryce, may significantly increase rendering time, depending on their size, complexity and the number of objects in the group.

What Kind of Time Difference Will Materials Make?

Figure 5–4a through c shows the lighthouse image rendered using Bryce's different render options. Besides the normal render (part a) and the Texture Off render (part b), there is the quick preview for seeing how the scene looks with textures (part c). The quick preview has small blocky-pixel artifacts, but is great for a peek while work is in progress.

So what kind of time differences does the rendering of materials make? The lighthouse was rendered by different machines under different rendering conditions. In Table 5–1, the results of each of the render reports are listed for comparison. The left column lists different types of computers, to show the relative speed of different types of processor—three Macintosh and one Pentium processor.

Figure 5–4 Lighthouse at Twilight, rendered under different conditions: a) Normal render; b) Texture Off; c) Fast Preview.

CPU	Accelerated Raytesting				Standard Raytesting			
	Txt Off	Fast	Both	Regular	Txt Off	Fast	Both	Regular
Mac PPC 8100/100	6:04	5:32	2:50	12:24	9:02	6:31	3:30	16:09
Mac Clone 604/132	4:17	4:47	2:15	9:49	5:12	5:06	2:27	11:03
Mac 68040/66	47:20	1:06:14	22:24	2:35:36	55:23	1:10:06	25:06	2:48:37

CPU	Spatial Optimization Maximum				Spatial Optimization OFF			
	Txt Off	Fast	Both	Regular	Txt Off	Fast	Both	Regular
Pentium 200Mhz	18:35	6:20	10:36	16:11	1:19:12	24:04	36:58	1:11:40

Table 5–1 Render time comparisons.

The scene has some materials set for the objects, but not all. The distant terrains are plain old green, since their detail does not show. The foreground terrains do have materials, though. More importantly, the water, with its transparency setting, is a render hog. Added to those are the light sources—a radial light inside the lighthouse, and a round spotlight emanating from it. Then there's a tricky glowing fuzzy cylinder to add more oomph to the light beam located closer to the lighthouse. Top it off with a couple of imported DXF models—the chairs, and you've got a scene with some expensive objects. As you can see from the time comparison, materials—and lights— roughly double the render time from no texture to texture. If you're rendering on a 68K Mac, the time is more than tripled from no texture to texture.

The results vary under Macintosh and Windows. Each version offers slightly different options. The Macintosh renders were tested comparing Accelerated Raytesting and Standard Raytesting. Under Windows, the scene was rendered using two different Spatial Optimization settings. (Windows rendered a scene that was originally created on the Macintosh and then imported into the Windows version of Bryce.)

On the Mac, the results of the Fast Preview are telling. They are roughly in the same range as the No Texture option. So, as you begin working with textures, use the Fast Preview option. Use it as an intermediate means of checking the overall look of your scene. Once your scene passes muster, then use the regular render method to do the final honing of your scene. The other thing that is obvious from this is that the Accelerated Raytesting does shave considerable time off of rendering. Use it as well. In fact, since I've used Bryce 2.1, I have used Accelerated Raytesting almost exclusively.

Under Windows, the use of Spatial Optimization drastically affects render time, especially in this scene with imported 3D polyhedron objects. Windows doesn't offer the same time savings for No Texture as the Mac. Additional test renders showed that No Texture did not remove certain surface material properties of surfaces, specifically Reflection and Transparency. This bug in the No Texture render mode skewed the results using the Lighthouse scene. Tests with simpler scenes, which used basic primitives without light objects or imported 3D polyhedrons, resulted in similar time savings as the Macintosh. The Texture Off, Fast Preview, and combined render modes were all faster than the standard render. Look at the CD-ROM's folder for this chapter; the folder called "WinTests" has more information.

Now that I have discussed the general approach to the working order to maximize efficiency in Bryce, I'll turn the topic of discussion to areas of Bryce other than rendering where you can shave your work time.

DISPLAY CONTROLS

The small palette to the right of the scene window holds two sets of controls. They're there to make life easier. The top part controls the displays, and the bottom half controls wireframes. (See Figure 5–5.) For this discussion, I'll talk mostly about the Display controls, since I covered wireframes in Chapter 4, Objects. I briefly will discuss eking out as much from wireframes as possible here, though.

Interface Max/Min

The top Display control, Interface Max/Min, determines where the Bryce palettes will be. You have two basic options with Bryce: snuggled next to the scene window, or huddled next to the edges of the monitor.

Which one do you choose? It's a personal preference, so choose whatever suits you. If you have a large monitor, you'll find that you're forced to choose between a long mouse journey to the menu bar (Interface minimum) or a long mouse journey to the controls surrounding the scene (Interface maximum). I'm using Bryce on a large monitor and find that I need to use the Selection controls more than I access the commands from the menus, so I keep things set to Interface Minimum.

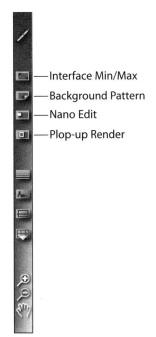

——Interface Min/Max
——Background Pattern
——Nano Edit
——Plop-up Render

Interface Max also provides you with the option of a full screen view of your scene. On the Macintosh, Interface Max has an option of a window with a title bar. (⌘-F takes you there; in fact, if you invoke ⌘-F when you're in Interface Minimum mode, you'll snap to Maximum as well as show the window with the title bar.) Under Windows, Interface Max snaps the palettes to the

Figure 5–5 The Display Palette, with controls labeled.

perimeter of your monitor, but you have no option to see Bryce in a Windows window. I'll discuss more of the window revision for Macs later in this chapter, under the Palette section.

Background Pattern

Background patterns are a matter of personal preference. Choose the one you want from the pop-up menu. (See Figure 5–6.) You can have a textured or a smooth background appearance. Or, choose another color altogether. On the Macintosh, you can also select the options by pressing the Control key while typing the numbers: Control-1 is paper, the first on the list. Control-3 gives you the old Bryce 1 gray. Although there are nine items on the list, the numbers only work up through 6, for some strange reason. (Seven is my background of choice, white. I get to choose it from the pop-up menu each and every time I work in a scene.) Windows Brycers may access the background options from the pop-up menu only.

Background patterns are not saved with the scene file. When the application is open, background patterns are defined for the present. When you open or create a new scene file, your background is inherited from whatever the current settings are. The background preferences will stay that way until you change the settings in the pop-up menu. This works in the case of all the textured and lined background patterns, and in the case of smooth black and gray. It does *not* work, however with white, nor with any custom colors you establish. Each time you create a new scene, or open up scenes when white or custom color is your selection of choice, you get a slightly lighter gray (the same as if you'd chosen No Texture from the pop-up menu when you had the texture set to the default Paper).

Figure 5–6 Background Pattern pop-up menu.

If I sound whiny about this Brycean prejudice against a white background, it's only because I have to manually set the background for each scene I work on whenever I create wireframe images for this book. Your situation probably differs from mine, so your overall experience with background patterns will probably be hunky-dory. If for some reason you do need to set all your backgrounds to white, then beware of the button above, to toggle the interface between minimum and maximum. It's all too easy to set up the interface palettes the way you want, and then go to create yet another white background and, if perchance you click the wrong control… SNAP! your interface now hugs the edges of the monitor (or the scene).

Nano Edit—Dainty (and Fast) Manipulation

The Nano Editor will allow you to make all of your camera adjustments in a smaller view. What does a smaller view mean? It means that instead of having to display a wireframe at 480 x 360 in motion, the Nano Editor only displays it at a fraction of a size (usually 1/4 the size). And what does a fraction of the size mean? Not as many calculation cycles. And what do fewer cycles mean? Fewer cycles mean speed! The Nano Editor is a way to work faster in Bryce. When you have a complex scene file, with many objects in it, working in the Nano Editor will compensate for the slowdown in the regular-sized window display.

There are two ways to access the Nano Editor. The first, of course, is by switching it on using the control on the Display Palette. Then, when you use the camera controls—the Camera Crosses, Banking, Field of View, and the Trackball controls—you'll be working with a smaller window while you make your adjustments (see

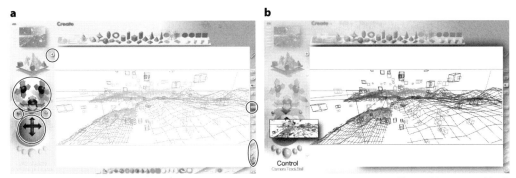

Figure 5–7 a) When Nano Edit is switched on, the encircled controls will be affected. b) As Trackball control is activated, a small window appears showing Trackball camera movements.

Figure 5–7). Similarly, the Flyaround and all panning will occur in a smaller window. (The Flyaround rotates at a nice clip!) In addition, when making adjustments to the wireframe in the wireframe depth cueing, you'll be making the adjustments to a smaller version of the scene.

The second way is the on-the-fly method. Hold down the space bar and Option key (Macintosh) or space bar and Alt key (Windows) and position your mouse inside the main scene window. The cursor changes to a rotation arrow (see Figure 5–8a). Once you press and drag the mouse there, a small window appears, showing you live motion of the adjustments you make (Figure 5–8b). You can release the space bar and Option key (or space bar and Alt key) once you've begun dragging the mouse. The range of motion is the same as for the Trackball. Dragging left and right rotates the scene, dragging up and down adjusts the tilt up and down. When you press the Command key (Ctrl key for Windows), you can move closer or further

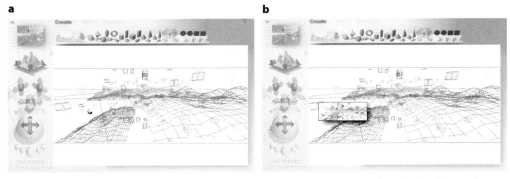

Figure 5–8 On-the-fly Nano Editor: a) Cursor changes to rotation arrow when Option key and space bar are pressed; b) When mouse is pressed, the Nano Edit window appears.

from the center of the scene by dragging up and down (the tilt up and down is suspended while the Command or Ctrl key is pressed).

Space bar and Option key (Macintosh) or space bar and Alt key (Windows) with a mouse click on any of the palettes resets them back to their default position, so don't try this indiscriminately.

Plop-Up Render

The last option on the Display Palette to the right of the scene window is the Plop-Up Render. When this is on (the Display icon is red), your rendered area will plop up from the rest of the scene, separated from all the rest by a drop shadow. Next to the marquee are three controls. The large sphere is for Clear and Render. The smaller sphere is to resume rendering inside the marqueed area. The triangle yields a pop-up menu for two more options, Zoom to Selection and Hide Selection. (See Figure 5–9.)

Figure 5–9 Plop-up Render with its accompanying pop-up menu.

You can still render in small areas if you don't want to have the Plop-Up Render window showing. You'll have to use the Clear and Render button on the main Render Palette or use that ol' ⌘-Option-R (Macintosh) or Ctrl+Alt+R (Windows). The advantage to the Plop-up, once you get used to it (it does take a bit of getting used to, in my experience), is that you'll like having the render button right there.

The state of the marqueed area is fragile, and it's all to easy to inadvertently drag a new one elsewhere in your scene area, especially when you don't intend to. It's one of those irritating things that won't occur when you want it to and will occur precisely when you don't want it to.

Well-tempered Wireframes

Working in wireframe view is the fastest way to view your scene, right? Well, yes and no. Viewing in wireframe is certainly faster than completely rendering the scene, especially while the scene is still evolving. But there are things you can do to make your computer draw the wireframe on-screen as quickly as possible. You also can reduce the clutter of wireframe objects when you have many of them placed in your scene.

Set up your wireframes so that they don't take more processing than they need to. Check out the wireframe section in the Objects chapter (Chapter 4) for many of the gory details, but the basic idea is that the higher the wireframe detail, the more your computer has to think about what it's showing, and the longer time it takes to display things. Here are the signs that things are too slow: After each move you make, when Bryce transitions from wireframe in motion to wireframe that's static, the pause while Bryce thinks about redrawing grows longer and longer. When you have three terrains and a handful of primitives, it won't matter, really. But when you get up there in the dozens, or even the hundreds (or thousands) of objects, Bryce will slow to a moribund crawl. Make all your settings as low-detailed as possible.

Another strategy for pepping Bryce out of a torpor is to change wireframes so that they show as boxes (Objects > Show as Box or ⌘-B on the Mac; Ctrl+B on Windows). Rather than having to draw all the details of a terrain, or torus, or other shape, Bryce only has to draw twelve straight lines to define the edges of the

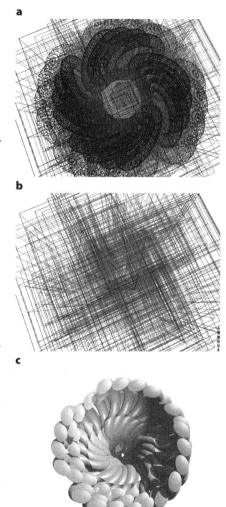

Figure 5–10 Bill Ellsworth wireframe series: a) Wireframe in Lattice mode; b) wireframe in Box mode; c) completed render.

box. Figure 5–10 shows a comparison between the wireframes when shown as boxes and as lattices in this image by Bill Ellsworth. To create the image, with 385 objects, Ellsworth changed all his wireframes to boxes. Even at that, it was slow going in Bryce.

The other advantage to having some wireframes show as boxes is that you can have the highest detail wireframe resolution for those objects you're currently working with, and make everything else the lowest—box form. Along with static and selected, you can place the lowest of the low—box—into your list of wireframe options. So change into boxes the objects that you can ignore for now. You can always change them back later.

Finally, you may do the same lattice-to-box action to a set of grouped objects. (More on grouping in Chapter 6.) The group will be changed to a single box.

Make this Scene as Efficient as You Can!

Here's a scene for you to practice all your newfound display shortcuts to make work in Bryce as streamlined as possible.

1.   Open up the scene file NANO RENDER ME! from the CD-ROM. It is quite a scene, with nearly 200 spheres, close to 50 tori, and a handful of the requisite terrains. In addition, just for kicks, it's in a lengthy wide format, just so you can see how the Nano Edit always displays the wireframe in the aspect ratio (and, incidentally, you can see that the Nano Preview, in the top of the Master control palette, does not).

Try to make this scene work as smoothly on your computer as possible. There are three areas to make adjustments:

2.   Viewing Efficiency. Make the wireframes as efficient as possible. Reduce the detail. Change objects to boxes. Group the tori and change the group to a box. See Figure 5–11.

Figure 5–11 Wireframe shown as lattices and as boxes.

3.   Working Efficiency. Work in Nano Edit mode. Compare how Trackball or other camera motion works in Nano Edit versus the normal wireframe scene.

4.   Render Efficiency. This scene also happens to have a set of render doozies to it. All those lovely spheres are transparent, reflective, and slightly refractive, making them render hogs. Until you have everything placed just so, try rendering without textures to work on placement only. See Figure 5–12.

BATCH MANAGEMENT

Figure 5–12 Render a) With textures switched off; b) with normal rendering.

Once you've completed your work on that scene, or a group of scenes, render them all later, when you're asleep or at the gym, or watching your favorite soaps. You can do this by batch rendering. Batch rendering is similar on Macintosh and Windows. But there are differences. The basic method to batch render scenes is to drag multiple scene file icons and drop them onto the Bryce application icon. You can use an alias (Macintosh) in place of either the scene file or the application icon. In Windows, you can use a shortcut in place of the Bryce application icon. (The Windows Explorer's shortcut for a scene file does not work.)

On a Mac, you can begin a batch render whether Bryce is unlaunched or is already running. (When you launch Bryce with a batch render, the render progress information is displayed in eentsy type.) Using Windows, you must start a batch render when Bryce is not launched.

Suppose you created several scenes and set them all to render overnight. In the morning, you return to your computer × and the renders aren't finished. Here's a way to remember which ones still need rendering. It's a technique for the Macintosh Finder that doesn't have an equivalent in the Windows Explorer, since the means of listing and sorting files differ between the two platforms' operating systems.

1. Before doing your first batch render and while you're in the Finder, change the label of all of the scenes to "Essential" for the scenes that you want to render. Then select View > By Label. All of your Scene document icons are now grouped together. (See Fig. 5–13.)

2. Drag the Scene icons to your Bryce Application icon, shut off your monitor, and go to sleep (or leave the office).

3. When you return to your computer, Bryce will have rendered, say, half of the six scenes. The fourth is halfway through the anti-aliasing pass. Save the

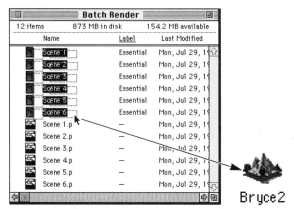

Figure 5–13 Batch render list in the Macintosh Finder—before rendering.

scene in progress and go to the Finder. All of your scene icons are still labeled "Essential" except for scene four; its label changed back to None when you saved it. Change it back to "Essential," since you know you have some more rendering to do. See Figure 5–14a.

4. Unlabel the scenes that were completed so that you don't drag those to the Bryce application icon the next time you do a batch render session. Select View > By Date. A series of PICT icons appears near the top of the folder (along with the scene icon for the fourth scene you just saved). You can see from this list those scenes whose labels you want to change back to None. Figure 5–14b shows the pared-down list, ready for the next batch session. Although the scenes shown here are for a medium- to small-sized list, when you get a scene backlog of some two dozen images, this technique comes in extremely handy.

As a result, you have kept your icon labels up to date. The next time you want to do a batch render, all you need to do is simply view by label, select the labeled scene document icons, and drag them to your Bryce application icon (or its alias).

Variation on this theme. (For Macs only.) If you are working on several scenes which have documents residing in different folders on your hard drive, create a To Be Rendered folder. Make aliases of your scenes in progress and put them in that folder. Drag all the aliases onto the Bryce application icon (or alias) to batch render. The originals stay in their own folders, and you get your batch rendering done.

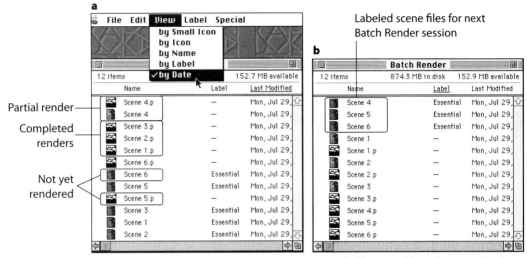

Figure 5–14 Batch render list a) After rendering three-and-a-half scenes; b) ready to render the remaining scenes.

Variation for System 7.5.x. (Again, Macintosh only.) System 7.5.x has a folder called Recent Documents. The system creates aliases for the 10 most recent documents you have had open. Access Recent Documents from the Apple menu. Select the entire folder. There you will find your recent scene document aliases, all ready to be dragged to your To Be Rendered folder for later batch processing.

GENERAL BRYCEAN BEHAVIOR AND OTHER TECHNICAL CONSIDERATIONS

This last section of the chapter turns the focus away from making you a "Bryce efficiency expert" to simply being a Bryce expert. Here I discuss general things about the way Bryce behaves.

Option-clicking: Revert and Variations

Here is something worth mentioning as a standard all over the Bryce software. After you have manipulated things, and you want to reset something to its default state, try Option-clicking (Macintosh) or Alt-clicking (Windows). This works with some camera controls; it removes saved camera views and saved skies (both camera and sky memory dots), it resets wireframe depth cueing, it resets panning and zooming, it works within the Preset previews and Terrain Editor to place objects in standard position, it resets the brackets in the Terrain Editor clipping, and perhaps there is another case or so where it reverts to the default state (alas, it doesn't work in the Materials Composer to reset the refract index back to the default setting of 100).

Option-clicking or Alt-clicking is not completely consistent across the board, however, for a revert-to-default. Option-clicking or Alt-clicking, in the case of all color swatches, brings up a different color picker, and in the Materials Composer texture sources, it brings up the Deep Texture Editor.

Naming Scene Files

When you name your scene file, Bryce names your rendered image file for you, adding a suffix to the image file name. In Bryce for Macintosh, the rendered PICT file will be assigned a suffix of .P. For the file name GROOVY SCENE FROM OUTTA SPACE, Bryce will assign the PICT image the name GROOVY SCENE FROM OUTTA SPACE.P. The maximum number of characters in a Mac file name is 31. The example here just happens to hit the upper limit. What happens if you were to go over that limit, say, in assigning a scene name A GROOVY SCENE FROM OUTTA SPACE? In cases where your scene file name is 29 or 30 characters in length, Bryce will truncate the name (at the end) in order to add the .P suffix. The resulting PICT name will become A GROOVY SCENE FROM OUTTA SPA.P. The only problem with this is that since the names don't match up, Bryce will not automatically open up the image file when the scene file is opened. Here's how I ensure that I keep the last two characters for the .P suffix: When I name scene files with a long name, I type two extra spaces at the end. When you try to add the thirty-second character to a file name, the Mac doesn't allow it, and gives you a system alert. If I get no alert while typing the two extra spaces, I know that I'm "home free." Then I delete the two spaces (since I didn't want them, but used them just for a test), and save the scene with the name I gave it. If I do get an alert, then I remove characters elsewhere from the name (vowels are good things to delete), until the scene passes the two-spaces-at-the-end test.

In Windows, Bryce assigns extensions to both the scene file and the image file (.BRC for scene files, .BMP for rendered image files). When you save the scene file, Bryce automatically writes the rendered image file. Users of Bryce under Windows do not have to be as circumspect as Mac users about the characters at the end of the file name, since Windows 95 and Windows NT allow for file names with up to 256 characters. If you cannot manage to keep your file names under 256 characters (well, 252, actually, but who's quibbling?), than I can offer you no further advice. You can choose whether to show the file name extensions by selecting File > Option, then clicking the View tab, and clicking the checkbox next to the text that says Hide MS-DOS file extensions for file types that are registered. If you do so, the extensions will be automatically added to the files without possibility of your inadvertantly overtyping a part of the extension.

If you are transferring a Macintosh Bryce scene file to Windows, make sure to add the .BRC extension so that Windows Bryce will recognize it. (Depending on the networking software to connect your Mac and PC together, or the utility to make one type of computer write to or read from the other kind of computer's diskettes, you'll probably have to limit the file name to the old boring utilitarian eight-plus-three file name structure.)

Preset Libraries

There is a Bryce Preset Library that exists for each of the three main palettes: Create Palette, Edit Palette, and Sky & Fog Palette. They hold settings for objects, materials, and sky settings, respectively.

Click the triangle next to the name to access any of the preset libraries. That palette needn't be active in order to access the library. In Figure 5–15, although the Sky & Fog Palette is currently active, a click on the triangle next to the Edit title will bring up the Edit Preset Library.

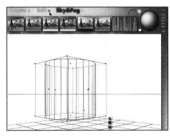

Figure 5–15 Accessing the Edit Preset Library when another palette is currently active.

Once inside the Preset Library, there is a list of categories for the objects. The Sky & Fog Library has no categories, though. Figure 5–16 shows an example of each of the three types of Preset Libraries. To view a type of category, simply click the name in the left column. The presets from that category will show up. If there are more presets than there are preset image tiles, then the last tile will be replaced by an arrow or set of arrows for scrolling through the entire list.

If you see one that you'd like, how do you apply it? Click the preset tile. The frame surrounding it turns red and its image shows up in the preview window. (In these illustrations the selected tile is an exaggerated white.) If there is a title and a text description for the preset, it shows up to the right of the main preview. Now it is the active one. To apply it, click the OK check mark. Depending what type of library you were in, you will have either a new material surface for the selected object, a new sky setting, or you will have introduced a new object or group into your scene.

a

b

c

  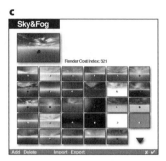

Figure 5–16 Preset Libraries: a) Object Presets; b) Materials Presets; c) Sky & Fog Presets.

When you're inside the Objects and Materials Libraries, you can change your views of the object. For the Objects Preset Library, you must have selected an object or group before entering the library in order to change the view of the object. If you have no object selected in your scene, you are limited to only looking at the different options in a slightly enlarged (and pixellated) view. If you have more than one object selected, they must be grouped in order for all of them to show up in the Objects Library.

Figure 5–17 Objects Preset pop-up menu.

From the pop-up menu, you can choose whether the object is viewed close up or at a normal distance (see Figure 5–17). The object can render against a neutral sky or the sky that you currently have established in your scene. (The current sky will affect the appearance of the object or material. Later on, under a different sky, you may select that preset and wonder why it doesn't look like the one you saw in the preset tile. The sky made it different.) Besides choosing these options from the pop-up menu that resides under the preview window, you can click directly in the window to momentarily see the corresponding wireframe and drag to customize your view of the object.

Dragging horizontally to the left and right rotates the object in front of you. In fact, you are moving your position around the object. This means that you can check your surface texture in direct sunlight, in shadow, and lit from the side. Dragging down vertically moves you above the object, or even over to its other side. Keep going and you'll be below it. Pressing the Command key (Macintosh) or Ctrl key (Windows) while dragging vertically moves the object closer or further away from you. Pressing the space bar while dragging allows you to pan around to change the framing of the object in the preview window. Pressing the Option key (Macintosh) or Alt key (Windows) while clicking the window restores the object to its default position.

Do these settings seem familiar to you? They should… or, if they don't, they will soon. These are the same shortcuts for moving your position in relation to the object (or scene, or terrain) that you find elsewhere in Bryce 2. The Nano Edit, Flyaround, and Terrain Editor preview share most or all of these same manipulations.

For the Materials Preset Library, the pop-up menu has another set of options for viewing your object. You can change the object being shown, from the current selection to the following primitive types: box, sphere, cone cylinder, terrain, ground, torus. (See Figure 5–18.)

Figure 5–18 The Materials Presets Library pop-up menu.

You know the options for manipulating the object inside the Preset Library. You know how to get a preset from a library into your scene. How about getting something from your scene into the library?

For Objects and Materials Presets, you need to have something selected before opening up the library. The Sky & Fog Library does not need an object selected, since it is not paying attention to *objects* anyhow. (It will place a sphere in each preview, as an added reference so you can tell the direction of the sun or moon.) To add a preset, let the preview render. It will take a few passes to completely render (see Figure 5–19a). (If you don't like the appearance, and want to move the object, this is the time to do so. Render again. To force a render from scratch, click in the preview window.) At that point, click the Add button. You'll be presented with a dialog box into which you may type your pithy description of the preset. The description allows you to add comments and reminders to yourself about it. The description typed in Figure 5–19 and shown in the resulted added texture in part c provides a memory jogger to use the preset smartly or do further manipulations later on. You can, if you want, add to your description. Simply click the text area and it becomes editable (see Figure 5–19d).

To delete a preset, simply select it and click Delete. You'll be asked if you're sure you want to do so, just in case you accidentally clicked Delete. After I explain some more about libraries, you may *never* be sure that you want to Delete. Stay tuned.

What if you want to import or export a set of presets? You can transfer them and trade them with your friends. How do you move them about? First, I'll talk about exporting presets, followed by a discussion of importing them.

In order to export presets, you need to select them. The Preset Libraries obey standard conventions for selecting in a list of items. Select one item by clicking it. There are two ways to select multiple items. To select everything between two objects, click the first object, and Shift-click the last object. Everything in between is selected. To select here and there, press the Command key (Macintosh) or Ctrl (Windows) while clicking each item you want to select. Figure 5–20a through c show the different results of these selection options.

You can only select objects from one category at a time. You cannot select some presets from, say, Rocks & Stones and keep Command-clicking or Ctrl-clicking to add presets from the Waters & Liquid category.

So, once you have your preset or presets selected, click Export. You get a standard Save dialog box, and you can name your preset file whatever you'd like to. When you click that Save button, Bryce will write the exported preset file. As it does so, it will momentarily display each preview that you had selected in the preview window.

If for some reason you forgot to select *any* preset, Bryce will merrily lead you through all the steps of saving, complete with a bit of disk-writing cogitation at the end, but no exported preset file will be written. Never cry wolf.

To import objects, the process is reversed. Click import, and you are presented with a dialog box. Select the Preset Library you want to import. As Bryce imports, watch all the new imported presets flash in the preview window

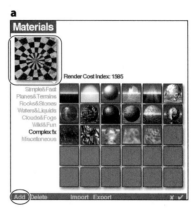

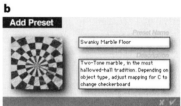

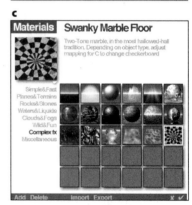

Figure 5–19 Adding a preset: a) Rendering the preset before clicking Add; b) text entry for preset; c) the result. d) To edit text later, click it.

as it's brought into your library. At the conclusion of the import, all the newly imported presets are selected with red frames showing. There are, however, some things to watch for. You cannot import into more than one category at a time. And you cannot import into a different category than the one you're in at the moment. If you want to import boolean objects, then you'd best be in boolean objects, not Rocks & Stones. But most awkward of all, if you import more than you need, deleting one or more presets is chancy. I'll explain the dubious nature of deletion—and the best way to work around it—after a bit more background explanation of how the preset files work.

There are three preset file types. They are found in the Bryce2 Support Files folder inside the Bryce application folder. They have different names:

- NAME.OBJ

- NAME.SHD

- NAME.SKY

The first part of the file name, NAME, is a file for the category. You'll see different ones that correspond to different categories, e.g., EFFECTS.SHD. The second part, .OBJ, .SHD, and .SKY, identifies which library it belongs to, objects, materials shaders, or sky presets. The files are standard Bryce scene files; you can open them up and render them (.SKY doesn't work exactly the same way, so you won't see anything meaningful in the scene). These library files have a data structure; for each preset, there is information for the objects or materials or sky, and there is a small thumbnail preview image—the one you see in the Preset Library. Bryce keeps track of them by number, with the image preview matching the data set. When you delete a preset, the image is purged,

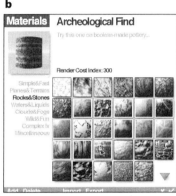

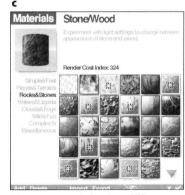

Figure 5–20 Selecting different presets: a) Selecting one preset with a single mouse click; b) clicking again with the Shift key held down selects all presets in between; c) clicking here and there with the Command key or Ctrl key pressed selects non-adjoining presets.

but the data set is not. Or at least, given the underlying numbering scheme, the purge isn't clean; Bryce doesn't take too kindly to renumbering. So it's very easily possible to import settings, and when deleting, delete the image thumbnail, but not the data, so that when you exit the Preset Library you get the preset next door to the one you selected. For you Macintosh Brycers, if you used Bryce 1.0, you may remember the Recycle button for replacing a preset with another one. The "replace" of Bryce 1.0 addressed the limits of the numbered file structure in a way that Bryce 2.1 does not.

In light of the shakiness of Preset importation, devise a strategy. If you want to import presets from one Bryce application to another, say, from Bryce on your home computer to Bryce on your office computer, do a bit of advanced planning to make sure you'll import only the presets you want. Instead of importing *everything* from the other version (where no doubt there is overlap between some presets), open that other version and export only the presets that you will want to have. Yes, it requires a bit more painstaking effort, and it's not as graphically intuitive as you were led to believe, but you also won't need to tear the underlying structure of your presets to shreds and risk having to build your presets from scratch, either.

Here are my recommendations for Preset Libraries. The Objects libraries are nice places to start. The Boolean Objects section of the Objects Library has quite a clever tutorial built into the thumbnails and descriptions. It's a great place to get some trees, too. But is this the place where you want to store all your carefully built objects? I'd say not. There are some objects from the Objects Preset Library—the ones that ship with the product—that lamely enter Bryce with one or another element marred. If it could happen to those objects, it can happen to the ones you built, too. It's much safer to keep your own object library on your hard drive with the one object in one scene file. (Remember, in the Preset Library, one category file houses *all* the objects in that category. The higher you go, the harder you fall.) If you want to both save a scene file and create an object preset, then give the preset a name that matches the scene file name. Scroll through your Objects Library, see the one you want, note the name, and then use your conventional Macintosh Finder or Windows Explorer's Find command to hunt down that scene file. Turn the Objects Preset Library into your reference library.

The Sky & Fog Presets are good places to store different options for skies. Be careful about importing and then deleting, though. If worse comes to worst, you can always create a separate scene file for the Sky Preset and re-save the presets.

The preset library that I find to be the most helpful is the Materials Preset Library. It's more robust than the others, as it's not so easy to overload. (Beware bulk importing, though. Import-then-delete has been known to tear this library to shreds, too.) It also happens to be a dual-purpose library, accessed from the Edit Palette as well as from within the Materials Composer. You lucky Windows Brycers get a bonus: two additional Material Preset Library categories—Glasses and Metals. Throughout the rest of the book, I'll refer to the Materials Preset Library the most, followed by the Sky & Fog Preset Library. The Objects Library… well, I mentioned it here, didn't I?

Save Prompts When Closing Files

Aside from the Preset Libraries, Bryce has greatly improved the forgiving ability of the application and the scene files in general in Bryce 2. Whereas Bryce 1 was shaky in its allowance of Undos (limited to Edit actions only) and skimpy with its prompts to save scenes (it only recognized edit actions as being worthy of a "Do you want to save?" prompt, but didn't do so at the end of a long render), Bryce 2 provides a lot of cushion room for you while you work. Gone is the need to be hyper-vigilant about saving a scene after rendering, because if you forgot, Bryce wouldn't remind you. Now it does. Here, then, is a small list of occasions when Bryce will prompt you to save the scene.

The standard Macintosh and Windows convention is to present a Save dialog box when you first save a scene document, so you can give it a name. Thereafter, whenever you save, it merely saves to that same file, without presenting a dialog box, unless you specifically request one by selecting Save As… from the File menu. Bryce has a few special instances where the request to save automatically brings up a Save As… dialog box. If you merge your scene with another one, when you choose File > Save or type ⌘-S (Macintosh) or Ctrl+S (Windows), Bryce will present you with the Save dialog box so that you may rename the new merged scene. (More about scene merging in Chapter 7, "Booleans and Multiple Object Construction.") If you change the resolution of the scene or the render in the Document Setup dialog box, the next time you go to save the document Bryce will present you with the Save As… dialog box. At that time you may rename the differently-sized document or save it over the old one. (Use this technique when you make high-resolution scenes based on smaller originals. The first one could be called something like SCENE NAME and the new one, when you are given the chance to rename it, could be called SCENE NAME.HIREZ.)

This next instance is a Bryce-prompt-to-save that's worth rejoicing over. When you have completely rendered a scene, and close it (by quitting the application, opening another scene, or by creating a new scene), Bryce will ask whether you want to save the scene, (whew! yes, after all that time rendering, yes, yes, yes!) and, if so, it will present you with a dialog box for naming the scene. In this case, you can save the scene as is and confirm that you *do* want to replace the old one with this one.

The only time the "Revert to saved" function is grayed out in Bryce is when you have created a new scene and have not yet saved it. When you change from one resolution to another, Bryce treats the situation the same as if you had just created a new document.

Because of Bryce's habit to prompt at various times, you might be confused. Although you have opened a scene, checked to see that a particular object's material is set to thus-and-so, and then want to close it again and move on to another scene, you will get a prompt asking if you want to save changes. If you select an object, or enter any separate dialog boxes to edit objects, terrains, or materials, even though you've made no changes, Bryce will ask you if you want to save. After a while you get used to these seemingly bogus queries and appreciate the genuine ones (especially at the end of a render!).

Preferences

In the Preferences dialog box (Edit > Preferences…), you have the option of choosing different states under which Bryce will run. Figure 5–21 shows the Preferences dialog box. It is slightly different for each platform.

Preferences can be divided into two categories: global preferences that affect the entire application, and "local" preferences for that particular scene file. The global

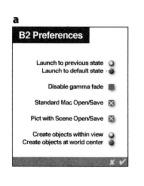

Figure 5–21 The Preferences dialog box: a) Macintosh; b) Windows.

preferences are kept in a small file in your system's Preferences folder, and the local preferences for the scene file are kept with the scene file.

The first of the global preferences, a Macintosh-only option, is gamma fade. Some computers work better without any gamma fade. Gamma fade, which takes place from the Finder when you first launch Bryce, makes the monitor behave like a theater, where the house lights are brought down and fade up when the performer, Bryce, has now come on the stage.

Also global—and exotic, perhaps, is the option not to have Mac standard Open and Save dialog boxes. (This, obviously, is a preference option available only on Macintosh computers.) The Brycean non-Mac alternative version is a bit more hip, as well as nicely functional. When opening scene files it displays the image preview for the accompanying PICT file. That way, in case you forgot, you'll know what the heck "My cool scene" is *really* about.

Then there are the local settings common to both Mac and Windows versions of Bryce: Launch to previous state and launch to default state. This setting primarily affects the sky in Bryce (for Bryce on Macs)—will you get the previous sky or the default sky? Will the sun be linked to view or not? Launch to Previous also affects the render options under the Render pop-up menu—whether anti-aliasing is off or on (under Windows there is another Fine Art option for anti-aliasing), whether there is a render report, and/or whether—under Windows—spatial optimization is off, medium or high.

What's a bit surprising is what is *not* part of the default state: The display controls—Interface Minimum or Maximum, Background Pattern, Nano Edit, and Plop-up Render—are not affected by the preferences. Whatever state you left Bryce when you last quit will be the state it launches to the next time. In this way, you can truly customize your settings and keep them from one Bryce work session to the next.

This explains, too, the function of the two commands in the Edit menu that are located above the Preferences… command. If you have moved any of the palettes to another position by space bar-dragging them, Reset Palettes will straighten them out and send them back to their original positions. If you have set the Interface to maximum (hugging edge of monitor), then Reset Palettes will make them once again hug the edge of the monitor. Likewise, if you have set the Interface to minimum (hugging the scene window), then they'll snap back to that position.

Reset to Defaults will take you back to the original pristine state of Bryce, complete with original paper texture, palettes that hug the scene window, and a plain blue sky with the sun linked to view. It's the same as when you first launched Bryce right after installing it on your hard drive.

So now that I've told you what the Preferences' default or previous state does *not* include, let me tell you what it does include. "Previous" is best thought of as the settings from the previous scene file that you had open.

These settings change from scene to scene as different ones are opened, changed, and saved: Launch to Default/Launch to Previous; Pict (or Image) with Open/Save; Create Objects at World Center or within view of your scene.

Now, normally, you won't go changing preferences between each and every scene file that you save, like I did when researching their function for this section of the chapter. So you won't have the opportunity to notice or be confused by their strange capricious behavior.

No matter what happens, Bryce launches to a default sky (unless you launch Bryce by double-clicking a scene file, in which case it launches to the sky from that scene). If you have set Preferences to "Previous," if you're on a Mac, the next new scene file you create will inherit the sky from the previous scene file. Under Windows, you will always get a default sky, whether or not you have Default/Previous selected. However, if you change the preferences to default and then save that scene, the next time you create a new scene file, it will inherit the sky from the previous one, which will mean it will have a default sky.

Similarly, the setting for a new Bryce scene inherits the Create objects at world center/within view setting from the last scene file you had open. The same thing goes for the Open/Save Pict (Image) with scene (which, incidentally, I always leave on unless I purposely want to save a scene file separate from the rendered image). It makes you wonder what a default state is, or what kind of preferences are global enough to counteract the scene file.

Here, then is a concluding remark about preferences. You'll probably set them up and forget about them. It's certainly smart; I do the same thing, except for the times when I futz around with them because I have to write about them. Since you can click the Memory Dots to return sky settings to default, and since Bryce launches to a default sky no matter what, I'd recommend keeping your preferences set to "previous." It's far easier to make a sky turn back to default than it is to go back and get a sky from another scene that you just closed (unless you're in Windows, in which case, I'd recommend clicking a Memory Dot before you start a new scene, if you want to bring over the sky from the previous scene).

Windows Memory Structure

In the Windows version of Bryce, the preferences have an option for assigning Physical Memory. It lists the total RAM available on your computer, and then allows you to decide what percentage of that available memory you want to assign to Bryce. For reference, it tells you the amount of memory that is currently being used by Bryce. What is available RAM? It is the amount of memory not in use by the operating system or by disk caching software. You can assign anything from 0-200% of the available RAM to Bryce. When you assign more than 100% of available RAM, you'll be calling upon virtual memory to do so.

Palette Principles for the Proficient Person

As I mentioned, Bryce has one Interface control that lets you decide whether you want the palettes to hug the scene or to hug the edge of the monitor.

There are yet other options: dragging them around to reposition them. Hold down the spacebar and drag. This is different from the normal Macintosh or Windows "drag by the title bar" behavior. If you want to reset everything back to normal, then press the Option and space bar (Macintosh) or Alt and space bar (Windows) keys and click a palette. Back they go, hugging the edge of your scene. Wait a second. Didn't we talk about that Option (or Alt) and space bar combination earlier? Yes, when you hold down the Option (or Alt) key and space bar and click *inside* the scene area, you get the Nano Edit window. The same key combination applied to a palette brings all the palettes back to their standard home spots. Needless to say, don't click the palettes when you want to elicit the Nano Editor, and vice versa.

Oh, and speaking of the palettes and the black area surrounding, that *is* active area. If you have a larger monitor, try this: create a new scene, with a new ground plane in it. Now click in the area below where the wireframe for the ground "extends." Wait just a second, you say. What's that? It turned red! Yup, you clicked outside the scene window and selected one of your objects. Your outside area may be black, gray, or even a striped legal pad, but it's still active area. So don't drag out there thinking it's no man's land. It's your Bryceland, actively. All of it.

Keyboard stuff

Unless you have concocted your custom setup by dragging palettes this way 'n' that, you'll have only one of the Create, Edit, or Sky & Fog Palettes showing at a time. (And, of course, every time you open or create a new scene file, you'll pop back to the Create Palette.) No doubt by now you've discovered that you can make one of the other two palettes active by clicking its title. You can do the same thing using keyboard shortcuts as well. Here are their keyboard equivalents:

⌘-1 (Mac) or Ctrl+1 (Windows)	=	Create Palette
⌘-2 (Mac) or Ctrl+2 (Windows)	=	Edit Palette
⌘-3 (Mac) or Ctrl+3 (Windows)	=	Sky & Fog Palette
⌘-4 (Mac)	=	Control Palette
⌘-5 (Mac)	=	Select Palette
⌘-6 (Mac)	=	Display/Wireframe Palette
⌘-Tab (Mac) or Ctrl+Tab (Windows)	=	Toggle Palettes off
⌘-F (Mac)	=	Full Screen

Under Windows, you cannot get the Control, Select, or Display/Wireframe Palettes to appear using key commands, nor can you invoke the full screen command.

The ⌘-Tab/Ctrl+Tab toggle is good to use in combination with the others. Suppose you have a smaller monitor, and a larger scene, one that's going to take a while to render. You want to watch the render's progress while seeing as much of the scene as you can. Toggle all of the palettes off, then use the key command sequences to bring back only those you absolutely need—most probably ⌘-4, the Control Palette. Then use the space bar drag to move it out of the way so that only the render time and render buttons show. Your particular working situation may suggest other alternatives; go to it.

Full Screen Command (⌘-F; Macintosh Only)

Bryce's default method of displaying on-screen is to black out everything but the scene and the palettes. If you have a cluttered desktop or other open applications and windows, this enables you to concentrate solely on Bryce. But there may be times when you want your scene to appear in a regular window. An apply of ⌘-F will toggle you back and forth between Full Screen mode and Window mode. When you switch to Window mode, you'll automatically jump to Interface Maximum (palettes hug edge of monitor) as well.

Why would you want Bryce to be in Window mode? There are at least two possible reasons. First, if you are working on several versions of a scene and discover that you've lost your place ("Wait a second, which scene was this?"), then by having Bryce in Window mode, you can see the file name on the window's Title bar. (Additional alternatives, especially helpful for Windows Brycers, who have no access to title bars: You can do the same by selecting Save As... from the File menu. Bryce automatically puts the current file name in the Save dialog box. Once you've found out the name, click Cancel. Or, bring up the Document Setup dialog box—double-click the Render sphere or type ⌘-Option-N (Macintosh) or Ctrl+Alt+N (Windows). The name of the scene is displayed in there, too.)

Second, you may want to toggle between two applications. Say you are carefully working on a terrain and need to change it in Photoshop. You can toggle between Bryce and Photoshop with a mouse click on any of the background application's open windows. You can see the other application beneath the current one when you are in Window mode.

A third alternative, for those with two monitors, uses Window mode. I'll describe it in more detail in a little bit.

Full screen and Mac-Style Windows (Macintosh Only)

When you are in Window mode, you get a standard Macintosh document window, complete with Title bar, Zoom box, Size box, scroll bars and arrows—but no Close box (grrr. . . I've always wanted one of those). You'd think that a click on the Zoom box in the upper right of the document window would make the box snap down to the size of the scene file, right? Wrong! It will enlarge to fit the size of your monitor. In Bryce's way of thinking, the two sizes the Zoom box will jump to are the present size and maximum size. Or, the size of the area just inside the palettes and the size of the monitor. Oops, forget I said toggling. Once you have expanded the window, the Title bar hides under the palettes, making it all but unusable at that point. (⌘-Tab will hide the palettes so you can click the Zoom box to reduce it to fit just inside the palettes. Then ⌘-Tab to bring those palettes back.) I'd rather see it so that it toggles between the render size, say, 480 × 360, and the maximum amount of space that can be there inside the palettes. *That* would be logical, and even useful. If Bryce knows the area of the active scene in order to make its palettes hug up against it, why not have the document window be able to do the same?

The practical uses for the Macintosh document window rests with the Title bar, the Size box and scroll bars. Use the Size box to make the window smaller, so that you can see what you need to see elsewhere on your monitor. The Title bar, besides allowing you to reposition your scene, also allows you to do something way cool—activate WindowShade (A Control Panel available under System 7.5 or later) to make the scene disappear momentarily. Click (or double-click or triple-click, depending on your settings for WindowShade) the scene closed for a moment so that you can see your desktop. Progress at last!

Palette Placement tricks and Two-Monitor Brycing

When you have a larger monitor that displays 800 × 600 pixels or better, you can drag out the other palettes (Edit, Sky & Fog) to other places on your screen so that you can see different palettes simultaneously. If you do that, it's probably better to work in Interface minimum size, so that the palettes maintain the smaller width, matching the width of the scene. However, if you change your scene from, say, default (480 × 360) to, perhaps the 640 × 386 option, the palettes next to the scene will rearrange themselves around a new center, and the extra palettes placed elsewhere on your screen will widen accordingly, extending to the right by whatever the new size is. Figure 5–22 illustrates how this works, using a monitor that measures 1152 × 882 pixels.

a

b

Figure 5–22 How palettes change when the scene size is changed: a) Bryce default scene size; b) after enlarging scene size to 640 x 386.

A different alternative is to work with palettes in two monitor setups (far more prevalent on Macs). Assuming that one monitor is larger than the others, as in this setup shown in Figure 5–23, you cannot see the full length of the Master Palette when it is on the smaller monitor (the menu bars and font are different due to customization of this particular computer). Its size is determined by the size of the main monitor; though it has been moved to a smaller monitor, the Control Palette still thinks of itself as hugging the edge of the larger monitor. Because of this delusion of grandeur, the bottom text display—the one that tells you what's what—is missing. (The diagonal stripes represent what is not viewable because there is no monitor there.) Likewise, the positioning of certain dialog boxes and the preset libraries takes its cue from the position of the main Control Palette and the Nano Preview location, so they must show.

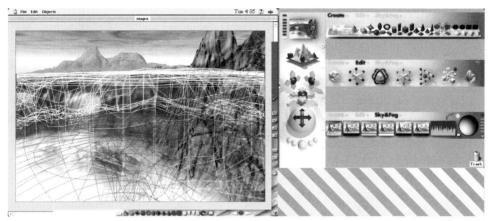

Figure 5–23 Screen shot of a two-monitor working situation, with all palettes arranged on the second, smaller monitor.

Plop-Up Dialog Boxes

Bryce's plop-up dialog boxes have dual-access controls. The plop-up dialog boxes are the Object Attributes dialog box, the Family Attributes dialog box, and the Preset Libraries. They act like both of two Macintosh standard user interface items: pop-up menus, and dialog boxes. When they are pop-up menus, you press the mouse on the switch that opens it up (either a triangle or an Object control icon), drag to change the setting, and when you release the mouse, they disappear. To access the same thing as a dialog box, click the switch. The dialog box opens until you send it away by the usual OK or Cancel routes.

Similar to the plop-up dialog boxes is the plop-render display. It shares the drop shadow with the plop-up dialog box, but none of the other "It behaves like a dialog box! It behaves like a pop-up menu! It's two, two, two functions in one!" attributes.

Monitors: What to Do with Screen Savers, Clocks, and Other Details

You will probably have Bryce render during the time you are away from your computer, for example when you are asleep or on your lunch hour. So, you will inevitably run into the question of what to do with your monitor. Should you keep it on and let your screen saver run?

Some screen savers have been known to interfere with the rendering process because they are continuously asking for the computer's attention. Bryce wants as much of the processor as it can get while rendering. It "concentrates" on the task at hand and does not constantly monitor for keystrokes and mouse clicks. Clocks are continuously updating a portion of your screen. Screen savers are also watching to see how long it has been since the mouse was last moved or a key was pressed.

Who's going to get the upper hand in this situation: Bryce, which wants to ignore all outside stimuli, or the screen saver and/or clock, which prefer to stay aware of the outside stimuli? I'd rather give Bryce the upper hand. My recommendation here is to disable the screen saver and then shut off the monitor while you're away so that there will be nothing on a system level that interferes with the render process. And, if you're the one that pays the utility bills you'll save some nickels.

CHAPTER SIX

Editing and the Internal Bryce Grid

The Caterpillar was the first to speak. "What size do you want to be?" it asked.

"Oh, I'm not particular as to size," Alice hastily replied; "only one doesn't like changing so often, you know."

"I don't know," said the Caterpillar.

Alice said nothing; she had never been so much contradicted in all her life before, and she felt that she was losing her temper.

"Are you content now?" said the Caterpillar.

"Well, I should like to be a little larger, sir, if you wouldn't mind," said Alice: "three inches is such a wretched height to be."

"It is a very good height indeed!" said the Caterpillar angrily, rearing itself upright as it spoke (it was exactly three inches high).

"But I'm not used to it!" pleaded poor Alice in a piteous tone. And she thought to herself, "I wish the creatures wouldn't be so easily offended!"

"You'll get used to it in time," said the Caterpillar; and it put the hookah into its mouth and began smoking again.

…Then it got down off the mushroom and crawled away into the grass, merely remarking as it went, "One side will make you grow taller, and the other side will make you grow shorter."

"One side of what? The other side of what?" thought Alice to herself.

"Of the mushroom," said the Caterpillar, just as if she had asked it aloud; and in another moment it was out of sight.

LEWIS CARROLL, *ALICE IN WONDERLAND*

IN THIS CHAPTER…

- World Space, Object Space, and Camera Space

- Bryce's internal grid

- What it takes to change a single object—resize, rotate, reposition, flip, align

- Changing object type

- The Torus Editor

- Go from one object to more objects—duplicating and replicating

- Work with a number of objects—aligning, randomizing, and grouping objects

What goes on in the editing process? Editing is the precision adjustment. This is where all your objects get tweaked, and otherwise primped, prodded, and poked into the proper position and presentation. To understand what takes place in the edit process, think in terms of several main areas.

- Awareness of the Bryce Space and units. What are the units and measures of the Brycean Universe?

- Adjusting a single object. Think back on that object matrix and the three R's from Chapter 4.

- Special edits that are unique to an object. The terrain, symmetrical lattice, polyhedron, light, and torus all have special Edit controls. The particulars of each will be discussed in other chapters. Terrain and lattices are discussed in Chapter 8, "Terrains, Symmetrical Lattices, and the Terrain Editor," polyhedrons in Chapter 13, "Bryce and Other Software," lights in Chapter 11, "Bryce EnLightenment," and the torus later in this chapter. The torus is not significant enough to merit a chapter of its own, so I'll discuss it here.

- Edit materials. Change the surface appearance of each object. This, too, is covered in a chapter all its own, Chapter 9, "Material World."

- Changing object type—transforming from one object type to another.

- Generating multiple objects from one object.

- Adjusting a set of objects. This includes aligning, randomizing, and grouping a set of objects.

- Shortcuts—nudges and key nudges abound.

These are the things that will be discussed in this chapter on editing Bryce objects.

The Edit Palette is where most of the object-oriented activity in Bryce takes place. This palette has eight main controls. Figure 6–1 shows them all. The Edit Materials and Edit Terrain/Object controls will be handled in other chapters. This chapter will focus on the inner controls: Resize, Rotate, Reposition, Align, Randomize, and Object Conversion.

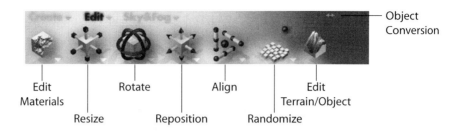

Figure 6-1 The Edit Palette: Edit Materials, Resize control, Rotate control, Reposition control, Align control, Randomize control, Edit Terrain/Object control, Object Conversion control.

THE UNDERLYING STRUCTURE OF THE BRYCEAN UNIVERSE

Once you select an object, you can do something to it. You can change its size, its position, its attributes, or change its orientation in the world. This is what the Resize, Rotate, and Reposition controls are for. I'll take a look at them in turn, but first, I want to discuss the Brycean Universe, the *xyz* space, and the underlying grid.

XYZ Axes

Let's do a bit of *xyz* review. By now, you're aware that there are three dimensions. If you're reading this book in order, you've run across discussions of *xyz* in the Camera and Scene chapter (Chapter 3) and in the Objects chapter (Chapter 4). When thinking editorially about Bryce 2, you'll be dealing with all three varieties of *xyz* space. (Does that make Bryce 9-dimensional? Ouch. Forget I asked that...)

There is the *xyz* space that is World Space. This is the absolute World Space. It's analogous to the compass directions. The *x* axis is east-west, the *z* axis is north-south, and the *y* axis is altitude. You can no more change what the *z* axis is than you could capriciously shift the direction of north by 28° or so. The *xyz* axes in World Space are inviolable. Yes means yes, no means no, North means North.

Then there is the *xyz* that is Object Space. This is the object's own width (*x*), height (*y*), and depth (*z*). After you change the object's position, the width part of that object may face Brycean northeast. But you can still expand the object along its own width dimension (*x* axis), making it wider or narrower. Object Space is inconsistently consistent; the *x* axis will always be the object's *x* axis, no matter

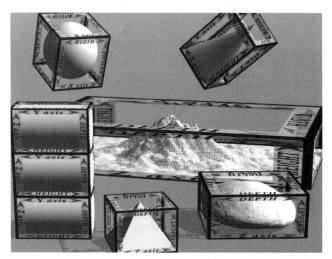

Figure 6–2 A smattering of Bryce objects with Object Space axes showing.

which way the object is facing. Figure 6–2 shows a series of objects and identifies their axes in Object Space.

Finally, there is the *xyz* that is Camera Space. The directions of Camera Space are always from the perspective that you view a scene. So the *x* axis is left-right, the *y* axis is up-down and the *z* axis is forward-backward. Those refer to the camera movements, or, since *you're* the one looking through the camera, you could also think of it as your own point of view. Camera Space is, then, completely subjective. This holds true even when you are looking in views other than "current view." If you were to look at your scene from, say, top view, enlarging an object along the *x* axis will enlarge it left-to-right *as you are currently viewing it* from top view. This is true no matter where the main camera position is. Consider Camera Space the most ephemeral and inconsistent of Bryce Spaces. Once you rotate the camera, *xyz* space has changed.

World, Object, and Camera Space Edits

When Resizing, Rotating, and Repositioning objects you can work in any of the three Bryce Spaces. The object will be changed a little differently, depending on which Space you're in. How do you know which space you're in? The pop-up menus for each of the Three R controls have options for changing space (see Figure 6–3). When it comes to switching from World to Object to Camera Space, it's "all for one, and one for all." Once you change the state under one menu, say, the Resize menu, the other two menus will reflect that state.

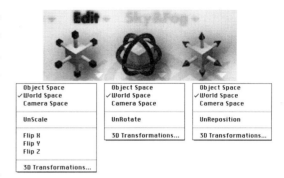

World Space

When World Space is selected, an object will be adjusted along the Brycean Universe's x, y and z axes.

Figure 6–3 The pop-up menus for Resize, Rotate, and Reposition.

If an object is not lined up along those axes, resizing along the x axis will seem as though there's an external x force that stretches or squishes an object, no matter what the object's own orientation. The same holds true for rotation. Repositioning will move an object north, east, south, west, or up and down only, regardless of the object's own orientation in space.

The wireframe for World Space is a bounding box with dimensions that are always in alignment with the World Space xyz axes.

Object Space

When Object Space is selected, the selected object is transformed based on the object's own x, y, and z axis. This is a new feature for Bryce 2, and a very welcome addition at that. Working in Object Space is very advantageous, as an object that has already been put into place and rotated one way or another can be made "wider" without losing the integrity of the object's shape (as would happen if the object were "widened" in World Space).

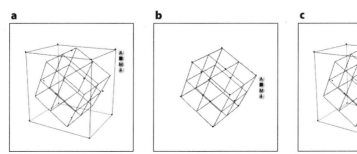

Figure 6-4 Comparison of a) World Space, b) Object Space, and c) Camera Space wireframe bounding boxes.

Camera Space

When Camera Space is selected, all object transformations take place along the camera's orientation. The wireframe is the same as World Space. When resizing or repositioning the selected object, the x axis is left-right, the y axis is up-down and the z axis is back-front as you look at the scene. Rotation around those axes is established by the camera's orientation.

When you pick up an object and drag it elsewhere, you are working in Camera Space. This has been true from Bryce 1.

The Grid

Inside the Brycean Universe is an invisible internal grid. It is referred to in the Snap to Grid command under the Alignment pop-up menu. What is the grid? Bryce has no command for making the grid visible, yet it is the underlying structure of the Brycean Universe, and many of the Edit controls occur in relation to the grid. Figure 6–5 depicts the grid points. You can work more efficiently in Bryce when you are aware of the grid.

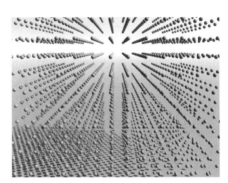

Figure 6–5 Bryce's internal grid.

The grid's unit of measurements are different from those units or measurements that correspond to our world. No inches, picas, miles, kilometers, or anything like that. Bryce is a world unto itself and the Brycean Units and Measurement Council devised this particular set of units by their own internal logic for our use and pleasure. The grid and units of measurement correspond to the sizes of objects as they come into being in the Brycean Universe. The units are measured in Bryce units, or B for short. You'll see the B symbol for dialog boxes (Object Attribute, 3D Transform, Replicate)—B, Bryce units. Since those measurements are shown for each axis, Bryce units (and my discussion of size in general) describe the linear size of an object on a given dimension. (The real-world counterpart to this is to say something is *n* inches in size, not *n* cubic inches.)

When you create a primitive in Bryce, it comes into a certain defined space. I will call that defined space a *unity unit*. The unity unit is the size and orientation that objects snap to when you invoke Unity using a key command. (I discuss the concept of Unity later in this chapter.) Figure 6–6 shows the unity unit and the grid points that are part of the unity unit. When you create a terrain, the object comes into Bryce at four times the size of a unity unit. Although terrains pop into the scene covering four times the width and depth of a unity unit, they remain one unity unit high. When you create a ground or infinite plane, it comes in four times as large again as a terrain. However, although their wireframes

Figure 6–6 The unity unit and the grid points that occupy the space of a unity unit.

are sixteen times the size of one unity unit in size, they aren't literally at that scale; both ground and infinite planes render on an infinite scale. Figure 6–7 compares the size of the unity unit, a terrain, and the size that an infinite plane wireframe occupies in Bryce Space.

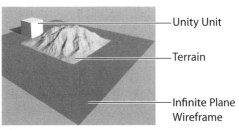

Unity Unit

Terrain

Infinite Plane Wireframe

Figure 6–7 Size comparison of a unity unit, terrain size, and infinite plane wireframe.

The unity unit is the foundational unit of measurement, though. For each unity unit, there are four *grid units*. Grid units are significant because they comprise the underlying structure of the Bryce World Space. They're also tied to the arrow "nudge" keys on the keyboard. For this reason, a grid unit may also be referred to as a nudge unit. Then, for even further fine tuning, there is a smaller scale increment—the Option-nudge (Macintosh) or Alt-nudge (Windows) unit. (The unit's name is derived from the action of holding down the Option or Alt key while nudging objects. Hereafter I'll refer to it as the Option/Alt-nudge unit.) There are are 64 *Option/Alt-nudge units* to one grid unit. Although I am currently discussing the units of space in Bryce in terms of an action—nudging, I'll discuss the actual process of and strategies for nudging later in this chapter.

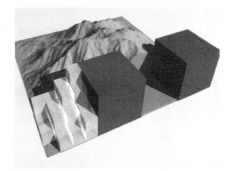

Figure 6–8 The different units of the Bryce grid: four nudge units to a unity unit; four unity units to match the width of a terrain

Bryce has numeric values for each of these units, and so many of one type equals one of another type of unit. The chart below and Figure 6–8 show you how all of these units fit together.

Bryce unit	=	.01
Nudge unit	=	5.12
Unity unit	=	20.48
8 Bryce units	=	1 Option/Alt-nudge unit
64 Option/Alt-nudge units	=	1 grid unit/1 nudge unit
4 grid units	=	1 unity unit

Don't blame me for the strange proportions. It's like wondering why there are 12 inches in a foot, 36 inches in a yard, and 5,280 feet in a mile. (And how many inches are in a light year, anyhow?) Once you live in this world, it makes sense. Or at least you get used to it. Here the same scale is presented again, this time using Bryce unit numbers.

1 Bryce unit	=	.01 B
1 Option/Alt-nudge unit	=	.08 B
1 nudge/grid unit	=	5.12 B
1 unity unit	=	20.48 B

Since Bryce is a world that ultimately depends upon ones and zeroes, its numbering units are inherited from them: 1, 2, 4, 8, 16, 32, 64, 128, etc. Bryce units, however, have placed the decimal point in a different place, so that the 2048 becomes, instead, 20.48. This is why a single Bryce unit is represented by a Bryce unit number of .01B.

I will refer back to these standards of measurement in my discussion of other Edit controls in this chapter.

Other Units of Measurement in Bryceland

In Bryceland, the other unit of measurement is the degree. This is used for measurements of rotation. There are 360° in a complete circle, so the Bryce standard of measurements matches ours for dividing a circle into certain units. Thank God for small mercies. Can you imagine if Bryce measured it so a circle was divided into 16384 equal units? Happily, there are but 360. Yay!

CHANGING ONE OBJECT: RESIZE, ROTATE, REPOSITION

Now that I've told you about the units of measurements in Bryce Space, I can move on to the Edit controls themselves. The first set of Edit controls I'll examine are those that change the attributes of one object. They're located together on the Edit Palette, roughly occupying its left half (remember, we're ignoring the outside controls on the Edit Palette, since they get their own chapters), as shown in Figure 6–9. The "Three R's" are Resize, Rotate, and Reposition. They work with single objects. Of course, they can also work with multiple objects, but unlike the two controls to their right, they do not *require* a multiple object selection in order to perform their editing magic. These three edit the attributes that are part of the object's matrix (matrix was discussed in Chapter 4, "Brycean Objects").

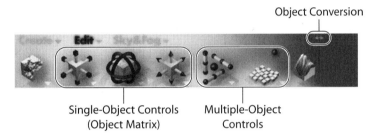

Object Conversion

Single-Object Controls
(Object Matrix)

Multiple-Object
Controls

Figure 6–9 The Edit Palette's controls broken into their logical control groupings: Single Object controls, Multiple Object controls, and Object Conversion controls.

There are four ways to change an object in Bryce.

- *Edit Palette Control.* In the Edit Palette, you can use the Edit Palette control by dragging the appropriate part of the Resize, Rotate, or Reposition controls.

- *Direct Manipulation.* You can directly change the object in the scene work area by dragging the control handles or dragging the entire object.

- *3D Transformations dialog box.* The pop-up menus for each of the Three R's controls gives you access to the 3D Transformations dialog box.

- *Object Attributes dialog box.* Related to the previous option, the Object Attributes dialog box enables you to make changes to the object using absolute coordinates.

Although the Edit Palette presents them in the left-to-right order of Resize, Rotate, and Reposition, I will discuss Reposition first, since there are concepts in repositioning that are more basic to both it and Resize.

Repositioning Objects in Bryce

The first and most basic thing you can do to edit your object is to change its position. Move it from here to there. There are four ways you can move objects around in your scene.

In the direct drag method, you select the object and then drag it to some other location in your scene. Drag it from there to here. Simple. Select and drag. Drag in the main view, or, for more precision, in top, side, or front view.

You can also use the Reposition control to move an object in a particular direction along an axis. There are times when attempting to drag the object directly will be vexing. The Reposition control will come in handy.

A more precise means of repositioning is to use nudge keys to move the object in one direction by a certain amount.

The final method is to change the numerical value for the object's position using one of the dialog boxes that have numerical input. (I'll discuss numerical input later in the chapter in its own section.)

Direct Dragging a la Constrain Key

Although the Macintosh generally uses the Shift key to constrain the movement of the cursor, there are only two directions involved—horizontal and vertical, as you look at your monitor. Because Bryce works in three dimensions, it departs from the limitations of one constraining key. It has three keys, one for each dimension, as follows:

- The *Control key* (Macintosh) or *Ctrl+Alt* keys (Windows) constrain along the x-axis.

- The *Option* (Macintosh) or *Alt* (Windows)key constrains along the y-axis.

- The *Command* (Macintosh) or *Ctrl* (Windows) key constrains along the z-axis.

For the most perfectly aligned movement, make sure you hold down the constraining key *before* you begin dragging. You can press the constrain key after you begin the drag, but the constrain won't kick in from the point where the object was when you started dragging. It takes effect somewhere in between. For instance, if you were to move an object along the x axis and then constrain it a bit later, the object might stray too far up or down from its starting position before the constrain takes place and then be locked into a constrained position along the x axis—only higher or lower than where it was before. Bryce seems to pick some arbitrary levels along the grid for constraining in those cases, so make sure that you constrain at the outset.

When you press down the constraining key, the cursor changes to a double-arrow. (This occurs in the Macintosh version of Bryce only; the Windows cursor remains the 4-way arrow. The object *will* still move in a constrained fashion, however.) Then when you drag, the object will move only on that one axis.

The constrain keys work in any of the views. However, each view has one axis on which a constrain key won't work. That axis is whichever axis you are peering down in order to see the scene, as follows:

• In top and bottom views, the y-axis (Option or Alt key) does not work.

• In left and right Views, the x-axis (Control or Ctrl+Alt keys) does not work.

• In front and back views, the z-axis (Command or Ctrl key) does not work.

When you are in main view looking straight down any of the axes, Bryce will not constrain on that axis, unless the camera happens to be peering exactly down any one of the three axes (that is, mimicing the angle used for any of the orthogonal views). Since the default position is not directly along any axis, you probably won't enounter this much.

Reposition Control

The Reposition tool, like direct dragging, gives you the option of moving your object along all three axes. There are no constrain keys for the Reposition control. The movement itself is already constrained. The Reposition control is especially good for moving small objects or moving objects that are positioned in such a way that they're hard to move. The Reposition control, as a member of the Three R's group, can move an object along, say, the x axis of World Space, Object Space, or Camera Space.

To move an object along the x axis, drag the Reposition control from either end of the x axis point. The direction you need to drag varies a bit from Macintosh to Windows. For the Macintosh horizontal axes (x and z) and for all three axes under Windows, dragging horizontally changes the object's position. On the Macintosh, to move something up along the *y* axis, drag *up* or *down* when using Reposition control. Here is a caveat, though: Your range of motion is limited to the monitor's edge. So if you are using a small monitor (640 × 480 pixels), or if your Bryce interface is set to hug the edge of your monitor (rather than the edge of your scene), then you'll probably run out of upward mousing room before your object reaches its destination. Make the palettes hug the scene if you have a larger monitor by clicking the Interface Min/Max switch (discussed in the previous chapter).

Repositioning and World/Object/Camera Space

So, you are repositioning objects. You can work in one of Bryce's three Space orientations. Which one? How? For starters, any time you directly drag a selected object, you are working in Camera Space. You can drag up, down, left or right along the camera's orientation.

When you use the nudge keys on a Macintosh, you are working in World Space, moving your objects north, east, south west, or higher or lower in altitude. When using the nudge keys in Bryce for Windows, you will be working in whatever Space orientation you choose in the Three R's pop-up menu.

When you use the constrain keys or the Reposition tool, the objects will move according to what type of Space is selected in the Three R's pop-up menus.

Try It Yourself!

Take a look at the difference between the three different Spaces.

1. Open up the scene file MOVE AND CONSTRAIN from the CD-ROM. The object is rotated so that its axes do not match up with the world's axes, nor is the camera aligned on the Bryce World's *xyz* axes.

2. Select World Space from one of the Three R's pop-up menus. The bounding box around the object changes to align itself with World Space. Hold down the Control key or Ctrl+Alt keys (to constrain on the *x* axis) and drag the cube. Notice that it moves in the same orientation as the bounding box.

3. Select Object Space. Notice that the bounding box changes to align with the object. (The scene should have been this way when you first opened it.) Hold down the Control or Ctrl+Alt keys again, and drag. This time the object moves in a different direction.

4. Select Camera Space. The bounding box changes to World Space. (If it were a true Camera Space bounding box, it would have straight lines top and bottom and you could see the distance perspective to the box. Oh well.) Press the Control or Ctrl+Alt keys and then drag the object. It moves precisely right and left in your monitor orientation.

Change your camera position with the Trackball and try it again.

5. Try the same thing, only use the Reposition tool this time. You needn't use the constrain keys with the Reposition tool, since the tool is "pre-constrained" for you.

6. Mix and match constraining movement on the other axes.

Moving Things That Are "Hard to Move"

If you're in side or front view and you want to drag something that's flat, such as a square, disk, ground, or infinite plane, you might have a bit of a problem. Those are very difficult objects to select from those angles because Bryce "sees" objects in a ray-traced fashion. In other words, almost all of the rays pass above or below the flat object, so it's hard for Bryce to "see" at that angle (see Figure 6–10a). But there are times when you must look at your scene from that angle in order to make your adjustments; the other angles simply won't do. There are two options to make your hard-to-move object movable. The first is to use the Reposition control. Once your object is selected, it will go in whatever direction you drag with the Reposition tool. The second option is a sneaky trick for those times when you just gotta get in there and do it directly by dragging about in your Bryce scene. This recipe presents another way to have complete control over that flat object.

Recipe for the Hard of Moving

1. Create a small sphere to use as a "moving buddy." Make it a different color from all the other objects in your scene (see Figure 6–10b).

2. Select the sphere and flat object as follows: First, cycle through with the Tab key until your flat object is selected. Next, hold down the Shift key and select the sphere either by directly clicking it or by selecting by its unique color in the Family pop-up menu.

3. With both objects selected, drag the sphere. The flat object will go along for the ride! (See Figure 6–10.) Place your flat object wherever it needs to go. When you're done with your sphere moving buddy, delete it.

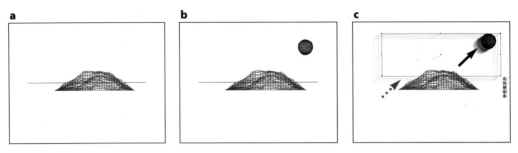

Figure 6–10 Moving using a moving partner: a) The flat object; b) create a sphere; c) moving the sphere with the flat object following along.

Never again will you be eluded by an object that doesn't want to move!

Moving Objects by Nudging

Move your selected object or objects by tapping the arrow keys. You've been introduced to them already in the discussion of the grid: When you press any of the arrow keys to nudge an object, the object will be moved by increments of one grid unit. That doesn't necessarily mean they will move *on the grid,* however; they will move over by that grid amount. Of course, if your object is already aligned to the grid, it will stay on the grid as it moves.

You can use the arrow keys and the Page Up and Page Down keys to move objects by one grid unit, as summarized:

• The *left* and *right* arrow keys move objects horizontally along the x-axis.

• The *up* and *down* arrow keys move objects horizontally along the z-axis.

• The *Page Up/Page Down* keys move objects vertically along the y-axis.

Figure 6–11 shows the orientation of the arrow keys in Bryce's World Space. The most intuitive position is from top view, where they work to move things "front back left right" as the arrow keys themselves are positioned. Since Bryce 2's default camera angle is diagonal to the *x* and *z* axes, sometimes the right-left and up-down arrow combinations are confusing. The arrow keys are tricky when looking at your scene in side view, because the objects move in the opposite direction from what is indicated on the arrow keys. So here, from every view, are the arrow keys pointing in the direction things will move in Bryce Space when that particular key is pressed. The arrow keys are locked inside of Bryce World Space; they do not move things any differently if you have set things to move in Object Space or Camera Space.

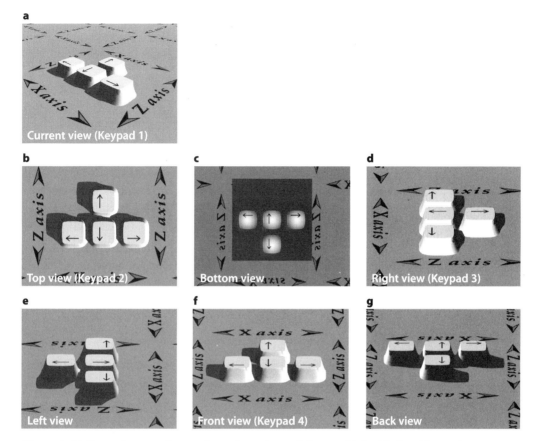

Figure 6–11 Bryce Space and arrow key orientations: a) Current (default) view; b) top view; c) bottom view; d) right view; e) left view; f) front view; g) back view.

Now I'll move on to inventory the abundance of alternatives for how much distance is covered in one arrow key-nudge.

Commanding Your Control Shift Options

Bryce is teeming with modifier key combinations to push an object twice or half the distance that a simple nudge will move it, as elaborated in this list:

Shift-nudge	2 nudge units (1/2 unity unit)
Plain ol' nudge	1 nudge unit (1/4 unity unit)
Option-Shift nudge	1/2 nudge unit (1/8 unity unit); not available under Windows.
Option/Alt-nudge	1/64 nudge unit (1/256 unity unit)

So, as modifier keys go, Shift makes a move bigger, and Option/Alt makes it smaller. Option and Shift together (on a Mac) make the size of the move larger than the minuscule size of the Option key move alone. Figure 6–12 shows the relative size of the nudge units, with each key combination identified.

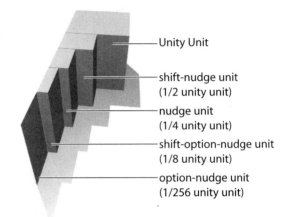

Unity Unit

shift-nudge unit
(1/2 unity unit)

nudge unit
(1/4 unity unit)

shift-option-nudge unit
(1/8 unity unit)

option-nudge unit
(1/256 unity unit)

Figure 6–12 The lengths an object will travel when modifier keys are used along with the arrow (nudge) keys.

I will revisit this list of modifier keys when I discuss the numerical entry in the Edit dialog boxes later in this chapter.

Nudge Fluency Exercise

If you thought that the "practicing scales" exercise for the Flyaround in Chapter 3 was wacky, then welcome to more scale practice. This will help you gain some fluency with all the Control Shift Option Alt Command keys. Roll up your sleeves and dig right in.

1. Start with the basic nudge arrow keys. If you haven't already played around with moving an object, do so. Create an object and move it this way and that with the arrow keys and the Page Up and Page Down keys.

With a bit of practice, you'll find that knowing which key moves in which direction in which view becomes completely intuitive, although you may still get a bit tangled up in side view.

2. Nudge in larger increments. Press the Shift key down, use the nudge keys, and watch the objects move twice as far as they did before.

3. (This step is for Mac Brycers only.) Nudge in smaller increments. Press both the Shift and Option keys down and watch the objects move around in half the space as the nudge units.

4. Nudge in tiny increments. Press only the Option or Alt key while tapping those arrow keys. You'll have to tap a few times before you really see any significant object displacement on your screen.

Resizing

Using the Resize controls, you can take objects that start out symmetrical (a cube or pyramid) and create objects that are far different from their original shape. Bryce 2's Create Palette, with its addition of "preprocessed" stretched and squashed shapes, is a nod in this direction. Once you change the shape of the original object, the possibilities for modeling objects widen considerably. By resizing, a cube primitive becomes a flat "board," a square tile, or a rectangular brick. A cylinder can be a column, a teeny tiny tube, almost a piece of string, or a flat coin. A flattened pyramid becomes a flag. This object flexibility is yours with the Resize controls. Figure 6–13 shows several objects created from primitives using the Resize control.

Figure 6–13 A ridiculously simple scene in which all objects were created from primitives.

Objects can be uniformly reduced or enlarged, or they can be resized along one axis only. The Resize control and the handles of the selected object work similarly to change the selected object's size.

The Resize control will make a selected object grow or shrink. Press the mouse on the control and drag. Keep dragging; when you like what you have, let go. Depending where you first "grab" the control, you will make it grow or shrink in different ways. As you move your mouse over different parts of the control, you get two sources of feedback to tell you how the object will be resized. The Object control itself changes, showing you how the object will be changed. The pointer cursor changes, too, to four different possible cursors. When your mouse is over the object's center, you see the uniform resize cursor. The object also is uniformly enlarged. Roll the cursor over any of the edges of the control, and the cursor changes to tell you which axis you'll be affecting: x, y, or z.

To increase the size of an object, drag to the right. Drag to the left to decrease it. This holds true no matter which axis you are working with; it does not matter if you are trying to increase the object's size along the y axis (vertically); you still drag to the right to increase, and to the left to decrease the size.

You can increase the object in either direction. In Figure 6–14, a simple cube is resized along the x axis. The cube grows "out" in one direction—toward the side where you dragged it in the first place. So if you drag the closer control (on the right), it grows out on the right.

The same thing happens when you directly drag the selected object's resize handles. The cursor changes to tell you which axis you'll be affecting. Note how the Resize control has little cubes on each end, to match the shape and position of the handles on the object's bounding box. (The interface design here, with the corresponding look of

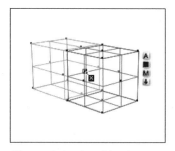

Figure 6–14 An object growing out along the *x* axis.

handles and Resize control "handles" is quite handsome!) Here, too, the object will grow or shrink in the direction of the side of the handle you picked. Or, to put it more simply, the edge that you do not touch stays in the same place.

When you drag from the center of the Resize control, the object grows or shrinks uniformly from its own center. Since the direct-drag approach does not have a control handle at the object's center from which to drag, the direct approach acts a bit differently. The object is resized uniformly when you drag from any of the corners of the object. Rather than growing out from the center, though, the object grows toward the corner where you commenced your drag. In Figure 6–15, the cube was "grabbed" from the upper left corner and enlarged proportionately. The three-step image shows how the opposite corner on the lower right stays stationary. The cube grows up and to the left as it increases in size.

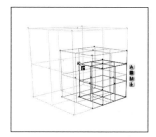

Figure 6–15 Proportional resize by directly dragging an object: The object grows out in the direction where the grab started; the other corner stays stationary.

A Shift-Clicking Drag

What happens if you want to make the object grow along a certain axis on both directions from the center? For that, you'll need to use a modifier key. This next section will allow you to familiarize yourself with the dizzying array of modifier options to make your object resize every-which-way.

For this section, when I say "grow" I mean either grow or shrink. While focusing the discussion on the different modifier keys, I figured it's best to simplify matters: objects grow. Also, I refer to the origin point and the grab point. The origin is the part of the object that stays still. The object grows or shrinks from the origin point. The grab point is the point of the object from which you drag.

Option (Macintosh) or Alt (Windows) Key. Holding down the Option or Alt key will enlarge or reduce the object from the object's center. The center-option is consistent with some other applications that change from edge to center when the Option key is pressed (e.g., Photoshop, Illustrator). See Figure 6–16b.

The Option key (but *not* the Windows Alt key) also makes the resize happen more smoothly and with more minute increments. The object will resize along a certain axis differently if you press the Option key *before* you commence your drag than if you begin dragging *and then* press the Option key. Pressing Option before dragging results in a smaller, more pre-

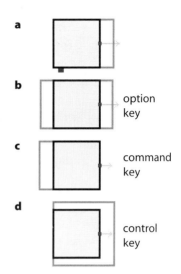

Figure 6–16 How modifier keys change resizing (top view, resizing along *x* axis): a) No modifier key; b) Option (or Alt) key; c) Command (or Ctrl) key; d) Control key (or Ctrl+Alt keys).

cise range of motion—from the object's center, of course. When you begin resizing and then press the Option key, the object will resize at a normal rate, and then, as soon as the Option key is pressed, the object snaps to center-resize, but maintains the faster rate of change.

Pressing the Option key for precise movement is a throwback to the way that the Option key functioned in version 1 of Bryce. There, too, Option would make for smaller, more precise movements. But resizing from the object's center was regulated elsewhere in version 1, so that each element —precise movement and center orientation—could be controlled separately. In version 2, you will always move from the center with the Option/Alt key. On a Mac, you can do so slowly, by pressing the Option key first, or more quickly, by pressing the Option key after you begin dragging. But if you want to slowly resize along one axis moving from the object's other end, well, I'm afraid the Option key's precision mode won't do you any good. Oh well.

Shift Key. When you press the Shift key, the object will be constrained by 50% increments as it shrinks or grows. When enlarging, the object will snap to 150%, 200%, 250%, and so on. Reducing happens a little differently in Macintosh and

Windows versions. When reducing on a Mac, the object will snap to 50% of its size before coming to rest at 12.5% of its size. (I'll talk some more about this pause point on the reduction end further on in the chapter). Under Windows, the object reduces in consistent 50% increments: 50%, 25%, 12.5%, etc. The Shift key can be used in conjunction with the other key combinations mentioned here. For instance, when the Shift and Option (or Shift+Alt) keys are pressed, the object's size increases or decreases from its center, jumping in 50% increments.

For the next two modifier keys, it makes all the difference in the world whether you press the modifier key *before* or *after* beginning your drag-to-resize when working directly on the selected object's control handles. You needn't pay attention to the before/after distinction when you're working with the Resize control, since the Resize control has no control handles.

Command (Macintosh) or Ctrl (Windows) Key. When you press the Command/Ctrl key *after* beginning a drag from a certain point, it changes the origin of the resize to the opposite side. The point that you "grabbed" to begin your drag will stay still, and the rest of the object will grow or shrink from that place. See Figure 6–16c.

For kicks, to make your objects do a wireframe dance, begin a drag of an object, and, after you begin dragging, press and release the Command/Ctrl key at intervals. If you really get good at it, try it to music! (But please, make the music something other than scales!)

Pressing the Command/Ctrl key *before* beginning to drag the object will put the object in rotation mode. That is a different kind of dance. I'll discuss it more in the Rotation section below.

Control Key (Macintosh) or Ctrl+Alt Keys (Windows). Press the Control key or Ctrl+Alt keys *after* you've started your resize drag. Use this when you want the object to grow or shrink uniformly, but from a certain edge. Drag on an axis and the object will grow from the other side of that axis. See Figure 6–16d, where, looking down at the object from top view, the object is enlarged along the x axis. It is enlarged uniformly, and the origin point is opposite the grab point.

Pressing the Control key or Ctrl+Alt keys *before* clicking any control point will result in snapping the object back to unity unit size.

And now, a review. All the modifier keys that are located on the bottom row of the keyboard (Command, Option, Control or Ctrl, Alt, Ctrl+Alt) change the resize manner and the origin point from which the object shrinks or grows. For your reference, the places to remember are the origin point (what part of object is stationary) and grab point (what point you dragged from).

Standard (Look Ma! no keys!) object grows toward the grab point; origin point is opposite the grab point.

Option or Alt changes the origin point to the center. The object grows toward both (or all) sides.

Command or Ctrl changes the origin point to the opposite end. The grab point becomes the origin point, staying still while object grows toward the other side.

Control or Ctrl+Alt enlarges uniformly; the object grows toward the grab point; the origin point is opposite the grab point and stays put.

The other modifier key, Shift, makes the object grow or shrink by leaps and bounds of 50%.

Resize Controls and the Grid.

I said that I'd get back to that 12.5% place. When you shrink your object, the Resize control reaches a pause point: It stops when the object's size is one-eighth what it was (12.5%). (This is a change from the way that Bryce 1 worked, where the natural stopping place was at exactly one-fourth size.) Bryce 2 for the Mac added the Option-Shift nudge to move an object one-eighth of a unity unit. Under Windows, there is no pause point when reducing; an object shrinks until you cease moving the mouse.

If Bryce for Windows does not have a natural pause point, then how do you resize objects with precision? The Shift key's size constraints will allow you to choose your pause point. Since Bryce for Windows does not have an equivalent to the Option-Shift grid unit that moves an object over by one-eighth of a unity unit, use the Shift key to resize to one-fourth size (grid unit), and use the basic nudge to move objects by that amount. You can, of course, still reduce to one-eighth size if you care to.

The beauty of the pause point coinciding with the grid units is that you can move and resize objects and ensure that they're in perfect alignment with one another. Once your object is in half-grid unit size, you can make copies of it with full assurance that each copy will neatly stack next to or on top of the others. This is the source of those brick walls and tiled floors with the repeated object.

This pause-point rule (whether induced by the Mac's one-eighth size or the Shift key constrain) assumes you shrank the object from its native unity unit size.

If you enlarge it first prior to shrinking it, the shrunken version will be one-eighth whatever size it was enlarged to. It won't necessarily be consistent to grid size. When you enlarge an object, there is no pause point at which the object reaches a certain size, unless of course, you're using the Shift key to constrain.

You can also work with an object at one-fourth size. This was the place where Bryce 1 would naturally stop when reducing. Bryce 2 takes an additional step. For at least one useful action, though, it's essential. (See Getting Out of A Terrain Jam, below.) To make an object go to one-fourth size, you'll have to use the Shift key. Begin your drag to reduce. Press the Shift key. Here, Windows users are at an advantage: simply drag until the object snaps to one-fourth size (the second snap). On a Mac, it's more tedious, since the Shift constraint doesn't stop right at 25%. After pressing the Shift key, the object will jump to 50% (one-half) size. Release both the drag and the Shift key, and do it again to jump to one-half again, which is actually one-fourth the original size. You do need to release both the mouse and the Shift key in order for this to work. (Sorry. I wish that I could offer you Mac users a better shortcut; I yearn for the old drag-to-one-fourth size at times.) Of course, if you went too far on the first reduce, and stopped at one-eighth, you could press the Shift key after beginning to enlarge the object, and it will pop into the 200% position, or one-fourth the original size.

The one-eighth pause point doesn't occur only when the Resize tool is used proportionately. When using the Resize tool to reduce along the x-, y-, z-axes, the object will also stop at one-eighth size along the particular axis. When you want to make one primitive fit with another, pause points enable you can make objects that fit together very quickly. Let's take a look at how the grid works with both Resize and nudge units to create a composite object.

Resize and Nudge Recipe

Follow these steps to create a composite object (see Figure 6–17):

1. Create a cube and a pyramid. (See Figure 6–17a.)

2. Use the Resize control and drag left on the z axis to bring the depth of the pyramid to one-eighth size. If you're using a Mac, drag until it stops. It will be precisely one-eighth its depth. If you're using Windows, press the Shift key while reducing, and reduce until the cube snaps the third time (first snap is one-half, second snap is one-fourth, third snap is one-eighth). (See Figure 6–17b.)

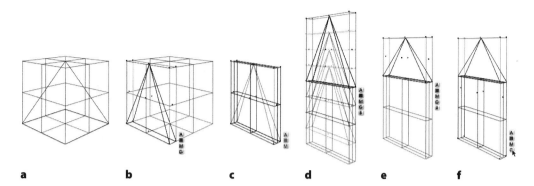

Figure 6–17 Composite object from a cube and pyramid: a) Create cube and pyramid; b) resize pyramid; c) resize cube; d) nudge pyramid up; e) reduce height of pyramid; f) group both objects.

3. Select the cube. Do the same thing (reduce it to one-eighth). See? It's an exact match! No need to "eyeball" it. (See Figure 6–17c.)

4. To set one object exactly on top of the other, make sure that you've selected the one destined for the top (in this case, the pyramid). Press the Page Up key four times; this will put the pyramid on top of the cube. Was that easy or was that easy? (See Figure 6–17d.)

5. Extra credit: Flatten the pyramid by dragging left on the top *y* axis control. Then group both objects. (See Figure 6–17e and f.)

Sure, you could've selected both objects and resized them simultaneously. But the point here is that with the internal grid-resize structure, when you get that great idea to add a new object to an already-existing object, you know your resize options.

Multiply and Divide

There is a key combination that will do proportional enlargements and reductions. In fact, if you want to get to 25% of your original size, and you are reducing along all three axes, then this is the way to go. To double the size of the object, press the multiply (★) key. To halve the object's size, press the divide (/) key. Pressing the / key twice will, of course, reduce the object to one-fourth its size. You can use the / and ★ keys located on either the keypad or the regular keyboard. (When you're using the ★ on the regular keyboard, make sure that you press Shift; otherwise you'll type 8 and mistakenly change camera views. Ow.)

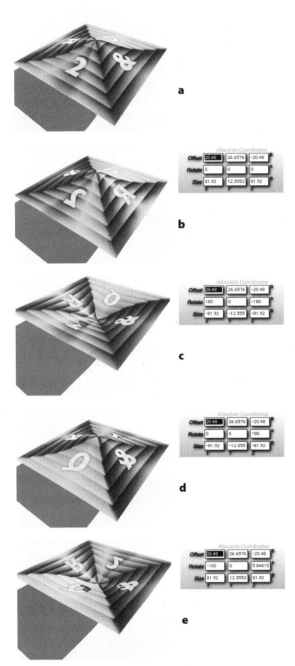

Figure 6–18 Flipping a terrain: a) Before any flipping; b) flip x; c) flip y; d) flip z; e) flip x and y.

Flip

The Flip controls are found in the pop-up menu under the Resize tool. Flip does just that—flips your object along the axis described. From Figure 6–18 you can see the effect of flipping along each axis—*x, y,* and *z.*

Flip X swaps the object's orientation along the east-west axis—what was facing east is now facing west. However, what faced up still faces up and what faced bottom still faces bottom. But the object is inverted. Notice in Figure 6–18b through e that the letters and numbers are wrong-reading as they're flipped.

Flip Z flips the object along the north-south axis. Flip Y flips the object vertically.

Why do the commands for flip live under the Resize menu? A peek in the Object Attributes dialog box provides the clue. The object doesn't really change *size* per se, rather it changes orientation, or is inverted. Compared to a regular object, the flipped counterpart's size numbers are all negative. Size numbers are either positive or negative. Unlike offset and rotation, there is no mix 'n match for positive and negative. If all numbers are positive, the object is regular. If they are negative, the object is flipped, an inverted mirror image of itself.

When to Use Flip

When positioning objects, Flip works well. You don't like it facing in *this* direction? Flip it so that it's now facing *that* direction. That's fairly self-evident. However, when you're creating more-complex objects from a series of primitives, then Flip is an excellent tool in your toolbox.

1. ⌘-D (Macintosh) or Ctrl+D (Windows) duplicates the object.

2. Then select Flip. The copy will be flipped.

What if you want to flip an object when you are aligning or sizing it carefully? To create the *x*-, *y*-, and *z*-axes arrows in Figure 6–19, I altered a cube primitive object. Then I created a pyramid and positioned it on one end of the rectangle, squashed it, and got it *just right*. When one arrow was finished, it was time for the other one. Stop. Think about this for a moment. Would you want to go through all that positioning and squashing to get yet *another*

Figure 6–19 Arrows for Axes, created by aid of the Flip command.

primitive to be "just so?" No! Neither did I. So I copied the pyramid, pasted it, flipped it, and then moved it to the other end of the flattened cube.

Resizing in World Space /Object Space/Camera Space

The significance of resizing in Object Space versus resizing in World Space cannot be underrated. This is one of those features, which, when put into the Bryce, has caused an outbreak of riotous thanksgiving and merrymaking. If you haven't joined the celebration already, then try out this resize practice.

Try It Out

Once again, open up that same scene file that you used for Resizing: MOVE AND CONSTRAIN. (Or, if it's still open, select File > Revert to Saved.)

1. Change the Space setting to World Space. The bounding box is aligned with World Space, no matter how the object is oriented. This is the first clue that a resize along the world's *x* axis will warp the cube. Resize along the *x* axis using the Resize control, by dragging to the right from the Resize *x* axis. See?

It warped the cube. Undo. Try the same thing by directly dragging the *x* axis control handle. Undo. (Undo after each move.)

2. Change the Space setting to Object Space. The bounding box changes, hugging the object. Here's your first clue that the resize will behave differently. Again, resize along the *x* axis using the Resize control. Undo. Now try the direct method on the object's bounding box. Notice how the object, though rotated, is enlarged along its own width. Try the other axes, too. (Undo after each move.)

3. Try out Camera Space. After changing the setting to Camera Space, try the Rotate control and the direct drag-the-control-handle method. Try all three axes. The resizing takes place in relation to your point of view. Try, say, resizing on the *x* axis, undo, move the camera position, then resize *x* again. Camera Space allows you to be completely subjective when resizing an object.

What Does It All Mean?

The difference between what happens when you resize in World Space and resizing in Object Space is striking.

In World Space, resize works from the outside, stretching or pulling on an object along the particular axis. The *x*-Force (not to be confused with a popular science fiction TV show) pays no attention to the object's orientation. In Object Space, the resizing works from within an object, changing the size of the object without destroying the basic integrity of the shape. Figure 6–20 shows the difference between the two. In Figure 6–20a, the World Space *y*-force is pushing down on the rotated cone. In Figure 6–20b, the rotated cone is being reduced along its *y* axis.

Obviously, the adage "resize before you rotate, or you'll regret it" no longer applies in Bryce 2. You can work more intuitively, positioning (and rotating) an object, adjusting its size, rotating it a bit more, and resizing again after that. Most of the time you'll want to work in Object Space for additional resizing if your object has been rotated at all.

However, there may be cases when World Space shape distortion is the desired end. Rotate the object and then make it grow or shrink in any of the three directions to make it into that shape you want. A pyramid can be forced into a right angle, a cone that is off-base makes a nice oblique source of light rays, and with judicious use of the Rotate controls, you can coax terrains to have overhanging edges. For more on the thrills of terrain overhangs, see Chapter 14, "Superlative Nature Imagery."

Occasional Resize Axis Amnesia (Macintosh Only)

After working on an object after resizing it this way and that for a time, the handles may become confused as to which is which axis. This is more apt to happen when an object is reduced greatly or when the size on one axis is proportionately much smaller than the other axes. When you thought you were dragging upward on the *y* axis handle, the cursor shows a z handle, and the resize takes place on the *z* axis. (Sometimes instead of a switch from *y* to z, Bryce will switch from *y* to proportional resize. Scary.) Try changing the space you're working in, say from World Space to Object Space (or vice versa). Or, if you were dragging directly from the object's handles, try using the Resize control instead. Usually a combination of one or both of those alternatives manages to get the object

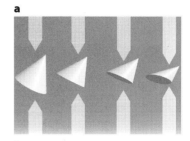

Figure 6–20 Resizing along the *y* axis: a) In World Space; b) in Object Space.

to move the way you want it to. If those don't work, then change the numbers in the Object Attributes dialog box. Why does it do this? Beats me.

Rotation

The Rotation control is in the center of the Edit Palette. It is the intriguing-looking control with rings around a cube nucleus. When you rotate, you rotate around the axis. The object will always move around its center. Think of the axis as a skewer piercing the object (see Figure 6–21). The object rotates around that skewer or axis. Of all the Edit controls I discuss in this chapter, the Rotation controls are the one set that has no relation to the grid units.

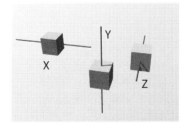

Figure 6–21 Each axis depicted as a skewer.

The beauty of Bryce 2 is that you don't have to complete all your resizing before you do any rotation. Since you can work in Object Space, you can freely move back and forth between resizing and rotation to get your object into place just so.

Like the Resize and Rotate controls, there are a number of ways to control an object's rotation. You can directly rotate the object, you can use the Rotation control, and you can use the 3D Transformation and Object attributes dialog box (see the 3D Transformation section below for rotation using this method). Unlike the other two R's, there are no keypad equivalents for rotating an object. However, there are, of course, modifier keys.

Direct Rotation

Place your mouse pointer over a selected object's control handle. When you press the Command (Macintosh) or Ctrl (Windows) key, the cursor changes to a little rotate arc. Now when you drag the handle, you will rotate the object. Make sure that you press the Command or Ctrl key *before* you drag. (Incidentally, this is the counterpart to my earlier admonition—when resizing an object—to press the Command or Ctrl key *after* the drag had begun.)

Which way will the object rotate? It depends which control handle you grabbed. Grab one of the face control handles—where the cursor changes to x, y, or z—and you will rotate around that particular axis. Grab one of the corner handles, and you will rotate freely this way and that. If you somehow manage to drag upward in a straight line (the cursor disappears, so you cannot see anything to help with your eye-hand coordination), the object will rotate around one axis. But since hand movement without any visual feedback does not go in straight lines, the object will teeter and reel around freely. Whee!

The Rotation Control

The Rotation control on the Edit Palette works the same way as the direct rotation method, only instead of grabbing a control point for an object's face to rotate, you drag on the control for that particular axis. Like the other controls on the Edit Palette that deal with matters of x, y and z, the cursor will tell you which axis you're going to rotate around, so you know which axis you'll be affecting. The Rotation control has no counterpart to the direct-drag-from-a-corner to rotate every which way.

Like the Resize tools, rotation works by dragging in a left-right direction. Depending on the direction the object is facing, and depending on your camera perspective, the direction of the rotation can be completely counter-intuitive. Figure 6–22a shows how, for each axis, there is a clockwise rotation when you drag to the right (yes, I know, it's a right-handed bias; lefties get the upper hand in interface design elsewhere in Bryce). "Clockwise" is determined by the camera's position, however. The x axis rotates clockwise if you look at it from the left as in

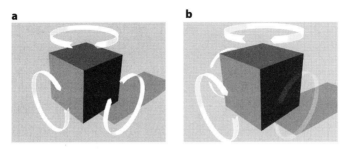

Figure 6–22 a) Rotation occurring in a clockwise direction;
b) the same "clockwise" perspective from default camera view.

the figure. In contrast, Figure 6–22b shows the same configuration from roughly the default camera view. From that perspective, the *x* axis rotates counter-clockwise. It can be bewildering to those who need to make sense out of the object-movement-in-relation-to-the-drag-movement.

Constrain keys

Bryce 2 has added a constraining key that will enable you to rotate by precise increments. Press the Shift key as you rotate and the object will pop to 45° positions.

The Option (Macintosh) or Alt (Windows) key, when pressed, provides you with more precise, controlled movement for fine-tuning. In cases where you need to precisely position an object, the Option key will greatly aid you as you "eyeball" the object as it rotates.

> **TIP:** You can see what is going on better for rotating if you have your depth cueing set so that the wireframe is fainter on the far sides of your object. If not, you'll be susceptible to those figure-ground optical illusions where you can't tell the near edge from the far edge of the object.

Rotation and World/Object/Camera Space

Rotation, like the other two R's, operates differently depending on the Space setting. Rotate the object around the world's *x* axis. Or around its own *x* axis. Or even the camera's *x* axis.

Try It Yourself

For practice, try it out, using that same scene file that you used for Resizing: MOVE AND CONSTRAIN.

1. Change the Space setting to World Space. Rotate along the z axis using the Rotate tool by dragging to the right. Undo. Then find the z axis on the object's bounding box. Press the Command (Macintosh) or Ctrl (Windows) key and drag to the right. Try the other axes, too. (Undo after each move.)

2. Change the Space setting to Object Space. Notice how the bounding box changes, hugging the object. Rotate the object using both the Rotate control and by directly Command- or Ctrl-dragging on the control points.

    Change your camera perspective while you are in Object Space. Rotate on the x axis, and notice how what is clockwise in one direction becomes counterclockwise when viewed from the other side. The object rotates consistently; it's just that your perspective on it changes.

3. Try out Camera Space. After changing the setting to Camera Space, try rotating using both the Rotate tool and directly Command- or Ctrl-dragging on the x axis.

    As an alternative, see how rotation on one particular axis changes depending on which Space you're in.

3D Transformations and Other Dialog Boxes

The Object chapter (Chapter 4) first introduced you to Object Attributes and the underlying Object matrix. The three Edit tools that we have been discussing, Resize, Rotate, and Reposition, work directly with the Object matrix. They are all related. Further, there is one more dialog box for editing your objects using numerical values instead of clicks, drags, and keyboard constraints. Under each of the three Edit tools' pop-up menus there is an option called 3D Transformations. In this section I'll discuss editing your Bryce objects using numerical values in the 3D Transformations dialog box.

But first, here's a quick review of how the tools and dialog boxes are related.

The two dialog boxes—Object Attributes and 3D Transformations—have settings for Offset, Rotation, and Size. These settings correspond to the three Edit controls I've been discussing. Figure 6–23 shows the relationship between the two dialog boxes and the Edit Palette controls.

Offset is the same as Reposition tool.

Rotation is the same as Rotation tool.

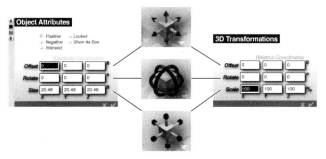

Figure 6–23 The relationship between the Object Attributes dialog box, the Three Rs' Edit Palette controls, and the 3D Transformation dialog box.

Size is the same as the Resize tool.

Object Attributes and 3D Transformations each work a little differently. Object Attributes expresses its values using absolute coordinates. When you want to know what the object is, you check Object Attributes. It is thus 'n' such a size and is rotated like so, and is offset from World Center by such 'n' such Bryce units. Those are specific numbers.

3D Transformations has coordinates in relative values. When you want to change the object, in 3D Transformations, you enter a relative number to determine *by what amount* you will change it. The 3D Transformations starts from where the object is currently located. Move it over this way *by this amount*. Rotate it on that axis *by that many degrees*. Reduce it on two of the three axes *by half*. Offset is figured in terms of B, that is, Bryce units. Rotate is in degrees, and Scale is in terms of percent. The 3D Transformations dialog box will always open up with the first two rows blank and the third set at 100% size. That is the status quo, and the numbers you put in there will change the object relative to the state it was in.

Choose, then, from the two dialog boxes depending on what you want to do. Do you want the object to be bigger and to be rotated by some amount? Then go to the 3D Transformation dialog box. Do you want the object to be a specific size (say, the same as that other object over there)? Then use the Object Attributes dialog box to enter the precise number.

You can use either dialog box for another handy trick—resize along two dimensions simultaneously. Or, very closely related to that, reduce in two dimensions while enlarging the third. Figure 6–24 shows three cylinders. The top one is there for reference, as the basic unity unit size. The middle one has been enlarged on the *x* axis.

(In this case, it's handy to get a head start by manually resizing so you know which axis is which.) Its corresponding Object Attributes values are shown. The bottom one has been resized in the Object Attributes dialog box. The two axes that control the width of the cylinder, x and z, were reduced. The y axis that controls the height (or length, since the cylinder is now "lying down") was enlarged. These two processes took place simulta-

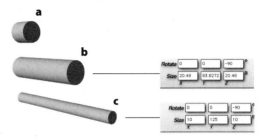

Figure 6–24 Enlarging a cylinder on two axes by using the Object Attributes dialog box: a) Cylinder at unity size; b) manually enlarged with attribute numbers; c) numbers entered into "size" to reduce on two axes and enlarge on the other.

neously in this dialog box. You can use either one to do so; in the 3D Transformations, you would have entered, say 75% in both the x and z numerical entry boxes and perhaps 130% in the y numerical entry box.

Object Attributes, 3D Transformation, and World/Object/Camera Space

How are each of the settings in both dialog boxes affected by the different types of Space in Bryce?

In the Object Attributes dialog box, the Offset value is always calculated in absolute World Space terms. (How else could you measure an object's distance from World Center?) In the 3D Transformations dialog box, the Offset value is relative when it changes the object's position; an object moves over by n units from its present position. But does it move based on its own coordinates, that is, in Object Space? If you're on a Macintosh, then yes, it does. If you're using Bryce in Windows, no, it does not; the object moves according to World Space orientation.

This table compares the two dialog boxes, listing which Space Bryce is operating in for each of the different functions.

Function	Object Attributes	3D Transformation
Offset	World Space	Object Space (Mac), World Space (Windows)
Rotation	World Space	World Space
Size	Object Space	Object Space

So, for both sets of dialog boxes, the following can be concluded:

Size is *always* expressed in terms of *Object Space.*

Rotation is *always* expressed in terms of *World Space.*

Offset changes; Offset is expressed in terms of World Space when measured in specific units from World Center in the Object Attributes dialog box. Using Bryce for the Mac, when changing the object position in 3D Transformation, the reposition act of offset always takes place in Object Space. Bryce for Windows always has offset in World Space. The implications of offset always taking place in World Space under Windows will be spelled out as I go along (and it's not good news).

Figure 6–25 compares a simple 3D transform under Mac (6–25a) and Windows (6–25b). A cube was rotated on all three axes so that it was not aligned with any axis. (For this example, in top view, the objects are shown in World Space; the same results occur when Object Space is selected.) The original cube is the left object in each image. In the 3D Transformations dialog box, a value of 35 was entered for Offset X. The resulting position of that transformation is the cube on the right in each image. Notice the difference in movement for each image. The Macintosh version moves in Object Space; the line of motion (indicated by the arrow) is parallel to the object. In contrast, the Windows version moves straight to the right along the x axis of World Space, heedless of the object's own x axis.

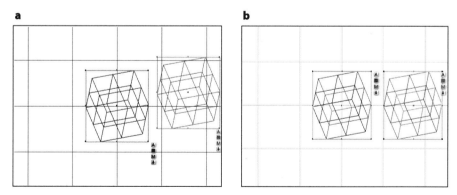

Figure 6–25 Comparison of 3D Transformation for offsetting: a) Macintosh version shows offset parallel to the object's x axis; b) Windows version is offset parallel to the x axis of World Space.

Numbers in the Boxes

Now that I've told you a little about how the dialog boxes work, which space gets affected by which attribute and how, I'll delve into some specific ways to change numbers in the dialog boxes.

Of course, you can click in the numerical entry box you want to change, type in the number and that is that. Slightly higher up on the food chain is the Tab technique: tap on the Tab key until the particular numerical box you want is selected, so you can then type the number. But wait! There's more! In the survival of the fittest, Bryce power users who master this next technique will evolve into a naturally select group of Bryce Lords and Bryce Lordettes. Here is the realm of the Up and Down arrow key and all the minion modifier keys. Let Bryce do the numbers for you.

Use the up and down arrow keys to increase or decrease the numbers. When you press the arrow keys along with certain modifier keys, then the numbers will jump up or down in different fashion. A dizzying array of options exists for you. I'll break 'em down as best I can into all the logical groupings.

The first way to group the numbers logically is by the different types of units. All of the numerical entry dialog boxes have but three different kinds of numerical units.

First there are Bryce units. This number is used to describe offset in both the 3D Transformation and Object Attributes dialog, and to describe size in the Object Attributes dialog box.

Then there are degrees. That's a degree [°] sign at the end of row, not a minuscule o! Oh! Degrees are used to describe rotation in all dialog box types.

Finally, there is percentage. That one is fairly obvious, with the % sign. You'll find it in the 3D Transformation and Multi-Replicate dialog boxes, where the change in size is being described.

So, there are three different types of numerical units. And an up arrow or down arrow will increase or decrease those numbers. Further, there are a host of modifiers to make the numbers increase or decrease in different amounts. The amount that the number will jump depends on both the modifier key and the type of units. The same key combination will affect degrees differently than it will Bryce units. So hang on and follow closely.

Changing Bryce Units

If you recall from earlier in the chapter, Bryce units are characterized by their binary numbering: 1, 2, 4, 8, 16, 32, 64, 128, 256, and so forth.

Table 6–1 delineates how the numbers change when you press different modifier keys in addition to the up/down arrow keys.

Mac modifier key	Windows modifier key	How numbers change	Numerical result
{Starting point}			20.48
No modifier		increase/decrease by 1	21.48
Option	—	increase by .1	20.58
Shift	Shift	increase by 10	30.48
Command	Ctrl	increase by 5.12 (nudge)	25.6
Command-Option	Ctrl+Alt	increase by .08 (Option-nudge)	20.56
Command-Shift	Ctrl+Shift	increase by 10.24 (Shift-nudge)	30.72
Command-Option-Shift (Option-Shift-nudge)	Ctrl+Alt+Shift	increase by 2.56	23.04

Table 6–1 Changing Bryce units in numerical entry dialog boxes: Modifier keys and up/down arrow keys produce the results shown here.

How in blazes do you make sense of all of these number units and key commands? Think of it this way: the up and down arrow keys increase and decrease the numerical values (this is true for all the new-style numerical dialog boxes in Bryce). Add refinement to the arrow keys by using the Option and Shift keys. However, since there's an overlap between what the arrow keys do when you're moving selected objects in the Bryce scene window, and what the arrow keys do when they're in a numerical dialog box, there is yet another level of modification. By pressing the Command or Ctrl key, you can imitate the moves that happen when you directly nudge—at least so far as the units are concerned. Similarly, pressing the Command key while Option-nudging (or the Ctrl key while Alt-nudging) in the numerical dialog box increases or decreases the amount by Option-nudge (or Alt-nudge) units. The same holds true for Shift-nudging and Option-Shift (or Alt-Shift) nudging. When you use the Command or Ctrl key with those sequences, the numbers will change by the same increments. The Command or Ctrl key turns the units into the nudge units; otherwise, you're working with different tenths, ones, and tens places.

Changing Degrees

That was for Bryce units. Now how about degrees? Table 6–2 lays them all out for you.

Mac modifier key	Windows modifier key	How numbers change	Numerical result
{Starting point}			90°
No modifier		increase/decrease by 1	91°
Option	—	increase by .01	90.01°
—	Ctrl+Alt	increase by .1	90.1°
—	Shift	increase by 10	100°
Shift	—	increase by 15	105°

Table 6–2 Arrow keys and modifiers for object rotation.

What modifier do you use for constraining rotation when using the Rotation control or directly manipulating the control handle? The Shift key. Therefore the Shift key will make the numbers jump up or down by increments of 15°. (Under Windows, for some odd reason, the Shift key constrains by ten degree amounts. Go figure.) On the Macintosh, if you start at 0, then each tap of the up arrow key (with the Shift key pressed) will change the number to 15, 30, 45, 60. This gives you an added level of precision that you don't get when dragging the Rotation control while holding down the Shift key. (Normally your constraints are limited to 45° increments.) Under Windows, you'll change the number by ten degree amounts, which may or may not coincide with the more precise rotation increments you may want.

Changing Percentages

When it comes to changing percentages, Table 6–3 delineates the modifier key combinations.

Percentages work the same way. Increase by 1 with a simple arrow, increase by a fraction of 1 with the Option or Ctrl+Alt key, and increase by 10 using the Shift key. Now, why does the Option key move in eight-one hundredths of a point increments rather than one-tenth? That's the amount of an Option-nudge unit. But this is percentage, not Bryce units, right? Anyway, you get the gist.

Mac modifier key	Windows modifier key	How numbers change	Numerical result
{Starting point}			100
No modifier		increase by 1	101
Option	—	increase by .08	100.08
—	Ctrl+Alt	increase by .1	100.10
Shift	Shift	increase by 10	110

Table 6–3 Arrow keys and modifiers for changing object size.

Matrix Pasting and Other Variations

The other practical use for changing the object's matrix was already covered in the Objects chapter, Chapter 4, where I discussed the Object matrix. Copy Matrix and Paste Matrix are excellent ways to adjust your object's size, position, and rotation when you want to place something inside of another object (this is how the light was placed in the lighthouse in Chapter 14) or in close alignment with it, or if you want to replace an object. I discussed it already, but it bears mentioning here, since it's an Object matrix thing and you'll use it when you're in your "Edit Objects" thinking mode.

I will touch on another subset of the 3D Transformation Object matrix controls a bit later in this chapter. The Replicate commands are specialized 3D Transformation commands. Since they are part of the process of going from one object to many objects, I will cover them in that section. So, until then, I'll stick to matters pertaining to editing a single Bryce object.

Starting Over: Shades of Undo and the Unity Command

By now you have been resizing and rotating and repositioning your objects. Inevitably, as you hum among the different controls to poke and prod your object into its proud position, it's highly probable that you will warp it the wrong way. All of a sudden you realize, too late, that you mangled your beautiful object out of alignment. How do you get it back into alignment?

Pause right here for a moment and give thanks that you are using Bryce 2. Bryce 2 has several available options to undo, go back, or start over. I'll discuss them all as we traipse down the hall of Bryce forgiveness. Bryce 2's added latitude merits some gratitude.

If you warped it just one action ago, there's always Undo (⌘-Z on a Mac, Ctrl+Z under Windows). That's the simplest option. From the advent of the Macintosh and the Windows adoption of the same, that's been a perennial source for gratefulness!

Most probably you'll call upon the faithful Undo after a resize or a rotate, when you realize that you actually wanted to do it in Object Space, but for some reason, you are actually in World Space. Undo. Change Space. Try again.

If you warped it by more than one action, it gets a bit trickier. Bryce 2's options for undoing became more robust this time around, but it's still only one undo. Under each of the pop-up menus for the Three R's is a command to undo that particular R. Under the Resize Control, it's UnResize. Under the Rotate Control, it's UnRotate. Under the Reposition Control, it's UnReposition. So, if you tweaked the Rotation, you can undo Rotation and start from scratch, without having to change the size of the object. (Undo Reposition is a redundant command; its identical twin, Snap to World Center, can be found one pop-up menu over to the right, under the Alignment pop-up menu. Use whichever one you want.)

If you want to scrap things completely, then there's the Unity command. Start over. The Unity command pops your object back into unity unit shape. It is the equivalent of selecting both Undo Resize and Undo Rotate. The Unity button is the "All ye all come free free free!" yell in the hide-n-seek of Bryce. (Regional yells may vary.) It pops the object back into its original size, shape, and alignment. It aligns it with the grid.

So how do you use the Unity command? There are two ways: First, hold down the Control key (Macintosh) or Ctrl+Alt keys (Windows), then click on one of the control points of the object. The cursor should change to a small "1" in a box when the mouse is hovering over a control handle prior to clicking. The second way is to press the = key. Beware when attempting to go for the + key on the standard keyboard. (The + key, with Shift key held down, acts as Zoom In; without the Shift key, it is the = key, and invokes Unity.) You may hit the = key accidentally. Here's another reason to be grateful for the Unity command. In Bryce 2 Unity is undoable with a ⌘-Z or Ctrl+Z. In Bryce 1, Unity was the end of the line.

If you had made a nice little brick out of that cube and found yourself in need to activate the Unity control, you'll no longer have a brick. It's a cube once again. The object has popped back into the space defined by the unity unit. In the case of the pre-squashed and stretched object primitives, Unity returns them to the standard shape. The square, disk and the torus will lie down flat when Unity is invoked. Under Windows, the torus will not only lie down flat, but it will grow vertically to fill up the entire unity unit area. Windows Brycers, get yourself in the habit of choosing UnRotate when you want to make your tori lie flat.

The other object that does not exactly go back to its originally-created shape after you go back to Unity is the terrain. Terrains are four times larger than the unity unit size. When Bryce brings a terrain back to Unity it will scrunch the terrain into the unity unit space (see Figure 6–26).

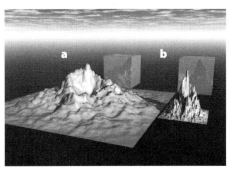

Figure 6–26 a) Terrain at its original size; b) terrain after clicking the Unity button.

Getting Out of a Terrain Jam

If your terrain has been hopelessly warped beyond recognition, you can, in a few easy steps, make it the exact size it was when it first appeared in your scene. Follow these steps:

1. Click the Unity button.

2. Reduce on the *y*-axis, holding down the Shift key. In Windows, reduce until the second snap which will put the terrain at one-fourth height. On the Mac, reduce until the first snap—that's 50% height. Then repeat that step again. You've just made it one-fourth height, thereby making the terrain the same proportion it was when first created, only smaller.

3. Press the multiply key (★) twice to enlarge it back to its original size.

There. Good as new!

The Final Resort

The last option is good to use when you find yourself saying something along the lines of "oh, the hell with it!" The Revert to Saved command lives under the File menu. Send everything away that you've done this Bryce session (or since you last saved) and go back to what the scene was like before. If there are things you'd like to bring along with you, select them and copy them. After the revert, you can paste them into your scene, and they'll pop right back in. Now, that wasn't so hellish, was it?

What? You didn't save your scene and now it's mangled beyond hope? In that case, the only advice I can tender is that when you express your disappointment, use very colorful language with rich, original metaphors. Fie on thee, Bryce!

Change Object Type

This section offers a genuine reason for appreciation (what a contrast!): the Object Conversion control. This is the "quick switch" in Bryce, where you can change one object into another object type. It lives on the upper right hand section of the Edit Palette. The double-arrows lead to a pop-up palette. If you have a sphere selected, you can change it to a torus. Or a cube. Or a light. Or a terrain. You can change any object to another object type. The only thing that changes is the basic shape. Position, orientation, size—these all are inherited from the object. So you can be working over in this one corner of your Bryce world. Get your object all positioned. Then, duplicate it. (⌘-D; I'll talk a bit more about Duplicate below.) Change the duplicate to another type. A few taps on one of the arrow keys and the object is positioned nicely.

This is an *extremely* handy little tool. It is immediately addicting—in the best sense. Once you start using this, you'll wonder what you did without it. The duplication recipe (later in the chapter) incorporates object conversion, so you'll have the opportunity to become addicted, if you weren't already.

One note: If you are using Bryce 2 for the Mac and taking the daring route of creating any of the Easter Egg object primitives, you won't be able to find them here in the object conversion section. You can convert a sphere set to another primitive type, but not the other way around. You'll have to Copy Matrix, create one of the "non-existent" objects, and then Paste Matrix to position it just so.

Edit Terrain/Object—Focus on Torus

Before moving on to the process of editing multiple objects, I want to discuss the control on the right of the Edit Palette, the Edit Terrain/Object control, specifically as it controls the torus. (The other objects that are edited via the Edit Terrain/Object control are covered in other chapters.)

What is a torus? It is a circular tube. In what ways can you adjust the size and shape of a torus? Of course, there is the regular Resize control for adjusting its size—its height, width, and depth. But in addition to that, there's that tube. How big is the tube? Is it skinny? Fat? The Torus Editor is the place to control the width of the tube.

There are a few methods to access the special object editor. These ways hold true for all object types that have a special editor. When your object is selected, you can click the Edit Terrain/Object control. Or you can click the E next to the object. Under the Edit menu there is Edit Object… command, with the keyboard shortcut of ⌘-E (Macintosh) or Ctrl+E (Windows). Do that with a selected torus, and up pops the Torus Editor, in its resplendent glory.

Fine! It looks pretty, but how does it work? To change the tube width, drag from the center of the rotating torus. (See Figure 6–27.) Dragging right increases the width, dragging left decreases it. To accept changes, click the central jewel-like thingie, tap the Return or Enter key, or (on a Mac) click outside of the Torus Editor in the main scene window. To leave the Torus Editor without accepting changes, type ⌘-period (Macintosh) or hit the Escape key, or (under Windows) click outside of the Torus Editor in the main scene window. (And, after the fact, there's always ⌘-Z or Ctrl+Z.)

Figure 6–27 Torus Editor with rotating torus.

The text readout area on the Control Palette displays numbers corresponding to the tube's fatness. The text readout is available for the Macintosh version only, so the rest of this section discussing the numbers won't apply for the Windows version of Bryce. The numbers range from 0-512, with the default being 256, exactly in the middle of the range. The higher the number, the fatter the tube. What do the numbers really mean?

The numbering for the Torus tube fatness is set in Bryce units. However, the Bryce units of the Torus Editor are unlike those of the Object Attribute dialog box, in which the numbers have been shifted over by a couple of decimal places. So the 256 you see in the Torus Editor readout is the same as the 2.56 that you see in the Object Attribute dialog box. If 256 torus units = 2.56 Bryce units, does that mean that a setting of 256 in the Torus Editor will be equivalent to the size of, say, a disk that is 2.56 Bryce units? Not exactly. A default torus set at 256 will need a disk that is twice that size, or 5.12, to precisely match up the tube width. The 256 setting in the Torus Editor is not the complete width of the tube. It is the radius, or the distance from the center of the tube to its edge, or one-half of the tube's width.

Figure 6–28 shows the relationship between all the numerical units of the torus. This cutaway view represents a torus set to the maximum tube radius, 512. The overall object's size (unity unit) is 20.48. Each tube is half the width of the object, or 10.24. The radius of the tube is the distance from its center to the edge. That number is 512.

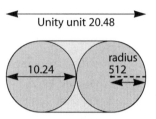

Figure 6–28 Top view "cutaway" of torus with numerical units shown.

The four tori in Figure 6–29 are set to different Torus Editor settings. The top one is at maximum (similar to the one just described), and the others are reduced by 25% increments. The measurements for disk and radius amounts are shown.

So what? Why all of the numerical details? Though math mayn't be your strong suit, it's probably good to know *exactly* how large to make a torus to fit some other shape.

What if, for instance, you want to create a hollow cylinder that has a rounded edge at the top? One cylinder hollows out another one (for more on booleans, see Chapter 7, "Booleans and Multiple Object Construction"), and a torus atop them will make the rounded edge. Is there a way, other than trial and error eyeballing, to determine exactly what the number should be for the torus so that it fits *perfectly* atop the hollow cylinder?

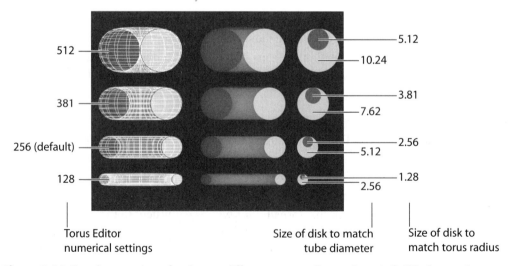

Torus Editor numerical settings

Size of disk to match tube diameter

Size of disk to match torus radius

Figure 6–29 Top view cutaway of tori set to different torus radius settings. Left: Wireframe view; Center column: rendered view with matching disk size; Right: disks that match tube size with disks that match tube radius.

First, there is the outer size of the cylinder. Both this object and the cylinder will share the same size: unity, or 20.48.

The next question—how wide is the lip?—determines both the size of the cylinder that will be subtracted from the outer cylinder, and the tube radius for the torus.

These are the dimensions:

Outer Edge	=	[your choice]
Size of Lip	=	[your choice]
Outer Edge – 2(Size of Lip)	=	Size of inner edge
1/2(Size of Lip)	=	torus radius to fit the lip

So, for a lip size of 1.28 on a unity-sized cylinder:

Cylinder x, y, z size	=	20.48
Torus x, y, z size	=	20.48
20.48 – 2(1.28) *or* 20.48 – 2.56	=	17.92 (Size of inner edge)
1/2 (1.28) *or* .64, er... 64	=	torus radius

Figure 6–30 shows the "cup" made using those dimensions. There is also an arch, where the torus is at default size and radius (256), and each cylinder column is 2 × torus radius size, or 5.12. The torus was sliced in half by a boolean operation.

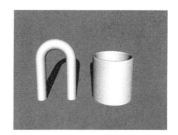

Figure 6–30 Torus at top of cup and as part of arch, the result of calculation of torus tube radius for precise fit.

You don't need to keep your dimensions in the strict binary format. But if you do, using the nudge keys to align will be much easier, since everything coheres to Bryce's internal grid.

One thing to bear in mind about the 0-512 scale: it is fixed. If you double the size of the torus so that instead of being 20.48 it is 40.96, you will *not* double the range of the radius to 1024. You have 512 torus radius units to play with, and that's it. They are calculated for the torus at Unity size and the entire torus is scaled up or down from that point. The obvious implication, then, is that if you want to do precise mathematical alignment of the torus with the cylinder or other objects, do it at Unity size. When you're finished with the alignment, group your objects together and resize them as a whole.

Torus orientation

When the torus comes into Bryce Space, it is already rotated so that it stands upright. When you tap the=key to invoke Unity (or select UnRotate from the Rotate Options… pop-up menu), then it lies flat. Figures 6–31a and b show the torus in World Space, upright (Figure 6–31a) and flat (Figure 6–31b). Note that although the orientations are different, the *xyz* axes are the same. Figure 6–31c is upright in Object space, and Figure 6–31d is flat in Object Space. Here in Object Space *y* and *z* are changed in overall world orientation, but are consistent with the object. Because the torus lends itself to uses in one orientation as easily as the other, be aware of where *y* is; you'll usually want to enlarge or flatten the torus on that axis. Knowing whether you're in World Space or Object Space will make a difference in which axis you'll be affecting to resize the torus.

a   **b**   **c**   **d**

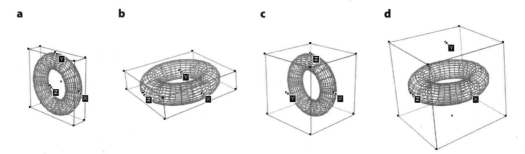

Figure 6–31 Torus and *xyz* axes: a) World Space, upright; b) World Space, flat; c) Object Space, upright; d) Object Space, flat.

GOING FROM ONE TO MANY OBJECTS: DUPLICATING OBJECTS/REPLICATING OBJECTS

Thus far, the discussion has been limited to the Edit controls that work on one object. Of course, you can also resize or rotate more than one selected object; Bryce will perform the edit action on each object individually and simultaneously. If you select several objects and rotate them, you'll have a rotation ballet, with all objects synchronized.

Unfortunately, under Windows, you will not get a synchronous resize ballet, where a group of objects are individually and simultaneously reduced or enlarged. Instead, when multiple objects are selected, resizing acts the same as if you had the objects grouped—the whole selection is resized. This is true no matter whether you're in Object, World or Camera Space. If you reduce uniformly, the entire selection is reduced from the center of the bounding box. Figure 6–32 compares how the different platforms work. In Figure 6–32a and b, the Macintosh multiple selection is reduced uniformly using the Resize control. Notice how in Figure 6–32b the location of each object's center has not changed; each object has grown smaller. The Macintosh method is an example of individual and simultaneous resizing. Figure 6–32c and d shows the same process in Bryce for Windows. A selected set of objects (6–32c) is resized uniformly. In the result in Figure 6–32d, the objects were reduced "as a group" (the objects were not grouped using the Group command). They maintain the same distance to each other, which means that the location of the center of each object has changed. They were not individually reduced. Compare the results of each of the resize actions—the objects are basically the same size, but in drastically different locations. Is there any way to simultaneously resize a set of objects without selecting each individual object and resizing? Fortunately, there is a solution. The 3D Transformation dialog

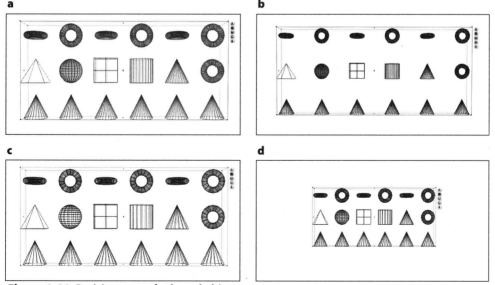

Figure 6–32 Resizing a set of selected objects:
a) Macintosh version, before reducing; b) Macintosh version after reducing;
c) Windows version before reducing; d) Windows version, after reducing.

box will transform each object. Enter the same number (expressed as a percentage of the current size) into the numerical entry boxes for the *x*, *y*, and *z* axes. The Object Attributes dialog box will also resize each object, if all of the objects are an identical size to begin with (If the size of objects is dissimilar, no numerical value will show in the Object Attribute dialog box).

Now that I've gotten that multiple-platform difference in editing multiple objects out of the way, it's time to make a full transition from one object to many objects. The first step to go from one to many objects is to duplicate or replicate the exising object. Once there is more than one object, there are edit functions for working with multiple objects.

Duplicating Objects

Bryce has a command for duplicating objects (⌘-D for Macintosh, Ctrl+D for Windows). It's under the Edit menu, of course. The Duplicate function creates a copy of the selected object(s) right in place. The newly duplicated object is selected. From there, you can nudge the new object into a new place (⌘-D or Ctrl+D, followed by a nudge-key).

With a flurry of Duplicate-nudge moves, you can build all sorts of things in Bryce. Build walls by laying a row of bricks: Duplicate-nudge right, Duplicate-nudge right to the end of the row. Select all the bricks in that row, and Duplicate-nudge-up to make the wall (see Figure 6–33). I'll return again to this Duplicate-nudge method for the Brycean mass production method of building things. But first, I'll focus on the Brycean hand-crafted method of construction using Duplicate in this tower recipe.

Figure 6–33 Brick wall built by the Duplicate-nudge method of construction.

Duplication Recipe

This tower recipe involves creating only one object from the Create Palette. All other objects are created by duplication and object conversion. While this recipe focuses on duplication and object conversion, it integrates several of the concepts presented so far in this chapter.

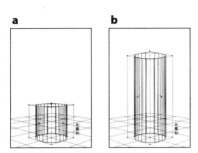

Figure 6–34 a) Cylinder created and b) resized.

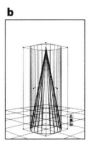

Figure 6–35 Duplicate cylinder is changed to a cone: a) Before and b) after selecting the cone icon using the Object Conversion control.

1. Create a new scene. Create a cylinder, and then ground it by clicking the down arrow. (Figure 6–34a.) Make the cylinder taller by enlarging on the y axis. To double the height while dragging directly on the y axis, press the Shift key. By the second snap, the cylinder will have doubled in height. (Figure 6–34 b.)

2. Make a new object from this one. Duplicate the cylinder by selecting Edit > Duplicate or typing ⌘-D (Macintosh) or Ctrl+D (Windows). Then convert it to a cone, by selecting the cone icon in the Object Conversion control. See Figure 6–35a. The result is shown in Figure 6–35b.

3. Make the cone go back to Unity size by either pressing the = key or Control-clicking (or Ctrl+Alt-clicking) one of the handles on the bounding box. See Figure 6–36a. Move the cone up by using the Page Up nudge key a few times. See Figure 6–36b.

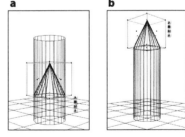

Figure 6–36 a) Cone resized to Unity and b) nudged upwards.

4. Flip the cone so that it's upside down. Select Flip Y from the Resize pop-up menu. Figure 6–37b shows the result. Then enlarge the cone uniformly using the Resize tool. (See Figure 6–37c.) To get more of a squat appearance, reduce it along the y axis. Grab the y axis control handle on the cone's top and drag to the left to reduce it. (Figure 6–37d.)

5. Duplicate this cone, and move the duplicate up using the Page Up key (Figure 6–38a). Then convert the object to a cylinder using the Object Conversion

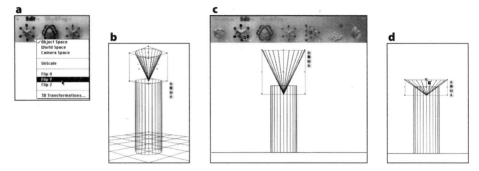

Figure 6–37 a) Selecting the Flip command; b) the result; c) enlarged uniformly then d) reduced on *y* axis.

tool (Figure 6–38b). It's a squat cylinder. Make it taller by enlarging it on the *y* axis. Enlarge from the center, using the Option key. See Figure 6–38c.

6. Now for a roof. Another cone. Duplicate and convert to cone. (Figure 6–39a, 6–39b). Select Flip Y to orient it just so (Figure 6–39c). Move the cone down. To constrain on the *y* axis, press the Option or Alt key before moving the cylinder down.

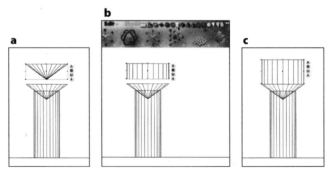

Figure 6–38 a) Duplicated cone is b) converted to cylinder; c) then is enlarged on *y* axis.

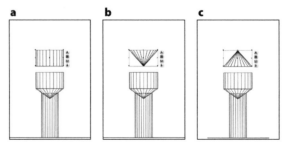

Figure 6–39 a) Cylinder duplicated and nudged up; b) converted to cone and then c) flipped.

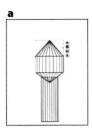
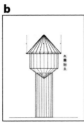

Figure 6–40 a) Cone enlarged and then b) shortened on *y* axis.

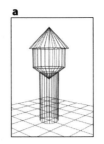

Figure 6–41 a) Final wireframe in current view; b) final rendered result.

7. Enlarge the cone slightly so that it has an overhang. Pull the bottom edge of the cone up by resizing along the *y* axis. (See Figure 6–40a, b.)

8. In the main view, the proportion of the bottom cylinder and the remainder of the tower is a bit extreme. The bottom cylinder needs a bit of thickening. 3D transformation will allow enlargement on two axes. In the case of this object, the vertical axis needs enlarging as well. Figure 6–41a shows the final wireframe result. Then render it. Figure 6–41b shows the finished rendered result.

It may not be completely gorgeous (yet), but it's a fine start. More importantly, all the objects are aligned with one another and are automatically centered on the *x* and *z* axes. You only used the Create icon once, and built from there, using different Edit controls to duplicate, convert, flip, resize and otherwise finesse each different object for this tower.

Stop for a moment and consider what you would have had to do if you had created each object from the Create Palette. Each object would have to be aligned with the others. The more individual objects you have along that one vertical axis, the greater the possibility that you'd mis-align one or more with each successive attempt to align the new objects. This method completely sidesteps misalignments.

Replicate Once

Recall the earlier mention of the brick wall, created by Duplicate-nudge. Bryce's Replicate commands automate that process. (Henry Ford, take note!) Replicate is a combination of Duplicate and 3D Transform. Bryce remembers the values of the last transform you did—the last reposition, the last rotate, the last resize. When you select Replicate, Bryce will duplicate the object and do the what you last did—reposition it, resize it, rotate it.

So, once you've done the first Duplicate-nudge, Replicate will do both actions. Actually, you don't even need to duplicate the object first. Bryce sees what the 3D transform settings are, and instead of duplicating an object in place, it replicates it—in the new place, position, size. Continue replicating to build the wall, or to create curlicue spiral natural abstracts.

Now is the time to discuss the implications of Windows Bryce using World Space for offsetting. The Macintosh version, which automatically offsets in Object Space, takes the rotation position into account as it computes the next offset. Each offset is based on the previous object's orientation. This results in a series of objects arrayed in curves, making circles and spirals. The Windows version, which offsets in World Space, will not accommodate each object's relative position, so that a series of objects will be replicated in straight lines.

Try it out!

1. Create an object.

2. Using the direct controls, change the object's location, rotation, and size. Make sure that the size change leans more toward the subtle side, not drastic.

3. Then select Edit > Replicate, or type Control-D (Macintosh) or Ctrl+Alt+D (Windows).

4. Continue typing Control-D or Ctrl+Alt+D and watch a new form emerge.

Try it again, only this time make the movements more infinitesimal. Then try it again and make the movements larger. For extra credit, select all those objects, and then do an object conversion to a different primitive type. Fun!

Multi-Replicate

Multi-Replicate is the same as Replicate, except it adds access to a dialog box. (See Figure 6–42.) Rather than accepting the last 3D Transformations you just performed on your selected object, you can directly enter numbers there. The Multi-Replicate dialog box is the hands-on executive management response to the *laissez faire* come-what-may approach of the simple Replicate. The dialog box is nearly identical to the 3D Transformations dialog

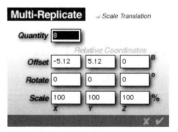

Figure 6–42 Multi-Replicate dialog box.

box, with two additions: Quantity and Scale Translation. Quantity is fairly self-explanatory—how many times do you want the object to be replicated? Scale Translation is more complex; I'll discuss it in a bit.

If you've just moved, resized, or rotated the selected object prior to accessing the Multi-Replicate dialog box, you'll see the values of your last move there. If you simply click the check or press Return, your object will be replicated in the same way as if you'd selected Edit > Replicate. Similarly, if you enter a number, say, 3, for quantity and then hit return, you'll have created three new objects, each transformed from the previous one. But if you invoke the plain ol' Replicate command after that, you'll replicate three again. Why? Replicate is the eyes-closed version. Multi-Replicate, with the dialog box, allows you to see and to determine what types of changes take place. *But they both perform the duplicate-transform actions described by the numbers in the Multi-Replicate dialog box.* It's not so much that Replicate will do only one and Multi-Replicate will do many, but that Replicate doesn't let you choose and Multi-Replicate does. And, at the outset, a quantity of 1 is the default, so Replicate will create one new object at a time.

The brick wall cited earlier is a fairly simple, highly utilitarian example of the way Replicate works. How many objects do you want? How far over do you want each one to be? Enter those values into the Multi-Replicate dialog box. How much space between objects? 20.48? How many objects do you want in that horizontal row? Twenty? Now *that* is mass-production!

The Scale Translation option is a special case function for scaling and offset when both take place on the same axis. When Scale Translation is activated, the size scale also operates on the offset, making for a cumulative effect. Although the Scale Translation control is available in both the Mac and Windows version of Bryce, it functions only in the Macintosh version of Bryce. I'll discuss how it works first, and then describe the exceptions.

Figure 6–43a shows the difference between a plain vanilla offset, a plain vanilla offset with scaling, and a Scale Translation offset with scaling in Bryce on a Macintosh. The original cube was reduced to 90% of unity size. Then, in each case, it was offset on the x axis by a value of 20.48 (unity unit). In the top row, there was no scaling. The second row scaled the cube by 90% on each axis, but Scale Translation was *off*. The third row was identical to the second, only Scale Translation was *on*. Notice how the top two rows have identical placement of objects along the x axis. In the bottom row, with each successive diminishing in size, the amount of offset is diminished as well.

a

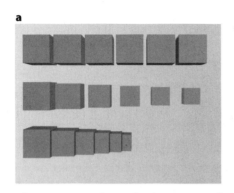

b

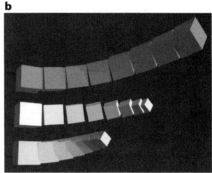

Figure 6–43 Multi-Replication in Bryce for Macintosh. a) Multi-Replication on the x axis; top row: no scaling; center row: scaling, Scale Translation off; bottom row: scaling, Scale Translation on; b) adding rotation to the mix: Multi-Replication on the x axis; top row: no scaling; center row: scaling, Scale Translation off; bottom row: scaling, Scale Translation on.

Add rotation to the process. The settings in Figure 6–43b are identical to those used in Figure 6–43a, only rotation has been added to each one (x 5°; y 10°; z –5°).

As you can see, the rotation numbers are small; the arcing effect takes place with the addition of many objects, each with a small rotation. A pattern develops. Too much rotation and the emerging pattern is more higgledy-piggledy.

All right, I just told you how Scale Translation works, and showed you examples. That was the good news. Now for the bad news. The Macintosh Bryce bad news is this: the Scale Translation switch works only on the x axis. On the y and z axes, *Scale Translation is on, perpetually*. On those axes, you'll never get the scale offset effect from the center row. You'll always get the effect from the bottom row. (Of course, if you scale on one axis and offset on another, the point is moot, since Scale Translation works when offset and scale are on the same axis.) So, the Multi-Replicate dialog box gives you the option to switch off Scale Translation— but only on the x axis.

The Windows bad news is this: Scale Translation does not work. Figure 6–44 depicts the Windows equivalent to the Macintosh Multi-Replicate and Scale Translation examples shown in the previous figure (Figure 6–43). Notice that in the third row of Figure 6–44a, where Scale Translation is supposed to scale the offset, nothing happens. The third row is identical to the second row. If Scale Translation affects the offset of an object, and the Windows version of Replicate and Multi-Replicate takes place in World Space, then there is no way that the object's size can affect the offset. This is the sad corollary to the inability of Bryce

a
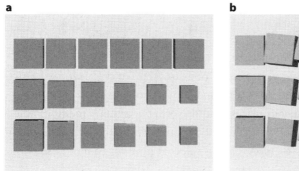
b
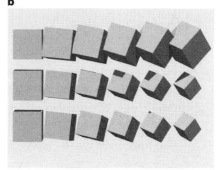

Figure 6–44 Multi-Replication in Bryce for Windows. a) Multi-Replication on the *x* axis; top row: no scaling; center row: scaling, Scale Translation off; bottom row: scaling, Scale Translation on; b) adding rotation to the mix: Multi-Replication on the *x* axis; top row: no scaling; center row: scaling, Scale Translation off; bottom row: scaling, Scale Translation on.

Windows to Multi-Replicate an arc of objects, since the object's rotation cannot affect offset. Figure 6-44b is the Windows equivalent to the Macintosh Multi-Replicate from Figure 6–43b. The same rotation settings are used. Although each object is rotated in succession, the array of objects describes a straight line, rather than the arc from the Macintosh version.

When offset takes its reference in World Space, neither rotation nor scale can have any effect on successive objects. When the two "bad news" scenarios are combined, the result is quizzical. On the Mac, you are forced to live in Scale Translation for two out of three axes. Under Windows, you cannot get a Scale Translation result, no matter how hard you try. Far more detrimental is the Windows inability to offset based upon the object's rotation, and the tutorial examples from the next chapter's "Boolean Objects and Multiple Object Construction" will suffer as a result.

Figure 6–45 shows an abstract image generated on a Macintosh by using the same settings, and varying negative or positive numbers in the offset and rotate categories. This sends four different strands in four different directions. In this chapter's folder on the CD-ROM, there is a Replication folder that has all manner of additional examples of replicated images.

Figure 6–45 Replicate abstract created using same basic settings and varying positive and negative values to branch into four directions.

CHANGING MORE THAN ONE OBJECT

Now that there is more than one object in the scene, the Edit Palette has two controls for working with sets of objects: Align and Randomize. As their names imply, they are complements to one another, one brings certain objects into nice neat gathered organized places, and the other is a quick method for distributing a number of objects helter-skelter about your scene. Whether gathering or scattering, you must have two or more objects selected in order to use these two tools.

To help you conceptualize the organization of the Edit Palette, consider this. Of the Three R tools, the Reposition tool is closest to these two gather/scatter tools. Even though I discussed the Reposition tool first among its three, its central position between the other R's and the gather/scatter controls is no accident. The Align and Randomize tools are both specialized Reposition tools as well.

Following the discussion of the Align and Randomize controls, I'll discuss the Group command, since group works with more than one object.

Alignment

Alignment precisely lines up two or more objects along a specified axis. The Align control has a rod for each axis—*x*, *y* and *z*—with three spheres on each rod for the three options for each axis: the center, and either edge. In the center of the control there is a sphere that aligns all objects' centers to one place. See Figure 6–46. Alignment also snaps the object to the invisible grid. (If you have one object selected and press one of the Align controls, then the object will snap to the grid.)

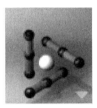

Figure 6–46
The Alignment control.

What does it mean to align "on" or "along" an axis, for instance to align on the *x* axis? Aligning on an axis means that all objects will travel on that axis to end up being in alignment with one another. Figure 6–47 examines alignment "on" the *x* axis. In each of the three cases, the objects travel along the *x* axis to arrive at a common point along that axis. They share a common Offset X position. (Assuming that the objects are the same size, when aligned on the *x* axis, they'll share the same Offset X setting in the Object Attributes dialog box.) To Align X Left, the objects travel left on the *x* axis to a common point (Figure 6–47a). To Align X Center, they travel in either direction on the *x* axis to reach a common point at the center (Figure 6–47b). To Align X Right, they travel right on the *x* axis to reach a common point (Figure 6–47c).

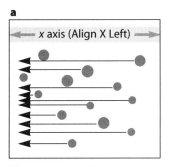 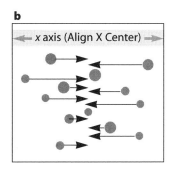 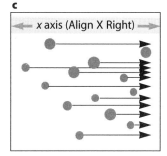

Figure 6–47 Aligning on the *x* axis moves objects along the *x* axis to a common point:
a) Align X Left; b) Align X Center; c) Align X Right.

When you are deliberating over which axis to choose, think of it this way: Usually you want everything to align either horizontally or vertically. If you want everything on the same horizontal plane, you'll need to make the objects move vertically—along the *y* axis—until they reach a common point. If you want to stack things up vertically, then you'll need to align on the two horizontal axes, *x* and *z*.

When aligning objects, they move along an axis to a common point. How do you determine what that common point is? The Macintosh and Windows versions of Bryce use uncommon methods to determine the common point for alignment on a given axis. Charitably put, both versions are not in alignment with one another. Each version has imperfections, and the imperfections of the one are not shared with the other. Bear with me as I spell everything out.

The Macintosh and Windows versions of Bryce differ in the way they answer the question, "How does Bryce determine the common point for aligning the objects together?" The Macintosh answers it in what I believe is the more logical fashion: If you want to align all these objects along an edge, then "the edge"—the common point—is actually the edge of the bounding box of *all the selected objects*. Align them vertically at the top (click the Align Y Top), so that they all jump to the top edge of the highest object of the bounding box of all the selected objects. The schematic diagrams in Figure 6–47a through c represent the way that the Macintosh determines the common point.

The Windows version answers the "how does Bryce determine the way it aligns objects together?" question differently. What is the common point for "the edge?" It is the edge of the eldest object in the selected set of objects. Recall from the discussion of creation order (from Chapter 4) that there are times when the "eldest" object takes precedence. For Windows users of Bryce, this is one of them. Of the set of selected objects to be aligned, the eldest of those objects becomes the common point. For instance, selecting Align Y Top will align all objects along the top edge of that eldest object, even if the eldest object is the lowest object in the selection. It's the eldest, so it bosses all the other "younger" objects around. (I'll refrain from making any saucy Bryce-imitates-Life comments here, since my oldest brother forbade me to!) Figure 6–48 shows all the alignment options for Windows. For each rendered image shown, the Align control used to get that particular result is shown, as well as the wireframe view. For objects aligned horizontally on the x or z axes, the wireframe is shown from top view. For objects aligned vertically on the y axis, the wireframe is shown from front view. The eldest object is the larger, darker sphere.

If you want to determine which object is the eldest of the selection, simply deselect all objects and then tap the Tab key. The first one selected is the eldest. (Keep tabbing to find out the next eldest object, etc.) If you have a complex scene with many more objects than the multiple object selection, take that multiple-object selection to Solo mode. Deselect, then tap the Tab key, and you'll identify the eldest object. You may have to move the eldest to the desired location in order to get the alignment results you want. Another option available to you is to demote the eldest by cutting it and pasting it back. It goes to the bottom of the list. The second eldest is promoted to eldest and becomes the common point.

I mentioned imperfections in both versions of the software, and have discussed the Windows imperfection (well, the not-so-logical interpretation). What is the Macintosh imperfection? The Macintosh version wins the hum-dinger award; it has the horizontal axes—x and z— swapped. Compare the different Macintosh alignment examples in Figure 6–49. When you click any point of the Align X control, the objects actually travel along the z axis. You'd think that clicking Align X Right would make objects move to the right. The result? They are lined up in back, arranged parallel—not perpendicular—to the x axis. When the control Align Z Back is clicked, shouldn't everything pop to the "back"? Nope, they travel on the x axis, jumping to the left. The result is an arrangement of objects parallel to the z axis. The top wireframe views show how the Align X objects are gathered at the front, center, and back. Likewise, the objects in the Align Z wireframes are gathered at the right, center and left.

Compare those results to the Windows versions in Figure 6–48. In the Windows version, the Align control gives a reliable clue how the objects will be arranged. The highlight on the Align X Left control looks similar to the result of clicking Align X Left. When you've studied the Windows example to see how the x and z axes *should* behave, take a look again at the Macintosh Align controls and the

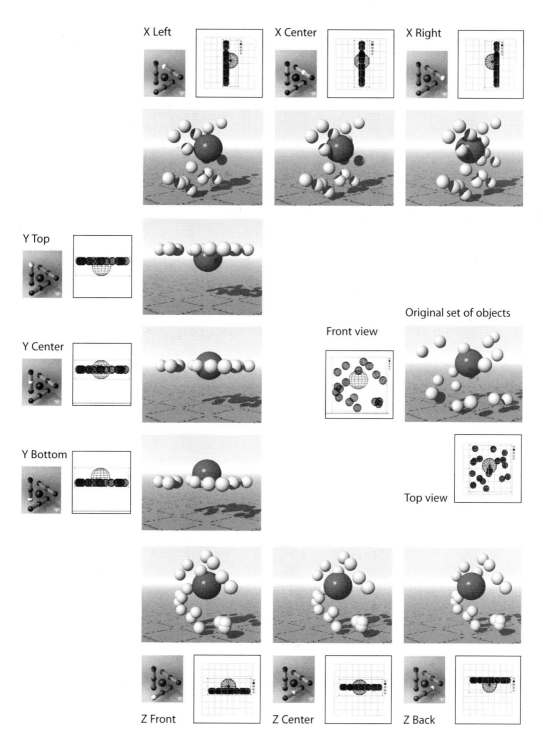

Figure 6–48 Alignment options using Bryce for Windows.

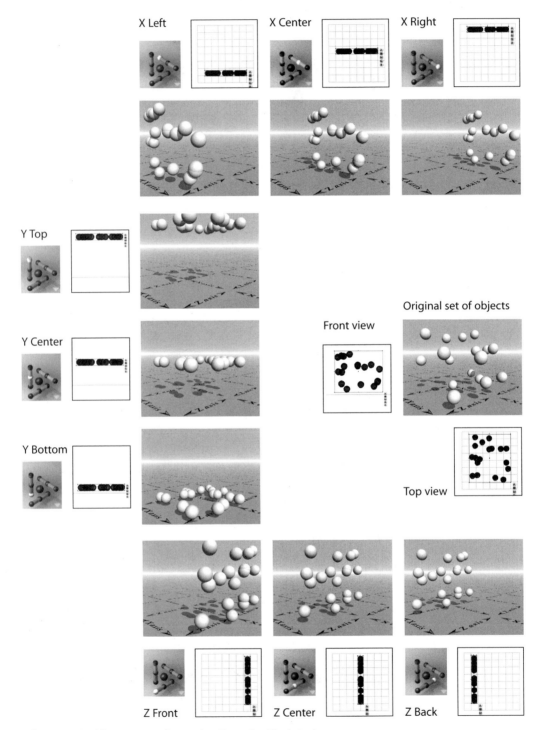

Figure 6–49 Alignment options using Bryce for Macintosh.

results. Compare the control for X Left with the result of Z Back. Compare the control for X Center with the result of Z Center. Compare the control for X Right with the result of Z Front. Is "the world as it should have been" starting to make sense? Welcome to the seedier side of Real World Bryce. To complete the comparison, now take a look at the controls for the *z* axis and the *x* axis results. Compare the control for Z Front with the result of X Left. Compare the control for Z Center with the result of X Center. Compare the control for Z Back with the result of X Right.

Here is the list of controls and the Macintosh real world (ahem) results:

When you click...	You actually get
Z Front	X Right
Z Back	X Left
Z Center	X Center
X Left	Z Front
X Right	Z Back
X Center	Z Center

The x and z axis controls are rotated around. How do you deal with it? Go slowly, look at the empirical results, use ⌘-Z, and hope that MetaTools has made all this information out of date by producing an update to Bryce 2.1 that fixes Alignment on the *x* and *z* axes.

Is this all too confusing? There is a bit of sweet relief in store when you examine the controls and results for the *y* axis. Both the Mac and Windows versions of Bryce operate as expected for alignment along the *y* axis. Top is top. Center is center. Bottom is bottom. (Of course, there is still the difference between the Macintosh edge-of-bounding-box and the Windows eldest object as the means to determine the common point of alignment for all axes.)

Now that I've gotten those nasty surprises out of the way, let's dust off our hands and get into the real uses for alignment by looking at a couple of examples.

Center Alignment

When would you want to align objects by their centers? Align objects by their centers when you have round objects and want them to share a common center.

Figure 6–50 features two objects: a cone and a cylinder. When you first create them, they pop into the world already in alignment (see Figure 6–50a). Suppose you want to alter their sizes and then align them to create a cylindrical tower with a cone-shaped roof. If you align all, you get the results in Figure 6–50b. That's not the solution, though; the solution is to keep them aligned centered on the *x*- and *z*-axes (those are the horizontal axes) and have each on a different position on the *y*-axis (the vertical axis). (See Figure 6–50c.)

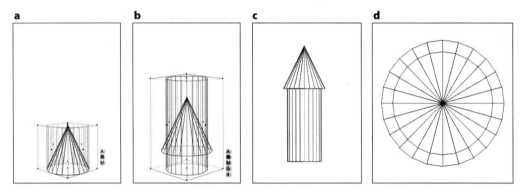

Figure 6–50 Aligning a cone and cylinder: a) Cylinder and cone as created (main view); b) cylinder and cone after resizing and alignment (main view); c) cylinder and cone positioned (side view); d) cylinder and cone aligned both on *x* center and *z* center.

> **NOTE:** When aligning objects in this type of centered fashion, hop on over to top view to confirm that everything got properly aligned. See Figure 6–50d. Or, depending on the relative size of your objects in your view, set the Nano preview to top view wireframe.

Edge Alignment

When would you want to align objects flush with one another on their edges? You'll typically use this with square-shaped objects: cubes, squares, and pyramids (pyramids have square bases).

Here are the steps for aligning a series of smaller cubes along a larger horizontally stretched cube. The smaller cubes become a set of checkerboard turrets at the top of a castle or fortress wall. (Note: Due to the confused way that the Macintosh aligns axes, I will break my customary habit of mentioning Macintosh prior to Windows. Here I'll mention the Windows controls first when it comes to which Align control to use.) Follow these steps:

1. Create one cube. Shrink it to one-half size by tapping the divide (/) key. Create another cube and enlarge it on the *x* axis from the center, holding down the Option (Macintosh) or Alt (Windows) key. The top view of the results of the two cubes is shown in Figure 6–51a.

2. Now it's time for alignment. Make sure you're in top view. Select both cube objects. You'll need to perform two align steps to make the cubes flush on two edges. To align them both on the left, click the Align X Left control (on the Macintosh, you'll have to click Align Z Back to actually accomplish this.) See Figure 6–51b.

3. Next, you'll align both objects to the front. Click the Align Z Front control (on the Macintosh, you'll have to click the Align X Right to actually accomplish this). See Figure 6–51c.

4. Extra Credit: Complete the turret-wall. The top cube is flush with the two outside edges of the wall. Now that you've aligned them, you can easily duplicate the top (small) cube along the top of the wall. Select the small cube and then Duplicate-nudge-nudge-nudge using the right arrow. Keep doing this to finish the wall. (See Figure 6–51d.) Of course, to complete the wall, you'll also need to adjust the vertical placement of the turrets in relation to the wall, and heighten the wall accordingly. In front view, the final result should look something like Figure 6–51e.

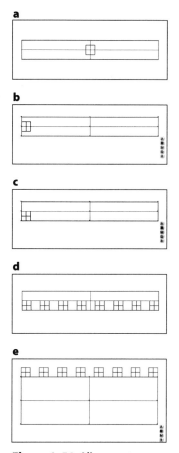

Figure 6–51 Alignment on the edges: a) Two cubes, top view, after initial resizing; b) after Align X Left; c) after Align Z Front; d) after replicating smaller cube; e) front view after height and size adjustments for turret wall.

TIP: You can also use Replicate. Once you've done the first Duplicate-nudge-nudge-nudge, Replicate ought to do both actions.

Make it Snappy

The pop-up menu under the Align control has a series of snappy options. These will work just as well with a single selected object as with a number of selected objects.

Snap to Grid. This option takes your object or set of objects and aligns each one with the internal grid. If you have one object selected and click any of the Alignment controls, Bryce will snap that object to the grid as well.

Snap to Ground. Snap to ground aligns your entire object (or its lowest edge) with Bryce's ground in your scene. (Bryce's ground level is distinct from the ground primitive; a ground primitive is created at ground level but can be moved above or below the ground level.)

Land Selection. This is the same as the down-arrow button that shows for selected objects. When you choose Land Selection, the object will drop to the next lowest object. Figure 6–52 shows a set of objects before and after landing. This is an excellent way to start having things rest upon others. Why do I say "start" and not complete it? For one thing, as soon as the object touches the surface of the other object, Bryce considers it done. For heavy materials like rock, just barely touching is not good enough. Those rocks need to sink into the softer dirt surrounding them; this lends a realistic look to the scene.

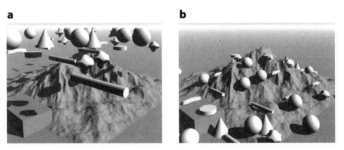

Figure 6–52 Many objects a) In the air; b) after landing on terrains and lower objects.

Land Selection can act funky at times. The object drops to the next lowest object—but there are a couple of mitigating (or was that aggravating?) circumstances. First, if the first object is not completely above the lower object, it will drop below to the *next* object (or ground). Sometimes it will drop *up* if it is not low enough to drop down. Second, Bryce takes into account the volume of each of the two objects. The volume of the top object must be equal to or less than the volume of the lower object. This explains why some object types, no matter how

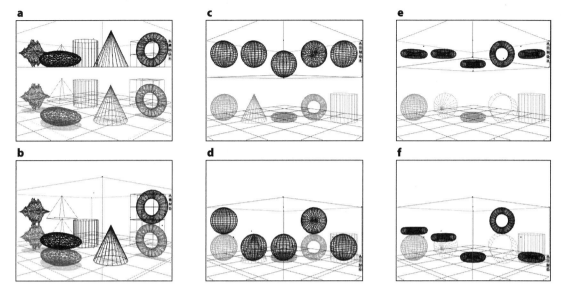

Figure 6–53 Land selection, showing normal and abnormal landing behaviors: a) Different object primitives b) landed on themselves; c) spheres landing d) on round objects e) torus object primitives f) landing on round objects, including rotated cone and cylinder.

perfectly aligned, will never land properly on an object below them. Further, objects that describe a circle on the ground or horizontally won't support objects. In Figure 6–53, various objects are landed onto various other objects. Note that the cone, cylinder, and flat (unrotated) torus do not support other objects. Once they are rotated (torus in Figure 6–53a through d; cone and cylinder in Figure 6–53e and f), they will support objects.

Snap Together. This aligns all selected objects together so that they share a common center point. What determines where that center point is? The order of creation. Of all the selected objects, the first one that was created will take precedent in saying "This is the center that all of you other objects will snap to."

Snap to World Center. This command is the same as the UnReposition command under the Reposition Tool. All objects will be snapped together with the centers lined up at World Center.

Randomize

Now that you've got all your ducks lined up in a row, I'll talk about the opposite process—Randomize. Randomize will take your selected objects and scatter them, changing their location, rotation, and size. Lest you think that

Randomizing is a completely random process (!), Bryce 2 has a set of eight options for chaos control.

The Randomize control has three parts. (See Figure 6–54) The Randomize mode preview and the Randomize Options... pop-up are tied to one another. The menu provides a verbal description of what you may change, and the mode preview supplies a visual representation. They answer the question, "How will you randomize?" Once you've

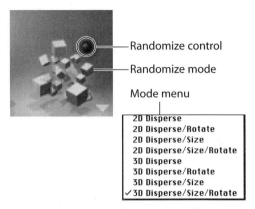

Randomize control
Randomize mode
Mode menu

| 2D Disperse |
| 2D Disperse/Rotate |
| 2D Disperse/Size |
| 2D Disperse/Size/Rotate |
| 3D Disperse |
| 3D Disperse/Rotate |
| 3D Disperse/Size |
| ✓ 3D Disperse/Size/Rotate |

Figure 6–54 Randomize controls with pop-up menu.

decided how to do it, the Randomize Selection control (the green sphere to the upper right) is the means to activate the randomization. It tells Bryce, "Do it!" You can click or drag the Randomize Selection control, with different results.

The Eight Randomize Options

So, what are the eight options and why would you want to use one or another? There are actually fewer options, five. Slice 'em and dice 'em different ways, and you end up with eight options.

The one thing common to all is Disperse. Every option includes it. I suppose you could say that Disperse is not an option; it's mandatory. Disperse takes all those selected objects and moves them every which way.

The additional options allow you to make each object change slightly while it's being dispersed. There are two options for changing each object: change its size, or change its rotation. (Hey! Including Dispersion, there are the Three R's!)

So, by now there are the following options:

• Disperse

• Disperse and Size

• Disperse and Rotation

• Dispersion, Size, and Rotation.

Finally, to add a fifth option to the other four, determine the number of dimensions into which you'd like the objects to move—2D or 3D. The dimensions serve as a major subset. Each of the four categories appears in each of the two subsets, for a total of the eight Randomize options. Do you want the randomize actions to happen in 2D where objects are dispersed across a flat, horizontal plane? Or do you want them to happen in 3D, where objects can be dispersed to different altitudes as well?

You can select the eight options from the pop-up menu, or you can cycle through the options by clicking the Randomize Mode display. (Dragging works as well for cycling through the options.)

Working the Randomize Control

To start the dispersion process, drag from the Randomize Selection control. The objects move from their original positions into new, random ones. If you drag a little, they move a little. The more you drag, the farther the objects move. Once you let go of the mouse and begin another drag, they will move again—into new directions. You can't go back along that dispersion path once you've released the mouse. There *is* ⌘-Z or Ctrl+Z, of course, to undo. But while you're dragging back and forth in the midst of dispersion, pause for a moment *with the mouse held down* to see if this is where you want the objects. It's been more than one time I've wanted to move the objects back a bit along the paths from whence they came, and was not able to.

Once you have dragged a set of dispersed objects, you can click the Randomize control and it will pop the objects into a new position. (Using Windows, you may only drag the control; it does not respond to clicking.) Actually, you can click the control any time you start with objects that are not in the same place. But when they all are starting from the same place (as would happen if you clicked the Create Sphere icon a dozen times, or typed the Duplicate command several times), Bryce wants you to determine how much they should be randomized. This allows you to make subtle scatters as well as widely scattered scatters.

Additional Notes on the Randomize Options

Randomize Size is not uniform. When you change the size of objects, they do not keep the same proportions. If you wanted to create a Lawrence Welk-esque scene filled with bubbles, and you tried the Disperse/Size option, you would get some tall bubbles and some squat bubbles (see Figure 6–55). When you want to randomize size, but keep a uniform shape, you'll have to try a different approach.

The "Lawrence Welk Bubble Show" recipe will walk you through a solution for this.

Randomize Size operates in World Space. This has implications for the order in which you do things. Back in the good ol' days of Bryce 1, when everything occurred in World Space, it was imperative that you made all your size adjustments before doing any rotation. . . *if* you wanted the option to adjust the object's size after that first rotate. Resizing while in World Space pushes or pulls an object from an external force, regardless of its rotation. Although Bryce 2's Resize and Rotation controls and the different World/Object/Camera Spaces free you from the tyranny of a heedless Xternal *x*-Force (or *y*-Force or *z*-Force),

a

b

Figure 6–55 Randomizing using Disperse/Size resizes objects non uniformly: a) 2D Disperse plus Size; b)3D Disperse plus Size.

there are pockets of World Space tyranny that remain in Bryce 2. (Can't you just hear the sound effects? There are strains of a martial music theme here, with a whole corps of snare drums.) The Randomize control is such a place. Therefore the old rules apply: Resize before you rotate!

You will get different effects if you first Disperse/Size, then Disperse/Rotate than if you reverse the order or if you Disperse/Resize/Rotate simultaneously. The next two figures show the results of three different processes to disperse, randomize size, and rotate the objects: Figure 6–56 shows the 2D process, and Figure 6–57 shows the same processes for 3D. First, there is a regular disperse in part a of each figure. Disperse/Size is shown in b, followed by a Disperse/Rotate in c. The order in which these processes occur makes a difference. If you start the process with Disperse/Rotate in d and then follow with a Disperse/Size in e, the results differ. Finally, f shows the results of Disperse/Rotate/ Size when all occur simultaneously.

Use Align along with Randomize. Rotation and Resizing in 2D tend to move objects off the 2D plane. The mechanics of randomizing rotation combined with 2D Dispersion actually do move the objects off a strict horizontal plane. There is a combination of World and Object Space taking place here, as the objects move in Object Space, but with rotation thrown in, the 2D horizontal plane, along which the object moves, is slightly changed in space. The more you drag, the more extreme both the dispersion and rotation are. Here again, the Windows method of offsetting in World Space means

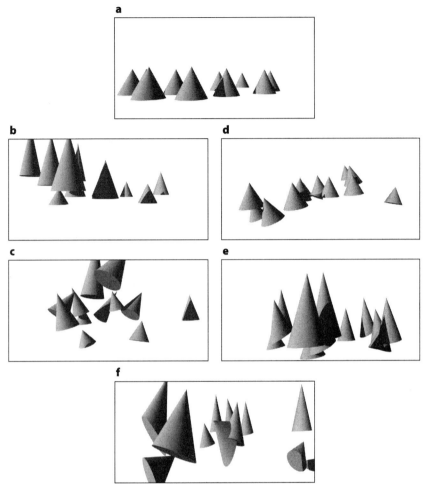

Figure 6–56 Dispersing in 2D: a) Simple Disperse; b) Disperse/Size followed by c) Disperse/Rotate. d) Begin with Disperse/Rotate followed by e) Disperse/Size. f) Disperse/Rotate/Size applied simultaneously.

that the results differ. The objects are moved and rotated, but their centers stay at the same horizontal level.

Figure 6–58 compares side views of both 2D Disperse/Size (a) and 2D Disperse/Rotate (b) for Macintosh. Figure 6–59 shows the same side view of the same processes taking place in 3D Disperse. Though there is movement in the 2D processes, they aren't as extreme as the 3D dispersions are.

Of course, at any time, if you want to return your objects to a horizontal plane, then a swift click on the Align Y control will return all objects to the same level.

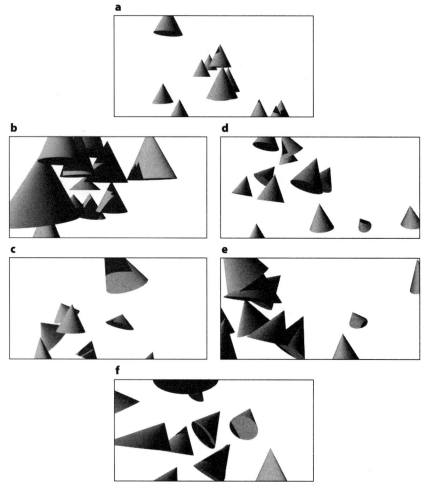

Figure 6–57 Dispersing in 3D: a) Simple Disperse; b) Disperse/Size followed by c) Disperse/Rotate. d) Begin with Disperse/Rotate followed by e) Disperse/Size. f) Disperse/Rotate/Size applied simultaneously.

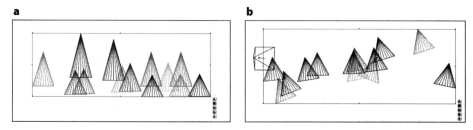

Figure 6–58 2D Dispersions from side view: a) Disperse/Size; b) Disperse/Rotate.

(This is unnecessary in Windows after a 2D Disperse/Rotate.) In fact, at any point along the way, use alignment to help shepherd your objects into certain formations, for "controlled chaos."

If you want to make all your Lawrence Welk bubbles float along in a narrow corridor, first disperse them widely into space, and then align them on two axes—*y* and one of the others. They'll all be in a row. Then a subtle disperse 3D will move them out from that place.

Recipes:

Here are a few related recipes for two different kinds of bubbles, and a variation.

a

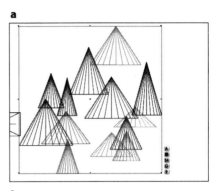

b

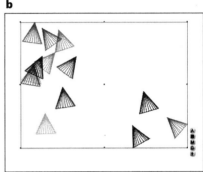

Figure 6–59 3D Dispersions from side view: a) Disperse/Size; b) Disperse/Rotate.

"Lawrence Welk Bubble Show"

1. Create a new scene file. Select the ground and delete it. Create a sphere. Make many spheres, by either creating more or by duplicating (⌘-D on a Mac, Ctrl+D in Windows). Ten to twelve is a good number to start. See Figure 6–60a.

2. Select all spheres by using the Sphere Select icon on the bottom Select Palette.

3. Randomize: Change to 3D Disperse, and drag to the right on the Randomize Selection control. See Figure 6–60b.

a

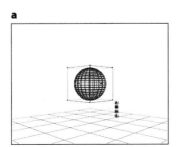

b

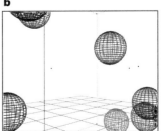

Figure 6–60 a) Create many spheres; b) select all and disperse.

4.   Now, to create more spheres that are a different size, duplicate the set that you have ⌘-D or Ctrl+D (or Edit > Duplicate). You now have a new set of spheres selected. Make these part of a different family. Change their Family color to a new color. See Figure 6–61a.

5.   Reduce their size. Use the Resize control and reduce the size uniformly. (See Figure 6–61b.) (Windows Brycers: Since you'll be randomizing location immediately afterwards, you don't need to use the 3D Transformation dialog box to reduce the size; simply use the Resize control.) Then click or drag the Randomize control to change their location. (See Figure 6–61c.) If they all disappear from view when you click the Randomize button, you can start over by selecting Snap to World Center from the Alignment pop-up menu. Then start your randomizing from there.

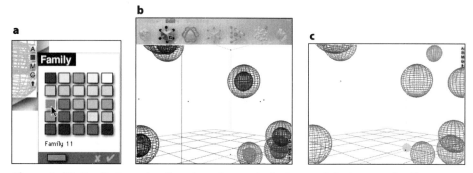

Figure 6–61 Duplicate and uniformly resize a set of spheres: a) Assign new family to duplicated spheres; b) resize new spheres; c) disperse new spheres.

6.   Do you want to have yet a third size? Then repeat the process again: Duplicate, a new family/wireframe color (see Figure 6–62a), followed by a resize and finally, a randomize (see Figure 6–62b). At any time you can select all the spheres of the same size by using the Select by Family pop-up menu. The completed render is shown in Figure 6–62c.

> **TIP:** If you want to add more sets of objects to the mix, here's a quick way to do so: Duplicate. Group the objects. Rotate the group. This repositions the entire group. Ungroup. (More on grouping follows.)

Save this scene file; you'll come back to it in a bit.

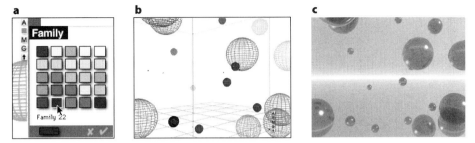

Figure 6–62 Repeat the process a third time: a) Assigning unique family; b) resize and disperse spheres; c) completed render.

Confetti Variation

All this randomizing and we've only used Disperse. How about Resize and Rotate? Sure, let's do so! The reason that rotation doesn't work with bubbles is that, being spherical, it doesn't matter whether they are rotated. If we change the object to another object type, then rotation will matter.

1. Select all spheres. Under Object Conversion, select the 2D square object icon. See Figure 6–63a. Now all your spheres are square pieces of confetti. They are all oriented identically, a most unrealistic effect, as you can see in Figure 6–63b.

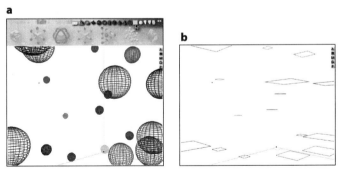

Figure 6–63 a) Change spheres to squares; b) the resulting flat squares.

2. Randomize using the 3D Disperse/Rotate. Voila! A ticker tape parade! See Figure 6–64a. The confetti may be a bit big, so reduce the size using the Resize tool. (Using Windows, try the 3D Transformation dialog box to simultaneously reduce the objects.) Though all the confetti is randomly rotated,

the objects may still be flattish. Rotate all objects on one axis for better visibility. Figure 6–64b and c shows the wireframe and resulting render.

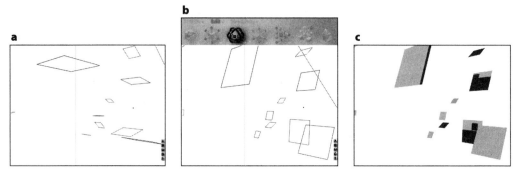

Figure 6–64 a) Randomized squares; b) rotating all on one axis; c) rendered result.

3. How about a bit more complexity? Select one of your wireframe families. You can make round "hole-punch" confetti by changing these to 2D disks in the Object Conversion control. Do so. See Figure 6–65a. Figure 6–65b shows the rendered result of the conversion (with some additional resizing thrown in for good measure) and Figure 6–65c shows the same scene with the objects all rotated.

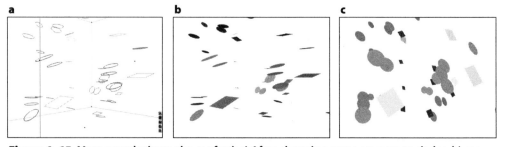

Figure 6–65 More complexity to the confetti: a) After changing some squares to circles; b) rendered result; c) all rotated and rendered.

4. Now that you've done this, under the File menu, select Save As and give this scene file the name Confetti.

"Lawrence Welk Bubble Columns"

How about a little alignment in the process? Make those bubbles travel in a narrow column.

1. Open up that Lawrence Welk bubble file again.

2. Select all the spheres. Align them vertically, to set them all on the same horizontal plane. Click one of the Align Y controls. Figure 6–66a shows before alignment, b shows after alignment, and c shows after a few taps on the down arrow key to center the plane of bubbles.

a
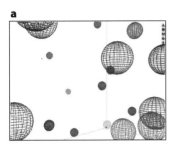
b
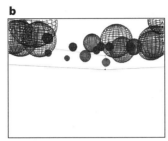
c
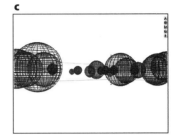

Figure 6–66 Aligning bubbles: a) Selecting all; b) align Y top; c) move down.

3. Now align on the horizontal axis. Click either Align X Center or Align Z Center. (Because of the horizontal axis anomaly in Bryce for the Mac, I'll let you choose which one. For the sample shown in Figure 6–67a, I clicked Align Z Center using a Macintosh which is the same as clicking Align X Center using Windows.)

4. After a bit of assessing, these bubbles seem a bit big. Plus, there aren't enough of them. First reduce by half (Tap the / key or—for Mac Brycers—use the Resize control with Shift-constrain). See Figure 6–67b. Then Duplicate and move them slightly along the z axis (or, if you aligned the other way, then move along that axis). Figure 6–67c shows the result. Now you have a lot of different sized spheres that are aligned into one column.

a
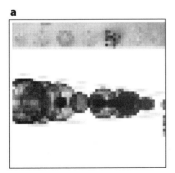
b
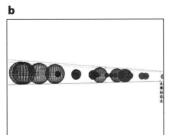
c
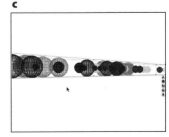

Figure 6–67 More alignment: a) Aligning on z axis; b) reduced by half c) duplicated and moved along the z axis.

5.   Select all the spheres. Change the Randomize mode to 3D Dispersion. Drag on the Randomize control ever so slightly. Easy does it. The spheres are now roughly in a column, but are meandering a bit, as bubbles will do. Figure 6–68 shows the randomizing and the rendered result.

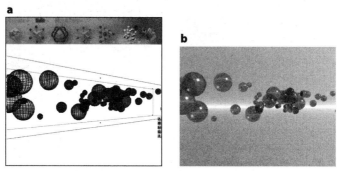

Figure 6–68 Finishing up: a) Disperse 3D slightly; b) rendered result.

6.   Assign a bubble material setting, and you're ready to polka! (The bubble material setting is on the CD in the Material Resources folder.)

Randomize. Align. Randomize again. This is an excellent technique to get controlled haphazardness.

Group Grope

Group is a kinda sorta hybrid between an object type and an edit action. If you were to think in terms of object as nouns and edit as verbs, group is both. Once you select a set of objects and Group (edit-verb) them, they become, well, a group (object-noun). As a hybrid, Group lives under the Objects menu, and has a selection icon on the Selection Palette. At the same time, it has its own little icon in the lineup of controls for selected objects.

First, I'll cover the basic edit-verb: how to group. Grouping as an action is very simple. When there are two or more objects selected, there is a G icon with the Edit Objects controls. Click the G to Group (or select Object > Group, or type ⌘-G or Ctrl+G). Ungroup is the counterpart; there's a U icon displayed when there's a group. You can click the U, or type ⌘-U (or Ctrl+U) or select Object > Ungroup. Now that you know how to group, I'll branch out and discuss why you'd want to create that object-noun thing called a group.

Uses for Groups

What are the different uses for groups in Bryce? There are four main types of functions for groups.

The first one is a logical one—to keep objects together that belong together. When a series of primitives comprise a conglomerate entity (such as a model of a tower, as in the Edit controls exercise earlier in this chapter), grouping them keeps them together.

The second one is an extension of this—boolean objects. In order for booleans to work in Bryce, the objects must be grouped. More on both of these types of group functions will be discussed in Chapter 7, "Booleans and Multiple Object Construction."

Third, grouping objects aids rendering time in some cases. Chapter 12, "Render unto Bryce," discusses this aspect of groups.

The fourth—last but not least—function of grouping is to take a set of objects and make them act as one object for some other editing process. This last type of grouping—group to perform intermittent edit actions—is one that I will discuss here in more detail.

How Groups Work

What happens when you group and ungroup a set of objects? When they are grouped, they are no longer a number of selected individual objects; instead they act as *one object*. Any Edit function you can perform on one object can be performed on a group. You can change the group's size or its orientation. You also can land or ground the group. All Rotation and Resize operations will work on a group of objects as though the group were one object. This means you can go back and forth between Grouped Object Conglomerate and Ungrouped Selected Plethora and perform different actions as you desire. (Recall from earlier discussions that the Windows Bryce is unable to simultaneously resize the Ungrouped Selected Plethora unless you use the 3D Transformation dialog box.)

Complex Composite Objects

The other important use of grouped objects is to control object clutter. In the earlier tower creation exercise, many primitives were used to comprise a complex structure. Grouping allows you to work with all of the objects easily so that they function as a unit.

Another advantage to grouping is that all the grouped objects are selected when you click on any one of them (or anywhere on the group's bounding box). In Figure 6–69, the towers were created with the same basic process used in the earlier exercise. But there are additional objects in there: small, hard-to-select objects, tiny easy-to-overlook objects. The tiny cylinder for the flagpole and pyramid for the pennant could easily be overlooked. Grouping all of the objects ensures all will be selected, so that when you move or resize them, you will move all of them, and they will be resized together, not as individual elements.

Figure 6–69 Two towers grouped for convenience.

Cone Campground Recipe—Grouping

When you are in Edit mode working on adjusting the geometry of your scene, and positioning objects, there are times that it will be necessary and prudent to group a set of objects in order to do a different kind of resize or rotation that will affect the set of objects as a whole. This recipe, to create a cone campground, uses grouping to rotate a set of objects in a certain way. It also reviews many of the other Edit controls explained in this chapter, and so gives you an opportunity to try them out together.

1. On the CD-ROM, in the Edit Chapter folder, open the scene file CONE CAMPGROUND START. (Figure 6–70a.)

2. Create multiple cones. For this, I clicked the Create Cone icon 18 times. You may use Multi-Replicate to create 17 additional cones (Figure 6–70b).

3. Disperse those cones! Select all cones using the Select Cone icon. Under the Randomize pop-up menu, select 2D Disperse. Then drag the Randomize tool to scatter the cones. See Figure 6–70c.

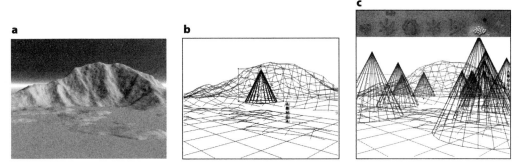

Figure 6–70 Cone Campground: a) Beginning scene; b) created multiple cones; c) dispersed.

4. They're a little too big. Reduce them in half. There are at least three ways to change their size: Tap the Divide key; select the 3D Transformations dialog box and enter 50% in all three numerical entry boxes for Size or Reduce using the Resize tool, constraining with the Shift key. (Figure 6–71a.)

5. Duplicate and disperse an additional set of cones. Select Edit > Duplicate (⌘-D or Ctrl+D), then click or drag the Randomize tool. See Figure 6–71b.

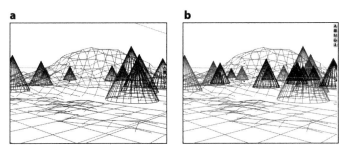

Figure 6–71 a) Reducing; b) duplicating and grouping.

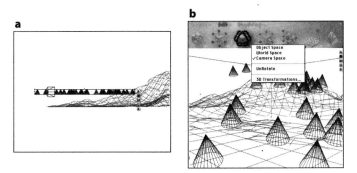

Figure 6–72 Rotating the group: a) Side view of group for reference; b) in Camera Space rotated on the *x* axis.

6. Select all cones by clicking the Select Cones icon. Group the cones by either clicking the G or selecting Objects > Group Objects.

7. Note in the side view (see Figure 6–74a) that the cones are on a horizontal plane. Change to Camera Space. Rotate the group on the *x* axis so that the close cones are lower and the far cones are higher, descending toward you. See Figure 6–72b.

8. Now it's time to realign the individual cones so that they aren't rotated. First, ungroup the group by clicking the U. All objects are selected, but any Edit actions will operate on each object individually. Then select Unrotate from the Rotation Control pop-up menu. See Figure 6–73a.

Other alternatives: In Object Attributes, for all the still-selected cones, change the rotation to 0° for all three axes. See Figure 6–73b for the Object Attributes dialog

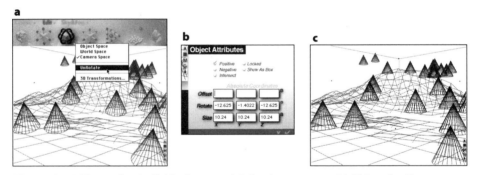

Figure 6–73 Unrotating individual cones: a) Selecting unrotate; b) Object Attribute numbers for still-rotated cones; c) result.

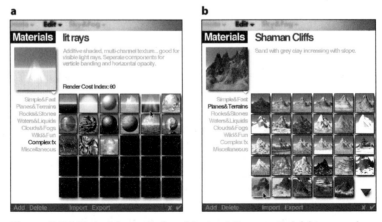

Figure 6–74 Material presets for objects: a) Cone material; b) ground and terrain material.

box *before* unrotating. Or, in the 3D Transformation, enter the amount you want to unrotate. (This option is too cumbersome in this case, but it might be *just* the solution for another time, so I mention it as a possibility here.) The unrotated result is shown in Figure 6–73c.

9. Assign textures to your objects. While the cones are still selected, make them otherwise worldly by selecting a a preset from the Materials Preset Library. Click the triangle to access the presets, and select "lit rays" from the complex f/x category. (See Figure 6–74a.) Click the OK check mark to get back to your scene. Then select the ground and terrain. (The Edit menu has an option to select inverse. Or type

Figure 6–75 Final rendered result.

⌘-Option-A on a Mac, or Ctrl+Alt+A using Windows.) Go back to the Materials Preset Library. In the Planes & Terrains category, select "Shaman Cliffs." (See Figure 6–74b.) Or, select another preset that tickles your fancy. Click the check to okay the Material selection, and render your scene. The final result is shown in Figure 6–75.

Disclaimers Regarding Groups

The "when grouped, all objects act as one object" rule does not apply when using the Unity command. Whether grouped or not, Unity will make all objects pop back to unity size. Figure 6–76a shows a camera, made of a series of groups. In the wireframe view (Figure 6–76b) , you can see the groups. Once Unity is invoked, mayhem breaks loose, with the sad (but morbidly interesting) result in Figure 6–77.

a

b

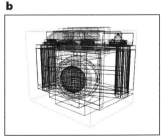

Figure 6–76 Camera: a) Rendered and b) wireframe.

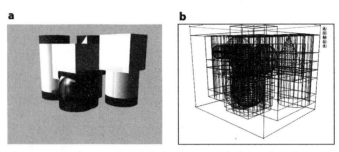

Figure 6–77 Grouped with Unity command: a) Rendered, b) wireframe.

Bryce 2 happily supports alignment and groups. It hasn't always been this way in Bryce history, so aligning grouped objects with other objects will be thrillingly simple to accomplish now.

Congratulations! You now know how to thoroughly edit your objects. Where this chapter ends up—editing multiple objects and groups—is where the next chapter, "Booleans and Multiple Object Construction" begins.

CHAPTER SEVEN

Booleans and Multiple Object Construction

"[Michelangelo,] how did you come to make that astonishing figure of Night?"
"I had a block of marble in which was concealed that statue which you see there. The only effort involved is to take away the tiny pieces which surround it and prevent it from being seen. For anyone who knows how to do this, nothing could be easier."

IRVING STONE, *THE AGONY AND THE ECSTACY*

IN THIS CHAPTER...

- Simple ways to make complex shapes and non-nature objects using multiple primitives and multiple terrains

- All about boolean object construction

- Architectural objects: temples, pillars, and principles

- Circular complex objects, such as spiral staircases and gears

- Merging scenes

Although the original purpose of Bryce was to be a landscape modeler, there is potential for far more complexity when different objects are constructed together. In developing Bryce 2, the MetaTools development team recognized the modeling potential of Bryce and created additional features for more robust modeling. Aside from new primitive types, the ability to combine primitives together using boolean operations gives you, the Brycer, many more options for generating fascinating objects and images. This chapter introduces you to complex objects, booleans, and more in-depth multi-replication in Bryce.

BUILDING BLOCKS: USING PRIMITIVE OBJECTS TO CREATE CONGLOMERATES

First, some term clarifications: When I talk about the creation of an object made from multiple objects, I use the term *conglomerate object* (or simply conglomerate). I do not use the term *group* to refer to a conglomerate, since group has a specific meaning in Bryce. A conglomerate object can be grouped or ungrouped. Since boolean objects must be grouped together in order for the special boolean properties to be apparent, I do refer to booleans as groups or boolean groups.

A conglomerate object is a bigger something that is created using many littler somethings. Bryce primitives are the basic building blocks to create conglomerate objects. Most objects in the real world work this way, also. Very few objects come prefabricated fresh from a mold. Using this method, you can create all manner of objects—household items, brick walls, gadgets, buildings, whatever your creative eye envisions—using Bryce primitives.

You can also create complex objects in a separate 3D modeling application and then import the object into Bryce. Modeling in applications other than Bryce goes beyond the scope of this book, however. This chapter focuses on pointers for working within Bryce to model objects.

Build a Little, Duplicate a Lot

When building your conglomerate object, there are a lot of shortcuts you can take. You can duplicate elements to facilitate your construction. To create two sides of a symmetrical conglomerate, build one half first. Then group the objects in the first half, duplicate, Flip X (or Z) and put the second half in position. The same thing works for top and bottom—duplicate and Flip Y. "Build a little, duplicate a lot" works at all stages of the process—from the beginning with one or two objects, to later on, duplicating a conglomerate many times over.

This technique is great for architectural objects. Put on your Frank Lloyd Bryce hat and build buildings and other fantastic edifices to place into your Bryce world. As a classic (literally!) example, build a column. Create a cylinder and stretch it up high. Add architectural detailing at the base and at the capitals through the use of other object primitives, placed just so. Then, when you have that one pillar, group it, duplicate it and create a row for a portico or arcade. Later in this chapter there is a walkthrough for creating cylinders. It takes you through the major sections of the chapter—booleans, multi-replicate, and merging scenes.

When on your duplicitous duplication spree, remember the Brycean universe grid, units of measure, and Object Conversion tool from Chapter 6.

Now that you've built the set of columns, why not build an entire building around them? Figure 7–1 shows the end result of the process of building a complex object—first a column, then a portico, then a roof, a frieze, a bizillion steps and other things here and there to create an Ode to a Grecian URL (especially if you put an image like this on your web page). Modeling conglomerate objects in Bryce 2 is made all the more fun and versatile using the boolean functions.

Figure 7–1 Greek Temple.

WHAT IS BOOLEAN?

What is a boolean? A boolean has nothing to do with a traditional chant sung by loyal throngs devoted to their beloved Ivy League school. A boolean is a computer term that refers to mathematical or logical combinations of more than one object. In the case of 3D, a boolean is the process of combining two different objects in the same mutual space (or at least space that overlaps in one or another area) to result in a new and different shape.

The Macintosh and Windows versions of Bryce each treat booleans slightly differently. They differently define the number of mathematical combinations available. Though there are three possible boolean combinations—positive, negative, and intersection, the Windows version starts out in a quasi-fourth state, neutral, which is the equivalent to what the Mac version considers to be positive. The Macintosh positive and Windows neutral is very simple, where two objects overlap in space.

The Windows positive combination actually joins the two (or more) objects into a union—they are considered one object.

Besides positive (or addition), Bryce has two other boolean operations at work: negative (subtraction) and intersection. Negative removes the shape of one object from the shape of another. Intersection takes away everything but the area where the two intersect. Figure 7–2 shows an example of each type: addition, cone is negative and combined with cylinder, cylinder is negative and combined with cone, and intersection.

Bryce has an excellent "on-line primer" for booleans. It lives in the Object Preset Library. Select the preset tile by clicking it, and read the description. After perusing the first few rows, you get a good idea of the way booleans work. I will briefly reiterate the basics, then elaborate on implications and techniques. At the end of the chapter there's sample walkthrough for you to construct your own conglomerate object.

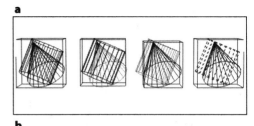

Figure 7–2 Four boolean constructions a) Wireframe and b) rendered on a Macintosh; c) rendered under Windows.

How to Set Up Booleans

Setting up booleans is simple. Assign the boolean property to your object(s), group the set of objects, and render.

To assign the boolean property, open the Object Attributes dialog box by clicking the A button next to the object's wireframe or typing ⌘-Option-E (Macintosh) or Ctrl+Alt+E (Windows). The three boolean options are there on the left side. Select one of them. If you select negative or intersect, the wireframe changes. Instead of a solid line, the wireframe will change to a dotted outline (negative) or to a dashed outline (intersect). Figure 7–3 shows the three different wireframe states for individual objects. If you are using Bryce for Windows, you must also assign the remaining object or objects to be positive. Otherwise the boolean operation does not take effect. Since the Macintosh default is already positive, this extra step is not necessary. Windows users, if you think that this extra step is meaningless drudgery, it is balanced out by two or three extra Windows Bryce boolean features (descriptions to follow!) that are way cool.

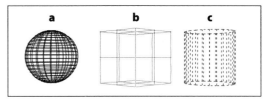

Figure 7–3 The wireframes for each boolean state: a) Addition (solid), also neutral under Windows; b) subtraction (dotted); c) intersection (dashed).

TIP (WINDOWS): Assign the object attributes to the selected object without going into the Object Attributes dialog box using key shortcuts. Type the P key to make the object positive, the N key to make the object negative, the I key to make the object intersect, and the O key to turn all attributes off and return to neutral.

Once you have two or more objects where one has a boolean property assigned, group the objects together. Select them and click the G or from the menu, select Objects > Group Objects or type ⌘-G (Macintosh) or or Ctrl+G (Windows). Then render.

It's All in the Renderer

In the more advanced 3D modelers out there, boolean operations are used to *permanently change the underlying geometry.* When you have a sphere take a bite out of a cube, the result is a new geometric shape that is neither cube nor sphere but something that shares characteristics of both. Bryce's boolean functions differ from those of complex modelers: Brycean booleans *do not change the underlying geometry.* Sure, you take that sphere and tell it to take a bite out of a cube, but the result is not a new geometrical shape. The resulting render sure makes it look that way, but what you are seeing is a snazzy render sleight of hand. The boolean operation does not change the geometrical shape of the resulting boolean group, but it changes the way the renderer *interprets* the shapes that it encounters when rendering.

The ray-tracing renderer sends rays out into the scene to see what is there and what it looks like. The ray tracer first sees a group, and asks, "What's in this group? Aah! A sphere and a cube. But wait, the sphere is negative—it's taking a bite out of the cube!" Then the renderer goes to work, calculating both the sphere's and the cube's placement. It interprets what portions of those objects will be rendered. "The sphere is not here, but its shape is subtracted from the cube at this location, like so. . ." The boolean operation takes place during the render, not during the modeling.

What are the implications of this ray-traced render-based boolean operation?

- *Booleans are editable.* The individual objects stay what they are. The sphere remains a sphere. After you have assigned boolean properties and grouped the objects, you can still select and manipulate the sphere individually, changing its size, position, and rotation, and so update the look of the entire boolean object. This provides you with editing flexibility throughout the entire scene-making process.

- *All component objects are still visible in wireframe mode.* This next implication mayn't be so pleasant. Since each shape is maintained through the end, each shape is visible in wireframe view. If you have an extremely complex object, you will have a far more complex morass of wireframe bits and pieces than if you had said, "Okay, now that my sphere has taken a bite out of the cube, change the shape forever and be done with it!" Unfortunately, you'll have to look at all the wireframe bits 'n' pieces that are non-objects in all their dotted and dashed wireframe glory.

- *Selectability is based on boolean attributes.* Here's another implication that follows from the first two. If all individual object wireframes still show even though they're now representing "non-objects" or "non-object portions," directly clicking a non-object (i.e., negative boolean attribute) will not select it. Even though you are viewing your scene in wireframe view, that wireframe information is being interpreted in a ray-traced fashion, and if the object is "not there," well then, by golly you can't select it. (Selecting by color, object type, and directly clicking an object in solo mode *will* select a negative object.)

- *Surfaces are based on individual attributes.* The final surface of the grouped boolean object is based on the surfaces and boolean attributes of the member objects. This implication is true on both platforms, but it takes slightly different forms for each. On the Macintosh, the surface appearance of the resulting boolean object depends on how the combination took place. Back in Figure 7–2b, the cone and the cylinder each have a different surface appearance. Whichever is the negative object loses its surface type; the surface type of the remaining positive object is the surface setting for the grouped result. Under Windows, each object maintains its own individual appearance, as shown by Figure 7–2c. Maintaining individual surface appearance also takes place in Bryce for both platforms for the other boolean operation—intersection (where the common areas of the two or more objects remain and everything else goes away). Each object retains its own surface setting. Planning the surface attributes with this in mind will make for some boolean objects that are simply fetching.

- *Booleaned objects are limited to certain types.* On the Macintosh, if it is necessary to have a basic geometric solid in order to be negative or to intersect, then those objects that aren't basic solids will not work successfully as boolean objects. Stones, which are constructed from polyhedrons, will not work. Likewise, any imported object (DXF, 3DMF) won't work in a boolean object relationship. The terrain *does* work, but the symmetrical lattice, which is a special double terrain object mirrored back-to-back and clipped, will *not* work. And lights don't work, either. (Besides, why would anyone *want* to boolean a light?) All Windows objects (even lights!), no matter how polyhedronous or geometrically complex, participate fully in boolean operations. (This is one of the way cool Windows-only features I hinted at earlier.)

Booleans in Depth

With this background in mind, are there any special techniques for using booleans during the construction process? Yes! Use objects as tools for construction. Use a sphere to scoop something out. The results of using objects as tools can become widely varied, as numerous as are the objects in the world. I cannot discuss them all, but I can discuss some principles of construction. You take it from there, being your own architect, contractor, foreperson, and master craftsperson.

Positive

All Macintosh objects begin as positive, whereas all Windows objects begin as neutral. For clarity's sake, I'll refer to the default state as "positive/neutral," and the Windows state as "Windows positive." For positive objects to be combined with other objects, I will refer to the object as the positive object type, such as "positive cone."

Positive/neutral is the most basic of object combinations. When you combine positive objects they just comprise a more complex shape than either of the two are when alone. You do not need to group a set of objects in order for the positive/neutral combinations to be visible. With the exception of a minimum of the fancy trickery in the temple image shown in Figure 7–1, most of the objects for the foundations and the steps are positive objects, positioned just so. They may or may not be grouped.

When you are working with transparent objects, the benefit of the Windows positive boolean state becomes clear (pun intended). Since Bryce considers each object to be a distinct element, two overlapping transparent objects will look like two overlapping transparent objects. If you want to combine different objects to make something such as a wine bottle (see Figure 7–4), you could run into some problems, as the complex object on the left demonstrates. The complex object on the right, however, doesn't suffer the same fate. All the objects have been assigned positive and then grouped, making for a nice glass bottle.

Figure 7–4 Windows grouping of positive objects results in uniting primitives into one shape; object on left is not grouped positive; object on right is a grouped positive.

Negative Noodlings and Subtraction Strategies

When you make an object negative, you subtract its shape from another one. Since it's far easier to talk about "subtracting the sphere shape from the cube," I'll speak of negative boolean in those terms rather than the more awkward "make the sphere negative and then group it with the positive cube."

Many consecutive subtractions make for an interesting construction. Follow the fate of the first object as it gets subtracted and re-subtracted again and again. Like math, it's a positive number then a negative number then a positive number, then a negative. . . ad infinitum. Figure 7–5 demonstrates this, starting out with a simple two-object subtraction, and then adding to it with an additional boolean subtraction process with each object to the right. (Each step is shown in front and side view.)

If the object you have isn't big enough to subtract from the other object (due to the shape you want to achieve), then create a larger subtraction group. Create the two objects to use in tandem; together they'll subtract from another object. If you're using the Windows version of Bryce, you'll need to ensure that the two objects are positive before grouping them. Combine two objects together and group them. Make the group negative. Then assign the negative group to subtract from your positive object. In Figure 7–6, a pyramid that is scooping out a shape from a cylinder needs to bore in deeper to the cylinder than the pyramid is tall. To do this, the positive pyramid and a cube are grouped together. The group is assigned negative, and is grouped with the positive cylinder to carve out a shape.

This is the technique used with terrains to cut areas out of other objects. I'll elaborate on terrain boolean strategies later in this section.

Of course, you can use booleans to create your subtracting object, for a two (or more) step process. To create the obelisk in Figure 7–7, where there are two pyramid shapes, the positive object is the tall, tall pyramid. But in order to cut it short with another pyramid shape, a double-negative is required. In Figure 7–7 the progressive building of the top boolean object is shown. First, a pyramid is placed in the bottom of a positive cube. The pyramid is assigned negative. Then the two are grouped. The resulting cube has a pyramid-shaped hole beneath. After creating and enlarging another pyramid so that it stands very tall, the cube-pyramid boolean is nearly ready to chop off the top of that tall, tall pyramid to finish the obelisk. But first, the cube must grow in height so that it occupies all the area of the top of the tall, tall pyramid (see Figure 7–7b). Once it does that, it can be aligned with the positive pyramid (Align X and Z; both centered) and then assigned negative, grouped, and rendered for the result shown.

Intersecting

Intersection takes away everything but the area where the two objects overlap. The surface properties of each object are retained, however, resulting in an object that has two or more different materials. In Figure 7–8, the obelisk is built with intersection, using only two objects that encompass a much wider area than did the subtraction example.

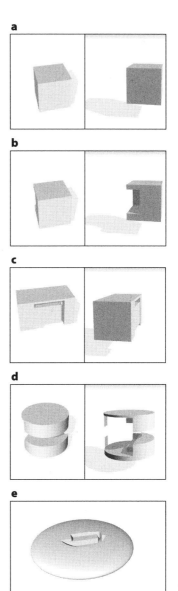

Figure 7–5 Cumulative subtraction.

When you go to create an intersection boolean group, you cannot create a group comprised solely of intersecting objects. There must be one object in the group that is positive. This is true whether there are two objects or more than two

a   b

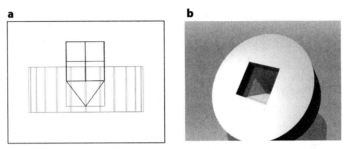

Figure 7–6 A pyramid and cube combined to make a negative object.

a   b

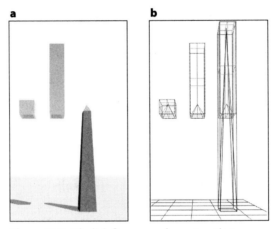

Figure 7–7 Obelisk figures and construction.

objects. It doesn't matter which is positive and which is intersecting, since the result will show only the area that is common to the two. You can have multiple intersecting objects as a part of the group. Figure 7–9 shows identical results from two different sets of boolean intersect operations. There are three objects to the boolean group: a cone and two pyramids. The pyramids are offset by 45° from each other. In the set on the left, the cone is assigned to intersect and then grouped with the two positive pyramids. In the group on the right, the two pyramids are assigned to intersect, then grouped with the cone. The net result is the same. You can also group a set of positive objects together and then assign the intersect attribute to the group before joining it with yet another object. Figure 7–27c, later in this chapter is the result of that technique.

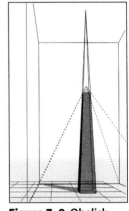

Figure 7–8 Obelisk with intersection wireframes.

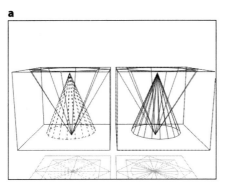 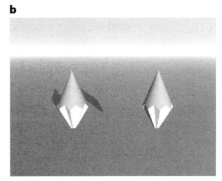

Figure 7–9 Two approaches to intersection: a) Two wireframe boolean object groups; b) the rendered results of those groups.

You can alternate between subtraction and intersection in your boolean groups. But you cannot have both a negative object and intersecting object in the same group. If you are at all mathematically inclined, you're aware that mathematical equations will first solve one part, and then another. You cannot subtract and divide simultaneously, you have to choose to do one first and then the other. The different parts are separated by parentheses. Grouping works in an analogous fashion. If you were to put boolean operations in a mathematical way, you might look at the operation like this:

(Cube minus sphere) intersected with cone.

The first group is the cube minus the sphere; the sphere is set to negative. The second group is the intersection.

Booleans and Groups

When you create a group of positive objects and then assign a boolean property to the group, the group's bounding box is changed in wireframe view to reflect the boolean status, not the individual objects themselves. Check out the two wire-frame examples in Figure 7–9. In the example to the right, the boolean property is assigned to the group, making the bounding box dashed.

Note how, once you have grouped an object, the bounding box changes. If you have selected one of your attributes to be negative, then the resulting bounding box reflects the new size of the object. The bounding box surrounds only the positive object. In the case of intersection, the objects are not trimmed in the bounding box; they are together as a group. Strangely enough, the combination of the two using intersection results in an object that is smaller than subtract (usually). In the obelisk example cited earlier, the group bounding box encompasses the object that has the positive attributes. With intersection, the bounding box encompasses both objects, since both objects are positive to some extent.

Terrains and terrains; terrains and grounds

Terrains are full-fledged citizens of Booleanable Objects in Bryce. Since terrains are not the simple geometric shapes that cubes and cylinders and spheres and the like are, there are some special shape considerations to bear in mind for proper boolean results using terrains. Although a terrain is hollow when you look at it, for boolean purposes, the terrain gets closed off at the bottom to become a solid object. The bottom edge is defined by outside edges of the terrain square. In order to create a clean terrain-shaped cutout of another object, you need to stay aware of the location of the edges of your terrain.

In order for a terrain to cleanly slice out of another object, its edges all have to be clear of that object's edges, otherwise you'll get an overlap. In Figure 7–10, a terrain is biting a corner out of a sphere. It has been rotated around so that its bottom (where the square edges are) is facing out, and its top is the part subtracting the object. Part a shows the side view, and part b shows the front view for the wireframes. Notice how the terrain's "bottom" edge doesn't clear the sphere. The result is the leftover sphere part of the terrain.

a   **b**

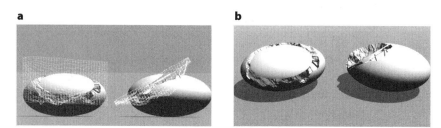

Figure 7–10 Terrain being subtracted from sphere.

To solve this kind of problem, group the terrain and another object together to make a bigger object. Since a terrain is square at its base, I like to set a cube there. Here's my quick positioning technique.

First make sure everything is ungrouped.

1. Duplicate the terrain and change it into a cube using the Object Conversion tool.

2. In the Edit Palette, change to Object Space and use the Reposition tool (on the *y* axis, most probably) to move the cube so that it extends off of the bottom of the terrain.

3. Make sure that they are both positive, then group the terrain and cube together. Assign negative to the group. The bounding box wireframe changes to dotted lines.

4. Group the negative terrain-cube group with the positive sphere.

5. Render.

Simple!

Another aspect of terrain booleans is the terrain's height information. Since a terrain changes shape based on the grayscale information, it's good to know how height information affects the boolean process.

The bottom of the terrain's area is defined by the its lowest points—in the grayscale information. Usually that also is the outside edge. If you want a terrain shape to take a gouge out of another primitive or the ground plane, there are seemingly two ways of doing so. You can position the terrain so that it is upside down, taking that bite out of the object. Or, conceivably, you could invert the gray map so that what's high is low and what is low is high. But those two actions do not yield the same result. Figure 7–11a through d shows two terrains positioned with two cubes. Parts a and b show wireframes. They seem identical. But they're not. Part a is a terrain that has been flipped on the *y* axis, and part b is a terrain whose gray map has been inverted. In wireframe mode they appear the same, but when they are rendered (Figure 7–11c and d), the differences are strikingly obvious. The terrain in part c gouges out the area, whereas the terrain in part d lies inside the cube. The outside edge will

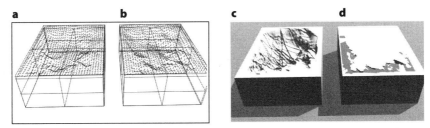

Figure 7–11 Terrains set to negative: a) Wireframe view of a terrain that has been flipped *y*; b) terrain wireframe with inverted height map; c) rendered view of wireframe from part a; d) part b rendered.

Figure 7–12 Ground Canyon: Many negative terrains grouped with ground.

always define the bottom. (The Terrain Editor preview also gives a nice clue about what is bottom, even for an inverted terrain.)

Clipping has no effect on a terrain that has been booleanized; the clipping will be ignored and all the terrain will show.

This same type of treatment is effective for taking a gouge out of the ground. In Figure 7–12, this "ground canyon" was created by duplicating several terrains that were flipped on the y axis, positioning them just above the ground level, then making them negative and grouping them all with the ground. Notice how the highest level in the scene is all one level—the ground plane.

a   **b**   **c**

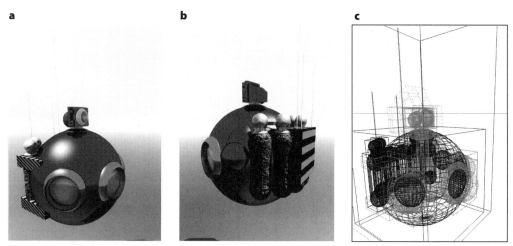

Figure 7–13 Rodney L'Ongnion's Planetary Traveler Probe a) Rendered view; b) rendered view; c) wireframe view.

a

b

Figure 7–14 Escher House a) Wireframe and b) render. *Art by Hilary Rhodes.*

A FEW BOOLEAN EXAMPLES

Boolean variety is the spice of Bryce. Here are a few example images that show the type of modeling abilities using Bryce. In the first, the Planetary Traveler Probe by Rodney L'Ongnion (see Figure 7–13), a flying ship is created using almost all spheres and cylinders, with a cube thrown in here and there for good measure. Compare the image of the final render with the wireframe view.

Hilary Rhodes' Escher House in Figure 7–14 is a Brycean reconstruction of the impossible room that is rightside up and upside down and every which way when viewed from every perspective. Though there is a lot of good old fashioned addition going on here, judicious subtraction makes the illusion of unreal reality possible.

Harald Seiwert's fairy-tale castle in Figure 7–15 is a study in architectural details. (I must say that European Brycers have a home-turf advantage with the local castles nearby for study!) The double-placement of pyramids and cubes (in diamond

a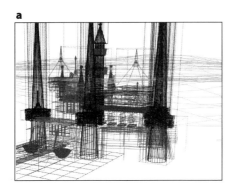

b

Figure 7–15 A fairy-tale castle a) Wireframe and b) render. *Art by Harald Seiwert.*

shape) for the two-sloped roof, the boolean cut-outs for the architectural details on the castle walls, towers, and turrets, and the overall detail in construction make this an exemplary study of the conglomerate Brycean object.

REPLICATING OBJECTS

When you are creating a conglomerate object or using many objects to create something bigger, make sure to use Multi-Replicate. It's excellent for creating objects in circles of one or another sort. I'll discuss how.

Circular Logic: Multi-Replicating into a Circle

With all the opportunities to use numbers in Bryce, it's helpful to know *how* to use them and under what circumstances. Here's the formula for setting a number of objects in a circle. It depends on the number of objects you want to have. Suppose you want to have 12 objects. As you probably already know, a circle has 360 degrees. In order to get a complete circle, you need to know the total number of objects and then divide 360 by that number. 360 divided by 12 equals 30. Enter 30 as the value for rotation. (You can also enter –30°.) As for the number of objects, enter the number you want minus one. If you want 12 objects total and you already have one (you have to have *one* to multi-replicate!), then you want to make 11 *new* objects. How big do you want the circle to be? The amount you enter into the offset determines the circle's size. Figure 7–16 shows three different circles created using different offset values in Bryce for Macintosh. (I'll discuss a Windows workaround for Multi-Replicate and offset in a bit.) The offset value for the cones is 10.24 (half unity unit size). The offset value for the cylinders is 20.48 (unity unit size, same as the object's size). The offset value for the pyramids is 30.72 (one-and-a-half unity unit size). Whatever axis (or axes) you offset the object, do not also rotate on the same axis. (If you do, you won't get a circle.)

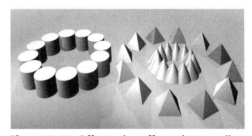

Figure 7–16 Offset value affects the overall size of the circle (Macintosh). Three circles created using the same rotation amount but different offset amounts.

Which axis do you want your circle to rotate around? If you want a circle of objects flat on the ground, then choose the *y* axis for rotation. In Figure 7–17a and b, the rotation takes place on the *y* axis, but the offset is on different axes. For all

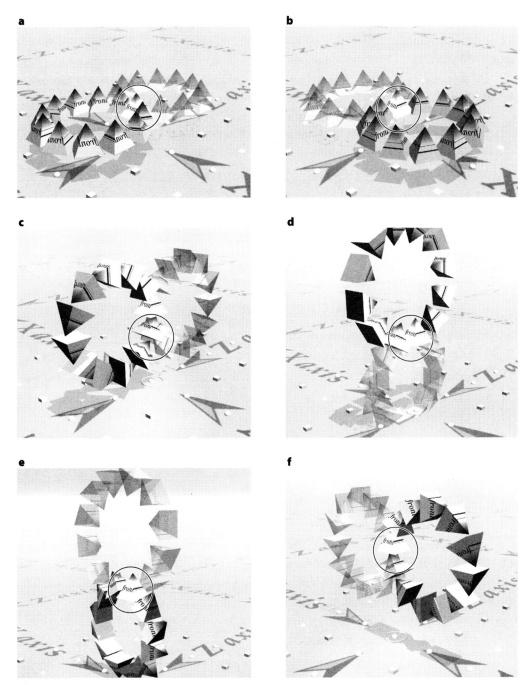

Figure 7–17 Multi-Replication into a circular form, by rotating around the *x*, *y* and *z* axes. Top Row: Horizontal rotation around the *y* axis, a) offsetting *x* and b) offsetting *z*. Middle Row: Rotating around the *x* axis, c) offsetting *y* and d) offsetting *z*. Bottom Row: Rotating around the *z* axis, e) offsetting *x* and f) offsetting *y*.

these images the opaque objects are rotated at 30°, and the transparent ones are rotated at –30°. The encircled pyramid is the original starting place.

Remember, in the Multi-Replicate dialog box, the offset is relative—for Macintosh, at least. It offsets from the previous position. This is most apparent by seeing the "front" of the object in relation to the previous one. Notice the difference in the rotation style for each axis. As each object is rotated, what is "front" differs from the *x* rotation (where all the fronts face inward) to the *z* offset, where the fronts line up one behind the other.

Figure 7–17c through f shows the same type of rotation variations for the *x* and *z* axes, where the circle shape is vertical, like a ferris-wheel. Again, the opaque objects are from rotating 30° and the transparent ones are from rotating –30° from the same original pyramid.

To summarize multi-replication for circles:

Quantity: Enter the total number of objects you want, minus 1.

Rotate: Divide 360 by the total number of objects you want. That's the degree of rotation.

Offset: Enter a number that's larger than the object size. Do not enter a number into the same axis as rotation. You can enter numbers into one or both of the other axes.

The multi-replication feature of Bryce allows for immense diversity. As another circular variation, take an object and rotate successive copies with no offset whatsoever.

In fact, for the crippled Windows version of Multi-Replicate, this is the starting point to get a decent circular shape. The process is broken into two steps. First, create several objects with successive rotations, and then later follow that with the reliable method to offset in Object Space, using the Reposition control. This is not only a solution for Windows users, it is a good all-around cross-platform solution to make the objects the proper distance from one another, rather than blindly guessing whether the value you entered into the Multi-Replicate dialog box's offset area was the proper one.

The calculations for number of objects—360° divided by the total number of objects—is the same for this two-step method. You simply enter 0 for the offset amount, since you'll manually offset using the Reposition control. Sounds manageable, right? Figure 7–18a shows the result using a Mac, where it works

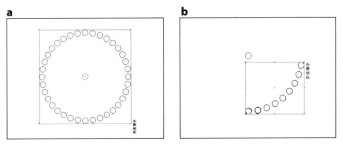

Figure 7–18 Multi-Replication to rotate 36 objects (at 10° each),
followed by use of the Reposition control to place them:
a) Macintosh result; b) Windows result.

according to the theory. There is a problem with the Windows version, however. Under Windows, if you Multi-Replicate a quantity of 36 objects and set the *y* axis rotation to 10°, followed by a manual Reposition in Object Space, you don't get an entire circle. You get a quadrant, literally. The objects describe only one-fourth of a circle. (See Figure 7–18b.) There are 36 objects there, though. Bryce Windows calculates the numberical values for rotation in such a way that the objects only show up in one-quarter of the circle. Fooey.

All is not lost, however. There is a workaround. It requires that some extra steps be taken—four steps, to be precise. If you can successfully distribute a quarter of the circle, then break the process down into four steps and offset each set of objects in a different direction. Of course, doing this requires some sort of a placeholder guide circle to judge each of the four successive offsets. Here's a recipe.

Windows Multi-Replication Workaround In Four-part Harmony

1. Create a cylinder. Duplicate it. One of the two cylinders should be selected. In the 3D Transformations dialog box change the size. Enter 20%, 200%, and 20% for the size numbers to increase the height and reduce the width and depth.

2. Select the other cylinder. This will become the template, or marker. Reduce its height until it is nearly flat. Go to top view. Hold down the Alt key to constrain from the center, and proportionately enlarge the cylinder until you reach the size you want your circle of objects to be. Reduce the cylinder's height again, if necessary.

3. You now have the original cylinder in the center, and a guide for your reposition (see Figure 7–19a). Next, decide the total number of objects you want to replicate.

To make life easy on yourself, decide on a number that is divisible by 4. How about 24? Good idea. 24 divided by 4 is 6, so you'll replicate 6 cylinders at a time. Select the inner cylinder, and select Edit > Multi-Replicate (Ctrl+Opt+ Shift+D). When you enter the dialog box, there are numbers there already. The numbers represent what happened to the cylinder since it was created. Bryce Windows does not provide numbers for the last edit move you made, it gives you something of a current status report of the object since it was created. It won't take you very long to grow irritated with this habit of Bryce Windows, since you'll have to change those numbers all four times you replicate the cylinders. Enter 6 for the Quantity, 0 for all Offset values, and 100% for all the Size values. What about Rotation? 360 divided by 24 is 15, so the rotation for the *y* axis will be 15°. Figure 17–19b shows the Multi-Replication dialog box. After you've entered those numbers, click OK.

4. You now have 6 selected cylinders. Make sure that you're working in Object Space, and then use the Reposition tool to move the objects. Drag to the right on the *x* axis until your set of cylinders just touches the inside edge of the template cylinder. See Figure 7–19c.

5. So far, so good. Repeat this process again. Re-select the center cylinder, open the Multi-Replicate dialog box, enter the same values again, click OK, and

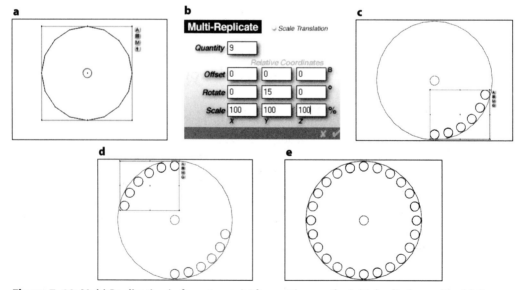

Figure 7–19 Multi-Replication in four steps: a) After setting up the initial cylinder and "guide" cylinder; b) Multi-Replication dialog box settings; c) after repositioning the first quadrant; d) after repositioning the second quadrant; e) after replicating and repositioning for all four quadrants.

then drag to the left on the *x* axis of the Reposition control to place the arc of cylinders in the opposite quadrant (see Figure 7–19d). Repeat two more times, and use the *z* axis of the Reposition control to place these last two arcs into the remaining quadrants. Figure 17–19e shows the final result.

Torus Multi-Replication Variations

Using Multi-Replicate to rotate only (without offset) works nicely with the torus. The torus, with its hollow center, can be used to create a delicate interwoven form resembling a basket or ball of twine. Start with a flat, unrotated torus. As with the circular rotation just discussed, the torus conglomerate follows the formula of number-of-objects × rotation amount = 360. Figure 7–20a through f shows several examples. Part a shows the torus rotated on the *x* axis by a constant amount, 15°, and there are 23 replications. This holds true for all of the examples, though the others add more than the *x* axis rotation. Parts b through d add rotation on the *z* axis, uniform, lower and higher amounts respectively (the final resulting conglomerate torus object in Figure 7–20d is rotated slightly so that the side detail is visible). The last two, parts e and f, add rotation on the *y* axis as well. Generally, the size of the opening corresponds to the size of the rotation amount on the secondary and tertiary rotation amounts; the smaller the amount of rotation, the smaller the opening. The larger the amount, the larger the opening. You can have a lot of fun with this one.

How about one more twist before we're through? What happens if you offset each value slightly? (Obviously, with the rotate-and-offset combination for Multi-Replication, the Macintosh and Windows results will vary widely. This paragraph

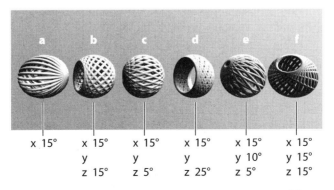

Figure 7–20 Different set of tori duplicated and rotated, but not offset.

features the Macintosh version.) Figure 7–21 experiments with an offset on the x axis, scale translation off and on. In the four examples there are different settings for the replications. The first is offset on the x axis by 10. The size stays the same. The next three sets of tori have scale translation on. The size is reduced to 90%, so each newly replicated torus is 90% of the size of the previous one. The second and third set have identical settings, except that scale translation is *off* on the second and it's *on* with the third. The offset amount is also determined by the scale of the object. The last sample on the right has scale translation on for all axes, with an offset of 10 on all three axes.

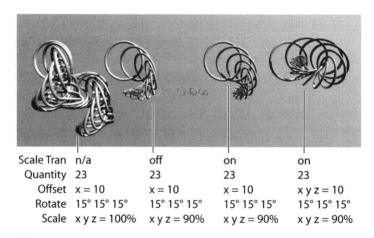

Scale Tran	n/a	off	on	on
Quantity	23	23	23	23
Offset	x = 10	x = 10	x = 10	x y z = 10
Rotate	15° 15° 15°	15° 15° 15°	15° 15° 15°	15° 15° 15°
Scale	x y z = 100%	x y z = 90%	x y z = 90%	x y z = 90%

Figure 7–21 Scale translation and offset for tori conglomerates.

(Not So) Vicious Circles

There's an older way to create a circular set of objects in Bryce. It doesn't require numbers and calculations and the Multi-Replicate dialog box, but it does do the trick. There are times when it's preferable to use this method to create something in a circular form. And, if you're using Windows, it will be one of your staple techniques.

To create a circular form without using the Multi-Replicate dialog box, duplicate the first object, move the duplicate object elsewhere and then group two objects together. Now these objects, being grouped, will move around a common center when you rotate them. Duplicate. Then rotate. See Figure 7–22a. Select both groups, duplicate the both of them, and then rotate again. To get even spacing between objects, rotate the new duplicates until they're positioned halfway between the older sets of objects. Keep duplicating and rotating until you have

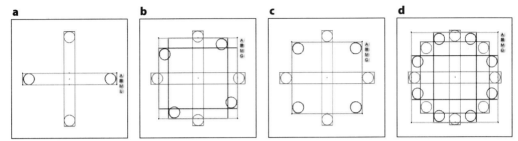

Figure 7–22 Creating circles by duplicating then rotating: a) After the first duplicate-then-rotate; b) the bounding boxes aren't yet aligned during rotation; c) now aligned bounding boxes indicate the completed rotation; d) completed circle after another duplicate-then-rotate step.

filled up the circle. You can reselect all the objects, copy and paste to fill up the circle faster. The position of the bounding box will help you judge when you've rotated enough. Figure 7–22b shows the subsequent rotate in progress, before it has reached the next place. Compare it with Figure 7–22c, where the two sets of bounding boxes are in alignment with one another. Of course, if you want a circle with 12 objects in it, you'll need to deliberately mis-align the bounding boxes while finishing the duplicate-then-rotate process. Under Windows, the Shift key constraint does not work for 45° angles. The Shift key constraint also tends to stagger the "snaps," so all the selected groups won't jump to the next constraining place simultaneously. Figure 7–22d shows the final step for this 16-object circle.

Figure 7–23 shows a set of spiral stairsteps made by this method. After the cylinders were placed in a circle (the original cylinder was lengthened on the z axis and shortened on the y axis), each cylinder was placed at a different elevation. To place them, all but one of the cylinders were selected, then nudged up by a tap on the Page Up key, then the neighboring cylinder was deselected, and the remainder nudged up once, and so deselecting and nudging the remainder up until each cylinder was located at a separate elevation.

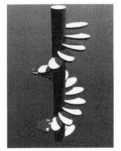

Figure 7–23 Spiral stairway created using the duplicate and rotate method.

Gear Variation

For another variation, make gears! Instead of flat stair objects, make these upright. Cubes are good for this. Use either method, the "duplicate and rotate" on the fly method or the Multi-Replicate dialog box and calculator method. See Figure 7–24. Once you have your set of gears, you can make them do all sorts of fascinating or sick and twisted maneuvers with rotation. Choose between Object Space and World Space to get a variety of effects.

While they are still selected, rotate them. The top row of Figure 7–25 shows a set of gears rotated on each axis in World Space. The ones for the x and z axes look bizarre in a fascinating way. The bottom row is a set of gears that have been rotated on each axis in Object Space. After singly rotating the gears on one axis, have some more fun! Figure 7–26 are gears that have been rotated on all three axes.

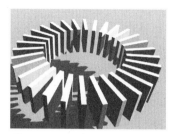

Figure 7–24 Freshly-created gear.

 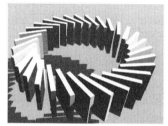 

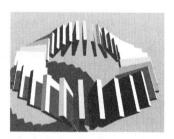 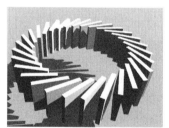 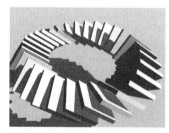

Figure 7–25 Gears rotated on each axis. Top Row: Object Space; Bottom Row: World Space.

a 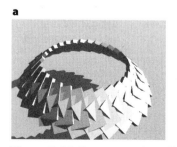 **b** 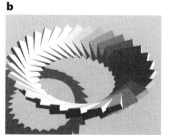 **c**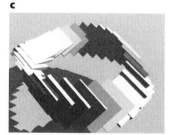

Figure 7–26 Gears rotated on all three axes: a-b) Rotated in Object Space; c) rotated in World Space.

a
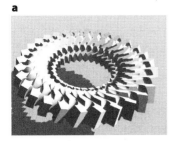

b
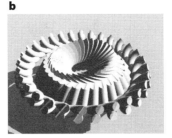

c
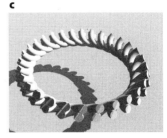

Figure 7–27 Some duplicate boolean object changes. a) Negative tori; b) additional set of booleans; c) intersect with tori.

Finally, for more abstract fun, create a set of gears. Duplicate. Change the duplicate to another object type using the Object Conversion tool. (Variations: change size or rotation only and not object type.) Then set the new objects to negative, group the whole thing and check out a new intriguing abstract. Use all of the Three R's tools in Object Space to set each of the new objects in a uniform relation to each of the old ones, even though they are rotated and facing in every direction to begin with. Figure 7–27 shows some samples. Part a has negative tori. Part b gets more complex, with an additional set of boolean objects (created by the duplicate and convert method). Part c has the tori intersect. The tori needed to be grouped together as positive objects, then the group was changed to intersect in order to get this effect.

TERRAIN MOLDINGS

If you want to get fancier with the construction of your model, include terrains and symmetrical lattices as a part of your conglomerate object. The terrain objects do not function as a mountainous surface but as a component for a conglomerate object. A grayscale-to-height map, combined with terrain clipping, gives you two powerful features for creating unusually shaped objects.

Figure 7–28 shows the famous "Bryce Big Rig," by Jackson Ting and Robert Bailey of ArtEffect. Though created in Bryce 1, it stands as a classic example of the versatility of grayscale-to-height maps. The figure includes several wireframe views of the scene if only to convince you that this was indeed generated using terrains. Notice the enormous amount of detail in this model. There are a mere 174 objects and a paltry 94 terrains. (It's safe to say that this was not created on a Macintosh with 8 MB RAM!) Many of the different elements were created in Adobe Illustrator and imported into Bryce via Photoshop.

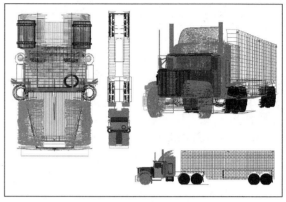

Figure 7–28 The Bryce Big Rig: Tractor-trailer truck constructed in Bryce from terains and primitives—174 objects total and 94 terrains. *Art by Jackson Ting and Robert Bailey, ArtEffect.*

This next example uses Bryce's symmetrical lattices to create architectural details. The Tower, by Chris Casady, has a number of different elements that use grayscale information to define the shape. In Figure 7–29 the construction is broken down, complete with a wireframe view of all the symmetrical lattices in the scene and a couple of samples of their grayscale information.

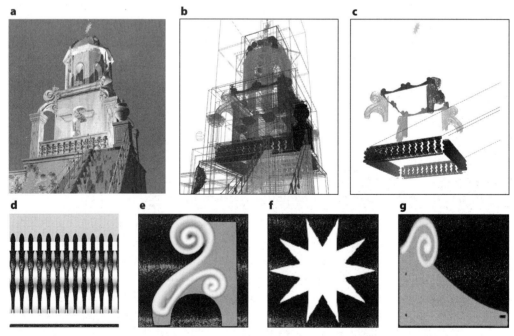

Figure 7–29 Tower and symmetrical lattices: a) Rendered image; b) wireframe; c) wireframes for symmetrical lattices. Bottom row: Graymaps for d) balustrade; e) curlique cornice; f) star; g) decoration. *Scene by Chris Casady.*

MODEL MANAGEMENT

When you are working on a conglomerate object scene, embrace a strategy for isolating each task into a manageable portion. Although you could work in one scene file and keep adding to it and save as you go along, it's a good idea to create a separate scene file for each element of your colossal conglomerate object scene. Save the pillar over here. Save the initial temple over there. Then put them together. That's a third scene file. If there are additional buildings, keep them in a separate scene file. You can merge them later.

One advantage to keeping the different elements in different files is that you don't have to juggle *all* of your objects while you are still working on construction. As you continue adding here and there—and Bryce has a tantalizing way of leading you on to "create *just one more* thing to get that bit of detail"—you will be placing more and more objects in your scene. The greater the number of objects, the slower Bryce will behave. Also, with a greater number of objects, Bryce's occasional tendency toward forgetfulness during resizing, swapping the y and z axes, will grow to become a frequent tendency. By working on separate elements, you prolong the state of manageability and the fleetness of Bryce's response to you until you can no longer delay the inevitable convergence of all your glorious creations into one triumphant but lethargic scene file. The temple scene file shown in Figure 7–1 is a handful shy of 1000 objects. With each exciting improvement, the temple, the pillars, the base, the steps, Bryce responded to the building tasks with a growing fatigue. (Of course, if your idea of a conglomerate scene is a mere hundred objects to the temple's thousand, then you'll be spared the anguish of waiting after each move.)

MERGING SCENES

So, you've created this splendid conglomerate object. It's in this document over here. And over there, in another document, is another exquisite conglomerate. You want to put them together. For extremely simple objects, you can copy an object (or several objects) from one scene and then open another scene and paste those objects. They'll be placed in the new scene file in the exact place they occupied when they were copied from the previous scene file. But Bryce gives you another option—merge scenes.

Merging in Theory

What happens when you merge scenes? Here's the theory behind merging. You already have a scene open. This is the host scene, as it will invite another scene (the guest) within. The invitation is extended via the Merge... command. All objects from the guest scene are brought into the host scene in the same position they previously occupied. For example, a terrain at World Center in the guest scene comes into the host scene at World Center. However, sky, camera, family, and render settings of the guest scene stay behind; those of the host scene prevail.

Merging in Practice

What happens when you merge scenes in practice? By this, I do not mean to imply practice deviates from theory, as in "do as I say, not as I do." Rather here is the sequence of events you'll discover when merging:

1. To bring one or more scenes together, use the Merge... command in the File menu. If your current (host) scene has not been saved after you have manipulated some objects, Bryce asks you if you want to save your scene. If you do save, you are presented with a dialog box in which to change the name of the scene, if you want. Click OK to save the scene if you want to.

2. You are immediately presented with what seems to be the same dialog box as in step 1. It's not. It's an OPEN dialog box. Bryce is asking you which document to open, that is, which guest is being invited into the merge. Select the guest scene and click OK.

3. Bryce merges the scenes. All objects from the guest scene come in selected (red wireframes). You may want to group objects if they are not already grouped. You may want to deselect or move them. You may want to change all items to one color. But host and guest are both together now in one scene.

> **TIP:** If you want to make any adjustments to the newly merged scene, activate Solo mode immediately after merging. The entire guest scene will be there, and you can select objects, delete superfluous objects (the ground plane?), rename families, and make other adjustments without worrying about mixing the guest and host scene components.

If you had assigned custom family and wireframe color settings for the guest scene, the family names and custom colors will take on the names and colors of the host scene. So in your guest scene you might have a family called "foothills." (Formerly it was, say, Family 12, and you changed the wireframe color.) When it comes into the host scene, it takes on the host scene's name and color for Family 12.

Here's a forward-thinking strategy if you plan to use Bryce's Merge… command to join different conglomerate object scenes into one master scene that will contain all the objects. Don't build any extra objects into the individual scene documents. When you merge scenes, all guest objects (including grounds) will be imported into the host scene. You don't need several grounds or other extraneous objects in your final scene, do you?

COLUMNAR CALAMITY: A BOOLEAN PRIMER

This exercise is an opportunity to create an object using the techniques discussed in this chapter. In creating the column, you'll work with both negative and intersecting booleans, multi-replication, merging scenes, and the fine art of making a terrain boolean work properly. Starting from a basic cylinder primitive, you'll carve out flutes, and then create a base, and merge scenes to put it all together.

The Main Column

In the beginning there was the cylinder. And it was tall. It had a base and it had a capital. This is very good.

1. Start by creating a cylinder. Enlarge it along the y axis so that it is somewhat tall. See Figure 7–30a. This is the main cylinder.

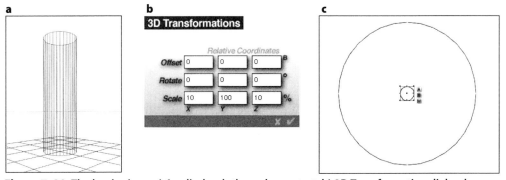

Figure 7–30 The beginnings: a) A cylinder doth a column start; b) 3D Transformation dialog box settings for duplicated flute cylinder; c) result of resize, top view.

To make this column fancy with fluted cutouts, a series of narrower cylinders will be used to scoop out column portions. First you need to create the first flute cylinder, change its size, and then replicate the newly-sized flute-cylinder to create a set of flute-cylinders that are evenly spaced in a circle.

2. Duplicate the main cylinder (⌘-D on a Mac, Ctrl+D in Windows). Now you are ready to change this new cylinder to the flute-cylinder size.

3. In the Edit Palette, under any of the Three R's controls pop-up menus, select 3D Transformation… . Here you'll maintain the height (*y* axis) but narrow the cylinder on the *x* and *z* axis (see Figure 7–30b). Enter 10% for each of those and click OK. From top view, your wireframe view should resemble Figure 7–30c.

4. Now it's time to multi-replicate that narrow column. If you're using Bryce on a Macintosh (Windows users go to Step 4a), select Edit > Multi-Replicate… or type Control-Option-D. How many flutes should there be? In this example, I used 24. So 23 is the quantity, with 15° rotation for *y* (15 × 24 = 360). For offset *x*, use a value of 2. The Multi-Replicate dialog box is in Figure 7–31a, and the results (from top view) are shown in Figure 7–31b.

4a. If you're using Bryce for Windows, you'll have to do a four-part multi-replication process. Refer back to the steps in the Multi-Replication in Four-Part Harmony tutorial earlier in this chapter. (Multi-Replicate 9 cylinders at a time, with a *y* axis rotation of 15°. Offset in Object Space using the Reposition control.) For your cylindrical guide, use the first cylinder that you created in Step 1 of this tutorial. When you have replicated all 24 flute cylinders, select the original flute cylinder from the center and delete it. Select the remaining 24

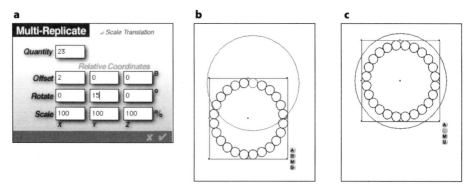

Figure 7–31 Making many flutes: a) Multi-Replication dialog box and values (for Macintosh); b) results shown in top view; c) main column cylinder aligned with the group of flute cylinders.

flute cylinders and give them a unique family color and name. Change back to World Space, and group the cylinders (a group's bounding box in Object Space behaves weirdly; avoid it by switching to World Space). Go to step 6.

5. If you're on a Mac, the circle of flute cylinders isn't aligned with the main column. To align them, first group the circle of flute-cylinders. You'll have to select the first flute cylinder before grouping. While you're at it, assign the flutes to a unique family color and name. After grouping the flute-cylinders, then add the main cylinder to the selection. Look at the scene from top view. Align by clicking the Align X and Align Z tools at the center points. See Figure 7–31c. Now that they're aligned, deselect the main cylinder.

6. The circle of flute-cylinders is not quite big enough. While the fluted cylinders are still grouped, enlarge them uniformly using the Resize tool. See Figure 7–32a. Then ungroup and reduce all cylinders uniformly. (Windows users, use the 3D Transformation dialog box to reduce uniformly. Try 80% for all three axes.) Each individual cylinder will be reduced simultaneously, though each centerpoint will remain the same. When they're just nicking in the main cylinder, stop (see Figure 7–32b). This is the home stretch for flutedness! In the Object Attributes dialog box, assign negative. (In Windows, also assign positive for the main cylinder.) Group the flute cylinders with the main cylinder. Render. Figure 7–33 shows the side view wireframe and the rendered result. Note: With the enlarge and reduction, the flutes stop a bit shy of the overall height of the column. Since the ends will have fancy-schmancy base and capital treatments, this is just fine for now. The Windows version of flutes may be slightly taller than what is shown in the figure. You may reduce the height along the y axis (press the Alt key to centrally constrain) so that what you have matches the proportions shown in Figure 7–33a.

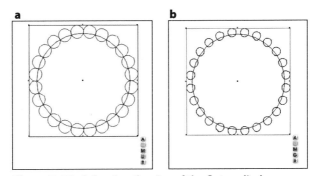

Figure 7–32 Adjusting the size of the flute cylinders:
a) After enlarging the grouped cylinders (top view);
b) after ungrouping and reducing the cylinders (top view).

At this point, you may look at the top and bottom edges of the flutes and say, "But they cut off abruptly rather than gently scooping in!" (See Figure 7–33b.) Yep. I said that, too. Working in Bryce is filled with "Do-something-cool; Render; Hmmmm...; Finesse" procedures. Here's how to make a nice gentle scoop.

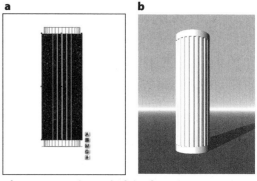

Figure 7–33 The end of the first phase: a) Side view of wireframe; b) rendered result of flute cylinders, with ugly abrupt endings at top and bottom.

7. Ungroup the group. Select the flute cylinders. Duplicate. Change the duplicated cylinders to spheres using the Object Conversion tool. Now the spheres are perfectly aligned with the flutes, however elongated they are.

8. Reduce the spheres along the *y* axis. Use either the direct manipulation handle or the Resize tool. Make the spheres slightly oblong. Then align them at the top of the flute cylinders so that the center equator of the spheres matches up perfectly with the top edge of the flute cylinders. See Figure 7–34a.

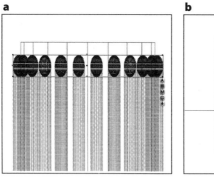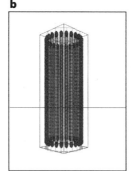

Figure 7–34 Fluted spheres: a) Spheres reduced and aligned with cylinders; b) main view of column with sphere sets at top and bottom; c) rendered result.

9. Duplicate those spheres and move the new set to the bottom, as shown in Figure 7–34b. (Hint: Remember to press the Option or Alt key to constrain movement along the vertical *y* axis if you are directly dragging the objects.)

10. Once you have the cylinders placed top and bottom, select the cylinders and the spheres and group, then render. As you can see in Figure 7–34c, there are

pretty smooth scoops on those flutes! (Note: Since you duplicated an object assigned to a negative attribute, the duplicates, the spheres, were also negative. Once they were grouped with the main positive cylinder the spheres began their scoop action!)

There. You've successfully made it through step one. I trust you are none the worse for wear with all this circuitous advice and negativity! Save this scene file and set it aside for the moment.

Column Base Basics

Now that you have a basic column, how about a fancy base for it? The options here are numerous; I'll show you a few different directions you *could* go and then pursue one in particular.

If you weren't using any boolean operations, you could make a base using a cube or a cylinder. (Do you want your base to be round or square?) Figure 7–35 shows a half dozen non-booleaned simple bases in rendered and wireframe form, so that you can make out what was used to create them. (The scene file is also on the CD-ROM.)

a   b

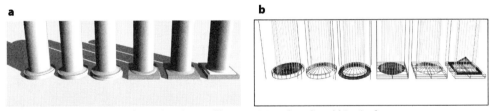

Figure 7–35 Examples of non-booleaned bases: a) Rendered and b) wireframe.

Once you get into booleans, though, you can get a bit more tricky. Intersection is good here for taking other shapes and combining them with cylinders. Cones and spheres come to mind here. See Figure 7–36.

a   b

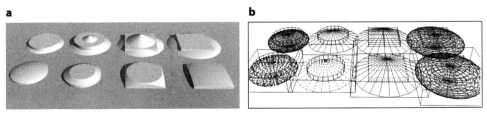

Figure 7–36 Column bases created by boolean combinations of objects: a) Rendered and b) wireframe.

Flattened cylinders and flattened cubes make the basic form, and cones and spheres make up the secondary shape. Choose whichever one tickles your fancy.

1. In a new scene file, create the basic shape (cylinder or cube). Flatten it to one-eighth height by reducing it along the y axis until you can no longer drag it.

2. Create your secondary shape. Make the secondary shape wider than the first by enlarging on both the x and z axes. If it's a sphere, its top point shouldn't be higher than the top of the cube or cylinder. See Figure 7–37.

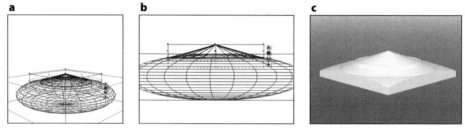

Figure 7–37 Making a column base: a-b) The primary shape (here, a cube) and a sphere, intersected in a) main and b) side view; c) the rendered result, with the addition of tori.

3. Assign one of the shapes to intersect and then group them. This is the beginning of your base. Now you can add some decorative elaboration. The torus is excellent for this purpose. In the base in Figure 7–37c, the tori have had their tubes reduced in thickness in the Torus Editor.

4. Create your own elaboration using the torus. When placing the torus, match the center of the tube of the torus to the point where the column and the cone intersect. If a torus is being used as a decorative edge for a vertical and horizontal object, only a quarter of the tube should show. This is true when the torus is positive, or if it is negative, as in Figure 7–38. This figure is a variation on the theme, and not a direct result of the steps described here. But then again, I told you that this portion of the walkthrough has more "dealer's choice" options in it.

Figure 7–38 Tori used to subtract portions from the base.

5. Once you have completed a base, save the scene file.

Merging the Two

Now it's time to put the column and the base together. For this, you'll use Bryce's Merge… command.

1. Open your base scene file if it is not open already. Under the File menu, select Merge…. In the dialog box you are presented, find your fluted column scene file. When it is selected, Click OK (Open).

2. Your fluted column scene comes into your base scene file. All the elements are selected. Most probably, you brought in a ground plane, too. You'll need to delete that, since only one ground plane is necessary. Go straight to Solo mode to edit any object that is in the newly imported scene. In this case, once you're in Solo mode, select the ground and delete it. Exit Solo mode.

3. Match the position of the fluted column with the column base. Go into orthogonal views. Unless you moved either one during the making, they probably match up horizontally. However, the fluted column probably needs to be moved up along the y axis so that you can see the bottom fluted edges. (If you need to align them horizontally, make sure that the base is grouped together. The fluted column should already be grouped. Select both and click the center options of the Align tool on the x and z axes.)

4. You may need to make some adjustments to your base in light of the position of the fluted column. A torus may need a bit of tweaking. Do this from side or front view. See Figure 7–39 for some non-verbal pointers on fine-tuning.

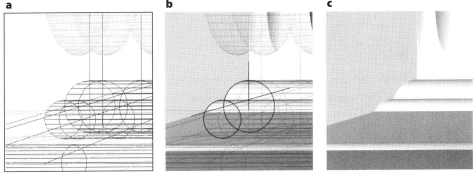

Figure 7–39 Precision alignment for tori at column base (all side view): a) Wireframe view; b) wireframe superimposed on rendered view, with tori, cone and cylinder position emphasized; c) rendered side view.

5. Group the objects together. Render. See Figure 7–40a

Once you have created a base, you can duplicate it and position it on the top. After duplicating the base, select Flip Y from the Resize pop-up menu. Depending on the shape of your base, you may need to reduce the top one for better proportions' sake (see Figure 7–40b).

Figure 7–40 Column and base rendered together: a) Base only; b) base duplicated, resized slightly, and positioned at top of column.

Make It a Relic

If you want to forego the capital altogether, then use boolean combinations with the terrain to antique the column. The terrain will carve out bits of broken column fragments. In order to bite off a nice chunk of column, you'll have to group the terrain with a cube and then make the terrain group negative.

1. Start with your column and base. Create a terrain. Move it to the side so that it does not overlap the column. Reduce it to half size by pressing the / key.

2. Duplicate the terrain (⌘-D for Macintosh, Ctrl+D for Windows). Move the terrain up by tapping the Page Up key. Select the bottom terrain. Use the Object Conversion tool to change it to a cube. (See Figure 7–41a.)

3. Make any adjustments to your terrain's shape in the Terrain Editor. Make sure that the terrain edges stay black, so they stay in contact with the cube object below.

4. Group the two together. Now move them to the top of your column and rotate the terrain so that it's more or less upside down. Position the group so that it takes a bite out of the column, similar to the position shown in Figure 7–41b. You may need to make adjustments to each of the objects in the group at this point. The cube may need to be elongated, or the terrain may need to be squashed flatter. Although you *could* adjust each one if you worked in Solo mode, once you have grouped objects, you cannot adjust any members of the group in Object Space. So ungroup the group and change to Object Space. Enlarge or reduce along the y axis as needed.

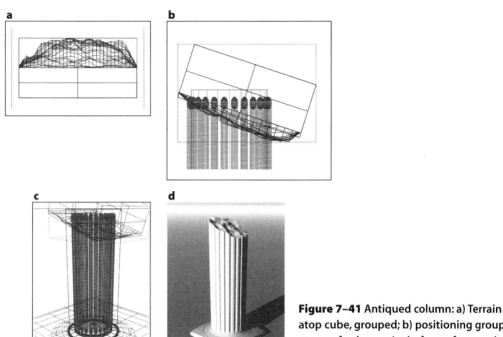

Figure 7–41 Antiqued column: a) Terrain atop cube, grouped; b) positioning group at top of column; c) wireframe from main view; d) completed render.

5. Group the terrain and cube again. Change the group to negative. Then add the column to your selection. Group. Render.

6. You may need to make other changes; this step requires some finessing. The cube and the terrain may need to overlap a bit more, or you may need to enlarge the entire terrain-cube group or reposition it.

7. When you're finished making your tweaks, render. Figure 7–41c and d show my completed wireframe and render.

OTHER STRANGE AND FANCIFUL EXAMPLES

The incredible thing about multiple object construction and boolean operations is that you get an infinite variety of objects. This is a place to let your imagination go wild! The few samples presented here and there in this chapter barely scratch the surface of multiple object construction. Check out the conglomerate object studies in the folder for this chapter on the CD-ROM. Also, check out the Gallery section as well; there are many talented Bryce artists who've contributed works ingeniously created using very constructive means.

CHAPTER EIGHT

Terrains, Symmetrical Lattices, and the Terrain Editor

"I only wanted to see what the garden was like, your Majesty—"

"That's right," said the Queen, patting her on the head, which Alice didn't like at all: "though, when you say 'garden,' I've seen gardens, compared with which this would be a wilderness."

Alice didn't dare to argue the point, but went on: "—and I thought I'd try and find my way to the top of that hill—"

"When you say 'hill'," the Queen interrupted, "I could show you hills, on comparison with which you'd call that a valley."

"No, I shouldn't," said Alice, surprised into contradicting her at last: "a hill can't be a valley, you know. That would be nonsense—"

The Red Queen shook her head. "You may call it 'nonsense' if you like," she said, "but I've heard nonsense, compared with which that would be as sensible as a dictionary!"

LEWIS CARROLL, *THROUGH THE LOOKING GLASS*

IN THIS CHAPTER...

- How to work with the Terrain Editor controls to make terrains and symmetrical lattices

- How to make clipped terrains for waterfalls and special effects

- How to create unusual terrain forms from words and images

- How to create terrains using United States Geological Survey (USGS) Digital Elevation Models (DEMs)

Each time you click the Create Terrain icon in the Create Palette, a terrain is randomly generated from a Fractal Noise map. No two Bryce terrains are alike (unless you duplicate the actual wireframe, of course!). The same is true for symmetrical lattices in Bryce; the same random generation process happens when you click the Symmetrical Lattice icon, and each one is unique unless the object itself is duplicated.

You control the terrain information in the Terrain Editor by clicking the E edit icon next to the wireframe, typing ⌘-E (Macintosh) or Ctrl+E (Windows), ⌘-T (Macintosh) or Ctrl+T(Windows), or clicking the Edit Terrain/Object icon on the Edit Palette. Bryce 2 has a much expanded Terrain Editor, rich with features and controls for making mountains, molehills, or other monuments (see Figure 8–1). Though the Terrain Editor is the place to edit both terrains and symmetrical lattices, I'll primarily talk about terrains in the editing process. When I discuss some editing procedures that focus more on symmetrical lattices I will refer to the object as the symmetrical lattice.

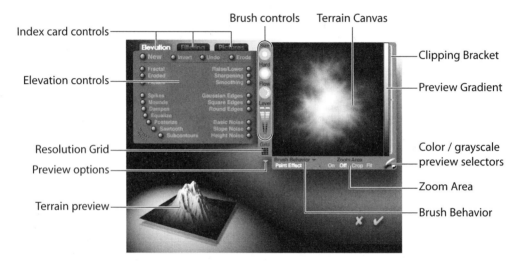

Figure 8–1 The Terrain Editor.

GEE TOO AITCH

The Terrain Editor is the master source of Bryce's land formations. How does Bryce control the shapes of a terrain? It generates them from grayscale image information. Different levels of gray correspond to different heights. The lowest elevation is represented by black and the highest elevation by white. This is called a grayscale-to-height map (G2H for short).

The G2H map is a two-dimensional grayscale representation of a three-dimensional entity. As you look at the G2H terrain image in the Terrain Editor, you need to make a mental shift away from looking at a two-dimensional image as a picture of something in which lights and darks are shadow and highlight. Think of light and dark as different heights. If it's darker, it's at a lower altitude; if it's lighter, it's higher.

THE TERRAIN EDITOR CONTROLS

The grayscale *image* determines the shape of the terrain, so the Terrain Editor is actually a specialized *image editor.* There are numerous controls for adjusting and shaping the grayscale image to make your terrain.

Overall Structure

The Terrain Editor is divided into several major areas. The main area, the Terrain Canvas, shows you the G2H information for your current terrain. To the left of the Terrain Canvas are three sets of controls, organized by index tabs. They are the Elevation controls, the Filtering controls and the Picture controls. Click the word on the tab to make that set of controls active (see Figure 8–2). Also, if you're using the Windows version of Bryce, you can step through the different sets of controls by tapping the Tab key. Immediately surrounding the Terrain Canvas are the Brush controls, the Zoom and Crop controls, and the Clipping and Color Mapping controls. In the lower left hand corner there are a couple of pop-up menus including the Grid pop-up menu, where the terrain resolution is set, and some other general controls that affect the preview. See Figure 8–3.

Resolution in the Grid

Terrains come in different resolutions. The Grid at the lower left of the Terrain Canvas panel, immediately surrounding the gray map editing area, has a pop-up menu for editing the terrain's resolution. (This Grid, with its pop-up menu, does

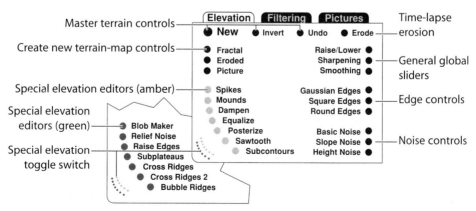

Figure 8–2 The Terrain Editor file card controls: Elevation, Filtering, and Picture.

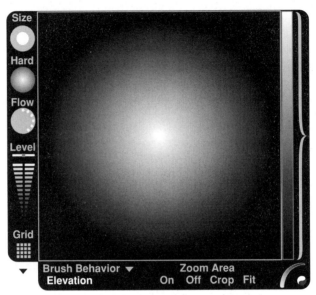

Figure 8–3 The controls surrounding the Terrain Canvas.

not have any relation to the internal grid discussed in Chapter 6, "Editing and the Internal Bryce Grid.") Like any other image editor, you determine how much image information you want. The numbers in the pop-up menu refer to the number of pixels along one side of the terrain G2H map. Each pixel represents a datum, or point of information. The higher the number for resolution, the more detail you have for transitions from one point to the next. The default size, 128, stands for 128 × 128 pixels. Under most circumstances, 256 is the minimum terrain size I use. However, I don't always start out with 256; I may do some manipulations at one resolution and then enlarge or reduce the resolution a bit later. There are times when a 16-sized terrain is adequate. (Andrew Pennick, who used customized terrains to build leaves for a plant, used terrains set to 16 to create the mesh shape. See Figure 14–27 in "The Greening of Bryce" section in Chapter 14.)

The largest terrain resolution is 1024 (1024 × 1024 pixels). Although Bryce's Terrain Editor works with that resolution internally, it does not copy and paste grayscale maps of that size. If you have a 1024 terrain, copy it and attempt to paste it in Photoshop, you'll get a 512 × 512-sized grayscale image.

More discussion of when to use large or small terrain resolution is covered in Chapter 14, "Superlative Nature Imagery." I'll discuss more about changing resolution as part of the terrain shaping process later in this chapter.

Preview

The preview in the lower left part of the Terrain Editor shows you what your gray map looks like as a real honest-to-goodness elevation. Like the other previews in Bryce (in the Preset Library windows, in the Materials Composer preview window, and in the Flyaround view), you can manipulate the preview to change your perspective. Here's a brief recap of the controls:

Drag right and left to rotate the terrain.

Drag up and down to move your perspective up and down.

Command-drag (Macintosh) or Shift-drag (Windows) moves the terrain closer to and farther from you.

Option-clicking (Macintosh) resets the terrain to its default preview position. There is no equivalent for this in the Windows version.

Space bar-drag scrolls around to change the position. It will move the entire terrain's position in the preview area. (It comes in handy for the times when you're zoomed closer to the terrain.) There is no equivalent for this in the Windows version.

Control-drag (Macintosh) or Ctrl+Shift-drag (Windows) heightens or flattens the terrain.

In Windows, when both the Ctrl key and the mouse are pressed, the preview will rotate.

You can also select from the preview pop-up menu to make your preview respond in real-time to your edits to the Terrain Canvas, spin around, or fill your screen with a higher sized preview.

Elevation Controls

There are many different options available to you in the Elevation controls window, what with all the different buttons you can click on and drag from. Since the preview gives you immediate feedback on your actions, and since the particulars of each are well documented in the Bryce 2 *Explorer's Guide*, it's not necessary for me to go through the list and provide individual descriptions of each Elevation editor. Rather, I shall categorize the controls and describe the ways to work with them.

The Different Types of Elevation Editors

On the Elevation index card, there are a series of different buttons for the different types of elevation edits.

At the top, above a dividing line, there are the master terrain buttons: New, Invert, and Undo. These operate with a single click. They also have key command equivalents. New is ⌘-N (Macintosh) or Ctrl+N (Windows). Invert is ⌘-I (Macintosh) or Ctrl+I (Windows). Undo is ⌘-Z (Macintosh) or Ctrl+Z (Windows). The key commands work all the time when you are in the Terrain Editor. In the Windows version of Bryce, Ctrl+I inverts as well as stepping through the three different sets of controls—Elevation, Filtering, and Pictures.

Two master terrain buttons that could be on the Elevation index card but are not are Copy (⌘-C for Macintosh or Ctrl+C forWindows) and Paste (⌘-V for Macintosh or Ctrl+V for Windows). The standard key commands work for copy and paste at all times in the Terrain Editor.

The last button on the top row is the time-lapse Erode. This control erodes for as long as you have the button pressed. Think of the eons of geological change you can make just by holding that button down for a few seconds!

Underneath the dividing line are the remainder of the Elevation editors. They are grouped into different categories which I'll describe momentarily, but they all have one thing in common: they apply both by clicking and by dragging. Each button works as a slider. A drag to the right gradually applies the effect one way, and a drag to the left applies it another way. A click on the button is equivalent to dragging the slider all the way to the right.

The first set of controls creates new terrain shapes. There are three main sources: Fractal, Eroded, and Picture. Fractal and Eroded comprehensively apply their respective procedures to the terrain map based roughly on the existing image information (in contrast to the way that the other Elevation controls make slight alterations on the existing image.) You can click to fully apply the effect or slide to partially apply it. (If you're using Windows, there is a key command shortcut to apply Eroded: Ctrl+Shift+E.) The Picture create tool is the one exception to the each-button-is-also-a-slider rule (there always has to be *one* exception, right?). The Picture button brings up an open dialog box for you to select any picture file (Macintosh: PICT format; Windows: BMP, TIF, and PSD formats). Make any grayscale image the basis of your terrain elevation data. Since the slider-approach to gradually merge two image sources is so useful, the Terrain Editor has an entire section devoted to it—the Picture controls. I'll discuss the Picture controls later in the chapter.

> **TIP:** *Option-clicking the Open Picture dialog box's Okay button when importing a picture will make the image's color information display in the preview. Tra la la! (This works only for the Macintosh version of Bryce.)*

The Elevation controls on the right side are more basic editors. At the top of the right side are a set of global editors: Raise/Lower, Smooth, and Sharpen. To remember which way to drag for the desired raise or lower effect, let the placement of the words be your guide. Drag to the right (the word "lower" is on the right) to lower and to the left to raise. The Windows version of Bryce has key command equivalents for raising and lowering the terrain. Lower the terrain by typing Ctrl+X. Raise the terrain by typing Ctrl+Shift+X. The amount the terrain will be raised or lowered is determined by the placement of the red dot in the Levels control. When the control is high (light end) the terrain will move in smaller increments; when the control is low (dark end) the terrain will move in larger increments. For more on the Levels control, see the Brushes section later in this chapter.

Below the global editors on the right are the editors for shaping the terrain edges: Gaussian, Square, and Round. Be sure to use the sliders for these; you'll get better results with Square and Round edges by an extreme drag to the right than by a mere click.

Below the edges are the noise editors: Basic, Slope, and Height. Basic applies noise all over, Slope applies noise only on the transitions from high to low (it makes for great cliff faces!), and Height only applies at higher altitude.

The last set of editors, the special editors, is the largest and most exotic group, located in the lower left hand corner. Switch from one set to the other using the smaller rows of buttons in the corner. (Windows users may also toggle between the two sets by pressing Shift+Tab.) One set of editors has amber buttons, the other set has green. The special editors utilize a variety of image processing algorithms that'll put some fun (and convincing!) geological phenomena on your terrain maps.

Within the two sets of special editors there are two main types of effects. The first effect type takes the existing image information and transforms it in some way. The amber button editors and a couple of the green button editors transform existing information. When your mouse is positioned over the buttons for these editors, the cursor changes to a double arrow for dragging left and right. The second effect type adds completely new grayscale information to the terrain map. Most of the green button editors, the ones with "blob" and "ridges" in their names, add new information. When your mouse is over those buttons, you see a four-way crosshair for positioning. As soon as you begin dragging, you're determining where the effect will be placed in the grayscale map.

Dragging the Elevation editors

There is a wealth of variety in the elevation editors. Not only is there a plethora of algorithms, but you can create subtle effects by repeated applies using slight drags and adding one effect after another. For the editors that work by left/right dragging the effect applies differently depending on the direction you drag.

The default drag direction is to the right. It applies the effect in the same manner as simply clicking the button. In most cases, it does so with a lighten apply mode. Drag to the left for a darken apply mode. Figure 8–4a through c shows a basic erosion terrain map and an apply of Subcontours when dragging to the right and to the left. Figure 8–4d and e shows the same thing using a different special editor—Sawtooth.

There is at least one notable exception to the drag-right-to-lighten rule: the Raise/Lower editors. Also, the noises tend to apply the same type of noise whichever the direction of the drag, as does Posterize. The smooth and sharpen also work differently when dragged to the left. For the most part, though, the right/left lighten/darken applies to the special editors.

Once you begin dragging, the cursor disappears entirely, so you must rely on your visual memory of the original state of the terrain, as well as muscle memory of the original mouse position. When you have a larger resolution terrain, it takes Bryce a moment to shift to "real-time" display of the changes, so it's all too easy to drag too far, lose your place, and undo to get back to your previous place and try again. For large resolution images, press the mouse on the button for the editor you're using and wait until the cursor arrow appears. When you begin to drag from that point, you'll be able to see exactly the degree of change you are making to the terrain.

When you drag to make changes, try out small distance drags. If you are trying to make ever-so-subtle alterations, you will probably pass the subtle "mark" before you can really see the changes in the Terrain Canvas. Once you are able to see the changes, they've gone beyond subtle toward exaggerated.

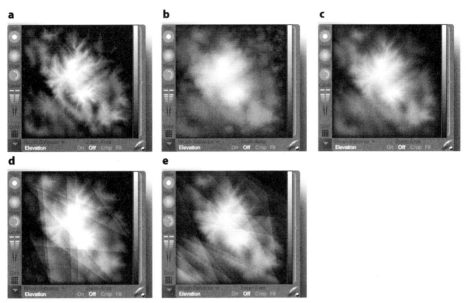

Figure 8–4 Dragging to the left and the right applies different lighten and darken effects: a) Subcontour dragging left; b) Subcontour dragging right; c) the terrain before the effect. Different Sawtooth applies: d) Sawtooth dragging left; e) Sawtooth dragging right.

Brushes

I will continue my exploration of the Terrain Editor based on the elements plainly visible when you first enter the Terrain Editor, and return to the other index card controls a bit later. Between the Elevation controls and the Terrain Canvas are the Terrain Editor Brush controls.

On the left and bottom edges of the Terrain Canvas display area are controls for the brush. The controls on the left side determine the brush's behavior. The first three, Size, Hardness, and Flow, are increased by dragging to the right and decreased by dragging to the left.

When you begin to drag within the Terrain Canvas, the crosshair cursor changes to a circle, indicating the brush's size. In Windows, it doesn't matter whether you are pointing the mouse or dragging the mouse; the cursor is always a circle when the mouse is in the Terrain Canvas. Size is fixed; a given brush size represents the same number of pixels. So a brush that is very large on a 128 terrain will be much smaller on a 1024 terrain. Figure 8–5 shows the same brush size applied to a terrain that has been set to different resolutions: 128, 256, 512, and 1024. The size control is not particularly smooth; the brush size tends to jump from one increment to the next without all the in-between sizes. If you need to brush a certain size and it isn't working, try changing the resolution and use a different sized brush.

Hardness determines whether the brush has a soft or hard edge; a soft brush allows you to do subtle effects without betraying your moves with "brush-tracks."

Flow can also be thought of as opacity. (Although the interface indicates different flow amounts by placing dots along the circle, a circular motion of the mouse will not change anything; the control works by dragging right and left.)

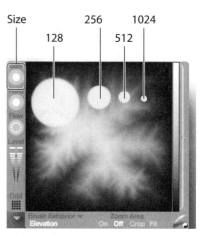

Figure 8–5 The same brush size when applied to a terrain that is 128, 256, 512, and 1024.

The default Brush Behavior setting is for Elevation (the Brush Behavior pop-up menu is located on the left side of the panel below the Terrain Canvas). The Level control, located on the left panel underneath the Size, Hardness, and Flow controls, sets the elevation—or gray level—for the brush. Drag the little red indicator up or down to the desired level. To move the red indicator, press anywhere in the Level control; you don't need to aim right for the couple of pixels of the indicator itself. As a shortcut, you can also paint the inverse level (black instead of white, dark gray instead of light gray) by pressing the Option (Macintosh) or Alt (Windows) key before or while dragging the mouse to make a brush stroke. In Windows, you can use key commands to set the indicator to the highest and lowest levels. Ctrl+L sets the red indicator to the highest (white) level. Ctrl+Shift+L sets the red indicator to the lowest (black) level. (There is no Macintosh key equivalent to set the red indicator to a particular level.)

Brush Behaviors

Not only does the brush paint in certain elevations, but the Brush Behavior pop-up menu has other options: Paint Effect/Unpaint Effect, Minimum/Maximum, and Erosion.

The most powerful of these by far is the Paint/Unpaint Effect set. Rather than painting a certain gray level, you can paint a portion of an effect you previously applied. After applying and then undoing, say, mounds, you can now paint the mounds effect only in the places you want, rather than applying the effect to the entire terrain. Paint the mounds in the darker, lower places. The east facing slopes. The heights. You choose. Then you paint.

Brush Behavior Walkthrough

Try it out.

1. Create a new Bryce scene document. Create a terrain. Go to the Terrain Editor. Click Eroded to create an eroded terrain (see Figure 8–6a).

2. Press the Option key (Macintosh) or Alt key (Windows) and drag slightly to the right on the Posterize special editor until the terrain pattern looks slightly pixellated. (Note: this is a variation on the usual Posterize; see Figure 8–6b.)

3. Click Undo or type ⌘-Z (Macintosh) or Ctrl+Z (Windows).

4. Switch the Brush Behavior pop-up menu to Paint Effect. Now you can paint the pixellated terrain in places on your eroded terrain (see Figure 8–6c).

5. If you painted too much, switch to Unpaint Effect and "erase" the pixellated effect so that the eroded terrain shows.

> **TIP:** You can switch between Paint and Unpaint on the fly by pressing the Option key (Macintosh) or Alt key (Windows) while you paint. Unlike the Elevation Brush Behavior mode, you must press the Option or Alt key while the mouse is pressed to toggle between Unpaint and Paint. It will not work if you press the key before you begin painting the same way that you do with elevation. Why is this? Since Bryce is looking for the previous action to undo, it's overly sensitive to mouse clicks. The Option-click/Alt-click is ambiguous; was that the action to undo? Don't ask me to spell it all out, though. Bryce just gets confused since it's looking for a prior state. Begin brushing then press the Option or Alt key.

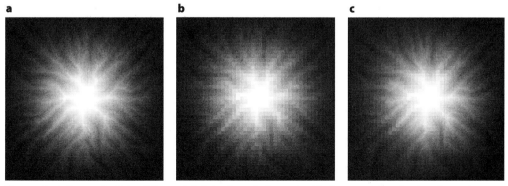

Figure 8–6 Do-undo-Paint Effect: a) Original eroded terrain; b) after applying Option-Posterize; c) after undoing then painting using Paint Effect.

This do-undo-paint-only-where-you-want-to technique is extremely handy in Bryce. I use it all the time. Keep in mind that you can combine it with a light apply of the brush, with a very soft edge. Between the gradual apply sliders and the do-undo-paint-only-where-you-want-to, you can add layer upon layer of subtlety. This technique also works with the other two types of terrain edits, from the Filtering and Pictures sections of the Terrain Editor (explained later in the chapter). Look at some of the "Fave terrain routines" later in the chapter for some additional techniques.

> **TIP:** *Under Windows, there is an additional shortcut method for Paint Effect. Press the space bar while clicking an Elevation Effect button. The Brush Behavior mode is automatically switched to Paint Effect and you may begin painting that effect. Of course, if you want use the slider to determine how much of an effect to apply, use the normal do-undo-Paint Effect method.*

The Brush Behavior also has another pair of options, Minimum and Maximum. This is analogous to the lighten only apply mode or a darken only apply mode in Photoshop. For Maximum (lighten only), once you choose an elevation level, you can paint the elevation. The result will be whichever is lighter—the brush color or the existing terrain (see Figure 8–7a). For Minimum (darken only) the result will be whichever is darker, the brush color, or the existing terrain (see Figure 8–7b).

The final Brush Behavior option is Erosion. Paint erosion wherever you'd like it. This is a splendid idea—don't erode everything uniformly, but erode it here and there, as you see fit. Unfortunately, the Brush Erosion is not sensitive to the Flow amount, so you cannot brush subtle applies of erosion. Although the terrain resolution does affect the outcome (the erosion is more subtle on a 1024-sized terrain than on a

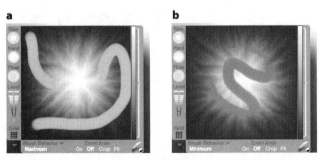

Figure 8–7 a) Maximum and b) Minimum Brush Behavior mode.

128), I prefer to paint my erosion using the do-undo-Paint Effect method using an apply of the Erode button. You can control the softness, the size of the brush, and the all-important flow, too.

Filtering

The second of the index card controls in the Terrain Editor are the Filtering controls. The title of the control is "Filtering." To avoid confusion between the *action of filtering* and a *thing* called a *"Filtering" control,* I'll use the word "Filter" when referring to the control. Filter allows you to change the shape of your terrain.

Like the old computer-ese saying GIGO (garbage in garbage out), referring to a special event (or, in GIGO's case, a lack of it) that occurs between incoming and outgoing information, the Filter control places you between the incoming gray values and the outgoing gray values. It allows you to tweak the gray values to your heart's content. If you've worked with the Arbitrary Map/Curve control in Photoshop, the Terrain Editor's Filter control will be familiar to you.

The Filtering control has several parts. The Filter is at the left of the card, bisected by a diagonal line. To its right is a small preview of your terrain, showing how it looks based on the Filter setting. Across the top of the Filtering index card are nine presets. Below the Filtering control are the Reset and Smooth buttons. The Apply button is located at the bottom of the index card. There is also a pop-up menu accessed under the Filtering control. See Figure 8–8.

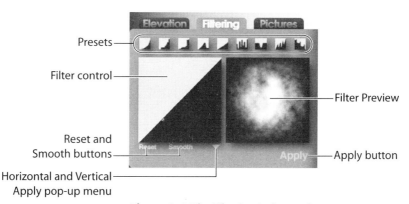

Figure 8–8 The Filtering index card.

Filter as a "Side View"

Think of the Filter section as a cutaway of your mountain terrain. The terrain's shape will be determined by the shape of the diagonal. In its default (reset) state, the straight diagonal line moves from black to white, smoothly. Change the Filter to other shapes by dragging in the area (see Figure 8–9). The cutaway follows as you drag.

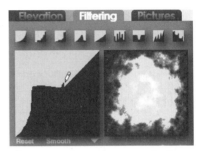

Figure 8–9 Drag the cursor in the filter to change the Filter's "shape."

When you look at a G2H map, you may be fooled into trying to read a three-dimensional illusion in that two-dimensional depiction. The image in Figure 8–10a looks to be a sphere. It's not a sphere, however; it's a cone (see Figure 8–10b). The gray values move evenly from black to white. Your eyes need to undergo a bit of retraining if you are going to work a lot with the grayscale terrain maps (and, if you like this thing called Bryce, you probably will!). The Filter portion of the Terrain Editor may help take the edge off of this visual illusion.

Let's look at a series of terrains and their Filter adjustments. Figure 8–11 has three rows: The top row shows G2H terrain maps, the middle row shows the filters for the G2H maps, and the bottom row shows the rendered terrains. The left G2H map has a black-to-white-to-black gradation. To help shift you away from seeing this as an illusion of a three-dimensional tube, notice how the Filter and the rendered terrain correspond to the G2H's linear transition from black to white. This is no tube; it's a straight diagonal wedge. This wedge terrain map is the starting place for every other G2H map in this figure. To create the other maps in the series, the Filter shapes in the middle row were created first. They were then applied to the wedge-

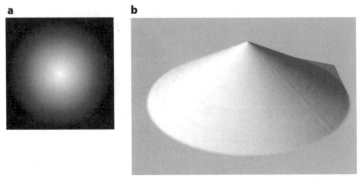

Figure 8–10 Cone or sphere? a) G2H map appears to be a sphere; b) when rendered, it is a cone.

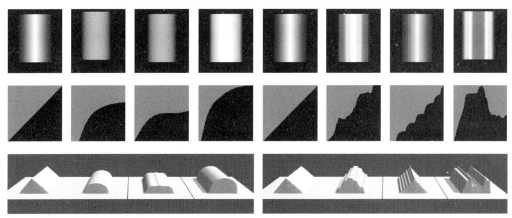

Figure 8-11 Filters as cutaway views. Top row: G2H maps; Middle row: the corresponding filters that shaped them; Bottom row: rendered results.

shaped G2H map to result in the other G2H terrain maps in the top row. The rendered terrains in the bottom row show the final result. Each filter in the middle row is a cutaway view of the corresponding rendered terrain below it.

Of course, a terrain won't precisely follow the Filter's shape, since terrains aren't conical in shape. Terrains go down in some places and up in others. (That's all a part of their charm!) The terrain will roughly follow the Filter's shape, complete with all those charming irregularities. But once you apply the Filter, the terrain itself changes. After any change, the new terrain shape acts as the straight diagonal wedge once again. If you continue to apply the same Filter over and over again to a terrain, you will get widely differing results (depending on the original image, the Filter, and the subsequent images).

Smoothly Reset the Apply

When you have changed the Filter, you have three options. Reset to get back to the default, Smooth to soften harsh transitions, or Apply to use the current settings to change your terrain. When you apply the Filter, you can undo the action and paint effect or unpaint effect, if you so desire.

Reset pops the Filter back to its normal diagonal state. Also, if you change your terrain's preview color, reset will display the colors in the diagonal ramp and the preview, so that you can more precisely refine your Filter shapes. You can also change the color to the preview color (if, say, you have already drawn a portion of a Filter and want to keep it, yet also display the Filter using the preview color) by exiting and re-entering the Filtering controls area.

> **TIP:** *Windows Brycers have an additional option to try before you apply— make the Filter effect temporarily apply in the terrain preview. To do so, click in the Filter Preview. The terrain preview will display the Filter effect for as long as the mouse is pressed.*

Filter Presets

The Presets are at the top of the Filtering area. Clicking any of them will apply them to the Filter ramp. Once you change your filter, you can't undo it; you will lose what was there before. You can, however, undo any change made to the terrain map itself.

Also, you cannot place your own custom filter into the filtering area. (This would be handy for production type work, where you do the same filter action to a series of terrains.) If you want to do that, you'll need to copy and paste terrains from Bryce to Photoshop and save an arbitrary map/curve there and apply the curve to a series of images. With one or two possible exceptions, I find that most of the presets are fairly worthless for normal Filter use.

Horizontal and Vertical Options

The pop-up menu below the Filter control has options to take the Filtering information and apply it differently to your Terrain Canvas. The additional options are Apply Vertical, Apply Horizontal, Apply Vertical Add, and Apply Horizontal Add.

At this point the Filter control changes. In the GIGO analogy, the horizontal and vertical options are GO (garbage out). These options do not process any input information; they apply the Filter map as output information only. So the Filter becomes a directional height generator.

When using the horizontal and vertical applies to the most beneficial ends, there are two standard conceptions that you need to discard. The first concept, the preview window, no longer provides you with any meaningful feedback. The preview window assumes that you'll hit the Apply button. But you won't. You'll be selecting an option from the pop-up menus. So ignore the preview.

The second concept to discard is the input-output diagonal ramp analogy. Because it's no longer an input-to-output function, the diagonal-as-default is no longer necessary. In other words, all the stuff I just carefully explained to you about the Filtering control being a side view of your terrain is meaningless for the

Vertical and Horizontal applications of the Filter. Forget diagonals (though they do have their uses). A rough scalloped map will generate bumps that you can apply in one direction or the other.

When the filter is applied horizontally, it results in vertical bands of some sort. That's because the filter was applied across the horizon of the terrain. The same holds true for the vertical apply; vertical apply creates horizontal bands. If this is confusing to you, remember the key combination for Undo. It applies here. The Add algorithms are not the classic Add calculation mode, but a special way to intensify what is there already. Darks get darker and lights get lighter.

So what are these options good for?

To generate a basic ramp, create a new gray map. Then click Reset to make sure that the filter is a straight diagonal line. Then select Apply Horizontal or Apply Vertical (one, not both). You get a basic ramp. Repeated applies (especially using the Add option) will make the ramp climb from black to white. This is good for creating terrain shapes where you need a one-sided ramp. As a variation, try using the same filtering curve, first horizontal and then vertical. The symmetrical plaid effect in Figure 8–12 was obtained by using the last preset on the right, one apply of the Horizontal Add, and one of the Vertical Add.

Figure 8–12 A strange symmetrical plaid effect created by applies of the Add Horizontal and Add Vertical.

The vertical and horizontal applies are seemingly meaningless when you are working on a normal terrain that rests upon the ground. Sure, you can make your trippy Madras plaid and all, but that's not what this control is good for. The horizontal and vertical applies are better put to use on terrains that stand up vertically, such as sheer cliff faces, or for symmetrical lattices. For the vertically-placed objects that take advantage of this type of construction, some of the previously meaningless presets now have become slightly useful.

The hoodoos in Figure 8–13 were created using a symmetrical lattice that stands upright. Starting with a new (black) terrain, some bumps were

Figure 8–13 Scene with hoodoos created using the Vertical and Horizontal Applies for the Filtering control.

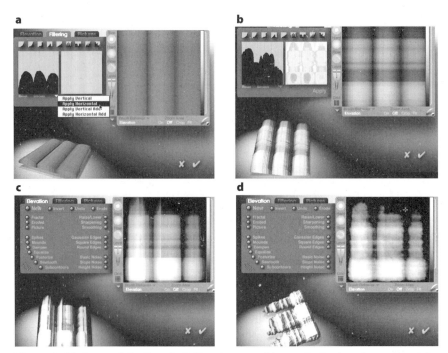

Figure 8–14 Some of the Terrain Editor steps used to create the hoodoo symmetrical lattice: a) After applying horizontal; b) after applying vertical repeatedly; c) after adjusting contrast; d) final terrain map.

drawn across the middle of the Filter control. The basic G2H shape was created by repeated Apply Horizontal and Apply Vertical filtering. Repeated applies accentuated the shape; the Add mode exaggerated the lights and the darks to make the top thinner and the bottom fatter. Figure 8–14a through c shows the first few steps used to create the shape of the individual hoodoos (the entire sequence is on the CD-ROM in the "Hoodoo Howdunnit" folder). The last step is shown in Figure 8–14d. The entire gray map was created in the Terrain Editor, in one editing session. No other imaging applications were used, and brushing was limited only to do-undo-paint-where-want-to applies of the algorithmic elevation effects.

Pictures

The third index card is for adjusting pictures. You can take any two images and blend them together in some way to create a resulting image from your Terrain Canvas and, ultimately, your terrain.

There are three preview windows in the Pictures portion of the Terrain Editor. Your existing terrain (from the Terrain Canvas) is in the left window (Figure 8–15)

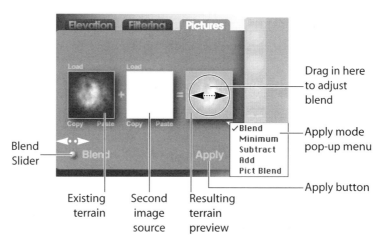

Drag in here
to adjust
blend

Apply mode
pop-up menu

Apply button

Blend
Slider

Existing
terrain

Second
image
source

Resulting
terrain
preview

Figure 8–15 The Pictures index card with
the Apply mode pop-up menu showing.

and the middle window is blank. Your result is in the right window. There are two ways to bring in a second image to the middle window—you can paste it from the clipboard, or you can load an image from elsewhere on your disk. The Mac version will open a PICT document format, and Windows will open BMP, PSD, or TIF document formats. (You can also paste or load an image into the left window, if you want to.)

Once you have pasted or opened an image, it appears in the middle window, and a blend of the two images shows in the right window.

In order to finetune the blend, adjust the slider button at the bottom of the Pictures index card, or slide directly in the third window to adjust the weight of the blend.

There are a couple of things I miss from the old Bryce 1 Merge PICT dialog box: the slider with visible feedback, so you can see where your slider is, and larger preview windows, so you can better see what the heck you're doing. If you don't like the blend, just release your mouse and then type ⌘-Z or Ctrl+Z to undo it.

You can adjust the mix of images in five different ways using the Blend modes in the pop-up menu. There's a standard Blend, Minimum, Subtract, Add, and Pict Blend. To adjust the mix between the two images, either drag the slider below or drag within the result window on the right. There's immediate feedback, so you can see how each method will work out. As you move the slider, the weight shifts between the two images.

- *Blend.* Does a simple average combining of the two images.

- *Minimum.* Compares the two images and accepts the darker regions.

- *Subtract.* Does a calculation between the two images where the value of one pixel is subtracted from the other. In grayscale, 0 equals black and 255 equals white. Subtract will tend to get lower (or even negative) numbers, so the image will get darker and move toward black. You end up with terrains that have more area that is "flat on the ground."

- *Add.* Takes the values of individual pixels and finds their sum. The larger the number, the lighter the images. At 255 or more, the result is white. Add is a fine way to create high plateaus.

- *Pict Blend.* The Pict Blend is an alternative algorithm. When you drag to the left it multiplies the two sources together, and when you drag to the right, it does a weighted subtract of the two (the second source becomes inverted and then some). When you're in the middle, between the multiply and the weighted subtract, it's pretty ugly.

Clipping Bracket

The Clipping Bracket, on the right of the Terrain Canvas, cuts an adjustable portion off the top or bottom of the terrain so that it won't render. (See Figure 8–16a through f.) In the preview (Figure 8–16e), the top is shown flat when clipped, although it will not render when in the actual scene. (See Figure 8–16f.) This enables you to create grayscale-to-height forms that aren't necessarily square. For symmetrical lattices, the bottom clipping point defines the place where the two back-to-back terrains join.

These are all the ways you can adjust the Clipping Bracket:

- Drag either end to adjust the end

- Drag from the center to reposition entire bracket

- ⌘-A (Macintosh) or Ctrl+A (Windows) selects all (resets the bracket); though on a Macintosh it doesn't work once you exit the Terrain Editor

- Option-clicking (Macintosh) or Alt-Clicking (Windows) the center resets the bracket (the only viable solution for Mac users).

(I have a minor quibble with the bracket's functionality. The developers at what was then HSC Software invented the bracket in the KPT Gradient Designer. The

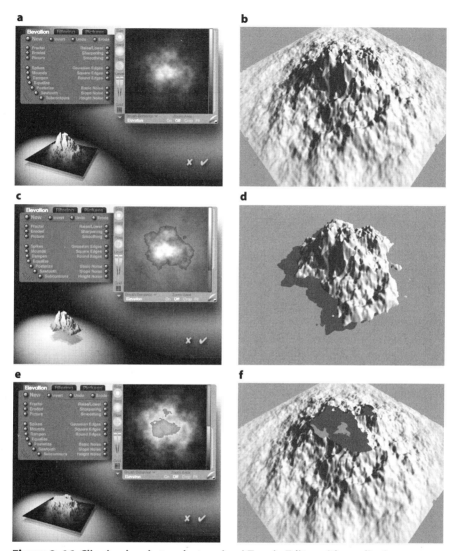

Figure 8–16 Clipping bracket and a terrain: a) Terrain Editor with no clipping; b) rendered result; c) Terrain Editor with bottom clipping; d) rendered result; e) Terrain Editor with top clipping; f) rendered result.

bracket's behaviors included a way to reset the entire bracket to include everything again—double-click the center. Everyone who has used the KPT Gradient Designer already "knows" how a bracket works, and can quickly get to work using this one, right? Wrong! For what seems to be no good reason, the double-click was omitted from the design, replaced—and not augmented—by the Option/Alt-click. This is no partial adoption of some other user-interface standard; this is a user interface about-face from the developers' own front yard.)

A second function served by the Clipping Bracket is the behavioral result of the clip—when it comes to grayscale editing in the Terrain Canvas, clipping creates a "selected area." Whatever elevation edits you make will not be applied to the area that lies outside the Clipping Bracket. In the terrain map shown in Figure 8–17, the higher elevations were clipped and then an erode was applied. Afterwards, the bracket was returned to the default position. Notice how the highest areas are smooth and erosion begins below.

Figure 8–17 Terrain edited using the Clipping Bracket to apply effect to a portion of the terrain.

The good news is that you can isolate certain elevation special effects to particular elevations. Make the top half eroded and the bottom half sawtooth. All you have to do is isolate the portion before applying the effect. If your effect lowers or raises the terrain so that it fits into the clipped elevation, the clipping preview will change accordingly. But although you can add to the clipped area, it's extremely rare that you would take away from it (exceptions to the clip rule: Posterize, Equalize, the Bubbles and Ridges in the special editors). There are a whole set of terrain edits that can be created by taking

Figure 8–18 A terrain form created by clipping top and bottom, applying an effect, then unclipping.

advantage of this. Figure 8–18 is a terrain made from clipping top and bottom, dampening the center (by dragging left), unclipping all, and then finishing up with touches of Slope Noise, Erosion, and Smoothing (not necessarily in that order).

The bad news is that you may have a clipping effect in place already and when you go to apply something new, whoa! It doesn't apply as expected. I've often discovered this when I have a terrain clipped at the bottom, and add an effect, say, Dampen. The new effect changes what was in the center, but the outer information is caught between being changed by the dampening and being clipped and is therefore "unaffected" by the change. Figure 8–19 shows the same symmetrical lattice before and after dampening. Note the tiny fringe of terrain on the dampened version. In order to drive that fringe away, you'll have to retouch your terrain map

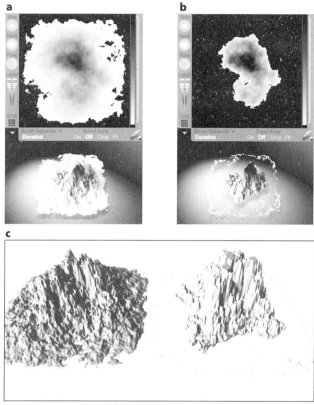

Figure 8–19 Clipping affects area near clip boundary: a) Terrain Editor for symmetrical lattice before and b) after applying Dampen; c) rendered results of the before and after states.

by painting black or by enlarging the clip area to include everything, making your adjustments, and then resetting the clip to what it was before. The first one is time-consuming, and it's too easy to forget to do the second one.

Oftentimes the little leftover bits on the outside stay there, and a pile of rubble accumulates at the outer edges of the object. See for yourself. Create a symmetrical lattice, then open the Terrain Editor. Flip the gray map so you can see light at the lower end (⌘-F for Macintosh or Ctrl+F for Windows). Click the Fractalize button repeatedly and watch how the detritus gathers.

If you are creating and clipping a series of symmetrical lattices, you may notice that subsequent symmetrical lattices emerge into Bryce slightly deformed. When you edit—and clip—a terrain or symmetrical lattice, and then create a symmetrical lattice, you'll be able to see tell-tale ghosting from the previous clip in the gray map of the new symmetrical lattice. If you're making many clipped terrain adjustments, then the best way to create a "normal" symmetrical lattice is to first create and then immediately delete a terrain. That terrain will "reset" Bryce's terrain map generator and exorcise the clipping ghosts.

Preview Color

Related to terrain clipping is the color of the terrain preview. The default is black when low, white when high. By holding down the mouse on the rainbow icon, you can make a set of colors appear. Choose any of the color sets to show different color schemes for the terrain. Different colors are good for working on things at certain elevations. The default dark-gray tends to obscure the details at that level, so you're not completely sure what is happening at low elevations. A different color scheme brings out the detail. Or you can flip any gradient by typing ⌘-F (Macintosh) or Ctrl+F(Windows). There is a third option as well for changing the gradient. Dragging up or down directly in the gradient area cycles the gradient around so that a different color corresponds to a certain elevation.

This third option is good for marking certain areas. For instance, if you have clipping set to a certain level, you can cycle the gradient around so that the sharp transition matches that level. Change the clipping in order to perform certain edits and then change the gradient back again (Option-click or Alt-click resets the position). If you need to clip a series of terrains all to the same level, you can use the cycled gradient as the marker, since the gradient's position stays where you put it until you change it back again or quit Bryce.

When the Terrain Canvas is displayed in color, you may also adjust the Filter using colors. Click the Reset button and the diagonal Filter ramp will display in color. There are times when this is very helpful to isolate a certain level for making adjustments. The sharp transition between the top and bottom of the gradient makes an excellent marker. Position the gradient so that the transition is right where you want it. In Figure 8–20, note how the color gradient has been repositioned to mark a valley in the foreground. In the Filtering area, the gradient matches, so that it's easier to make adjustments to the terrain.

Many of the alternative color gradients have black in them, making it difficult to see detail at certain elevations. Since the *Explorer's Guide* mentions that you can create alternative gradients, I have done so (for the Macintosh). Look on the CD-ROM in the "Bryce Utilities" folder for a folder called "PICT Resources for Bryce." There are several changed gradients, none of which have black in them. You'll need to use ResEdit to make your changes; this is not for the faint of heart and should be done on a spare copy of the application. Unfortunately, you cannot tinker with the Bryce Windows application resources. All of the user interface image resources were built using MetaTools' proprietary Axiom resource editor, which is not available to the public.

Zoom Area

The Zoom Area controls enable you to change the Terrain Canvas. Essentially, they help you redefine what is a part of the Terrain Canvas, so that the canvas can include more or less area.

There are four buttons: On, Off, Crop, and Fit. The default is Off, and the preview represents the entire Terrain Canvas. When you click the On button, a square marquee appears in the Terrain Canvas. The preview changes to show only what is within the bounds of the marquee. To change the position of the

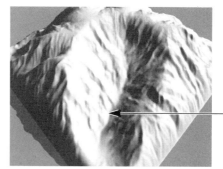

Chosen area to work on

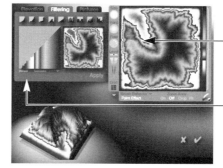

Gradient cycled to mark chosen area

Filtering applied to chosen area

Result of Filtering

Figure 8–20 A cycled gradient marks the exact position of a certain part of the terrain, making adjustment using the Filter much more precise.

marquee, drag it by its sides. To change the area, drag from any corner to enlarge or reduce the size (see Figure 8–21).

Why would you crop a terrain? If your perspective calls for a high-detail terrain but a very limited camera perspective, you can cut away the parts that are off-camera and devote all the terrain's size to the portion that faces the camera. Or use it as a step in the whole terrain shaping enterprise. You don't want a basic Gaussianized

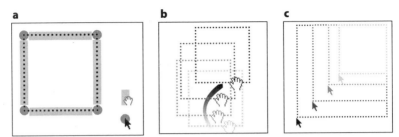

Figure 8–21 Working with the Zoom Area: The corner changes the size of the area and the hand positions the tool.

version, but one shaped differently. Use the Cropper to change the overall basic shape of your terrain and then go back and finesse from there.

The Fit function is more interesting. Take all your existing terrain data and fit it into the area described by the marquee. In other words, put your existing terrain into a smaller area surround by more black lowlands. Why would you want to do this? Say you're working on a terrain and the combination of a few edits (Stones, Dampen, and other lightening special editors) makes your terrain perilously high, perilously close to the edge of the terrain. You can't have any dramatic drop-offs to nothing; the terrain has to go from way up high down to ground level without falling off the edge of the terrain square. Use Fit to make the entire terrain into a smaller space. Figure 8–22 depicts the basic problem and solution, with sufficient space surrounding the terrain to add transitional terrain detail.

> **TIP:** The Crop and Fit functions are sliders as well as buttons in the Macintosh version. Try out your crops and fits by incremental drags as well as decisive button clicks!

FAVE ROUTINES

Now that I've introduced the Terrain Editor, it's time to discuss a few of the fun things you can do while you are in it. I will briefly describe the few steps to get each type of terrain, with the idea that in 1-2-3-4 steps or so, you can have a respectable shape that is not the normal humdrum terrain. Step 1 begins after creating terrain and opening the Terrain Editor. By the time you get through this, you'll also get a feel for some of the "Zen" of working in the Terrain Editor. For these (and more!) steps to create terrains, look on the CD-ROM in this chapter's folder for the "Step-by-step" folder.

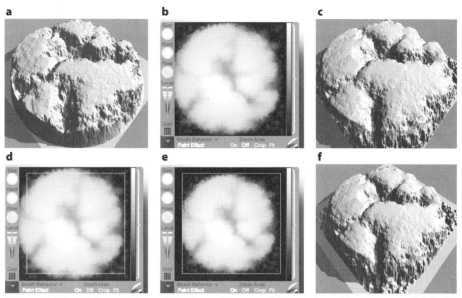

Figure 8–22 Fiddle as a Fit—using Fit to give a terrain some breathing room: a) Original terrain, in danger of "falling off the edge;" b) an apply of Mounds raises the terrains edge off the ground; c) rendered view of too-high terrain; d) positioning the Zoom area; e) after "Fitting;" f) The new terrain, with room all around.

Resolution Fluency

When you are working in the Terrain Editor, your fluency in changing resolutions—depending on the task you are doing—will help you obtain certain types of terrain effects.

The lower the resolution, the more powerful the erosive prowess of the Erode (time lapse) button. Conversely, when it comes to creating a terrain, the higher the resolution, the more refined and detailed the original erode. Figure 8–23a shows a set of terrains from the same starting place. A click of the Eroded button was applied at each of the four higher resolution settings: 128, 256, 512, and 1024. Using a slightly different approach, Figure 8–23b represents four steps in a terrain creation process. First, the Eroded button is pressed for the 128-sized terrain. Then that terrain is changed to 256 resolution where it becomes the basis for the next Eroded terrain. The result of that is the basis for another Create Eroded at 512, and the result of that is used to create Eroded terrain at 1024. It's not necessary to end up with a high resolution result, though. Figure 8–23c shows the 1024 terrain beside the exact same terrain reduced to 256.

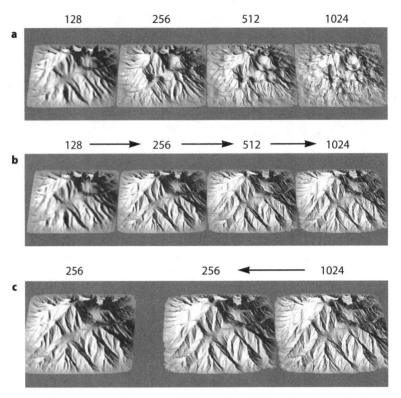

Figure 8–23 Terrain resolution and visible detail: a) Clicking the Eroded button to create new terrain form at different sizes; b) starting at 128 and clicking Eroded, each terrain is the basis of the eroded terrain to its right; c) eroding at 256 versus eroding at 1024 and then resizing down to 256.

So what does this mean? You can enlarge the resolution in order to perform some specific action in the Terrain Editor and then reduce the resolution afterwards. Or, you pack as much detail as you can into a 256 terrain.

For each of the next set of quick-terrain-tips, I'm assuming that you're in the Terrain Editor and that your terrain resolution is 256.

Brushing Beauties

For subtle terrain effects, or for effects only-where-you-want-them.

1. Click the Eroded button to make an eroded terrain.

2. Click the Mounds button.

3. Undo.

4. Change Brush Behavior to Paint Effect, and paint mounds only in the lowlands. See Figure 8–24.

Raise and Lower

The "Brushing Beauties" technique is excellent for selectively lightening (raising) or darkening (lowering) a terrain. Use it when you need to darken a terrain portion. I explain it here for raising a terrain.

1. Decide which portion of a terrain you want to lighten.

2. Drag the Raise/Lower slider to the left (lighten), keeping your eyes on the part you want to lighten. Don't worry if other parts become solid white.

3. Undo.

4. Using Paint Effect, brush in the lightened, raised terrain.

Rough Rough Rough

1. Apply Sawtooth with a subtle drag to the right (see Figure 8–25a).

2. Apply Sawtooth again, this time with a drag to the left (see Figure 8–25b).

3. Drag to the right again (see Figure 8–25c).

4. Drag again to the left (see Figure 8–25d).

5. For better definition of the blocks, apply Subcontours very gently (until you just see darker contours between gray levels. See Figure 8–25e).

Rice Paddies

1. Click Eroded to create a terrain form.

2. Apply Posterize to get a terrace effect; drag until there are about a dozen levels.

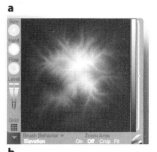

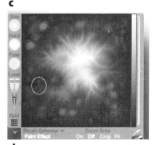

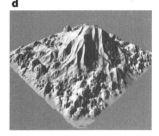

Figure 8–24 Brushing Beauties: a) Eroded terrain; b) after clicking Mounds; c) Brushing mound effect in the lowlands; d) rendered terrain.

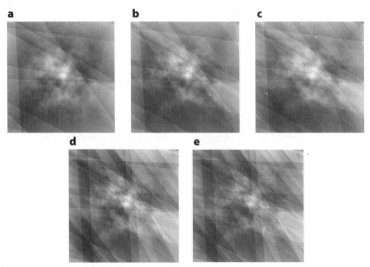

Figure 8–25 Sawtooth roughness: a) Drag right; b) drag left; c) drag right again; d) drag left again; e) subtle apply of Subcontours.

3. Click OK to exit the Terrain Editor. In the scene, duplicate the terrain.

4. Go back to the Terrain Editor with one terrain selected. Change resolution to 512. Apply Subcontours with very slight drag to the left (so the edges are barely higher, see Figure 8–26a). Click OK to go back to scene.

5. Select other terrain. Give the second one a water appearance, adjust the height positioning, and plant some rice. Add mist and brush calligraphy for a terraced rice paddy. See Figure 8–26b.

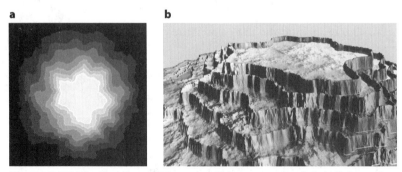

Figure 8–26 Rice Paddies: a) After using Subcontours to slightly lighten the edge; b) the rendered rice paddy.

Rivers and Deltas

1. Click New, then Invert to get a white terrain.

2. Brush basic path into the terrain (see Figure 8–27a).

3. Enlarge to 512. Clip off bottom and Drag Eroded slider to erode the top part (see Figure 8–27b).

4. Copy terrain.

5. Clip off both top and bottom and Dampen left (see Figure 8–27c).

6. Option-click or Alt-click bracket to select all. Switch to Pictures.

7. Paste terrain into center (second) source.

8. Switch Blend mode to subtract. Move slider all the way left, then to the right slightly until river area darkens (see Figure 8–27d).

9. Add Slope Noise and Erode (time lapse).

10. Reduce terrain's (wireframe) height slightly and render (see Figure 8–27e).

Game Over, Man

After trying something in the Terrain Editor, do you ever just want to start with a new terrain form without creating a new terrain? To start over from *within* the Terrain Editor:

1. Click New

2. Invert.

3. Click Gaussian Edges. Do so again.

4. Click Fractal.

All of these steps are illustrated on the CD-ROM. In addition, there are more step-by-step procedures to create original terrain forms. Let these be an inspiration to guide you into new areas for exploration.

Waterfall

A waterfall is a multilevel entity. When water's at rest, it is flat, then it falls to a lower level, where it is flat again. To make a waterfall in Bryce, use a terrain. But the water

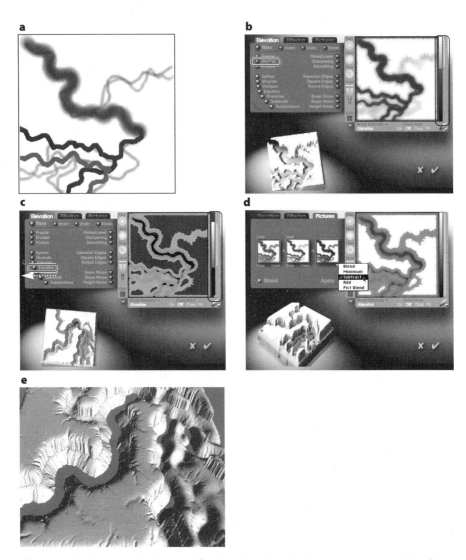

Figure 8–27 Rivers and deltas: a) After brushstrokes; b) clipping bottom and eroding top; c) clipping top and bottom and dampening left; d) merging eroded river and dampened river using subtract; e) the rendered terrain.

also must fit inside a container of some kind—there is a bank or a shore of land on all sides. The land-container is also a terrain. So a waterfall, then, is a water-terrain tucked within a land-terrain. To make an exact fit of the water within the land requires some intricate work, since the two terrains are very closely related.

In order to be convincing, the rock terrain needs the following characteristics:

- Suitably-shaped pockets to hold water.

- A bank that is higher in elevation than the flat water level.

- Dual-level rock; there must be a precipice over which the water falls to another level below.

- A bank below to contain (or partially contain) the lower water level.

The water-terrain needs to have the following characteristics:

- The water terrain is two basic gray levels—one for high water, another for low water, and all else is black (clipped).

- The flat areas of the water need to be wide enough to completely fit within the rocky area, otherwise it's not convincing, as shown in the one-level lake terrain in Figure 8–28.

- The flat areas need to be the proper shade of gray to match the rock elevation and fit within the rock terrain.

- The transition between the two levels is sudden.

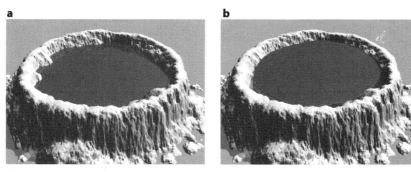

Figure 8–28 Making a water terrain wide enough to fit within a rock terrain: a) Water terrain that is wide enough; b) water terrain that is not wide enough.

Terrain Process Overview

Here's an overview of the process to create the two terrains. First, the land-terrain is created and edited. It determines the *shapes* and *heights* that will hold water.

Second, the terrain is duplicated to be the basis of the water terrain.

Next, the water terrain is edited based on the information from the land terrain. The area of the water terrain needs to match the *shape* of the rocky riverbed. The grays used to define the flat water levels need to make the water at the right *height* so that it will be above the ground.

After the basic gray levels of the water are created, the river bed on the rock terrain is lowered a bit. Finally, add fine tunings and tweaks and application of materials, and there's your waterfall! Add additional stones and other river-type objects to complete the scene.

Because of the close relationship between the two terrains, I find that the Terrain Editor's brushes are inadequate for the job. One serious limitation of the elevation brushes in the Terrain Editor is that you cannot precisely match gray levels using the gray selection slider. You cannot go back and decide to brush in some gray right *there* and match the exact shade of gray using an eyedropper sampling process. The Terrain Editor's gray slider is hit or miss. This type of job requires the heavyweight of an image processor like Photoshop.

Step-by-step Waterfall

1. First, create your land terrain. In the example shown here (see Figure 8–29), the upper and lower pools aren't completely enclosed. There's a higher side and a lower side, and the rocky enclosure forms a bank.

   Start by opening up the scene file WATERFALL START on the CD-ROM.

2. Open the Terrain Editor. Copy the terrain. Click OK. Then open Photoshop. Select File > New (Photoshop automatically assigns a size for new document based on the contents of the clipboard. Accept the size suggestions Photoshop offers to create a grayscale document). Paste into your new document window. Your terrain map should now be in the window.

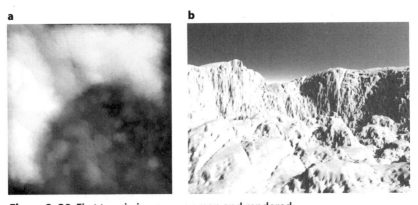

Figure 8–29 First terrain image: gray map and rendered.

3. In Photoshop, duplicate the terrain by creating a duplicate layer. (Drag the layer name to the New Layer button at the bottom of the Layers Palette.) Name your two layers. Name the new layer "Water Terrain" and the background layer "Original Terrain." The first thing you will do to the Water Terrain layer is create a separate selection that defines the area, or *shape* of the water. You can do this in at least a couple of ways. You can select a certain gray level by using the Magic Wand, or you can switch to Quick Mask mode and paint a selection area.

4. The Magic Wand method requires a bit of painstaking care, but yields better results, since you're getting exact elevation levels. For the Magic Wand Options, set the Tolerance to 10 and make sure that the Anti-aliased box is unchecked (see Figure 8–30a).

    Concentrate on one major puddle area at a time. Select the lower area. Click in the dark areas. Shift-click to add to the selection (see Figure 8–30b). When you have determined the perimeters of the selection, switch to Quick Mask mode (see Figure 8–30c). From there you can do some of the last bits of cleanup by painting out the little islands to leave a clear selection area. When you have finished cleaning up the little islands, switch from Quick Mask back to selection.

5. Take your selection and create a separate channel for it. Select > Save Selection and make the destination a new channel. Name the channel "lower level selection."

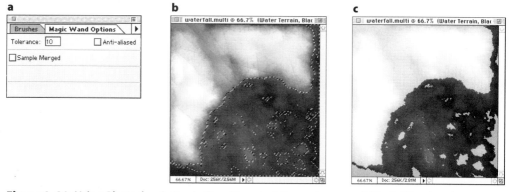

Figure 8–30 Using Photoshop's Magic Wand to select the water area: a) Magic Wand settings; b) Magic Wand selection marquee in progress; c) Quick Mask mode ready to clean up last little bits of selection area.

6. When you are finished with the lower selection area, deselect it. Now go back and do the same process for the upper selection area. Select with the Magic Wand and clean up the edges with the paint tool in Quick Mask mode. Save the selection and name it "Upper level selection."

7. Join up the two areas into one selection to create the water area mask. Create a new channel (which should have a black background). Load the selection channel for the lower pool and fill with white. Then load the upper pool selection and fill with white. Using white, paint in the transitional area between

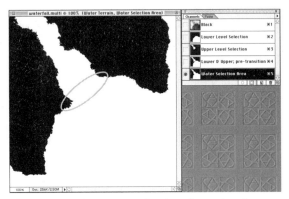

Figure 8–31 Water area selection channel and Channel Palette.

them, indicated by the encircled area in Figure 8–31. Name the channel "Water Selection Area."

You'll use this mask for several things. It will be the basis for creating the flat area in the water terrain. It will also select the area in the rock terrain that will be lowered (darkened) slightly later on.

If you haven't done so before now, save your Photoshop file. Make sure you save it using the Photoshop 3.0 format (In Windows, .PSD) to keep the layers intact.

8. Now that the Water Selection Area channel has been created and saved, make the Water Terrain layer active and load the Water Selection Area channel. Since you must ensure that the water is wide enough to fit snugly into the rock, the selection needs to be expanded. Under the Select menu, choose Modify > Expand… and enter 3 pixels for the expansion amount. The selection size will grow ever so slightly. (For all of these selection areas, make sure that you select with anti-aliasing switched off.) Save this selection for reference. Select > Save Selection… Save it into the same document as a new channel and name it "Larger Water Selection."

9. This expanded selection is what you'll use to paint the flat areas of your water terrain. Now that you know the area you'll be painting into, it's time to decide

what level of gray to paint. Look at the rocky area within the confines of the selection. Sample a gray level that is from the lighter values there, say, near the "shore" where the selection area meets the rocky part that is above ground. Select the gray and then paint in the lower water area with solid, normal brush strokes (see Figure 8–32a). Paint the lower level just over the water spill.

10. Repeat the process for the upper area. Select a gray level from among the lightest of the area enclosed by the upper pool. Paint the entire water terrain upper pool area that solid gray (see Figure 8–32b). When you are done, you

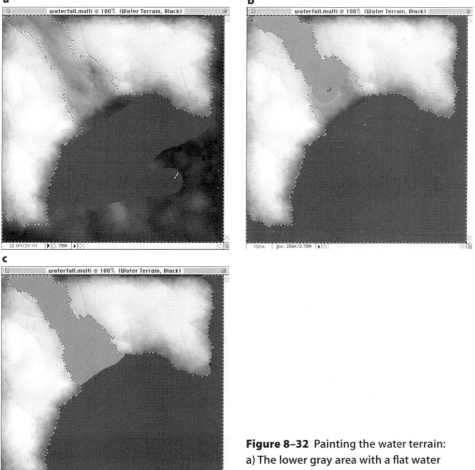

Figure 8–32 Painting the water terrain:
a) The lower gray area with a flat water
surface gray; b) painting upper water area;
c) after painting all water levels.

should have something like what is shown in Figure 8–32c. Outside the selected area is the same old terrain data, and inside the selected area are two levels of gray, with a place of transition.

11. There are two remaining things to fix here. The first is the transition. The water should spill out *over* the rocks, not cut under the edge to go *through* the rocks. Therefore the lighter area should project out ever so slightly into the darker pool area. Set the layer blending mode to Lighten to help you judge how far to project the water. If you see rocky area peeking through at the waterfall transition, then the water will be cutting under the rocks. It's okay if there is rock peeking out elsewhere from the water, but not at the waterfall's edge. The transition should be sudden. Use the Smudge tool to create the transition. See Figure 8–33a. However, a couple of judicious smudges here and there make for a wall of water that's not perfectly uniform.

12. You'll also need to fix the rest of the terrain area. Whatever isn't water (what is still rock) should be at the darkest level. Select inverse, so that all the extra non-water area is selected. Then fill it with black. You'll clip the black part so that the water does not even show in those areas. (See Figure 8–33b.)

13. In the Layers Palette pop-up menu, select Duplicate Layer… and where Photoshop asks you to specify the destination, select a new document. Save that

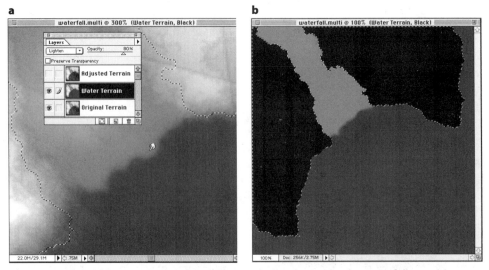

Figure 8–33 Finishing touches: a) Using the Smudge tool to make the waterfall transition between the two levels; b) filling all non-water areas with black to finish the water terrain gray map.

new document as a PICT file (Macintosh) or TIF file (Windows). You may need to delete the extra channels in order to do so. Name the new file "Water Terrain" and close it. Hang onto your master Photoshop file with the layers and selection masks. (In fact, save it again.)

14. Now you have one terrain map completed. Hooray! The second terrain map you'll make is a variation on your original one, the rocky terrain. Make your original terrain layer active. (Make sure no other layers are visible.) Load the water area selection channel. This smaller selection is the exact area the water will fit into.

Since you sampled an elevation from here for your water, the water is now too shallow. Deepen it by darkening this selected area where the water will be. Access the Levels dialog box (Image > Adjust > Levels or ⌘-L on a Mac or Ctrl+L in Windows) and move the middle gray (gamma) triangle slider ever so slightly toward the white end. The numerical readout should change from 1.0 to something in the .90's. This darkens your selection a

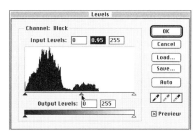

Figure 8–34 Using Photoshop's Levels dialog box to lower the rocky pool area.

bit. Remember, it doesn't take much to make the elevation fall off. If it's subtle for your eyes, it will be significant in elevation. (See Figure 8–34.)

15. Duplicate this layer into a new document and save it as a separate PICT or TIF file. Call it "Adjusted Terrain." Save your multi-layer multi-channel scene file and head on back to Bryce. (Quit Photoshop.)

16. Select your terrain (actually, it should still be selected). Open the Terrain Editor. Click the Picture button or type ⌘-O (Macintosh) or Ctrl+O (Windows). Select the image file "Adjusted Terrain." (When it loads, it shouldn't change much, just darken the current one in places.) Click OK to exit the Terrain Editor.

17. Duplicate the terrain. Open the Terrain Editor and click the Picture button again. This time, select the image file "Water Terrain." Once it loads into the Terrain Editor, slide the clipping bracket up from the bottom so that the low black terrain disappears (see Figure 8–35). Your body of water should be trimmed to the dimensions of water. All those sixteen steps led up to this single drag of the Clipping Bracket for this waterfall! Click OK.

18. For the sake of clarity when the terrains render, change the surface of this waterfall to the basic blue option in the Preset Materials library. Now when you render, you'll know what is water and what is not. See Figure 8–36a.

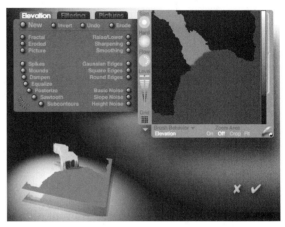

Figure 8–35 Clipping off the bottom of the water terrain.

19. Render and see if all works according to design. Make any necessary adjustments. Do not adjust the placement of the terrains, since they fit snugly together. If you need to make adjustments to ensure that the water is higher than the land or some other tweak, do so in Photoshop and adjust the gray map. If you need to move or resize the terrains overall, group them together before committing yourself to any move.

Assign surface materials and tweak. Be sure to check out the special waterfall material file in the Waterfall folder on the CD-ROM. Congratulations! You've just made a waterfall in Bryce! Figure 8–36b shows a completed render, with all the material settings. (The color image for this scene is Figure C14–21, in the color section for Chapter 14 "Superlative Nature Imagery.")

a

b

Figure 8–36 Rendered waterfall: a) With water changed to flat, dark color; b) complete with materials.

SYMMETRICAL LATTICES

The symmetrical lattice is a fine way to create "injection mold" objects. The symmetrical lattice is the equivalent of placing two terrain halves back to back. In nature scenes, you can create freestanding rocks, arches, and rocky-slab forms. The hoodoos shown earlier (Figure 8–13) in the discussion of the Filtering controls were created using symmetrical lattices. For modeling, you can create pretty much anything you can imagine! The tower architecture image by Chris Casady, at the end of the previous chapter (Figure 7–28) uses symmetrical lattices to construct architectural elements.

Symmetrical lattices require clipping at the bottom in order to be their respectable symmetrical selves in wireframe view. If there is no bottom clipping, you will not see both halves of the lattice, although it will render as such (and have square edges, too). There will be times when the symmetrical lattice wireframe extends one stray straight wireframe in some wayward direction. Figure 8–37 depicts both seemingly scary circumstances. Don't fret if you see it; the stray wire does not indicate that something's wrong or broken. Bryce just does that sometimes. If you clip the lattice at the upper end, the wireframe preview will not show the lattice as

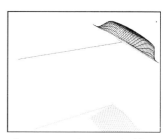

Figure 8–37 Symmetrical lattice as half-a-wireframe when gray map has no bottom clipping, as well as the strange stray wire—it looks a lot worse than it is.

a clipped object (nor will you be able to move the object if you drag it from a clipped part of the wireframe), but the symmetrical lattice will render clipped at the top.

When making objects with the symmetrical lattice, the most critical thing is to create the gray map in such a way to minimize the seam where the two halves join. The Filter is excellent for making a curve to minimize it; see the example in Figure 8–38. The trick is to make a very sudden transition from black to a lighter color.

WORKING WITH OTHER IMAGE EDITING APPLICATIONS

Of course, since the Terrain Editor is a special-case image editor, you can also use other image editors (such as Photoshop) to create or alter images to use as terrains. The Picture import option and the Pictures index cards are admissions of the fact

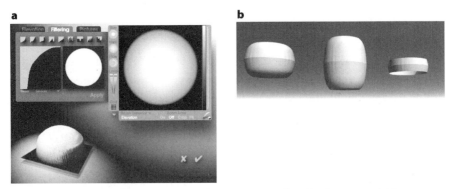

Figure 8–38 Minimizing the seam: a) The settings on the Filtering control; b) rendered result with different object height settings and with clipping at the top, too.

that images created elsewhere make good terrains. Of course you can start from scratch in the other image editing application (such as these sun-baked mud cracks shown in Figure 8–39, which were created using a technique developed by Chris Casady), or you can import terrain image information and further manipulate it using additional options available elsewhere. Figure 8–40 is a series of the same terrain manipulated using various Photoshop filters. More samples are also available on the CD-ROM.

Another idea in Photoshop is to create your own custom brushes to paint your terrains, whether they are footprints, geological phenomena, or some other wonderful invention.

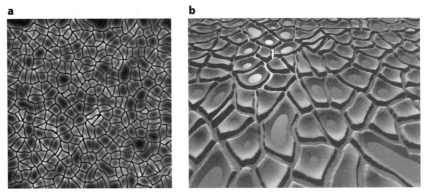

Figure 8–39 Mud-baked tiles a la Chris Casady, with the terrain created in Photoshop.

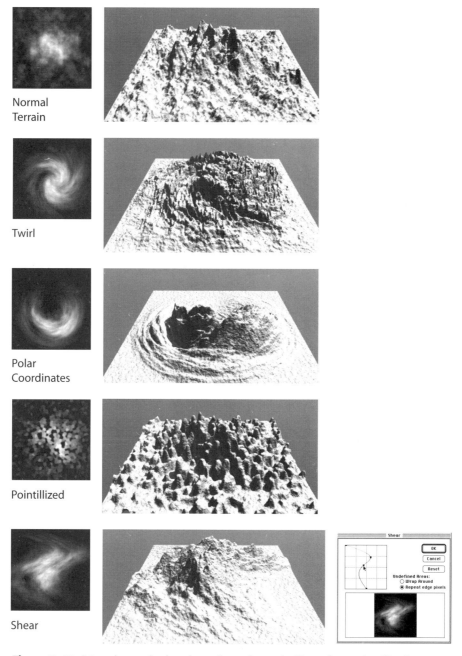

Normal Terrain

Twirl

Polar Coordinates

Pointillized

Shear

Figure 8–40 A terrain manipulated a variety of ways in Photoshop using filtering techniques.

Picture Terrain Tricks

Any image is game to become a terrain. Some of the more interesting (and, at times, horrifying) terrains are those created from an image source. Save the image as a PICT (Macintosh) or as BMP, PSD, or TIF (Windows), and then import it into the Terrain Editor using the Picture option. Bryce will create the terrain based on the values of the image. This works well when the image is also mapped onto the terrain as the 2D Picture texture.

When you want to make the image-as-terrain recognizable, lower the terrain's overall wireframe height in the Edit Palette. In the Terrain Editor, the Smooth button comes in handy, as sharp transitions from light to dark take on a more mellow, melted appearance.

Two sets of images in Figure 8–41 show examples of this process. The clock parts image is the basis for a terrain shape. It illustrates the pleasing way that images create abstract forms. And Phil Clevenger's "Necrofelinia" sets the standard for using Bryce's Terrain Editor to make sinister Mr. Hyde transformations from sweet furry adorable Dr. Jekyll images. For more particulars on the way to use picture images to create these transformations, see the section, "2D Picture Textures" in Chapter 9, "Material World," and the section "Strange Terrain-Based Images in Chapter 15, "Brycing Out of This World."

THE LOST CONTINENTS OF TEXT-LAND-IS

By now, the implications of using the Terrain Editor as a special image editor to create different heights might be working its way into your brain. Besides allowing you to exercise your mad geological creativity to make mountains, there are other things you can do. Create terrains out of words. Here are the basic steps and issues for making literate land from text terrains.

Use this technique with hand-lettering (my personal favorite), typography, and logos. If your logo is in a Postscript format, rasterize it directly into Photoshop and take it to Bryce from there.

Text Terrain Recipe

1. Create the text itself as line art. In this case, I wrote out the words by hand with brush, ruling pen, and ink on paper, then vectorized it in Adobe

Figure 8–41 Using a picture to create a G2H map: a) Original kitty image for "Necrofelinia"; b) G2H map; c) rendered "Necrofelinia" (image by Phil Clevenger); d) Clock Parts images for "GlockenFondue"; e) rendered "GlockenFondue."

Illustrator. From there I rasterized it in Photoshop and saved it as a PICT. (In Windows the rasterized image would be saved as a BMP, TIF or PSD format.) You can start with a scan, type created in Photoshop, or rasterized from Illustrator. I prefer an original that has a resolution of 512. 1024 is even better. If it's 256 or smaller, you risk losing some detail in the actual letter forms. The terrain will be square. If your words do not fit into a square format (the likely case), pad your word/image document with empty white space to make the format square.

2. For a little flexibility in manipulating your image, create two more variations. Besides your original, create a slightly blurred and an extremely blurred version

of your word or logo. Figure 8–42a shows three variations used for this text terrain.

3. Once you have all of your variations created as image files in the proper format, create a new scene file with a new terrain. In the Terrain Editor, change the resolution to 512 or 1024 and then click Picture to import your text image. (If you do not change the resolution before importing the picture, the imported image information will be interpolated down to the default resolution of 128. Ick.)

4. Now make the word more terrain-like. Notice in Figure 8–42a that as a black-on-white image, it will be initially translated to an inverted "valley" position in the Terrain Editor. For this technique, you may be doing a lot of work-then-invert, since the terrain needs to be merged with fresh source copies in order to maintain legibility.

    Invert the image so that the text is white (higher) (see Figure 8–42b). Click the Eroded button to make an eroded land mass based on the text-based information already there (see Figure 8–42c). At this point, you can continue working with the terrain for a while or try another merge in the Pictures index card area. Use any and all of your favorite tricks with the Terrain Editor.

5. When you are ready to merge the image again, you can invert it or not as you see fit. The keyboard combination, ⌘-I (Macintosh) or Ctrl+I (Windows) works the entire time you're in the Terrain Editor. Load the original image again and blend the two together.

    The new Pict Blend actually works quite well in this situation. Choose whichever method you want to use: normal terrain (white letters on black lowlands) and Pict Blend (drag all the way to the right, see Figure 8–42d), inverted terrain and Pict Blend (drag all the way to the left, see Figure 8–42e), or inverted terrain and Minimum blend mode (drag to the middle to evenly weight the two).

    For this merge variation, use one of the blurred versions of the original image. The merge will "beef up" the terrain heights just around the edges of the word. Make your adjustments so that the text form is the most extreme value—the whitest of the whites or the blackest of the blacks, depending which of the three blend mode methods you chose.

6. Go back to the Elevation controls and continue working with the terrain. Add whatever effects you want. Beware the Mounds, Relief Noise, and Subplateaus controls, which all tend to shift the terrain's bulk to the left. If

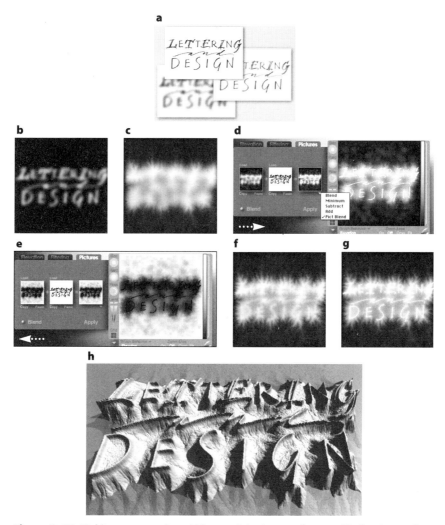

Figure 8–42 Making text terrains: a) Three original source images; b) after importing to Terrain Editor and inverting; c) after clicking Eroded; d) re-merging with the original using Pict Blend and sliding to the right; e) and to the left; f) additional erosion; g) after merging one last time; h) completed render.

you shift too much, the land mass will be out of alignment with the text form. Figure 8–42f shows the terrain after erosion is added.

7. When you have completed the exploration process (please feel welcome to do intermediate merges, too!), do one last blend merge to make the text stand out from the rest of the terrain ever so slightly. (See Figure 8–42g.)

Why this last blend-merge? It makes the word itself easily visible. Even when you have the word blurred or mostly light, any irregularities in tone will create elevation differences in the terrain that will make the word more difficult to read. Remember—for the umpteenth time—you're translating grayscale information to height. You may be able to "read" it fine in the Terrain Editor preview window, but it will be harder to "read" once you've rendered the terrain. After you've made the word the final flat top plateau surface, you can, of course, add a last touch of erosion for a more "natural"-looking word. The rendered result of this process is shown in Figure 8–42h.

Variation—Sloping Letters

Another variation doesn't use the image processing power of the Terrain Editor beyond assigning text and gradations to a terrain. Figure 8–43 shows three different gradations on words, where the lights to darks flow in different directions with differing results in the rendered terrain.

In Photoshop, make a document and fill it entirely with black. Create a text selection. Fill the text with a gradation. Try using gradations that run from left to right,

Figure 8–43 Three different text-gradient graymaps and the resulting three terrains.

front to back, or a radial depression. The three text gradients (with their respective G2H maps) show both. Save your terrain as a PICT (Macintosh) or BMP, TIF, or PSD (Windows) to import using the Picture control button.

Beefing up Serifs

When working with text terrains, you must take pains with serif fonts. The font shown in Figure 8–44a (Bodoni Poster) has thick portions joined together by very delicate branches. Normally, when font like this is rasterized into Photoshop, the delicate joins show up as grayed aliased transitions. This presents no problem when the text is a flat two-dimensional image; the grays help convey the shape of the letter.

However, you aren't thinking two dimensional here when you're looking at the G2H map. (At the risk of bordering on the repetitive wheeze, "howmanytimesdoIhaftatellya?" you'll often encounter the ingrained manner in which you rely on two-dimensional image information to perform three-dimensional optical illusions. Only after a few nasty surprises when the terrain doesn't "behave" properly do you start to see G2H maps for what they are.) In a G2H map, those delicate, slightly blurred branches between letter portions will end up at a different height. The joins *will* be there, but far below the level of the rest of the letter surface (see Figure 8–44a). Compound this by the fact that you're going to make the letter surface a variable gradient, and you've got a tricky situation. You can't simply work exclusively in the world of sans-serif type, with its more uniform widths. (I can just see that client looking over your shoulder, saying, "But I want you to use that other typeface!") So, how do you navigate through *this* one?

First adjust the word so that it will live on the same level. In Photoshop, "beef up" the joins and serifs. I prefer using the Burn tool (set to shadows) or the Levels command to darken the serifs, which provide results similar to what is shown in Figure 8–44c. You'll need to perform this step prior to adding any gradients.

To complete the process for this circular serifed type extravaganza, two circular gradients were applied using the KPT Gradient Designer. The first one was set lower in the image to bend the letters so that the open ends of the "horseshoe" were lower than the top of the circle. A second gradient was applied to make the tops of the letters higher than at the baseline (see Figure 8–44d). The text face is slightly curved as a result, and all the serifs are there (see Figure 8–44e).

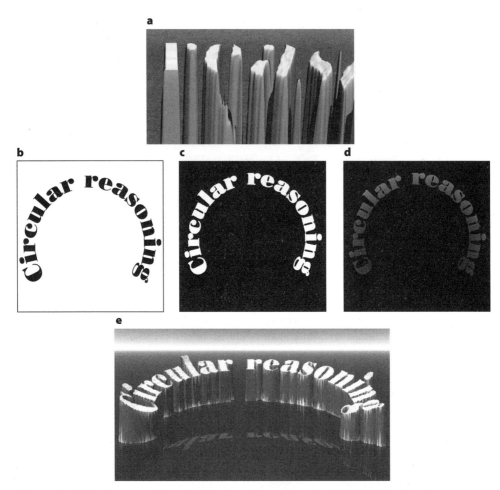

Figure 8–44 Beefing up serif text: (a) terrain with collapsed serifs; (b) original text in Illustrator; (c) beefed-up text; (d) additional gradients sculpt text levels; (e) final render.

DISTANCE OR ALTITUDE RENDER

Bryce's Distance Render is a good way to create a terrain from a render of top view objects. Create a new terrain based on objects that are already in your scene. This is especially good if you are trying to align several terrains in a mountain-valley formation. Alignment of the valley terrain with the mountain terrains can be tricky. This technique allows you to get the alignment "close" and then take a slightly different tack to get it "right." When in Distance Render mode, Bryce renders things according to the formula: "Whatever is closest to the camera is rendered as black. Whatever is farthest is rendered as white." When doing a Distance Render from top view, the image is the opposite of a G2H map, which says that the highest point is white and the lowest point is black. All you need to do after creating a Distance Render is to invert the image in an image editing application or in the Terrain Editor. See also the Distance Render section of Chapter 12, "Render Unto Bryce."

Recipe: Using Distance Render to Create a Terrain

1. Set up a scene with multiple terrains. Make one terrain the rolling valley floor if you like.

2. From the Master Palette's Views pop-up menu, select top view.

3. In the Render Palette, select Distance Render If you are using Windows, select Altitude Render, since Distance Render doesn't work in top view.

4. Render the scene.

5. Under the File menu, select "Save As..." and give this file a different name. You will open this up from Photoshop or an image editing application to set the proper size of the file.

6. In Photoshop, open up the file. Crop it into a square format. Crop out all the unnecessary image area.

7. Invert the image in Photoshop (⌘-I or Ctrl+I), if necessary. You now have your terrain map. Save the file or else copy it, ready to paste into Bryce's Terrain Editor.

DIGITAL ELEVATION MODELS (DEM)

To create terrains based on already-existing land forms, use what is called a Digital Elevation Model (DEM). DEM is the electronic file format used by the USGS for topographical information. The DEM file is a text file describing the elevation for each point on a mesh for a map. Imagine a grid laid over an area of land. The question "What's the elevation here?" is asked at each point where there's a grid intersection. This is called a sample. Samples are taken for each point on the grid, resulting in a text description of the actual terrain. If you convert this DEM information to a grayscale image, where each point on the grid is represented by a pixel, you have a G2H map. The pixel color indicates the elevation, so you can build a terrain based on real data from the real world.

DEMs come in different types of resolution. If you adjust the grid so that more points are sampled in a fixed area, you have a higher resolution map with more detail. It's the exact same principle as changing your terrain resolution from 128 to 512. There is more information about the terrain contained in the 512 map than in the 128.

DEM measurements are discussed in two ways: the amount of area covered and the amount of detail for an area. For the amount of land area covered, the measurements are conveyed in terms of Earth's basic measurements: latitude and longitude. Units of latitude and longitude are expressed in degrees, then minutes, then seconds. If you see reference to a two-degree map and a 15-minute map, the 15-minute map takes in a smaller area than does a two-degree map.

The other way of discussing DEM measurement, amount of detail, is referred to as meter samples. How many meters do you travel between one elevation sample and the next? A 100-meter sample is not as detailed as a 30-meter sample, since the 30-meter sample obtained just over three times the amount of data as a 100-meter sample did. There is a relationship between the amount of area in a DEM and the amount of detail in a DEM. For any number of data points in a DEM, questions of scale and resolution are asked. "Is this a highly detailed map of my four little acres?" "Is this a moderately detailed map that spans four big counties?" The larger the area, the less detail. The smaller the area, the more detail.

So how do you get from DEM to Bryce? There is a freeware Macintosh application on the CD-ROM that will convert USGS DEM data to grayscale PICT data. DEM View, created by Ken Badertscher, allows you to look at a DEM and save the entire thing as a PICT or select Bryce-sized terrain morsels to save as PICTs. Then all you need to do is use the PICTs to create terrains. For Windows users, there is a freeware application called DEMvert, which similarly converts Digital Elevation data to grayscale information. On the CD-ROM in the DEM Info folder there is a small sampling of DEM data as well as information about where you can go to download more by Anonymous FTP from Internet sites.

The ability to take real-world topographic data into Bryce has its scientific uses for visualizing planetary surfaces at times or in places where humans cannot visit. Bryce has been used to generate models of past geology as well as using elevation samples taken from spacecraft orbiting neighboring planets to enable earthlings to place themselves on Martian and Venusian soil and take a look around. (See the Mars images in Chapter 17, "Professional Images and Real Bryce Projects.") Not only can you make any land forms you have imagined or seen in Bryce, but also you can Bryce boldly where no one has gone before.

CHAPTER NINE

Material World

The lava, very porous in certain places, took the form of little round blisters. Crystals of opaque quartz, adorned with limpid drops of natural glass suspended to the roof like lustres, seemed to take fire as I passed beneath them. One would have fancied that the genii of romance were illuminating their underground palaces to receive the sons of men.

"Magnificent, glorious!" I cried, in a moment of involuntary enthusiasm; "what a spectacle, uncle! Do you not admire these variegated shades of lava, which run through a whole series of colors, from reddish brown to pale yellow,—by the most insensible degrees? And these crystals,— they appear like luminous globes."

"You are beginning to see the charms of travel, Master Harry," cried my uncle. "Wait a bit, until we advance farther. What we have as yet discovered is nothing—onward, my boy, onward!"

JULES VERNE, *A JOURNEY TO THE CENTRE OF THE EARTH*

IN THIS CHAPTER...

- What object surfaces are made of—illumination, optics and bump, and color

- Bryce's ten channels for controlling surface appearance

- Texture Sources and how they drive combinations of the ten material channels

- Different methods for combining multiple sources into one material channel

- The Materials Composer interface and general organization of the Editor

- A deeper explanation of each part of the Materials Composer

- Discussion of some basic approaches to working in the Materials Composer

- 2D Picture textures—description, how-to's, and pointers

- 3D Textures and the "shallow" Texture Editor

- The Deep Texture Editor—a dissection of each part

- How to analyze any material

- Building a couple of material settings from the ground up

Bryce allows you to make pictures of a virtual world. In order to give that world a sense of reality, you have to make the objects' appearances convincing. Since you cannot leave the chair in front of your computer and jump inside your monitor to wander around that world, all of your cues and clues about what makes up that world are visual, represented on that rendered two-dimensional image. How can you tell what the objects are? What are they made of? Are they metal? Granite? Glass? Steam? Wood? Sand? Crystal? The surface appearance of the object provides substantial clues to the nature of the matter. The Materials Composer is where you compose the matter of your objects. (The relation of the two words, material and matter, is no coincidence.) Here you blend your artistic vision with a type of mad-scientist (or is that "mat" scientist?) observation, bringing as much from the disciplines of geology, chemistry, and physics as you can muster into your crafting of the surface appearance of the Brycean objects in your world.

This chapter will unfold the concepts that comprise an object's surface material and the Materials Composer user interface controls, starting with the simple and introducing additional levels of complexity as we go along.

Instead of the exercises that I have been offering in other chapters, this chapter has lots of illustrations which show all of the Materials Composer settings. You can follow along and recreate the combinations that you see in these pages and use them as a starting place for your own material explorations.

INTRODUCTION TO THE MATERIALS COMPOSER

This is the object that Jack built.

Before I discuss what the Materials Composer does, I'll review our setup. There is an object in the scene. The renderer will shoot a ray (actually, many rays) into the scene that will intersect the object. What happens at that point? What information about the object is discovered? Where does the ray go after that? It will bounce off and go somewhere—to a light source or to other objects, eventually deriving a color for that pixel.

The Materials Composer is where you determine the surface properties of each object so that it has its own particular appearance. Settings in the Materials Composer determine the answers to these questions: How will the ray bounce? Will rays of certain colors be absorbed and others be reflected? Will the ray bounce directly, creating a specular highlight, or will it bounce from all directions, an indication of diffuse light? Is the object transparent, with some of the rays passing through the object to what is on the other side? Or is the object reflective, bouncing the ray to that other object over there, which is reflected on the surface of the primary object? Is it matte or shiny? What color is it? Are there patterns of colors? What are the shapes of those color patterns? Is the actual surface smooth or are there indentations?

The Materials Composer controls the sum total of the object's surface properties—the way it absorbs, reflects, or transmits light, surface texture, color, and small indentations (bumps). More than a uniform means of coloring the object, the surface appearance may change depending on altitude, orientation, or slope (how level or upright the surface is), as well as incorporate all the additional information about lighting and surface qualities. The Materials Composer is the place to define *every aspect* of the object's surface.

When discussing how the surface of an object appears, it might be tempting to use the words "Materials" and "Texture" interchangeably. Don't. Each has a specific meaning; Materials and Texture aren't identical. Material is the *overall* appearance of the surface of an object. Texture is *a part of* the object's surface appearance.

THREE SURFACE PROPERTIES

Here are the three elements to the surface of the object that Jack built.

So what are the surface properties, anyhow? All the surface properties can be broken down into three categories: illumination, color, and optics. See Figure C9–1 in the color section.

Illumination refers to the way that the object's surface responds to atmospheric light. Ranging from a glossy shine with bright highlights to a duller, matte surface, to self-illuminating glow, the object surface's response to lighting gives you information about what material comprises the object.

Color is what reaches your eyes when light rays bounce off of objects. In the real world, a green object absorbs all but the green rays in the light spectrum. The green light rays reach your eyes, causing you to see "green."

Optics are special-case situations where the renderer's ray is divided as it hits the object's surface. If the object is reflective, then you'll be able to see the likeness of the surrounding objects and environs in the object's surface. If the object is transparent, then light rays pass through the object, and you'll see what lies behind it. Depending on the nature of the substance, the light might refract as it passes through the object. There is another surface "special event" that is lumped together with optics: bump. (So the category is optics & bump.) Light rays encounter bump— the surface indentations that tell your eyes about the tactile qualities of the object's surface. Is the object nubbly or smooth, pitted, or wavy?

These three areas comprise all of the object's surface properties. In the course of this chapter I'll delve into the complexities with which Bryce's Materials Composer enables you to determine the object's appearance, but it boils down to these three. If you find yourself getting lost or confused amid the myriad details, hang on to these three as your organizational life preservers.

Adding Ten-Channel Complexity

Here are the ten channels that comprise the three elements to the surface of the object that Jack built.

The first unfolding of the three basic properties will introduce you to two parts of the Materials Composer interface. There is obviously more to each of the three categories I just named. Each one is comprised of additional parts. They are called channels.

To discuss the basic elements of the three surface properties at the most basic level, it's as if the user-interface has collapsed so that only the elements in Figure 9–2 are showing. (This and other figures where the user interface is collapsed are my reconstructions for illustrative purposes; don't even try to find the secret key ingredient to collapse the Materials Composer into the form you see pictured here! If you want to see the Materials Composer labeled in its entirety, see Figure 9–39.) There is a preview window, a set of sliders and color pickers, and two additional names with numeric settings off to the left. Look at the central set of controls. Thicker dividing lines separate the list of properties into three groups. The top group, Diffusion, Ambience, and Specularity, constitutes the first surface property I mentioned—illumination. The second group, Transparency, Reflection, and Bump Height, is the optics and bump group. The first two groups have sliders that extend out to the left, ranging from 0 to 255. The third group does not have numbers or sliders, but little color swatches. This last group is, surprise! color: Diffuse Color, Ambient Color, Specular Color, and Transparent Color. The swatch shows the currently selected color.

These are the ten basic channels. If they seem confusing to you, remember—they boil down to the three basic surface properties: illumination, optics and bump, and color.

Figure 9–2 The controls and sliders for the ten channels along left side of Materials Composer.

About those sliders…

When you make adjustments with the sliders, be careful to limit your mouse movements to the horizontal level where the particular slider lives. If your mouse strays above or below, you'll end up adjusting those other sliders, too. The usual user interface standard is that once you have pressed the mouse button and started adjusting the one control, all other controls are "off-limits" while your mouse remains pressed. This standard is upheld throughout the rest of the application, but not here with the sliders; they're all "live." One vertical drag of the mouse will leave a trail of ravaged settings in its path as you inadvertently readjust the sliders for all six channels. Happily, ⌘-Z or Ctrl+Z undoes the last move you made, so the destruction needn't be permanent.

Also, you can use the Tab key to cycle through the numbers to type in your own numbers.

Illumination

These are the three illumination channels, which tell how the object reacts to light; as part of the ten channels that comprise the three elements to the surface of the object that Jack built.

The illumination channels allow you to control the way light interacts with your object. Light bounces off the object and hits your eye. Or, in the ray-tracing analogy, once the ray hits the object, it bounces from the object to the light source. The three illumination channels determine how that ray will bounce and thus how the object is lit.

Diffusion

When light strikes a rough surface, it doesn't bounce in a particular direction; it bounces away in all directions. Consequently, the surface appears matte (flat). The object is in direct light or it is in shadow, but there is no hot highlight. Figure 9–3a shows a sphere with maximum Diffusion and Figure 9–3d has Diffusion mixed with Ambience and Specularity.

For many of the objects created in Bryce, especially ground and terrain surfaces, a high Diffuse setting is the norm. Much of the natural world has rough surfaces, and light bounces away from a matte surface in all directions.

Ambience

When an object has Ambience, it is self-illuminating. It resists shadows. At the extreme end, it "glows in the dark." Figure 9–3b shows a sphere at a maximum Ambience setting. Although the path from the light source is obstructed by another object, the sphere is not in shadow. When Ambience is mixed with diffuse illumination, the shadows falling on the object will not be as dark and pronounced (see Figure 9–3e). Most natural objects (terrains and such) have little to no ambient light. A low setting (Bryce's default is 50) will allow you to see some surface detail for portions of the object that are in shadow.

Important Note: It's crucial that the Ambience setting be consistent for most of the objects in your scene (stay tuned for exceptions). If you have one object that has a low Ambience setting placed next to an object with a high Ambience setting, they will not appear natural. The edge between the two objects will seem artificial, especially when the edge is in shadow.

In cases where you want an object to be especially bright, such as snow (atop a darker, rocky surface) or for a glowing object, the Ambience setting should be different. Also, when you have an object with a 2D Picture for its surface, and you want the details of that image to be readily apparent, give the object a higher Ambience setting.

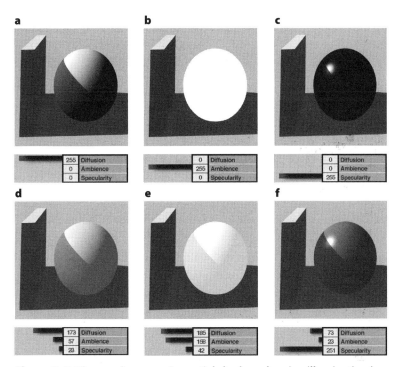

Figure 9–3 These spheres are in partial shadow, showing illumination in direct light and shadow: a) Maximum Diffusion; b) maximum Ambience; c) maximum Specularity; d) Diffusion mixed with Ambience and Specularity; e) Ambience mixed with Diffusion and Specularity; f) Specularity mixed with Diffusion and Ambience illumination channels.

Specularity and Specular Coefficient

When light hits a hard, polished surface and bounces directly off it, what is seen is a "hot spot," or specular highlight. Figure 9–3c shows a sphere with maximum Specularity, and Figure 9–3f shows a sphere with some Diffusion and a tad of Ambience added to the high Specularity setting. An object with a high Specularity setting appears very shiny, glossy, or wet. In its most basic form, the size of the specular hot spot is set using the Specular Coefficient control.

The Specular Coefficient control is located to the left of the Materials Composer grid. Think of the Specular Coefficient as a second slider, where black is minimum (very small, pinpointed) and very light gray-to-white is maximum (very large). Of course, you've probably noticed that the sliders all have a range from 0 to 255. Likewise, the gray values in Specular Coefficient range from 0 to 255. (Surprise!) Figure 9–4 shows three spheres with three different Specular Coefficient settings for otherwise identically illuminated objects. The small highlight has a Specular Coefficient of 0; the large highlight has a Specular Coefficient of 250, just shy of the maximum. The size of the highlight changes (note how 205 is seemingly closer to zero than 250). In Figure 9–5, the nuances of maximum are shown with every setting from 255 down to 246 for both the Macintosh and Windows versions. Obviously, a Specular Coefficient of 255 is brilliant, with maximum illumination on the entire hemisphere of the object that faces the sun and/or light sources. Just below maximum is a level I call "pretty dang bright," where the crisp edge of light is distinguished from shadow. As the setting moves down into the high 240's, the crisp edge disappears. The mid-to-high 240's are acceptable for bright highlights if you want to avoid that crisp line. If you've ever wondered why the bright line is on some of your objects, now you know. Crank down the Specular Coefficient a tad. I'll revisit more of this when I discuss Specular Color.

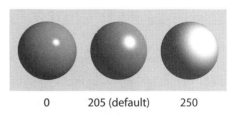

0   205 (default)   250

Figure 9–4 The setting for Specular Coefficient changes the size of the specular hot spot.

Macintosh

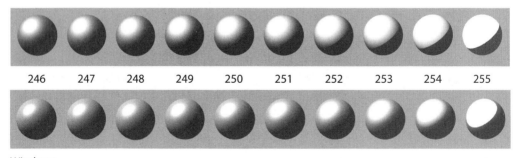

246   247   248   249   250   251   252   253   254   255

Windows

Figure 9–5 A detailed examination of the high end of the Specular Coefficient. The sharp border is visible above 249 or 250 or so.

Optics(and Bump)

Here are the optic and bump channels; the light ray will split into two directions, or a snazzy emboss makes tactile surface; as part of the ten channels that comprise the three elements to the surface of the object that Jack built.

Optics are the special case situations when the object's surface is not your normal basic opaque. The optics channels allow you to determine if light passes through or reflects off the object. Transparency and Reflection each determine the manner and amount in which the renderer's ray is split—the ray is traced to the object itself, and the ray is traced *through* to the other side or *mirrored* to the surrounding area for additional information to calculate the image of the object in the scene. Naturally, adding more complexity by splitting light rays means a longer render time, since there are more calculations that must be made in order to chase down those rays to their sources.

Transparency

In Transparency, one part of the ray will be traced through the object to what lies on the other side (and, further, if there is refraction; the ray will be bent as it bounces). The other part will bounce off the object until it reaches the light source. How much light passes through the object? The Transparency slider determines that amount, balancing the strength of "the surface" information with the "on the other side" information. A low Transparency setting casts the weight toward the information about the surface, while a high Transparency setting will swing the weight to the other side, with more of the objects beyond showing through.

Of course, once the light passes "through" the object, the question arises: "Do the light rays bend as they pass through?" That's where the Refract Index comes in.

Refract Index

Refract Index determines how much light bends as it passes through an object. Adjusting the number scale (located to the left of the Materials grid, next to the Specular Coefficient) will suggest what the transparent object is composed of. In the real world, different types of physical matter refract light differently depending on their molecular structure and other physical and chemical properties. In this virtual 3D world that you're creating, you get to play molecular physicist by tweaking the numbers. Want air? Set it to 100. Want water? Set it to 133. How about glass? Take it on up to 152. The higher the number, the more light bends.

You'll reach a point where the world turns upside-down through your refracted object. (This is especially true of spheres.) If you want to play virtual mineralogist, check out a paper written by Linda Ewing (a geologist, of course!) about the refraction index for different gem and mineral substances. It's on the CD-ROM in the Tips folder.

Changes in refraction can be quite dramatic taken in the small increments. This is a control to use with subtlety. Also, despite the Refract Index given for certain materials, there may be times when you want to "cheat" a little and have a lower refraction rate in the interest of allowing the viewer to see more easily through the object.

Figure 9–6 shows a sphere at different Refract Index settings for both Macintosh (top row) and Windows (bottom row). The Refract Index for these spheres changes by a factor of 5. 100 is the neutral Refract Index; it's the same as air. As the Refract Index moves up, the world turns upside-down. When the Refract Index goes below 100, there will be a halo around the edge of the object. The lower the number, the bigger the halo. The light bends differently, like it does when passing through a concave lens (think of glasses for nearsightedness). The Refract Index below 100 phenomenon in Windows is slightly different. There's that ring-like halo at the edge of the object, but it is not bright. It appears as though there is no refraction in that ring. (It makes bumpy glass look much better.)

With judicious use of refraction, a couple of intrepid Bryce users have set up telescopes to take advantage of the laws of physics inside their ray-traced worlds! Whatever you do, don't create a magnifying glass to burn holes in your Brycean ground. No screen saver will help in that case!

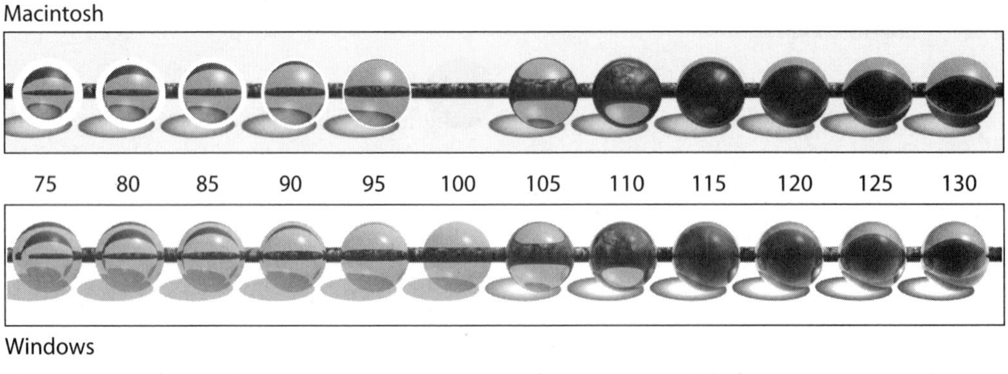

Macintosh

75   80   85   90   95   100   105   110   115   120   125   130

Windows

Figure 9–6 Refract Index settings: Top row: Macintosh; Bottom row: Windows.

Macintosh and Windows Differences

When it comes to Transparency and the Refract Index, the Macintosh and Windows versions of Bryce operate a little differently. In the Macintosh version, there is a radical jump when the Refract Index changes from 100 to the next higher or lower setting, 101 or 99. The Windows version is far more subtle, and the change from 100 to 101 or 99 is not so jarring. There's some background explanation for how each version of Bryce operates. Since the explanation requires an understanding of textures and alpha channels—concepts I will explain shortly—I discuss the larger picture for these differences later in the chapter, in the Shading Modes section, under the heading "Blend Transparency." In the meantime, I'll weave the Macintosh and Windows differences into my ongoing explanation of the Materials Composer. Look for more sections entitled "Macintosh and Windows Differences."

Reflection

In the case of Reflection, the ray will bounce off the object to other surrounding objects—and the light source—in the scene. The Reflection slider determines to what extent the object reflects light. Like Transparency, it's a weighted matter— low Reflection results in little reflected surroundings in the object's surface, and high Reflection results in more surrounding area than object surface. Those rays of light bounce off that reflective surface and go elsewhere, to another surface. Of course if that other reflected surface is an object that also has a lot of complexity, then the renderer will take its sweet time calculating all that detail. If that object is also reflective, then the "bounce rays into surrounding areas" process begins all over again. The maximum number of reflective bounces is six; after that the "reflection" is black. Unlike a real world, where light rays can travel infinitely down a "hall of

mirrors," Bryce would be brought to its knees by infinite recursion. You'd never see the watch cursor go away during your render! Figure 9–7 is set up as an infinite hall of mirrors, as two reflective surfaces face one another. At the sixth reflection, the object turns black. Water, mirrors, and metals are reflective. Adjust to taste.

Figure 9–7 Bryce's six-reflection limit.

Top Row:
Transparency 175

Bottom Row:
Transparency 150

Refract Index: 150

Reflectivity: 30   70   110   150   190

Figure 9–8 Combining reflectivity and transmitivity makes the object brighter—more light comes from the object to the camera.

Macintosh
Spec
+ Trans
+ Refl
= 320

Windows
Spec
+ Trans
+ Refl
= 320

Macintosh
Spec
+ Trans
+ Refl
= over 320

Windows
Spec
+ Trans
+ Refl
= over 320

Refract Index = 100

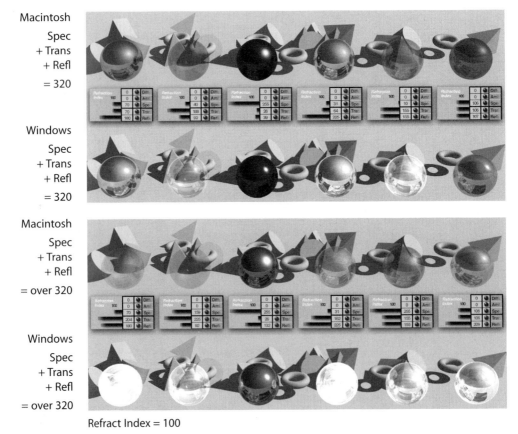

Figure 9–9 Crossing the optical brightness threshold, where Specularity plus Transparency plus Reflection equals or exceeds 320; the Macintosh version does not cross the threshold of brightness unless the Refract Index is higher than 100.

When you have a high degree of both Transparency and Reflection, the object will appear brighter, since more light reaches the object (see Figure 9–8). When it reflects, the surrounding light bounces toward the camera. When it's transparent, light passes through, so you see light from the other side and also light from everywhere else. If your object is a primitive with an enclosed shape, such as a sphere, there may be additional reflection as light bounces around inside. To get the right appearance, you will have to noodle with your settings some.

For an object with high Transparency and Reflection settings, make sure Diffusion is set to 0. If you don't want the object to be too bright, make sure that sum of Specularity plus Transparency plus Reflection does not go above 320—especially if you're using Bryce for Windows—or if you're using Bryce for

Macintosh

Spec
+ Trans
+ Refl

= 320

Windows

Spec
+ Trans
+ Refl

= 320

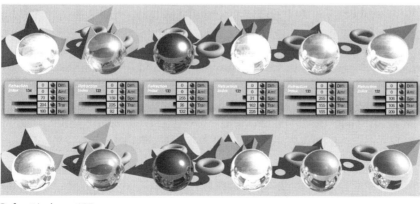

Macintosh

Spec
+ Trans
+ Refl

= over 320

Windows

Spec
+ Trans
+ Refl

= over 320

Refract Index = 133

Figure 9–9 *continued*

Macintosh and have a Refract Index set at anything other than 100. Figure 9–9 compares a set of spheres. There are four different conditions shown—the sum of Specularity plus Transparency plus Reflection *equals* 320, the sum *exceeds* 320, the Refract Index *equals* 100, and the Refract Index *exceeds* 100 (it is 133). The settings are shown for each sphere, with the Macintosh version above the Materials Composer grid inset, and the Windows version below.

Macintosh and Windows Differences

Since the Windows version treats Transparency differently, allowing diffuse and specular illumination to register while the object is transparent, even when there is no Refract Index, the object will be brighter than its Macintosh counterpart. The limit of 320 for Specularity, Transparency and Reflection is more crucial in Bryce for Windows, whether or not the Refract Index is set to 100 or any number other than 100. It's all too easy to set the sliders for those channels so high that more light reflects off the object than would be physically possible in the real world. You'll be able to recognize a too-bright object when you see it.

Also, when it comes to Reflection, there is an additional difference between the Windows and Macintosh versions. The Windows version has an additional control called Metallicity. Metallicity modifies the manner in which an object reflects light. Since Metallicity concerns itself with the object's color, I'll tell all in the next section when I discuss color.

Bump

Bump is lumped together in the optics & bump category because it, too, is not a normal-basic-opaque surface. In order to convey the impression that the surface has tactile texture, the Bump Height channel tells the renderer to create an optical illusion. But it doesn't split the ray during rendering. Mostly Bump Height is in this category because it doesn't easily fit in anywhere else. Like the optics, Bump Height can be render-intensive. Since Bump Height requires additional texture information to wield its effect, and since we've not yet talked about Texture Sources, then that's all I have to say about that for now, Forrest Bump. Would you like a chocolate?

Color

Here is the color of the object; whether RGB, or yellow-magenta these four of ten channels that comprise the three elements to the surface of the object that Jack built.

The color channels determine how the object's surface will be colored. What color bounces off the object and to your eyes? The color channels echo the illumination channels, with one addition: Transparent Color. Transparent Color determines the color that passes through the object when the Refract Index is set to anything other than 100. For each of the different illumination types, determine a color. There is a color swatch for each.

Of course, the colors you set for your object in the color channels depend also on the amount of illumination for that corresponding channel. If you wanted to have, say, shocking pink Ambient Color but the Ambience slider is set to 0, then you won't see any shocking pink, since the object is not responding to ambient lighting at all.

Before I discuss the different individual color channels, I want to discuss the Bryce color picker.

The Bryce Color Pickers

There are two types of color pickers in Bryce. The first is the pop-up color picker. Press the mouse on any of the color swatch areas in the Materials Composer (as well as the Sky & Fog Palette and the Edit Lights dialog box, both introduced in subsequent chapters) and up it pops. Drag to your desired color and release. The left half is a fully saturated spectrum, and the right half is a desaturated spectrum, very handy for more subdued coloring in nature scenery.

To access the second color picker, hold down the Option key (Macintosh) or Alt key (Windows) and click again on the color swatch. (Although the Windows version of Bryce will access the second color picker from the Sky & Fog Palette, the changes made in the color picker will not "take.") This one adjusts with sliders and gives you a choice of four different color models: Red Green Blue (RGB), Hue Luminance (Lightness) Saturation (HLS), Hue Saturation Value (HSV), and Cyan Magenta Yellow (CMY). For Brycean color subtlety, I like the HLS and HSV pickers, and of those, prefer the HLS (see Figure 9–10a).

Drag on the Saturation (S) slider to pull the saturation back (see Figure 9–10b). With dark colors, that's probably all that is needed. With lighter colors, de-saturating

Figure 9–10 De-saturating light colors: a) Original saturated color; b) pulling back saturation; c) increasing lightness.

the color will make it darker, and you may need to bring up the Lightness (L) to get back in the same general range (see Figure 9–10c).

You may continue to go color-shopping at this point if you like. Once you find an acceptable level of saturation and lightness, drag around the Hue (H) slider to find a different hue in the same general range.

For those who are CMYK oriented, the CMY color picker is not a CMYK picker with a missing K. It is the complementary side of the RGB picker. Red's complement is cyan, green's is magenta, and blue's is yellow. Select a color and look at it with the RGB slider and then the CMY slider. They're opposite. If there's a color that will be outside of the CMYK gamut by RGB standards, it will also be outside the CMYK gamut in the CMY color picker.

Color Picker Gripe

When using the pop-up color picker, you can also select a color from anywhere on your screen, assuming that you can get out of the Materials Composer to do so (this is easier if you have a two-monitor setup, or when selecting colors from swatches available elsewhere in Bryce). The Materials Composer is a separate room so you're cut off from anything else on the Mac. Although the color picker— in theory—allows you to select a color from anywhere, you cannot select from anything other than the Materials Composer interface. (There is a way to get around this for textures, however. I'll discuss it later when I discuss the Texture Editor.) I have a gripe about the color picker and its limitations to only the Materials Composer user interface. There is no significant white area to choose from. If you want to choose black or middle gray it's easy enough. Granted, the color picker has white but you have to aim for a very small area that's one pixels wide. (Actually, while double-checking the white strip, I discovered that there is no absolute white anywhere in the color picker. You can select 254 254 254 but not 255 255 255 using the color picker. Yikes!) My solution has been to modify the look of the Materials Composer user interface slightly. Figure 9–11 shows my personal Materials Composer, with a white strip below the title area. Dragging precisely to sample white (pure white, at that!) is no longer a major drag. (If you're on a Macintosh and want to make your Materials Composer look like mine, the altered PICT resource is on the CD-ROM in the Bryce Utilities > Pict Resources folder. You need to use ResEdit to change it; the standard ResEdit disclaimers apply. Windows users cannot make a change to the software's user interface.)

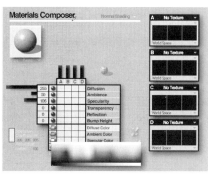

Figure 9–11 My customized Materials Composer user interface, with a white strip at the top for easy white color picking.

Diffuse and Ambient Color

Diffuse Color is the color of the object when it is lit by diffuse light. This is the color of the object when it is directly lit. Ambient Color is the overall color, but primarily the color that you see when the object is in shadow. These two colors, as a rule, are the same when you want to convey the sense of a uniformly colored object. However, you needn't limit yourself to making the Diffusion and Ambient Colors identical. Setting a different color makes an interesting color shift, much like the fabric weave that shifts between two colors. Figure C9–12 shows a set of objects with identical illumination settings but different Diffuse and Ambient Color settings. The colors are mixes and matches of blue, pink, and white. The most brilliant pure colors are the objects with identical Diffuse and Ambient Colors. The outside objects are Diffuse Color and Ambient is white. The center two are a mix of Diffuse and Ambient.

When you use two different colors, a darker Ambient Color will give the object more contrast. When the Ambient Color is lighter, the object looks washed out and flatter—as opposed to strikingly dimensional. (You'll revisit the advantages of a darker Ambient Color when you adorn your entire environment in the Sky & Fog Palette settings, in Chapter 10.) In Figure C9–13, there are sets of objects whose Ambient Colors range in the grayscale, for a diffuse that's blue and diffuse that's the default gray. The outside set of objects has an Ambient Color of white. The Ambient Color gets darker for the objects located closer to the center.

Specular Color (and Specular Coefficient)

The hot spot's color is not the object's color so much as the color of the light that strikes the object. Of course, depending on the nature of the surface you are trying to create, the Specular Color adds a nuance of surface texture, polish, or sheen. In Figure C9–14, the brightly polished objects have high specular sheens or gloss that suggest either wetness or shellac. Adding a touch of Reflection heightens the effect.

Specular Color and the Specular Coefficient color interact to make the size and color of the hot spot. The colors are combined, and, depending on the specific colors, one may augment, complement, or counteract the other. Diffuse and Ambient Colors also play parts in the interaction.

To understand the color interaction dynamics of the Specular Coefficient and the object, it helps to understand additive (RGB) color theory. The sum of all colors is white. Earlier you saw that if you have the Specular Coefficient set too high, you'll get a bright white highlight with a crisp border between "lit" and "unlit." So how can you get a nice strong white without that harsh border? Use the complementary color. In Figure C9–15, Top Row, the Diffuse and Ambient Colors are red. There are different Specular Coefficient settings for the objects. The left two are gray shades. The center two are cyan shades. The right two are the other RGB complements: yellow and magenta. But those center two don't show any cyan at all; they look to be a nice, bright white. Why? Red plus cyan equals white! This is a way to tiptoe around the "if it's too bright, you'll get a harsh border" situation. Notice that in the halo around the two on the right there is a more intense red. That is because yellow is red plus green, and magenta is red plus blue. The red of the Diffuse and Ambient is intensified by the red in the yellow and magenta.

The middle and bottom rows of Figure C9–15 are variations on the top row. The Specular settings (both Specular Color and Specular Coefficient) are identical, but the middle row's Ambient Color is white and the bottom row's Diffuse Color is white. When the Specular Coefficient is not the exact complement of the Diffuse and Ambient Color, you can see a bit of the Specular Coefficient color. Notice the center two objects in the bottom two rows. Because there is white as either the Diffuse or Ambient Color, you can notice an ever-so-slight tint of cyan.

When setting the Specular Coefficient and using the alternative color picker, use the HLS slider. HLS stands for Hue, Luminance, Saturation. Hue is separated from the others. If you want to create a bright specular highlight, then set the L and S sliders no higher than the low-to-mid 220s. If one of the sliders is lower, in the middle of the range, then the other one can go as high as 235. Any higher than that and you'll end up with your friend the harsh-edged highlight.

The same extreme highlight as the white is generated when one or two of the RGB values exceeds the 250 threshold. See Figure C9–16a.

In the same way that the Specular Coefficient interacts with the Diffuse and Ambient Color, the Specular Coefficient color and the Specular Color also interact. In Figure C9–16b, an object with a blue Specular Coefficient interacts with a "neighbor" Specular Color, cyan (cyan is the combination of blue and green). The entire intensity range of that hue is shown. Conversely, Figure C9–16c demonstrates the interaction of the blue Specular Coefficient with its complement, yellow. As the intensity of the hue decreases, the combination of both colors sucks any hue out of the Specular Coefficient.

Transparent Color

Transparent Color is the color of the object when light passes through it. Transparent Color will be applied to an object when there is a Transparency setting. The higher the setting, the more you will see the Transparent Color. Not only does the Transparent Color affect the color of the transparent object, but the shadow that is cast by the transparent object will be the Transparent Color. (The Sky & Fog Palette setting for global shadows determines the strength of the shadow.)

Transparent Color does not operate on its own. As already mentioned, it is tied to the Transparency setting. In addition, Transparent Color is tied to the setting in the Refract Index. The Diffuse Color is also incorporated into the object's color, *even if there is no Diffusion setting!* The manner in which Diffuse Color is applied to the object depends both on the Refract Index setting and which platform you're working on. The Macintosh and Windows versions treat Transparent Color a little differently.

Macintosh and Windows Differences

For the Macintosh version of Bryce, Transparent Color will show only when light bends as it passes through that object. Transparent Color will have no effect on an object when the Refract Index is set to 100 (air). But once you set the Refract Index to 99 or below or to 101 and above, the Transparent Color will have an effect on the object's color.

For the Windows version of Bryce, Transparent Color will always have an effect on the object's color, as long as the Transparency setting is something other than 0. The mix of Transparent Color to Diffuse Color changes depending on the Refract Index.

For both versions of Bryce, when there is a Refract Index setting above 100, the Transparent and Diffuse Colors combine to form a new color. In Figure C9–17a and b, there are several sets of transparent spheres. You can always tell what the Transparent Color is, since that is the color of the shadow cast by the object. The same Diffuse Color is used for the entire row of objects. The object at the right end of the row is the Diffuse Color only; the Transparent Color is white. So use it to evaluate all the other color interactions for that row. For Diffuse and Transparent Color, complementary colors combine to make the object darker. In Figure C9–17a, where there is a row each of red, green, and blue, three of the color variations are extremely dark. The dark ones are the other primaries and the secondary that is the combination of the two other primaries. So for red, the dark ones are green and blue, and the combination of green and blue, cyan, which so happens to be the complement of red. Notice that the front row is a pleasant mocha-brown, a color that liberally mixes each of the primaries. There is no complementary cancellation, so all six Transparent Colors interact with the Diffuse Color in a pleasing way. Figure C9–17b is a similar set of spheres, only the colors are more of the secondary range—orange, purple, and aqua (yellow, cyan and magenta).

If you were to take those objects, change them to cylinders, and make them taller, the result on a Macintosh has Diffuse Color at the top and there is a bit of the Transparent Color at the bottom. (See Figure C9–18a.) If the object is shallow, then you'll see more of the Transparent Color, and not the Diffuse Color. This is the basis for Bryce's water coloring that responds to depth. In Figure C9–18b, the same colors are used as in C9-18a. Each terrain indentation is covered by a disk. The disk is set to maximum Transparency, with a Refract Index in the 130's, and the same Diffuse and Transparent Colors as in the cylinders in part a. The Transparent Color is more noticeable in the shallower areas, and the Diffuse is strongest where it's deep. When you are experimenting with your own waters, make the Transparent Color lighter than the Diffuse. If you set them up so that they're complementary, you won't be able to see as much of the Transparent Color through the darkened Diffuse Color.

The Windows version of Bryce shows both Transparent and Diffuse Colors, but there is *no* transparent depth effect. Compare Figure C9–18b (Macintosh depth version) and Figure C9–18c (Windows version); there is no shallow transparent color in the Windows version. The Windows version modulates the Transparent

Color and the Diffuse Color depending on the Refract Index setting. Figure C9–19 shows a series of objects in the Windows version, with the Refract Index settings indicated. The Transparent Color (yellow) is present when the Refract Index is set to 0. As the Refract Index increases, the two colors are mixed together as the Diffuse Color (magenta) gains in strength. The Refract Index indicates that the substance changes—the higher the Refract Index number, the harder the substance. When the substance is harder, it slows down the light as it is passing through the object. The result is more of the Diffuse Color.

Metallicity (Windows Only)

The Windows version of Bryce has an additional Easter Egg control—Metallicity. Access it by pressing the Ctrl+Alt keys and clicking to the right of the preview window (see Figure 9–20). The control will appear, with the word Metallicity and a numeric setting that ranges from 0-255. Dragging left and right on the control changes the numbers.

Figure 9–20 Access the hidden Metallicity control in Bryce Windows by Ctrl+Alt-clicking in the indicated area.

So what does it do? What is the significance of Metallicity? As the name implies, Metallicity provides additional controls for metallic effects. It works in conjunction with two other controls in the Materials Composer—Reflection and Diffuse Color. The inclusion of Reflection is rather self-evident, because metallic surfaces are generally reflective. Not all reflective metallic surfaces provide exact mirror-images of the world around them. Copper, gold, steel, bronze, and brass all reflect their surrounding environs, but the reflection includes the color of the metal, too. This is where Diffuse Color comes in. Metallicity acts as a filter controlling how much the Diffuse Color is included in the reflection. When Metallicity is set to 0, the Diffuse Color does not show at all. So the reflection is like a mirror. When there is a Metallicity setting, the reflection takes place through the Diffuse Color. A Metallicity setting of 255 provides the strongest color cast by the Diffuse Color. When Metallicity is active, it doesn't matter whether there is any setting for Diffusion channel (illumination); Diffuse Color will still be seen through the reflection. (It's similar to the way that Diffuse Color is seen in an object with Transparency when the Refract Index causes the two colors to interact.) Figure C9–21 demonstrates the range of Metallicity. There are two rows; the bottom row has some diffuse illumination in addition to maximum Reflection; the top row has no diffuse illumination. The range of Metallicity settings is shown. The objects on the left have no Metallicity, so the reflections are mirror-like. The objects on the right have maximum Metallicity, and reflection takes on a gold cast.

NON-UNIFORM SURFACE APPEARANCE

This is one of the four Texture sources, containing color and alpha and bump; these will drive any of the ten channels that comprise the three elements to the surface of the object that Jack built.

So far, everything I've said has concerned an object with a uniform surface appearance. How do you get from uniform to non-uniform, where all the power of the Materials Composer lies? Right there in the grid, in a slightly more unfolded form (see Figure 9–22)! The grid has expanded slightly to include an A column. A black box with a corresponding A has shown up to the right of the grid. That black box with three windows to the right is the Texture Source. No doubt you've noticed that there are a

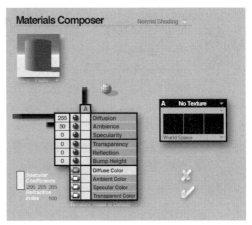

Figure 9–22 The Materials Composer user interface, unfolded a step to show the grid for column A as well as Texture Source A.

total of four windows in the actual Materials Composer interface, but for the unfolding explanation of the Materials Composer, I'll focus on the first one.

The Texture Source

The Texture Source allows you to select a texture to drive some or all channels of your surface material. There are several parts to the Texture Source (see Figure 9–23). There are three pop-up menus and three windows. The first pop-up menu is the Texture Source's title bar. The title bar identifies which source it is (in this case, A), and the pop-up menu allows you to select what type of texture to use: None, 2D Picture, or 3D Texture. You know all about None already; up to this point this chapter has discussed nothing but None. (Don't confuse this with a chapter that has gone many pages in the attempt to describe nothing.) The 2D Picture source uses images from the Pictures Library, and the 3D Textures uses textures created by Bryce's powerful texture generator.

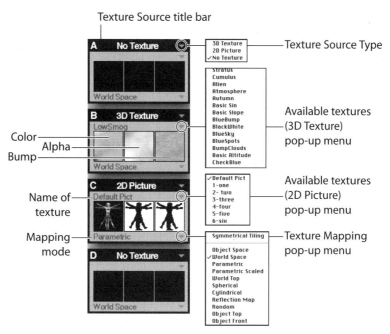

Figure 9–23 The Texture Source, with all pieces identified.

The three windows show the three properties of the texture. The left is color, the center is alpha, and the right is bump. These three texture properties are used in the ten different material channels to drive the amounts or colors using the non-uniform aspects of the texture. Figure 9–24 shows which Texture Source properties provide the information for which channel. illumination and optics are driven by the texture's alpha information, Bump Height is driven by the texture's bump, and the color is driven by the texture's color.

Textures created in Bryce's 3D Texture Generator have the three different output types that correspond to the three texture properties. I'll delve into all the gory details of creating and editing 3D Textures in the Deep Texture Editor in the latter half of this chapter, but will mention here that there are some terminology differences with the texture output types. Color is color (no difference). What is called alpha here in the Materials Composer is called Value in the Deep Texture Editor. What is called bump here in the Materials Composer is called Normale (from the term "surface normals," but in the DTE it has an *accent français*, as this application is the brainchild of a Frenchman). The 2D Picture textures have both color and an alpha channel; alpha is used for both alpha and bump information.

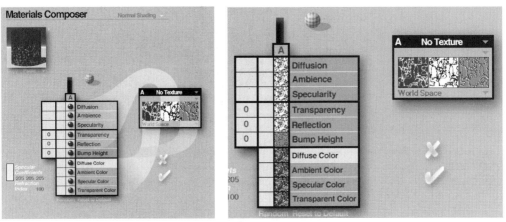

Figure 9–24 Three texture properties—color, alpha, and bump, supply the information to the color, illumination and optics, and Bump Height channels of the texture.

(You may want, then, to duplicate your picture source if you require different alpha and bump information for a given texture.)

Hang onto your alpha hats for a moment, because there's a very confusing twist to the alpha settings. There will come a point where the alpha's grayscale values determine certain matters (I begin to tell all in the next section). If alpha is white, it means one thing. If it's black, it means another. So when you are trying to wrap your mind around the significance of what does what, Bryce throws a banana peel on the floor for you to slip on if you're not careful. The alpha information for the 2D Picture is the reverse of the alpha information for the 3D Texture. When 3D Texture alpha equals black, the identical alpha situation for 2D Picture is alpha equals white. Watch your step!

The pop-up menu underneath the title bar allows you to choose the particular Texture Source: If 3D Texture is selected, then the pop-up menu will list all of the possible 3D Texture Sources. If 2D Texture is selected, then the pop-up menu will list all the available pictures from the Picture Library. If None is selected, the pop-up menu will list the 3D Texture Sources. So for a quick way to select a 3D Texture Source, go straight to this menu; you'll select both the type (3D Texture) and the particular texture you want.

The third pop-up menu below the three black preview windows selects the mapping of the texture. Mapping answers the question, "How will this texture be applied to my object?".

For 3D Solid Textures, the default answer is World Space (the Texture Sources will display "World Space" even if no texture is selected).

In World Space, the texture has an orientation in the world. Any object that uses the texture—no matter what its position, rotation, or elevation—will take on the texture for that coordinate in the world. Move the object, and the object's texture will change to reflect what the texture is like in that other part of the world. This explains why Bryce provides seamless textural transitions between the ground plane and the terrain that rests on the ground. They both use the same texture in World Space. (It also explains why your objects change when they move if you are attempting to do stop-motion animation in Bryce.) The objects in Figure 9–25a are all mapped with World Space using Sine Layers. Notice how the stripe changes as the objects are higher or lower in elevation. There are ghost images of the objects as they are moved

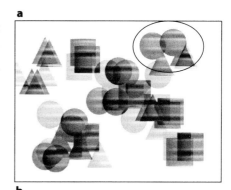

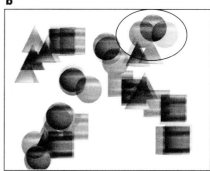

Figure 9–25 Mapping spaces: a) The surfaces of objects mapped to World Space change when the objects are moved; b) The surfaces of objects mapped to Object Space do not change when the objects are moved.

around in the World Space. The texture belongs to the world, and the object's surface changes as its position in the world changes.

In contrast, the same set of objects mapped in Object Space will display the texture the same way no matter what the position, as Figure 9–25b shows (with the same ghosted moved images, for comparison).

A corollary to World Space is World Space Top. This reorients the direction of the overall space. It comes in handy in cases where a perfectly decent texture is oriented toward the "front" in World Space so that a flat surface, like a ground plane, has only variegated stripes. In Figure 9–26a, a set of objects facing in all directions has had the texture "Mushrooms" applied to it in the standard World Space mapping. Notice how the "front" has the full benefit of the texture but on flat horizontal surfaces, all you see are stripes. Figure 9–26b has the same texture

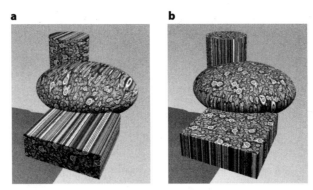

Figure 9–26 A texture mapped in a) World Space and b) World Space Top.

mapped to World Space Top, which reorients World Space from "Front" to "Top," and the texture is visible on horizontal flat surfaces. Make World Space Top your first recourse when you find a great texture for your ground plane, but the texture turns out to look like an incomprehensible set of lines.

The answer to the "How will this texture be applied to my object?" question for 2D Picture textures is Parametric. Parametric mapping is proportional to the object. Figure C9–27 shows a set of Bryce objects with a picture texture mapped to them. The picture is different at top, bottom, left, and right, so that the mapping manner is clear for all the different objects. If the object gets larger, the picture is enlarged as well.

With the list of options in the mapping pop-up menu, no doubt you notice some old friends: World Space and Object Space. (No, there is no such thing as mapping a texture onto an object based on Camera Space!) Are these identical to the World and Object Spaces of the Edit Palette? Well, no and yes. They are similar in that World Space is oriented according to the Bryce world. Object Space is oriented to the object. They are not, however, sensitive to whichever option is selected in the Edit Palette pop-up menus.

Also found in the Mapping pop-up menu is the Symmetric Tiling option. If you will have more than one image on the face of an object, then choose from symmetric tiling, which makes smooth transitions between edges, or the default, non-symmetric tiling, which butts bottom against top, left against right. In Figure 9–28, both options are shown in the cubes with the Bryce skates. Brrr!

For the sake of explanation and demonstration from here on out, I will be drawing from a set of 12 3D Texture Sources. Each one is quite distinct in color and value. Figure C9–29 shows them with their three properties and provides the names so that you may follow along and match the examples you see in these images.

Figure 9–28 Tiling for 2D Picture textures, non-symmetric and symmetric tiling.

Texture-Driven Illumination

How does the texture's alpha property correspond to the texture? If the blue marker is in the left column of the Materials Composer grid (no texture), then the slider for that attribute will control the amount. When you click in the A column to place the marker there, your slider goes away. You may have a global setting for, say Diffusion, or your object's response to Diffuse light may be driven by a texture. It's an either/or relationship; the lighting is determined *either* by the slider for global illumination *or* by the texture for non-uniform illumination, but never by both.

When a marker is placed in the A column (or one of the other columns) then the alpha of the texture(s) will control where and how much of that lighting property affects the object. Where the texture's value is white, there is the maximum

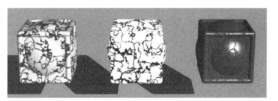

Figure 9–30 Texture-driven illumination: Diffusion, Ambience, and Specularity.

response to lighting effect. It's the same as pulling out the slider to the 200 and higher range. Where the texture's value is black, the response light is at a minimum, the same as if the slider were at 30 or below. See Figure 9–30.

For the most part, illumination channels set to global amounts make the majority of Bryce objects. When would you want to use textures for illumination?

- *Terrains that are "wet."* Driving Diffusion with a 2D Picture texture that matches the terrain's form will make terrain darker at lower elevations, giving the appearance of wetness near a body of water where water has seeped into the ground. The mud in Figure 8–39 and the water pond in Figures 9–49 and C9–50 both have their wet edges created by a Diffusion texture.

- *Dirty or scuffed surfaces.* Driving Diffusion with a lower-contrast texture (such as Low Smog) will result in surfaces with a mottled, dirty appearance. The objects in Figure 9–41 use texture-driven diffuse illumination for a dirty, industrial look.

- *Blinding snow.* Driving Ambient with the alpha information of certain textures will make brilliant snow. The ground (non-snow) is generally dark, with low Ambience. But snow is brilliantly white. To make the white snow bright, assign a high ambient lighting property only to the area that has the snow. So, having the snow texture's value drive the amount of Ambience will result in the snow that is blindingly light, while the rocky places that peek through the snow stay darker and dimmer. The snow in the Brrryce skates image (see Figure 9–28) uses a snow with texture-driven Ambience.

> **ULTRA POWER-USER TIP:** *Bryce's already-created snow texture presets were made back in a day where the development version of the software allowed for a small bit of global Ambience in addition to texture-driven Ambience. The current result is that the snow is fully ambient and that areas without snow have no Ambience. The rocky part of the terrain cannot be seen in the shade, as there is no residual Ambience there. Create a second texture based on the first, and adjust the value so that the darkest output is not black, but a dark gray, allowing a bit of ambient illumination to show in the rocky areas. Check out several examples in the folder "Snow Cone" in this chapter's folder on the CD-ROM. If this was Greek to you, read the second half of this chapter several times and then try to make the second texture yourself. You're welcome to peek at the material on the CD-ROM, Greek or no Greek.*

- *Textured Sheen.* Driving Specular with the alpha information of certain textures provides additional detail. For a brushed metal surface without the render cost of Bump Height (or in addition to Bump Height), a textured Specular highlight provides clues to the nature of the object's matter. It can be dewy and wet, or textured, or something else besides. Figure 9–31 shows a sphere and a torus, each with different Specularity textures. See how much information is conveyed in the different pattern of shiny highlights?

Figure 9–31 Texture-driven Specularity provides additional clues about what the object is made of.

Texture-Driven Optics

The optics channels likewise use the texture's alpha properties as the basis for non-uniform Transparency or Reflection in an object's surface. The optics channels do not have an either/or relationship between the slider and the texture when it comes to what drives the intensity of the effect. They are "both/and," where information about the optic channel is derived by *both* the slider *and* the Texture Source. Figure 9–32 shows an example of each type of texture-driven optic material.

Figure 9–32 Texture-driven optics: Reflection, Transparency, and Bump Height.

In Transparency, the object is transparent when the texture's value is black. When the value is white, the object is opaque. (The meaning of black or white is reversed for 2D Picture textures.) No matter where the slider is set, black value equals a transparent object. The slider affects the Transparency of the *remainder* of the object. Or, to state it differently, the slider affects the global Transparency of the object, but, since part of the object is already transparent, it can't affect that. In the case of Reflection, when the texture's value is black, the object is immune to the actions of the Reflection slider. When the texture's value is white, the object is sensitive to the amount of Reflection determined by the slider. In addition to being sensitive to the Reflection amount, the white areas are no longer responsive to diffuse illumination. In order to see the reflection, however, the slider must be invoked. The strength of the slider determines the amount that the reflect areas (white alpha) will reflect. For 2D Picture Texture Sources, the situation is reversed.

Figure 9–33 How Reflection looks under different circumstances. The two objects on the left are for reference; the center two objects have standard high Diffusion with maximum (top) and minimum (bottom) Reflection; the right two objects have Reflection settings identical to the center objects, using low Diffusion settings.

The objects in Figure 9–33 show the range of possibilities for the Reflection slider. The left column of objects is for reference. The top object shows the alpha information for that Texture Source. The bottom object shows a plain-jane object with Diffusion. The center row of objects places the texture in the Reflection channel. The bottom object in that row has the Reflection amount set to zero and the top object has the Reflection amount set to maximum (255). The right row is identical to the middle row, except that no Diffusion is set. The bottom object is uniformly dark. Notice how the gray shade matches the dark areas of the bottom object in the center row. The reflection area has no Diffusion, and the normal area has no Diffusion. Of course the top right object has Reflection set to maximum.

Texture-Driven Bump Height

Bump Height determines how much your surface will have perturbances. Of all the ten channels, Bump Height stands alone when it comes to certain matters. Bump Height is the only channel driven by the third texture property, bump. (In the case of picture based textures, it is driven by the image's alpha channel.) In addition, this channel *requires* a Texture Source to affect the object's surface. There is no such thing as a global bump in the same way that there is global Diffusion or global Reflection. It doesn't matter if the slider is pulled all the way out to a maximum of 255; if there is no texture driving bump, the net result will be nothing. Flat. Smooth. Plain. Your tactile illusions require that the marker move from the left "home" position to one of the texture columns. In addition to requiring a Texture Source, you must also set the slider to something other than zero in order to see the bump effect. You can set the bump to be positive (drag to the left for the red slider) or negative (drag to the right, the slider turns green and what was poked out now pokes in). In Figure 9–34, an object is bumped positively and negatively.

Figure 9–34 Object with four different Bump Height settings.

The actual surface geometry of the object is not changed in bumping. Bryce takes the bump information and very smartly "embosses" the surface appearance to create the illusion of all those perturbances. Bump Height makes rendering costly, since information is used to tell Bryce to move a texture on the y-axis, as well as on the x- and z-axes. Additional calculations occur in order to create the appearance of displacement on the object's surface. When working with the non-terrain primitives, you won't see little perturbances if you look closely at the edges of objects. (This is also an excellent argument for creating a terrain, no matter how flat, for extreme foreground ground when you have anything more than a mild bump.)

Texture-Driven Color

In the color channels, texture-driven color allows you to color your object using different Texture Sources. You can pick and choose which color will show for which type of illumination. Where the object is lit by diffuse light, there is one type of coloring. Where the object is illuminated by Ambience, there is another (or the same) type of coloring. Where the object is lit by Specularity, there can be a third type of coloring. If the object is transparent and the Refract Index is set to anything other than 100, then the color of light that passes through the object can be set using the Transparent Color.

The color of the object for any color channel is an either/or situation: Either you have a uniform color set by the color swatch, or you have a color driven by one or more of the Texture Sources. (When you render your scene with Textures Off, any texture colors "go away" and the object is rendered using the uniform color set in the color swatch.)

Of course, texture-driven color is the same as uniform color: the amount of illumination for that channel will also determine the strength of the color for that channel.

Figure C9–35 is a series of studies for placing a single Texture Source into the different channels. In the top row, the Red Fractal Texture Source is first placed in the Diffuse Color channel, then the Ambient, then Specular. Each channel is shown twice with a larger Specular Coefficient and a smaller one, so that you can see how the amount of Specular Coefficient interacts with the other illumination and color parameters.

To see which is doing what, you need to know where ambient, specular, and diffuse illumination fall on the object. You see the Ambient Color where the object is in shadow. You see the Diffuse Color where the object is lit by the sun (or light source). The specular highlight is the hot spot, though the hot spot can grow or shrink depending on the coefficient.

The Specular Coefficient can be used in conjunction with the color controls to get effects that you wouldn't first think of as shiny and glossy. As you can see by the figures identified as Specular Color in the top row of Figure C9–35, when the Specular Color channel is driven by the texture, you can have a nice brightly lit area. This technique was used to get the high contrast between sunlight and shadow in the image of the globe in Figure C10–35 (in the Sky chapter's color section). Specular Color was driven by the texture, with a bright Specular Coefficient to create the nice, crisp boundary between sunlight and shadow.

The bottom row of Figure C9–35 shows texture-driven color for two out of the three channels. The third channel's color is a uniform color. For most of the typical Bryce objects, the same Texture Source drives both the Diffuse and Ambient Color channels, with a uniform color for the hot spot.

What's this about three color channels when there is plainly a fourth—Transparent Color—in the Materials Composer grid? Since Transparent Color responds to an optic situation, Transparency, along with the presence of a Refract Index set to something other than 100, I don't automatically include it in with the Big Three illumination makers. But I do include it: Figure C9–36 shows texture-driven Transparent Color in addition to two other texture-driven color channels as an adaptation of Figure C9–35b.

Like uniform Transparent Color, texture-driven Transparent Color interacts with Diffuse Color to create a new hybrid color. Figure C9–37 shows the interaction of colors. The samples demonstrate how the Transparent Color can be the only texture-driven color channel, where others are uniformly colored. In order to see the Transparent Color in the Macintosh version of Bryce, it's necessary to have both Transparency, and a Refract Index setting. The sets of objects in Figure 9–38a and b (rendered on a Macintosh) have different Refract Index settings and different Transparency settings. In part a, the diffuse and Ambient Colors are not texture driven (note what happens when the objects are opaque, and when the Refract Index setting is 100!). Part b shows the same settings, but with the Diffuse Color channel also being driven from the texture information. Note that when there is no refraction, but there is Transparency, the Diffuse Color casts its own shadow. The Windows version will show the Transparent Color even at a Refract Index setting of 100.

Frequency

At the top of each Texture Source column in the grid is a Frequency slider, along with the numerical equivalent for the frequency. Frequency determines the texture's size. Drag up on the slider to increase the frequency, drag down to decrease it. Or click in the box where the number is, to directly type in numbers from the keyboard.

Although the slider range is from 0-99, you can enter negative numbers and numbers higher than 100.

In a sneak preview of the discussion of multiple Texture Sources (see the next section) you can adjust frequency for each Texture Source individually, and then adjust the global frequency using the Frequency control (small sphere).

Frequency usually needs to be set higher for objects that are closer to the camera than for those that are far away. With certain textures that have snow, the frequency amount will also determine the snow's altitude. The higher the frequency, the lower the snow level descends.

BUT WAIT! THERE'S MORE!

There's more to the grid than what I've described. There are four Texture Sources in the grid, to be precise. (See Figure 9–39, an image of the Materials Composer interface that actually matches what *you* see when *you* access it.) When it comes to those four Texture Sources and placing the markers to have textures drive certain

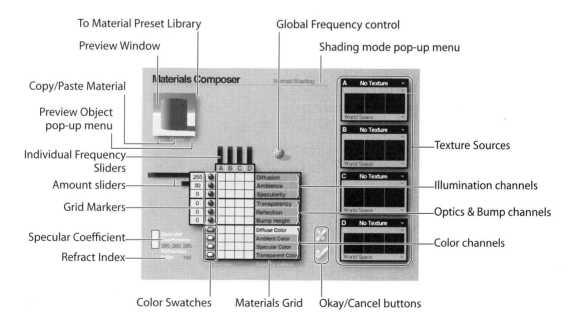

Figure 9–39 The bona fide real honest-to-goodness Materials Composer. Accept no substitutes (unless they are interpretive illustrations that help you understand how the whole thing works!).

channels of the surface material, you can invent all sorts of interesting ways to mix and match them. There are three strategies for combining your Texture Sources: mix and match, A-B blend, and A-B-C blend.

Mix and Match

This is the mix and match multiple method to use willy-nilly all four Texture Sources to drive the ten channels that comprise the three elements to the surface of the object that Jack built.

Combine different Texture Sources to drive different channels. For instance, you can choose one Texture Source to drive the Transparency of the object, while choosing another one to drive your Bump Height, Diffuse Color, and Ambient Color. Combine that with, say, a 2D Picture-based alpha to drive the Diffusion channel, and you've got yourself one interesting complex surface material. This is the mix and match method.

Taking up the texture color refrain from the earlier section, you needn't necessarily have both the Ambient and Diffuse Color channels driven by the same texture. Figure C9–40 shows some different mix and match possibilities between two Texture Sources—Marble and LowSmog.

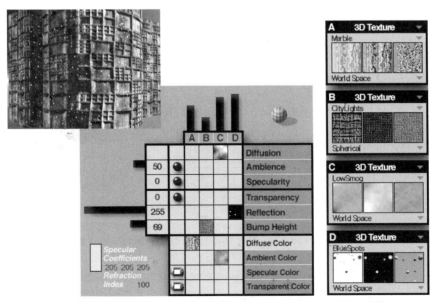

Figure 9–41 The mix and match method of assigning textures to drive different material channels.

Figure 9–41 shows a possible set of options for a material. For this I have taken liberties with the user-interface in hopes of reinforcing the idea that the different sources are called upon to do different things when they are selected.

A-B Blending

The is the blend mode A to B, that mixes two Texture Sources according to height, drawing from two of the four Texture Sources containing color and alpha and bump; these will drive any of the ten channels that comprise the three elements to the surface of the object that Jack built.

The second and third methods of combining your Texture Sources get a bit craftier. No doubt you look at the grid and say, "But is there any way to combine more than one source into the same channel?" There certainly is! There are two possible combinations: A and B, and A, B, and C. Press the Control key (Macintosh) or Ctrl+Alt keys (Windows) and click in the B column. Markers are placed in both the A and B columns. Or press the Control key or Ctrl+Alt keys and click in the C column to place markers in A, B and C. Why are there only those two combinations? Why not B, C, and D? Read on!

When two Texture Sources are combined into one material channel, the sources are blended together. The two possible combinations correspond to the two blending types. But don't think that two mere blending types constricts you unnecessarily. The possibilities are vast. For the first A-B combination, the two Texture Sources are blended together via altitude. Source A is in full effect at ground level. Moving up in altitude, A begins blending into B. At the highest altitude, B is in full effect. In Figure 9–42, the Texture Source A (Mushrooms) and Texture Source B (City Lights) are combined.

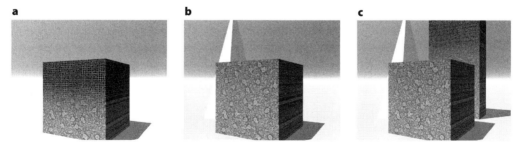

a **b** **c**

Figure 9–42 Combining two textures in an A-B Blend: a) The A-B blend applied to one existing object; b) the presence of another object skews the blend between textures A and B; c) the pyramid shows where and how the blend has been skewed.

What constitutes the lowest point? The highest point? It is not the height of the object. The lowest and highest points are calculated based on the total altitude of objects in your scene. In Figure 9–42b, the only thing that changed from Figure 9–42a was the addition of a pyramid that was higher, forcing the total altitude higher, and remapping the blend between the two Texture Sources. Depending on your scene composition, you might run the risk of adding just that last one object and ruining your altitude-blend-mapping.

Figure 9–43 shows the grid with the textures and the blend mode pre-interpreted for you.

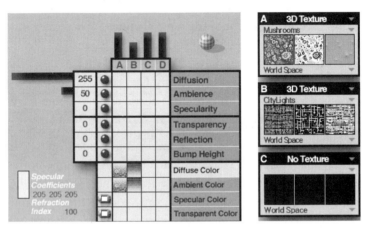

Figure 9–43 The A-B Blend in the Materials Composer, with the blend directions indicated in the Diffuse and Ambient Color channels.

A-B-C Blending

This is the blend mode A-B-C, that takes the alpha from Texture Source C as the basis to blend A and B to create a more complex multi-source texture drawing from three of the four Texture Sources containing color and alpha and bump; these will drive any of the ten channels that comprise the three elements to the surface of the object that Jack built.

The second multiple Texture Source blend option (and the third grid strategy overall) is the A-B-C blend. Like the A-B method, it is a blend between two Texture Sources. Instead of a straight altitude blend between them, the A-B-C blend uses the alpha information from the C source as the means to blend between the two A and B sources. In Figure 9–44, the placement of textures in the grid for the Diffuse Color and Ambient Color channels reflects which goes where. The A and B source textures are color, and the C texture is alpha information.

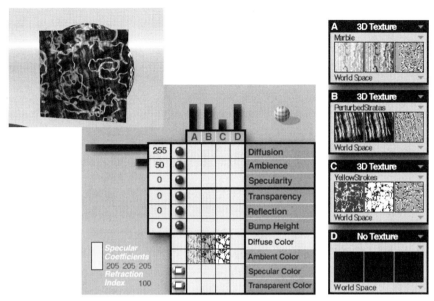

Figure 9–44 A-B-C blending: An A-B-C blend in the Materials Composer along with the rendered result.

This means that where Source C's alpha is black, the color from Source A is applied. Where Source C's alpha is white, the color from Source B is applied. Of course, in the case of 2D Picture textures, the black-white A-B is switched.

The A-B-C blend is extremely powerful. Consider that your 3D Texture Sources can also pay attention to altitude, slope, and orientation. Combine that with the basic textured noise and you have random patches of two different textures on your object.

When creating A-B-C textures, you needn't limit yourself to keeping the same mapping for all three Texture Sources. The marble tile steps in the Water Temple at Night image (shown in chapter 3, Camera and Scene, and in Chapter 11, "Bryce EnLightenment") use an A-B-C texture blend. The two marbles in A and B are set to map in World Space, but the Check Blue texture in Source C is set to Spherical Mapping. (The Texture Sources for that material are shown in Figure 9–48.)

Analysis of the "Mountain" Material Preset

The "Eternal Lake" image by Eric Wenger (on the application's splash screen) uses a by-now famous A-B-C Texture Source material. Indeed, I've seen this material preset used a lot in Bryce imagery; it's a beautiful surface material. Knowing how it was created will give you the courage to alter it and to come up with your own texture creations.

Create a terrain. Open the Materials Composer. In the Preset Library, select Planes & Terrains > Whole Mountain. Click OK to leave the Library and go back to the Materials Composer.

Take a look at what you've got here. There are three

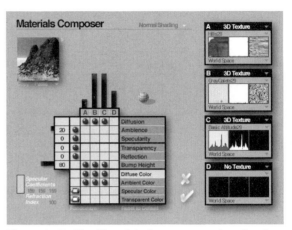

Figure 9–45 The Materials Composer settings for the Material Preset "Whole Mountain."

Texture Sources. Source A is a greenish, brushy texture. Source B is a pebbly light sandy texture. Source C has some spiky things and is colored wildly. (See Figure 9–45.) By now you know that when there are A-B-C blend textures, the color of C matters not a whit; the C source is there for the alpha information.

Just so you get a feel for what Source C is doing, try changing it momentarily. Select another texture. Try out Check Blue and Sin Layers. You may need to lower the frequency for Source C in the Materials Composer grid.

In Figure C9–46, I have created two additional terrains, and for each, I have replaced the Source C texture with Check Blue and Sin Layers. Both new textures are complex A-B-C textures. The new Source C texture determines the manner of variation between the sandy pebble texture and the green hill texture. Although the new variations are bizarre, they're instructive. The C Source is *the* switch for the two other textures. In the case of the original Whole Mountain preset, the C Source determines where it's pebbly and where there's vegetation. Mostly the pebbly part is lower and the vegetation is higher, but there are higher pockets where the pebbly part peeks through.

The Source C switch works for all three of the basic surface properties for this Whole Mountain material. (Reminder: the basic three properties are illumination, optics and bump, and color.) In Figure C9–47a through c, the three surface properties are isolated. The left terrain shows only the illumination, the center terrain shows bump, and the right terrain shows color only. In this way, the illumination, bump, and color information for Texture Sources A and B are consistent. If Source C determines that "A shows here" then A's Diffusion, Bump Height, Diffuse Color, and Ambient Color will all be there together.

The illumination example in Figure C9–47a has changes in the light and darkness of the terrain. The combined alpha channels of the A-B-C textures determine where the object responds completely to light (where it's white) or where it resists diffuse light (dark). At the bottom of the terrain, near ground level, the alpha is dark. The darkness corresponds with the bottoms of the green vegetation and the pebbly areas. The pebbles, when they reach ground level, are dark, or wet. This surface material was designed to be used with water.

The terrain in Figure C9–47b has only the bump information applied to it. Notice that it, too, changes according to the placement of the A Texture Source or the B Texture Source. The Bump Height information is varied from one texture to the other.

The terrain on the right (see Figure C9–47c) shows the color information. The lower part is sandy, and the higher part is green with streaks of brown. (Also, in places where the terrain is vertical, there is a brown rocky cliff color.) See how the entire bottom portion is a consistent sandy color? Compare how portions for the diffuse illumination example correspond to the same places for color. (Since these textures are mapped to the object in World Space, you won't see an exact correspondence of streaks to dark places from one terrain to the next.)

Figure C9–48a and b focuses on the coloring and diffuse illumination for each texture. Part a is the hilly texture and part b is the pebbly texture. For each of the two images, the left terrains show the texture color with uniformly bright diffuse lighting. The center terrain shows the texture color and also includes the texture-driven diffuse lighting, with lights and darks. The right terrain shows the final result, combining both Source A (hills) and Source B (pebbles) with illumination, bump, and color all combined.

> **TIP:** If you want to isolate one part of the surface properties to analyze which is doing what, then place all the other markers in the default "home" column in the Materials Composer grid. If you want to look at a texture for alpha only (to see what is driving illumination and optics for the object), then set the Diffuse and Ambient Colors to white (no textures), and have the textures drive the Diffusion and/or Ambience information. All other channel markers are in the home position. Include or omit texture-driven Ambience depending on whether you also want to see shadow portions of the object. In Figure C9–47, I wanted to show shadows, so I didn't include texture-driven Ambience. You can do the same thing to isolate the Bump Height information, or the color information. Each of the scene files for analysis of this material are in a folder called "Whole Mountain" in this chapter's folder on the CD-ROM.

I've already said that some portions are such-and-such close to sea level. But why are they so? Why is the area closest to sea level dark? Why does the pebbly texture fall mostly at the areas closer to sea level? The alpha information for each texture is paying attention to altitude. Herein lies the genius of the complex 3D Texture generator: your texture information is intelligent, and knows how high or how flat or which direction that part of the object's surface is, and the texture is adjusted accordingly. The altitude sensitivity is very integral to the final look of this texture. I won't go into the particulars of creating a texture with altitude sensitivity here; the second half of this chapter discusses that.

I will be examining the underlying textures in depth when I get to that part of the Deep Texture Editor.

You can adjust the different frequencies independently. This will become important when you use this texture. Depending on the scale of your terrain, the pebbles may be too big or too small. Since they're Source B, you can adjust the frequency for Source B and it will change the scale.

What about D?

Here's the forlorn Texture Source D—The Maverick of textures who goes it alone—
It will do whatever it pleases to apply color and alpha and bump; to drive the leftovers among
the ten channels that comprise the three elements to the surface of the object that Jack built.

In all this discussion, poor Source D has been neglected. Isn't there any special blend combination for D? No. D stands alone. The advantage to having one last Texture Source available is that you can tie up three textures for certain purposes and then tie up a fourth for a different purpose. A-B-C together can drive the color and bump information for a texture, while D drives, say, Diffusion. If you want a complex set of textures on a terrain to show wetness near a water source, then you have one remaining Texture Source card to play—Source D. Figure 9–49 shows the Materials Composer for a material where Texture Source D is used to drive Diffusion. (Again, I have taken liberties with the user-interface to show which Texture Source is being applied where.) Texture Source D is a picture (a dampened variation of the terrain map) that is driving the Diffusion channel to convey moisture. The results of the A-B-C and D combination is shown here in grayscale. In Figure C9–50a and b (in the color section), the result is shown in color, along with the identical scene *without* the Texture Source D. Figure 9–50b lacks the extra Diffusion information and there is nothing to give the impression of moisture seeping through the ground near the mudhole. What a difference a D makes!

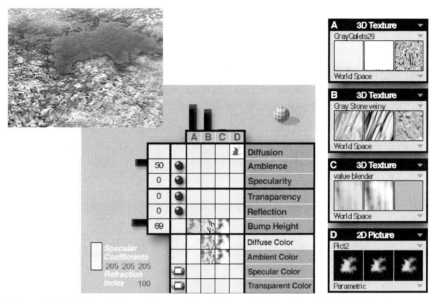

Figure 9–49 Using Texture Source D for diffuse illumination: Materials Composer that includes A-B-C texture combination with a D source to darken the ground near the water puddle, along with rendered result. (Color image of rendered result is shown in Figure C9–50a).

Texture Source Revisited: Practical Tips

Once you place any of the ten channel markers into any of the columns to drive that channel, Bryce randomly assigns a 3D Texture to the source. So if, say, you place the Diffusion marker in column D, then Bryce will assign a 3D Texture to Source D.

If you want to quickly change to a 2D Picture, you can change the Texture Source title bar pop-up menu from 3D Texture to 2D Picture, then select the picture that you want. Changing two pop-up menus in succession gets old quickly. A quicker way to change to a 2D Picture is to Option-click the gray area underneath the Texture Source's title (where the current texture name is displayed). That will toggle between the 3D Texture name and a 2D Picture name, thereby switching to the 2D Picture type.

If you exit the Materials Composer, you'll lose any Texture Source that isn't actively placed into one of the channels. Sometimes I like to momentarily get rid of a texture and see how the material—minus that one Texture Source—renders in the scene. But I don't want to lose the texture entirely. For that, I'll place the marker into an unused channel as a holding spot. Assuming that there is no other Texture Source in these two channels, two of my favorite places are Bump Height (with the slider set to 0) and Transparent Color (with Transparency slider set to 0). The Texture Source will still "stay" there, but won't affect the render.

When you open up the Materials Composer, there is a priority order in the rendering of previews. First, the Preview Window renders. When that is finished, then each Texture Source previews will render. Naturally, the order of preview rendering differs from the Macintosh—which I just described—to Windows. Windows happens in the opposite order. Of course, once you click anywhere in the Materials Composer user interface while the Preview is rendering, the Preview stops (click inside the window to resume). To force the Texture Sources to render, click immediately above the Texture Sources. That will force a quick, one-pass rough render of the contents. To force an update of any particular Texture Source, click in the area above the color-alpha-bump preview windows, where the texture name is. The click tells Bryce, "render this preview first."

To edit either of the Texture Source types, click in the color window for the property. That brings up either the Texture Editor or the Pictures Library. If you want to perform major texture surgery, Option-click (Macintosh) or Alt-click (Windows) the Source color preview window to access the Deep Texture Editor. (I devote the second half of the chapter to the ways and means of editing both 2D Picture and 3D Textures.)

Figure 9–51 shows the Texture Sources and indicates the places to click to change certain Materials Composer behaviors.

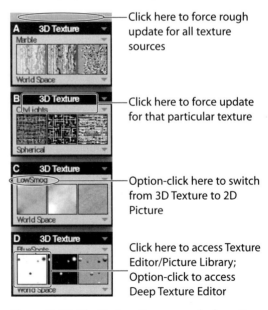

Click here to force rough update for all texture sources

Click here to force update for that particular texture

Option-click here to switch from 3D Texture to 2D Picture

Click here to access Texture Editor/Picture Library; Option-click to access Deep Texture Editor

Figure 9–51 The Texture Sources and where to click to change things.

SHADING MODE

Here are different shading modes where special effects are used by the ray-tracer to render the color and alpha and bump that drive the ten channels that comprise the three elements to the surface of the object that Jack built.

There is one last major part to the Materials Composer that needs describing. At the top of the Materials Composer, at the rule underscoring the title of the Materials Composer, there is a pop-up menu for you to choose the Shading mode for your object's surface. The default listed is Normal Shading. In the pop-up menu there are additional options: Additive, Fuzzy, Fuzzy Additive, and Light. Under Windows, there is also Blend Transparency. I'll treat the discussion separately from the other Shading modes. Below that are two additional options, Shadowable, and Distance Filter.

The Shading mode allows you to select different effects. To understand a bit about how these work, consider again the render process. As the renderer encounters objects in the Brycean world, it doesn't necessarily stop when it reaches the one sphere. With a rendering "X-ray" vision, the renderer, if directed, will also find out about the objects beyond the object, calculating what lies behind the sphere. What is the advantage to that? There are different ways to combine the object and what lies behind.

There are five different options, four of which are combinations of two different parameters (Fuzzy and Additive). The four combinations are neither parameter (Normal Shading), one (Fuzzy), the other (Additive), or both parameters (Fuzzy Additive). The fifth, Light, is a special case. Figure 9–52 shows a cylinder rendered in each of the effects shading modes.

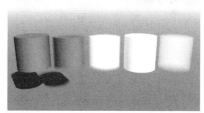

Figure 9–52 A Cylinder rendered using each of the shading modes: Normal, Fuzzy, Fuzzy Additive, Additive, and Light.

Fuzzy Options

The Fuzzy options will give your object a diffuse edge for a soft look. To create a fuzzy edge, the renderer calculates the surface of the object, and then blends in the calculated result of the area beyond the edge of the object. Use the Fuzzy options on any primitive object aside from flat objects, polyhedron-based objects, and terrains. Fuzzy is excellent to use on spheres that will be free-standing clouds, planetary atmosphere, or fake glowing pseudo-light sources. The Fuzzy options are not available for use with terrains, polyhedrons, or lights.

Additives

When this option is selected, Bryce uses a special process when rendering the object. The ray finds the object, and determines its surface appearance. It then finds whatever is *behind* the object, whether an additional object or atmosphere. When it determines the final pixel color for each, it adds the two together—the object and what is behind the object. Essentially, adding things together makes them brighter. You have probably seen this if you've worked with Add in other image processing situations or when you used the Add option in the Pictures portion of the Terrain Editor. This brightening effect gives the object the appearance of glowing. (See Chapter 11, "Bryce EnLightenment," for more on creating glowing objects.) When this is combined with fuzziness, you can create glowing atmospheres and light bulbs. When it is not combined with fuzziness, you can create moons. Make sure Diffuse is your only illumination. (See Chapter 15, "Brycing Out of This World," for more on planetary and lunar effects.)

Lights

The Light Shading mode is automatically selected when you create light object primitives. It calculates the mass of the object in a semi-glowing fashion. When an object is set to Light, it does not respond to any of the illumination controls. The only channels that affect the appearance of a Light object are Transparency and Diffuse Color. Both global and texture driven variations can be used to good effect. You probably won't be surprised to learn that more discussion about this particular Shading mode is found in Chapter 11, "Bryce EnLightenment."

Blend Transparency

Blend Transparency is an option included in the Windows Shading mode pop-up menu. It is there because the Materials Composer for the Windows version was constructed slightly differently from the Macintosh version. You've already noticed how the Macintosh and Windows versions behave when the Refract Index is set to 100. There are times, however, when emulating the Macintosh version is desirable.

So, then, what is it? When Blend Transparency is selected (and, indeed, for Macintosh Transparency when the Refract Index is set to 100), the renderer calculates the appearance of both the object and whatever lies behind it. The final result will be a mix of the two, as determined by the setting for the Transparency slider. It's a two-step process—first, the renderer's computation of both objects, and second, creating the final result by weighing the two in a blend. This is why a Transparency setting of 1 is just as costly as a setting of 254; both require that double render of the object and whatever lies behind it.

The other method for calculating the appearance of transparent objects is used all the time when the Windows version is set to Normal Shading, and when the Macintosh is set to any Refract Index number other than 100. In those circumstances, Bryce uses a different, more complex ray-tracing routine to bend the rays and create refraction. Under Windows, the normal state will add lighting highlights to the object rather than creating a straight blend between the object and the background. Figure 9–53 is a Bryce Windows-created scene with two nearly transparent cubes. The Refract index is set to 100, Diffusion is set to 100,

Figure 9–53 Transparent cubes rendered using different shading modes: a) Blend Transparency (Macintosh method); b) Windows Normal Shading mode.

and Transparency is set to 233. The left object has Blend Transparency for a Shading mode, and the right object has Normal Shading. The Normal Shading more closely follows the actual behavior of light from the physical world.

If that's the case, then what's the good of Blend Transparency? Blend Transparency struts its stuff when alpha information is used to make a portion of the object transparent. When there is a 2D Picture texture or a 3D Texture including some type of alpha-driven Transparency, the Blend Transparency Shading mode (and Macintosh Refract Index 100 method) works beautifully. There are portions where the object shows, and other portions where the background shows. The alpha information determines which part will show.

When you import a Macintosh scene file with Transparency and a Refract Index at 100, the Windows version automatically sets the Shading mode to be Blend Transparency. When you create a picture object, Bryce Windows also sets the Shading mode to Blend Transparency.

Figure 9–54 Distance Render and bumped surface material: a) No Bump Height setting; b) Bump Height, normal; c) Bump Height, with Distance Filter.

Distance Filter

Distance Filter is a special case shading mode that accompanies the use of Bump Height in your surface appearance. The Distance Filter tells the renderer to ignore Bump Height as the object moves into the distance. This reduces excessive noise (and render time) in the distance. Figure 9–54a through c compares three different views of the same ground. Part a is the standard color apply of the texture, without any bump. (There is no difference between an object rendered with or without the Distance Filter for this situation.) Part b is the same material texture, with considerable Bump Height applied. The bump makes the ground darker overall, as the indentations of the bumps contain shadows. Part c is the bump applied with the distance filter on. In the close foreground, shadows from bumped surface are noticeable, but those fade as the object moves back into the distance. The ground is lighter than the completely bumped version. (Incidentally, the render times for each of these three scenes are: a) No bump, 4:45; b) bump 5:57; c) bump with Distance Filter, 5:20. The Distance Filter cut 10% off the render time of the bumped version.)

Shadowable

Unlike the real world, where you either have shadows or you don't, you can choose whether to have shadows on Bryce objects. The default state will have the surface of the object accept shadows cast from other objects. There are times, however, when it's better to have an object that resists shadows (February 2 is one of them!). This is different from the resistance of shadows that takes place with a high Ambience setting, as shown in Figure 9–55. The left and right sphere have the default Shadowable setting checked. The center sphere has it unchecked. There is a difference between whether the object accepts a shadow (the outer ones do and the center one does not) and whether the underside of the object lies in shadow. The right sphere's Ambience setting is fairly high (200), and the object as a whole is lighter in shadowed areas. But it still receives shadows from other objects. The left and center spheres' Ambience setting are at the default, and the lower part of the spheres are identically shadowed.

Figure 9–55 Does the Shadow know? Shadowable switched on and off: a) Default settings, including Shadowable checked; b) Shadowable unchecked; c) Shadowable checked and a higher Ambience setting.

When would you shut off the shadow? At times when you want to reduce the shadow clutter. The objects in Figure 6–2 have the Shadowable setting switched off, since there's sufficient visual detail in the "frames" already without their shadows getting in the way, too.

A BIT OF HOUSEKEEPING

Warning: In the Windows version of Bryce, you'll get unreliable results when creating or adjusting materials settings for grouped objects. For some reason, Bryce Windows won't remember the group's setting when you enter the Materials Composer. Instead, the Materials Composer will display whatever state the Materials Composer was in when you were last there. Say you create a set of objects and assign a metallic-looking material. Then you create some terrains and give them a rocky appearance. If you select the grouped metallic objects (it doesn't matter when you grouped them; what matters is that they *are* grouped) and enter the Materials Composer, the settings that will be displayed will be the last thing you set when you were there previously—in this case, the rocky material setting. (The normal expected way Bryce *should* operate is to display the metallic settings that are assigned to those objects.) You may cancel out of the Materials Composer and render; the renderer correctly remembers the objects' settings. They just won't be displayed in the Materials Composer. If you ungroup the group and enter the Materials Composer, the settings will correctly reflect what you previously assigned to them. Of course, if you enter the Materials Composer with a group, and accept the settings with the checkmark, then you'll have just assigned the wrong settings to the group. Undo comes in handy at that point.

2D PICTURE TEXTURES

Here's the Picture Library, that holds up to thirty two—scuse me, thirty one—pictures with their alpha masks: An image for your Texture Source containing color and alpha (and alpha for bump) to drive the ten channels that comprise the three elements to the surface of the object that Jack built.

Bryce's 2D Picture options allows you to wrap images (Macintosh: PICT; Windows: BMP, TIF, or PSD) onto any object. You can have a texture that repeats again and again or you can place a single photographic image into your scene as a separate object.

A Basic How-To

To put a photograph into your scene as a cutout, two image files are required: the object itself and a mask. The mask trims away extraneous image area so that your image retains its own shape inside the Bryce scene. The mask or alpha channel can be viewed in the Bryce Picture Library; it can drive any of the illumination or optics and bump channels in the Materials Composer. There are other uses that Opacity Maps can be put to with the aid of the Materials Composer, but I first focus on the basic transparency model.

How to Create a Photographic Two-Dimensional Image with Alpha Channel

1. Click the Create Picture Object icon (Leonardo's little man) in the Create Palette.

2. Bryce opens the Picture Library. Select an available picture or click Load to import an image from your hard disk to the Picture Library. (See Figure 9–56a and b.)

3. Click the picture preview so that the red border shows around the image. (This indicates that it is selected.)

4. The selected picture should show in the previews at the top of the Pictures Library. If the image has an alpha channel, it will show in the second window. Click the black and white circle above the center preview window to clip the background but not the object. The window on the right previews what is clipped and what is not. See Figure 9–56c.

a
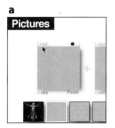

b

c
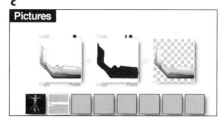

Figure 9-56 Loading pictures into the Picture Library: a) Clicking the Load button; b) navigating in the dialog box for the desired image; c) the selected image shows in the Picture Library preview windows.

You may need to run the Minimum filter (in Photoshop) to make the alpha channel fit more snugly to the image. Do this if you find that your image has a minute "halo" where the background image information leaks into the image. (This is something you'll discover in Bryce while doing a test render.)

Images courtesy MetaPhotos.

5. Click the check mark. Your image is applied to the object. Bryce takes care of the Material settings automatically.

6. Render.

Figure 9–57 is a series of many picture images brought into a Bryce scene using this method.

Figure 9-57 "Occupational Hazard," a series of picture objects.

The Picture Library

Bryce keeps all of the images in a Picture Library. The little walkthrough indicated one way to access it. There are several others. In the Materials Composer, click the Texture Source color preview window. In the Edit Palette, select Edit 2D Pict Textures from the pop-up menu underneath the Edit Materials icon. Under the Objects menu, select 2D Pictures (or Control-M on Macintosh, Ctrl+Alt+M using Windows).

The Picture Library (see Figure 9–58) has two main parts. The top part, with the larger windows, is the place for working with the active picture. Below are holding places and thumbnails for up to 32 pictures.

To make any of those pictures active, click the thumbnail. The outline is red, and that image (if there is one) appears in the top windows. If there is no image, then you can load an image through an Open dialog box to that spot, or paste an image into that spot.

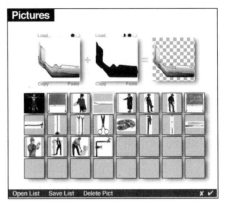

Figure 9–58 The Picture Library.

The three windows are previews for the active (or selected) picture. The left two windows correspond to the first two Texture Source properties: color and alpha. The third window is a combined view of the way that the alpha information will affect the object. (The alpha information also determines the bump information; there is no third information source that drives Bump Height.)

Both the color and alpha windows have sets of controls for setting up and manipulating the picture. Though the controls seem identical (with the exception of the black and white button above the alpha preview window), and function similarly to one another, there is a hierarchy. The controls for the color preview take precedence over information in the alpha window. Copying and pasting information in the color preview will also affect the alpha information. Being aware of this from the outset saves you from potentially nasty surprises.

The Load button, above the window, accesses an Open dialog box for you to find any picture image to load into the Picture Library. Also above the window are the plain black and plain white buttons. Those will delete the current contents of the picture and leave a solid black (or white) field.

For all three of the controls above the Picture color preview window, the action of loading or deleting to solid black (or white) will act for both the color and the alpha information.

Underneath the preview window are the copy and paste options for copying and pasting to another picture in the Pictures library, or for copying and pasting elsewhere in Bryce (to the Terrain Editor.) The black-and-white circle above the picture alpha preview will invert the alpha channel mask. You can see the results of the flipping in the third window to know whether your mask will cut out everything else but your image, or cut out the image and leave everything else. As mentioned previously, Bryce's picture alpha information is flipped. Therefore the usual mask that works to select the particular area in other applications (such as Photoshop) will need to be inverted in Bryce in order to work properly. The third combination preview helps keep you straight.

Picture Resolution

When you load an image containing a fourth (alpha) channel mask, the mask will automatically be loaded into the Picture Library—provided that the image resolution is 72 pixels per inch. Other software applications that work with images may prefer more densely packed image information. If you're thinking in terms of preparing images for print, then resolutions of 288 ppi or 300 ppi are the norm. Bryce, however, is not that way. Bryce wants to render images, and does so at a resolution of 72 pixels per inch. Bryce wants to establish the relation between this object over here, with its geometrical shape, and this image in here, in the Picture Library. Bryce wants to take the image and put it on the object, and have a nice pixel-per-pixel relationship between the picture map and the rendered image. When using pictures that have alpha channels, Bryce is happiest with images that are set to 72 pixels per inch. (Resolution is not so critical if you won't be using an alpha channel.) Stock photo disks ship with images (including alpha channels) set to higher resolutions as a matter of course. To use them in Bryce, you'll have to adjust the resolution in an image editing application. Figure 9–59 compares two sets of picture objects which came from a stock photo CD-ROM set to (you guessed it) 300 ppi. The chalkboard and teacher with dunce cap on the left were unchanged from the 300 ppi resolution. The chalkboard on the right and the teacher were changed to 72 ppi—for a much nicer result. Although the images set to 300 ppi had alpha channels, they did not automatically import into the Picture Library. If the quality of your rendered picture image is funky, blocky, squared, fuzzy, or icky, check to make sure that the image is set to 72 pixels per inch!

Figure 9–59 Comparison of 300 ppi picture images and 72 ppi picture images. This teacher—and Bryce—prefer 72 ppi.

The other resolution matter concerns the actual size of the image. Is it 128×128 pixels? 256×256? 512×512? Bigger than that? In the earliest days of Bryce, you couldn't possibly have an image larger than 512×512 pixels. The image needs to be held in memory while you're working. (An image 1024×1024 that has RGB + alpha channel is four megabytes in size). The rule of thumb is to keep the image the smallest size without sacrificing quality. Before you make the image larger, make sure that it's at 72 ppi. The final render size will also determine the resolution of the image for the picture texture; if your final render is going to be 640×480, then there's no sense in having a source image that's 1024×1024. Not only will you have to keep that huge image in memory, but during the render, Bryce will have to interpolate the image to a smaller size. (Note: This discussion concerns the total number of pixels to use in a picture texture. Render resolution and changing the final render to be something other than 72 ppi is a different subject entirely. See Chapter 12, "Render Unto Bryce," and Chapter 16, "Printing Bryce Images," for more about image resolution that is something other than 72 ppi.)

Library Capacity

There are 32 images that can be put in the library. The first image place holder is occupied by the default Golden Leonardo image. Although you can theoretically place 32 pictures in the Picture Library, I advise against it. Since Bryce starts out with one placed already, it's best to give the library some breathing room—in the amount of one picture placeholder—to keep its own picture wits together. Filling all 32 pictures will result in a Picture Library case of addled Bryce-brains. Bryce performs a wacky switcheroonie, as the picture that you placed in spot number 32 later occupies the first "Default picture" spot the next time you open up the scene file that contains objects with all those pictures. Figure 9–60a shows how the 32 images looked in the library when they were first loaded. Later, after quitting and re-launching Bryce and opening up the scene file again, the Picture Library changed. (See Figure 9–60b.) This funky displacement does not occur when there are only 31 pictures in the library.

Picture Library Behaviors: Cancel and Delete

Make sure that if you are pasting a new image into the Library, you paste to an empty slot! Otherwise you'll be pasting over your previous image, sending it to file heaven. Your actions in the Picture Library cannot be undone with a ⌘-Z or Ctrl+Z. So what good is the Cancel button when you leave the Picture Library? While you are in the Picture Library, you're living on the edge. Everything you do

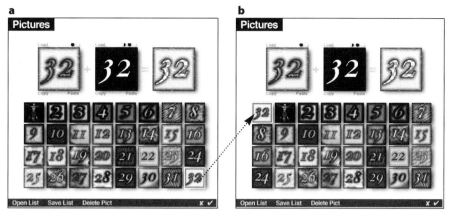

Figure 9–60 a) What the Picture Library *should* look like when filled to capacity; b) what it actually looks like after reopening a scene file that contains all 32 images.

matters. You can keep the Picture Library in the shape you just made it, but by canceling to leave, you will make no changes to the 2D Picture texture for your object. All your changes to the library are immediately permanent, but you can decide not to change the object itself. Of course, if you changed the picture that is being applied in the Materials Composer, the changes to the picture will "take." Clicking the check mark indicates that the selected image will be applied to the object.

There are two different forms of delete in the Picture Library. At the bottom, there is an option called Delete Pict. This will completely remove the selected image from the library. You are asked if you're sure you want to delete. (Remember, *nothing* is undoable in the Picture Library!) You can also delete the contents of either the color or alpha information and replace it with white or black. When you click the black button or the white button to do so, you are presented with the very same alert box that asks you if you're sure you want to delete. If you click the OK check mark, then there is still something in that picture spot; you've merely removed the picture information.

> **TIP:** *Deleting the color (to replace with flat black or white) will also delete the alpha information. To make a blank color that contains alpha information, first copy the alpha information, then delete the color, then paste the alpha information back in.*

Image Names, Library lists and Disaster Avoidance

When importing an image into the Picture Library, Bryce will remember the name of the image. The name will show up in the list of available 2D Picture textures in the Texture Source pop-up menu. That name information is saved in the scene file. This is not a publish and subscribe situation, though. You've brought the image into the scene and there it stays, no matter what changes you might make to the original image. The presence of the name will help if you want to reimport an altered image.

You can also save the contents of the Picture Library into a separate document on your hard disk. This is called a List file. When you save the list Bryce will suggest the name 2D Textures in the Save dialog box. Saving a list is a good precaution; it keeps all your resource images together in one place in a form that Bryce can easily deal with, should it become necessary to reassign the images to your objects. Do not open up the scene file and then reimport the picture list as a matter of course, however. The List file does not remember the images by name; your pop-up menu in the Texture Sources will only say "Pict, Pict, Pict." So why should you create a list, then? Like backing up your drives, it's an action to do just in case disaster strikes.

When might disaster strike? Disaster will strike if your working situation requires more RAM than you have allocated to Bryce. (This disaster recipe is not limited to pictures!) All those images are stored in your computer's memory for the duration that they're in the Picture Library when Bryce is launched. Even if you have closed the scene file with a couple dozen pictures in it, the Picture Library with the couple dozen pictures will remain in RAM for the duration of your current session in Bryce. If you are running Bryce in lower memory situations or with heavy picture texture content, watch the status of the Picture Library. Quit and relaunch Bryce if you need to flush the memory, or create a List file with just the default Leonardo image in it. Open that list to purge the pictures from Bryce's memory.

What is the other situation that spells disaster? Too many images. Stay away from that thirty-second image.

Opacity Maps and PICT Textures

Now that you have the basic idea for how to wrangle picture textures, what sort of cool tricks can you try with images? Remember the Texture Sources in the Materials Composer— you can use the alpha information to drive illumination and optics, and you can have bump information, too. The alpha information is used for creating bump information.

Here is a class case of using an alpha channel to create some optic and illumination. The dome of this tower by Chris Casady (see Figure C9–61) features a cobalt-blue flat surface with gold stars. The Texture Source is a picture and alpha channel. The alpha drives both Reflection and Specularity, giving the impression that the stars are gold foil applied to a matte cobalt-blue surface.

To create picture-driven bump information, place bump information in the alpha channel for the picture. You can also create a different image for bump information only. Figure 9–62 uses two different methods to create bump information for the objects. For the tile floor, the color image was pasted into the alpha to provide luminosity-driven bump information. For the celtic scroll medallion, a second picture was created from the color of the first, after blurring and adjusting the contrast. The original alpha information was necessary to outline the shape. (The source for the images is The Grammar of Ornament, by Direct Imagination—a CD-ROM with a wealth of historical ornament and decoration.)

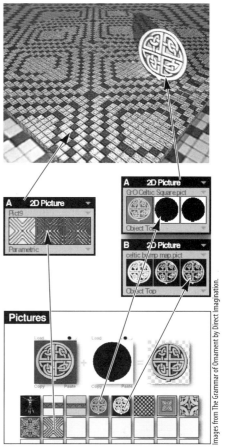

Images from The Grammar of Ornament by Direct Imagination.

Figure 9–62 Tiles and Medallion scene and Picture Library show different methods to create bump information from picture sources.

TIP: *Here's a way to do some quick picture editing without leaving Bryce. Copy your picture and then select (or create) a terrain. Open the Terrain Editor, paste the image, and then alter it using the tools available in the Terrain Editor. When you are through, copy the completed image, cancel out of the Terrain Editor (to leave the terrain unchanged), open up the Picture Library and paste the image back into the target spot.*

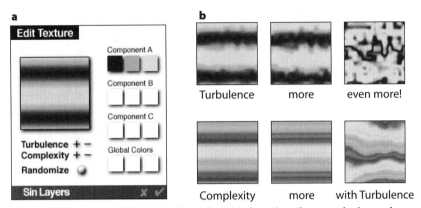

Figure 9–63 a) The Edit Texture dialog box; b) changing the complexity and turbulence alters the look of the texture.

3D SOLID TEXTURES—THE REAL MEATY STUFF

3D Solid Textures are what underlie all those natural-looking terrains and Brycean landscapes. This is where you can set textures that respond to altitude, slope, and orientation. In this way, your Brycean landscape will differ depending on whether there's a sheer cliff face, a flat lowlands or highlands, or north-facing rocks that have lichen growth.

In the next sections, I take you through the Texture Editors—the places you access by clicking the Texture Source color in the Materials Composer—first the Shallow Texture Editor and then the Deep Texture Editor.

Edit Texture—Level I, or the Shallow Texture Editor

This is the shallow texture editor to preview and choose from Texture Source types; Complexity, turbulence and color adjustments containing color and alpha and bump; these will drive any of the ten channels that comprise the three elements to the surface of the object that Jack built.

When you click the color preview in the Texture Source for any 3D Texture, you will arrive at the Edit Texture dialog box (see Figure 9–63). Here you can do the following:

• Look at the texture in two dimensions, devoid of other material setting.

• Scroll through the entire range of texture options using the arrow keys (Macintosh only), or access the entire list from the pop-up menu.

• Change the colors of the textures.

Figure C1–1 Bryce Canyon National Park at sunrise. *Photograph by the author.*

Figure C9–1 The three surface properties of an object: illumination, optics (and bump, not shown here) and color.

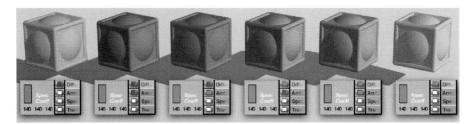

Figure C9–12 The Diffuse and Ambient Color settings for each object are below that object.

Figure C9–13 The Ambient Colors for these objects range from white to dark gray.

Figure C9–14 A set of objects with the color settings shown. Objects have high Specularity and also some Reflection.

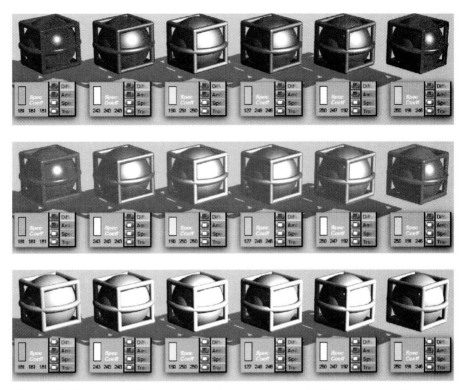

Figure C9–15 Specular Coefficient colorings for red objects. Top row: Interacting with Diffuse and Ambient Color; Middle row: white Ambient Color; Bottom row: white Diffuse Color.

Figure C9–16 Specular Coefficient interaction: a) Each hue pushed over the bright line threshhold; b) detail of blue Specular Coefficient with neighboring hue cyan Specular Color; c) detail of blue Specular Coefficient with complement, yellow, for Specular Color.

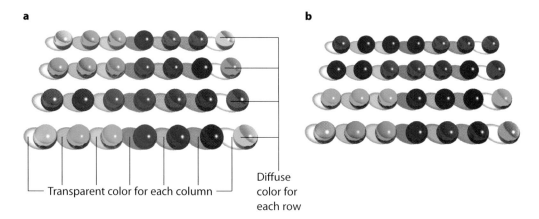

Figure C9-17 Transparent Color interacts with Diffuse Color: a) Diffuse Colors are mostly the primary colors (red, green, blue); b) Diffuse Colors are mostly secondary colors (magenta, cyan, yellow).

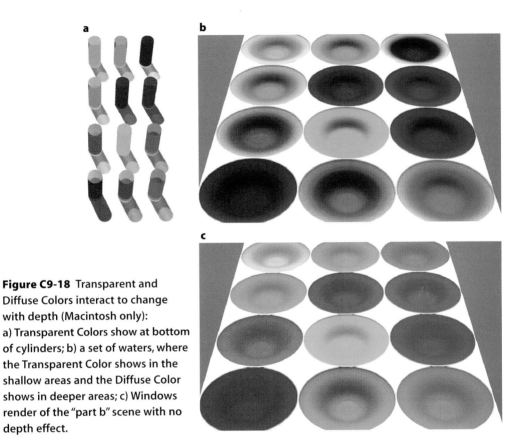

Figure C9-18 Transparent and Diffuse Colors interact to change with depth (Macintosh only): a) Transparent Colors show at bottom of cylinders; b) a set of waters, where the Transparent Color shows in the shallow areas and the Diffuse Color shows in deeper areas; c) Windows render of the "part b" scene with no depth effect.

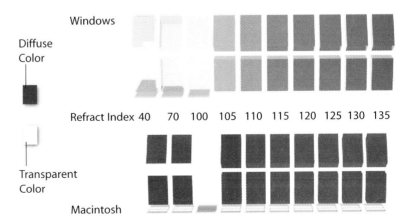

Figure C9–19 The interaction of Transparent and Diffuse Color at different Refract Index settings.

Diffusion 0

Diffuse Color

Diffusion 146

Metallicity   0   51   102   153   204   255

Figure C9–21 Metallicity settings (Windows only). Top row: No diffuse illumination; Bottom row: diffuse illumination.

a   b

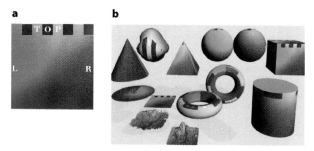

Figure C9–27 Parametric mapping places a) the image b) onto the objects in proportion to the object's shape.

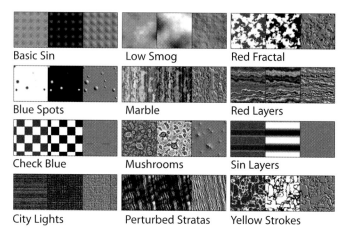

Basic Sin   Low Smog   Red Fractal

Blue Spots   Marble   Red Layers

Check Blue   Mushrooms   Sin Layers

City Lights   Perturbed Stratas Yellow Strokes

Figure C9–29 The 12 Texture Sources used as the primary examples for this chapter.

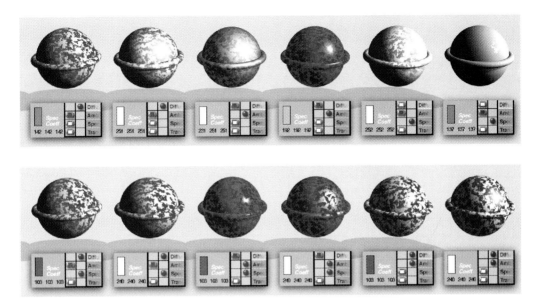

Figure C9–35 Object colored by a texture-driven color: Top row: Texture drives one channel, while the rest of the channels have uniform coloring; Bottom row: texture drives two of the three channels.

Figure C9–36 Texture-driven color for Transparent Color and two other channels.

C8

Figure C9–37 Texture-driven Transparent Color interacting with Diffuse Color.

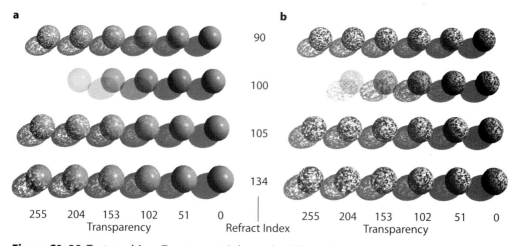

Figure C9–38 Texture-driven Transparent Color under different Transparency and Refract Index settings: a) Transparent Color is the only texture-driven color; b) Transparent and Diffuse Colors are both driven by a Texture Source.

Figure C9–40 Marble and Low Smog driving the different color channels.

Figure C9–46 Changing the Source C texture changes the way that textures A and B are blended together.

a   b   c

Figure C9–47 Whole Mountain material broken down into the three surface properties: a) Illumination; b) bump; c) color.

a

b

Figure C9–48 Whole Mountain color breakdown: a) Hills color only, color and diffuse illumination, combined colors and diffuse illumination; b) pebbly color only; color and Diffusion, combined colors and Diffusion.

a

b

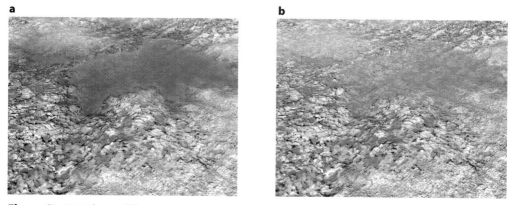

Figure C9–50 What a difference a Texture Source D makes! a) Terrain with material settings as shown in Figure 9–49, including a Texture Source D to drive the Diffusion channel and provide the appearance of moisture; b) the same scene without any Texture Source D.

Figure C9–61 "Tower Blues," by Chris Casady, made from a picture Texture Source.

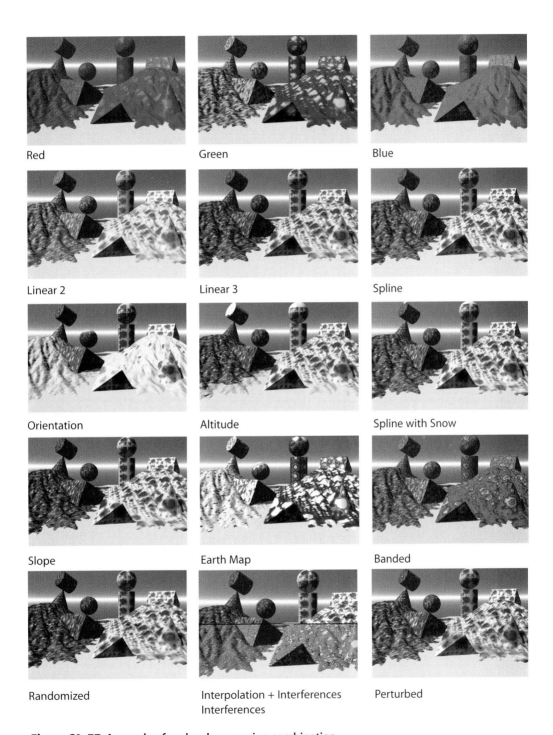

Figure C9–77 A sample of each color mapping combination.

C12

Add

Subtract

Average

Multilply (Bump Only)

Minimum (Bump Only)

Blend Minimum

Combine

Maximum (Bump Only)

Blend Maximum

Blend Value 1

Blend Value 2

Blend Random

Blend Altitude

Blend Slope

Fast Slope

Figure C9–79 Blend options in the Deep Texture Editor for combining texture components.

Component 1   (Value)   Component 2   (Value)   Component 3 (for Parallel)

Parallel

Procedural Blend

Difference

Blend Orientaton

Figure C9–79 *continued*

a   **b**

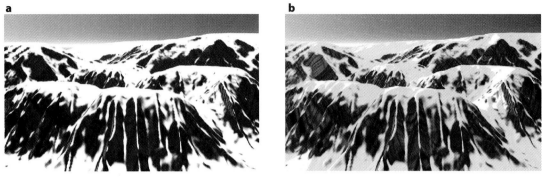

Figure C9–86 The Snow rendered: a) The Snow preset; b) with the Ambient Color modified.

Figure C9–87 Puddlebumps, final result of a Deep Texture Editor recipe.

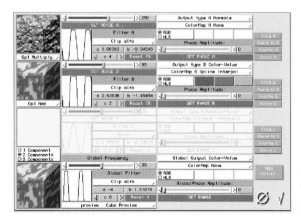

Figure C9–93 The Deep Texture Editor with final settings for Puddlebump.

Figure C10–6 Opposite Sun control behavior with night skies: a) Centered Sun control; b) Sun control on right, moon on left; c) Sun control on left, moon on right.

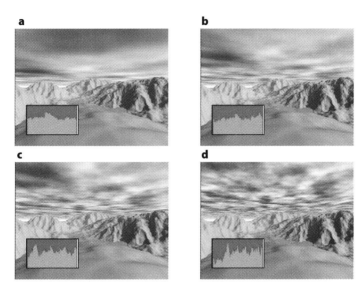

Figure C10–11 Clouds and frequency adjustment: a) Lower frequency; b) default frequency; c) higher and; d) still higher frequency.

Figure C10–12 Adjusting cloud coverage with the Cloud thumbnail changes cloud amounts so they range from daintily decorating the sky (left) to dominating it (right).

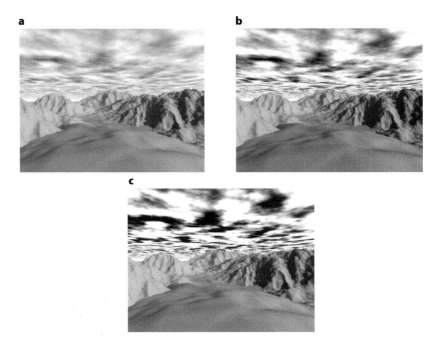

Figure C10–13 Amplitude and cloud definition: a) Lower amplitude; b) moderate amplitude; c) high amplitude.

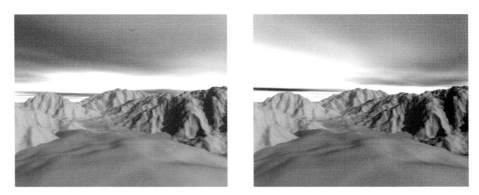

Figure C10–14 Clouds with a) Positive and b) negative amplitude.

- Adjust the complexity for a texture.

- Adjust the turbulence for a texture.

- Randomly shuffle through different combinations to create a completely new texture.

- Create a new name for your texture (when you create any changes to the current texture).

You will also encounter information about the Deep Texture Editor later in this chapter. The Shallow Texture Editor and Deep Texture Editor are related and concepts will be described in a mutual frame of reference.

Changing Color

There are 12 possible colors you can use in a texture. When you take a peek here and see a texture that has one row of colors, it may mean either that there is only one component or that only one component has color and the others are assigned to other output methods. (More on components and output in the Deep Texture Editor section.)

Clicking on any color swatch accesses the pop-up color picker, or, with the Option (Macintosh) or Alt (Windows) key held down, the numerical slider color pickers. This is good for selectively changing the colors of textures. Change one color and watch how the entire color scheme of the texture is changed. If you cannot access the color picker for a particular color swatch, that swatch is not being used to create the texture.

Since you can access the Shallow Texture Editor from the Edit Palette, use that access method to sample colors for your texture directly from your scene. If you're Brycing on a Mac, you can also rearrange your scene window in order to access other reference images or palettes that might be floating on your desktop.

Sometimes the resulting color of the texture is not the direct result of the colors you see in the swatches. There are blend modes that determine how the final texture is mixed. The different sets of colors can be added, subtracted, and multiplied, as well as combined in other ways. To get to those apply modes, you'll need to go to the Deep Texture Editor. The fourth set of colors are for assigning color to the texture on a global basis.

Complexity

When you click the Texture Complexity+ button, you are adding the same type of texture noise to itself in larger increments. It's the same thing as increasing the Octaves in the Deep Texture Editor. The texture gets more complex when you generate additional octaves of the original texture noise. (More on this in the Deep Texture Editor.) Figure 9–63b shows different complexity settings for a texture.

Turbulence

Turbulence introduces an additional texture noise to offset the original one. The more Turbulence you set, the more vigorously the additional noise interferes with your original texture. In the Deep Texture Editor, this is introducing phase on a global level to all noises. The more Turbulence you add, the greater the amplitude of this additional noise you're introducing (see phase later in this chapter for more explanation).

Adding more Turbulence and Complexity increases the cost of your render time, as you're asking Bryce to do more calculation to generate that texture.

Random Shuffling

Clicking the Shuffle button randomly generates entire textures. Any combination can be generated. Just in case you were curious about the total number of possible combinations of 3D Solid Textures, the number is:

1,097,135,300,000,000,000,000,000,000,000,000,000,000,000,000,000,000,000,000,000,000,000

(The calculator stopped filling in specific numbers after the first eight decimal places.) This is a 1 followed by 72 zeroes, give or take a few zeroes. Some new options have been added in Bryce 2, providing more options than those originally calculated here. But when you have a number of that magnitude, what's a few zeroes among friends?

Once you find something within one of those random combinations that interests you, you can adjust the colors, complexity, and turbulence in the Shallow Texture Editor. To carefully fine-tune a promising texture, however, you'll need to go to the Deep Texture Editor.

Naming New Textures

After making any changes to the texture and clicking the Okay check mark, Bryce presents you with a dialog box for renaming your texture. If you keep the name as is, you'll forever change the underlying texture—at least for as long as the software is launched. Once you restart, Bryce reverts back to all the original texture settings. In the same way, unless you use that new texture in a material setting for an object, or create a preset using that new texture, your carefully named and saved texture will go to the Great Texture Graveyard somewhere between the Great Zero and the Great One.

Deep Texture Editor

Here is the Deep Texture Editor, the heart of Bryce, the Procedural Mecca. Noise that's sythesized six ways to Sunday—with Octave and Mode, using Filter and Blend. Color and Value and Normale become the familiar color and alpha and bump to drive the ten channels that comprise the three elements to the surface of the object that Jack built.

Access the Deep Texture Editor by pressing the Option (Macintosh) or or Alt (Windows) key while clicking the Texture Source color preview. This editor is the heart of Bryce. It evolved over years of Bryce's development while Eric Wenger shaped the application. From time to time, he'd work on how to be able to create such-and-such an effect, devise a solution, write it up in some code, and put it in the Editor. Bit by bit, it has grown into what it is now.

It's a personal solution, much as your own method of keeping track of your files, or how you organize your socks or kitchen utensils is a personal system. It's there. It works. All the complexities are self-evident to you, the creator. But it's not really meant for public attention or distribution.

When Eric Wenger's application was undergoing transformation into the software KPT Bryce (version 1.0), there was the question of what to do with the Deep Texture Editor. It was written for personal use and simultaneously was a central driving power of the application, so what was to be done? Should it be included in the commercial software? Should it operate deep inside Bryce, yet users would have no way to access it? The decision was to put it in but not to document it. It's high on the revamping list, and indeed, between version 1.0 and 2.1, Eric rearranged his sock drawer so that he could see everything at once, and that is now what is in Bryce. But MetaTools still does not document nor provide technical support for it. For the great explorers, the tinkerers, and the terminally curious, here is an explanation for how the Heart of Bryce works.

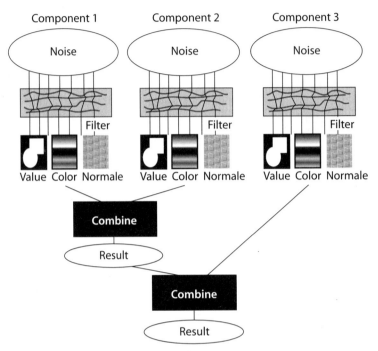

Figure 9–64 The logical sequence used by the Deep Texture Editor to create textures.

Overview

The Deep Texture Editor is analogous to a musical synthesizer. A synthesizer sends a tone through one or more filters to produce a new variation with unique qualities. Bryce's Deep Texture Editor does the same thing, only instead of synthesizing sound, it synthesizes visual noise. The result is visual texture.

The schematics in Figure 9–64 show the logical order of the Deep Texture editing process. Figure 9–65 shows the Deep Texture Editor's interface for both the Macintosh and Windows versions. Although they have cosmetic differences, the layout of the interface is basically the same. The Deep Texture Editor is broken up into four horizontal areas. The first three appear identical except that they are identified by the letters A, B, and C. The fourth is slightly different and is referred to as "global."

Those first three areas (A, B, and C) are controls for the three texture components. Before launching into the overview explanation, a little clarification of terminology is in order. Though the texture components are referred to as A, B, and C in the Deep

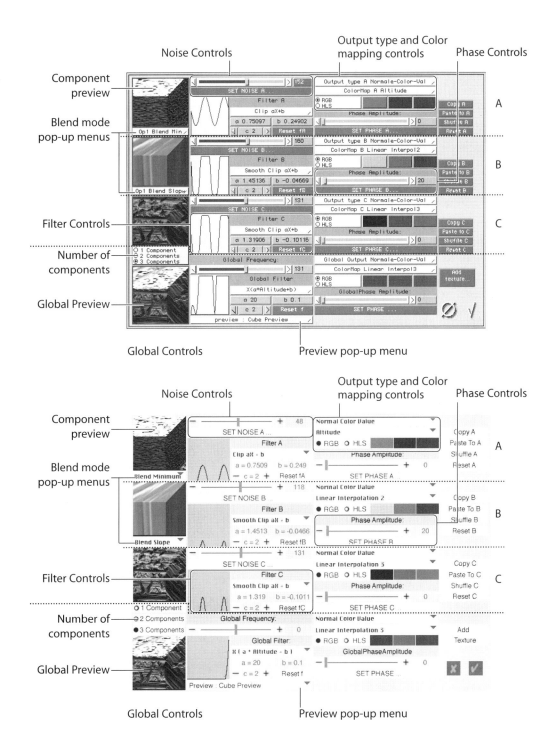

Figure 9–65 Both the Macintosh and Windows versions of the Deep Texture Editor with everything labelled.

Texture Editor, they do not correspond directly to the A, B, C, or D of the Texture Sources in the Materials Composer. The result of the combined components in the Deep Texture Editor will become *one* Texture Source in the Materials Composer. The example texture in Figure 9–65 uses a three-component texture—Hills 29, which joins with two other Texture Sources to create the Whole Mountain material. You could even have a surface material that uses four Texture Sources, each with three components. (MetaTools, in offering access to the Deep Texture Editor while forgoing the process of documenting it, hasn't concerned itself with using precise terminology that is consistent for both the Materials Composer and the Deep Texture Editor. Although their software documentation refers to the Texture Sources as "components," perhaps you've noticed that I have not. The Deep Texture Editor, with its three texture components, has been around longer than the four-Texture-Source Materials Composer. Therefore the Deep Texture Editor takes precedence when it comes to what is called a component.)

Here in the Deep Texture Editor you can start with either one, two, or three components (and now we all agree on the term!). For each component, assign a noise. Then put the noise through a filter. At that point, there's a choice to be made between three output options. Will the component be output as Value (alpha channel), Color, or Normale (bump map)? Or will the output be some combination of the three? When there is more than one component, how are they combined? The first two components are combined together to form a new hybrid. If there are three components, the hybrid of the first two will be combined with the third component.

Finally, you can apply some global settings to the combined result of the component process. Overall frequency, a final color scheme, a final apply of global phase—and you're on your way back to the Materials Composer for fine-tuning and additional tweaking to create that perfect surface appearance for your object.

This has been a quick take on the process; there are plenty of eddies and pools of complexity at each step along the way. I'll stop and explore them all as I go through the Deep Texture Editor part by part.

Noise

Noise is the source for textures in Bryce. Inside the Deep Texture Editor, clicking the Set Noise A… (or B or C) button takes you to a dialog box, which I call the Noise Editor (see Figure 9–66). There you'll find the following controls:

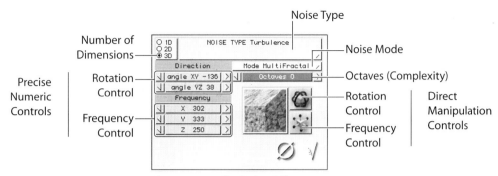

Figure 9–66 The Noise Editor.

- Type of noise

- Number of dimensions

- Frequency

- Spatial orientation

- Octaves

- Noise modulations

First, there's the type of noise that is generated. Choose from 27 types. Random (RND) Continuous is the default noise.

The Noise Editor renders the noise in two steps, first rough and then detailed. The length of time it takes to render the preview gives you an indication of the processing time involved. Different noises will take different amounts of time to compute. RND Continuous does not take a long time to compute. The most expensive of the lot is Vortex noise, followed by Waves and Fractal Stone and Spots, and perhaps some others. Don't avoid the costly ones altogether; after all, they're there for a purpose. But if you're just experimenting around, don't use them cavalierly, unless you have all day—and then some.

Number of Dimensions

Set the number of dimensions for your noise with the radio buttons. Noise that is 1D is a one-dimensional noise, 2D is two-dimensional, and 3D is three-dimensional. The number of dimensions for the noise is an integral part of the two controls described next: Frequency and Orientation.

Frequency

There are two ways to adjust the frequency of your noise to shape the look of your texture. The first, on the right of the Noise Preview, controls frequency proportionately. Drag to increase or decrease the frequency on all axes. The other method adjusts frequency independently on each dimension. The numeric tools on the left accomplish that. Click the arrows or, if you're using a Macintosh, type numbers directly. You can also drag the numbers to quickly adjust them. (On the Macintosh, the number area turns blue to indicate that it is selected.) Although all three are constantly available for adjustment, you won't always need them. To determine which ones you'll need, check to see how many dimensions your noise has. One-dimensional texture is the x-axis. Two-dimensional adds the y-axis. Three-dimensional adds the z-axis. Don't try to fiddle with the z adjustment if you have a 2D Texture. If you do, the Noise Editor will take the time to recompute the noise, but nothing will change. When changing frequency on an individual axis basis, drag the numbers or type them directly.

At least one exception exists. The Leopard noise (new to Bryce 2), when set to one-dimensional, will also receive input from the y and z frequency amounts. It's as if, for this noise, 1D defines the direction of the grain, and the noise itself will vary by frequency adjustments from all three axes. There is a Leopard Noise slide show on the CD-ROM (More Info > Chapter 09 Materials > DTE > Leopard Noise Slide Show).

Besides adjusting the noise frequency proportionately using the control to the right of the preview, you can use the Frequency slider in the Deep Texture Editor proper. The advantage to using the outer Frequency slider is that you can render a preview in the window and make an adjustment without having to go back and enter the separate dialog box. However, for the Windows version of Bryce, the outer Frequency slider will only change the noise frequency for x. If you want to change the noise frequency for all three dimensions, you'll need to do so in the Noise Editor.

When previewing the noise inside the Noise Editor, the part of the cube that faces front is the same as the two-dimensional preview in both the Deep and Shallow Texture Editors. (You can switch this by ninety degrees in the Materials Composer by selecting World Top for mapping, and what is facing front here in the noise editor will face up in Bryce.)

When you set the frequency of the noise, the x, y, and z axes are established first. After that, you can rotate the noise in any general direction using the Rotation controls, which are discussed next.

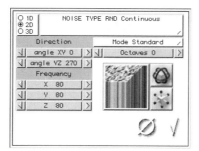 

2D Noise with uniform texture along the Y axis

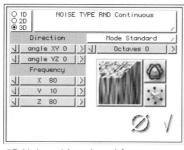 

3D Noise with reduced frequency on one dimension.

Figure 9–67 Three-dimensional noise with two-dimensional look to it.

> **TIP:** To make a noise that's generally consistent across two dimensions, but without the rigid uniformity of a two-dimensional noise, use three dimensional noise and vary the frequency along one dimension. For noise that has a vertical grain, reduce the frequency on the y axis. For noise that has a horizontal grain, reduce the frequency along both the x and z axes or increase it along the y axis. Figure 9–67 compares a two- and three-dimensional noise.

Orientation

Noise, whether it comes in one, two, or three dimensions, has a grain, or a fixed spatial orientation. In your scene, the direction in which that noise "points" will stay consistent no matter what the objects are or how they are oriented in space. The default mapping for 3D Solid Textures' World Space is based on this orientation. Here in the Noise Editor, you can change the orientation of the noise by rotating it. To rotate, use the control to the right of the noise preview. Drag to change direction. For precision (or to start over), use the numerical controls to the left. Click the arrows to increase or decrease by single increments, or drag up and down for very quick adjustments. On the Macintosh, when the number is blue, it's selected, and you may directly type in a number.

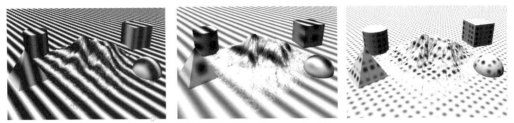

Figure 9–68 One-, two-, and three-dimensional noise oriented in space.

Figure 9–68 shows one-, two-, and three-dimensional noise at Noise Editor settings 0 and 0. Settings at 0 and 0 favor the front. If you want to change the orientation to the top of your object, then you need to rotate so that the cross-hatches appear on the top.

Octaves

Octave in Bryce's Noise Editor is similar to musical scale octaves. The C an octave below Middle C is the same note, but lower. (Mathematically, the frequency is half.) Adding an octave in Bryce is analogous to playing both Middle C and the C below it at the same time. The result is more complex than if you played only one note. (In fact, in the Shallow Texture Editor, when you are adding *complexity,* you are increasing the Octave setting for the noise.)

Each time that you set the Octave to a higher number, you are introducing more processing time, as the noise has to be run through more frequencies for each octave that is computed.

When you add octaves to your noise, you can modulate the noise in one of the several options available in the Mode pop-up menu.

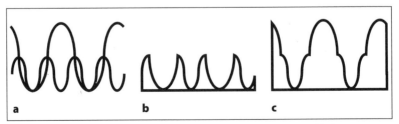

Figure 9–69 Octave and modulation: a) A noise wave and its higher octave cousin; b) Minimum modulation; c) Maximum modulation.

Noise Modulations

When you add an octave, the noise is also generated at a lower frequency with longer wavelengths. Figure 9–69 shows a wave and its higher octave relative. So what happens when there are additional octaves? The Mode menu allows you to tweak these in different ways. For instance, Maximum and Minimum will take the combined noises and select only the "top" and "bottom" values for the scale. This is analogous to Lighten Only and Darken Only.

Here are brief descriptions of each of the noise modulations. Figure 9–70 shows examples of octaves and modulations. Two different noise types, RND Continuous and Sine, are shown at four octave settings. RND Continuous noise is shown in each modulation option. To make modulations work, make sure you set Octave higher than 0. Remember, the higher the Octave setting, the longer the processing time, so set Octave judiciously.

- *Standard.* This default modulation adds the new octave at half the frequency and twice the amplitude (see Figure 9–69a).

- *Irregular.* The same as Standard, but more weight is given to the higher frequency noise, resulting in a noise with more detail.

- *More Irregular.* Same as Irregular, only more so.

- *Maximum.* Analogous to Lighten Only, takes the highest (lightest) values together to produce the resulting noise. See Figure 9–69c.

- *Multi-Fractal.* Lighter values mean more high-contrast noise.

- *With Rotation.* Puts a spin on the noise so that each additional octave is rotated in space. This is most easily seen in linear noises, such as a one-dimensional sine or in the RND linear.

- *Minimum.* Darken only. (See Figure 9–69b.) Selects the lowest (darkest) values of the combined noises.

- *Multiply.* Also a darker result. The different values are multiplied together.

- *Difference.* When the values are identical the result is black. When the values are different, the lightest value inverts the other. A darker value lets the other remain as is. Gray values are weighted accordingly. Difference works even at 0 Octaves. The higher the number of octaves, the darker the resulting noise.

- *Minimum 90.* Repeats the noise at a 90° angle from its original orientation, and combines the two, finding the maximum. Say what? How come it's maximum

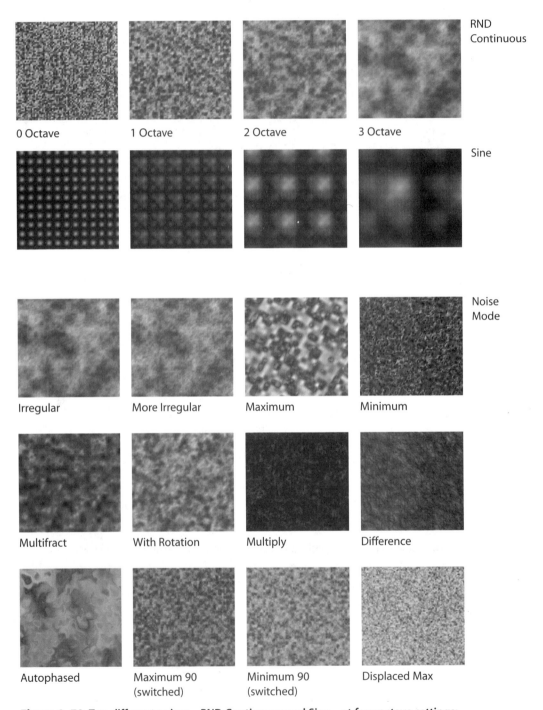

RND
Continuous

0 Octave   1 Octave   2 Octave   3 Octave

Sine

Noise
Mode

Irregular   More Irregular   Maximum   Minimum

Multifract   With Rotation   Multiply   Difference

Autophased   Maximum 90   Minimum 90   Displaced Max
             (switched)   (switched)

Figure 9–70 Two different noises—RND Continuous and Sine—at four octave settings; RND Continuous noise in all modulation options.

combination when it says minimum? Because the Minimum 90 and Maximum 90 are switched. Someone at MetaTools got mixed up. This is good for woven patterns, where woof and warp are used.

- *Maximum 90.* Repeats the noise at a 90° angle and combines the two, finding the minimum. Its name is switched with the noise above.

- *Auto-Phased.* This automatically introduces phase to the noise modulation itself, rather than using the separate Phase control (see the "In Your Phase" section for more about phase).

- *Displaced Max.* This displaces, or offsets, the noise by a small amount, and shows the lightest of the two places where they overlap. This is good for pebbles and stones.

In Your Phase

At the end of the fast overview of the Deep Texture Editor, I briefly mentioned phase as something that can be globally applied to the entire combined texture. Phase is an added level of turbulence. (In the Shallow Texture Editor, you are calling on phase when you click the More Turbulence button.) However, you can apply phase to any one of your individual components or to the combined texture (or both!). When you are working with the Deep Texture Editor, you usually work for a while and then decide later that a bit of phase would do the trick. However, as Bryce's Deep Texture Editor processes things, it looks at phase first to see how the turbulence displaces everything else. So first Bryce will look at the global phase, then phase settings for individual components, and then individual noises and so on through the loop.

How does phase work? When you click the Set Phase... button, *surprise!* You find yourself in the Edit Noise dialog box. All the particulars for editing noise apply to creating and editing phase as well, with two important distinctions:

1. The only place that you can set the phase frequency is in the Edit Phase... (Edit Noise) dialog box. The little slider on the face of the Deep Texture Editor allows you to adjust amplitude. This slider determines how much phase will interfere with the component's noise. I'll elaborate on this in a moment.

2. There is no such thing as filtering a phase. The filter applies to the noise. Once you have introduced phase into the equation, the combined phase-noise will be percolated together through the filtering process.

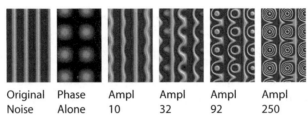

| Original
Noise | Phase
Alone | Ampl
10 | Ampl
32 | Ampl
92 | Ampl
250 |

Figure 9–71 Phase amplitude adjustment: Original noise is at left; phase is next to it; phase is applied with increasing amplitude settings.

Since my entire discussion of filtering follows this section, I'll let the filter matter rest here and take up again with this amplitude business.

The amplitude of the phase refers to the degree of phase's effect. The higher the amplitude, the more "offset" the original noise is. Figure 9–71 shows a sample of this. As amplitude is increased, there is more interference with the original noise. You don't need to set amplitude very high in order for phase to have a marked effect. In fact, restrain yourself to the lower parts of the amplitude scale until you've got a good grasp of what is happening.

Of course, by now you're starting to get a feel for the costliness of the process. Once you have introduced another element to offset all other elements, you're asking Bryce to process more, and so your rendering time will increase. Phase in your cost! Have a care when using phase. By all means, use it when the situation calls for it, but don't use it willy-nilly because you think it will be cool to run into the Deep Texture Editor and tweak a few dials.

> **TIP:** This is a phase housekeeping tip. Check each component to see that phase isn't called upon unnecessarily. Even if your phase amplitude is set to 0, check the Edit Phase… dialog box for each component, as well as the final combination, to ensure the noise type is set to Nothing. If you have some noise type selected, even if there's no amplitude, you will still force Bryce to think about that noise type before it gets the "all clear" from the zeroed amplitude slider. When Bryce is forced to think about things needlessly, your render time increases.

Filtering

This is an extremely powerful part of the Deep Texture Editor. When you refine a noise through a filter, you alter it in some fashion. Make the noise more contrasty, posterize the noise, pull out additional details, or make the noise occur only at certain altitudes or other spatial orientations.

Filter Area—The ABCs

The Filter is in the area to the right of the preview. (See Figure 9–72.) There is a graph and some numbers for *a, b* and *c*. Choose which of the filter functions you want to apply from the Filter pop-up menu. The filter has a Reset button. Clicking that in the Macintosh version changes the values and graph to show no effect, or the equivalent for None for that particular filter. When first exploring what these filters do, use Reset as a starting point. Clicking the Reset button in the Windows version is the same as a partial revert; it restores that filter's settings to what was present when you first opened the Deep Texture Editor. Also, the Windows version of the Deep Texture Editor does not allow you to directly type numerical values for *a, b*, or *c*. Being forced to always drag the filter graph while being unable to reset the filter to a neutral state puts the Windows user at a disadvantage in the Deep Texture Editor. But hey, this is the first go-round for Bryce on Windows. The first Macintosh version didn't allow you to see everything at once.

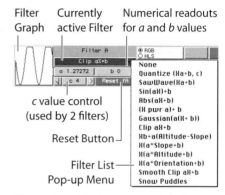

Figure 9–72 The Filter area of the Deep Texture Editor.

The Filter area has a graph with numeric readouts for *a* and *b*. Drag the graph to change the filter. Dragging horizontally changes the *a* number and dragging vertically changes the *b* number. There is also a *c* variable. In a couple of filters, *c* is also an option in the filter equation. Generally the *a* control adjusts the intensity of whatever the effect is, while *b* adjusts the overall height. In some filters, *a* and *b* may stand for other things. Visualize the top part of the range as being white and the bottom part as black. (This works well for Macs; I'll address the Windows situation shortly.) Figure 9–73a shows the filter graph next to a gray ramp. Or think of the graph's range as a side view cutaway of a bump map. The deepest dents are at the bottom and heights are at the top.

There are two sets of number schemes in the filters. In the graph, which you should visualize as a continuum from black to white, the bottom (black) is 0 whereas the top (white) is 1. The graph will not go lower than 0 or higher than 1. The other set of numbers are for *a* and *b* (and *c*, in the couple of instances where *c* is used). They range all over the place.

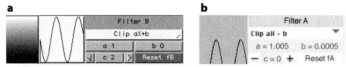

Figure 9–73 a) Macintosh version of the graph (visualize white at the top, black at the bottom); b) Windows version of graph for comparison.

As previously hinted, the Windows version of the filter graphs works differently. The graphs have a different appearance than do their Macintosh counterparts. Notice in Figure 9–73b that the Windows filter graph (with nearly equivalent numerical values) does not occupy the entire range of the graph area. Instead, it occupies the bottom half. It's more problematical to visualize the graph with a simple rule such as "visualize white at the top, black at the bottom" since the graph is inverted. If you drag up, the result is the same for both Mac and Windows versions—the noise will get lighter. However, the graph moves down in the opposite direction of the mouse. So is the "white-is-up" rule connected to the direction of your drag—in which case it would be true— or is the "white-is-*down*" rule connected to the placement of the graph? I agree, it's confusing!

One way that I will address the cross-platform filter graph confusion is to provide screen shots for the Windows filter graphs for every example I illustrate. Otherwise, you Windows users would look at the Mac screen shots and say to yourself, "But *my* version of Bryce doesn't look like *that!*"

Also, although the drag-horizontally-to-adjust-item-*a* and the drag-vertically-to-adjust-item-*b* rules apply to Windows, you must drag in the opposite direction to get a similar result. To lower the value for *a* using a Mac, you drag to the left. But dragging to the left will raise the value for *a* under Windows. The difficulty is compounded by the fact that you cannot directly type in numerical values for *a*, *b*, or *c*. When it comes to dragging the graph vertically to change the value for *b*, it gets more complicated. As previously mentioned, a drag up results in the graph moving down in the opposite direction, even though the results of an upward drag are the same for both Mac and Windows.

The last difference betwen the Macintosh and Windows versions of the filter controls concerns the Reset button. The Reset button on the Mac sets the filter back to the neutral position for that filter. In all cases, the numberical settings for reset are *a* 1, *b* 0, *c* 2. Under Windows the Reset filter button is a limited revert function—it will return you to the filter setting that was present when you first entered the Deep Texture Editor. If you want to get back to a neutral place, drag the graph until the numbers are as close to *a* 1 and *b* 0 as you can possibly get. They'll help you get yourself oriented in the Deep Texture Editor.

> **TIP:** When exploring in the Deep Texture Editor, set the output to Value. Value has the fastest processing time, and you'll see everything in plain grayscale. Later you can change the output to one of the others, if need be.

Now let's get down to specifics. The following descriptions will show the relationship between the filter formula, the graph appearance, and the final noise result. The discussion will take them in a logical sequence, not necessarily the order they're listed in the pop-up menu. I'll begin with Clip aX + b because it is the most basic of the filters.

The most often-used, ubiquitous contrast filter, Clip gets its name from portions of the noise being clipped at the upper and lower ends for higher contrast. When adjusting the sliders, *a* controls the contrast and *b* controls the overall brightness.

Clip aX + b

For a low-contrast effect, make the wave smaller. Decrease *a* to reduce the size of the wave and increase *b* to move the entire wave up. This one is a mid-gray. All the noise information will be output as expressions of middle grays for low-contrast noise. See Figure 9–74.

For a high-contrast effect, adjust so that the graph hits the top and bottom edges—for the Macintosh version. Windows users, let the graph illustrations in Figure 9–74 be your guide. When the wave hits the top, it clips at white; when it hits bottom, it clips at black. The wave actually ascends above and descends below the limits, but if the top represents white you can't get any whiter than white once you go "beyond" white. Give *a* a large number for a higher range of wave motion; give *b* a negative number to move the entire curve down (Mac) or up (Windows) and then "center" it so that portions clip at top and bottom.

To invert the noise (white changes to black), make *a* negative and adjust *b* to the corresponding level.

Figure 9–75 shows examples of all filter types as they are applied to two types of noise—RND Continuous and Linear Sine.

Smooth Clip aX + b

Smooth Clip is the same as Clip aX + b except that it smoothes out the hard transitions.

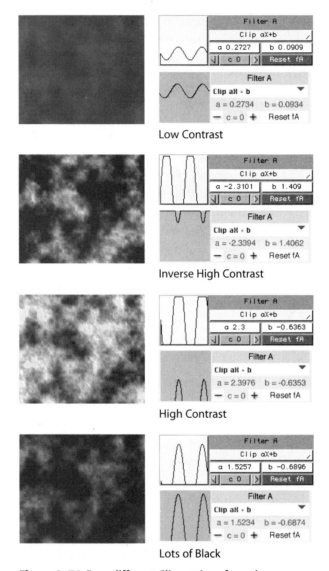

Figure 9–74 Four different Clip settings from the same texture demonstrate the range of possibilities.

Quantize

Quantize, analogous to the Terrain Editor's (and Photoshop's) Posterize, creates discontinuities as gray values stair-step from one level to the next. The setting for *c* determines the number of levels between black and white, and the settings for *a* and *b* determine overall contrast and height.

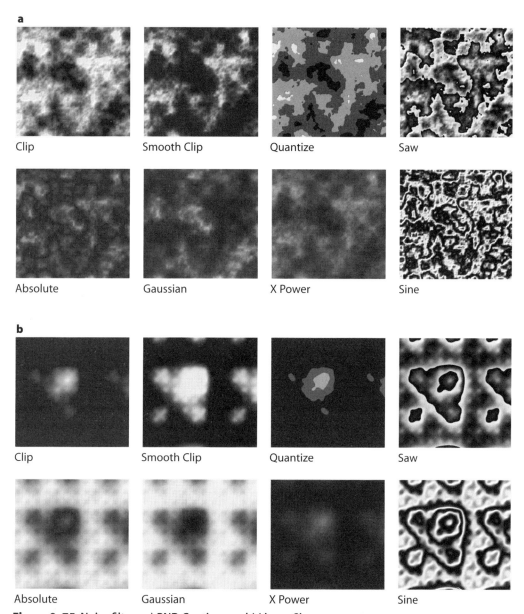

Figure 9–75 Noise filters: a) RND Continuous; b) Linear Sine.

Saw Wave

Saw Wave starts as a contrast filter (when there's a small curve in it). When the curve reaches the limits, instead of the top and bottom being clipped, the curve is "bounced" back in the other direction. The result is high-contrast discontinuity, like a saw. (Happily, the Windows version uses the full range of the graph in order to create the bounced curve.) Use this with color output to get portions of high-contrast alternating color. When you set *a* high, so that there are many waves bouncing top to bottom, you'll get areas where there is a lot of noise. Take care how high you set *a* when using this to filter noise for Normale bump output.

Sine Wave—Sin(aX) + b

This filter gives you a high number of lines that follow the same path. Use it for creating things such as wood textures or perhaps desert sand. The number of lines is determined by *a*. This filter is continuous. As *a* increases, the curve maintains its curved shape as it bounces back down from the top. Higher numbers, say, 10 or 20, are better. On the Mac, you'll need to type these in by hand, as the slider will let you set numbers only up to 4; the Windows version has no limits to how far you can drag. (The Macintosh-drag-stops-at-4 and you-can-drag-forever-in-Windows are both true for all of the filters, not just Sine Wave.) The value for *b*, as usual, adjusts the entire curve and will determine clipping at top or bottom.

Absolute—Abs(aX + b)

This filter, analogous to Photoshop's Difference calculation, takes the absolute value of the noise sine wave. So where the curve would otherwise clip at black, it ends up popping back up. This results in more light areas and additional complexity for bump maps, especially in those places where the bump would be flat (or 0). Absolute will clip at white if given the opportunity. To get twice the bump information, enter $a = 2$ and $b = -1$.

X Power—(X PWR a) + b

X Power is similar to Gaussian. Both smooth out the darkest areas as they get to the bottom. However, X Power clips at white, whereas Gaussian "bounces" the curve back down. X Power's curve is offset halfway from Gaussian's, so what Gaussian clips is what X Power actually shows.

Gaussian—(a(X + b))

Gaussian creates a bell curve and clips at 0. The variable for *a* determines how spiky or pinched the curve is; *b* determines the upness and downness of it (whether toward white or toward black). You get smooth areas near 0 and bump when the value is higher, toward white. When the value is up at white, Gaussian bounces it down, thereby resulting in noisier areas in the light range.

The next five filters adjust the noise and apply it depending on the object's orientation in the three-dimensional World Space. Their curves move in a diagonal direction. Figure 9–76 shows each filter applied to Sine and RND Continuous noise.

Altitude— X(a★Altitude + b)

The Altitude filter modulates the noise according to altitude. The setting for *a* determines how fast the noise is scaled by altitude. A lower number will result in a gradual transition, whereas a higher number will result in a sharper transition. For noise applied at high altitude, *a* is a positive number. The *b* setting determines the onset of the transition. The higher the onset of transition to noise, the lower the number. For noise applied at high altitude, *b* is usually a negative number. To apply the noise at low altitudes, reverse the settings so that *a* is negative and *b* is positive.

Slope—X(a★Slope + b)

Slope works the same way as the Altitude filter, except that it uses slope. It applies the noise according to the object's position, from flat and

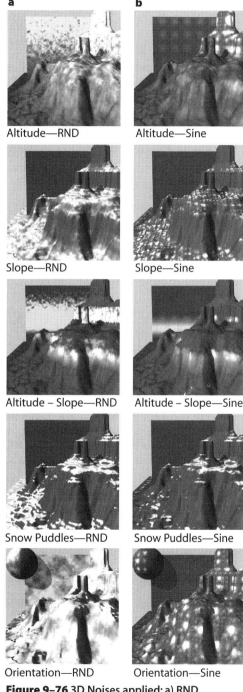

a   **b**

Altitude—RND   Altitude—Sine

Slope—RND   Slope—Sine

Altitude – Slope—RND   Altitude – Slope—Sine

Snow Puddles—RND   Snow Puddles—Sine

Orientation—RND   Orientation—Sine

Figure 9–76 3D Noises applied: a) RND **Continuous; b) Sine.**

horizontal (no slope, or graph at 0) to sheer and upright (high slope, or graph at 1). This is the filter to use to isolate textures to vertical cliff surfaces or flat surfaces.

When looking at 2D Preview of the texture, the left side represents no slope (or flat areas) and the right represents high slope (or upright areas). The best preview to look at, however, is the Spherical Preview, since you can see all of the transitions from flat to vertical.

The value for a determines the steepness of the noise; –4 is completely flat, while 4 is sheer upright. The value for b adjusts the starting point of the transition and controls clipping at the sheer vertical or flat horizontal extremes. When the slope is 0 (as determined by the graph), only the setting for b acts on your noise. So if you want a little noise where there are flat places, set b slightly above 0 (0.1 or 0.075).

Noise on upright surface: $a = 4$ (or high 3's); $b = -2$ (or 2.5).

Noise on flat surface: $a = -4$ (or high –3's); $b = 1.5$ (or 2 or more).

Altitude Minus Slope—Xb+a (Altitude–Slope)

Altitude Minus Slope puts the noise only at certain combinations of slope and altitude. When a is positive and b is negative, the result will be noise at high altitude and flat surfaces. When a is negative and b is positive, the result will be noise at low altitudes on upright surfaces.

Orientation—X(a★Orientation + b)

Orientation operates similarly to Altitude and Slope, only instead of change being oriented to degrees of height, it is oriented to degrees of "east" and "west."

Snow Puddles

This filter turns noise into snow patches. The value of a determines how much snow is affected by the noise. When $a = 0$, the noise doesn't apply at all, so the snow is uniform. When a is higher, the snow takes on the look of the noise. The value of b shifts altitude, or the snow level. The Snow Puddles filter has a c value, too, which determines the slope. The higher the number, the flatter the surface needs to be for snow to stick to it.

Output Types

Now that the noise has been generated and filtered, it's time to determine the output type. The three options are Value, Normale, and Color. You can also combine them so that a component can have any one, two, or three output types. Value here in the Deep Texture Editor corresponds to the alpha for the Texture Source, and drives the illumination and optics channels. Normale corresponds to the texture's bump information, to drive the material's Bump Height channel. Color output corresponds to the Texture Source's color, and will drive the color channels in the Materials Composer.

Value and Normale both take their information from the gray values of the noise. In the Windows version of Bryce, you'll need to select Normale as one of the options for Global Output in order to see the Normale information in the preview for a particular noise. Otherwise the "Normale" preview will look the same as Value.

But if the output will be Color, then how will the colors be chosen? It should come as no surprise that Bryce provides plenty of options!

Color Combinations

Here is a description of each color combination option. Figure C9–77 (see color section) shows a sample of the results of each. For all but the red/green/blue, the same set of colors was used. Also, there are two sets of textures for each image comparison: The objects on the left used a texture generated with Random Continuous noise; the objects on the right used a texture from Sine noise.

- *RGB/HLS.* The Red (Hue)/Green (Light)/Blue (Saturation) (RGB/HLS) options will set that one component to output for that one channel only. So you can have three components, each set differently for Color (or Color-Normale or Color-Value). Make one a Red Channel, another a Green Channel, and the last a Blue Channel. Click the radio button that changes the color model to HSV, and your noises are Hue, Saturation, and Light, respectively.

- *Linear Interpolation 2.* Creates a linear blend between the two chosen colors.

- *Linear Interpolation 3.* Creates a linear blend between the three selected colors.

- *Spline.* One of the more common color mapping options, it is similar to Linear Interpolation 3.

- *Spline with Snow.* Same as Spline, only it adds snow on top according to the altitude of the object.

- *Altitude.* Puts white snow level on your colors. Vary the snow level using the Material Editor's Frequency control. Anything below ground level is automatically colored blue.

- *Randomized.* Applies color using standard interpolation and randomized afterwards in RGB space by means of a noise that Bryce generates internally.

- *Earth Map.* Generates color according to the bump map. Besides the colors you've selected, which are applied in the middle of the bump range, blue is applied at the lowest values. There are also white polar ice caps. Use this with Normale-color on spheres in outer space for planets.

- *Perturbed Map.* This applies colors with additional irregularities.

- *Banded.* This version applies the colors in bands. Rather than the normal trek through the lowest-midpoint-highest color associations, this one will have cycled back through the color again, so that it looks like low-middle-high-middle-low.

- *Interferences.* The individual red, green, and blue values for the *first* color create a repeating pattern around the contours of the noise. It's wild n' crazy.

- *Interpol+Interferences.* A combination of Linear Interpolation and Interferences.

- *Slope.* Gives an object a different color depending on its slope.

- *Orient.* Assigns the colors to the object according to east-west orientation.

Global Changes

What happens to the textures when they are combined? That is determined in a couple of places; the Global changes and the Blend mode pop-up menus that are between the two.

Normally, with an explanation like this, I'd continue on with a how-it-works explanation and then, toward the end, provide some housekeeping practical tips. However, the current state of the Deep Texture Editor is such that I must mention the practical tips at this point. There is at least one nasty gremlin that lives in the Global changes section of the Macintosh Deep Texture Editor that can make your life miserable. So I'll describe my work-around. (This is a ticklish part of the Deep Texture Editor because in order to fix one problem, you have to tiptoe around another one. It *can* be done, however. Just keep thinking of this as someone else's way cool sock drawer, and you'll learn to live with the quirks.)

If you have worked with changing the individual component noise(s), and then go on to change the global output type and/or the color type and/or the colors, you will commit an unintentional "revert" action. Those noises and filterings that you have so carefully worked on will all go away, and your noises will be set to what they were when you first opened the Deep Texture Editor. Rather than letting this inspire a colorful swearfest after you've lost your work, beat the Deep Texture Editor to the punch and save the texture that you're working on before you make any global edits.

To save the noise, you can do one of two things. Click the check mark to leave the Deep Texture Editor, or else click the Add Texture button. I prefer the latter, since, by the time I've been hanging out in the Deep Texture Editor for a while, I don't know which texture I started with anymore. Unlike the Shallow Texture Editor, where you are presented with a text input dialog box for renaming your texture or else overwriting it, the Macintosh version of the Deep Texture Editor assumes that you know what the heck you're doing. (Sock drawer! Sock Drawer! Keep thinking about that sock drawer—only it's the drawer belonging to Jack with his Amazing Technicolor Dream Socks.) In assuming so, it's assumed that you know that you are overwriting the texture that is there. If you don't want to do that, you rename it by adding it. Of course, once you get to the Add dialog box, you can see the Cancel button all right, but the OK button is, well, hanging off the right side. But you know where to put those socks, right? On your feet! And no one has to tell you where your feet are, nor put a label on your foot that says "foot." Likewise the OK button. Click the half-a-button on the right. (See Figure 9–78.) If you don't like it, deal with it! (Or fix it in ResEdit; look on the CD-ROM in the DTE folder for some ResEdit fixer-upper hints!) Incidentally, the Windows version of the Deep Texture Editor presents the normal Add Texture dialog box; its appearance is the same as the one presented in the Shallow Texture Editor.

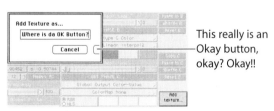

Figure 9–78 The Add Texture dialog box, with the Okay button on the right (Macintosh version).

So, now that you've added and named your texture, you can work in the global edits with impunity. (Sorry, I wish there were a way to fix the Global Editor in ResEdit, too. I know of none. We take what we get, and are thankful.)

At this point, you can do several things with your combined output. The options should be familiar to you, since you could also do them working on the individual texture components:

- *Preview Combined Components.* When you look at a preview, you'll see the combined texture.

- *Adjust Frequency.* This presumably adjusts frequency on a global basis. It is broken in the Macintosh version, so don't bother. In the Windows version, the Global Frequency adjusts the individual component frequencies accordingly, but since the individual component frequencies adjust only on the *x* axis, this control is not much use. It's a good idea, though.

- *Assign Output Type.* Assign an output type for the color, Value, Normale, or combinations of those.

- *Filter Combined Output.* Choose a filter and settings for the combined texture. The Filter will affect the combined Value for the texture.

- *Add Global Phase to the Combined Texture.* This is the same as adding turbulence in the Shallow Texture Editor and similar to adding phase to any of the individual components.

If the final output type is something that is not matched by any of the individual components, those individual components will be converted to the final output type. So if you have one component that is Value and the final combined output is Color, Value will be converted to Color. (Parallel is an exception to this; see later in this chapter.) If you have a one-component texture and set the component's output type to Normale and then set the combined output type as Color, you'll get a scary color combination as your Normale information is converted to color information. (This explains the strange behaviors you see when you are creating textures and it just doesn't look right.) Likewise, if you do not have a color setting for the texture but use the texture to drive color information in the Materials Composer, you'll get the funky coloring of the psychotic texture.

On the Macintosh, if you have more individual output types (say, Normale, Color and Value) in the individual components than you do in the combined (which is, say, Color-Value), but at least one output type is shared between the combined and individual, the individual components won't be changed. Under Windows, in order to both *see* the Normale preview in the individual texture component, you must have Normale set as part of the Global Output option. If you have set

Normale to be a part of your texture and activate it in the Bump Height channel, it will drive the Bump Height even though you cannot see it in the Deep Texture Editor preview.

Combining Components—Blend Modes

By now you have generated noise, filtered it, assigned an output type of Value, Normale, or Color (or a combination of those), and assigned color maps for your color components. Assuming you have more than one component, now is the time for you to choose the parameters for the combined output and choose the way that the individual components interact with one another. The parameters can be set in the pop-up menus between the previews for each of the three components.

Although the Macintosh version of Bryce calls them Op 1 (an abbreviation of the French term Operations Interactions—the second one *should* say Op 2, but oh well), I call them Blend Modes. The Windows version of the Deep Texture Editor has entirely rid itself of the Op1/Op2 label. Figure C9–79 shows the result of each of the different blend modes.

Maximum/Blend Maximum

In Maximum, Bryce compares the two components and whichever is lighter is the final result. If you are familiar with channel operations or apply modes, this is the same as Lighten Only. Blend Maximum is the same as Maximum, except it creates blurring at points of harsh transition.

When you use Blend Maximum for basic bump mapping, the resulting bump map will generally have more high points and dip into low points only occasionally. When it's used with a Color output type, it's not the lightest color that determines the maximum result, but the value. Temporarily change the output type to Value to check. You may have a result where a darker color is actually "lighter," since the dark color was assigned to an area of light value.

Minimum/Blend Minimum

Minimum is the complement to Maximum. Instead of the lighter portions of noise prevailing, the darker ones do. It is analogous to "Darken Only" in two-dimensional imaging blends or channel calculations. Blend Minimum smoothes out any abrupt transitions between the two.

When creating Normale bump maps, use Minimum when you want areas that are generally lower with some higher points. The same situation about so-called darker and lighter colors holds true for Minimum as well as Maximum. These combination modes work better for components that use Normale as an output type.

Parallel

This is a non-blend mode. Use it when you have Normale in one component, Color in another, and Value in another. If you have one output type that is shared by components, such as Normale-*Color* and Value-*Color*, you won't get your desired result for color. The color will be taken from the first component only.

Combine

Combine is a blend mode for color only. For each component, you can assign three colors. I'll call the first of these Color 1. Combine uses Component B's Color 1 as an alpha channel. Wherever that color is located, you see Component A in the combined result.

Average

Average is a normal blend between the two components, where all elements are mixed with equal weight. If one is black and the other is white, the result will be gray. This is a good, all-purpose output type for Bryce textures, another Normale combination workhorse. In fact, there are other blend options here (such as Add) that combine the Color and Value information using that blend procedure, but the Normale information is blended with a straightforward Average. I'll mention the Blend options that work in this fashion as I go along.

Multiply

Multiply combines both components in such a way that they get darker. In the case of Value or Normale, when one is black, the result is black. When one is white, the result is whatever the other one is. Where both are shades in between, they are proportionately darkened.

When using Multiply with Normale output type, the result will be a smaller bump map. Black is "flat" and, when multiplied, gets darker. However, use Multiply when one component has patches of black and white. The black will completely flatten the other map, and the white lets all the rest stay as is. (I've seen this successfully used on a bump map when the first component is set to Normale, and the second, high-contrast component is set to value. The second component also affects the Normale of the first, without its being set to Normale. The Puddlebumps recipe at the end of this chapter is set up that way. I've yet to have two Normale components successfully combined using Multiply, however.)

Add

Add combines colors so that they are dramatically lighter. However, it does not alter Normale information in the same dramatic way. Add uses a basic average for the bump information.

Subtract

Subtract is a Blend mode that, in grayscale, tends to go toward black. In color, subtract results in brilliant and bizarre combinations that lean toward the complement of the original color. Be adventurous with color here and remember that the Normale information is averaged together in the same way as Add and Average.

Blend v1; Blend v2

Since you are never blending more than two components, you always choose between the first or the second. These modes blend the two components according to the Value of the first one (v1) or of the second one (v2). Essentially, these allow you to use one or another of your noises as an alpha channel for blending.

Blend Slope/Fast Slope

These modes blend two different components according to slope. The first component is applied to areas that are flat; the second is applied to areas that are upright (or have high slope). Fast Slope is a variation that blends in a more abrupt manner.

Blend Altitude

Blend Altitude blends the two different components—the first one at lower altitude and the second one at higher altitude.

Blend Orientation

This blend mode will put one component facing all directions and blend the other component on one direction only (used for such things as moss or something that grows only on north sides of trees and rocks).

Blend Random

Here's another alpha channel type of blend. A low-frequency random noise becomes the alpha channel. It chooses one component here and the other component there for the final version. Of course, since you're adding another layer of noise, it means you get that much more noise for your two or three components. But it's costlier, too.

Difference

Difference finds the difference between the noises of the two components. It operates only on the output types common to both components. If the first component is color-value and the second is value, then the first component's Color will be passed on "straight" while the Value will be "differenced." Normale is combined using the straightforward average.

Difference is too complex to go into here, but it does some pretty wild things to your colors. A light color combined with another color will invert the other color; so you'll find a lot of complementary-color relationships using difference.

Procedural Blend

Procedural Blend combines the two textures so that the color and value of the first is applied to the second based on the gray values of the second. Where the second's is light, the first is not applied. Where the second is dark, the first's is made darker. Where the second is a straight medium gray, the first is applied without change. Blending using this method usually results in colors that are more saturated. You may need to adjust your original colors to get the right combination. Normale information is interpreted as a straightforward average when noises are combined using Procedural Blend.

3D Texture Practicalia

At last it's time for the real housekeeping hints! Here's an assortment of important things to know that don't fit into the overall conceptual information I previously explained.

Some Deep Texture Editor Mechanics

Sometimes after making a change, the preview does not update. At other times the filter graph may fail to update (especially in response to typed numbers in the Macintosh version). This usually happens after you've been working in Bryce for a while. To force an update, click inside the preview window for that particular noise component. To force the graph to update, click to increase or decrease the value for c by one number, then click to return it to its former state. The graph will have updated. I've found that after a time of working in the Windows version of the Deep Texture Editor, Bryce as a whole becomes more unstable and prone to crashing. If you're working in the Deep Texture Editor for a prolonged amount of time, be sure to go back to the scene and save it (your texture-in-progress will be saved with the scene) in case Bryce decides to die on you.

By now you Macintosh Brycers may have noticed that when a section of the Deep Texture Editor is colored blue, it means it's selected. For most numeric adjustments, you can directly type the information (Macintosh only!). If you've begun typing and need to start over, click the box again and start over. Otherwise your 10—oops, I wanted that to be a 12!— will turn into 1012. If worse comes to worst, click elsewhere and then click back again to enter numbers. Both Macintosh and Windows users may drag from the number to increase or decrease. Up is higher, down is lower. Bryce Windows allows dragging only for certain numerical controls, though. Dragging to change the number works in the Noise Editor (and Phase Editor), and for the Frequency and Amplitude sliders. It does not work for adjusting the numbers for the Noise Filter.

> *TIP: When working in the Deep Texture Editor, choose bright saturated colors (at first) so that you can clearly see what each color is doing. When all is balanced to your liking, then you can go back and make fine-tuning adjustments to your color.*

Frequency

There are several places where you can adjust texture frequency. They are all related to one another, from the individual noise frequency in the Edit Noise dialog box, to the Frequency slider for that component, to the Global Frequency control—assuming that it works, of course, to the Materials Composer's frequency control for that texture source and for all the textures combined. (Previous warnings about the Windows Frequency sliders apply.)

Add/Copy/Paste Texture

These three types of buttons on the right-hand side of the Deep Texture Editor are used for general housekeeping.

- *Add Texture.* Add a texture to the list of 3D Solid Textures in the Materials Composer. Click the button, name your creation, and click OK. Your texture has joined the list *for as long as Bryce stays open.* When you quit Bryce, it will go away. Remember, the path to Texture Permanence travels through the Valley of the Saved Preset or through the Valley of the Object Saved in a Scene.

- *Copy A (or B or C)/Paste A (or B or C).* Use these buttons to copy one component and paste it to another. Do this to shuffle around components within the same texture. Or, copy a component from one texture, close the Deep Texture Editor, select another texture, open up the Deep Texture Editor for *that* one, and paste the component.

Shuffle Texture

If you find all of this Deep Texture Editor detail too much to deal with, you can submit yourself to the random muse by clicking the Shuffle Texture button. 'Round and 'round and 'round it goes, and where it stops, nobody knows. Whee!

Component Order

The order in which the components are created sometimes makes a difference. How? In the way things are blended together. Depending on the output type, you may need to change them around. I'll talk about this type of situation when I talk about the "Snowed Under" material exercise at the end of this chapter.

Names in the List

The textures are listed in a certain order. The default ones are listed first and in alphabetical order. For some crazy reason in the Macintosh version of Bryce, there are repeats of a subset of those textures. They look the same. They're named the same. But they're in the list twice—permanently. Why? Heck if I know. I just told you this so that you won't think that you are the only crazy one with that crazy setup. If *I'm* the only one, though, you can write me and tell me that the last laugh's on me!

Following the default list are the ones that have been accessed through the Presets, or contained in any scenes you have opened during your current Bryce work session. When you add a texture from the Deep Texture Editor, it goes to the bottom of the list. Incidentally for you Mac Brycers, when you add those textures, do not use slashes (/) in your names. They'll be interpreted to tell Bryce to use the following character as a ⌘-key symbol. Windows doesn't seem to have any illegal characters.

ANATOMY OF A TEXTURE AND MATERIAL

By now, I have poked into every nook and cranny of the Deep Texture Editor. But what does it all mean? How do you use it? This Journey-to-the-Center-of-the-Earth has shown what everything is, but so far it hasn't provided a look at a real-live texture and how it was put together. That time has now arrived! I'll take a look at some specific textures and examine them in the Deep Texture Editor to discuss how they work, paying attention to how they'll be used in the Materials Composer.

I'll bite off and chew six separate Deep Textures:

- The three textures in the Whole Mountain Preset examined earlier;

- Planet Rings: Variations on an existing Materials Preset;

- Snowed Under: Snow atop a rock;

- Bump and Reflections: bumps with reflective puddles.

Analyzing Textures

"Okay," you say. "All of those mathematical equations were simply lovely, Susan. Do you have any more like them? Any more that will help me get just that right look to my terrain that I want?" Look, just admit it. Your eyes were glazed over during that section. I don't blame you. Mine were rather glassy the first time I encountered the explanation for how they work. The explanations I provided are a resource for you to turn to when the right time comes. Once you get to working with the textures a bit, you'll turn back to refer to them. "But how do I *start* working with the textures?" you reasonably reply. The first thing you do is analyze the textures that you like. I'll do a bit of that here. There is enough depth and complexity to the Deep Texture Editor to merit a book all its own, and so as a thick part of a very thick chapter in a rather thick book, I cannot go into all the lurid details for every one of those options. The next best thing is to break down a few textures and analyze how they work. Before I do so, however, I'll provide a few clues for how you can do your own exploration, just in case the texture that has caught your eye doesn't happen to be one that I discuss here.

- *Orient yourself to orientation.* Look for the overall orientation. Is the texture doing something in Bryce's World Space that relies on altitude or slope or orientation? You can see the orientation effects in the filtering (for the individual component, or in the global), in the blend mode between components, and in the color mapping.

- *Simplify multi-component textures.* When there's a texture that has two or three components, switch down to a lower number and look at the combination preview or exit the Deep Texture Editor and go back to the scene and see how it renders. You'll be able to see how—by its absence—that second or third component interacts with the first (or combination of first and second), and how the Blend mode does what it does. You needn't worry about the texture component going away and getting lost somewhere. After you're through poking at the simpler texture, click the proper button to bring all the components back again.

- *Look at the different preview views.* The menu at the bottom accesses the different methods of previewing the texture. The default preview on the Macintosh is the cube preview; the default for Windows is the 2D preview (though once you select another preview option, Bryce remembers it until you change it to something else for the duration of your current work session). Remember, there are two other options besides the default preview. Although the cube preview will show some slope qualities—the flat part will show on the flat part, and the upright parts will show on the uprights—you cannot see the subtle shifts at differing slopes. The 3D sphere will show you that. In other cases, seeing what occurs at low altitude will show up best when looking at the 2D preview. Altitude runs from bottom to top, slope runs at an angle, and orientation runs from left to right. This is also helpful to understand the previews when scrolling through textures in the Shallow Texture Editor, where the preview is the flat 2D version.

- *Explore the noise.* It's fairly easy to see what's going on with noise without necessarily changing the numerical settings (frequency and direction). You can change the noise, you can change the number of octaves, and you can change the modulation. If you don't want to keep your exploratory changes, click cancel when you leave the Noise Editor.

- *Switch off the filter momentarily.* When looking at the filter graph accompanied with numbers out to the fifth decimal place, it's easy to be intimidated. You may find yourself fearing, "if I touch it, I'll ruin it!" and thereby talk yourself out of exploring the filter. There are at least two ways to explore safely without budging a thing. First, you can switch the filter from its present form to None. The numbers won't change, you'll just momentarily deactivate the filter. Then you can see how the noise operates alone. When you're done looking at that, select the filter again. All the numbers are still there, down to the last decimal place. Whew!

- *Levels of undo.* The second option is also sneaky; it allows you to get your hands dirty with the Filter controls and still emerge from the Deep Texture Editor unscathed. At the right of each component area are a set of buttons for copying that component and pasting to that other component. So, before you tweak the filter for, say, Component B, just click the Copy B button. When you're through with your mad scientific ramblings through all the different options in the Filter B menu, click Paste to B and all is restored.

- *The ultimate undo.* Of course, you can always cancel out of the Deep Texture Editor after you're through, and none of the changes you have made will affect the texture.

This set of options should make your own explorations easier.

- Look only at the value output type, especially for the global texture.

If you want to branch out on your own, you can copy a texture and then paste it into one component as a starting place. Then add your own noisy textural explorations and see what kind of new hybrid you come up with!

Another place to go exploring, after you're through here, is to Hilary Rhodes' Deep Texture Editor website (http://www.cadre.nepean.uws.edu.au/~hilary/Brycehtm/Cats.html). Hilary created the site as an elective project for her master's degree—and received a high distinction for it!—at the University of Western Sydney, Australia. The site is also mirrored at the Terraformer's Guild (http://www.terraformers.org). It's an excellent compilation of the different elements that go into creating a texture in Bryce. You can start in any direction and browse through noises, modes, filters, differing number of components, and more. There are rendered samples for each type.

Altitude Adjustment: Whole Mountain, continued. . .

Having performed a thorough exegesis of the Whole Mountain material in the Materials Composer, let's take up the discussion once again with the underlying textures. There are three of them: Hills 29, Gray Galets 29, and Basic Altitude 29 (The number 29 is the result of making a preset—Bryce adds a number to the texture, renaming it.) Hills is Texture Source A; Gray Galets (pebbly) is Texture Source B, and Basic Altitude is the Texture source that switches between them.

Hills 29 Texture

The Hills 29 Texture is a three-component texture (see Figure 9–80). Each component is set to Normale-Color-Value, with the Global Output also set to Normale-Color-Value (it should come as no surprise, then, that the render time on this texture takes a while). There are a couple of World Space orientations. The Color Mapping for Component A is set to altitude. The Filter for the global texture is set to altitude as well. The high numbers and extreme waves on the filtering graph also indicate that there's *something* going on with that altitude as well; it's pretty extreme. (Windows users, check out the Windows filter graph in the figure.) There is also another World Space orientation operating; the blend mode between Components A-B and C is Slope. So Component C applies only under certain slope circumstances.

How about the individual noises? Component A's noise is modulated to Displaced Max. This means that there is lots of detail, and it's lighter detail. Noise that is darker has been obliterated by the Maximum setting. Component B's noise swoops in wide, circular streaks. The Blend mode between the two, Minimum, makes sense when you see the filtering for each. The higher, lighter noise in Component A is filtered to stay in the mid-to-high range. The sweeping paths are

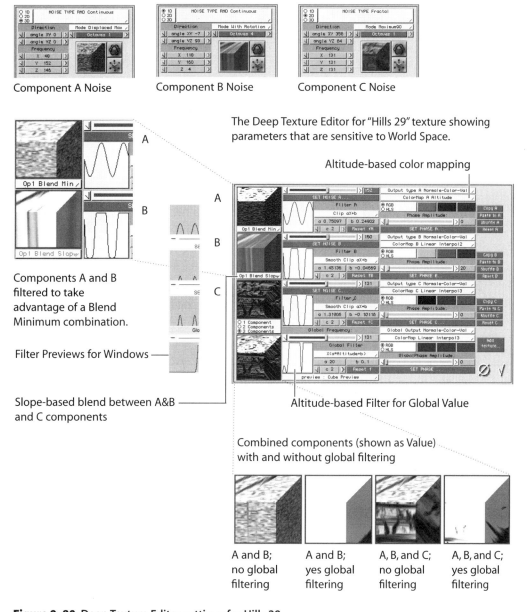

Component A Noise   Component B Noise   Component C Noise

The Deep Texture Editor for "Hills 29" texture showing parameters that are sensitive to World Space.

Altitude-based color mapping

A

B

Components A and B
filtered to take
advantage of a Blend
Minimum combination.

Filter Previews for Windows

Slope-based blend between A&B
and C components

Altitude-based Filter for Global Value

Combined components (shown as Value)
with and without global filtering

A and B;   A and B;   A, B, and C;   A, B, and C;
no global   yes global   no global   yes global
filtering   filtering   filtering   filtering

Figure 9–80 Deep Texture Editor settings for Hills 29.

filtered for smooth, high contrast, in the entire range. This filtering is for bump. Visualize the two filter paths superimposed, and you'll understand how those dirt scars (or clearings) show up here and there in the hilly texture. Wherever the two noises are lower, you get a scar. Therefore it's important that the second component is higher every place else. The mid-to-high range for the first noise ensures that it will be lower than the places where the second dirt noise is high. The dirt scars shouldn't show up all over the place, so the frequency for the second noise is much lower.

Component C is a departure from the foliage-and-dirt-scar combination. The third component is blended according to slope, so it provides the appearance to any vertical faces of the terrain. The noise modulation, Maximum 90 (remember, they're switched on the Macintosh it really is Minimum 90) applies the same noise to itself at ninety degrees, with the lower portions taking a bite out of itself. This accounts for the horizontal gashes.

Finally, the Global Filtering settings will determine the final Value—or alpha—information that will drive the diffuse illumination for the texture. Changing the Global Output to Value is instructive to see what is taking place. Compare the Global Filter with a preview of what the value looks like when there is no filtering. There are gray tones all over the place. The consequences of all that gray is that the diffuse illumination will be darker in those areas, making the Hills texture significantly darker. In order to have full diffuse illumination, the value needs to be made primarily white. However, there are spots for it to be dark, at low altitudes. Therefore the altitude filter is used and the numbers set to make the vast majority of the altitude range white, with only little rough dark patches at the bottom, as well as the most extreme of the horizontal gashes in the vertical cliff face.

Gray Galets 29

The second Texture Source, the pebbly one, has two components. (See Figure 9–81.) The first one uses the Leopard noise to create the pebble shapes. For shape, Normale-Color is the Output mode. The second noise is for determining color and value. Altitude comes into play here. For the noise itself, the lower altitude pebbles are a darker, richer beige than they are at higher altitudes. More than that, though, this second noise is the basis for the final Value, which will determine the diffuse lighting conditions for the overall texture. The Global Filter alters the texture's Value based on an extremely high-contrast altitude filter. This removes any traces of darkness at higher altitudes. In other words, the beach will be darkened only at the very lowest altitudes, although the color of those pebbles will be darker at higher altitudes. Refer back to the color images of the textures in Figures C9–44 and C9–46. Then notice how the higher the number is for *a* in the altitude filter equation, the more extreme the altitude contrast and the more white area when the noise is viewed as value only.

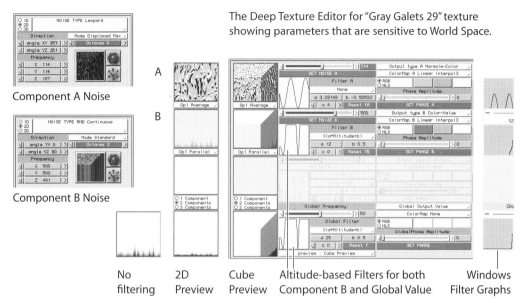

Component A Noise

Component B Noise

The Deep Texture Editor for "Gray Galets 29" texture showing parameters that are sensitive to World Space.

No filtering   2D Preview   Cube Preview   Altitude-based Filters for both Component B and Global Value   Windows Filter Graphs

Figure 9–81 Deep Texture Editor settings for Gray Galets 29.

Basic Altitude 29

The Texture Source C noise, Basic Altitude 29, is the texture that determines what's going to show at any point on the object—Source A (Hills) or B (Galets, er, pebbles). See Figure 9–82. Since the pebbly beach material is lower than the hilly vegetation, it's no surprise that the texture is based on altitude. Both noises are altitude noises. The first noise establishes a high-contrast, low-altitude barrier between light and dark value. This is for the boundary between the two textures. The second noise has lower contrast altitude filtering, allowing the lower texture to creep up into the higher regions at little spots here and there. When combined for the final output, the filter used is Clip, which creates an extremely high contrast between the two. A lower contrast would have fuzzy edges that are partially stony and partially hilly. A diffuse boundary between the two areas is not as dramatic—nor realistic—as two crisp edges. Hence the high-contrast Clip. The negative number inverts the value so that black is above and white is below. The usual altitude order in the Materials Composer is to have Source A for the lowest altitude texture and Source B for the higher altitude texture. Though this altitude texture adds noise, the white-above, black-below of the component noises follows suit. Only because the higher altitude texture was placed in Source A was it necessary to invert the final value. Since this material was created by Eric

The Deep Texture Editor for "Altitude 29" (Source C) showing parameters that are sensitive to World Space.

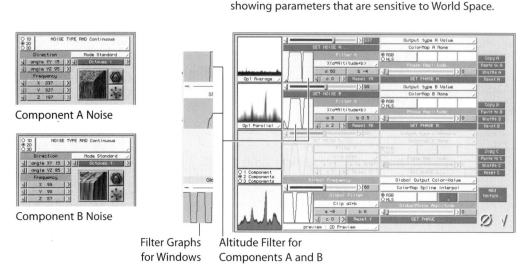

Component A Noise

Component B Noise

Filter Graphs for Windows

Altitude Filter for Components A and B

Figure 9–82 Deep Texture Editor settings for Altitude 29.

Wenger, for whom adjusting the clipping for a value is as simple as switching around Texture Sources, it's a trivial matter to change the filtering in order to accommodate the already-established Texture Source order.

Why does the output type also read color? Bryce probably kicked the color switch on when this was applied in the color channels. Try it yourself. Change the output type so that it's Value only (probably as it was first created, too). When you go back to the Materials Composer, the texture is used in the color channels, even though, as Source C, only the alpha is used. Being an active color-based texture is enough to trip the automatic "color" switch, though. The yellow-blue-red coloring is meaningless for what the texture is intended for: a texture-based alpha channel to switch between the hilly vegetation and pebbles.

Recipe for the Ringed Planet Material Adjustment

Chapter 15 ("Brycing Out Of This World"), which covers space scenes and other phenomena, contains a recipe for ringed planets. To create the planet rings, alter one of the existing presets from Bryce's Materials Library. The ringed planet recipe refers you back to here for the lowdown on altering the preset. This recipe is an example of how you might use an existing preset as a starting point to create some other effect. If you are following along from a cruise through the Deep

Texture Editor section, create a scene with a sphere, enlarge it, and flatten it (the squashed sphere won't work for this, since it's rotated 90°). Set up your scene so that Atmosphere is *off,* there's no haze, and the cloud color is set to black.

1. Begin with the Materials Preset Dali Bee Stripes in the Wild & Fun category. (See Figure 9–83a.) You'll try some successive attempts to get these to look like planet rings. First, in the Materials Composer, try to make the rings fuzzy by changing the Effects control to fuzzy. It softens the outer perimeter of the ring. But the rings themselves are too even and too regular. How would you make them irregular? By changing the underlying noise!

2. Next, change the noise. Go to the Materials Composer, and then to the Deep Texture Editor. This is a one-component texture. Click Set Noise A to access the Noise Editor. You will see that the noise is square and one-dimensional (see Figure 9–83b). Are there other noises that would do as well? Let's try Random (RND) Linear. Just by changing the noise, you get many different shades of gray. Click OK to get back up to the main level of the Deep Texture Editor. Check out the preview.

3. Look at the preview windows to see how the color works. (Incidentally, with the color settings here, the black is in the places where the transparent areas are going to be. Bear that in mind as you make adjustments.) Change the coloring of the other two swatches if you'd like. Two different yellows is, well, rather yellow. Click OK to exit the Materials Composer and do a little test render of your scene. (See Figure 9–83c.)

4. Go back and adjust the noise a little bit. I mentioned that black was the transparent part. You'll need more of it, somehow, to create "in-between" areas of your ring stripes. So go get it back in the Deep Materials Composer. For a quick route there that bypasses the Materials Composer, press the Option (Macintosh) or Alt (Windows) key and then under the Object menu, select Edit 3D Texture... to go straight to the dialog box. Proceed directly to Component A and play with the filtering. (See Figure 9–83d.) The filter is the ubiquitous Clip. Where the curve reaches the top, it clips at white, and where it reaches the bottom, it clips at black. Fine. But you want more black. So, get the curve to be more "bottom-y." (No relation to a lobotomy!) Drag the graph down. Drag far enough where you see the top of the curves, then drag to the right to increase the overall contrast range. (The figure has an arrow to indicate the overall direction of the adjustment drag for both Macintosh and Windows versions of the Filter.) The dark areas are larger now; that's good.

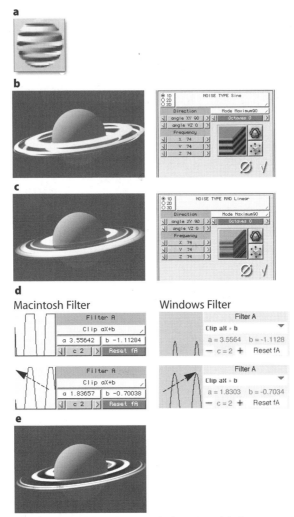

Figure 9–83 Adjusting an existing Materials Preset to create planet rings: a) The starting preset; b) Sine noise results in too-regular ring stripes; c) changing noise to RND Linear for irregular rings; d) Macintosh and Windows filter controls before and after adjustment; e) rendered image after adjusting the Clip filter.

Click OK to exit the Deep Texture Editor and also the Materials Composer and do a test render. (See Figure 9–83e.)

Now you're getting somewhere! The stripes are fainter and there is more "in-between" area.

5. Adjust the Mappings setting. Notice that the stripes are strange as they come around from behind the planet to the front. Perhaps the way the texture is mapped to the object could change a bit. Look at the Mappings control. Up to now, this one has been applied in Object Space. Other potential mapping candidates are: Parametric, Spherical, and Cylindrical. Try Cylindrical.

6. As a final noodle, try adjusting the frequency in the Materials Composer. And try again with those different mapping options. The one I was finally satisfied with was the Spherical mapping.

Snow Puddles Material

This next material description is not a walkthrough so much as an analysis of a material setting that already exists. In examining all of what goes into it, you'll get a feel for how the controls in the Deep Texture Editor work together.

Here's a material that uses two components to create a snowy terrain. It is found on the CD in the Bryce file entitled SNOWED UNDER. It is also the basis of the Material Preset called Mid Winter (in the Plains and Terrains category). See Figure 9–84.

I'll begin by taking a look at the Deep Texture Editor to see what is there.

The Snow Component

The first component, snow, has its noise positioned in such a way that the grain is visible on the top as well as in "front." The significance of this will be apparent shortly.

Now, take a look at the filter. It's Snow Puddles, the three-variable filter that makes snow occur at certain altitudes and slopes.

Remember that a determines how much the snow patches are influenced by the noise. The higher the number, the greater the noise's influence on the snow. Here, the number is 3.99221. Since the standard dragging range on the Macintosh is from 4 to –4, this is fairly high. (You can go higher than 4 on the Mac by typing the number; in Windows you may continue dragging past 4.) The b value shifts the altitude. The number is fairly close to 0, meaning the snow patches occur at pretty much any altitude.

The c value determines how much slope will influence whether the snow will appear. When c is 0, it does not matter whether the terrain is flat or upright; snow

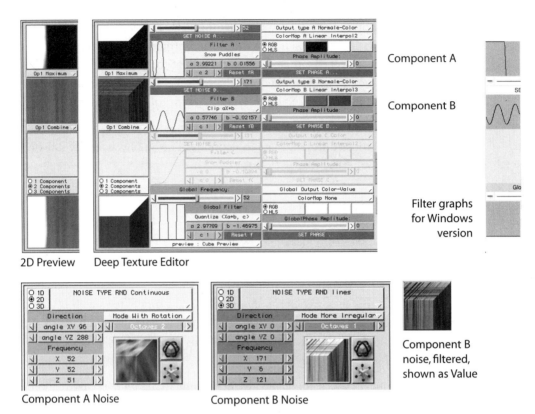

2D Preview   Deep Texture Editor

Component A

Component B

Filter graphs
for Windows
version

Component A Noise

Component B Noise

Component B
noise, filtered,
shown as Value

Figure 9–84 "Snowed Under" Deep Texture Editor settings.

will "stick" to the terrain. The higher the number, the flatter the surface needs to be for snow to appear. Here c is 2, thereby requiring that the terrain be somewhat flat in order for the snow to stick to the ground. Snow won't stick to the upright surfaces, and the rocky portion of the texture will show through.

Now, look at the output type. This component will output as Normale-Color. Normale is for the bump. Where the noise is white, the surface bump will be at its highest. This ensures the snow sits atop the terrain. Where there is no snow, the noise is black. The color for this is set as Linear Interpol2. This means that the color is linearly interpolated between two colors, black and white. The reason for the black will become apparent shortly when I discuss the interaction of the components. But first, take a look at your other component.

The Rocky Mountain Component

The second component is created from a three-dimensional noise, Random (RND) lines. Notice that the frequency for y is much less than that for x and z. This is a real-life example of how to make a three-dimensional noise with a vertical grain. It has a two-dimensional effect without the complete uniformity of a two-dimensional grain. Notice that there's no rotation to the noise and it's one octave with a More Irregular mode. So there's a bit of complexity to the noise and some random strains that aren't completely vertical or horizontal.

The noise has the same output type as the first, that is, Normale-Color. Normale is bump map, and Color, of course, provides the color for the object. Now take a look at the filter for this component. The filter here is set to make the bumpiness of the rock a certain height. The standard contrast filter, Clip aX+b, is used. The b value (which controls the height of the graph) is negative, thereby making the range of output about half height. Think about this for a moment. If the graph went from the bottom to the top, you would have a bump that goes the full range from lowest to highest. But this rocky texture will be combined with snow, and the rocky surface had better jolly well be located *underneath* the snow. So the filtering curve that determines the rocky surface bump keeps it in the bottom- to mid-range of the bump. The lightest (highest) values of the combined output is reserved for the snow. (See, it all makes sense, doesn't it?) The actual shape of the curve is not changed much. It goes to about 60 percent of its height ($a = .57746$), and the bottom edge just dips below the bottom black part, thereby making for more pronounced bottom edges.

Look at the result of this filtering. (In Figure 9–84, I show it using Value for the moment, a handy little trick for seeing the component solely in terms of the gray values.) The values shown are all middle to dark gray.

Component 2's output is Normale-Color. The Color Map is Linear-Interpol 3. The three colors are generally closer to one another, not widely divergent.

Combining the Components

Now that I've looked at each component individually, I'll talk about how the two components are combined. Each individual component has its output type set to Normale-Color. Look for a moment only at the Normale (bump). The snow needs to be higher than other elements. Maximum (analogous to Photoshop's Lighten Only) compares the two and takes the lightest one as the result. Where it's white, there will be snow with a higher bump. Everything else will be the underlying rocky matter.

The Global Output type is Color-Value. (The reason for including Value is to create an alpha channel to drive the Ambience channel for blindingly bright snow.) Although the first two components have Normale-Color as their output type, the final output type does not. The Normale information is there, available for the Bump Height channel in the Materials Composer. Here's another important little fact about how the Deep Texture Editor works. It isn't necessary to set the final output with everything in it. This is especially true if you are going to do any global filtering. In this case, there is a global filter, Quantize, that adds a bit of high contrast in a posterized fashion. This filter operates only on the Value portions of the noise. In this case, it is rather subtle. I'll come back to filtering at the combination stage in the next material exercise. For now, just remember that you don't need always to assign all the output types in the final combination. If Normale is included in the individual components, the Materials Composer will find it and know what to do with it.

Render the snow. Notice that there are little indentations in the snow, as if there were animal tracks or tufts of grass peeking out through the layers. This effect is a result of the two-dimensional noise rotation that included the "top" as well as the "front" orientation.

Suppose you wanted to add a third component to the texture. The rocky substance is rather uniform and might be nice with something else to break it up, perhaps some horizontal coloring of some sort. Think about this. If you add a third component, you'll want to change the order of the components, since you want the snow to come out on top. The snowy portions need to be highest, so Maximum is the blend setting. Any combination blend other than Maximum (Multiply, Add, Average) will result in funky snow.

If you don't believe me, try it out yourself. (You will anyway!) Switch the number of components to 3. For Component C, select some noise, give it some color, make the second blend Average, and see what kind of madness ensues. Recall from the overview diagram in Figure 9–64 how the results of the first two textures are combined with the third texture. In order for the snow-on-top-blended-using-Maximum to work, it must be a sole operator in the combination process, either as one of two, or as the third component to blend with the results of the first two components. It cannot successfully work as one of the first two components to blend with a third component. To rectify the situation, copy your snow component and paste it to Component C. Then create your rocky matter inconsistencies in the component where the snow used to be (in this case, Component A). Set the first blend to be Average and the second to Maximum so that the snow in combination with the result of the first two components will have a "come-out-on-top" result.

Snowed Under in the Materials Composer

Now, how is this snow texture worked in the Materials Composer? (See Figure 9–85a.) As a Texture Source, this texture is driving Ambience, Bump Height and Diffuse, and Ambient Color. To create the full illusion of height for the snow, Bump Height is set to a strong level (140). The texture's frequency depends more on the amount of detail you want to see in the object and is adjusted interactively while you are working on the particular object in the scene. (For objects closer to the camera, the frequency will need to be set higher than for those far away.)

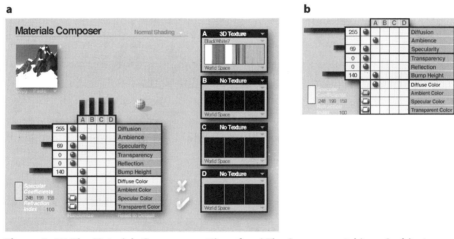

Figure 9–85 The Materials Composer settings for a) The Snow preset; b) my Ambient Color-changed "Snowed Under."

There is a problem with the existing preset. With Ambience being driven by this texture, there is either full ambient light (where the snow is) or there is little to no ambient light (where the rocky part is). This means where there are shadow areas, the rock will be black. If the Ambient color in the Sky & Fog Palette is white, then that no matter where the sunlight or shadow is, the snow will be uniformly blindingly white. To change this so that you can tell that there is shadow on the snow, you need to make the Ambient color darker. You can do this in the Sky &

Fog Palette, or you can change the Snowed Under material's Ambient Color to a uniform color and select a light blue or lavender. (See Figure 9–85b.)When snow is in shadow, you'll be able to see the shadow. Other solutions to this extreme Ambience problem are in the Snow Cones folder on the CD-ROM. Figure C9–86 compares the normal preset version of the snow with my Ambient Color modification.

Puddlebumps: Bump and Reflections

The last 3D Solid Texture that I will work with here uses the filtering in the combination output to get its result. It has a bump and also (you guessed it!) Reflection. (See Figure C9–87 in the color section.) If you're a Bryce 1 veteran, you might recognize an old preset that uses this technique, where rocky mass is interspersed with flat reflective puddles.

Do the Bump

1. For Component A, start by generating a noise. Open up the Deep Texture Editor for any texture, and click Reset A for the first noise. That gives you the start, a Random Continuous noise. In the Set Noise A dialog box, make adjustments so that the noise is three-dimensional, with three octaves, and is set to the Irregular mode (see Figure. 9–88a). Set Frequency to 250 for all three axes. In the Deep Texture Editor, set the filter to Clip and adjust it to be high contrast. Set the output to Normale for a gray bumpy surface.

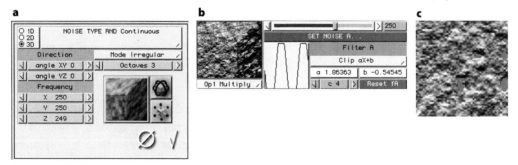

Component A Noise

Figure 9–88 Component A's a) Noise setting; b) filter setting; c) 2D preview.

2. For Component B, begin with the same type of noise as in Step 1 (copy Component A and paste to Component B) and then make adjustments. Adjust Component B's noise to have a lower frequency setting. Bring the Octave setting down to 2. (See Figure 9–89a.) Now, filter this with Clip. Adjust it to match the filter shown in Figure 9–89b. The filter is fairly steep, which makes for significant areas of black. Set Component B's output type to Value. Why Value? The Value information will be used as alpha information in the Materials Composer—in this case, it will drive Reflection. There, a Reflective setting will provide areas that will be reflective for the puddle surface.

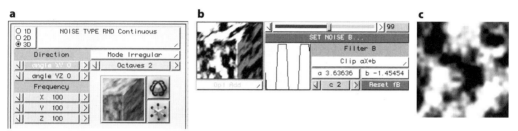

Component B Noise

Figure 9–89 Component B's a) Noise setting; b) filter setting; c) 2D preview.

3. Click the Add Texture button and name your texture Puddlebumps (or whatever else you'd like).

4. Now it's time to set up the blend between the two texture components. The first and second noises will be multiplied together, so choose Multiply. For the moment, make the final output type Value. The black portions of the Component B's noise, when multiplied with the Component A's bump map, will result in flat areas (no bump) in the combined final texture. This combination works on the Normale bump map, even though it's a Value component that's doing the "work." Now that you see where the large flat areas come from, you can see why the second noise was set to a smaller frequency than the first. Figure 9–90a compares a portion of the two components side by side with their multiplied result. You can see where the second noise is used to make flat areas.

5. In the Materials Composer, make the Texture Source drive both the Reflection and Bump Height channels. Be sure to set the Reflection amount, too! Make it at least 130. Set the Bump height amount to something moderate. Render. Take a quick peek at what's been created so far as it applies to the

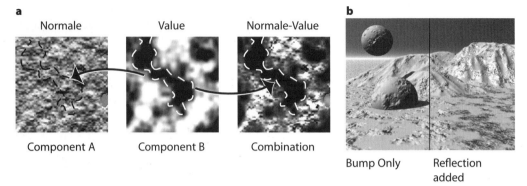

Figure 9–90 a) Multiplying the two components to get flattened areas; b) the result so far has flat areas interspersed with bump.

object's surface (see Figure 9–90b). The resulting image has areas of flat and areas of bump height. However, the alpha-driven reflections occur in the high portions, not the low portions.

Why is the reflective area in the bumpy area? Component B is set for Value. Where Value is white, you'll get reflective areas from using the alpha-driven Reflection. But where there's black, you're combining it with the Normale information in Noise 1 to flatten out the bump. You want portions that are flat and portions that are bumpy. You need the black to flatten the bump, but you also need to somehow swap the Value information so that the flat part is reflective.

You can't change anything in Components A or B. You *can,* however, change the final output. If you set the final output to be Value and somehow invert it there, then you will end up reversing the Value information without touching the interaction of the two components to create bumpy and flat areas.

6. Adjust Global Output filter to invert the Value setting. When Component B is set to Value and Global Output is set to Value, the textures look identical. So Component B's filter settings can be the basis for the Global filter. All you need to do is invert it. The filter is Clip aX+b, where a is 3.6 and b is –1.4. Now, before you invert it, a bit of background on Clip aX+b: The default values (no clipping) for this filter are $a = 1$, $b = 0$. A straight inversion is $a = -1$, $b = 1$. To invert *any* setting, change the value for a from positive to negative (or vice versa) and for b, change the number from negative to positive (or vice versa) and then add 1 to the number. So, in the filter for Combination, select Clip aX+b and provide the values of (roughly) $a = -3.6$, $b = 2.4$.

If you decide not to do the straight mathematical route, you'll need to tweak and preview. In order to see the results of your tweaking, you need to have the Global

Output set only to Value. Make sure that Component B and the Global Output previews are the inverse of one another. You'll need to play with this one a bit to make sure the white areas (reflection) are showing in the right place. If you make your white area grow a bit so that there's overlap, you'll have areas of reflectivity move up into the bump, thereby creating an illusion of wet land right where the two meet. See Figures 9–91 and 9–92.

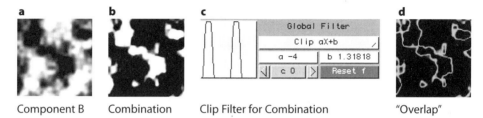

a   b   c   d

Component B   Combination   Clip Filter for Combination   "Overlap"

Figure 9–91 Changing the Value to make reflective area flat; (a) Component B; (b) Combination after inverting; (c) filter settings for inversion; (d) overlap to create "wet" edges.

If you leave the Deep Editor to do any test renders, select the menu item Objects > Edit 3D Texture.... You'll need to press the Option key before selecting it from the menu. For work that goes back and forth between a scene and the Deep Texture Editor to finesse the underlying texture, it's a handy shortcut.

Figure 9–92 The result of swapping the Value in Global Filter creates flat reflective surfaces.

Now that you've inverted the Value for your Global Output, take stock of this texture.

7. The color for this texture, which is something of a land mass, goes to Component B. Until now, the output type has been Value. Change the output type to Color-Value and set your colors for Component B. In this example, the Color Map is Spline. For the final combination, make the Color Map to be None (since you already set it in Component 2). Now you're set. Figure C9–93 shows the Deep Texture Editor with final color settings for Component B and for Global Output.

Finally, adjust the contrast for the Combination filter to fine-tune the partially reflective wet edge around the puddle. Semi-reflective areas are gray in the final value, and they overlap very closely on the "shores" of the other bumpy areas.

Congratulations! You've made your way through four different forays into the Deep Texture Editor as well as many explorations of the Materials Composer. With this as a foundation, and knowing how to analyze already existing textures, you've more than scratched the surface on creating realistic surface materials in Bryce.

CHAPTER TEN

Brycean Skies

The line of the horizon was clear and hard against the sky, and in one particular quarter it showed black against a silvery climbing phosphorescence that grew and grew. At last, over the rim of the waiting earth the moon lifted with slow majesty till it swung clear of the horizon and rode off, free of mooring; and once more they began to see surfaces—meadows widespread, and quiet gardens, and the river itself from bank to bank, all softly disclosed, all washed clean of mystery and terror, all radiant again as by day, but with a difference that was tremendous. Their old haunts greeted them again in other raiment, as if they had slipped away and put on this pure new apparel and come quietly back, smiling as they shyly waited to see if they would be recognized again under it.

KENNETH GRAHAME, *THE WIND IN THE WILLOWS*

IN THIS CHAPTER...

- Changing cloud shape and color

- Positioning the sun and moon in your Brycean sky using the Sun control

- Fog and haze—controlling water moisture in Bryce

- All about color—how each color setting for Sky & Fog affects your Bryce scene

- Advanced sky tricks

- Freestanding clouds and fog

In Bryceland, you can create an atmosphere to mimic the best day you ever had in your life—or any other kind of day. Working with the Sky & Fog Palette to make that atmosphere is a mixture of incredible ease and daunting complexity. The Palette's controls are easy to work with. Drag one of the controls to make an adjustment. Since there are so many interconnecting variables in the Sky & Fog controls, the complexity comes in knowing which control to drag at what time to get that certain result you want.

If you aimlessly drag here or there and watch the preview to see what comes out, you may get something you like; you may not. The hit-or-miss approach may work fine at the beginning, but it gets old quickly. It's better if you know how to go straight to a particular control to change some aspect of your Brycean sky.

In this chapter, I'll look at each Sky & Fog Palette control in turn, isolating each as it influences all the others. After that, I'll launch into a related topic, how to create freestanding clouds for incredible skies in Bryce.

THE SKY & FOG PALETTE

The Sky & Fog Palette has many controls, each with additional options (see Figure 10–1). There are a number of variables that you can manipulate to make your Brycean sky: six swatches for choosing color; two sets of cloud controls to manipulate Bryce's cumulus or stratus clouds, and controls for fog and haze and shadow. You'll find light source direction—both day and night—that influences the rest of the scene. Four different sky modes, including a "no atmosphere" with a color swatch and the custom sky option with yet another three color swatches brings the color swatch total to ten. Any one setting will influence the outcome of any other setting.

Because there are so many interconnected parts, a lot of this chapter's step-by-step directions will simply be exploratory exercises to help you become fluent with all of the Sky & Fog parameters. Once you see what each one does to the sky and the scene as a whole, you can go on to create more complex sky effects.

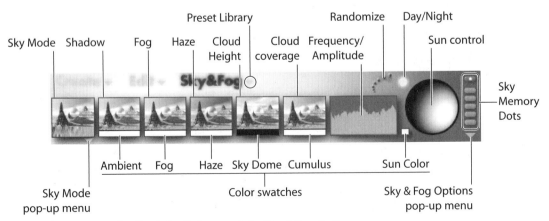

Figure 10–1 The Sky & Fog Palette and the Sky & Fog Options pop-up menu.

All of the exercises in this chapter use the scene called PLAIN VANILLA! from the Chapter 10 folder of the CD-ROM (see Figure 10–2). The scene has the Bryce default sky set among several terrains with default flat-gray surfaces. The mountain forms will let you see how changes to the sky affect the entire scene.

Figure 10–2 "Plain Vanilla!" scene.

This chapter's game plan for sky exploration is divided into two major sections. The first section covers all the elements that give "shape" to the sky, starting with the solar and lunar direction, then continuing with all the forms of atmospheric moisture—clouds, haze and fog. The second section explores all the different ways to put color in your sky, including Sky modes.

SOLAR AND LUNAR DIRECTION

At the outer limits of the Brycean world is a sphere. This virtual edge is Bryce's sky dome. On the surface of that sky dome are Bryce's light sources. The sun illuminates the world during Bryce's daytime, and the moon comes out during Brycean night.

Basic Bryce Astronomy

How do you set time of day? With the Sun control. Think of the Sun control's different locations as different times of day. There is a sunrise position, a high-noon position, late morning and early afternoon positions, and so on. With the Link Sun to View option, located in the Sky & Fog Options pop-up menu, checked, you will stand with your back to the sunrise when the Sun control is positioned at the bottom.

A different way to think of the Sun control is as the top view representation of the Brycean sky dome. You place the light where the sun shines in the sky. At the edges of the circle are different points along the horizon, and center is light from the top of the sky. In that case, the

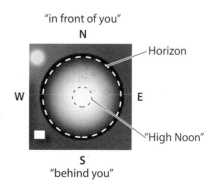

Figure 10–3 The Sun control with Bryce sky dome positions superimposed.

top edge is the northern horizon, bottom is south, and east and west are to the left and right sides, respectively (see Figure 10–3). No, this is not a strict "the sun rises in the east and sets in the west" situation. Remember, Bryce is another world entirely. You can make your sun rise and set wherever you want.

Of course, the north-east-south-west orientation can be relative or absolute depending on the status of Link Sun to View. Link Sun to View is checked (selected) as Bryce's default state. (See Figure 10–1.) No matter from which direction you look at your scene, the Sun control position will match your view. So "North" horizon will always be directly in front of you when it is checked. Recall from the Edit Chapter (Chapter 6) how you can edit your objects from World Space or Camera Space (or Object Space). This control is analogous to selecting World Space or Camera Space to orient your skies. When Link Sun to View is unchecked, the sun's position (and the entire sky) is oriented in World Space regardless of your camera perspective on the scene. When Link Sun to View is checked, the sky is oriented in Camera Space as the sun's position follows the camera position.

a

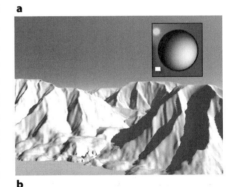

b

c

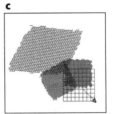

d

When you create a new scene, the camera is in default view, rotated 45° around the *y* axis. Link Sun to View matches the sun and sky to the camera position. If you uncheck Link Sun to View while looking at your scene from the default view, then the sun position will be "off" by 45°. Figure 10–4 compares the default view of the same scene, showing Link Sun to View on and off, with a top view wireframe and Sun control position for reference. If you are making a Bryce

Figure 10–4 Linking Sun to View changes the sky, depending on the camera's position. Scene from default camera view with Link Sun to View a) checked and b) unchecked. c) Wireframe view from top and d) Sun control position for both scenes.

scene as a single illustration, then it doesn't matter if you have Link Sun to View selected. But if you are creating a multiple set of Bryce renders of a scene, for, say, interactive game navigation, you'll need to make sure that the sun's position is oriented to World Space. That way, when you turn to the left or right, the lighting changes as it would in the real world.

When working on a scene, you may wish to render from top view and turn off Link Sun to View. Otherwise the areas of sun and shadow will be bizarre, since they are, of course linked to your view!

On the top left part of the Sun control is the Day and Night button. To change from day to night, simply click the sun. It changes to a moon, and it's now nighttime in Bryceland (where a certain king has been heard to croon, "Love Me Render"). Click again to change back to day.

You may have noticed in your explorations that the sun and moon are on the same continuum—they're in the opposite ends of the sky. If you create a scene that has no ground in it, change the day to night, set the sun in the direct center, turn off view linking and then point your camera down into the depths… peekaboo! There's the sun! (You cannot do the opposite, where you look into the depths to see the moon when the sun is out above your head.) In fact, anywhere you place the sun, the moon will ride along opposite it.

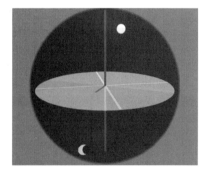

Figure 10–5 Bryce sky dome with the sun opposite the moon.

Figure 10–5 shows a miniature Bryce sky dome sphere, with sun above and moon below halfway around the Brycean world.

That moon, incidentally, will always be full. It makes sense; after all, it's always opposite the sun. Since the sun and moon are opposite one another, in order to place your moon somewhere in the sky, you will have to move the Sun control to the opposite place. It can be very confusing. Things may not seem predictable until you realize the following: *When using the Sun control, you are always controlling the sun's position; the moon follows along on the opposite side of the sky dome.* When the Sun control is centered, the moon is centered as well. But when the Sun control is placed on the left side, the moon appears on the right and vice versa. To place the moon left of center in your scene, you need to move the Sun control to the right (see Figure C10–6 in the color section).

Sun and Moon Secrets in the Sky & Fog Dialog Box

The Sun control on the Sky & Fog Palette was designed for pure intuitive play with your light sources. Drag the sun to the position you want, and there you are. You don't need to deal with numbers to get the sun's position just so. Deep in the Sky & Fog dialog box, however, you can alter the numbers for the Sun controls. This is good for precise incremental change for animations or other sequential events.

Here's what happens numerically when you drag the Sun control. Like the other controls in Bryce, the illumination positions have x, y, and z as well. (What a surprise! Another case of those ol' x-, y,- and z-axes! Well, for a three-dimensional application, Bryce is surprisingly consistent at assigning x, y, and z attributes to most everything.) The possible numbers range from –99 to 99.

Figure 10–7 shows the sun's position as if you were looking from top view. The horizontal position of the sun is expressed by the x- and z-axes. Noon is $x = 0$, $z = 0$; northern horizon is $x = 0$, $z = 99$; southern horizon is $x = 0$, $z = –99$; eastern horizon is $x = 99$, $z = 0$; and western horizon is $x = –99$, $z = 0$.

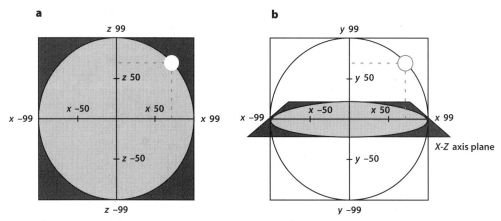

Figure 10–7 Light source position and corresponding numerical settings:
a) Top view representation; b) side view representation.

To include the y setting, look at Figure 10–6b. The y setting corresponds to the sun's height in the sky. High noon is $y = 99$ (or anything in the 90's), and at any place that the sun is on the horizon, $y = 0$. If y has a negative value, the sun is below the horizon, thereby making it night and placing the moon above the horizon.

It's possible to enter numbers that would seemingly make the light position fall outside the circle (99, 99, 99). Internally, however, Bryce calculates the numbers and places the light source at a point on that circle.

Solar and Lunar Fluency Exercise

To limber up your "Work with the Brycean sky" muscles, open up the PLAIN VANILLA! scene file from the CD-ROM. Limit yourself only to the Sun control for changing the sun's position and changing from day to night and vice versa. For this exercise and the others, the aim is to create as many "quick sketches" as possible. If you've ever taken drawing classes or tried drawing exercises, you've probably done quick gesture drawings, where you try to capture the basic pose or attitude with just a few quick strokes. When you've made those few marks on paper, you move on to the next one. The aim is not to complete a detailed drawing, but to work quickly with fluidity, going from one to another to another to another in rapid succession.

This exercise works in the same way.

1. Make sure that you have between 20 and 50 megabytes of disk space free on your hard drive for this exercise (and the exercises to follow in this chapter). Each version of the scene file and image file takes up about one megabyte. (There is also a lower resolution version on the CD-ROM that should be in the neighborhood of 600K, if your disk space is tight.) Later, when it's all over, you can trash the scene files.

2. Give yourself about 10-15 minutes for this exercise. Create between 10 and 15 (or more, even!) different versions of the scene, each with a unique sun or moon position. The idea is to create as many *different* versions of lighting as you can.

3. Make a move with the Sun control. Render a couple of passes. You don't need to have it finished.

4. Select Save As... and give the Plain Vanilla! scene a unique name (easy way: add a number). See Figure 10–8.

5. Then start again. Make another move with the Sun control. Render a few passes. Select File > Save As... and give this one a unique name and number. Continue on with your sky gesture drawings.

Figure 10–8 Save As... dialog box for giving each Plain Vanilla! scene file a unique name.

Put the sun in your scene so you can see it. Put the moon in your scene. When you're working on the moon, pay particular attention to the lunar opposition to the sun, and decide beforehand to make a lunar shadow from *some* direction. Then place the Sun control to make it so. (Remember, set the Sun control opposite where you want the moon to be.)

6. When you are finished, or the time is up, prepare them for a later batch render. On the Macintosh, select all the scene files and assign them a unique label in the Finder (you know the routine: Label > Essential, Hot, In Progress, etc.). Using the Windows Explorer, arranging icons by type will put all scene file icons together. That way, it will be easy to do a batch render later. To batch render, drag the scene file icons to your Bryce application icon, alias, or shortcut.

Note: As you work on your Plain Vanilla! scenes, please refrain from making any changes to the terrains that are already in the scene (unless you want to adjust the terrain resolution to make a smaller scene size). There are other chapters in this book for working on other parts of Bryce. Right now you are concentrating on skies, and the scene is provided so you can see how various changes in the Sky & Fog Palette will affect your scene. At the end of this chapter, you will have amassed a collection of sky variations, and it's valuable to have a common reference to the same set of terrains.

CLOUDS, CLOUDS, CLOUDS

In this section, I'll examine all the different ways to adjust and manipulate clouds in Bryceland. There are many different factors to manipulate. This section explores them individually so that you can be aware of which control influences which behavior.

Stratus and Cumulus

Brycean clouds come in two flavors: Stratus and Cumulus. You can set up either or both types of clouds in your scenes. Do so by selecting one or both from the Sky & Fog Options pop-up menu.

Here are the main differences between them:

Stratus	Cumulus
Higher, wispier cloud	Lower, more substantive cloud
Color comes from Sun Color	Color comes from Cumulus/Ambient Color
High amplitude, high definition	High amplitude, high definition
Low amplitude, wisps dissolve	Low amplitude, low definition into high-altitude haze

Cloud Shape

There are several ways you can adjust your clouds. In the Sky & Fog Palette, the four means of adjusting clouds are Altitude, Cover, Frequency, and Amplitude. (You can also adjust Cumulus Color in the Sky & Fog Palette as well, though I'm not focusing on color at the moment.) In the Sky & Fog dialog box, there are numerical settings for each of those controls. Figure 10–9 shows both the dialog box and the palette and indicates which is which.

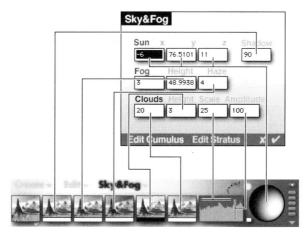

Figure 10–9 The Sky & Fog Palette and the Sky & Fog dialog box, with arrows indicating what corresponds to what.

This next exercise explores all that goes into creating cloud shape. Both stratus and cumulus clouds are included in this study of Brycean cloud shapes.

Exercise: Adjusting Cloud Shape

Set aside another 20 minutes or so for this exercise. First you'll learn to adjust specific controls in response to questions about which way to change the clouds. Later, after you've gone through each of the questions, spend some time freely playing with the different controls. Each time you create a unique look for your sky, select File > Save As... and give your scene a unique name.

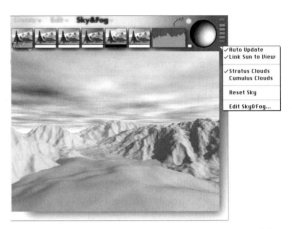

The scene file Plain Vanilla! starts with the basic default sky that ships with Bryce. Anytime you want to return to the plain default, simply click the highest Sky Memory Dot (it's perpetually green), and you'll return to the default state. You now have a blank

Figure 10–10 Sky & Fog Options pop-up menu with stratus checked; Plain Vanilla! with stratus clouds selected.

sky. To place clouds in that sky, go to the Sky & Fog Options pop-up menu. Select Stratus so that it is checked. Now you have your initial cloud setting for this exercise (see Figure 10–10).

Next, ask these questions:

1. Do you want more clouds?

   More clouds in the sky, that is, more individual cloud shapes, can be obtained via the Frequency control. Drag the graph to the right to increase frequency and to the left to decrease frequency. Figure C10–11 (in the color section) has a series of clouds with different frequency adjustments. Part b is the default frequency; part a is lower and parts c and d are higher. The frequency graph for each rendered image is inset on the image. You can also type in any value from 0 to 200 in the Scale section of the Sky & Fog dialog box.

2. Do you want more cloud cover?

   Drag the Cloud coverage thumbnail. Dragging to the right increases cloud coverage and dragging to the left reduces it. Coverage determines the amount of cloud cover in your sky. You can have the same number of cloud puffs (frequency), but you can change how much they cover the sky (coverage). By adjusting the Cloud coverage thumbnail, the same number of cloud puffs can grow in proportion until they dominate the sky or shrink back to daintily decorate it. Figure C10–12 shows a series that has lower (left) to higher coverage (right).

3. Do you want the clouds wispier or more defined?

    Adjust Amplitude to control how wispy or defined the clouds are. When you drag down so that the graph gets spikier, your clouds become more defined (see Figure C10–13). When you drag up, the graph becomes more leveled and the clouds become more diffuse at their edges.

    The Sky & Fog dialog box includes a section for numerical entry of the amplitude. The numerical range is 0–500. (Actually, it's from –500 to 0 to 500.) The higher the number, the spikier your graph; the lower the number, the smoother your graph. With an amplitude of 0, you won't be able to see your clouds at all.

    Note: With stratus clouds, a lower Amplitude setting—or wispier clouds— results in a high-altitude haze. The less defined the stratus clouds are, the greater the high-altitude mist, since the clouds are dispersed. Figure C10–13 shows the default stratus clouds at three ranges of amplitude—low, default, and higher. So if you want a hazy sky when you don't have haze elsewhere, use a lower Amplitude setting and stratus clouds.

4. Do you want the clouds to be placed differently in the sky?

    Would you rather your clouds changed places with the sky? You can swap your "cloud" and "sky" areas by setting Amplitude to be positive (see Figure C10–14a) or negative (see Figure C10–14b). The default is usually positive. Compare the images in the figure. The basic cloud shape is the same. But a positive Amplitude setting will put the cloud here and sky there, whereas a negative setting will swap the sky and cloud.

5. Do you want your clouds to be at a different altitude?

    Changing the altitude will change the way your clouds look in the sky. Change the altitude setting by dragging the Cloud Height thumbnail. The default setting, 3, is pretty low considering that the range is from 0-100. In some ways, adjusting the altitude is the same as adjusting the frequency of the clouds—the higher the clouds, the higher the frequency. Your eye is able to see more area farther away, so the clouds farther away (higher) seem to have a higher frequency. When the altitude is lower, you can see fewer clouds. However, lest you think that Cloud Height is merely another means of adjusting frequency, Cloud Height also affects the way that you see haze in your sky. (I wasn't kidding when I said that everything is tied to everything else!) I'll talk more about this when I discuss haze later in the chapter. Figure

C10–15 illustrates how different altitude levels affect the haze modulation. For each altitude level, the left half of the image is a cloudy sky, and the right half is a clear sky. The haze amounts in all cases are close to the default level of 4. The image is shown in five variations with altitudes throughout the possible range. The higher the altitude, the more clouds that can be seen. If you want to place your clouds higher in the sky, you may have to adjust the frequency afterwards to compensate.

6. Do you want different clouds?

Change from stratus to cumulus via the Sky & Fog Options pop-up menu. (Or, as a variation, select both. Try both on your own; this exercise continues by working with cumulus only.) Figure C10–16 shows cumulus clouds after switching in the Sky & Fog Options pop-up.

7. Do you want the clouds to look different?

To make your clouds depart completely from their current shape, adjust the underlying texture via the Sky & Fog dialog box by clicking the Edit Stratus or Edit Cumulus button (see Figure 10–17a). Doing this will take you to the Shallow Texture Editor (see Figure 10–17b), your friend from the Materials Composer. If you hold down the Option (Macintosh) or Alt (Windows) key when you click the Edit Stratus or Edit Cumulus button, you will access the Deep Texture Editor. In the Windows version of Bryce, changes made to the Stratus or Cumulus textures will not change the way that clouds appear. The rest of this step, then, pertains to Macs only.

Unlike the Materials Composer, which is designed to give you access to all of Bryce's

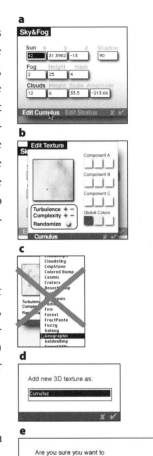

Figure 10–17 Editing cloud textures: a) Edit Cumulus Button highlighted in the Sky & Fog dialog box; b) the Shallow Texture Editor with relevant controls indicated; c) the texture list is meaningless for editing cloud textures; d) dialog box for renaming edited texture—but don't! e) final alert to confirm keeping the texture of the same name.

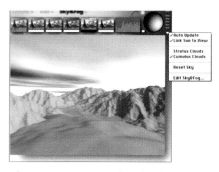

Figure C10–16 Cumulus clouds after switching.

Figure C10–15 Different Cloud Height settings change how many cloud forms can be seen, as well as modulating the haze amount.

Haze Amount: 4   Haze Amount: 35

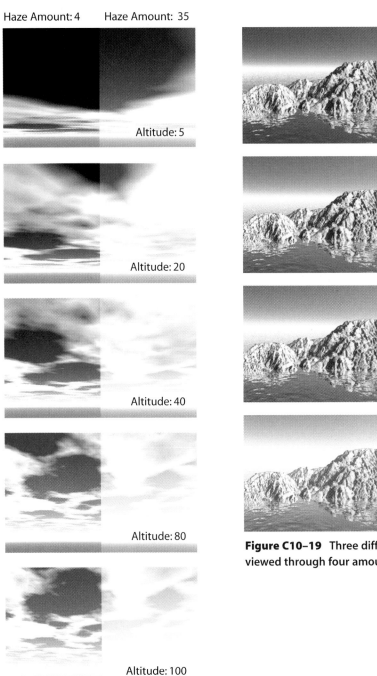

Altitude: 5

Altitude: 20

Altitude: 40

Altitude: 80

Altitude: 100

Figure C10–18 Haze and altitude.

Figure C10–19 Three different-sized terrains viewed through four amounts of Brycean haze.

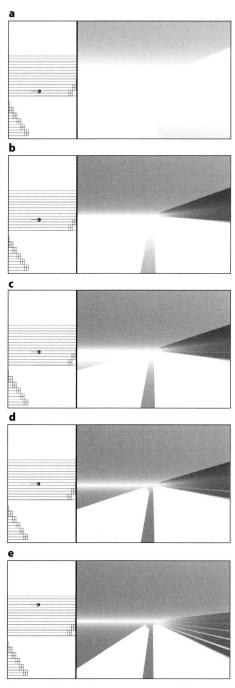

Figure C10–24 Localized fog from a uniformly transparent sphere.

Figure C10–25 Shadow at a) Maximum and b) minimum.

Figure C10–23 The appearance of fog changes depending on the camera position: a) Lowest position; b) low position, c) higher position; d) still higher position; e) high position.

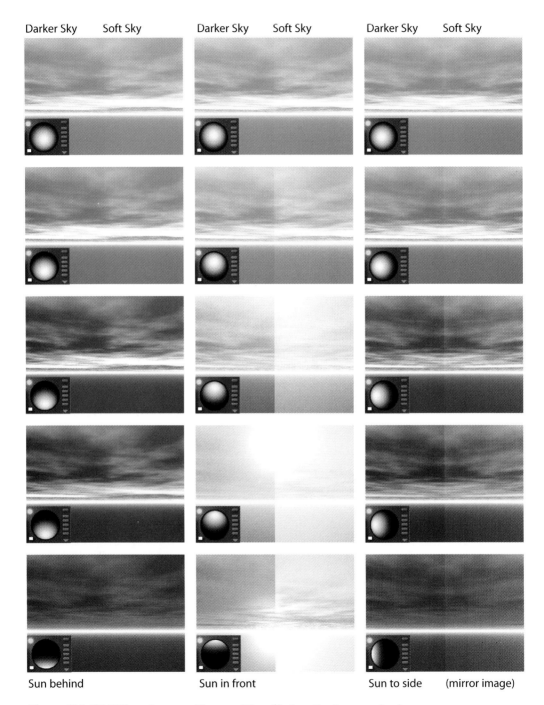

Figure C10–27 Different sun positions and the effect on the Brycean sky dome.

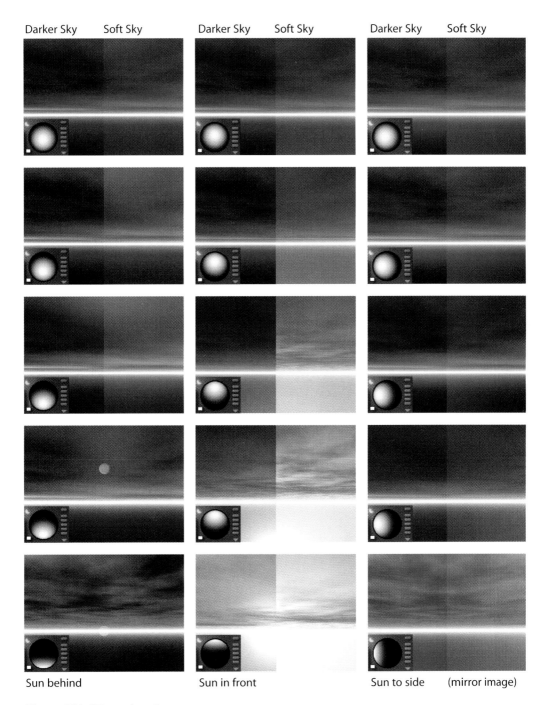

Figure C10–27 *continued*

Sun in high position

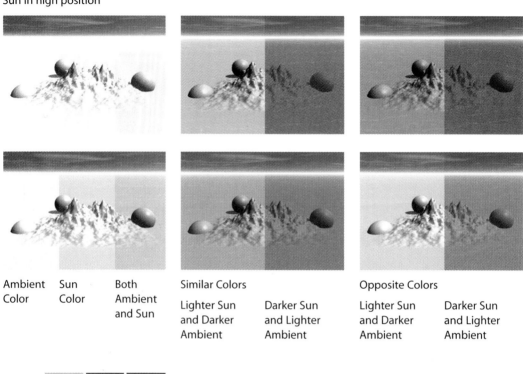

Ambient Color	Sun Color	Both Ambient and Sun	Similar Colors		Opposite Colors	
			Lighter Sun and Darker Ambient	Darker Sun and Lighter Ambient	Lighter Sun and Darker Ambient	Darker Sun and Lighter Ambient

Warm	Cool	Sunset	Moon-rise
R 255	R 183	R 254	R 47
G 245	G 203	G 32	G 197
B 183	B 255	B 16	B 255

Figure C10-28 This set of images compares different settings for Sun Color and Ambient Color.

Sun in low position

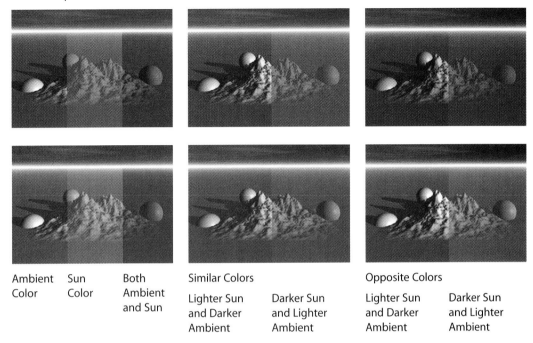

Ambient Color	Sun Color	Both Ambient and Sun	Similar Colors		Opposite Colors	
			Lighter Sun and Darker Ambient	Darker Sun and Lighter Ambient	Lighter Sun and Darker Ambient	Darker Sun and Lighter Ambient

Figure C10-28 *continued*

Altitude 3 (default)   Altitude 20   Altitude 40

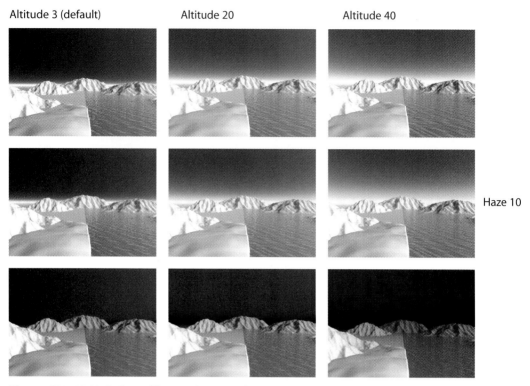

Haze 10

Figure C10–29 Variations of haze—changes of color (white, ivory, and black), amount (10, 33, and 65) and Cloud Height (3, 20, 40) affect the appearance of near and distant objects in this scene.

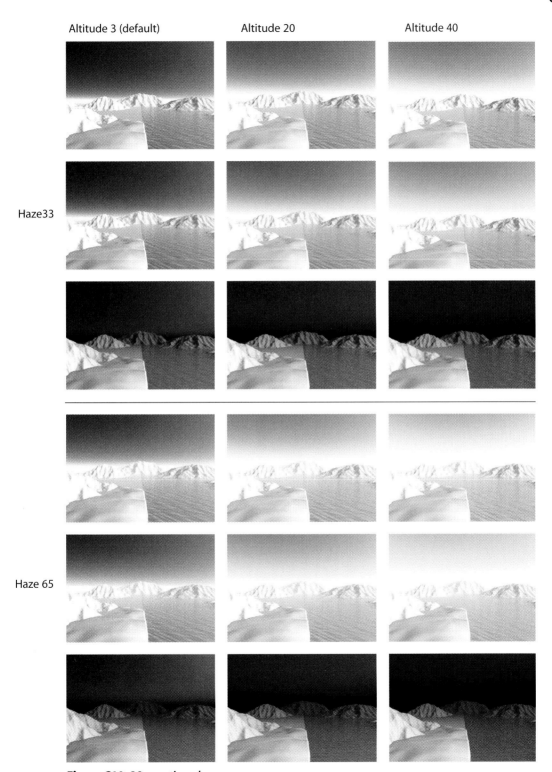

Figure C10–29 *continued*

C26

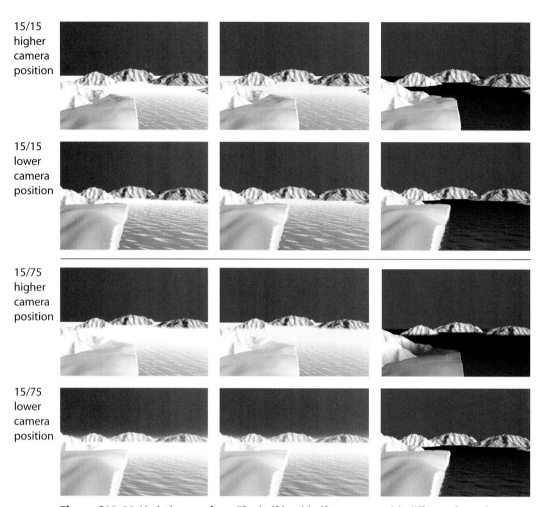

15/15 higher camera position

15/15 lower camera position

15/75 higher camera position

15/75 lower camera position

Figure C10–30 Variations on fog—The half-land/half-sea scene with different fog colors, heights and amounts, and varying camera perspectives.

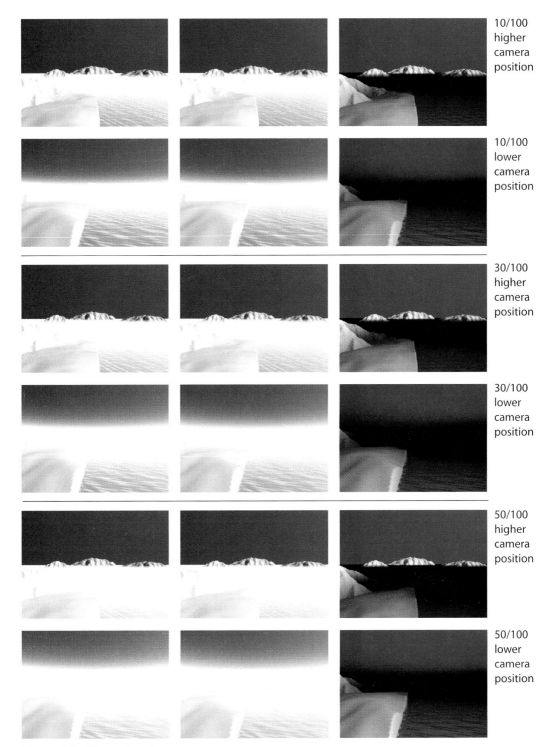

10/100
higher
camera
position

10/100
lower
camera
position

30/100
higher
camera
position

30/100
lower
camera
position

50/100
higher
camera
position

50/100
lower
camera
position

Figure C10–30 *continued*

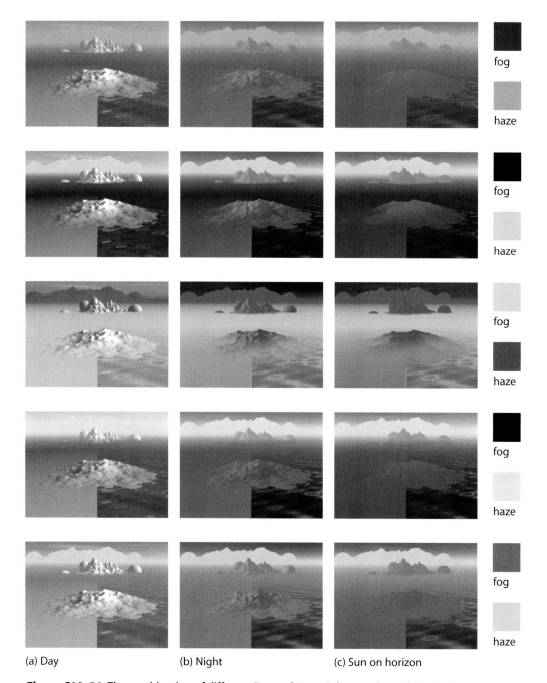

(a) Day   (b) Night   (c) Sun on horizon

Figure C10–31 The combination of different Fog and Haze Colors; each combination is shown at three different times of day.

Figure C10–32 Haze Shift Color.

Figure C10-33 Custom Skies in Panorama View with the custom colors as insets.

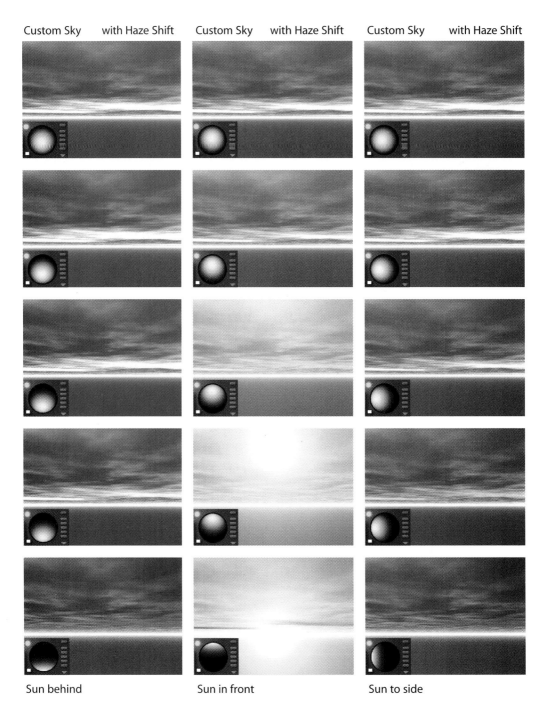

Figure C10–34 Custom Sky color and different sun and positions.

Figure C10–34 *continued*

Area in sun's shadow but
atmosphere above is lit.

Figure C10–35 A side view of a planet shows
how an area can be in the sun's shadow while
the atmosphere is lit by the sun and thus be
illuminated by the Sky Dome Color.

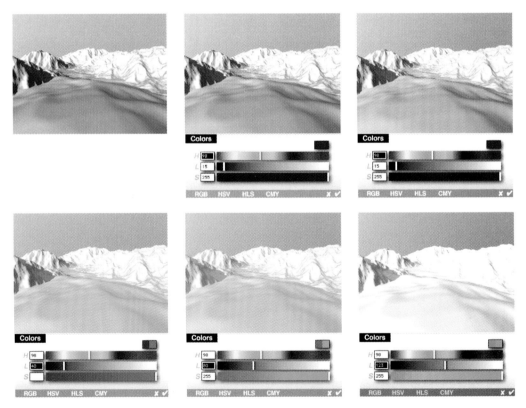

Figure C10–36 Sky Dome illumination: Color dialog boxes for the Sky Dome Color of the
corresponding rendered scene.

textures, the Sky & Fog dialog box's access to the textures is extremely narrow. One button takes you to one texture and the other button takes you to another. Any other texture will be ignored. So if you go to the Shallow Texture Editor for cumulus and decide to scroll in the list for another texture that you'd like to place in the sky, do not be surprised if the net effect is zilch (see Figure 10–17c). The stratus clouds will take their appearance only from the stratus texture. Cumulus clouds will take their appearance only from the cumulus texture.

But implicit in the limitation and focus for each of the textures is the fact that you *can* change them to alter the appearance of your clouds in the sky. The sky is hard-wired to work only with cumulus and stratus textures. So, then, if you cannot change the texture, what can you do? In the Shallow Texture Editor, you can use the other controls, the randomize, the complexity, and the turbulence controls. At the end of your efforts, you will no doubt wish to click the check mark to accept your changes. Bryce will present you with a dialog box giving you the opportunity to rename your texture (see Figure 10–17d). Give it the same name (otherwise it will not apply to your clouds!). You'll get an alert asking you if you're sure (see Figure 10–17e). Yes, you are. Even though it tells you that this cannot be undone, the permanence lasts only as long as your current Bryce session. The cumulus or stratus texture will be returned to its normal state the next time you launch Bryce.

Incidentally, if you get some wild colors in your texture explorations, those colors will not show up in your sky. Bryce takes the value information for the texture and applies it to the heavens. All the coloring comes from Bryce's sky and cloud creating model. If you're surfing for something new by using the Randomize button, look only at the texture's shape; the colors will not be applied.

When you click OK to leave either of these two editors and go back to your scene, you will have changed one of the textures from the 3D Solid Texture list in the Materials Composer. You can essentially make the same type of changes to your clouds by accessing the Texture Editors from the Materials Composer. (See Chapter 9, "Material World," for more information about the Materials Composer and Texture Editors.)

Note: If you are going to go on a texture adjustment spree, access the Sky & Fog dialog box by selecting it from the Sky & Fog Options pop-up menu, rather than double-clicking the Sun control. On some Macs accessing the Sky &

Fog dialog box by double-clicking results in a Type 1 error. (Windows users need not worry about this.) The Type 1 Error doesn't occur until the end of the process, after editing the texture. The crash happens when exiting the Sky & Fog dialog box to go back into the scene. Using the Sky & Fog Options pop-up menu makes the whole process more robust; your texture edits will "take." If Bryce up and quits on you when playing with cloud textures, try getting to the dialog box by a different route. If it doesn't, consider yourself fortunate.

8.   Do you want to create even more variations?

Continue creating variations on your Plain Vanilla! scene. Work with all of the cloud controls: altitude, coverage, frequency, amplitude, switching between stratus, cumulus, and both. Add the Sun control to the mix. Tempting though it may be, do not use the other Sky & Fog controls just yet. In the space of another 15-20 minutes, create as many different scene files as you can. Aim to create 15 in a 20-minute time span. (If you don't create that many, don't worry; the time and quantity are guidelines to help you to get onto a quick-quick-quick pace.)

Clouds and Sunlight

Whatever their size and shape, Bryce clouds never obscure the sun's light. You may not be able to directly see the sun, since the cloud cover covers it, but the sun will cast light nonetheless. If you've set a high amount of cloud cover to create dark threatening clouds, pull your Shadow setting (described in a few pages) back to make the direct sunlight less apparent.

FOG AND HAZE

Both fog and haze are manifestations of moisture in the air. Haze is overall moisture, whereas fog is localized, clinging to the ground. This section discusses the contributions haze and fog make to Brycean atmosphere.

Haze: On a Hazy Day, You Can't See Forever

Haze indicates distance. As you walk to and fro upon the earth, haze is one visual cue that something is far away. The farther away an object is, the more its details and color intensity are obscured by the water moisture in the air. Or, to put it differently, the more haze you have to look through, the farther away the object will appear. The Haze control is very simple—drag in the Haze thumbnail control to change haze amount. Assign the haze a color from the Haze Color swatch.

A little haze goes a long way. With just an infinitesimal Haze setting, you will see the haze line on your horizon. If your scene is just a plain blue sky, the presence of the tiniest amount of haze (.0001 in the Sky & Fog dialog box; you can set smaller amounts; the numbers will show up as scientific notation, such as 1e–6 for .000001) will make all the difference as you look off in the infinite distance.

If you have entered a very small haze amount (such as .001) in the Sky & Fog dialog box and later drag to 0 in the Haze thumbnail, the haze may not go away. The thumbnail's numerical readout is 0, but there is still haze present. Drag to a higher Haze setting, then back to 0 to rid your scene of those last little traces of haze.

Once you start adding objects to your scene, however, a higher Haze setting will give the appearance of distance. Take a look at the scenes by Eric Wenger on the Bryce CD (and on the book's CD, too). The Haze setting is often above 10 for a sense of distance and scale. (It can go much higher, especially when you're set to lower altitudes.) What was just a dinky-looking terrain swells to massive grandeur once all the haze is there to tell you that the mountain is really quite large.

Not only can you change the amount of haze by dragging the thumbnail to a different setting, or by typing a numerical entry into the Haze portion of the Sky & Fog dialog box, you can also modulate the height of haze by making adjustments in the Cloud Height control. Haze is the moisture in the atmosphere between ground level and cloud level. If the cloud level is higher, then haze exists in those higher areas.

Figure C10–18 shows some samples of the same cloud settings, where only the altitude is changed. The left half of each image has a Haze setting of 4 and the right half has a Haze setting of 35, so that you can see how altitude affects lesser and greater amounts of haze.

Other factors that affect haze: How much "distance" and size cueing you get from your haze also depends on the size of your terrains. This is something that's rather self-evident. The larger the terrain, the more space it occupies. The more space, the more distant portions to the terrain, and the more exaggerated the depth effect. In Figure C10–19 each image has three terrains at different sizes. The left of each shows the terrain at the default size (when it enters the Bryce scene). In the center of each image, the terrain has doubled in size. On the right of each image, the terrain has doubled in size again. The four images have different Haze settings. The larger the terrain, the more pronounced the distance effect. (This is really my underhanded way of urging you not to be shy; make your terrains bigger to get better haze effects!)

Fog

Fog, in real life, is a cloud layer that clings close to the ground. Bryce's Fog control allows you to create any color mist that clings to the ground. Aside from fog's color, there are two parameters that determine the fog's appearance—the overall amount of fog is set by Fog Amount and the height of the fog is set by Fog Height. In the Thumbnail control, there are two directions to drag to change either setting. Dragging right and left changes the amount of fog; dragging up and down changes its height. Two corresponding sets of number readouts tell you what you have. The Sky & Fog dialog box allows for precise numerical entry for either fog parameter.

Fog, like haze, is at maximum in the infinite distance of the horizon. This is true even when there's the slightest Fog Amount setting—1. But what determines the volume of the fog at places other than infinity, at points closer to you? The Fog Amount and the Height controls do.

Amount determines the fog's density as you look down the camera's depth (z axis) from the foreground to the infinite horizon. In Figure 10–20, there are three representations of fog density. (Here maximum fog is considered black.) All three are completely "socked in" at the horizon. Each one dissipates differently as it moves from the distant horizon to the near foreground. The left one dissipates in the distance, with very thin fog in the foreground. The center one still has some density in the mid- to foreground. The right one is quite thick, with some thinning in the foreground. Based on these simple illustrations, which one do you suppose has the lowest Fog Amount setting and which one has the highest? (Tick tick tick tick tick—beep! Time's up!) The left one has the lowest setting and the right one has the highest Fog Amount setting.

The second half of the fog volume equation is fog height. Height determines the vertical density or range. It answers the question: How much room is there for

Figure 10–20 Fog density—amount.

the transition from solid "socked in" fog (at the bottom of the fog bank) to no fog (at the top of the fog bank)? Figure 10–21 has equally simplistic representations of three different Fog Height settings. Which one do you think is maximum? How about minimum? (Insert the theme song from "Jeopardy" here!) If you matched up minimum with the left and maximum with the right, then you're right! ("Now tell our contestants what they've won, Jay!")

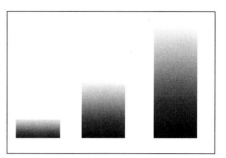

Figure 10–21 Fog density—height.

Now that we've established what the two halves of the fog volume equation are, it's time for some observations about the relationship between the two. Fog at low height settings is different above ground level than below ground level. In the first image in the top row of Figure 10–22, a setting of 5 and 5 with a bowl-shaped crater below ground level shows the fog below ground level solidly socked in whereas above it, it's not. (Note: All objects that are at ground level are just a teensy smidgen *above* ground level.) Why is this? The Fog Height settings tells how much vertical room there is to make the transition between solid fog (where fog covers every-thing) and no fog (where fog obscures nothing). With a low Fog Height setting, there's scant room for any transition between everything and nothing. So it will look like a very thin layer of solid fog. Above ground level, you get mostly nothing and below ground level you see everything. In the remainder of the images in the top row of Figure 10–22, there is more vertical room to modulate from solid fog to no fog. The same amount is shown at different heights. In contrast the bottom row shows different amounts at the same height.

> **TIP:** As a general rule, avoid low height levels unless you want to struggle with sudden socked-in layers of fog. As an emphatic rule, if you have any-thing in your scene that is below ground level, avoid low height levels like the plague.

Fog is calculated in the render as part of the shading process. There's a relation-ship between the Fog settings, the camera position, and the other objects in the scene. The appearance of fog in a scene changes radically depending on the pres-ence or absence of objects—especially a ground plane. At the same time, though, the position of the camera in relation to the objects—or to the horizon in gener-al—also affects the appearance of fog. In Brycean terms, the whole purpose of fog is to obscure objects in the scene. When there are no objects, there's nothing to

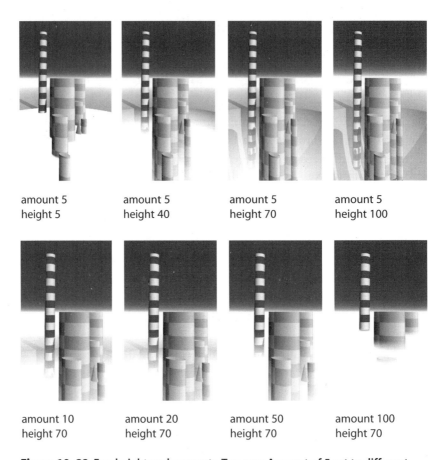

| amount 5 | amount 5 | amount 5 | amount 5 |
| height 5 | height 40 | height 70 | height 100 |

| amount 10 | amount 20 | amount 50 | amount 100 |
| height 70 | height 70 | height 70 | height 70 |

Figure 10–22 Fog height and amounts. Top row: Amount of 5 set to different heights; Bottom row: height of 70 with different amounts of fog. Bowl-shaped cutout is below Bryce's ground level.

obstruct. (This is a big departure from the way that fog worked in Bryce 1, where fog below ground level was at a constant amount, and fog obscured naked sky regardless of camera position.) In most scenes you'll have a ground plane. As it extends into horizontal infinity, the ground plane is obscured by the fog. But if you delete the ground plane, then fog acts differently, in what seems like a bizarre fashion. Figure C10–23 (in the color section) shows a series of scenes. There is a pseudo-ground plane on the right (it's just a square occupying the right hand side of the scene and it stretches way way back). There are steps on the left that descend into the infinite sky abyss, and steps on the right that ascend toward the sky. All of the scenes have an identical Fog setting: the amount is 37 and height is 100. What is different about each one is the camera placement. The cameras are at five different heights. (For reference, there is a side view of the wireframe next to each rendered image.) What the camera sees differs depending on the camera's height and, consequently, its viewing angle of each object. The camera's rotate settings (as set in the Camera controls dialog box) do not change. But as the camera's position is raised, its perspective of the foreground changes. The higher the camera position, the more directly the camera looks down into an infinite sky. Since it's hard to measure precisely how to obstruct "nothing" stretching way off into infinity, Bryce does not do so. What you see instead is the wild blue yonder—literally.

Freestanding Fog

If you want to create freestanding fog that is local to one particular area in your scene, you can use a sphere or cube primitive and give it foggy material attributes. Figure C10–24 shows a localized fog bank. It is made from a basic sphere. In the Materials Composer, the Shading mode is set to fuzzy. Diffusion is set to maximum (255), Ambient to medium (132) and there is some transparency as well (21). The Diffuse and Ambient Colors are white. To adjust the visibility of the edges, increase the Transparency setting or change the size of the sphere. Make the localized fog sensitive to shadow by ensuring that there is some diffuse illumination. You can do the same sort of thing with freestanding clouds to get localized fog effects. I'll talk about freestanding clouds at the end of this chapter.

SHADOWS

Bryce allows you to control the harshness of the shadows with the Shadow control. Shadow is a universal setting for your entire scene. It determines to what extent objects will block light from reaching other objects that lie in the sun's path. A setting of 0 results in no shadow, and a setting of 100 results in maximum shadow. Even if you have your Shadow setting at minimum, the part of the object that is not facing the sun will be darker, depending on its setting for diffuse and ambient illumination from the Materials Composer. In Figure C10–25, you can compare the maximum and minimum Shadow setting. In maximum shadow, the terrain on the scene's right blocks light from reaching other surfaces that lie "behind" the terrain in the sun's path. When shadows are set to minimum, the sun shines "through" the terrain to illuminate what lies behind it. However, in both cases the parts of the objects that do not face the sun will be in shadow regardless of the Shadow setting.

Since this is not the real world, but a virtual ray-traced world, you can make separate determinations about any object's acceptance or resistance to shadows. Related to the Sky & Fog's Shadow control are a couple of settings in the Materials Composer for the surfaces of objects. An object lit by diffuse light will display light and shadow, even on its shady side, when the Shadow setting is at a minimum. Besides the basic diffuse light setting to enable light and shadow on an object, the Materials Composer has a special control to determine whether any one object will accept shadows independent of the diffuse light setting. See Chapter 9, "Material World," for more on this Shadow setting. Also, if you are using any of Bryce's light sources, you can decide whether any or all of them will cast shadows. See Chapter 11, "Bryce EnLightenment" for more information about enabling or disabling cast shadows.

Shadows and Other Sky & Fog Elements

Bryce sky elements don't have object surface properties that are sensitive to diffuse, ambient, or specular light. Therefore their response to direct sunlight and shadow are different from what you'd expect of their real-world counterparts.

Bryce clouds do not cast shadows. Although you can adjust the amount of their coverage so that they'll block the sun or the moon (provided that either are in your view to begin with), they won't cast shadows on your Brycean world. It is easily possible to set your cloud coverage to 100% and have the sun still shine on your scene, bright as can be. This is advantageous for creating those days that have a front of dark storm clouds off in the distance while the sun is shining overhead. Or, if you want to have an overcast sky, tone down the harsh light by reducing the shadows. Adjust the degree of shadow in the Sky & Fog Palette.

In the same vein, Bryce's fog pays no attention to shadows. You can have a dark area completely shaded, and the white fog glows merrily in shadow as much as it lurks brightly in the sunshine. This resistance to shadow enables you to make some clever eerie fogs in dark Brycean places. When you're aiming for dead-on realism in sunlight and shadow, you'll have to augment Bryce's fog with additional effects.

Bryce's haze also has no sensitivity to light and shadow. Try though you might (and I have) to duplicate high moisture atmospheres in order to see rays of light passing through hazy air, you cannot achieve that effect using Bryce sky parameters alone.

In order to get atmospheric effects that are sensitive to light and shadow, you have to use actual objects which are editable in the Materials Composer. Fortunately, the diligent Brycer's efforts will be rewarded. The last section of the chapter covers freestanding clouds, and the sample images demonstrate solutions for each of the non-shadowed situations described here.

HAZE, FOG AND SHADOW WALKTHROUGH

Continue your walkthrough exercise with the Plain Vanilla! scene. No doubt by now you have the routine down.

1. Work with the three sets of controls—Shadows, Fog, and Haze—and create as many different scene files as you can with as much variety as you can.

2. Make sure to use the other controls as well—Sun control and the four Cloud controls. When it comes to haze, make sure that you work with the Altitude control! Steer clear of the color swatches and that funky set of beads (Randomize control) for now.

3. Save each scene variation as a separate scene file. Do so after a couple of render passes. Remember, the idea is to make as large an assortment as you can, and create as much variety as you can. Try for a 20-minute session working with the Fog, Haze, and Shadow controls.

COLOR

Until now, I've discussed the Sky & Fog Palette controls without introducing color. I've examined the shape of the sky— the type of clouds, the sun and moon, fog and haze, and the extra options in the Sky & Fog dialog box. Now is the time to focus on color. Bryce's atmospheric controls provide a rich and varied capacity for color to create the subtlety that is inherent natural landscapes. There are eleven different colors to mix and match: Sun Color, Ambient Color, Fog Color, Haze Color, Sky Dome and Cumulus Color. There is the color of the sky dome itself. You can select among two "normal" types of skies (Soft Sky and Dark Sky), set your own sky color in the Custom Sky (with its three color swatches), or if you don't want to have a sky with clouds, sun, or moon, you can select Atmosphere Off and determine a backdrop hue. In each of the three normal sky modes, the color of the sky dome also changes by the position of the sun (or moon). All of these colors interact with one another, resulting in sophisticated color combinations. We'll explore them here, one by one.

Of course, the best way to learn how these colors interact is to play with them to see what happens. This discussion will be a guided play time interspersed with discussion about the significance of each color.

If you need a review of methods for using the color picker, check in the Material World chapter (Chapter 9), where I discuss it in depth. In the Windows version of Bryce, the alternate color picker that has numerical values (accessed by pressing the Alt key while clicking any of the color swatches) does not work. Although you can work within the Color dialog box, whatever changes you make to the color will not be applied to the color swatch when you leave. Windows users are limited to the color picker eyedropper.

> **TRIPLE TIP:** *Here's a color picker tip. When you're choosing white, don't drag at the far end of the grayscale part of the gray ramp in the pop-up color picker. To get white, you'll be aiming for a tiny area. If you're set to Interface Maximum, where you can see the Macintosh menu bar, there's plenty of white just above in the menu bar, and the color picker samples from anywhere on your screen. Otherwise, in Interface Minimum (where the menu bar is hidden) aim for the area near the View controls on the Master Palette. There's quite an area of white available there. Figure 10–26 shows the area of pure white, with non-white areas darkened.*
>
> *Since you can select colors from elsewhere on your monitor, select colors from your partially rendered scenes or the Nano Preview. This technique will especially come in handy for Windows users whose color picking abilities are crippled by the non-functional Color dialog box. (Still, I've used this method long before Bryce 2 came along with its desaturated spectrum in the color picker.) Render a bit, and then choose your color from that rendered area. If you need to desaturate the color, mix it with some white haze or fog, render a portion again, and then send your eyedropper in search of a toned down color.*
>
> *This last variation will work in the Macintosh version of Bryce. If you need to select from a color swatch that will be common to several scenes (as I did to create some of the illustrations for this chapter), create a small image file— preferably a PICT. Set your interface to Interface Maximum, and invoke the full-screen command so you can see the scene file's title bar. Open up the color swatch PICT in Simple Text and position it near the Sky & Fog palette so that it doesn't overlap it. When you need to access the color swatch, close the scene file window using the WindowShade system extension (which needs to be loaded at startup). The scene is still active even though the window is closed, and when you drag the color picker to the swatch, you'll be sampling for that active scene. See Figure 10–26b.*

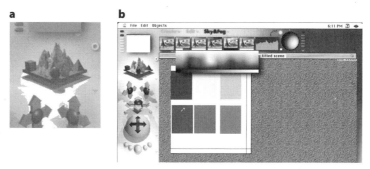

Figure 10–26 Color picking tips for Sky & Fog: a) The pure white area surrounding the Views Control, a fertile source for white color-picking; b) color swatch PICT file open in Simple Text, accessible after invoking WindowShade to hide current scene file.

Color and Bryce Atmosphere

The different controls for assigning color are the following:

- *Sky Mode.* There are four total sky types possible in Bryce. The "normal" ones, Soft Sky and Dark Sky, affect the sky color. Custom Sky allows you to set your own sky colors for a fully functioning sky. Atmosphere Off allows you to set a color for the sky, but there are no clouds, nor are the sun or moon visible. The first part of the exploration will assume that you have Soft Sky or Dark Sky selected; I'll discuss the other modes later in the chapter.

- *Light Position.* Not a direct color control, but sky dome, cloud, and haze color are affected by it nonetheless.

- *Sun.* The color of the actual sun (when it's visibly positioned in your sky) and the color of diffuse light as it falls on objects in your scene.

- *Ambient.* The color of indirect light everywhere in your scene, especially in shadow.

- *Clouds.* The color your cumulus clouds take on when in shadow. Also, when Atmosphere in the Render Palette is switched off, the color of your sky dome.

- *Haze.* The color of the general water moisture, dust particles, and all other airborne matter that's suspended in your Brycean sky.

- *Fog.* The color of the localized moisture that clings to the ground level in your scene.

- *Sky Dome Illumination*. This is another control new to Bryce 2. A general overall light source from the atmosphere illuminates your scene, if you so desire. (Unfortunately, it does not work in the Windows version.)

Color Exercises

In these exercises, I'll take you through alternating explanation and exploration. They are not intended to help you make that killer sky in three easy steps. Rather, they are to help you become fluent at navigating through all the complexities. This will be a guided exploration of colors while you work in your Plain Vanilla! scene. If you see anything you like, save it under a unique name, and then keep going in your explorations. At the end of this chapter you will have quite a body of work, showing you the variety of looks you can give your scenes simply by changing the sky.

To create your initial sky setting, open up the scene file PLAIN VANILLA! from the CD-ROM, then follow these steps:

1. Start again with Bryce's default clouds. Go to the Sky & Fog Options pop-up menu to select stratus clouds.

2. Drag down on the graph to increase amplitude slightly for better cloud definition (Spikier graph).

Time of Day

The first color manipulation is time of day. You set time of day with the Sun control. This control affects the color of Bryce's sky dome, which changes color according to the Sun control position. It also affects cloud color.

Recall the Sun control conventions mentioned previously. Bryce's high noon is the Sun control at the center. Place the sun at the top horizon (north) for sunset.

1. Let's explore stratus clouds and Sun control position. Drag the Sun control Preview to the bottom (south). The stratus clouds turn red. Drag up in increments toward the center, letting Bryce render between each little movement. The clouds change from red to yellow to white. Drag the Sun control up toward the top (to north, sunset, 12 o'clock). The clouds turn reddish again, although the glare of the sun may make it hard to see this. Compare Soft Sky and Darker Sky modes when the sun is visible. Drag along the horizon's edge off to either side. Change to Night View and look at the different colors again depending on the Sun control's position.

Make sure to save a few interesting variations in your Plain Vanilla! pile.

2. Adjust cumulus clouds and color. Before you change to cumulus, save the stratus cloud setting in one of the Sky Memory Dots to the right of the Sky & Fog Palette. Once you've done that (you'll come back to it later), change the cloud type to Cumulus in the Sky & Fog Options pop-up menu. To get decent and recognizable clouds, you'll probably have to increase the frequency and perhaps amplitude. (An increase in altitude helps, too.) Drag the sun position all around the sky, repeating the movements from the previous step. Does sun position act the same with cumulus as it does with stratus? How about when the sun is shining from behind the clouds when you drag the Sun control toward sunset?

    Keep those Plain Vanilla! variations coming! Save interesting scenes as you see them!

Figure C10–27 explores different sun positions as they affect sky dome color and cloud color. Each image is divided, comparing Darker Sky (left half) and Soft Sky (right half). The sun is shown at five different basic heights, from three perspectives: behind, in front, and to the side. Side and behind are almost identical. Although the Soft Sky on the right of each image is flipped, it is showing the the portion of the sky closest to the sun. When the sun is on the horizon, the haze and clouds are red. When the sun is near the horizon, the sky is violet and haze and clouds are orange-beige. When the sun is at mid-sky, the sky is a vivid blue and the clouds and haze are white. When the sun is directly overhead, all colors are washed out to a lighter blue. When the sun is facing you, the same is generally true, except the sky color is lighter and is reddened by the sun's presence. (Changing to Darker Sky in the Sky Mode pop-up menu deepens the sky dome color, especially for the half of the sky where you face into the sun.)

When the sun is closer to the horizon, all sky colors take on a reddish cast. This is similar to the way light works in real life, since the sun's rays have to travel through more atmosphere to reach your eyes. Longer distance draws out the longer red light wavelengths. Conversely, when the sun is positioned directly overhead, the sky is blue because the shorter light waves bounce about. The strongest red is when the light is "behind" you (bottom position).

Go inside the Sky & Fog dialog box to numerically manipulate the Sun control. Sky color is determined by the γ factor. The reddish horizon corresponds to a γ value of 0; the sun is on the horizon and the overall color is red.

3. Change from day to night and move the Sun control to different places. The right-hand spread of Figure C10–27 shows the same set of variations, but the Sun control set to night. The sky dome is noticeably darker and the cloud color stays in the same general range as it was during the day. Notice the continuity when the sun is close to the horizon. Whereas the biggest change in day is when the sun is in front, night's biggest change is when the sun is behind, and the moon is in front. In order to see the moon, the y value for the sun position must be a negative number. There is no such thing as –0; the position on the horizon for the bottom row is –.000001 (or –1e–06, the scientific notation for the same).

The Sun's Color

Now that you've played with the bare bones sky and light source position, it's time to give some color to that light. Sun Color affects the scene overall, primarily where light falls directly on objects. However, Sun Color also has an effect on cloud color.

1. Change the cloud type back to stratus. (Before doing so, save your cumulus cloud into a Memory Dot, then go back and click on your stratus memory dot.) Now assign a Sun Color. Switch the Sun control back to Sun (day). Sun Color is transferred to the clouds. Stratus clouds take on the Sun Color.

2. Drag the Sun control around. Notice that when the sun gets down toward the horizon, the cloud color mixes oranges and reds into whatever the Sun Color is.

3. Have an Amplitude adjustment hour. Place the sun closer to the center (close to noon) than to the horizon. Drag up the Amplitude graph to even out the spikes somewhat (that is, lower the amplitude) and notice that stratus clouds become hazier. The overall high haze takes on the Sun Color.

4. Change the Sun control to night, and drag it around. Sun Color has no effect during Bryce's deep midnight. Only when the sun nears the horizon does Sun Color creep into the clouds. Change back to daytime.

5. Alter Sun Color and cumulus clouds. Change the clouds back to cumulus and select a different color for the sun. Compared to the stratus clouds, there's only a subtle change in cloud color. Drag the sun all around to see how the color affects things at different times of day. Try the same thing for night. Set the sun to white again.

The stratus clouds easily pick up the the color of the sun. So to change the color of the stratus clouds, change the Sun Color. To a limited extent, there is an influence on the cumulus cloud color when a different Sun Color is chosen. But that's more of a little color lacing the edges than it is a pure color.

So far, this exploration has shown that a change in Sun Color affects the color of other objects in the scene. But it hasn't yet addressed the question of *which color*. Cast an overall tone in your scene by your selection of Sun Color. Warm up your scene with a warmer Sun Color. Likewise, cool it down with a wintry chilly color. At this point in time you may want to change the Diffuse Color of your Plain Vanilla! terrains from the default gray to a lighter gray, or white, so that they'll respond to the all the colors to be used in these exercises. Figure C10–28 shows two sets of warm Sun Colors and two sets of cool Sun Colors. When the sun is high in the sky, it's realistic to make the colors subtle. For that glowing sunset and the red rays just before dusk, change the Sun Color to a more intense red-orange and place it low on the horizon. (Of course, if you want to make a fiery red-orange sun at high noon, go right ahead. It's your world.) A deep blue sun casts a strong "moonlight." This is an effective color alternative, as long as you don't want to have much sky showing, or—heavens forbid!—the moon itself.

In the images for the figure, the ground, terrain, and sphere all have Bryce's basic white material setting. There is a bit of white haze, and the Cumulus and Ambient Colors are white. So you can see how much influence the Sun Color has on the entire scene. Portions of the images have an Ambient Color setting as well. I will discuss Ambient Color momentarily.

The Sun Color is apparent by the color of its light. When you position the sun so that you can see it directly, it is, well, the Sun Color! Think about making your sun ultramarine or black or day-glow green for skies that do not resemble our home world. You're not limited to the yellows, oranges, and reds that are associated with our own Earth's sun! The sun, when seen directly, is affected by the amount of haze and fog. With the presence of haze, it might lose its strength. So be gentle with it.

Incidentally, there is no corresponding control for the moon's color. It never changes.

Ambient Color

In the same way that Sun Color affects the overall scene, so also does ambient light. Ambient light is the sum total of all light in your scene. The color of ambient light affects the color of objects both in direct sunlight and in shadow, but it is far more pronounced in shadow. For the general color of light in your scene, think of the Sun Color as the color of direct light and the Ambient Color as the color of shadow. There are more subtleties to it than that, but that's the gist of the situation.

Figure C10–28, previously discussed as a part of Sun Color, uses the same set of warm and cool colors for Ambient Color. The set of images in the left column has a portion in which there is only Ambient Color and a white Sun Color. The presence of *any* Ambient Color is better than white, since white tends to make the shadows look washed out. When both the sun and ambient settings have color, the result is a richer-looking scene. Bear in mind, of course, that these samples are using the white matte material setting. Your mileage may vary with material settings that have different colors. You may not require Sun and Ambient Colors of this intensity to get a rich effect.

The RGB values for the four different colors are provided so that you can try out your own Ambient and Sun Color combinations. The top half has the sun in a high position, and the bottom half has the sun placed in a lower position. Compare the different images, especially in the shadow and highlight areas. The middle column compares warm with warm colors and cool with cool colors, whereas the right column compares mixtures of dissimilar colors.

For images with good lighting contrast, use a darker color for ambient light than for your Sun Color.

Bearing these points in mind, try out a bit of Ambient Color-choosing yourself.

1. Try different Ambient Colors in your scene. Change your cloud type back to Cumulus. Select a lighter Ambient Color and see how it influences the clouds and your objects. Move the sun into a high position and then to a low position.

2. Select a darker Ambient Color and look for the same things. (Of course, check out these colorings at night, too!) Then change the Ambient Color back to white. Make sure you save any variations that are interesting to you!

Cumulus Color

This is the first of the moisture-atmospheric color conditions. The following is self-evident: Setting the Cumulus Color swatch will affect the color of the cloud. But lest you think this is *too* simple, read on.

1. Set Cumulus Color and stratus clouds. Change your cloud type to stratus. For comparison's sake, select a deep color for the Cumulus Color swatch control. No change. *Stratus clouds are not affected by the Cumulus Color, only by Sun Color.*

2. Now change to cumulus clouds. Change the Cumulus Color. This time you will see a far more dramatic color influence on the clouds. Cumulus is strongly influenced by Cumulus Color.

Haze Color

Haze Color tends to put an overall color cast to a sky (and all objects in it).

When the haze amount is high enough, the Haze Color will interact with the Ambient Color. Your Haze Color will provide a secondary "ambient" color. In some cases, that little bit can be too much.

In most standard day-sky scenes (Soft or Darker sky, sun roughly overhead), a white haze gives the scene a bluish cast. When the sun is close to the horizon or in Bryce nighttime, the haze takes on a reddish cast.

Figure C10–29 shows different Haze settings in a scene that is half sea, half land. Notice the distance of terrains from the camera and how their details are obscured by haze.

All that I said earlier about the sun's position and sky color also applies to haze. Moving the Sun control will change the color of haze. In fact, there are two color changes occurring simultaneously: While the sky dome changes from a light blue to deep blue to violet, haze changes from white to light orange to red.

Now try this exercise.

1. First, modify Haze Color and stratus clouds. Then change the color (and amount) of haze. Increase the haze amount to somewhere in the 30-40 range and assign a color to the haze.

2. Try these settings for a night sky, too.

3. Adjust the altitude of clouds to see how it affects the overall color of the haze.

Fog Color

Here's another simple, self-evident statement for you: Set your fog's color with the Fog thumbnail color swatch. (Yawn.) Figure C10–30 shows some examples of different fog amounts and fog heights. The same three color variations are used as the haze example from Figure C10–29—white, ivory, and black. For each of the Fog Height/Amount settings, the scene is rendered from two different camera angles. The scenes with the lower camera position show less fog in the foreground than the higher camera position with the same Fog Height and Amount setting. Compare how the appearance of the other objects in the scene changes with the Fog Color.

Fog will also add a tint to the sky, assuming your camera position is low and your fog height is high. (See especially the examples in Figure C10–30 where the fog amount is 100 and the camera is lower.) Try this exercise. Give your scene some fog and give the fog a color. Drag the Sun control around and add colors for both sun and ambient. Notice that the Fog Color is not affected by the lighting colors. For that matter, fog is not affected by sunlight or shadow either.

Combining Haze and Fog Color

Combining Fog Color and Haze Color takes you to an interesting place. You can select a color to be distinct by itself or select one to mix with your Haze Color. Fog Color can be intriguing, yea, exciting when combined with the color of haze. Though fog maintains its color when mixed with lighting controls, the combination of haze and fog creates some very subtle and pleasing effects. If your fog is dark and the haze is light, then the resulting combination can be downright fetching. Try a light yellow haze with any dark color fog. Black fog provides a delightful surprise, as does dark green.

Figure C10–31 shows the same scene with different combinations of Haze and Fog Colors. For each color combination, the light source is shown in three different positions—daytime, nighttime, and dusk, with the sun on the horizon. The double combination of haze with sun position and Fog and Haze Colors results in a surprising new color. The result is not a straightforward mix of the Fog and Haze Colors, as there are other factors at work. Sun position, sky color, and Ambient Color all will enter into this delightfully complex area of atmospheric color.

Try this exercise free-for-all. Lay down this book, put *all* the Sky & Fog controls to work with all their colors, and simply play.

But by now this will not be hit-or-miss playing. When you tweak here and adjust there, your playing will have more direction to it. If you find yourself gravitating toward this or that control to move further in a particular direction, then congratulate yourself! You've started building an internal sense for all of Bryce's atmospheric controls. (If not, don't fret. Keep working and exploring. It will come.)

Sky Mode: Custom Sky Colors

After Bryce 1 came out, one of the most frequently requested new features was the ability to customize sky color. Sure, you could select Atmosphere Off and set a color for the overall sky dome, add some fog and haze, and fake your way through it. Since Atmosphere Off does away with clouds and a visible sun and moon, it required ingenuity and effort to create a custom color sky, complete with clouds. (Hint: infinite cloud planes are involved here.) All those options are still available in Bryce 2.

Far more applicable in those situations where the typical Bryce sky just won't work right is the Custom Sky. In the Custom Sky, you set your own colors for the sky. There are three color swatches to control the sky.

- *Sky Color.* The center swatch is the Sky Color. That's the overall color of the sky. Here's where you can create a soft faint blue, or an angry burnt orange, or a surrealistic aquamarine sky.

- *Solar Halo Color.* This is the color swatch to the left. This color is assigned to the area of the sky that surrounds the sun. Make it closer to a shade of the Sun Color, or warmer or cooler than the rest of the sky. Even when the sun is not in the sky, this color can become the partial sky color.

- *Haze Shift Color.* This is the color swatch on the right. It adds a tint to the haze in places away from the sun's location. It affects the color of stratus clouds, too. The Bryce 2 Explorer's Guide points out that the best way to see the influence of the Haze Shift is to create a scene with no ground plane and to see the abyss of sky below. To be sure, the abyss below lies opposite the sun. At the same time, though, there is an extra lingering source of Haze Shift Color that lives primarily below the horizon rather than above it. Figure C10–32 has two scenes with identical coloring, pale sky and Solar Halo colors, and a bright red Haze Shift Color. Even when the sun is below the horizon, there is still a strong influence of the red color—far more than you see above when the sun is above the horizon.

If you want to see the below-horizon effects with your Plain Vanilla! scene, simple select faraway terrains (but not the closest one) or no terrains at all, and enter Solo mode. When you render, you'll be able to see down into the sky abyss below.

The images in Figure C10–33 are 360° panoramas of custom skies, with different colors and positions of the sun. Since you can see the entire panorama, it's easy to note the color closest to the sun, furthest from the sun and everywhere in between. The custom color swatch is included in the lower left corner of each scene.

Exercises for a Custom Sky

1. Try the custom sky yourself! Open up that ol' Plain Vanilla! scene. Under the Sky Mode pop-up menu, select Custom Sky.

2. Change the Sky Color and move the sun around to different positions.

3. Assign a Solar Halo Color and continue moving the sun to different positions.

4. Add a Haze Shift Color and move the sun to different positions. Select stratus clouds and see how the presence of the Haze Shift Color affects the cloud color. Move the sun to different positions.

5. Increase haze, fog, altitude as you see fit. Add one or both type of clouds.

6. Assign colors for the sun, ambient, fog, haze, and clouds.

7. Change to night—the color shift is not so dramatic as with Bryce's Soft and Darker Skies.

8. Save lots of variations of your work. There are so many options here, from the beatific to the hellacious.

Figure C10–34 shows the same variations of solar position as in Figure C10–27, only a Custom Sky is used. Each image is divided in half; the left is with a Haze Shift Color of white; the right uses yellow. Like the previous example, there are spreads for both day and night. The sky does not vary as much with custom color. Though it may look subtle and perhaps boring in a two-page spread of images, think of the possibilities you want for that sky color when the sun is close to the horizon!

Sky Dome Color

There is a new illumination and color source in Bryce 2 sky. The Sky Dome Color is an extremely diffuse light source. Light falls from above, reflected through the atmosphere. By changing the color—and the value—of the Sky

Dome Color, you determine the color and strength of the subtle illumination that descends through the atmosphere.

Although there is a control for Sky Dome Color for the Windows version of Bryce, it does not work. It's a great pity; Brycean twilight will not be the same in Windows. The remainder of this section applies to the Macintosh version of Bryce.

What's all this about light reflected from the atmosphere, anyhow? If you've been outside before sunrise, or after sunset, when the sun is below the horizon and there is no direct sunlight shining on anything, you've probably noticed that there is a very faint diffuse light that comes from above. Though you are in the shadow of the earth, the atmosphere above is not. Light strikes the atmosphere above, descending to where you are after being thoroughly scattered in the atmosphere. The result is a soft illumination that comes from directly above.

Figure C10–35 depicts the earth, atmosphere, and the shadow of the earth to show what portions are in sunlight and shadow. If you are in the shadowed portion of the earth near direct sunlight, the atmosphere above is lit. Of course, you don't *have* to be at a dusky spot to take advantage of Sky Dome illumination. You can use it whenever you want to. But you'll notice it most for an overall light fill when you have your sun close to the horizon.

So how does it work? There are two dynamics taking place. Both are controlled by the color you select. The value of the color (or brightness) determines *how much* light falls onto your scene from above. The hue of the color determines the color of the light. (Saturation will determine how muddy or pure the hue is.) When you use the color picker, look at it for the two color dynamics. Move left to right to choose the color, and up and down to choose the amount of light. Dark, dark colors will still make a noticeable difference in your scene! Figure C10–36 shows five variations of green in the Sky Dome illumination, with a neutral reference scene. For each Sky Dome illuminated scene, the color picker values are shown. In the first variation, even though you cannot tell what the color the Sky Dome is, you see the result in a subtle green. A look at the numerical values behind it show that the green is nearly black. Yet see how much green has entered the scene from this Sky Dome Color! Each of the other variations is made by sliding the L (Lightness) slider toward white.

When the sun is overhead, you won't need very much Sky Dome illumination. In fact, as you can see by the last sample in Figure C10–36, too much will blow out your highlight areas of your scene. When the sun is overhead, use dark colors to provide color shift subtlety. When the sun is not overhead, a stronger Sky Dome illumination is more effective. Anything from dark to light color is appropriate here.

Now YOU try it!

Spend a little time playing with the Sky Dome Color.

1. Whip out that PLAIN VANILLA! scene file.

2. In order to make the ground more sensitive to the changes in the diffuse light, alter the diffuse setting for them a bit. Select all terrains (or simply select all objects).

3. In the Materials Composer, change the diffuse setting from 255 to something lower. Then change the Diffuse Color to white or very nearly white.

4. Try different colors. Experiment with all the lightness variations of any hue by using the HLS Color Picker. Option-click any color swatch on the Mac. Unfortunately for Windows, although an Alt-click accesses the alternate color picker, any changes made will not be applied when you click the check mark to leave the Color dialog box.

5. Try the same set of lightness variations with the sun in different positions.

6. Change the Sun control to night and see what kind of Sky Dome illumination you get.

7. You *are* saving interesting variations, aren't you?

Sky Dome Color and Different Sky Modes

It just so happens that the Sky Dome Color works differently when you use Custom Sky than when you are in either of Bryce's "normal" skies, Soft Sky and Darker Sky.

When you are in the normal sky modes, and you have Sky Dome Color switched on (anything other than absolute black), the Cumulus Color will leak in. It's not an issue if you have your Cumulus Color set to white, but once you set it to some other color, you'll see the color shift. Figure C10–37 shows a comparison of the same color settings in the Sky & Fog Palette, but different Sky Mode settings. The orange Cumulus Color does not affect the Sky Dome illumination of the scene when custom color is set, but when both of the normal modes are active, the Sky Dome Color is no longer green, but mixed with a muddy orange to result in a pinkish gray. Though the Cumulus Color is orange, there are no cumulus clouds present. This disagreeable color influence occurs even when the cumulus cloud option is unchecked in the Sky & Fog Options pop-up menu. Oops.

So what do you do about this? Well, you won't encounter it constantly; you'll get the two-color influence only when you are in the normal sky modes and only when you have assigned *both* the Sky Dome and Cumulus Colors. If you need to have both colors at work simultaneously, then create a custom sky to match your "normal" sky as closely as possible. (To aid you in the process, draw a selection marquee around a portion of the sky, so that you won't completely render over the old one and can tweak your custom sky to match the normal one.)

Sky Mode: Atmosphere Off

When you select Atmosphere Off, the sky's color is set by the color swatch in the Sky mode control. The clouds, sun and moon will no longer be visible in your scene. However, you can still see sunlight or moonlight reflections off of a reflective surface.

You can set haze and fog in a sky with Atmosphere Off. If you have haze in your scene, the position of the sun will change the color of the sky, the same as when Atmosphere is turned on.

The Sky Dome Color is inherited from whatever the previous state is. . . for a bit, anyhow. If you have a custom sky with a deep green Sky Dome Color, when you switch to Atmosphere Off, the previous deep green will be inherited. It doesn't matter if you up and decide that you want to change the deep green to hot pink or midnight blue for your Sky Dome Color. You'll have green. It will stay that way until you open up the Materials Preset Library or the Materials Composer. When you exit to go back to the scene, you'll now render a scene without any Sky Dome Color influence. This newfound absence of Sky Dome Color is probably the way Bryce was designed—after all, light from the upper atmosphere is contrary to a state where the atmosphere is turned off. This strange state of inheritance also holds true for the mix of Cumulus Color and Sky Dome Color that I mentioned earlier. If you switch to Atmosphere Off from a Soft Sky or a Darker Sky with a mixed up Sky Dome, you'll inherit the previous mixed-up state until you go to either the Materials Preset Library or the Materials Composer.

Exercise—Is It Midnight or Is It a Red Dusk?

Try this series of exercises to develop your "Atmosphere Off" fluency:

1. Open the your PLAIN VANILLA! scene file from the CD-ROM. Under the Sky Mode pop-up menu, select Atmosphere Off.

2. In the Sky & Fog Palette, make sure that fog and haze amounts are all set to zero. If they aren't already, set all of the colors (Fog, Haze, Cloud, Sun, Ambient) to white. Sky Dome Color should be black (off).

3. In the Backdrop Hue color swatch, select a color. (Make it a deep, dark color.) Change the sun's position a few times, just to see how it affects the objects but not the sky.

4. Add a bit of haze. You don't need much. A setting of 1 or 2 or so will do just fine. Now adjust the sun's position. Make sure you get it down toward the horizon, too. Switch from day to night and change the position around some more. You get reddish haze at midnight when the moon is straight up in the sky.

5. Change the color of the haze. Make the haze a lighter color, up toward the top of the pop-up color picker colors. Now adjust the sun's position again. When the sun is at high noon, switch to night. There's quite a difference in color.

6. Add fog. Make the amount less than 10 and the height more than 50. Make the fog deep blue, and the haze white, and the scene at night. Change the Backdrop Hue to black. You get nice reddish tones. Now change the haze to a light, light yellow. Beautiful! With night coloring and light color haze (the red effect tends to die out when you select greenish colors), you can get soft dusky peach-hued skies that are stunning in their subtlety. Try the Backdrop Hue as dark blue. Adjust the altitude to modulate the haze amount. See Figure C10–38 for a day and night example.

7. Add color to Sun and Ambient and compare day and night effects. See how the Sun and Ambient Color affects objects in your scene? The degree of effect differs depending on whether it's night or day.

Plain Vanilla! Conclusions

By now you have amassed quite a collection of Plain Vanilla! scenes that are by now neither plain nor vanilla. What will you do with them all?

1. First, finish rendering them. Select the scene file icons and drag them onto the Bryce 2 application icon. Then go outside and take a look at the sky or

visit people in the real world while your Bryce skies finish their rendering. Or, if it's late at night, go to bed and have a restful well-earned sleep.

2. Put them all in a folder together with a copy of KPT QuickShow or use another slide show application to view your rendered images. (QuickShow is on the Bryce application CD-ROM for both Mac and Windows versions, as well as this book's CD-ROM in the Software folder. It will display the PICT file format for Macintosh Bryce renders, but since it only displays JPG file formats for Windows, using it to display the BMP format won't work. I've included a couple of Windows slide show shareware applications on the CD-ROM; look for them in the Software folder.)

3. Let the slide show run while you look at all the scenes. Notice the incredible variety in the appearance of all your scenes. All the scenes have identical objects. You haven't changed their appearance. (Well, maybe you lightened the gray of the terrains for some of the Sky Dome Color scenes.) The only thing you have changed is the sky. See how much mood and feeling in a scene comes from your atmospheric settings?

(On the CD-ROM there is a similar slide show of sky work done by participants in the Corcoran School of Art Digital Multimedia Master's Class.)

4. No doubt there are some skies that you think are real "keepers." These are the ones you'll open up again and add to the Sky Presets (I discussed Preset Libraries in Chapter 5, "Streamline Your Brycing.") Since the file names are displayed on the screen with each image, you can make a note of which scenes you want to keep.

5. Once you have opened up all your "keeper" scene files and saved the presets, you can trash the scene files if you need the rest of your hard disk back! Keep the rendered images to look at for inspiration or to help get you out of a rut.

By this time you will probably have an internal gut sense about skies. Perhaps as you go through the slide show, you might see a scene and find yourself with an intuitive sense for how to fix it or tweak it, or to do something else to it. If you do have that sense, congratulations! You have managed to wrap your brain and your senses around a very complex set of interweaving controls, with ten shape parameters and eleven color parameters. This was no simple task!

Random Sky Control

"Now wait a minute!" you may be saying. "There's one sky control that this chapter hasn't covered yet." Yes, that funky doo-hickey little set of spheres is located just to the left of the Sun control. If you've worked with Kai's Power Tools, you know that it's a tiny version of the mutation marbles. Unlike the full-scale mutation marbles, these do not require you to click a specific marble for a weaker or stronger mutation—they're too small for that! Simply click the marbles-in-general to randomize the Sky & Fog settings. After a few clicks, you'll see a range of Sky & Fog fog, haze, cloud, sun, and color settings as Bryce zigs and zags through some seemingly improbable options.

You've probably already visited this bastion of random skyness before you cracked open this chapter, right? I saved the discussion of the Random Sky control until last, since you now know how you can use it. When you get a random sky, you may or may not have something useful. If you don't know what to change to make something weird and ho-hum into something that's Wow! Original! Spectacular! you may end up clicking many times until you get something moderately useful. Or you might have been tempted to abandon use of it altogether. If, after all the plain vanilla-ing, you've got the gut sense that tells you, "Tweak *this* (but not *that*; that is okay for now)" you can use the Randomize control to launch you into new directions.

Memory Dots

While exploring the sky controls, I told you about the bulk of the controls on the Sky & Fog Palette. Although I have briefly mentioned Memory Dots earlier in this chapter, there is need for more elaboration on this set of controls.

The Sky & Fog Palette has a set of Memory Dots for saving sky settings. The mechanics for working them are the same as those for the Camera Memory Dots. If you need a brush-up on how to save them, then go back to Chapter 3 where they're explained in detail.

The Memory Dots allow you to save a sky preset momentarily. Momentarily is the operative word here. Unlike Saved View Presets on the Master Palette, the Sky Memory Dots are not saved with the scene file. Any settings you store in the Memory Dots will stay with you throughout your Bryce session, but they'll disappear once you quit Bryce. So use them as much as you need to within a

Bryce session, but if you want to make any of them more permanent, save a full-fledged Sky & Fog Preset in the Preset Library.

Like the Camera Memory Dot, the current Memory Dot is the green-with-white-spot-dot. However, the Sky dots are a bit more flaky than their camera counterparts. If you use the Sky & Fog dialog box to change the numerical settings, the white dot remains afterwards, even though the current Sky & Fog setting is different from the saved one. If you click the white dot, the sky will change back to the previous settings.

> **TIP:** In the Windows version, the Preferences option "Launch to previous state" will not allow a sky setting to carry over from scene to scene (where you create a scene, change the sky, save that scene, create a new scene which inherits the sky settings from the previous scene). If you want to keep the same sky for a set of scenes you are creating in one Bryce session, save the sky settings to a Memory Dot before creating a new scene.

The Sky Memory Dots will save all the settings from the Sky & Fog Palette. However, they do not save the settings for the underlying cloud textures. If in the course of a Bryce session you create a Memory Dot for one sky setting, then you change the underlying texture of one or both cloud types, clicking the Memory Dot will not take you back to the previous cloud texture. When it comes to clouds, the Memory Dot will recall whether stratus or cumulus clouds are switched on, and their coverage, frequency, amplitude, altitude and color. But the Memory Dot retains no information about the underlying texture of the cloud. After you've changed the cloud texture, the previously saved Memory Dot will apply the saved settings to the new cloud texture. When you save a Sky Preset in the Preset Library, however, the underlying cloud texture is part of the preset. So you can use the Preset Library to change from one underlying texture to another, if dinking around with cloud textures strikes your fancy.

The top Memory Dot is the "revert to default sky" dot. The Sky & Fog Options pop-up menu also has a setting that's seemingly identical: Reset Sky. However, they differ in this one important way: You can use the Undo command with the top Memory Dot but not with the Reset Sky menu command. Typing ⌘-Z (Macintosh) or Ctrl+Z (Windows) after selecting Reset Sky will result in no change, whereas typing ⌘-Z or Ctrl+Z after clicking the top Memory Dot will take you to the previous sky.

ALTERNATIVE CLOUDS

Brycean clouds are wonderful inventions of a mathematical nature. However, there are some limitations. They do not cast shadows. "Real" clouds do. In this section, I explore real shadow-casting Brycean clouds in their two and a half forms—infinite planes and freestanding spheres (and sphere sets, for you adventurous Mac Brycers!).

Infinite Planes for Cloud Layers

Bryce 2 now has its own specialized infinite plane object for clouds. When the sky infinite plane is created, Bryce automatically assigns a material setting from the Clouds section of the Material Presets.

There are several infinite plane cloud presets in the Materials Preset Library to get you started. Note also that the infinite cloud plane object enters the Bryce world with a different family wireframe color than the default charcoal gray.

When tweaking the clouds in the Materials Composer, make sure to play with the frequency and the transparency sliders. Also, take a look at the mapping options for the infinite plane materials that are in the other presets. Object Mapping is frequently used. What happens if you change to Parametric? World Space Top? Figure C10–39 shows a basic cloud infinite plane with transparency adjustments (top row) and mapping and frequency adjustments (bottom row).

When you use a cloud infinite plane, you're not limited to one. In Figure C10–40, there are two cloud planes, above and below the camera level (each one is removed in the other images for comparison's sake).

Freestanding Cloud Structures

When creating clouds that cast shadows, you needn't restrict yourself to flat planes with clouds by using spheres. Bryce enables you to create freestanding clouds using spheres. This type of sky is a personal favorite. An effective freestanding cloud is not created with one sphere, though. Several spheres are needed to create that cotton-puffy, ice-cream-cone cloud shape.

The trick to creating good cloud structures is to use multiple spheres and to enlarge them to a size that has the right cloud dimension. Don't create clouds and limit their size to the small unity unit size. Enlarge the sphere. Enlarge it again. And again. And again. Brycean clouds work better when enlarged considerably.

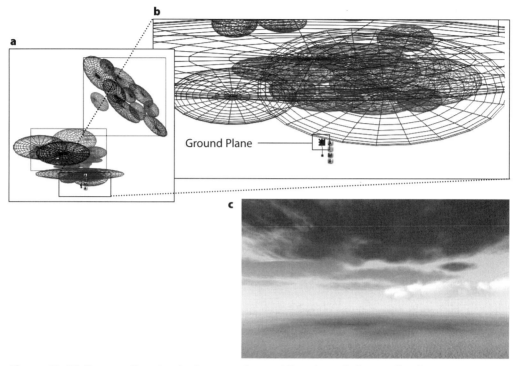

Figure 10–41 Freestanding cloud spheres are large: a) Top view wireframe of entire scene; b) enlargement inset with ground object indicated; c) rendered image. *Image by Eric Wenger.*

Figure 10–41a and b are top view wireframe views of the rendered scene shown in Figure 10–41c. Compare the size of the spheres in this scene to the size of the ground plane. Even in the more close up view of the wireframe it is still awfully small. Good freestanding clouds are large.

To perfect the freestanding cloud spheres, you'll have to liberally tweak the frequency and the transparency of your clouds . Also, because of the fuzziness and the transparency of the spheres, a scene with many freestanding clouds will take a big performance hit when it comes to rendering time.

Clouds needn't be always set in the air; in this Grand Canyon scene they act as low-lying fog, too. Figure C10–42a through c shows the wireframe views. Parts a and b are shown from top view, with the sphere clouds missing from part b so that the terrains are distinguishable. Part c is the wireframe view from the camera perspective. Figure 10–42d is the rendered result. Although there is some fog in this scene, much of the fog effect is created with freestanding clouds. Of course, the freestanding fog is susceptible to sunlight and shadow, too.

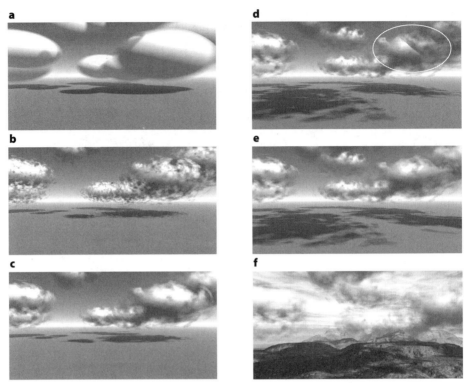

Figure 10–43 Steps to create freestanding clouds: a) Basic sphere placement with fuzzy spheres; b) texture applied; c) frequency reduced; d) spheres duplicated and rearranged with bad overlap where circle is; e) overlapping spheres moved; f) final rendered image with terrains underneath clouds.

When creating clouds of this sort, first create spheres that are default flat, gray, and fuzzy. This will help you in their general placement. When you assign the Cloud Texture (good ones are variations on Low Smog and similar textures; check out successful cloud scenery and use the Clouds & Fogs section of the Material Preset Library), the sphere size will shrink again. But at least you've gotten one set of positioning checks out of the way before moving on to the next phase.

In the series shown in Figure 10–43, the scene starts with basic spheres set to Fuzzy in the Materials Composer (see Figure 10–43a). Then the texture preset Smoke Stack is applied in part b. Thereafter follows some tweaking, reducing the frequency, and increasing the transparency (see Figure 10–43c). The clouds are duplicated and rearranged in part d and rearranged slightly in part e. Finally, a few terrains are placed to create a sweeping vista of land under the clouds, as shown in Figure 10–43f.

Here are some other tips for freestanding clouds:

• *Position of spheres in relation to each other.* If spheres overlap, the fuzzy soft edge effect will be destroyed by the rude reality shock of the sphere shape. (See encircled portion of Figure 10–43d.) Find the offending sphere and move, resize, or delete it. This problem is exacerbated when the camera is touching a sphere that is touching another sphere. You'll see half-sphere shapes and very crisp geometric edges.

• *Sky Ambient Color.* When freestanding clouds are in your scene, the cloud object's Ambient Color is very sensitive to the overall Ambient Color. Therefore watch that the Sky & Fog's Ambient Color setting is in the lighter ranger rather than the darker range.

• *Specular highlight coefficient.* If your clouds are bright, they'll have a high Specularity setting. Be careful that you do not have your Specular Coefficient set near 250 and above. If you do, you'll get a noticeable line where the high-light ends and the remainder of the object begins. See Figure 10–44a and b.

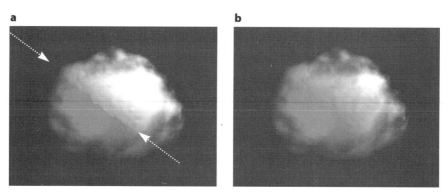

Figure 10–44 High specular coefficient contributes to a) Solid-appearing highlight indicated by arrows; b) reduced specular coefficient softens edge .

• The bright silver lining trick! You can do this with any of the clouds. Duplicate the clouds and offset them above and back from camera view. Change the duplicate to a separate family color. Then change from fuzzy to fuzzy additive. Where the edges of the clouds appear in view, you'll have a bright dazzling cloud. Figure C10–45, "Dazzling Light" uses this method to create the bright dazzling cloud edges. Note the side view perspective where there is a duplicate set of clouds, shown with darker wireframes (see Figure 10–46). They are the

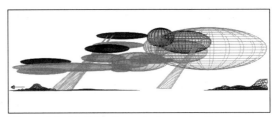

Figure 10–46 Side view wireframe for "Dazzling Light" scene.

same size and relative position as the first, but they are offset behind and above. They are set to fuzzy additive, so that the portions that show will be glowing.

All of these techniques work for creating clouds using the Easter Egg Sphere set object.

CHAPTER ELEVEN

Bryce EnLightenment

"What a very strange world yours must be!" the beast said, "that such a peculiar-seeming thing should be of such importance. Try to tell me, what is this thing called light *that you are able to do so little without?"*

"Well, we can't see without it," Meg said, realizing that she was completely unable to explain vision and light and dark. How can you explain sight on a world where no one has ever seen and where there is no need of eyes? "Well, on this planet," she fumbled, "you have a sun, don't you?"

"A most wonderful sun, from which comes our warmth, and the rays which give us our flowers, our food, our music, and all the things which make life and growth."

"Well," Meg said, "when we are turned toward the sun—our earth, our planet, I mean, toward our sun—we receive its light. And when we're turned away from it, it is night. And if we want to see we have to use artificial lights."

"Artificial lights," the beast sighed. "How very complicated life on your planet must be."

MADELEINE L'ENGLE, *A WRINKLE IN TIME*

IN THIS CHAPTER...

- Creating pseudo-light forms from glowing primitives

- Bryce's light primitives and how they work

- Practical tips for using light objects

- Different types of light objects and how they were created

- Sample lighting scenes

The addition of lights into Bryce 2 now provides the opportunity for you to be a lighting director. Dramatic lighting is what separates the ho-hum scenes from those eliciting an exclamation of "Wow! Incredible!"

There are pseudo-lights in Bryce, where special Shading modes give the appearance that self-illuminating glowing objects throw off light, even though they do not. And there are light sources that actually throw light elsewhere in the Bryce scene, as well as cast shadows. The chapter begins with a discussion of the glowing forms and then continues with discussion of the light objects and how to use them. The chapter concludes with several examples of lights as used in completed scenes.

GLOWING PSEUDO-LIGHT FORMS

The pseudo-light approach makes *any* Bryce primitive object glow. This is not the specialized light object, where light is projected and shadows cast. With a glowing object you can make suns and moons, light bulbs, tubes, and cones of light.

How do you make any Bryce primitive glow? The Materials Composer. There are three options that contribute to an object's glow: Shading mode, Ambience, and one or both of Ambient and Diffuse color. In Shading mode, you can select these options: Additive, Fuzzy Additive, or Light. Second, in the Materials Composer grid, hone in on Ambience and Transparency (the Ambience setting has no effect on the Light Shading mode). Third, select your color. When you've chosen the Additive Shading mode, the Ambient Color will determine the color of your object. When you've chosen the Light Shading modes, Diffuse Color will determine the color of your glowing object. Figure 11–1a and b shows the results of the three Shading modes for Mac and Windows. The top row has some transparency and the bottom row has no transparency. The left column is Additive. The edges are hard. The center column is Fuzzy Additive, with fuzzy edges. The right column is light. Although the edges are soft, you can see further to their edge. In the Windows version of Bryce, the Light Shading mode results in a different appearance. The object has a hard edge,

Figure 11–1 A torus made to glow using the three Shading modes—Additive, Fuzzy Additive and Light in a) Macintosh and b) Windows versions of Bryce.

is translucent, and appears to be a glowing, flat silhouette. Figure 11–1b shows the same objects.

Figure 11–2 shows a series of glowing objects made using the Fuzzy Additive mode. In all of them, the horizon intersects the object so that you can see the additive effect at work. As the ray passes through the object, it adds the value of the "glowing" object to the value of whatever lies behind it. Those values, when added together, become brighter, and the object glows as a result.

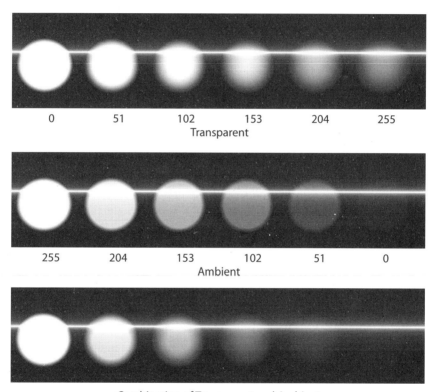

Transparent

Ambient

Combination of Transparent and Ambient

Figure 11–2 Different Ambience and Transparency settings for Fuzzy Additive glowing objects.

There are three sets of glowing objects. The top row shows different values for Transparency. Higher Transparency settings result in a fuzzier object. In the case of the spherical objects shown here, the Transparency setting causes the spheres to maintain their round shapes. The second row has different Ambient settings. As the Ambient setting is decreased, the object loses its glow. But the lesser glows appear flat. And a 0 setting is still barely visible! The bottom row adjusts both

Ambient and Transparency in proportion to one another. As the glow decreases with Ambient, fuzziness increases with Transparency to result in definite spherical shapes. The sphere on the right has now completely disappeared.

Since you can get different levels of glow, you can put one object inside another for a light-bulb-and-halo effect, that is, a light bulb in a frosted globe.

You can also use the Light Shading mode for some light-related effects. In the image of the slide projector shown later on in Figure 11–8, the dusty light beam from the projector uses a pyramid set to the Light Shading mode with the transparency information coming from a 3D texture.

LIGHT SOURCE PRIMITIVES

There are four types of light source primitives in Bryce. They are based on geometric primitives that already exist, but they project light. They are the radial light (sphere), the spotlight (cone), the square spotlight (pyramid), and the parallel light (square).

- *Radial light.* A sphere light bulb (or, more accurately, orb). It radiates light in every direction from the center of the radial light object. The light source can be made visible or invisible.

- *Spotlight.* A cone that projects a circle of light resembling the classic spotlight. This is a directional light; the needle emitted from the cone indicates the direction as well as distinguishes the light wireframe from the pyramid's wireframe for easier identification. The light source is the top of the cone. The spotlight can be made visible or invisible. The spotlight's edge can be adjusted so that it has a sharp edge, a very soft edge, or anywhere in between.

- *Square spotlight.* A pyramid that casts a square shaped light; the further away from the source, the larger the spread of the light. The light is projected from the flat square of the pyramid. This is good to use as a "slide projector" for projecting images or patterns onto other objects in the scene. In the Macintosh version, the square spotlight enters the Bryce world facing the ground. But though it is facing down, it is "pre-rotated;" it enters Bryce rotated 90° on the *x* axis (much like the torus enters Bryce pre-rotated). In the Windows version, the square spotlight also enters the scene facing down, but it is *not* pre-rotated; down is the basic position for the square spotlight. (If you are opening any Macintosh files in the Windows version, you may need to re-orient the square spotlight by 90° on the *x* axis to compensate for the differences in orientation.)

• *Parallel light.* A square that projects light without any spread. The final size of the area of light thrown matches the surface area of the light object, no matter how close or far the object is from the surface it's shining onto. So if your x and z size dimensions are 20.48 units apiece, it's impossible for the size of the light thrown from that parallel light object to be any bigger than 20.48 × 20.48. The source of the light is the square plane.

The Windows version of Bryce has an Easter Egg light object—a round parallel light! Press the Ctrl key while clicking the Create Parallel Light icon, and you'll get a round parallel light. Other than being round, it acts just like the square parallel light. (Hint: Think in terms of laser beams!)

EDIT LIGHT DIALOG BOX

All of the lights can be adjusted in the Edit Lights dialog box (⌘-E using Macs, Ctrl+E using Windows, clicking the Edit Terrain/Object icon on the Edit Palette, clicking the small E icon next to the selected object, or selecting Objects > Edit Object from the menu). When you have more than one light selected, even though you won't see the little E tile next to the wireframe, you can still access the dialog box by the key command or by clicking the Edit Terrain/Object icon on the Edit Palette. The Edit Lights dialog box contains all the controls for adjusting the lighting properties of every Brycean light type. (See Figure 11–3.)

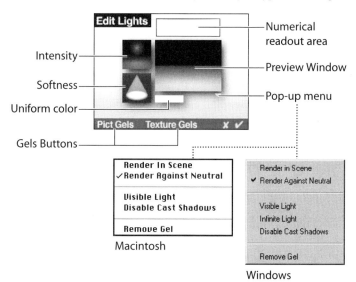

Figure 11–3 The Edit Lights dialog box, where lighting features are controlled.

a

b
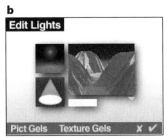

Figure 11–4 Two different types of previews: a) Neutral
Background; b) Render In Scene.

a
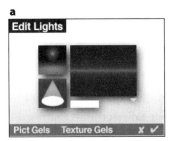
b
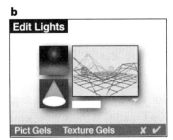

Figure 11–5 Render In Scene when Nano Preview on main
Control Palette is set to a) Sky Only mode; b) Wireframe mode.

Preview

The Edit Lights preview can be viewed in two forms, Render Against Neutral and
Render In Scene. Choose between the two in the pop-up menu. You can show
the illumination effect against a neutral background (default) or you can show the
light in the scene (see Figure 11–4). In order for the Render in Scene option to
work correctly on a Mac, you need to make sure that the Nano Preview on the
Control Palette is set to Full Scene. Otherwise, if it's set to Wireframe, you'll see
only a wireframe preview in the Edit Light dialog box, and likewise a setting for
Sky Only will show a sky in the Edit Light dialog box, as shown in Figure 11–5.
(The Windows version of Bryce does not tie the Edit Lights preview to the Nano
Preview state.) Depending on the complexity of your scene, the Render In Scene
option is a better preview. However, if you have a costly scene or so many objects
that you spend more time waiting for the preview to update than you do making
the changes to the light settings, Render Against Neutral is the better option.

> **TIP (WINDOWS):** *Preview while you work! When you're working directly in
> your scene and placing lights hither and yon, get immediate feedback on
> the light's placement. Make sure that the Auto Update option is activated in*

the Nano Preview pop-up menu. Then press the F10 key while dragging your light around, and watch the Nano Preview window update in real-time. Pretty snazzy, eh?

Intensity

How brightly does the light shine? Dragging in the Intensity control adjusts the amount of light. The numbers range from 0 to 100. In order to see the current setting in the Macintosh version, you have to move the mouse *ever-so-slightly* until a number shows, but not so much that the number changes. If you're doing a lot of production on lots of lights, you have my sympathies. In the Windows version of Bryce, you merely need to click in the Intensity control.

When it comes to measuring intensity, there are two different factors to consider. Of course, the first factor is the numerical setting for intensity. The second factor is the size of the light object—a given numerical setting will have a different brightness depending on the size. When any light is at the default unity size, the lower numbers are adequate for adjusting the light strength. Beyond a certain point, the light just doesn't get any brighter. But when the size of the light is doubled, tripled, quadrupled, or and-them-some-pled, the higher numbers become useful.

In Figure 11–6, a series of images shows how a range of light intensity settings affect lights of different sizes. All the images are top view renders of each of the Brycean light forms. In all these images, each light is twice the size of the one in front/below it, and the intensity setting is identical for all lights in that image. The intensity amount is indicated for each image. Notice how the larger lights are still dim when the smallest ones are at a maximum brightness.

Also, intensity has different results with different light forms. In the case of the square spotlight, when the light is still dim, the light has a round hot spot in the center while the square edges are slightly less intense.

In the case of the parallel light, intensity has two effects, from dark to light, and then, once there is light, intensity measures the size of the light. Note how a setting of 10 has the "spotlight" at the same size for all the parallel light objects (except for the three smallest lights whose size is smaller than the fixed size of the parallel "spotlight"). As the intensity increases, the spotlight becomes larger until it fills up the largest of the parallel lights.

What are the implications of all of these size and intensity studies? If you enlarge the lights you may be able to get a more subtle range of illumination intensities.

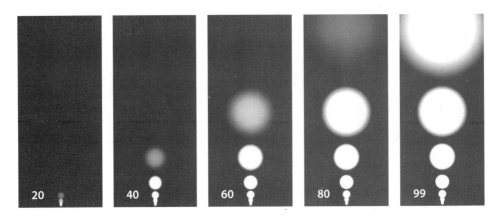

Spotlight

Parallel Light

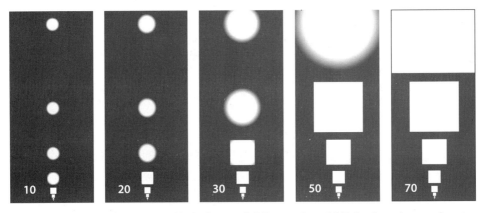

Figure 11–6 Top view renders of light forms of different sizes. All lights in an image share the same intensity setting.

If you find that your current light settings have too many jumps from one level of light to the next, then enlarge the light.

> **TIP:** *To enlarge everything in your scene, select all and group. Then enlarge using the Resize tool. All your objects will retain the same relationship, though they all will be bigger. You'll have to readjust the camera's position. You can anticipate this by creating a small cube and aligning it exactly with the camera before you group and enlarge the entire scene. Afterwards, align the camera to the new box position; it will precisely match the old one. Delete the box when you're through.*

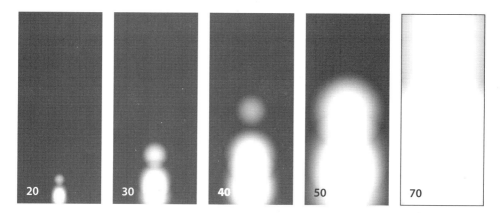

RadialLight

Square Spotlight

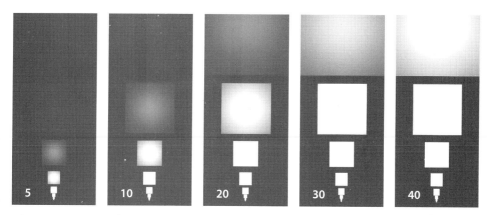

Figure 11–6 *continued*

Softness

The softness control determines how sharp or smooth the transition is from "all light" to "no light" at the edges of the light. Although the Bryce 2 *Explorer's Guide* states that this control is only for the spotlight, it also has an effect on the spotlight for the parallel light, when the size of the light is big enough. In Figure 11–7a and b there are some different softness settings for the spotlight and the parallel light.

The front row has the same settings, ranging from 0 on the left (completely hard) to 100 on the right (softest). The lone light in the second row is the default setting for that light. The Softness setting works with the parallel light as well. (It has no effect on the square spotlight or the radial light.)

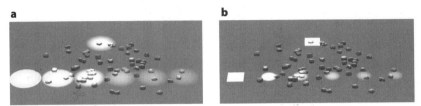

Figure 11–7 Softness settings for a) Spotlight and b) parallel light.

Uniform Color

What color is the light that you're projecting? The color swatch enables you to select the color. Like all other color swatches in Bryce, this one accesses the pop-up color picker, and accesses the Color Editor (with numerical values) when you press the Option (Macintosh) or Alt (Windows) key as you click the color swatch.

Setting the uniform color of the light is similar to setting the Sun color in the Sky & Fog Palette. The color is the color of diffuse light that emanates from that light source, and, if the light object is visible, it is also the color of the light itself.

Select Gel

If you do not want to have a uniform color but rather a variety of colors or a stencil effect, then use one of the gels. In real world lighting, a gel is a piece of film (the earliest ones were made of gelatin, hence the name "gel") placed in front of the light to give a light color. When you want a uniform color, use the Uniform Color picker. When you want multi-colored light, Bryce allows you to select from its two types of gels, Pict Gels and Texture Gels. When you select either of those, you'll go to libraries to select a texture from the appropriate type. Pict Gel takes you to the 2D Picture Library and Texture Gel takes you to the Materials Preset Library. The two gel types—3D Textures and 2D Pictures—are components of the Materials Composer. Even though this discussion revolves around the Edit Lights dialog box, when you work with gels you will possibly need to go outside that dialog box to the Material Composer. To complete the discussion of gels, I will definitely take you to the Materials Composer.

Pict Gel

A Pict Gel is any picture image that is loaded into the Bryce Picture Library. Here is the source for "slides" to project slide images. Load any pict image into the library and so into the light. The light will project in the pattern of the image. The square spotlight is a good one for the slide projector type image. A very literal application is shown in Figure C11–8 (see the color section). When your good friend's old college buddy gets you onto the White House lawn for 4th of July fireworks, you simply *must* take a picture to remember the moment, and be obligated to show it off at every opportunity. Bryce's slide projection ability gives you yet another means to bore your friends with your vacation snapshots. There are, incidentally, more lights in this scene besides the one square spotlight projecting the slide show image. For the terminally curious, the scene file for an earlier version of this image (the final scene file is too large) is on the CD-ROM in this chapter's folder, along with that entire boring slide show (in the Portfolio folder). Although square spotlights take to the Pict Gel the best, any light type can be used.

> **TIP:** When creating square spotlights that are true image slide projectors, it's best to make the square spotlight the exact aspect ratio of the image (Otherwise, the picture will be squashed to fit the square shape of the spotlight). To do so, try this handy trick: Make sure that you have your picture image all ready as a picture file, saved on disk. Then create a picture object. The first thing that happens is that you go to the Picture Library and select the picture. When you complete that step, Bryce creates a picture object that exactly matches the aspect ratio of the picture. Now all you have to do is change the picture object to a square spotlight using the Object Conversion tool on the Edit Palette. You'll have to readjust the rotation of the object, but your image will not be squashed or stretched.

The color of the projected light is determined by the Diffuse color. (It makes logical sense, since the type of light that is projected from all light objects is primarily diffuse light.) After assigning a Pict Gel, if you go to the Materials Composer, you may notice that Bryce has assigned the default picture configuration in the Material Composer for the light object. Parametric is the mapping style, the texture's Transparency will be driven by the picture's alpha channel, and the picture texture drives the color for both Diffuse and Ambient channels. Even though it seems as though there is alpha channel information affecting the Light Gel, and ambient color as well, the only thing that determines the color of light is the Diffuse Color. If the Diffuse Color is black, no light will be projected.

The options in the Materials Composer that you *can* adjust are texture frequency, mapping, and Diffuse Color. (Incidentally, these options are the same for Texture Gels, which I'll discuss in the next section.) Figure C11–9 in the color section shows some light variations using the same picture source with different mapping and frequency options.

Well, if there is alpha channel information that's available, what could it possibly be used for? The alpha/transparency information becomes meaningful when the light itself is visible. (See the discussion on visible light a bit later on.) In normal (non-gel) lights, the entire light is visible. When the alpha channel drives the texture, then you see the portions of the light that the alpha channel allows you to. You can mix and match the Diffuse Color so that the light object looks like the light it projects, or it has alpha channel holes cut into it while projecting. Figure C11–10a and b shows two variations on visible light of the Picture Gel variety. Part a shows the basic visible light. Part b shows what happens when you have a solid Diffuse Color with no Picture Gel driving the light but a picture that drives the appearance of the visible light. The Material Composer settings for each version are shown as well.

Texture Gel

The Texture Gel is similar to the Picture Gel, only it uses the information from a 3D Solid texture in Bryce to create the gel's color. Again, the diffusion color is all-important for determining the color emitted from the object. In order for the 3D Solid texture to work with a light, there needs to be enough color information in the texture itself to drive Diffuse Color. In other words, if you go to the Material Preset library and choose a solid color or a reflective optic effect, the net result from a light gel standpoint is nil. The texture takes its information from the 3D Solid texture's color information only.

Like the Picture Gel, you can make some adjustments in the Materials Composer to the Texture Gel for effects. You can adjust the frequency and mapping. And if you have a visible light, the Transparency information will affect the appearance of the light.

What about more complex multi-channel textures? If your mind works in wicked "what if" ways, then the thought has (or will) occur to you. Alas, creating a multi-source Texture Gel is impossible for lights. Source A is all you get. If you try for more, you'll be knocked back into uniform color land. Therefore the multi-source textures that seemingly are available for the choosing in the Material Preset

Library will be null and void. (In the Materials Composer, you can switch the markers so that only the A texture applies and you'll get a colorful result.)

Pop-up Menu Items

The Edit Light dialog box has a pop-up menu for certain selections. Choose the preview mode, the shadow and visibility, and clear your gels using this menu.

Clear Gels

Although it is not the first one listed on the pop-up menu, I mention it first since this discussion of the pop-up menu immediately follows the discussion of the gels. If you have 'em there, this one will get rid of 'em and get you on the straight and narrow again. (In the Materials Composer, you can do the same thing by clicking back into the default column for Diffuse Color.)

Render Window preview

This is the spot where you choose which of the two previews you will see in the Preview Window.

Disable Cast Shadows

The Disable Cast Shadows switch will disable the light from casting a shadow.

Brycean lights differ from real world lights because you can control whether or not they cast shadows. Since the Bryce world is visualized by means of ray tracing, the creation of shadows is a separate additional routine. Therefore you can decide whether or not you want the renderer to go through that routine in order to have shadows from lights. (If you want to explore all of Bryce's shadow side, check out the following chapters, Chapter 9, "Material World," Chapter 10, "Brycean Skies," and Chapter 12, "Render Unto Bryce.") Figure C11–11 shows a scene where the lights cast shadows and the same scene where those lights do not. When you do not cast shadows, other objects in the scene do not block light. This can have a wide variety of effects, from subtle (the additional light sources do not betray their presence with a shadow) to eerie (where is the light coming from?) to the bizarre.

The ability to disable shadows opens up a whole realm of possibility for lighting and coloring effects. Figure C11–12a through e shows a series of images I call "Boolean Potato Skins." This series explores a whole range of light possibilities. It starts with no special light source (part a), and adds a white radial light in the center that casts shadows (part b), and does not cast shadows (part c). Then visible yellow lights are placed in the bowls of each of the half-sphere objects, both casting shadows (part d) and not casting shadows (part e) to result in an ethereal glow.

Visible Light

Some lights have visible light sources. Not only will the object cast light, but you can see the light source itself when Visible Light is checked. The radial light, the spotlight and the parallel light all can be

Figure 11–13 Visible lights.

made visible. The Macintosh version of the square spotlight cannot, and the Windows version can. Figure 11–13 shows a sample of each kind of visible light.

In order to make a parallel light visible on a Mac, you need to assign a gel and have something in the alpha channel. The combination of the alpha channel information and diffuse information determines what is visible. In Figure 11–14, there are three different combinations. The squiggle object has white

Figure 11–14 Parallel lights that are visible with gels and alpha channels.

on black in the diffuse (color) channel and a completely opaque (black) alpha channel. The center solid square is a solid white color and solid black alpha channel opaque. The word poetry, right, has white on black color and an alpha channel that's reversed so that the alpha channel is black (opaque) where the words are.

Light visibility is separate from light intensity. In fact, a light can be set to 0 intensity and still be a visible object. Figure 11–15 shows a sample of each of the three visible light sources with intensity settings at 0. What determines the visibility of the light, then? Size is one thing, especially with the spotlight. In Figure 11–16, there are three rows of spotlights (again, they are set to 0 intensity). In the front row, each spotlight is wider than the one to its left. In the second row, each spotlight is taller than the one to its left. In the back row, each light is larger than the one to its left, though proportions are maintained. The Macintosh version of Bryce establishes visibility by calculating how much distance the ray has to travel to get to the other side of the object. The longer it travels, the more opaque or dense the object seems. This explains the size differentiation. It also explains why you can hardly ever see the peaks of cones and pyramids—the ray has barely entered the object's peak before it exits again.

The other thing that determines the strength of the visible light is the Transparency setting in the Materials Composer. In Figure 11–17 the lights at the same size (the maximum size from Figure 11–16) have different transparency settings. The one on the left is 0 (most opaque). Each one to the right adds 50, and the last one is 200. (These lights were created using the Macintosh version of Bryce.)

This "visibility" factor of the light can be assigned to any object in Bryce. As mentioned in the first part of this chapter, the Light Shading mode can be applied to any object in Bryce. Figure 11–18 shows some very unlight-object type objects that appear to be visible lights. They are objects assigned to the Light Shading mode. The only settings that affect them are—surprise!—Diffuse Color and Transparency.

Figure 11–15 Visible light sources with intensity set to 0.

Figure 11–16 Size and Visibility with the spotlight. Front row: Enlarging spotlight width; Middle row: enlarging spotlight height; Back row: enlarging spotlight proportionately.

Figure 11–17 The same size visible spotlight at different ransparency settings.

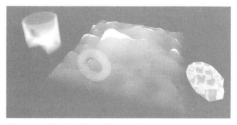

Figure 11–18 Non-light objects parading as visible lights courtesy of the Light Shading mode.

Infinite Light (Windows)

The Windows version of Bryce has an additional menu option—Infinite Light. It augments the Visible Light option for the lights which cast beams of some sort (all but the radial light). The visible portion continues on forever. Figure 11–19 shows each kind of light both as an infinite light and as a merely visible light. The wireframe dimensions are identical for each version. Use the Infinite Light option

Figure 11–19 Infinite lights side-by-side with visible lights—infinite lights keep going beyond the bounds of the wireframe (Windows).

with the secret round parallel light to create laser beams. (This figure also illustrates the difference in the rendering method for the Windows Light Shading mode; the object's edges aren't as soft as those using the Mac version.)

OTHER LIGHT PROPERTIES

Now that you've been introduced to the basics of the light objects and the means of manipulating them in the Edit Light dialog box, I'll discuss light in the real world, light in the Brycean world, and a few practicalities in terms of scene complexity and render time.

Inverse Brightness–Distance

Each light type has its unique attributes. The round spotlight acts like real-world light in that there's an inverse relationship between the brightness of the light on the object or surface, and the amount of space projected. The further away the light is from the object, the dimmer the light is as it falls on the ground. At the same time, the area that's illuminated increases in size as the light is moved away. Figure 11–20 shows a sample scene with different light positions, where the relationship between illuminated area and light strength is seen. The further away the light is, the larger the area and the dimmer the illumination. The closer the light is, the smaller the area and the brighter the illumination.

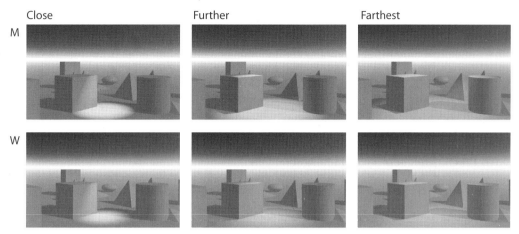

Figure 11–20 The relationship between distance, brightness, and the illuminated area with the round spotlight. Top row: Macintosh; Bottom row: Windows.

The other Macintosh light object types do not obey this inverse law the way the round spotlight does. However, the Windows objects do. See the comparisons in Figure 11–21 where the radial light (in Rows 1 and 2) and the square spotlight (in Rows 3 and 4) shine in the same scene as Figure 11–20. The positions are the same for each light: close, further, and farthest. Note that for the Macintosh version (identified with an "M" at the left of the row) the area of illumination changes with the square spotlight and the radial light, but the resulting illumination does not decrease. The Windows versions (identified with a "W") do change in brightness as the distance increases. The parallel light is not shown here since it does not change in size with distance. The Windows parallel light does grow dimmer with distance, though. (You might also notice slight differences in the size and softness settings for the lights from Mac to Windows versions. Adjust to taste.)

Caustic Attitude

There are a couple of real-world light conditions that are not captured in the ray-trace process. They both concern secondary illumination effects as light passes through objects or bounces off other objects. The first one, highlights from water, is the effect where the bends in the water's surface act as a lens to focus light. When that light passes through water to a solid surface below, there are wavy lines that shine on the solid surface. In the same way, reflections off the water's surface onto other areas also reflect those wavy lines. The wavy line refractions and

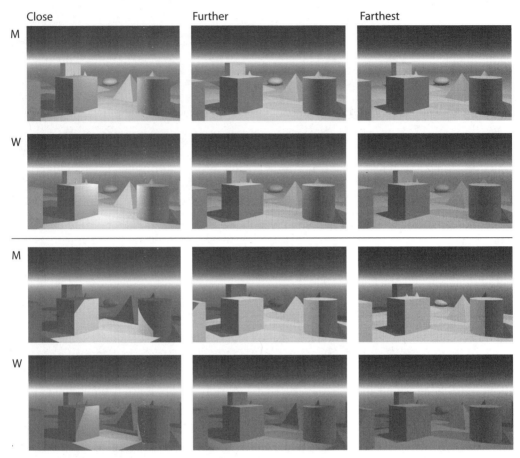

Figure 11–21 Comparison of other light objects that do not obey the inverse distance-brightness-area rule in the Macintosh version and do obey the rule in the Windows version. Row 1: Radial light, Macintosh; Row 2: radial light, Windows; Row 3: square spotlight, Macintosh; Row 4: square spotlight, Windows.

reflections are called caustics. Though caustics exist in the real world, they are not created by ray-tracing.

The second type of light condition is the reflection of light from an object. If light bounces off a brightly-colored object onto another object—especially one that's a light color—a bit of the bright color will be reflected onto the object. The rendering method that treats every object as a potential light source is called radiosity. With all the added rendering calculations, it is an extremely time-consuming method. (Radiosity is not used in Bryce.) The light bouncing off brightly lit objects is the subtle version. The more obvious version uses a reflective object, say, a mirror. If a light is shining toward a mirror, when you look into the mirror, not only do you see the light, but the light shines into your eyes. (A car rear-view mirror is a real-world example. The little switch that adjusts the tilt so that the glass is not as reflective as the mirror is an eye-saving invention that compensates for this light reflecting tendency.) But if you set up a rear-view mirror in Bryce, it will not work that way.

For any of these kinds of phenomena to appear in your scene, you'll have to find a way to create them.

In Figure 11–22a, my version of a caustic light is shown. There are two ways to generate the light; you can do so by using a picture, or you can do so using Bryce's texture generator. I prefer the latter, though I continue to search for that "just right" caustic wave pattern. (The cover image as well as the temple image in Figure C11–36 both use a caustic texture for water.) Depending on the situation, the type of light you select to illuminate the caustic will vary. If the light is shining down onto the surface below, such as a swimming pool, fountain or other shallow water, then use a parallel light. In the case of the rocks lit by the caustics reflecting off of water, I use a spotlight. Experiment for the best results. Look on the CD-ROM in the folder for this chapter to find a scene file that has several lights with different caustic textures.

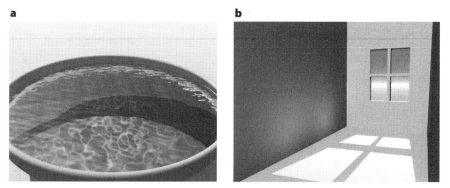

a **b**

Figure 11–22 Emulating real-world lighting conditions using Bryce lighting tricks: a) A parallel light with caustic texture throws fake caustics on the bottom of this pool of water; b) round spotlights cause the illusion of light "bouncing" off a brightly lit area and reflecting on a nearby wall.

To get a radiosity type of reflection from a light or brightly colored object, use a very weak radial light or spotlight. The spotlight can project on the surroundings, and since it has a narrow beam, it won't shed additional light on the object that's reflecting onto other objects. Figure 11–22b uses two round spotlights to create the illusion of light bouncing off the brightly lit floor onto the wall. For best results, give the light the color of the object that's "reflecting." Creating the bouncing light reflection is a painstaking extra step, but if you're going for drop-dead realism, the difference will be convincing and you'll no doubt be extremely satisfied with the results.

Increased Render Time

As with every other part of Bryce, there's a constant obsession with rendering time. Is this costly? Is it efficient? Lighting is no different. Each light source in the scene increases your render time. Why? Unlike the real world, where the addition of lights does not add to the time required to perceive objects in your environment, the addition of light increases the number of calculations required to render the scene. Each time a ray intersects an object, it then bounces toward the light source to determine its effect on the object and hence the object's color. Bryce always does this type of calculation for the primary light source, the sun (or moon). When there are multiple light sources, there are multiple calculations. When the renderer finds an object in the scene, it asks "What influence does the radial light have on this object?" If there are several additional lights, it asks the question for each one. Figure 11–23 shows a scene with some reflective primitives in it, and the render time and calculations for each successive light that's added to the scene. For this sample, where the longest render time is just under 6 minutes (on a Power Macintosh 8100/100; your mileage may vary), the times don't seem all that lengthy. But consider that the addition of each light adds nearly a minute of rendering time to a scene that took around two minutes to start with. That's half again as much time per light. When you have a whole host of them (see the Light Array section later in this chapter), the scene becomes very expensive. The real world analogy that fits, it seems, is electricity. When you have a whole wad of lights, *someone* has to foot the electric bill.

Of course, there will be times where you need each and every light source to create just that perfect look for your well-lit Brycean masterpiece. That's what they're there for! But if you've added a bunch of lights willy-nilly and wonder why your render has slowed to a crawl, consider the impeding effect of the addition of all those light sources.

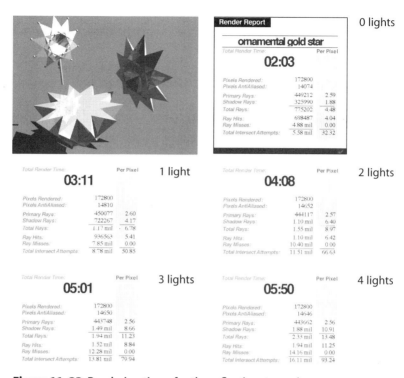

Figure 11–23 Rendering times for the reflective star series.

Lights and Solo Mode

When you go to Solo mode, you will see the influence of lights, even when the lights aren't there. If you have set your light objects to be visible (spotlight, radial light and parallel light), the light object must be in Solo mode in order for the visible part to render.

Lights are hybrid objects. They can be created, selected, and edited like objects, but once they're in the scene, the renderer treats them like skies and environment; their influence is global.

USING BRYCE LIGHTS: DIFFERENT TYPES OF LIGHTING CONDITIONS

This next section takes up the question, "But what do I use lights *for* in Bryce?"

There are all the technical considerations for lighting, most of which I've discussed so far, and then there is the aesthetic decision-making process. Betty Edwards, in her book *Drawing on the Right Side of the Brain*, makes the case that learning to draw is not so much developing eye-hand coordination, rather, it is a matter of learning how to see. Using Bryce is an extension of this process, and indeed, if you have found yourself more aware of the environment and atmosphere and lighting conditions outdoors, Bryce has been guiding you to look at the world a little differently.

If you've had studio photography experience where you need to light objects, you're at an advantage. If you haven't, there is a body of reference material about lighting from experts in that profession. John Alton's *Painting with Light* is a discussion of lighting for cinematography and is considered a canonical reference on light in motion picture. Though not all of it applies to Bryce, the discussion of the different lights and their uses in combination with each other will increase your awareness of ways to set up lights for your scenes.

In a different vein, Burne Hogarth's *Dynamic Light and Shade* discusses light and shade in drawing. Though nearly all of his examples are hand drawn—and what beautiful images!—his discussion of different lighting considerations throughout the book will help you to analyze the world around you. In short, this book will help you learn how to *see* light. There are plenty of landscape samples—all in grayscale, so you can see how much is conveyed in a reduced palette. Besides landscapes, Hogarth's book is filled with drawings of the human figure and other objects and environs.

These are not the only reference works available, but those are two from some of the best in their fields, and one emphasizes technical aspects of lighting while the other concentrates on making aesthetic judgments about light.

What Light Does Aesthetically

What else does light do in a scene? If you've gone through all the Plain Vanilla! series of Sky & Fog variations in the previous chapter, you know how much light and atmosphere affect the appearance and overall tone of a scene. Lighting is a continuation of the atmosphere process. Here are some of its important functions.

- *Lighting helps to define the full dimensions of form.* This is a three-dimensional world, rendered in a two-dimensional image. Lighting helps to establish a sense of depth. Light and shadow push objects out toward you and pull them away into the distance. Notice in Figure 11–24 how the flat overhead gray light makes the objects dull and flat. In the other examples with additional lighting, a sense of depth is added to the scenes.

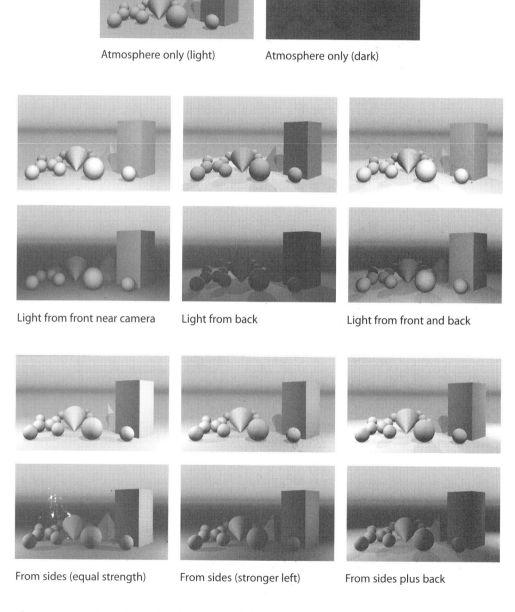

Atmosphere only (light)   Atmosphere only (dark)

Light from front near camera   Light from back   Light from front and back

From sides (equal strength)   From sides (stronger left)   From sides plus back

Figure 11–24 Three-dimensional forms and lights.

- *Lighting establishes mood.* Is the scene hot or cool? Is it happy or sad? Is it bright or drab? Is it commonplace or mysterious? Lighting helps establish the feel of a scene. Look at the scenes in Figure 11–24 again. Notice the difference between the lighter and darker versions. Do you get a different feeling from them? A different emotional tone? How about the difference between left and right lighting and front and back? The backlight adds drama and intrigue.

  This Wine Cellar scene by Gary Bernard (see Figure C11–25 in the color section) uses lights to help establish the environment and create a mood. The warm yellow lights —are they actual flame torches or lights made to resemble torches?—bespeak an indoor environment, and together with the rest of the scene, invitingly beckon the viewer to share a glass of the finest.

- *Lighting defines textures.* In the samples from Figure 11–24, the objects are primarily smooth. But when there is a tactile sense of the object, light is the means of conveying it to your eyes, which in turn tell your fingers what it would feel like to touch the object. Figure 11–26 shows a version of the scene using surface textures on all the objects.

Figure 11–26 Lighting shows the texture of an object.

- *Lighting emphasizes a focal point, or points of interest.* In Figure 11–27 the pyramid—which was the most lost in the other images—is shown highlighted. Once the single bright light is on it, your eye goes to it first. The emphasis on one object poses a question—why is the pyramid singled out for special notice? Lighting, then, can be used to help tell a story.

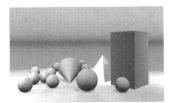 

Figure 11–27 Lighting serves to focus your attention on a particular part of the scene.

Ways to Use Lights

The previous section discussed ways to use light for the purpose of enhancing your composition and telling a story. This section discusses ways to use light in a more logical "what kind of light do you want" sense. This is a counterpart to the cinematographic guide for which light does what and under what circumstances do you use each. Although it's entirely probable that your fertile imagination will find uses beyond those mentioned here, I'll get you started with a basic list of uses.

- *The artificial light.* This is probably the most common form of light you'll create in your scene. It is the light form that is not the sun. Besides the primary light source, there is the additional light source, whether it's electric or flame or some other source. This is also the type of lighting you have in indoor environments, such as the Wine Cellar image. In the scene "Triad: Live at the Hammersmith Odeon" by Robert Mann, spotlights create the feeling of a live amphitheater (see Figure C11–28 in the color section). The variations on artificial lights are legion, from flame to lamp to incandescent light to spotlight. Go for it!

- *The augmenting light.* Augmenting light is a subtle addition to what is already present in the scene. Add to the light source that is already there, or use lights to make up for what is lacking in the ray-tracing procedure. In the moonscape over the water, a radial light adds strength to the light reflection on the water. The scene by Eric Wenger, on the Bryce software CD-ROM, has a radial light placed between the camera and the moon. It adds some subtle lighting to the shores as well as to the watery surface. In Figure C11–29, note the superimposed wireframe for the radial light, and compare the finished render with a version of the scene rendered without the light. Though the highlight still is there on the water, the subtle added moonlight created by the radial light is missing.

The earlier discussion of caustic lights and subtle reflection lights fall into this augment category.

- *Studio lighting.* For your still life Bryce image. Fill in shadows or add drama with additional lighting. Here is where you set up a scene with the keylight, or principal light (usually your sun, though not always), a fill light to fill in harsh shadows and a back light or kicker light to shine on the object from behind for added drama, or shine onto the background area to illuminate it adequately and separate it from the foreground object. Figure C11–30 shows a Brycean studio complete with studio lighting.

- *Stealth lighting.* Any lighting for added effect that does not have shadows. The advantage here is that you can carefully light a scene and highlight certain portions with lights without giving away the light source by shadows. In artificial environments multiple light sources might be perfectly acceptable. In nature scenes, the presence of artificial lights is, well, artificial. In "Cappuccino on the Rocks," two radial lights illuminate a cappuccino machine nestled in a rocky enclosure. The light to the right is the main one (shown as the only one in Figure C11–31a), and a second, weaker light, which serves to fill in the shadow is on the left (see Figure C11–31b). When the secondary light casts a shadow, there are a few places (note the top of cappuccino machine, the area behind the carafe, and the right part of the rock wall "behind" the unit) where the presence of a second shadow contradicts the impression that all light comes from the above right, cast by the primary light (see Figure C11–31c). For reference, there's an image (Figure C11–31d) where light comes only from the left.

Tips for setting up lights

If you are mixing different lights and want to see which one is doing what, try giving each a different light color. That way you can judge which one is lighting up what space. In a variation of the "Cappuccino on the Rocks" scene in Figure C11–32, here's a view of the forward light tried as a spotlight. The light is red. It's easy to tell where the light is falling and if it's aimed correctly.

The time to place lights in your scene varies. If your wild inspiration springs fresh from the Muse with an integral lighting plan, or the light is the main part of the scene, you may set up your lights early on in your scene-making process. On the other hand, lighting may be one of the final steps after completing many other steps to your scene construction. At either stage, you'll encounter the clashing of two expensive processes—rendering multiple light sources and rendering those beautiful material surfaces. When you're placing your lights, use the Textures On/Off switch on the Render controls (it's the one on the left) to turn your textures off. Lights will show up when the Texture Off render mode is active. Figure C11–33 compares a scene with several spotlights when Textures are turned on and off. Though the ground texture and presence of haze changes, the presence of the spotlights does not change. And the Textures Off can be significantly faster. Of course, the beauty of the final process is seeing how the presence of additional lights enhances the look of those beautiful expensive textures. But that's what sleep is for.

Gel Cookies

When designing your lights, make sure to consider Gel cookies. What is this, some new weird combination between chocolate chips and jello? (Eeeew.) No. Since the color of a Gel—specifically black—determines if light will shine on that spot or not, you can design color patterns to create a cookie. Cookie is the time-honored term used by cinematographers for an opaque stencil that blocks light in some shape and cast shadows onto a surface. Use a specific picture (or texture) to make certain types of shadows. Make a foliage shadow (see Figure C11–34 in the color section), or smoky eerie lighting effects. When it comes to shadow casting, Bryce creates hard-edged shadows. If you try to use actual objects to block the light, you won't get soft shadows. Look again at the foliage cookie image. The shadows are soft because you can create a nice fat blurry pattern by painting in Photoshop.

Another use for Pict Gel cookies is a bit of judicious touch-up for the lighting to shape the pool of light just so. In the highlighted pyramid back in Figure 11–27, a Gel cookie would have handily cut away the light that spilled beyond the pyramid itself. This type of situation calls for back and forth work in Photoshop and Bryce (or try it in the Terrain Editor with a "throw-away" terrain, and copy and paste), and a lot of top view renders, assuming that the light is being cast from above.

Light Arrays

In Bryce all shadows are hard-edged. If you want a soft-edge shadow you'll have to go to additional lengths to get it. One way is by using an array of lights. Figure 11–35 shows a series of images by Robert Mann that compares a light array to a single light source. Mann adapted a technique described in *3-D Artist* magazine (Issue #25, "Shadow of Doubt: Mechanics of Realism" by Timothy Wilson). A spiral light array (rendered as spheres for the purpose of illustration in Figure 11–35e) casts light onto the scene. There are two versions of objects, those with smooth edges and those with bumped edges. The array technique is more convincing with the bump, since the shadow pattern is obscured. With the number of additional lights in the scene, render time is tortuously prolonged.

EXAMPLE SCENES

This last section examines a few scenes containing lights. It analyzes different techniques, goals, and effects for lighting.

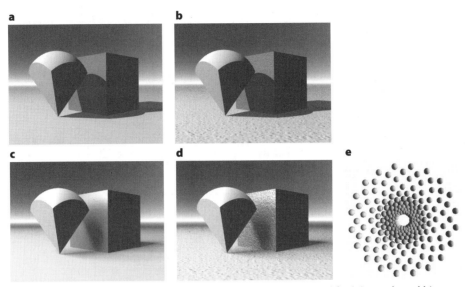

Figure 11–35 Light array for soft shadow: Single light source with a) Smooth and b) bumped surfaces. c) Light array with smooth surfaces and d) bumped surfaces; e) Light array pattern rendered as spheres.

Flames using Light and Pseudo-light

These two scenes, "Tiki Torches in Cave" and "Water Temple at Night" (see Figure C11–36) both employ the same type of flame and light effect. In addition, the "Water Temple at Night" has two other types of light sources. For each of the torches in both scenes, there are actually two spherical objects used to create the light effect. The flame itself is not a light source. The flame is a sphere with a fire texture on it and the Shading mode is additive. This is the Bryce pseudo-light technique. The actual light illuminating the scene comes from the radial light that occupies the same space. In the "Tiki Torches" scene, the lights are larger and visible. The visible part acts as the glow very close to the light "source," the flame. The glow is not as apparent in the "Water Temple at Night" scene. The light with pseudo-light is a tricky hack: The flame is not the light source, the glow is the light source while acting as the glow from the flame pseudo-"light source."

Besides the flame lights in in the "Water Temple at Night" scene, there are spotlights to highlight the objects in the temple's center and the pillar area. In addition, a parallel light projects the water caustics onto the marble floor.

Smoky Spotlight

To create a smoky spotlight, two different cone objects are used. (See Figure 11–37a.) One is a spotlight. It is large and visible. The texture that is applied to it is a variation on the preset for light streaks in the Bryce preset Library. (The texture has a higher frequency, and stays more in the gray midtones.) Although this is a texture that is applied to the Transparency setting of the visible light, the Diffuse Color has no texture driving it, and the uniform color is, well, whatever color the spotlight should be. See Figure 11–37b for the spotlight alone.

The second object is a normal cone. (Convenience tip: Duplicate and convert the light to a cone. Simple!) It has a modification of a cloud texture applied to it, and the Shading mode is Fuzzy Additive. The smoke alone is shown in Figure 11–37c. When put together, the result is a spotlight shining into a smoky area, whether a nightclub, ceremonial incense, or geothermal pool.

Figure 11–37 Smoky spotlight: a) The combined smoke and spotlight; b) the spotlight alone; c) the smoke alone.

Chambered Mace

In this scene by Robert Mann (see Figure C11–38a in the color section), an object—a mace—is placed in an environment and all are lit for maximum effect. The lantern is comprised of four spherical shapes of varying function. The innermost one is a radial light. Outside of that is an imported spherical polyhedron object that is a transparent and refracting globe. Outside of that is the cage, with a picture texture for transparency and a 3D texture for the color. Finally, outside of that is a sphere that is set to the Light Shading mode, to supply some extra "glow" around the light. There are additional radial lights to illuminate the room, and two spotlights, one on the mace against the left wall, and another focused on the shelf with ring decorative motif at the back. Figure C11–38b is a detail view of the lantern globe assembly set against a plain sky background.

The Castle Hall Scene

This extremely complex scene by Glenn Riegel, created for the Sanctuary Web-game project, uses lighting superbly. (See Figure C11–39.) The light sources are radial lights, and there are *many* of them in the scene. In some places two are doubled up at the same location to create extremely bright light. Notice how lighting establishes focal points and dimension in this hall. Although the camera is placed in the middle of the room, you don't really notice the ground you're standing on, since it's dark. The points of emphasis are elsewhere. Stairs lead up to a second level. A banner hangs from the wall in the center back. Lights located upstairs and downstairs against the wall not only define the building's dimensions, but they suggest places that you could walk to. There is light off to the right side. Don't you want to just turn to the right and see what's there? Lighting in this scene does three things. It establishes the full dimension of the place, establishes mood with warm flame lamps with yellowish glows, and suggests possibilities for further game play. The main focal points are the stairs, the flag, an undefined area to the right and places along the perimeter of the scene. Look at the scene again and notice how your eye moves from one to another area in the scene. When designing your own images, use light to establish priorities for the viewer and tell your story.

Make sure that you look through the gallery images on the CD-ROM to see what other light inventions have been created by other Brycers. ("The Castle View" image is there for the viewing in stereoscope 3-D glory!) Admire and analyze what the artists have done with light and let them be a guide to help you create your own beautifully lit environments.

CHAPTER TWELVE

Render Unto Bryce

"That was a very beautiful sunset," said Milo, walking to the podium.

"It should be," was the reply; "we've been practicing since the world began." And, reaching down, the speaker picked Milo off the ground and set him on the music stand. "I am Chroma the Great," he continued, gesturing broadly with his hands, "conductor of color, maestro of pigment, and director of the entire spectrum."

"Do you play all day long?" asked Milo when he had introduced himself.

"Ah yes, all day, every day. . . . I rest only at night, and even then they play on."

"What would happen if you stopped?" asked Milo, who didn't quite believe that color happened that way.

"See for yourself," roared Chroma, and he raised both hands high over his head. Immediately the instruments that were playing stopped, and at once all color vanished. The world looked like an enormous coloring book that had never been used. Everything appeared in simple black outlines, and it looked as if someone with a set of paints the size of a house and a brush as wide could stay happily occupied for years. Then Chroma lowered his arms. The instruments began again and the color returned.

NORTON JUSTER, *THE PHANTOM TOLLBOOTH*

IN THIS CHAPTER...

- How ray tracing works

- Grouped objects and rendering

- Tips and tricks for rendering while you are working on your scene and when you're done

- The Render Report

- Batch rendering

- Large format rendering

- 360° rendering

- Distance rendering

- Mask rendering

- Semi anti-aliasing tricks

Everything I've talked about in earlier chapters—objects, terrains, materials, and sky and fog—culminates in rendering, which is the creation of a two-dimensional PICT or BMP image of the scene. The main concern with the scene creation process is to make a great image. Very closely tied to making a good scene is making an efficient scene. This chapter begins with a deeper description of the mysteries of ray tracing, complete with some time-saver tips so that you can make your scenes render more quickly. Then it continues with discussions of rendering during the working process and rendering when the scene is complete. From there, the chapter treats batch renders and then launches into beyond-the-basic renders, ranging from large images to 360° renders to uses of the other render modes for post-processing of your scenes.

THE BASIC RENDERING MODEL

What takes place during ray tracing? For an image to render, Bryce shoots a ray into the scene for each pixel. What is rendered depends on what is or isn't struck by the ray. When the ray doesn't intersect an object, it renders sky. When it does intersect an object, it bounces off of the object. Then, depending on the surface features of the object, it bounces elsewhere until it finds the light source(s) that contribute(s) to that object's color. From that it determines one final color for the pixel. Of course, the area that Bryce considers a "pixel" changes with each progressive rendering pass. Recall that in the first pass, Bryce determines a color for an area that is actually 32×32 pixels. The second pass covers a 16×16 area, the third pass an 8×8, and so on until every single pixel has been rendered. The final anti-aliasing pass shoots nine rays to determine a color for each pixel (in those areas of high contrast), averaging together all the information to come up with a color for that one pixel.

If there are 16 objects in a scene, then Bryce must test for 16 objects for each ray that goes out in your Bryce world. Each ray "knows" how many objects are out there. It will 'ask,' "Did I hit 1? Did I hit 2? Did I hit 3? Did I hit 4?" and so on. The greater the number of objects in your scene, the greater then number of queries to see if it struck any of them. The more queries, the slower the render.

This happens for each ray that is shot out. The same 16 questions are asked each time. There are no shortcuts.

But what if there were some way to reduce the number of objects that Bryce has to test for at any one time? You could speed up your render time. Well, there is! You can do this by grouping objects.

Grouping Objects to Save Render Time

Consider that a ray is shot out into the scene that has 16 objects. Objects 1, 2, 3, and 4 are in one group (group A) and objects 7, 8, 9, and 10 are in another group (group B). The ray then will "ask" its questions like this: "Well, objects 1, 2, 3, and 4 are a group—group A. Did I hit that group? Did I hit 5? 6?... well, 7, 8, 9 and 10 form group B, so did I hit group B? Did I hit 11? 12?" and so on.

You can see that Bryce must ask fewer questions for each ray that is shot into the scene. When it asks, "Did I hit (anything in) group A?" the answer is either no or maybe. A maybe answer results if it struck the bounding cube for the group. At that point, it will ask, "Did I hit 1? 2? 3? 4?"

If the area of the bounding box is limited, then the ray must ask only the additional questions a few times, in comparison to all the times it would ask about 1, 2, 3, and 4 for the rest of the rays shot into the scene. Although you may lose a bit of speed when the ray must ask about the specifics of the group, you gain speed by it not having to ask about the specifics of that group everywhere else.

This process also works for nested groups. Say you have 10 objects. Three are part of one group, the next four are part of another group, and the last three are part of a third group. Those three groups are grouped together. Instead of a ray's hitting that group of 10 objects and asking, "Did I hit 1? 2? 3? 4? 5? 6? 7? 8? 9? 10?" the ray would ask, "Did I hit sub-group A? Sub-group B? Sub-group C?" Here, 10 objects are segmented into three questions. The specifics are asked only when a ray hits a group that has the specific objects. Fewer questions are asked overall, and so the scene renders faster.

When objects are grouped and groups are grouped (nested groups), Bryce is asking after only a few objects at a time. Rather than a scene with, say, 80 objects, Bryce is confronted with a choice of about 8 objects or fewer.

Setting Up Groups for Better Rendering

On the Macintosh, this discussion of grouping objects to save time continues here with practical tips. The Windows version of the renderer is different, and arranging objects in groups won't make any difference in rendering speed. The preceeding discussion is enough to enable you to understand the theory behind Spatial Optimization, which I discuss a bit later in the chapter.

There are three points to keep in mind when grouping objects for efficient rendering on the Macintosh: group objects that are close to each other, make each group distinct from its neighbors, and create nested groups. All three of these strategies depend on the camera position.

Group Close Objects

Make sure the objects you group are close to one another. A grouped box that stretches clear from one side of the scene to another has more "in-between" area than it has actual objects. In this case, Bryce won't gain in render time because any time a ray hits the group (including all that in-between area), the ray must ask whether it hit any of the objects that are part of the group. The more between area, the more wasted render time, since so many of those additional queries are for naught. When objects are close to one another, you have more object area than area in between. The more object area, the more efficient the render. The additional queries about the group elicit more positive responses. Of course, what is object area and what is in-between area will change depending on the camera angle. If you change the camera angle, you may need to ungroup and regroup to keep objects close.

Make Groups Distinct

By making each group distinct from its neighbors, you will gain in render time. When two groups overlap, Bryce asks about all of the contents of both groups. If the two groups overlap in "thin air," then all that extra querying is for nothing. Overlapping groups is unavoidable in some cases, but be aware of this strategy so that you can keep overlapping groups to a minimum. Again, camera angle determines what overlaps and what doesn't.

Group (Nest) Groups

Nesting groups within other groups increases efficiency. Avoiding overlap in the grouped groups is even better. Figure 12–1a shows a rendered scene of 20 objects. In Figure 12–1b, those objects are shown in their groups. When the ray tracer first looks at the scene, it asks if it hit any of the five objects or grouped sets of objects (see Figure 12–1c). When the ray strikes group A in Figure 12–1d, it asks if it hit the two subgroups. When it finds that it has struck one of the subgroups, it then asks if it has hit the specific contents (see Figure 12–1e). Instead of asking about all 20 objects at a time, it first asks about five objects/groups and then two objects/groups and then the three specific objects. Where the groups overlap (see Figure 12–1f), there is inefficiency, since Bryce tests for all of the objects of both groups without any constructive result. But in comparison to the overall time savings, the inefficiencies are negligible. A change in camera angle will probably change whether there is overlap.

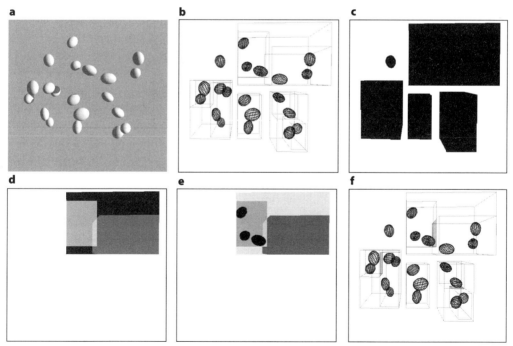

Figure 12–1 Rendering group strategy: a) The rendered scene; b) objects in groups; c) what the first ray sees; d) group of two subgroups; e) objects in one of the subgroups; f) where the groups overlap.

Render Options

All of Bryce's render options are on the Render pop-up menu on the Control Palette. (See Figure 12–2.) The Windows and Macintosh versions of Bryce differ in the specifics of rendering, but the render options have the same categories—Anti-Aliasing, Acceleration/Optimization, Render Report, render method, and some preset render sizes.

Though the names are different, there are rough equivalents between

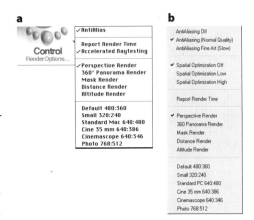

Figure 12–2 Render controls on Control Palette and Render pop-up menu: a) Macintosh; b) Windows.

methods. Accelerated Raytesting (Macintosh) is roughly the same as Spatial Optimization Low/High (Windows). Non-Accelerated Raytesting—what I call the no-name version (Macintosh) is roughly equivalent to Spatial Optimization Off (Windows).

Non-Accelerated Raytesting/Spatial Optimization Off

In the Macintosh version of Bryce, the non-Accelerated Raytesting is the original render method used in Bryce 1. It is the no-name version. (Simply uncheck Accelerated Raytesting.) If you want, you can change the method to the slower, no-name method. However, there's no way to get the menu to stay that way for scene after scene. Even if you have the Preferences set to Launch to Previous State to retain the attributes of the previously opened scene, Bryce will open each scene in the default render mode—Accelerated Raytesting. Naturally, I've long forgotten about the old, slower no-name render method in the Macintosh version.

The Windows verion of Bryce has the default set to Spatial Optimization Off. It performs the most infinitesimal bit of optimization. Bryce assigns everything in the scene into a bounding box. When rendering things outside that bounding box (sky), Bryce won't even test for objects. All it cares about is sky. For all practical purposes, this is not optimization. It works fine when you have fewer than five objects in your scene. Above that, you'll need to move up to real optimization.

Accelerated Raytesting/Spatial Optimization Low and High

So what is this default Accelerated Raytesting/Spatial Optimization method and how does it work? The render method works on the same principle as the grouped objects method described earlier. The goal is to divvy up the objects in the scene in order to cut down on the unnecessary part of rendering. I described the process as the renderer "asking" if something was there. If you're geeky enough to actually write the code for a ray tracer, you'd call the process "testing." The ray "tests" to see if something is there. To accelerate the process, arrange the scene so that the rays perform only the necessary tests. (Accelerated Raytesting. Get it?) You've seen already the theory behind grouping to accelerate the process, making it unnecessary to pay attention to a series of objects until it has to. In the Accelerated/Spatial Optimization method, Bryce is automatically performing a process similar to the grouping described earlier. Bryce subdivides the scene's bounding box into smaller bounding boxes, each containing a certain number of items. Bryce creates additional automatic groups, and doesn't perform any tests for objects in *this* part of the world when it's over there rendering *that* part of the world.

(That number is fixed in the Mac version and changes in the Windows version, depending on whether you've selected Low or High.)

The Windows version of Bryce has two additional options. Spatial Optimization Low and High operate in the same manner, only that bounding box of all objects is divvied up into different quadrants.

Each of the sub-divided quadrants for Low contain a lower number of items, and each of the quadrants for High contain a higher number of items. It may seem backward—for the same scene, there are fewer total quadrants for Spatial Optimization High than there are for Spatial Optimization Low. Consider it from the perspective of the number of questions each ray must ask. In a scene with 300 objects, it's better to require each ray to ask six questions about sets of 50 than it is to require each ray to ask 60 questions about sets of five objects.

This explains the rule of thumb for which option to use: When you have fewer than five objects, Spatial Optimization Off is fine. When you have more than five objects, but the numbers don't run up into the hundreds, Spatial Optimization Low is fine. In fact, you might as well make Low your own default render method. If you've gotten this far in this book, the majority of your scenes propably contain over five objects. When you create scenes with objects numbering in the hundreds, use Spatial Optimization High. By now it should be obvious that for medium-sized scenes, dividing the bounding box into fewer quadrants containing many more objects may be more truoble than it's worth.

Anti-Alias Options

The Macintosh version of Bryce has two anti-alias options, and the Windows version has three. They both share the "none" option, where anti-aliasing is not applied. The Macintosh Anti-Aliasing option is the same as the Windows Anti-Aliasing Normal. I'll refer to this as the standard anti-alias process. The third Windows option, the Fine Art option, works slightly differently and will be discussed separately.

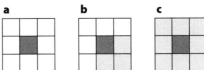

The standard process of anti-aliasing takes place after the six render passes. At the conclusion of those, Bryce conducts a special render pass. First it decides whether to anti-alias the pixel or not. To do so, it examines each pixel and the pixels below and to the right (see Figure 12–3a and b.) If there is a high contrast between the target pixel and the ones below and to the right, it then conducts a super sample. It shoots extra rays around

Figure 12–3 Anti-aliasing strategy— in order to determine if a) the center pixel will be anti-aliased, b) additional rays sample the area below and to the right of the center pixel; if there's high contrast, then c) the remainder of the eight surrouding pixels are sampled.

the rest of the eight pixels surrounding the one pixel (see Figure 12–3c). The result of the super sampling is weighed together with the center pixel to arrive at the final color for that pixel. The image is smoothed as a result. The basic process is to do a regular render for six passes, and then conduct a post-processing super sample pass at the end to smooth out the areas that need it. The areas that will be anti-aliased are areas of high-contrast, and high frequency textures.

The other Windows option, Anti-Aliasing Fine Art, approaches anti-aliasing in a different manner. Rather than conducting six normal render passes and saving the super sampling for the end, the Fine Art method conducts the super sampling during all six render passes. If you wondered why this method is slower than the others, this is it! Further, for each super sample, instead of shooting out a set of rays in a 3 × 3 formation, for a 9-times oversample, the Fine Art method shoots out sets of rays in a 4 × 4 formation, for a total of 16 rays per pixel. After six passes, the render is complete. After super sampling throughout the process, there is no need for an anti-aliasing pass to cap it off.

But wait! There's more! Each time those 16 rays are shot into the scene, they are randomly jittered. (Normally, the ray is shot out to sample the upper left corner of the pixel.) Figure 12–4 shows how the arrangement varies from one sample to the next. The result of this random

Figure 12–4 Windows Fine Art Anti-Aliasing pass randomly jitters the placement of each of the 16 rays that are shot into the scene in order to determine one pixel's color.

jitter is a better-looking final image. Additional detail that might otherwise be lost in the standard ray tracing is picked up by those jittered rays. The kinds of artifacts that create aliasing tend to occur from repeated patterns, rather than randomness. For those familiar with offset printing technology, the difference between the basic line screen half tone and the stochastic screen half tone is analogous to the regular render method and the jittered sampling method. The line art screen has artifacts (moiré). Stochastic screening lacks moiré and has crisper detail. (I want this method for the Macintosh, by golly!)

Report Render Time

Initially installed as a testing device when the developers were working on the rendering part of the software, the Render Report has remained in the software to indicate render time and recount what's transpired during the render process. I'll discuss the significance of items listed in the report after focusing on the practical uses for having the Render Report selected (or not).

Besides telling you how long it took to render the image, this feature provides another significant function. It will give you a system alert when the image has completed rendering. Anytime you're in a production environment where you need to actively attend a set of renders (on one or multiple machines), the system alert is your friend, telling you to come back after working on the other computer (or paying your bills or practicing your juggling) to save this image and go on to the next.

What is the significance of the report itself? Aside from the total render time, what additional meaning can be abstracted from the report and all those different numbers? (See Figure 12–5.)

As you look at the rows of items in the report, there are three main categories. The first has to do with the number of pixels in the scene. The second concerns

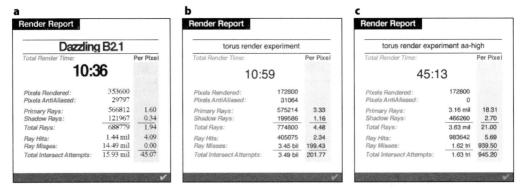

Figure 12–5 Render Report: a) Macintosh scene with Anti-Aliasing; b) Windows scene with Normal Anti-Aliasing; c) the same Windows scene, Fine Art Anti-Aliasing.

the number of rays that are "shot out" into the scene in order to render the image. The third tells how many of those rays hit objects and how many missed.

The first category concerns the number of pixels in the image. The first item, Pixels Rendered, is simply a count of the pixels in your scene. That number is fixed at the time you set the document and render resolution in the Document Setup dialog box. The second item, Pixels Anti-aliased, depends on the contents of the scene. If you have a completely smooth image where no anti-aliasing occurs (for instance, rendering a cloudless sky with no haze), then the number would read 0. An image with more complex surface detail will have a higher number. If you render using the Fine Art anti-alias method in Windows, the result will also be 0 pixels anti-aliased (see Figure 12–5c).

The next section concerns rays that are shot into the image. For each pixel, rays shot into the scene calculate that pixel's color. How many rays are shot out? Primary rays include the first set of rays and the anti-aliasing rays. Shadow rays shoot out from "found" objects to determine if a shadow is cast onto it. If you have the Shadow control in the Sky & Fog Palette set to anything other than 0, then Bryce will shoot out shadow rays as appropriate while it is rendering the scene.

The final set of items concerns whether the ray hits an object or not. For a sky scene with no objects, all you'll have is misses. Recall from the initial render discussion that when a ray is shot into a scene it either finds something (a hit) or it doesn't (a miss). In a scene where the camera looks down from above onto a ground plane, every one will be a hit. Between those two extremes of all-sky or all-object are all the hit-or-miss possibilities in Bryce.

By the way, if you're applying your mathematical due diligence to the report, adding up the numbers here and there to see if they reconcile (Ah! But you're reading this because you're an artist, not because you're an accountant, right?), you may have noticed that the total number of rays does not always equal the total intersect attempts. That's because there are other rays in the render process, but they aren't listed in the Render Report. What are they? Why, secondary, tertiary, and additional rays that are shot out in special optical conditions (reflection, refraction, transparency). Those additional rays are factored into the Total Intersect Attempt number. They result in many more misses, since they may bounce off an object and into the sky.

The Render Report is a good diagnostic tool for reducing the expense of a scene and making it render more efficiently. How do you conduct a diagnosis of a scene?

First, look at the number of pixels anti-aliased. The number can be no higher than the Pixels Rendered number. The higher the number is, the longer the rendering takes.

Next take a look at the total number of rays shot into the scene. In a scene created at Bryce's default size, the resulting numbers are in the hundreds of thousands and low millions. It's hard for numbers of that magnitude to be meaningful. But when they are divided by the total number of pixels, a baseline ratio emerges. It becomes meaningful when you consider the number of rays per pixel or the number of intersections per pixel. One ray per one pixel is extremely efficient (the lowest number I've seen is 1.03). The higher the number, the more complex and costly the scene is. I've seen scenes using the normal render method that hover near and even exceed 10 rays per pixel. (Of course, the Fine Art method *starts* at 16 and goes up from there, as Figure 12–5c shows.) Needless to say, those have longer render times.

Finally, take a look at the relationship between the total rays per pixel and the Total Intersect Attempts per pixel. The Total Intersect Attempts will be equal to or higher than the total number of rays shot. It can very easily be two, three, four, or five times as many. When you add lights and other optic conditions to your scene, then you're making that ratio higher.

I'm not saying to try to keep the numbers equivalent. Pretty scenes in Bryce will require expensive components. It's just that it's best if you choose to use the expensive ones rather than having the pricey render foisted upon you by a lack of familiarity with the software. If you need some measure of your scene's efficiency, you'll find it here in the Render Report.

Before leaving this topic, I'd like to briefly mention what types of Bryce settings affect the outcome of the Render Report.

- *Anti-aliasing.* The factors that determine anti-aliasing are the joining of one contour to another, the presence of a bump map, the presence of high-contrast color, and high-frequency detail.

- *Primary Rays.* These are determined by the total number of pixels, the total number of anti-aliased pixels, and a third category that's harder to quantify, the specialized optic conditions.

- *Shadow Rays.* These are determined by the shadow setting in the Sky & Fog Palette, as well as the presence and number of additional light sources in a scene.

- *Ray Hits and Ray Misses.* Will be significantly larger due to optical material surfaces and additional light sources. Also, hits and misses are determined by the overall structure of objects—how many there are and whether or not they occupy the greater part of the scene.

So reduce those numbers if you dare—or can. For better understanding look at several scene files and read their render reports. Check in the Render folder of the CD-ROM for a set of examples to study.

"While You Are Working" Rendering

Of course, in Bryce you don't simply build a scene, place objects hither and thither, and assign materials and sky settings without also doing many intermediate, "am I on the right track?" renders along the way. Bryce 2 added a couple of render modes just for working on in-progress renders: No Textures and Fast Preview.

No Textures Render

When this option is selected, none of the surface textures of any objects—nor the sky—will be rendered. This is good for determining the basic shape of your image, and setting up the geometry and composition. The colors of objects can vary widely, however. That's because they are taking their color information from the diffuse color in the Materials Composer. Even if the object's surface color is determined by a 3D Solid texture source, whatever color is in the color swatch for Diffuse Color will be the color of the object. (To double check, move the marker out of the Texture Source columns back into the color swatch column and see what the Diffuse Color is.) If you need to distinguish objects from one another, you can quickly sneak in a global Diffuse Color "under" the texture color.

As I mentioned in Chapter 5, "Streamline Your Brycing," the Windows version of the No Textures render does not rid objects of reflection or transparency. If you have assigned those to your objects, they'll render as such even when you select No Textures. By now you understand that those are two of the more expensive items contributing to your render time.

Fast Preview Render

This is a two-pass version of a basic render. It renders surface textures and fog, haze, and clouds, trading off speed for some imperfections in the rendered results. Use it while you are working on "in progress" renders, when you've moved from the basic composition to decisions about material settings. With its speed and imperfections, Fast Render's not the option of choice at the stage where you are checking minute details of your sky or objects. It won't provide meaningful feedback on, say, the detail pattern of the surface's bump map. But if you want to test whether the snow is falling where you want it, the quick render will do the job admirably.

Rendering "in Progress"—Earlier Stages

To get a better sense of overall image detail, zoom out while in render mode (click the Zoom tool or tap the minus key on the keypad) and then begin rendering your scene. Those first few passes will give you a general sense of the image. Reducing the image's size on screen increases the apparent resolution, so you can get a better idea after one or two passes how the image is developing.

Rendering "in Progress"—Later Stages

This render technique is good for the later stages of scene building, when you're doing some serious fine-tuning. You have done at least one initial render and you have come back to the scene the next day or after your lunch hour or…

Suppose you have a scene and PICT or BMP saved from a previous working session. You open up the image and decide it needs further tinkering. After tweaking it here and there and doing little test renders for each tweak, what do you have? Many subtle changes displayed in a fine mess of coarse pixels. What if you want to get a quick look at the changes—against a completely rendered background—before you leave your computer to complete its rendering work in peace?

Select File > Open Pict... (Macintosh) or Open Image... (Windows) to go back to your original rendered image. Think of this move as a partial revert to saved. With it, you revert to the saved image but retain all the intermediate changes you made to your scene document when you were having that fruitful dialog with the Bryce Muse. (Bryce will ask you if you want to save changes when you open the image. You don't.) Of course, if you had saved your scene document along the way, the newly opened image might not be as dramatic when you go to re-render over the image from when you saved the scene yesterday.) After you open your original image, simply drag a marquee around the area you want to render and then select Clear and Render. The rest of the image stays. You can clearly see the changes you made. Your scene document underneath keeps the changes.

You can render on top of *any* image, even if it's not an image created with Bryce. If you're looking for a new experimental medium for creating rendered abstractions, open any image file, drag a marquee around an area, and render. The Abstract Muse will tell you what to do next.

When you save the scene (and your Preferences are set to Open and Save Pict/Image with scene), Bryce will write the new image over the old image. Say you have opened a scene document called ORIGINAL SCENE (Windows: ORIGINAL SCENE.BRC). The accompanying image document is called ORIGINAL SCENE.P (Windows: ORIGINAL SCENE.BMP). Then you open an image from a variation on this scene that is named SECOND SCENE.P (Windows: SECOND SCENE.BMP). Opening a subsequent image closes the first one. You render over portions of the new image to see changes made since you worked in SECOND SCENE and SECOND SCENE.P (Windows: SECOND SCENE.BRC and SECOND SCENE.BMP). When you save the scene (⌘-S or Ctrl+S), then this new rendered image will be renamed ORIGINAL SCENE.P (Windows: ORIGINAL SCENE.BMP). The scene document that is open takes precedence in the writing and naming of the accompanying image document.

This technique of opening older images is good for seeing changes in a scene's object placement, size, materials, position, and sky. It is not as successful for seeing changes in camera position, since everything in your scene will have changed.

"When You Are Finished" Rendering

You have finished working with your scene. Now it's time for the final render.

For your final render, ensure you start from scratch. On the Control Palette, click Render Scene. Or, when you are in Render mode, select all and then select Clear & Render. You can select Clear and Render from the Edit menu by clicking the Clear and Render button on the Control Palette or by using the keyboard shortcut, ⌘-Option-R (Macintosh) or Ctrl+Alt+R (Windows).

Why do either of these? In all likelihood, you made minor changes since the first tentative pixels were rendered at the beginning of your session. Perhaps you moved the camera slightly or changed the orientation of the 2D Projection plane. If you just click Resume Render (or type ⌘-R or Ctrl+R), you will not completely overwrite the older rendered portion. In fact, the finished render will have ghosts of the old render. This is especially true in the Macintosh version, where the fourth channel of the PICT image keeps track of the render's progress. The fourth channel has different patterns for each stage of the render. During the render, Bryce looks at the fourth channel and says, "Yes, well, but that's been done already" and so overlook an area for the next couple of passes. That portion that's been "done already" may not be the most recent revision of the scene. The PICT's fourth channel remembers where the render left off, but it doesn't check to make sure that what it calls "rendered already" is, in fact, the *latest* version of the scene. That's for *you* to do. And it's easy enough to do by clicking that big Render Scene button on the Control Palette.

If you do not start a render from scratch, when things come down to the last 1×1 pixel pass and the anti-aliasing pass, there will be tiny rows of pixels in an orderly formation, but they won't fit in with the remainder of your image. Not cute. Figure 12–6 is an image that has been rendered over an old image. The original image had a black sky (see left edge of image). The new sky, with haze and horizon, was rendered on top of the black sky in progressive steps. With each

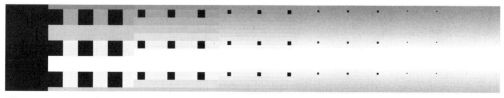

Figure 12–6 Rendering over an old image (Macintosh). As the render progresses, the old black sky never completely disappears.

subsequent pass, more of the new sky shows, but even after the final anti-alias (see right edge of image), the old black sky is faintly visible.

The Windows version does not have an alpha channel to track the render's progress, and the bitmap file format does not even contain a fourth channel. So where does the information about the render's progress reside? Bryce Windows keeps track of it and stores it in the scene file itself. The problem of old-leftover-render artifacts does not exist on the Windows side. The storage of the render progress in the scene file does have repercussions in batch rendering, however. I'll discuss them in the section on batch rendering in a bit.

Render to Disk

Bryce now does background renders. You can render an image to disk and the computer will be free for other tasks.

To use this, select the Render to Disk... item from the File menu. You'll be presented with a dialog box that enables you to select your final size (see Figure 12–7a). Unlike the normal rendering requirements, which require enough RAM to keep the Bryce application, the scene file and the number of pixels for the rendered image all in dynamic memory, the Render to Disk option enables you to render an image larger than your RAM would allow. So if you had, say, 32 MB RAM on your computer, and had a scene file that would render fine at, say 1:1.5 ratio, but chokes when you try to render it at a ratio of 1:2, 1:3, or 1:4, you can render the scene to disk and sneak around the memory limitation.

You can select the final size and determine the image resolution, that is, the number of pixels that are displayed in an inch (if you're a centimeter person, well, sorry!). Bryce calculates the total number of inches to the scene.

You can an also choose the QTVR option. I'll discuss that in a separate section on rendering 360° panorama views.

When you have set up your dimensions and click OK, you'll be presented with a dialog box for naming your image (see Figure 12–7b and c). The current file name is there for you Macintosh Brycers already (see Figure 12–7b). It is the name of your scene file. *Urgent Warning!* Make sure that you change the name slightly. Otherwise you'll overwrite your scene file and cause untold hours of frustration and misery as you wonder where in tarnation it went. (It was replaced by a rendered image.) If you've realized you just overwrote the scene file while the scene is yet rendering to disk, you still have an escape hatch. Re-save the scene file under a different name.

At the end of a completed render, Bryce will usually ask you if you want to save the scene (and image). Do so. Give it another name, just in case. Windows users need not worry about accidental overwrites since Windows automatically appends the file extension to the file name, and does not place the current file name in the Save As dialog box.

Once you've sent the render on its merry way, you'll see a modal window with a progress bar on it (see Figure 12–7d). At that point, you can put Bryce in the background, so that you can do other tasks on your computer. Just pray that the second software that you're using is not buggy or allergic to Bryce or vice versa. Because if something should go wrong, all your render is down the drain. In fact, you cannot save a partially-rendered render-to-disk image. It's all or nothing. Nor can you start a render and resume it. Once you commit yourself, you're committed (this is why you pray that all your software is very stable). Oh, and you wanted to move that progress bar to another part of your monitor so you could keep an eye on it while you wrote your novella to your email pen pal? Sorry. Despite the title bar that promises you it will allow itself to be moved, it will not budge.

At the end of the process, you will be presented with the beloved Render Report. This is helpful for, among other things, conducting tests of rendering capabilities. Seriously, though, the information is helpful if, say, you use this to render an image that's a rough… then you know approximately

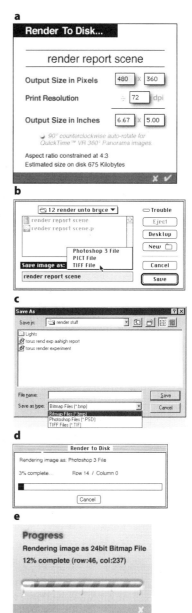

Figure 12–7 Render to disk:
a) The Bryce Render to Disk dialog box;
b) the File Save dialog box with file format pop-up menu and same file name as scene file (Macintosh);
c) the Save As dialog box in Windows;
d) the Render to Disk progress bar for Macintosh and e) Windows.

how long it took so when the client asks you to do some changes and then deliver it in *n* minutes/hours/days, you'll know exactly what you're up against.

BATCH RENDERING

One of the joys of Bryce is its ability to do batch rendering. It works through the computer system's Drag and Drop feature. Drag the scene icons (*not* the PICT or BMP icons) and drop them onto the Bryce Application icon (or alias or shortcut). I keep a Bryce application alias on the desktop and drag all of my scene icons onto it.

Of course, batch rendering, like other complete renders, should be started from scratch to ensure there are no weird anomalies left over from previous work sessions. Before you save your final scenes prior to rendering, hit the Render Scene button and let 'er go for a couple of passes. Then include the scene as part of your batch.

Sometimes the Macintosh version of Bryce seems unwilling to do a batch render when you drag and drop to the Bryce icon when Bryce isn't already launched. If that's the case, then launch Bryce first and then drag and drop to begin your batch render. Bryce Windows requires that the application not be launched when you initiate a batch render.

Of the selected scenes that are dropped onto the Bryce Application icon, how do you know which one will render first? On the Macintosh, that depends on how the scenes are listed in the Finder. If you select View by Date, then the most recent scene will render first, followed by the next most recent scene, and so on. If you select View by Size, the largest scene file will render first, followed by the next largest, and so on. View by Name scenes will render in alphabetical order, as will View by Kind scenes, in the latter case because all scene documents are the same kind. If you've selected View by Label, scenes that are labeled (such as Essential or Hot) will render according to the label pecking order. So if you want to ensure one scene renders before another (just in case you need to interrupt the render mid-batch), arrange the labels accordingly so that the high-priority scene is labeled "Essential," while the other ones are "Project 2" or "None." What about the order for Windows? Although the Windows desktop directory structure allows for file viewing using different criteria (alphabetically, size, date), I didn't recognize any discernible relationship to the order in which scenes were rendered and the manner in which the scene icons were displayed.

When batch rendering, Bryce opens a scene, renders it, saves it, and then moves on to the next one on the list. More to the point, what is saved is the rendered image. The scene file itself is not saved during the batch render. For the Windows version of Bryce, where the information about the render progress is saved with the scene file, the renders are completed during the batch process, but the scene files don't "know" that they're completed. If you batch rendered some scenes last night and you open up one of them today, when you make a change and begin to render, you'll begin from scratch—or wherever the render had left off when you saved the scene just before the batch render. The information stays in the scene file, and there's no changing it. You cannot "educate" the scene file about the render's completion short of entirely re-rendering it again.

BEYOND THE BASIC RENDERING MODEL

Everything I've discussed so far fits into the category of basic rendering—how Bryce operates during rendering and how you can make your trips to RenderLand more pleasant. In this section, I depart from the basic. First, I discuss rendering large images. Then I consider each of the other render options available on the Render pop-up menu: 360° Panorama and rendering for post-processing using Distance Render, Altitude Render, and Mask Render.

Rendering Large Images

How large can you make your Bryce images? Bryce 2 gives you an array of options in the Document Setup dialog box. It's very easy to proportionately enlarge an existing size to one of the available ratios: 1:1.5, 1:2, 1:3, or 1:4. To create render resolutions that are even larger, say 1:6, you can see what the resolution is at 1:3. Enter those numbers into Document Resolution section and then select 1:2.

(If you run into any memory ceilings, you will be told along the way that Bryce won't participate to your liking.) If you don't have enough memory to render at a large resolution, then you can always use the Render to Disk option.

Here are some image resolution and memory considerations to keep in mind. Bryce will limit your maximum image size according to the amount of memory available. If you have chosen a size larger than what Bryce will be able to accommodate, you will get the alert "Not enough memory, revert to default format!" Your custom size image will then be reduced to one of those listed in the Render Size pop-up menu. Changing the resolution will, in turn, change your 2D Projection plane (on a Mac;

the 2D Projection plane is left untouched in the Windows version), as Bryce does its "best guess" at fitting everything to the new size. So your old image may be shot. Therefore do as the wise and cautious do: Before making a drastic change in size, save your scene. If all "not-enough-memory-revert-to-default" hell breaks loose, you can simply revert to saved and then head on over to the Render To Disk option under the File menu.

You can gauge how much memory is leftover in the Bryce allocation by checking the text readout when the scene is in render mode. It should tell you how many megabytes are free and what the render resolution is.

The maximum size of a rendered PICT image (on the Macintosh) is 4096. Bryce—for both platforms—only goes up to 4000. That is the maximum size that Bryce will render or save an image. When you're in the Document Setup dialog box, you won't be able to enter anything higher than 4000 for sizes. You can, however, render larger than that to disk. The TIFF file format and the Photoshop 3.0 file format are not limited by a maximum size, so you can create sizes larger and actually save them. Although the Render to Disk dialog box for naming your file gives you the options of choosing between the three file formats, if you're using a Mac and have selected, say, a 6000 × 6000 sized image, you can still select PICT and Bryce will begin rendering away. I did not hang out long enough through a render that size to see what Bryce does at the end. If you want to try it for kicks, go ahead. It won't be pretty.

When you're rendering large format scenes (ones that take 12 to 24 or more hours to render), saving the scene from time to time is a good precaution. Then if a thunderstorm winks your electricity off and sends that big beautiful render to file heaven, you'll at least have the rendered image data from the last time you saved the render.

Also, any time you increase the render resolution, you may need to increase your terrain resolutions accordingly. Although a terrain with a resolution of 256 may serve admirably in the foreground of a scene that's at Bryce's default size, once you double or triple the render resolution you may get triangle-shaped pock marks in a terrain of that size. Increase the resolution of your terrains if you need to.

360° Rendering

To render the entire panorama encircled by the camera position, select 360° render. Whatever your current image size is, the 360° panorama will be squished into that space. And "squished" is an accurate word, especially if your image format is nearly square. See Figure 12–8. A 360° panorama is better for very wide images.

Bryce's Document Setup dialog box gives you a couple of options for panoramas. There's the simple Panorama aspect ratio, which is good for nice wide scenes. Then there's the QTVR Panorama aspect ratio.

a

b

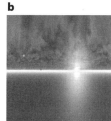

Figure 12–8 a) Wide and b) squished panoramas.

Bryce's 360° Panorama render is like projecting the entire scene onto the round vertical wall of a cylinder. The image comes to a stop at top and bottom; this is not a spherical render. In Bryce panorama renders, the vertical dimension of the image is distorted. When renders are complete, the sun, moon and other spherical objects appear oblong. In fact, the vertical dimension is twice as high as it is wide. So how do you make those oblong spheres round? There is no way to adjust Bryce's camera to make it undistorted. The distortion needs to be taken care of by image adjustment afterward. Here's my technique for first compensating for the distortion in the way that I set up the render in Bryce, and then making adjustments later in Photoshop.

1. First, determine the desired image size. For this example, I'll take the Document Setup's Panorama setting, where the aspect ratio is 8:3. On my large monitor, that amounts to an actual pixel dimension of 992 × 372 (if your monitor size is different from mine, you'll get different pixel dimensions).

2. Compensate for the distortion. Double the height. Simply double the aspect ratio number. Type 6 in the box where it says 3 (see Figure 12–9a). Bryce will

calculate the actual pixels for you. You've now given yourself an unusually high scene.

3. Render the scene and save the PICT or BMP image.

4. Open up the rendered image file in Photoshop. Go to the Image Size dialog box. Uncheck both Constrain options at the bottom of the dialog box. Under the Height area, select Percent from the pop-up menu. Enter 50 (percent) for the height option. Click OK (see Figure 12–9b).

You should now have an image that has no vertical distortion at the original size you requested from Bryce. In order to compensate for the vertical distortion, you added in twice the vertical space as necessary and then resized to bring it all back down to size. Figure 12–9c and d compare the original and the Photoshop adjusted renders.

Another critical point is to ensure your camera is level. An unlevel camera causes your horizon to undulate like a sine wave, as shown in Figure 12–10.

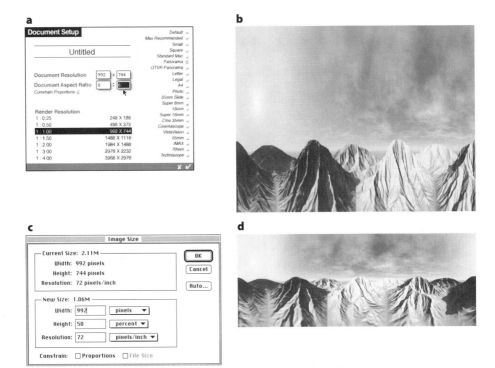

Figure 12–9 Fixing vertical distortion in 360° Panorama renders: a) Doubling the height ratio in the Document Setup dialog box; b) rendered image; c) reducing the rendered scene by half in Photoshop's Image Size dialog box; d) after reducing vertically.

Ensure the horizon is level by double-clicking the Camera controls on the Main Palette to access the Camera dialog box. There, the Camera Angle value of *x* and *z* should be 0. For a 360° panorama that takes

Figure 12–10 A wavy horizon resulting from an unlevel camera.

in what's below and above as well as both horizons, enter 90 for either the *x* or the *z* axis.

To have convincing image detail close to the camera and larger terrains far off (see Figure 12–11a), set up a whole series of small terrains very close to the camera. In fact, make sure that a terrain is placed *under* the camera. It needs, of course, to be a higher-resolution terrain. Figure 12–11b shows the top view of the scene with terrains on all sides of the camera.

Because you are creating a panorama that goes in a complete circle, you need to look at your scene from different perspectives as you set it up. Use the Camera Memory

a

b

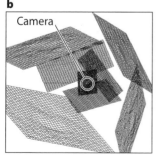

Camera

Figure 12–11 A 360° render where land surrounds the camera: a) 360° render; b) top view of wireframe.

Dots to add different perspective views so that you can move back and forth between them. Or go to top view and move the camera position (the needle end, not the box "base" of the camera—this works only using the Macintosh version). Then switch back to camera view and add that view.

Or enter the numbers in the Camera dialog box. Note that if you want to position your camera at World Center, then set the offsets for x and z to 0. Offset y refers to how far off the ground the camera is. The Camera Angle y points your camera to the four directions: 90, 180, 270, and 0 (or 360). Enter those numbers and save a view for each. You can work with developing your scene that way. In the end, your panorama will incorporate those views.

Here's another way to preview the placement of objects in a panorama: Use the Perspective Trackball. Press the Control (Macintosh) or Alt (Windows) key and then drag the Trackball. The camera will be constrained along the x-axis and rotate in a circle. You can check for object positioning in wireframe view.

The Zoom and Field of View controls have no bearing on 360° rendered scenes. Your placement of the camera in the 2D Projection plane, however, does affect the way the final render appears. In fact, if your image is rendering very strangely, and you're hard pressed to know how to fix it, pan up or down to change the placement of the 2D Projection plane. Often the wireframe view and the rendered view do not match. Make sure that the rendered view takes precedence.

Rendering Post-Processing

Besides Basic Perspective and 360° Panorama, the Render pop-up menu offers three other options: Mask Render, Distance Render, and Altitude Render. These are useful for creating post-processing effects after the initial render, as well as for other kinds of scene-building techniques. With them, you're not choosing either one or the other. Rather you can do both. First, do the Basic Perspective render. Then go back and render an additional image, a mask to use for special post-processing. The same is true for Distance Render. Since Mask and Distance Renders are both much faster than a Basic Perspective render, you can render them "live" and export the image. I'll discuss Distance and Altitude Renders first, since they have aspects in common, and then discuss Mask Render afterwards.

Distance Render

Distance Render creates a grayscale image based on the distance of the object from the camera. The closer the object is, the darker the value that is rendered; the further away the object is, the lighter the value. Sky far away is white.

The range of gray values is determined by the overall placement of objects in your scene. If your camera is located outside of the bounds of all objects, then will see a full range of black to white. (This includes the placement of the ground plane, even though it renders infinitely. Its placement in the scene will affect the overall tonal range.) Often your camera is placed within the scene, so the range of grays are more limited.

Distance Render is handy for creating selection masks that vary depending on distance for such things as motion blurs, depth-of-field focus, and so on. In the ray-tracing render model, all objects are rendered "in focus." To create a realistic unfocus, use Distance Render.

The object will *not* be a part of a distance render if any of the following settings are activated in the Materials Composer:

• Any Shading mode other than Normal (Fuzzy, Fuzzy Additive, Additive)

• Alpha-driven Transparency

• A Transparency setting other than 0 (opaque)

So, if you need to see if an object is showing or to do a quick test, make a note of your Transparency setting and your Shading mode. Change Transparency to 0, do your distance render, and then go back and change your Transparency setting when you're through.

Creating Blur Effects with Distance Render

Although in some cases you'll do a partial render without saving the resulting image, using Distance Render to create a selection mask requires that the entire scene be rendered and the image saved. (Use Export Image... from the File menu.) The naming convention I use on the Macintosh is a .DX suffix; resource documents on the CD-ROM with that suffix are Distance Renders.

In a Distance Render, the gray levels provide you with the means to create a blur based on distance from the camera. Although you see a grayscale image, the Distance Render is still an RGB image with four channels. In Photoshop, load one channel as a selection for the Basic Perspective image (see Figure 12–12a). If you invert the selection, the blur will take place in the foreground (see Figure 12–12b). If you leave the selection as is, the blurring will occur in the distance.

I find that several applies of the Blur More filter (see Figure 12–12c) are better than a single application of Gaussian Blur (see Figure 12–12d). In Gaussian Blur, the edges of the mask will prohibit the blur from being applied to the masked-off area. However, it will not prohibit the blur from picking up information from

Figure 12–12 Distance Render blurring: a) Distance Render mask; b) foreground blur; c) Distance blur using Blur More; d) distance blur using Gaussian Blur; 3) detail comparison of Blur More and Gaussian Blur.

behind that mask to mix with the neighboring pixels. The result is a strange, unnatural glow. See the close-up of the two types of blurs in Figure 12–12e. Blur More is on the left, and Gaussian Blur is on the right.

Another approach to blurring is to change the selection mask to create a depth-of-field blur. The blur is applied to the foreground and background, with the area "in the middle" staying in focus. To do this, you need to use Photoshop's Curves. The grayscale information in the selection mask is based on distance. So if you change the gray values to make portions lighter or darker, you will enable something that affects only that one area.

Figure 12–13a shows a grayscale image. In the middle ground is a cabin and waterwheel. Those objects need to be changed to black (or very dark gray) so that the image will be in focus and any blurring applied won't affect them. Change it using the Curves dialog box in Photoshop (see Figure 12–13b). Adjust the curves so that the darkest colors, up close, are lighter. Darken the tones where depth-of-field sharpness is important. The resulting blur is applied to the foreground and in the distance. See Figure 12–13c.

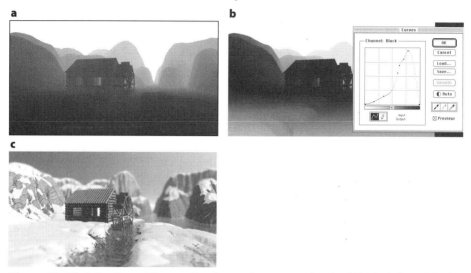

Figure 12–13 Adjusting a Distance Render mask to create depth-of-field: a) The original mask; b) masking adjusted with Photoshop's Curves; c) resulting blur.

Altitude Render

Bryce 2 has a new alternative render method. A cousin to the Distance Render method, Altitude Render takes all points at the same elevation and gives them the same gray or color value. Like the Terrain Editor's grayscale to height map, the highest points are white and the lowest points are black. Unlike the Distance Render where the camera angle has everything to do with the final render, Altitude Render's camera perspective doesn't have any affect on the ultimate values rendered. Everything located at the "light gray" elevation will be that light gray no matter which way you look at it.

Like Distance Render, Altitude Render determines the full range of gray from the highest point of the highest object in the scene to the lowest point. (Note: Beware the torus lying flat on the ground, since its overall object shape is smaller than the confines of the object's bounding box. You'll not see the full range of white-to-black if the torus is the only object in your scene.) If you add an object that's higher than all the rest and re-render, Bryce will have adjusted for this new "highest height" and reset the range of grays. Altitude Render is an equal alternative to Distance Render for the impromptu creation of terrain or other grayscale data from top view. In some cases it is better. For Windows users, it's the only option, since Distance Render doesn't work from top view.

Also like Distance Render, Altitude Render will not show an object that has transparency or special shading modes activated in the Materials Composer.

I mentioned that the final values rendered matched those of the Terrain Editor's grayscale-to-height map. That assumes, of course, that you have your Terrain Editor set to the default grayscale black-is-lowest-and-white-is-highest setting. If you have the Terrain Editor set to something else, it will be reflected in the Altitude Render. Figure 12–14 shows some variations on Altitude Renders based on different mapping colors and positions in the Terrain Editor.

Using Distance or Altitude Renders to work with terrains

When rendered from top view, Altitude Render and Distance Render on the Macintosh are good for working with the scene as a whole. This is something to use while your work on a scene is in progress. Suppose you need to take a look at a terrain's shape in the context of the scene. Your terrain is in place, resized, and rotated, and you don't want to touch its orientation. You do, however, want to shave off or augment a ridge for aesthetic balance. In order to know which part of the terrain to darken, you need to understand how the terrain

a

b
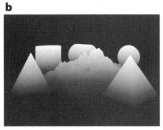

c

d
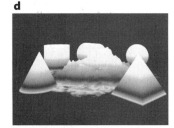

e
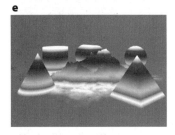

Figure 12–14 Different Altitude Renders reflecting different states of the gray map in the Terrain Editor.

is oriented. An Altitude or Distance Render from top view (see Figure 12–15a) will give you a grayscale image. For Distance Render, the gray values are inverted. Either way, you'll be able to recognize the landmarks so that you can alter the terrain as need be in the Terrain Editor (see Figure 12–15c). The figures shown here were made using Distance Render.

a   b   c

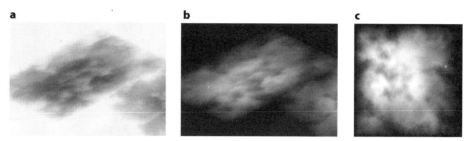

Figure 12–15 Distance and Altitude Render for terrain context: a) A top view render of the terrain in position; b) Altitude Render of same top view; c) grayscale-to-height map of that same terrain.

To create the Distance/Altitude Render, go to top view. Locate the terrain, then tap the Escape (esc) key to switch to render mode. Draw a marquee around the area to be rendered. In the Render pop-up menu, change to Distance Render and then click Clear and Render. After a few passes, you will see the orientation of your terrain.

You can also use Distance or Altitude Render to create a larger terrain comprised of smaller ones. When creating mountains and valleys, do a Distance or Altitude Render from top view. The render will become the image used to create the larger terrain that incorporates transitions between smaller terrains (see Figure 12–16).

In this scene, Distance Render was used to solve the problem of creating a smooth transition from mountain to valley (see "Superlative Nature Imagery," Chapter 14). Rather than the scene's having four separate terrains, (three as mountains and one as valley; see Figures 12–16a and 12–16c), the entire area was rendered from the top as a Distance Render in order to incorporate both mountain and valley. Again, although the example cites Distance Render, Altitude Render is perfectly acceptable as an alternative—especially if you're using Windows.

1. To create a new terrain map, the scene was rendered from top view using Distance Render. See Figure 12–16d.

2. Then, the rendered image was captured with a screen capture utility, which copied it to the clipboard.

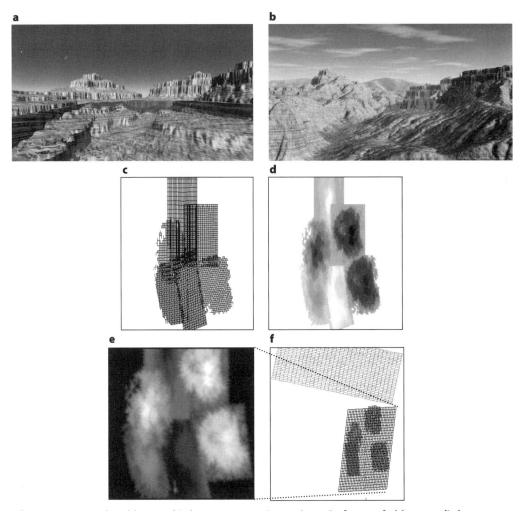

Figure 12–16 a) The old scene; b) the new scene; c) top view wireframe of old scene; d) the Distance Render; e) the new terrain grayscale map based on the Distance Render (note camera, too!); f) wireframe for the new scene.

3. The old terrain that had been the valley was selected and then the Terrain Editor was accessed. A paste brought the Distance Render into the Terrain Editor, where it was inverted to get the correct G2H orientation. (You can see the camera showing from the top view, too.) See Figure 12–16e.

4. Finally, the terrain was spread out over the area covered by the Distance Render screen capture. See Figure 12–16f.

I have been describing methods for using Distance Render as a temporary part of the scene creation process. The render is used to check something or to create something, but no Scene or PICT/BMP document is saved as a Distance Render.

Mask Rendering

Mask Rendering takes a selected object or objects and renders a mask. The selected objects (see Figure 12–17a) will be black and all else will be white (see Figure 12–17b). If the object is behind another object, then only the portion that is visible to the camera will render. If everything is selected (see Figure 12–17c), then all objects in the scene will be rendered as a mask. The sky will be white and everything else will be black. See Figure 12–17d. If nothing is selected, then nothing will render as a mask.

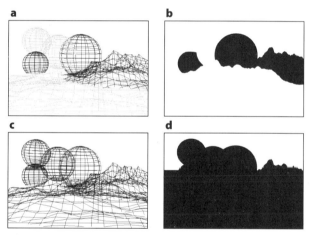

Figure 12–17 a) Objects selected and so b) are rendered as a mask; c) all objects selected and so d) all are rendered as a mask.

Mask Rendering for Work in Progress

Use a Mask Render while you work to determine if a particular object is showing and if so, how much of it is showing from a particular camera angle or from the object's placement. Mask Render helps you fine-tune the positions of the object and the camera. Like Distance Render, Mask Render requires much simpler computation by Bryce's renderer. Figure 12–18a shows Mask Render used to verify that the "waterfall" shows from the indicated camera position (see Figure 12–18b).

Figure 12–18 Mask Render used in progress: a) Mask Render; b) final render.

Mask Render is good to use in the case where one terrain (rocks) is poking out of another terrain. When the scene is viewed as a wireframe, you can see what part of an object is above ground level. But when both objects are above ground level, you can't easily see if one object pokes out beyond another object. Select the one underneath and use Mask Render.

Because Mask Render allows you to specify which object or objects will render, you can test certain things by selecting the objects and rendering. Suppose a scene with many objects appears on screen as a confusing jumble. You want to know whether object A has the same wireframe color as the others (you want to assign the same material setting to the whole set, and you want to ensure all are included). Select by family and then render as a mask. If you can see object A in silhouette, you'll have your answer. If the jumble of objects is sufficiently confusing, using this method may be faster than tabbing through the lot until the one is selected.

Mask Render and Transparent Objects

Rendering selected objects doesn't work in all cases as you'd like to. At least, if you have a picture object (like that Leonardo guy or the glasses shown in Figure 12–19a), and want to render a mask of the object in position in your scene, you won't be able to. The object is the square, and individual points of transparency as introduced by the image mask won't affect the rendering of the object's shape. (The same holds true for partially transparent objects in 3D Solid textures, which is why you'll never be able to make an accurate mask of freestanding clouds.)

There are workarounds for this, however painstaking. To render a mask of a picture object, you need to "fake" the mask part. You don't need to create a whole new scene for this; Solo mode will do admirably when combined with another trick or two.

1. Save your scene before you try any of the next steps. You won't save anything that you'll do to the scene file, and you can simply revert to saved to get back to where you were.

2. Save your current sky with a Memory Dot. Then change the sky mode to No Atmosphere and select white as your Backdrop Hue.

3. Select your picture object. In the Materials Composer, select source B (or C or D) and assign it to 2D Picture. Click the Leonardo image to access the Picture Library. When you're there, copy the mask from the source image. Select a new item in the library, and paste the mask in both the first and the second areas. (See Figure 12–19b.)

4. In the Materials Composer, assign the Ambient and Diffuse Colors to column B where your mask picture is. (The reason for not assigning the transparency as well is that you'll keep the old source. Later it's a matter of clicking in column A to revert your object to its former state.)

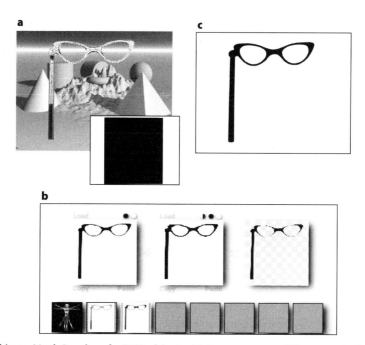

Figure 12–19 Faking a Mask Render of a PICT object with transparency: a) The scene before Mask Render with standard Mask Render inset; b) the mask image pasted in both the image and mask areas; c) the final faked mask rendered in Solo mode.

5. Go to Solo mode and render the black mask against a white sky. Export the image to a new mask file (see Figure 12–19c). Was that easy or was that… well, at least a way to get your desired result?

Also, if you need to create a mask of a partially transparent object, such as a cloud, create a separate scene file with different settings. Get rid of other objects in the background, and make the sky a flat color (black or white). Change your object's color to white with high ambience so that even shadowed areas render. A normal render will create an alpha channel mask that you can use for compositing transparent, wispy, cottony, or otherwise semi-visible objects.

Mask Render for Finished Rendering

Of course, Mask Render also creates a mask for selections to use in post-processing. Select all elements in your scene to render a mask that will have only your sky showing. If you need to do any post-processing of only the sky, then you can easily select just that one part of the scene with the mask.

Mask Render, Anti-Aliasing, and Compositing

What if you want anti-aliasing only on the edges of objects? Doing this involves a bit of extra work, but for the right scene, it's worth it. The scene in Figure 12–20, "Deep Undulating Canyon," has a lovely texture when seen in the last render pass. It's rough, and you can just sense the sandpapery texture of the rock face by the way the render looks. Once it's anti-aliased, the rock will have been metamorphosed into some other thing that, well, might be plastic (see Figure 12–20a). Needless to say, the un–anti-aliased is better (see Figure 12–20b). However, the edges of objects are a bit too rough. Those are the areas that need to be anti-aliased. How to do it? Combine Mask Render in Bryce with some Photoshop manipulation to create masks for the edges and then happily marry the two render versions, anti-aliased and rough.

Case Study: Anti-Aliased Edges in a Rough Rendered World

To create a Bryce scene that mixes anti-aliasing and non-anti-aliasing, follow these steps:

1. Use Mask Render to create masks of each individual object (see Figure 12–21a). This generally happens pretty quickly, so you can use the one scene document and export the rendered mask images, giving each one a different name.

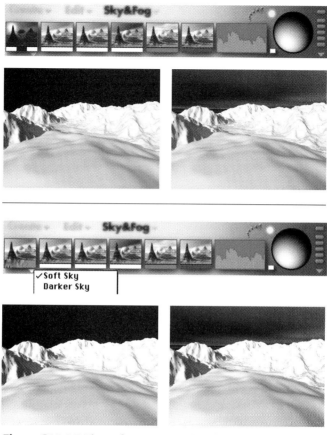

Figure C10–37 The unfortunate results of mixing Sky Dome and Cumulus Colors in normal Bryce skies. Top row: Custom Sky mode does not let Cumulus Color bleed into the Sky Dome Color, whether or not there are cumulus clouds present. Bottom row: Soft Sky (and Darker Sky, too) has a color bleed from Cumulus Color, whether or not cumulus clouds are present.

C34

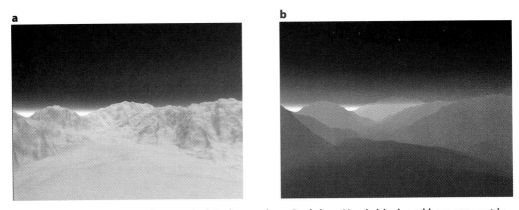

Figure C10–38 No Atmosphere and white haze, where Backdrop Hue is black and haze amount is set to around 40: a) Day and b) night.

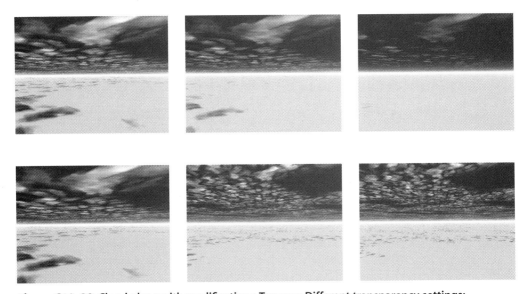

Figure C10–39 Cloud plane with modifications. Top row: Different transparency settings; Bottom row: change in mapping and frequency.

Figure C10–40 Night sky and infinite plane: a) Top plane only; b) both planes; c) bottom plane only.

Figure C10–42 Grand Canyon-like scene with many freestanding clouds: a) Top view wireframe; b) top view terrains only; c) wireframe from camera view; d) rendered result.

Figure C10–45 "Dazzling Light."

Figure C11–8 A square spotlight and a 2D Picture Gel make Bryce very good at projecting slides.

Parametric

Object Space

Spherical

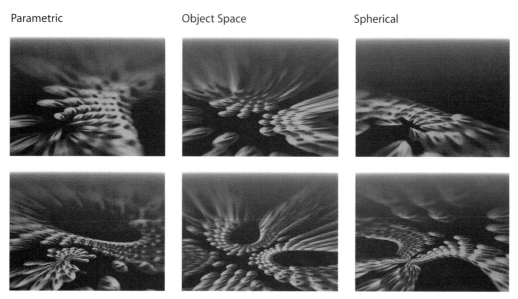

Figure C11–9 Mapping differences in the light. Top row: Frequency = 1; Bottom row: Frequency = 5.

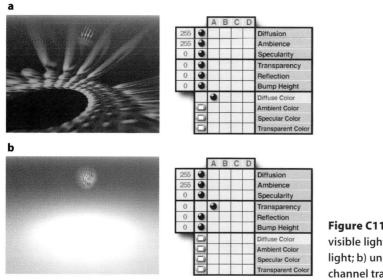

Figure C11–10 Picture Gels and visible lights: a) Normal visible light; b) uniform light with alpha channel transparency activated.

Figure C11–11 A light that casts a shadow and one that does not.

a

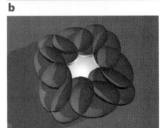

b

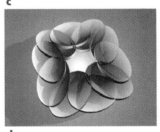

c

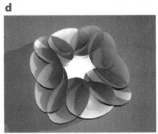

d

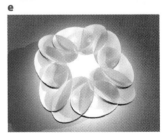

e

Figure C11–12 "Boolean Potato Skins." a) No lights; b) white radial light casting shadow; c) white radial light that does not cast shadows; d) yellow visible radial lights in each bowl, casting shadows; and e) not casting shadows.

Figure C11–25 "Wine Cellar." *Image by Gary Bernard.*

Figure C11–28 "Hammersmith Odeon."
Image by Robert Mann.

Figure C11–29 "Moon Water" by Eric Wenger: a) Scene rendered; b) scene with light wireframe; c) render without light.

Figure C11–30 A studio with the different kinds of studio lights.
Image by Chris Casady and Susan A. Kitchens.

right only

Figure C11–32 "Cappuccino on the Rocks" setup: Give one light a separate color to test its effect on the scene.

left light set to Disable Cast Shadow (stealth)

left casts shadows

left only

Figure C11–31 "Cappuccino on the Rocks." a) Lit from right only; b) lit from both sides, only light from right casts shadows; c) lit from both sides, only light from left casts shadows; d) lit from left only.

Figure C11–33 Scene with lights rendered with a) Textures On and b) Textures Off.

C42

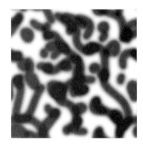

Figure C11–34 A hand-painted foliage Gel cookie used in two spotlights casts shadows onto the wall and ground, suggesting the presence of trees and moon above.

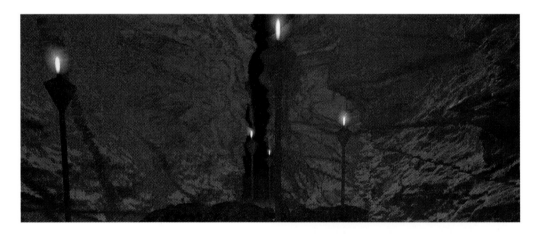

Figure C11–36 "Tiki Torches in Cave" and "Water Temple at Night."

Figure C11–38 a) "Chambered Mace"; b) lantern detail. *Scene by Robert Mann.*

Castle View v1

© 1996 Glenn Riegel

Figure C11–39 "Castle View." *Scene by Glenn Riegel.*

Figure C13–13 Garden Hose post-processing: a) A rendered scene; b) after adding more foliage with the Garden Hose. *Rendered scene by Susan A. Kitchens; Garden Hose by Dennis Berkla.*

Figure C14–3 a) "Fjord Mud"; b) "Abisko Pine Trees"; c) "Valley," all by Eric Wenger.

	Bkdrp	Amb	Fog	Haze	Sun
R	103	255	172	105	255
G	198	161	85	132	201
B	171	39	64	170	103

	Fog	Haze	Shadow	Cl Height
Amt	72	93	10	6
Ht	47.9			

	Bkdrp	Amb	Fog	Haze	Sun
R	103	255	172	105	255
G	198	161	85	132	201
B	171	39	64	170	103

	Fog	Haze	Shadow	Cl Height
Amt	28	96	10	13
Ht	92.9			

	Bkdrp	Amb	Fog	Haze	Sun
R	103	255	172	105	255
G	198	161	85	132	201
B	171	39	64	170	103

	Fog	Haze	Shadow	Cl Height
Amt	12	91	10	13
Ht	35.9			

	Bkdrp	Amb	Fog	Haze	Sun
R	103	255	172	105	255
G	198	161	85	132	201
B	171	39	64	170	103

	Fog	Haze	Shadow	Cl Height
Amt	36	81	10	11
Ht	55.9			

Figure C14–18 Four sea scenes with different colors set in the Sky & Fog Palette.

C48

Figure C14–21 Waterfall created by using clipped terrain to make the water cascade.

Figure C14–29 "Bushes," created by using lots and lots of small terrains and a picture texture. *Scene by Andrew Penick.*

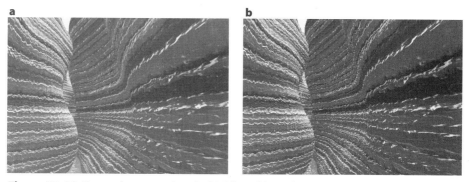

Figure 12–20 Scene shown rendered: a) With and b) without anti-aliasing.

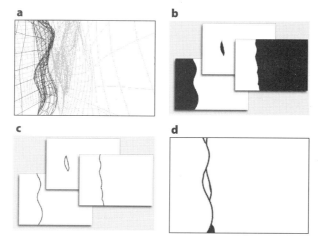

Figure 12–21 Creating a mask for compositing:
a) Selecting one wireframe; b) mask for each object;
c) Blurred and Find Edges; d) combined edges mask.

2. Change your render option to Basic Perspective. Then save the scene with a suffix that includes something meaningful, such as .NO AA. In the Render pop-up menu, uncheck the Anti-Aliasing option so that this first render will not have anti-aliasing. When the scene is finished rendering, save it again.

3. Immediately save the scene document with a different name, changing the suffix to .YES AA. Change the Render option so that Anti-Aliasing is *on* and then click Resume Render or type ⌘-R or Ctrl+R. (Don't start from scratch; you've already done the first six passes!) When the anti-aliasing pass is completed, save the scene/image combination again.

Continue in Photoshop or other image editing application with these steps:

4. Open up each of the mask images and change them to grayscale. Blur each one slightly and then apply the Find Edges filter (see Figure 12–21c).

5. Create a combined edges mask. Use Calculations and the Darken mode to combine them (see Figure 12–21d). (In this case, the area at the bottom where the water is located was added to the mask using a painting tool.)

6. Open up both of the rendered color images of the scene. Invert and load the combined mask as a selection into the non-anti-aliased version. The edges should be selected. In QuickView, check that the mask area has taken in sufficient border area and, if necessary, adjust using Levels.

7. Change back to the selection. Copy all of the anti-aliased version and paste it inside the selection. Adjust the opacity; this sample (see Figure 12–22) had the anti-aliased edges at 70% strength.

There you go! You have your beautiful, rough, rocky surfaces and smooth transitions from edge to edge.

Figure 12–22 Anti-aliased edges and non–anti-aliased everywhere else.

CHAPTER THIRTEEN

Bryce and Other Software

"Very true," said the Duchess: "flamingoes and mustard both bite. And the moral of that is— 'Birds of a feather flock together.'"

"Only mustard isn't a bird," Alice remarked.

"Right, as usual," said the Duchess: "what a clear way you have of putting things!"

"It's a mineral, I think," said Alice.

"Of course it is," said the duchess, who seemed ready to agree to everything that Alice said; "there's a large mustard-mine near here. And the moral of that is—'The more there is of mine, the less there is of yours.'"

"Oh, I know!" exclaimed Alice, who had not attended to this last remark. "It's a vegetable. It doesn't look like one, but it is."

"I quite agree with you," said the Duchess; "and the moral of that is—'Be what you would seem to be'—or if you'd like it put more simply—'Never imagine yourself not to be otherwise than what it might appear to others that what you were or might have been was not otherwise than what you had been would have appeared to them to be otherwise."

LEWIS CARROLL, *ALICE IN WONDERLAND*

IN THIS CHAPTER...

- Importing 3D objects into Bryce

- Working with the Polyhedron Editor

- Software for specialized terrain-making: Waves World, DEMView, and DEMvert

- Foliage for Bryce via The Garden Hose in Fractal Design's Painter

- Making Bryce QTVR movies

Using other software with Bryce can be broken down into two different categories: pre-processing, and post-processing. In the category of pre-processing, there are applications that create things that can then be imported to Bryce. The imported items are models, via the File > Import… command, and images for either terrain graymaps or for picture textures. With the exception of a couple of software applications that create graymaps for Bryce terrains, I will not discuss those image-type pre-processing software applications. (They were addressed in Chapter 8, "Terrains, Symmetrical Lattices, and the Terrain Editor," and Chapter 9, "Material World.") My discussion of pre-processing will be focused more on importing 3D objects into Bryce.

When doing post-processing, you can use all the tools that you normally would use to adjust any type of image. After creating your virtual landscape, touch it up or completely alter it in Photoshop, Painter, Live Picture, or other image-editing application. The other use for post-processing is to take a rendered image that Bryce created and imported it into another application, as a part of another project altogether, such as multimedia. Bryce works very nicely with Quick Time Virtual Reality (QTVR), for multimedia presentations.

PRE-PROCESSING

In pre-processing, something takes place in another application prior to working in Bryce. For 3D models, either you create the model yourself or otherwise procure a model that someone else created, and then use it in Bryce.

How to Import a 3D Object

To import a 3D model into Bryce, select Import Object… from the File menu. A dialog box will appear, allowing you to navigate to your object. There is a checkbox at the bottom of the dialog box. Checking it makes Bryce scan every item in the current folder to see if it is a legal object type to import into Bryce. This slows down your search considerably, especially if you have to navigate through some crowded folders to get to your target location for the model. I would suggest unchecking it and keeping it unchecked until you reach your destination folder.

After you've selected your object, Bryce imports it, complete with the ceremonial progress bar. If the object is a DXF file, there will be two progress bars. If it is a 3DMF format, there will be one progress bar. The larger and more complex the object, the longer it will take, and the more RAM you have to assign to Bryce to successfully import the object.

Once inside of Bryce, the object is considered a polyhedron (many-sided) object. You can perform the same type of edits that you would to any other object. Select it by type using the Polyhedron option in the Select Options pop-up menu. Change the object's size, position, or orientation. Duplicate it. Assign it a unique family identity. Give it a material setting. But most importantly, polyhedron objects (including Bryce's own stones) have an editor all their own for special polyhedron surface smoothing.

Polyhedrons dialog box

Since polyhedrons are faceted surfaces, your models *could* look quite hackneyed when brought into Bryce. Happily, Bryce supplies a means to get around the faceted look and round out the object. The Polyhedron dialog box enables you to smooth the object's surface. When Bryce smoothes, it doesn't add more polygons, but examines what is there and interpolates a smoother surface. The same routine is employed by the Terrain Editor for creating terrain surfaces out of grayscale data. (If you used Bryce in the 1.0 era, you may recall the option to have faceted polygons or smoother terrains.)

So, when you enter the Polyhedron Editor (⌘-E for Macs, Ctrl+E for Windows, or click the E button, or click the Edit Terrain/Object icon on the Edit Palette), there are two buttons and a slider. Although the thumbnail images look like preview windows, they are actually buttons (see Figure 13–1). To smooth the object, click the Smooth button on the left. To unsmooth, click the right button. The slider is for setting the amount of

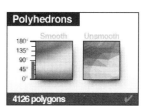

Figure 13–1 The Polyhedrons dialog box.

smoothness. The numbers correspond to the angle that will be smoothed. The default, at 82°, means that planes at less than perpendicular angles will be smoothed into a curve, whereas those at perpendicular angles (90°) and greater will remain sharp angles.

When you click the button, Bryce performs two passes. When it has completed those passes, click the check mark. If you change your mind, you cannot click a Cancel button. To leave the Polyhedrons dialog box, you *must* click OK. To change the polyhedron back to its former faceted state, you'll have to click the Unsmooth button. Also, once you set the smooth angle to an angle other than the default 82°, it is not automatically set back to the default position the next time you access the Polyhedrons dialog box. Other than knowing what the setting is and manually dragging the slider to that location, the only other way to reset it is to quit and relaunch Bryce (selecting Edit > Reset To Defaults will not reset it).

If you change the setting to a higher number, you'll get some interesting curvature to the image. In Figure 13–2, the water cooler model has gone through some different smoothing sets. The left is plain unsmoothed. Next to it is one that is set lower than the default. The center cooler is smoothed by the default settings. The fourth cooler is smoothed at near-maximum settings. The right cooler is smoothed at default settings, clicking the Smooth button twice.

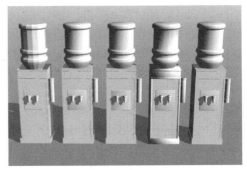

Figure 13–2 Different settings in the Polyhedrons dialog box to smooth the facets of this water cooler object.

Import Formats

Bryce imports 3D file formats based on the plug-ins in the Bryce applications plug-in folder. If there's a plug-in for that format in the folder, then Bryce can import it. With the release of Bryce 2.1 for Macintosh and Windows, there are two formats, DXF and 3DMF. This list may grow if and when MetaTools makes available additional import plug-ins for Bryce.

DXF

DXF stands for Digital Exchange Format, a 3D format invented by Autodesk, Inc. It's among the—if not *the*—oldest interchange file format used by 3D modelers. The file format is in ASCII text, and describes flat surfaces with polygons. There is no such thing as a curved line in a DXF format, just the presence of many polygons joined together in such a way as to appear curved. In a harsh way, a sphere is a multi-polygonal surface, a geodesic dome.

Although this popular format is ubiquitous, it is at the bottom of the 3D-model-format food chain, an unevolved file format creature. The type of information required to represent curved surfaces will require lots and lots of polygons. Lots of polygons calls for a larger file size, and a larger file size means more work for Bryce. But it's there, and it can be used to bring very non-landscapish objects into Bryce.

When you have multiple objects in a DXF format, they are imported into Bryce as a group of objects. To work with each one separately, ungroup. Or, bring the model into Solo mode, select each object, and assign them families and names for easier identification. You can also select each object and display as box (⌘-B or Ctrl+B). I find that this is a helpful way to keep track of all the objects right after importing them. After assigning a family label for an object, I change its wireframe to a box. It's helpful for knowing whether there are any parts to the model that are on my family identification "to do" list. Figure 13–3 shows a many-part model in a state of partial identification using this method.

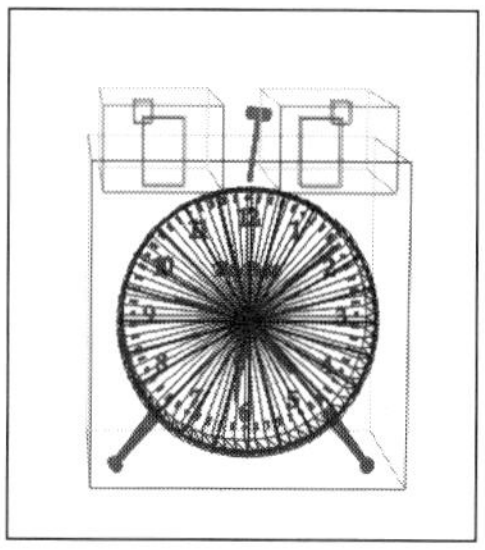

Figure 13–3 This clock model is comprised of several parts, some of which are set to Show As Box.

3DMF

Objects saved in the 3DMF (3D Metafile) format can be imported to Bryce. However, unlike DXF, the object is brought in as a cohesive whole. If it was made up of composite parts, they all were married together in some fashion between the time they left the modeling application and when they were imported into Bryce. The aforementioned multiple-object working tip used for DXF models does not work for 3DMF models.

Bryce's treatment of the 3DMF file format is incomplete. Bryce will not import texture nor color information from a 3DMF file. Also, Bryce will not successfully import an object that has a hole cut out of it (such as 3D text). Still, 3DMF objects tend to import faster into Bryce than do DXF objects.

Tips for Importing

So, before you import an image, are there any things you can do to make the process easier? More foolproof? Here are a few tips:

- *The Polygon-Memory ratio.* First, know that the greater the number the polygons in your model, the greater the amount of memory that is required to import and work with the model. Also, the more polygons, the slower Bryce will work when handling the model in both wireframe and rendering modes.

- *How you export can make a difference.* Different 3D modeling applications have different options to export a model. The options vary from application to application, but there are options that will result in models that import more successfully. If you find that a model is missing faces or is otherwise strange, then try re-exporting it from your modeling application using a different export option.

• *Selectively reduce model resolution.* While you're working on the model, reduce its resolutions in smart ways to reduce the overall polygon count. A cube needs only six faces, ever. If for some reason you have more detail in that cube, you'll force Bryce to deal with more unnecessary detail than it needs to. Find ways to make your models simpler where you can get away with it.

Other Modeling Applications

What applications create models to import into Bryce? Any modeling application that will enable you to save 3D objects as DXF or 3DMF.

Usual bevy of 3D modeling applications

If you have it, and it can make models and save them in either DXF or 3DMF format, then you can use it with Bryce. There are a couple of programs that merit special mention, since they go so well with Bryce.

Fractal's Poser

Fractal Design's Poser is an application for the creation and posing of three-dimensional human figures. (It is available for both Mac and Windows.) The posed figures can be exported in DXF or 3DMF format and then imported into Bryce. They can also be rendered inside of Poser and saved in an image file format, including a mask (Macintosh: PICT, Windows: TIF or BMP). Figure 13–4 shows the working process in Poser and the imported model in Bryce (unsmoothed and smoothed).

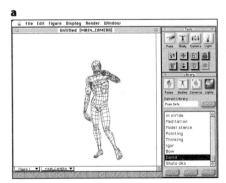

Figure 13–4 Poser and Bryce: a) Working with a figure in Poser; b) imported into Bryce and rendered with the model unsmoothed and smoothed.

Since Poser enables you to create surface textures to put on the body (more successfully than does Bryce), you may want to work in each application separately and then composite the results. Match the lighting in both applications, render the Poser figure, and import the completed Poser image as a picture object in Bryce.

Check out the CD-ROM gallery for many Poser uses in Bryce. The arrival of Poser 2 on the scene with better controls and clothing provides a nice evolutionary step in the Bryce-peopled worlds you can create.

Tree Pro

Tree Pro, created by Onyx Computing, is the flora to Poser's human fauna for Bryce. It is available in a Macintosh version, with a Windows version to ship during 1997. Tree Pro specializes in creating trees, in broad-leafed, conifer, and palm variations. Tree Pro is called a Parametric modeler, since you can control the different parameters of the tree, and it will generate a tree model from there. Figure 13–5 shows the interface with the different parameter controls for a broadleaf bush. Select and manipulate the individual parameters that go into creating a tree, from the size and height of the trunk, to the placement of the initial branches, their angle, how many branches and twigs emerge from each one, whether the branches are wavy or straight, and the number and shape of leaves.

Tree Pro will export the tree models as DXF or enable you to save them as PICT images.

The Tree Pro CD-ROM comes with quite a grove of already-created botanically correct trees. Unless husbandry is your obsession (and even if it is!), you can

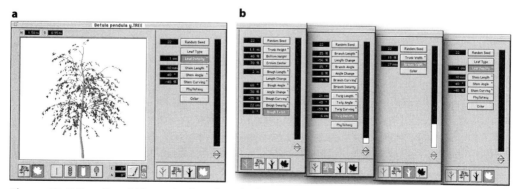

Figure 13–5 Tree Pro: a) The entire interface; b) detail of the parameter settings for different parts of a tree.

start with the trees provided on the CD-ROM. Then alter them to make your own trees. In many cases, the sizes of the tree models are a little high-powered for Bryce (unless you're aiming for the Guinness World Record in RAM). My random spot-checks of the resulting DXF tree files range from one to 11 MB a pop. Besides selecting the "pruning" function in the various parameter dialog boxes, the master export to

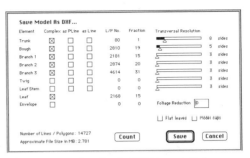

Figure 13–6 Tree Pro's DXF Export dialog box, with checkboxes for reducing the detail—and consequently the size—of the model.

DXF dialog box also has places where you can slim down the complexity—and therefore the size and render time—for the tree. The software's online documentation includes a section for reducing the size of tree models using that dialog box. (See Figure 13–6.)

If you're looking to create a series of flat image pictures, you can also make plain old PICTs using Tree Pro. (Since the Windows version is not out as of this writing, I don't know how the image file format will be handled.) However, the rendering that you see on the screen is the WYG of WYSIWYG. The PICT that is exported is an indexed color image (sad, but true). About the only advantage to that is that the background color is easily selectable in Photoshop in order to create an opacity mask, which, of course, is not automatically created by Tree Pro. Why use the rendered PICT image, then? You can take the same basic tree model, rotate it this way or that, generate a new random seed (what makes one tree look different from another), and each time save a PICT image. Placing those in distant parts of your Bryce scene will eat up far less RAM than if Bryce had to ray trace each of those lovely branches and leaves.

To make the test picture image shown in Figure 13–7, I first changed the image from an Indexed color to RGB, and put it on a separate layer (not the background). Then I deleted the entire background to change the old background to transparency. That was followed by a slight blur, to get rid of the "I am a pixellated bitmap image" appearance. The transparency area was saved as a separate channel, the background was made black, and the image was flattened. This transparency-then-blur ensures that the resulting selection mask completely matches the image area, and the black background will show up where the edges are, providing ever so slight enhanced contrast when the image renders.

Figure 13–7 Foreground tree models and background flat picture images of trees created with Onyx's Tree Pro.

Don't Model It Yourself

If you want to get your hands on a ready-made model, there are 3D data "clip art" companies that have a library of models available. In addition to the sets of models that are commercially available, there is an ftp site that has an extensive set of models created and uploaded by 3D artists from all over the world. It's called Avalon, and you can reach it by ftp or via the web. Usage rights for each model vary and are determined by the artist/owner who uploaded the model. Check it out at http://avalon1.viewpoint.com/. Contact information for the following companies is in Appendix A.

- *Viewpoint Data Laboratories.* Viewpoint has an extensive (and growing!) collection of models of just about anything and everything. They have a three-tiered level of detail: The Platinum Collection is the highest resolution, and is out of Bryce's league (unless, of course, you're that Guinness RAM Book of Records candidate). The Gold Collection are models that are lower in resolution, suitable for gaming environments. They also have a new collection, which is more suited for work using desktop machines as 3D Clip Art. There is a small selection of their datasets for you to check out in the Models folder on the CD-ROM.

- *Zygote.* Specializing in human forms and in characters, Zygote has a growing collection of models, many of which have been used in motion picture and gaming titles. Check out their sampling here on the CD-ROM.

- *Acuris.* This 3D model distribution company has set up a very special relationship with Bryce. Acuris has licensed Bryce and is combining it with a set of their own 3D animal and tree models to enable you to create an entire environment and populate it with 3D flora and fauna.

How 'bout Those Exports?

"If Bryce can import, then can it export?" you may wonder.

The unique look of Bryce is generated by the Deep Texture Editor, the Materials Composer, and the sky model and rendering engine. Theoretically, you could create something inside of Bryce and export it elsewhere, but that would only allow you to work with the geometry of the object, and not with those other important elements that make Bryce look like *Bryce*. However, there are times when you might want to do just that. So the question remains, can you export from Bryce?

The one thing that Bryce does uniquely and wonderfully—that *can* be exported— is create grayscale terrain maps. Any 3D modeling software that can take a grayscale image and generate a mesh model can use Bryce-made terrain maps. If you need to generate one outside of your 3D modeling application, then try out CyberMesh, by John Knoll. It is a Photoshop shareware plug-in (available for both Mac and Windows) that generates a grayscale-to-height DXF model based on the currently active Photoshop image.

To create an exported terrain, open up the Terrain Editor for your terrain. Copy the terrain. Exit the Terrain Editor. In Photoshop, create a new document. Paste. Then use the CyberMesh plug-in, located in the Export options under Photoshop's File menu. Depending on your RAM and the ultimate requirements in your target 3D application, you may need to reduce the size of the image. Then CyberMesh exports the image. You cannot export a set of already-positioned terrains as a whole, unless you view the entire scene from the top and do a distance or altitude render and then take *that* and export it to a DXF using CyberMesh.

Software Just for Bryce

Here are a couple of software applications that are created just for Bryce, or for similar grayscale-to-height-aware 3D software applications. They are both included on the CD-ROM.

Waves World

Waves World is Macintosh shareware created by Mark Hessenflow. (He's trying to get it ported to Windows, check his web site—listed in Appendix A—to see if there's a Windows version. If there isn't, and you write code for Windows—do it! The entire Bryce Windows community with be grateful.) Waves World addresses

the problem of creating waves that are meaningful for transitions between water and shore. A Brycean water infinite plane will have wave forms, but the waves aren't smart. They are unaware of land forms, and do not change in any way when they encounter Brycean shores. Real world waves *do* change their shape when they encounter land. Waves World creates smart wave forms based on the objects that the waves encounter.

Waves World's basic procedure starts when you load a PICT terrain graymap. From there, select the water level, add waves and adjust their direction, frequency and height (amplitude). Once you do that, Waves World will render wave forms, and will save the various image components that are a part of the wave. In Figure 13–8a, a terrain is in Waves World with a couple of waves (shown as circles with a direction indicator). When the wave is edited, a dialog box appears for changing the direction, frequency, and amplitude (see Figure 13–8b). Once you have placed your waves, render them to create a new PICT image form (see Figure 13–8c). When you save, Waves World will save any combination of the following PICT images: the original terrain, the land above water, the land below water, and the waves (water level).

When you have the completed wave map, import it into the Terrain Editor

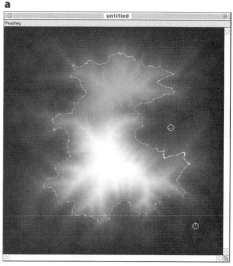

a

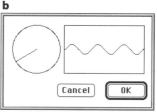

b

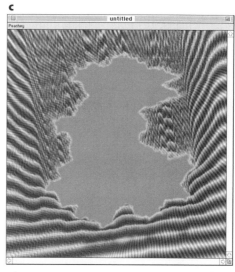

c

Figure 13–8 Waves World: a) The basic working window containing a terrain gray map, with shoreline and waves indicated; b) the Edit dialog box for the wave; c) the rendered wave (in Waves World) for this terrain gray map.

as a picture image. (You'll need to create a duplicate terrain object, of course!) The picture comes into the terrain editor way too tall, since the wave forms use the entire range of grayscale. So after bringing the wave image into the Terrain Editor, you'll need to reduce the overall height on the y axis. For this, I have been using numerical entries into the Object Attributes dialog box, and have been typing numbers between .5 and 1.0 (or so) in the Size y field. Your own situation may vary, but beware of an excessively high wave terrain wreaking havoc on your nice relaxing shoreline.

Before you spend much time in Waves World, two challenges pose themselves. The first is the placement, frequency, and amplitude of the waves. Once the waves hit one side of the object, they change. When they emerge on the other side, they become rather crazed. So think of Waves World as providing mostly one-sided waves. The second challenge is what to do about the relationship of land to water. Taken together, the one-sidedness and relation of the two call for terrains that have land on one side, water on the rest. In Figure 13–9, the land form is a crescent. This allows for some play with two wave forms that affect the water inside the crescent. But the crescent land shape also serves to contain the water. With a camera placement that's low enough, there's no need to worry about creating water on the other side of the terrain.

The close-up shoreline is one example of the way to incorporate a water terrain and a land terrain. For another solution to the same problem, I created a terrain, duplicated it, and then used the Terrain Editor's Zoom and Fit tools to increase the terrain area around the land forms. The first land form was a high resolution terrain. The terrain object was duplicated. In the Terrain Editor, I switched on the Zoom tool, then positioned the Zoom marquee. Once the marquee was positioned, a click on the Fit button caused all the existing terrain information to fit within that area, creating new virgin terrain outside of it. (That area outside became additional sea.) In order to take the newly-fit terrain information to Waves World, I copied the terrain, and clicked OK to leave the Terrain Editor.

Before switching to Waves World, I needed to make the newly-fit terrain match up with the first, high-resolution terrain. Enlarging on the x and z axes, and repositioning, aligned the two terrains. One was re-colored for ease of reference. (See Figure 13–10a.) The alignment steps were taken while looking at the scene in top view. The now correctly-positioned terrain with additional area is ready to have the waves applied to it.

In Waves World, I created a new document, pasted the terrain gray map from the clipboard, then created a wave terrain. (See Figure 13–10b.) Back in Bryce, I opened

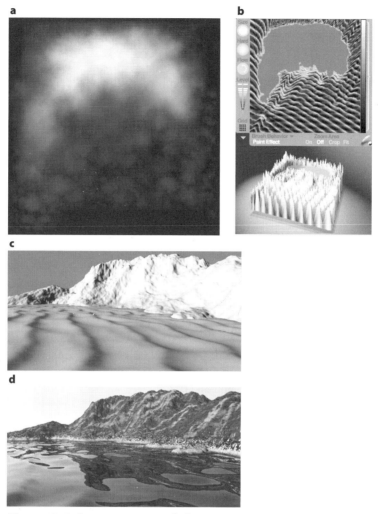

Figure 13–9 Crescent scene made from a terrain which allowed for lots of water on one side: a) Terrain gray map; b) resulting wave map shown in Terrain Editor; c) rendered scene with no textures; d) rendered scene with textures.

up the Terrain Editor for the newer Fit terrain, and imported the waves terrain. Changing the vertical scale and position of the terrain followed. Then I performed additional tweaks, including creating a duplicate of the wave terrain, applying the ocean floor terrain with additional detail, and resizing and repositioning it. The last technical problem to solve was to create additional water surfaces whether using squares or water-wave terrains without any land masses. The final image is shown in Figure 13–10c.

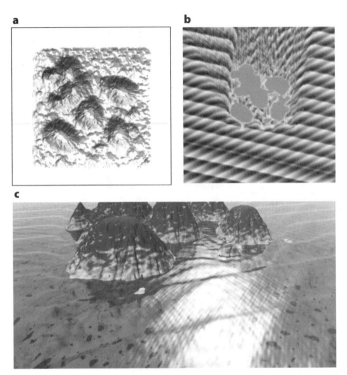

Figure 13–10 A wave terrain scene created by some Terrain Editor Zoom-tool-then-Fit trickery: a) Matching the fitted terrain (soon to be a wave) to the initial terrain in a top view render; b) the wave generated for the landmass; c) rendered image.

DEMView (Mac) and DEMvert (Windows)

As mentioned in the Terrain chapter, DEMView is Macintosh freeware software designed to convert DEM (Digital Elevation Model) files to grayscale picture images, so that you can create terrains that are based on actual earth elevation. Recreate actual places, especially in the United States from USGS (United States Geological Survey) topographic maps. Open up a nine-megabyte DEM file as a grayscale picture image and save portions of some or all of it. The software comes with an excellent ReadMe file for documentation.

One problem with the USGS data is that there are many more than 256 elevation levels (the number of grays in an 8-bit PICT or BMP). Likewise, Bryce can internally handle far more than 256 levels of gray. However, at this time, DEMView only works with the 256 levels of an 8-bit image. The 256 gray levels results in a terraced appearance to the terrain. In the future there may be a version of

DEMView that converts more information directly to a terrain form that Bryce can use. But the timing of that is at the mercy of those who hold Ken Badertscher's attention during his day job. In fact, this chapter would feature another cool Bryce utility that Ken has been working on, but the same day-job circumstances apply.

For Windows Brycers, there is a DEM conversion utility, DEMvert, that converts USGS DEMs into bitmapped images. It's here on the CD-ROM in the Dem info folder. Written by Tony Beeman, it takes a minimalist approach, allowing you to open the DEM and save the bitmap, without any selection tools or elevation analysis. If you want to work with some size other than the nine-megabyte DEM-sized area, you'll have to work in a separate image editing application. The previously-mentioned limitations with 256 gray levels applies to DEMvert as well.

POST-PROCESSING

You have your rendered Bryce image. Now that you have it, you can tweak it further in any image editing application.

Photoshop

Of course, anything that you can do to a digital image you can do to a Bryce render. The myriad options available to you in Photoshop can be applied to your Bryce image, from simple color correction to the lens flare (handy visual trick, that!) to compositing to a more radical image alteration.

When it comes to compositing Bryce images, be sure to use a mask render for the item you want to portray in other software. This technique is good as well if you want to create the same object with a different "states" (such as normal and highlighted) for mouse roll-overs in multimedia presentations.

There is something to watch out for, though. Bryce objects that have Transparency assigned in the Materials Composer do not render as masks. Look under the Mask Render section in Chapter 12, "Render Unto Bryce" for some tips.

Here's a fun Photoshop technique—it's the classic virtual photographic post-process to apply to a virtual landscape image. Scott Tucker (who wrote the sidebar at the end of Chapter 3, "Camera and View") paid an homage to the darkroom techniques for developing black and white photographic prints used by Ansel Adams. Far from a simple convert-to-grayscale, Tucker's image, "Ansel," employed some of the classic darkroom techniques—dodging and burning—to bring out the contrast and tonal range of the image, which began its virtual life as a full-color rendered image. (See Figure 13–11.)

Figure 13–11 A color Bryce image was converted to black and white using the virtual counterparts to traditional darkroom techniques in this homage to Ansel Adams, by Scott Tucker.

The DigARTS Garden Hose and Fractal Design Painter

Here's a post-processing technique that also fits into the "greening of Bryce" category. (More information on Bryce greenery is found at the end of Chapter 14, "Superlative Nature Imagery.") Use Fractal Design Painter and the Garden Hose, the brainchild of Dennis Berkla, to create foliage for your worlds. (The Garden Hose works with both the Macintosh and Windows versions of Painter.) The Garden Hose is a set of special Image Hose resources to paint foliage of many types. There are grasses, flowers, distant foliage, eucalyptus, jasmine, and more. You can use the Garden Hose to create foliage in a picture texture that is applied to an object before rendering, or to use on your completed render as some foliage-after-the-fact.

If you're creating image files to make as picture textures (the "before render" option), then make sure to activate the mask in the Nozzle palette. This paints the same image shape in your alpha channel, so that you can activate alpha channel transparency in Bryce and see only the foliage without the background. You may have to make some contrast adjustments, however, since most of the Garden

Hose options also paint a drop shadow in both the image and the alpha channel. For best results, you'll need to lose the shadow from the alpha channel.

In Figure 13–12b, the Image Hose has been used to create a seamlessly tiling image. (In Painter, selecting Pattern > Define Pattern will make brush strokes that wrap around the image. You may move your mouse or tablet stylus continuously in one direction as you paint, and when you reach the edge of the image area, the painted image wraps around to the other side as it applies.) The seamlessly tiled image is applied to a second terrain that's slightly higher in elevation than the first terrain, and rendered. (See Figure 13–12c.) Conversely, in Figure C13–13a and b (in the color section), after rendering a landscape image, the Garden Hose was used to add foliage detail to complete the landscape.

For more information and tips about ways to use the Garden Hose, check out the DigARTs website at http://www.dcs-chico.com/~digarts/.

Multimedia and QTVR

Multimedia is a post-processing event. After rendering is completed in Bryce, you take the result and further process the image to incorporate it into a multimedia product. Any multimedia authoring application that uses bitmapped images can use Bryce imagery. The one multimedia-type application that I want to focus on here is Quick Time Virtual Reality, since it ties in so well with Bryce renders.

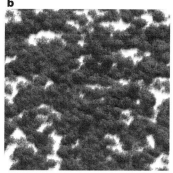

Figure 13–12 Garden Hose and pre-processing: a) Mountain image; b) picture texture; c) applied to upper terrain in rendered scene.

Quick Time Virtual Reality (QTVR) is a movie format available for both Macintosh and Windows. In a QTVR movie, you can navigate through areas at will. There are two different QTVR movie formats. The panorama movie places you in the center of a virtual cylinder. You can turn in any direction to look at any area of the cylinder. Zoom in or zoom out. Look up or look down.

When Apple first introduced QTVR, the technology was intended only for photography, and Apple offered specialized photographic equipment to create a perfect panorama and software that required stitching several image portions together. Some quick-thinking Brycers realized that the 360° Panorama Render would work beautifully to create a QTVR movie, merrily skipping the process of the careful photographic and stitch process. The Bryce QTVR process has been on the virtual reality creation scene ever since.

The second type of movie is an object movie. In an object movie, you can "pick up" an object and examine it on all sides by dragging vertically and horizontally. Object movies can be made for any two-axis animations, not necessarily an all-persepctive view of an object. On the CD-ROM there is an Adobe Acrobat document by Brian Strauss (dr. Zox) that describes how to make QTVR object movies by hand.

In more sophisticated multimedia presentations, the different views, called nodes, are linked together. When you have a multi-node movie, you can navigate through multiple QTVR panorama movies at will, exploring this part or that part as you see fit. Each node has a panorama view, and there are links to jump from one node to another. For an extensive example of this kind of interactive QTVR experience, check out Bill and Zox's Excellent Adventure on the CD-ROM (in the Gallery folder). It includes both types of QTVR movies. There are also plenty of other simpler single-node QTVR movies on the CD-ROM as well.

For those using a Macintosh, making your own QTVR panorama movies is quite simple. (If you're using Windows, you can prepare the Bryce image, but you'll need to get access to a Mac to turn it into a QTVR panorama movie.) In the first step, create a scene in Bryce and render it in 360° Panorama mode. Bryce even includes settings for easy rendering. When you have a completed render, take it into Photoshop and rotate it 90° (for this, rotate it counter-clockwise). This puts it in the vertical orientation that QTVR needs to create a panorama movie. You can also select File > Render to Disk... and check the rotate 90° option. If you've doubled the vertical dimension according to the directions in Chapter 12, "Render Unto Bryce," then do not let Bryce resize the image for you.

The Macintosh freeware applet Make QTVR Panorama allows you to make a panorama movie. It is located at http://quicktimevr.apple.com/sw/sw.html.

1. Launch Make QTVR Panorama. The applet gives you an open dialog box to load your PICT image. Load your image.

2. You do not see the image, but you get a dialog box for choosing options to make your movie. See Figure 13–14 for the Make QTVR Panorama dialog box. There are a set of options: Compression, Size, Horizontal Pan, Vertical Pan, and Zoom, along with options to name and choose the locations for the files that the panorama maker will create for you.

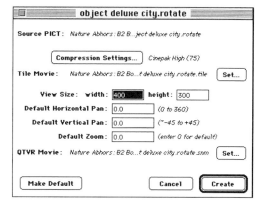

Figure 13–14 The QTVR Make Panorama applet dialog box.

3. Determine the Compression. The default option, Cinepak, will create cross-platform compatible QTVR movies.

4. Set the View Size. This option determines the size of your QTVR window when you open the movie. Make sure to choose dimensions that are no higher than the actual Bryce render image size.

5. Set the Horizontal and Vertical Pan. These options allow you to choose where the virtual camera focuses when you first open the QTVR movie. The horizontal rotation starts by focusing on the left edge (well, the right edge, too, since they end up being set next to one another). If the object you want to focus on is in the middle of your image (probably a more natural way to work when in Bryce, since Bryce's camera aim puts the part of the image that the camera sees in the center of the rendered strip), then you'll need to enter 180° to place the focal part of the render into the center part of your panorama movie.

Vertical Pan has a range of positive or negative 45° for looking up or down. Depending on your subject matter, you may find yourself wanting to adjust up or down.

6. Determine the Zoom. Since a QTVR panorama movie allows zooming in and out, you can set the default zoom. 100 is zoomed all the way in (very

blocky pixels, yuck!), and 0 is zoomed all the way out. For a nice pleasing look, start with something in the 0-50 range.

7. Once you have all those settings in place, click the Create button. After a bit of cogitating, you'll have a completed movie! Open it up in the QTVR Player and there you go!

ANIMATION

Since Bryce 1.0, bringing animation into the program has been a desire of most anyone who sees Bryce, including the developers. Until the animation version of Bryce ships, however, the only means to create animation is to do stop-motion animation, where objects or the camera is minutely changed frame by frame, and each frame is saved as a separate scene. A few zealous souls have devised the means to do so using tricky Excel spreadsheet calculations to map the position for each frame. On the CD-ROM in the Tips folder there is a file describing how to do so. It's for version 1.0 of the software, but the same rules apply. In fact, with the addition of the Object Attributes dialog box, some parts of Bryce's stop-motion animation have been made easier in version 2.1. (Yes, I know, I know, that's like comparing the relative speed of travel by horse to travel by foot in an era when many have their own private jets. Still, riding a horse is easier than walking.)

The developers have been at work on an animation version of Bryce. In the meantime, a full-length animation motion picture, "Planetary Traveler," has been created using a development version of Bryce (see more about the movie in Chapter 17, "Professional Brycing"). A trailer for the movie is on the CD-ROM, so you can see the state-of-the-art of Bryce animation a little before the animation version reaches the marketplace.

CHAPTER
FOURTEEN

Superlative Nature Imagery

They are wonderful to behold, and therefore in the summertime strangers come here from all parts of the world to see them. They cross snow-covered mountains, and travel through the deep valleys, or ascend for hours, higher and still higher, the valleys appearing to sink lower and lower as they proceed, and become as small as if seen from an air balloon. Over the lofty summits of these mountains the clouds often hang like a dark veil; while beneath in the valley, where many brown, wooden houses are scattered about, the bright rays of the sun may be shining upon a little brilliant patch of green, making it appear almost transparent. The waters foam and dash along in the valleys beneath; the streams from above trickle and murmur as they fall down the rocky mountain's side, looking like glittering silver bands.

HANS CHRISTIAN ANDERSEN, "THE GARDEN OF PARADISE,"
FAIRY TALES OF HANS CHRISTIAN ANDERSEN

IN THIS CHAPTER...

- At the feet of the Master—dissect some scenes by Eric Wenger, Bryce's creator

- Specific tips for certain nature effects

- Geology 101—how Earth formations occur and how to do them in Bryce

- Undersea worlds

- Rainy weather conditions

- How the "Lighthouse at Twilight" (Bryce default image) was made

In this chapter, we'll jump back and forth between the natural world "out there" and the virtual world of Bryce "in here." There is an interactive process of using Bryce and being outdoors. The best way to make natural-looking Bryce images is to spend some time outdoors observing the lay of the land. After you've worked in Bryce, you'll start noticing things about the environment—you'll observe geological structures, habitats, and atmospheric conditions. After inspecting the way things look in the natural world, you will apply your observations to your Brycean scenery. You'll set up your skies with haze and fog that's just so. Your terrains will benefit from all that careful scrutiny of the local land. Working in Bryce will give you a keener eye when you're out-of-doors.

To give you a head start on the reciprocal observation process, this chapter discusses some of the common solutions for making convincing nature scenery. Not all natural possibilities can be explored in detail in this (or any!) book. I will, however, explore some common tricks. With basic nature scene understanding and a few tricks as a foundation, you'll be able to continue on and more readily translate the outdoors to the inner workings of Bryce.

IN THE MASTER'S FOOTSTEPS: ERIC'S METHODS

The absolute master at creating nature scenes is Eric Wenger, creator of Bryce. After all, he wrote the software to tickle his own funny bone long before Kai, Phil, and Sree became involved with putting together a version for public consumption. Eric knows it best. The best school of instruction for getting natural-looking images is to study the methods of his Brycean madness. This section will do just that, exploring a few of his images and examining the characteristics common to superlative scenery. After reading this section, take a look at Eric's scenes on the Bryce application CD and on the CD-ROM for this book as well.

Here is a brief list of the principles that can be deduced from Eric's images. Each one is discussed in turn. If you want a master reference list of masterful techniques, then come back to this place.

• Create multiple terrains.

• Create a sense of relative distance from the camera with terrain size and resolution.

• Put all the detail right in front of the camera.

• Enlarge the terrains that go way off in the background (usually).

• Create a sense of scale with atmosphere and materials settings.

• Pay attention to those sky settings!

I'll explore these concepts by examining three scenes (see Figures 14–1 and 14–2). They are shown in final rendered state and in wireframe from top view. The final renders are also shown in Figure C14–3 in the color section. Figure 14–1, "Fjord Mud," is on the Bryce application CD-ROM in the Eric Landscapes folder. Figure 14–2 has two images, "Abisko Pine Trees" and "Valley." You can find the scene documents for both scenes on the Bryce software CD-ROM.

Terrain Placement: Create for Depth

Eric's placement of terrains—their position and size—provides a sense of scale in his nature scenery. Multiple terrains are placed in the scene, and their resolutions and wireframe sizes vary depending on the distance from the camera.

Wireframe Analysis from the Top Down

There is a top view wireframe for each of the three scenes in Figures 14–1 and 14–2. Notice how the camera is at one end and the small terrain sizes are closest to the camera in "Fjord Mud" and "Abisko Pine Trees." Farther away, the terrain sizes become gargantuan in comparison. In each of the figures, the ground is highlighted so that you can compare the relative sizes of the terrains. Nearly all of the terrains have been enlarged from their original sizes. The farther away from the camera, the larger the terrains are. This establishes a sense of scale.

Now that I've told you one thing, I'm going to contradict myself right here! You don't *always* have to have larger terrains in the distance. "Valley" (in Figure 14–2) successfully uses several terrains of the same size. Here, the mountains are all high detail and large size. With the proper camera perspective, the result is a nice sense of overall distance and grandeur from the heights of a snowy mountain top.

The figures have numbers indicating the terrain resolution set by the Grid pop-up menu in the Terrain Editor. Close to the camera, they are generally 256 or 512. But far away, the amount of resolution detail does not increase in proportion to the increase in wireframe size. The larger the terrain's resolution, the more RAM that is required to process your scene. When the terrain is far away from the camera, the detail is not required.

"Fjord Mud" has high detail placed right in front of the camera. The four terrains in the foreground (shown in an enlargement) are mostly medium- to high-resolution. Their wireframe sizes have been *reduced,* creating even higher detail (see Figure 14–1).

Fjord Mud

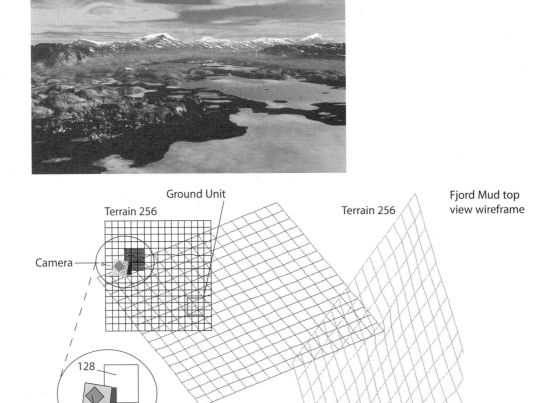

Ground Unit

Terrain 256

Terrain 256

Fjord Mud top
view wireframe

Camera

128

64

256

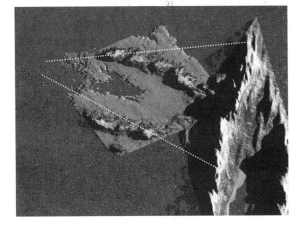

Fjord Mud top
view rendered

Figure 14–1 "Fjord Mud."

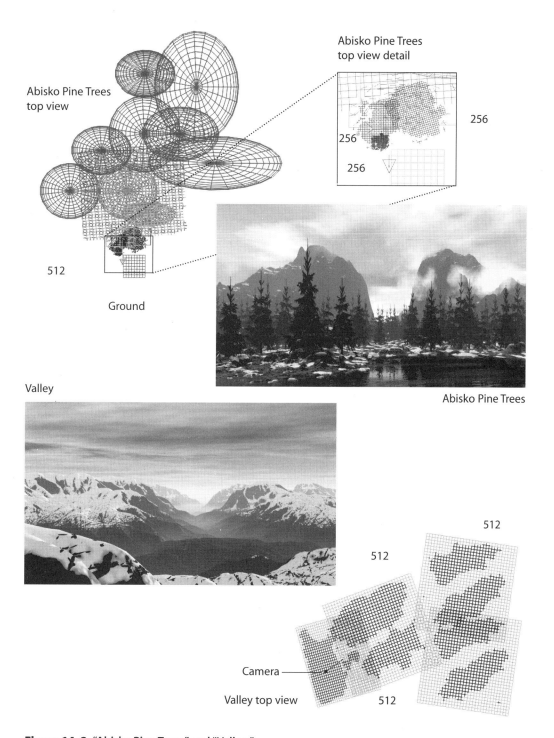

Abisko Pine Trees
top view

Abisko Pine Trees
top view detail

256

256

256

512

Ground

Abisko Pine Trees

Valley

512

512

512

Camera

Valley top view

Figure 14–2 "Abisko Pine Trees" and "Valley."

Open up the scene documents on the CD. Notice that the terrain maps for many of them are the same. You can also see this trend toward sameness in the top view render of "Fjord Mud" as well as the scene file for "Valley." You don't need to create and painstakingly perfect a separate G2H map for every terrain. You can use the same one and change the terrain's orientation (rotate it around on the y-axis). Or make it a bit different by a slight tweak, if you must.

Having analyzed the scenes from the top view, you may think that the general order of business is to create and place terrains from the top view. A potential top view formula would go like this:

Start in top view. Create a terrain. Duplicate it and move it away from the camera. Enlarge it some. Stretch it out on one dimension. Duplicate the terrain again. Move it over and back a bit. Enlarge it. Rotate it around. Now create a ground. Give the terrains and ground a material setting. Add haze to taste. Go back to camera view. Sashay the camera back and forth to get the right perspective. Render. Voilá! Instant natural scenery!

This will work, since it bows respectfully to the Major and Minor Deities of depth and scale. But the scenes shown here weren't created that way. Eric created them while in main view, with forays into top view to make adjustments. In the next section, I discuss camera perspective as part of the scene-building process.

Camera Perspective

Each of these scenes was created for a one-camera perspective. They were not meant to sustain the perspective of a complete circular panorama. In all of these, the camera's active image area determines the location of the terrains in the three-dimensional world. In the "Fjord Mud" example, shown rendered in top view, the lines roughly indicate the edge of the camera's field of view (see Figure 14–1). Like a movie set where all of the beams and frames can't be seen by the camera, Bryce terrains end abruptly off-camera. This is a natural outcome of the process of working in camera view; as long as the object looks right through the camera, it doesn't matter how it appears elsewhere.

If you are going to create a scene for a 360° render or for animation, you'll have to work a bit differently. Smaller, detailed terrains are close to the camera, with larger terrains spread out along the perimeter. (More on 360° renders can be found in Chapter 12, "Render Unto Bryce.")

In "Fjord Mud" and "Abisko Pine Trees," the camera is located close to the ground. If you were to somehow take a Fantastic Voyage and actually enter Bryce Space, your eyes would be located—you guessed it—close to the ground. The mountains would be huge in comparison—hundreds of times taller than you are. Be sure to select the Eye-Level Camera item from the Camera Option pop-up menu to put you in your humble place. As a result, those massive terrains will look just that—massive. In "Valley," the camera is on higher ground, atop a terrain. The same "be close to the ground" rule applies; it's just that you're close to higher-elevation ground. The Eye-Level Camera item does not work for higher elevations.

Material Frequency Detail

The terrain placement and camera position are adjusted to give an overall sense of scale. Perpetrate this illusion of realism in the Materials Composer. In these scenes, the amount of surface detail is adjusted to ensure authenticity. The adjustments are most critical when an object is right in front of the camera. When the object looks blurry in the foreground, increase the frequency to add more detail. There are a couple of ways to do so. In the Materials Composer, adjust the Frequency control. In the Deep Texture Editor adjust the Frequency sliders for each of the different components or adjust the frequency of the noise itself. These detail-increasing controls are covered in greater detail in Chapter 9, "Material World."

Material Setting: Ambient

For a sense of cohesion of all elements in these scenes, the objects' Illumination settings have been given identical Ambience amounts in the Materials Composer. If each of your object's ambient settings differs, the scene won't look natural. The discrepancy between objects will be most apparent in their shaded areas. On occasion you can beautifully exploit different ambient settings. If you have a terrain with dark rock and another with snow, the ambient settings will differ. However, in most cases, giving all your objects a consistent ambient setting will make them live harmoniously in your Brycean habitat.

Sky Settings for Depth and Realism

How did Eric set up his skies in these scenes? The sky settings contribute to the natural look. For my analysis of the three scenes, I'll focus on haze, sky colors, freestanding clouds, and the choice of atmosphere.

Haze and Sky Settings

The Haze setting provides a feel of true depth and perspective. All the strategic placement and sizing of terrains does nothing without adequate haze to infuse distance into the scene. The objects close to the camera are clear; the distant mountains *are* far away. The presence of haze—in generous proportions—is common to these and most of Eric's landscape scenes.

What differs from scene to scene is Haze Color. The Haze Color for "Fjord Mud" is a pale bluish gray, and "Abisko Pine Trees" has a pale azure haze. In "Valley" the haze is lavender. In these instances, the Haze Color generally matches the overall color tone of the image. Don't take this as a strict rule, however.

If you *do* want to take a color observation as a rule of thumb for realism, I offer you this one: The color of ambient light should be in medium values on the cool side of the spectrum. Not only does it influence areas in shadow, but it influences the color of other areas in the scene. In "Abisko Pine Trees," the Ambient Color is a medium blue. In "Fjord Mud," it is a pale aqua—most noticeable in the cloud layer above. "Valley" has a mauve-gray Ambient Color, which is most noticeable as the color of the snow when in shadow.

Shadow color depends on three things: the Shadow setting in the Sky & Fog Palette, the Ambient Color, and the Haze Color. In "Fjord Mud," gray ambient and blue haze mix to create the overall shadow color. The Shadow setting is set to maximum. Of course, you can have one color or the other dominate, depending on the amount of haze in your scene. An increase in haze will always make that color dominate the shadow area.

Clouds Are Huge

Freestanding clouds can add to a scene's sense of realism. Look at the top view of the "Abisko Pine Trees" image. The spheres are the clouds. They are huge, especially when compared to the terrains in the scene's foreground. This is not merely a matter of creating a sphere, flattening it somewhat, and then applying a cloud material setting to it. No, these puppies are grandiose. Remember, this is a *world* you're creating, and clouds are large-scale objects. Creating and seeding clouds is not something you've had day-to-day practice in—until now. So think big!

Eric's Scenery Recap

Here's a summary of all of the tips I covered during my examination of Eric Wenger's scenes:

- *Number of Terrains.* There is more than one terrain in these scenes, ranging from four to seven.

- *Terrain Proportions.* Close to the camera, terrains are relatively small; farther away, they are spread out and larger.

- *Terrain Size.* Terrains close up and far away use a size of 256 × 256. When the terrains are close to the camera, higher detail is needed. Far away, the same terrain resolution suffices even when the terrain wireframe is greatly enlarged.

- *Detail Right in Front of the Camera.* The greatest amount of detail is right in front of the camera.

- *Low Camera Position.* All of the camera views are close to the ground, whether at ground level elevation, or close to terrain level at a higher elevation. Since the terrains far away are large, the low camera position tells you that you are in a big, big world.

- *Carefully Calculated Material Detail Frequency.* The material setting frequency is finessed to give the proper sense of scale. If repeating patterns or bump maps are too large, it makes the object seem too small.

- *Haze to Create Distance.* Haze provides a visual cue that the object is located far away.

- *Cool Ambient Colors.* Make your Ambient Color cool and medium-valued for realistic outdoor coloring.

- *Huge Clouds.* Spheres used for freestanding clouds are not small. Make 'em big!

GEOLOGY 101: MOUNTAINS AND VALLEYS

Making landscapes in Bryce is not about creating things that you think up in your head (well, then again, yes it is!). Even a fantasy landscape looks impressive because it's based on some sort of reality, or at least a perception of reality. To aid your reality perception process, this section examines some basic matters of geology, or how Earth was formed. I'm not talking about the big plate tectonics stuff all the world over but rather what happens on a local level.

If you've ever been to a scenic spot, you may have wondered how Earth got to be the way it is. How were the canyons formed? Why do the mountains there look different from the mountains you're used to seeing at home?

How New Mountains Are Created

New mountains are created in four basic ways:

1. *Volcanic Activity.* Magma from inside Earth forces its way to the surface. Lava spills onto the surface, thereby creating successive layers that build a mountain. Volcanoes are known for the central hole or crater from which lava emerges at the surface. Mt. St. Helens in Washington state is one notorious example of such volcanic activity.

   Volcanoes in Bryce. Use the Filtering control in the Terrain Editor to draw a downward line to make the top portion of the terrain descend (see Figure 14–4a). Figure 14–4b shows two Bryce volcanic cones. One is level at the top; the other is jagged after applying Noise in the Terrain Editor.

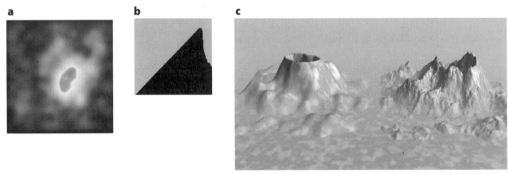

Figure 14–4 Volcano terrain map: a) The grayscale map; b) Filter settings to create volcanic dent; c) two rendered volcano terrains.

2. *Compression.* Land masses are forced together. Where they collide, Earth's crust shortens and becomes thicker. What Earth's crust would call "thick" is what we call mountains. This process gives us folding and faulting and earth-shattering experiences. The Grand Tetons in Wyoming are mountains created by the compression of Earth's crust.

   Compressed Land Masses in Bryce. There is no characteristic "look" to this type of mountain-making method. Just click the Terrain icon on the Create Palette and you'll be okay. However, bear this in mind: If land masses come together quickly, there will be a rapid rise with high relief faces where mountain-building vastly outpaces erosion. If the two land masses are compressed together more slowly, slopes won't be as steep and there will be more erosion.

3. *Extension.* Earth's crust is stretched apart. As it is stretched and thinned, cracks form, creating new faults. Some of the crustal blocks sag into the thinner crust along these faults (see Figure 14–5). Those crustal blocks that don't sag become mountains by default (pun intended!). The Basin and Range Province of Arizona and Nevada was created by extension.

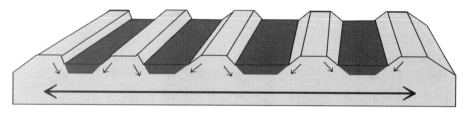

Figure 14–5 Extension: As Earth's crust is stretched apart, faults form and matter sags into the thinner crust along the faults.

Extension Mountains in Bryce. Extension mountains create an alternating sequence of parallel mountain ranges and basins. Set up a ground terrain with multiple terrains for a basin-and-range effect.

4. *Broad Upwarping.* A large mass of crust bulges upward, creating broad mountains. The Black Hills of South Dakota were created by broad crustal upwarping.

Broad Upwarping in Bryce. Enlarge your terrain with the Proportional Resize tool and then reduce it on the *y*-axis (height) for extremely broad rolling hills.

Then, on the other hand, there's the matter of valleys. Once the mountains are there, how are the valleys created?

Glaciers

Some landscapes have been formed by glacial erosion. During the ice age, massive ice sheets, drawn by gravity, crept downhill ever so slowly. In the battle between ice and land, these massive glaciers won. They carved a path for themselves, leaving behind huge sweeping U-shaped valleys as they retreated.

The "Abisko Pine Trees" scene in Figure 14–2 has a broad U-shaped valley. Although a peek at the terrain from top view shows that the valley does not extend over a long distance (proper glacier-formed valleys do), it has the right shape.

Create a Brycean glacier by using brush tools. In the Terrain Editor, use a brush tool with the elevation set to low (dark). Make the brush wide, soft, and set the Flow (opacity) to low-moderate. Or, use the brush tool in Photoshop and set the apply mode to Multiply. Either way, wield that brush and cut a wide swath in your terrain. Your brush is now the glacier. (How's that for being a virtual ice mass?) Figure 14–6a shows a normal terrain, which was taken into Photoshop. The terrain was then brushed with a large (150 pixel) brush in Photoshop using the Multiply mode (see Figure 14–6b). The final rendered terrain has the characteristic U-shape (see Figure 14–6c).

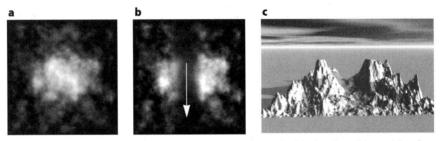

Figure 14–6 Brycean glacier making: a) A normal terrain; b) after brushing with a fat brush; c) the rendered terrain.

Faults

All the world over, Earth's crust has cracks, or faults. Add faults and diagonal roughness to your terrains by using the Sawtooth control in the Terrain Editor. When you run diagonal lines through your terrains, the land masses break up as though different layers of rock had shifted. It may be San Andreas running through your terrain, or it may be a little localized action.

Eroded Canyons

How are canyons created?

The Colorado Plateau, in the southwest United States, has over 30 wilderness areas set aside—either as national parks, national monuments, or national recreation areas—because of their scenic beauty. The Plateau is home to such wonders as Zion National Park, Bryce Canyon National

Park, the Grand Canyon, and Canyonlands National Park. When it comes to erosion, this region's geology beckons a closer look.

Go to your library or bookstore and peruse any publications that have pictures of the American Southwest (*Arizona Highways Magazine, Islands in the Sky, Tony Hillerman Country,* Time-Life books, and so on). There are many places with fascinating land formations that are worth studying.

How did this type of land come into being? Once, the entire area was under water, depositing layer upon layer of sedimentary rock. Eventually, the water receded. That was the beginning—layers of rocks.

Then along came some source of erosion— more water. Combine that with vast amounts of time, some wind, and Earth's gravity, and voilá! Layer cake geology!

How are canyons formed? At the base of the canyon is usually a river (or wash or arroyo). Depending on the hardness of the rock that the water cuts through, different types of canyons are formed. Figure 14–7 shows different types of valleys formed by erosion, depending on the hardness of rock. The darker substance is hard rock; the lighter substance is soft rock. Hard-rock valleys are narrow and V-shaped; soft-rock valleys are wide and V-shaped. Alternating layers of rock are called stair-step canyons.

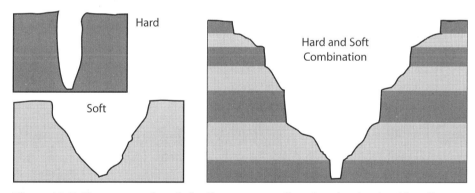

Figure 14–7 Three types of eroded valleys: narrow valleys from hard rock; wide valleys from soft rock; stair-step valleys from alternating layers of rock.

Soft Rock

Water cutting through soft rock will make canyons that are shaped like a wide V. As the water washes away portions of the ground, higher rock breaks off and follows gravity's inexorable pull down to the water source, where it is washed away. The process continues, deepening and widening the V-shaped valley.

Making Soft-Rock Valleys in Bryce

To make Bryce have soft-rock canyons, you don't have to do much to change the default terrains. Make the canyon walls the shape that you want them using the Terrain Editor's Filtering tool. That little diagonal line is like a cutaway side view of the shape of the mountain or valley (see Chapter 8, "Terrains, Symmetrical Lattices, and the Terrain Editor" for more details on this). Since it's already V-shaped (well, half of a V-shape), you don't have to do much else to shape it that way. To make the valley broader, stretch out the terrain using the Resize controls on the Edit Palette. In Figure 14–8, a terrain was widened via the Edit controls to make a wider valley.

Figure 14–8 Soft rock V-valley.

Hard Rock

Over time, water acts like a saw, digging a deep gulch into the rock. Canyons formed in hard rock will be deep, narrow, and V-shaped. Water cuts through just the one section of rock, but the newly exposed rock is more resistant to erosion. See Figure 14–7 for a side view diagram of this type of hard-rock valley.

Set up your Bryce images two ways. You can try to get all of these effects with one terrain. But there will probably not be enough terrain detail once you put your camera in there. So try the second alternative. Set up multiple terrains, where each terrain is a portion of the deep gorge walls. Four terrains, two on each side, is a good start. You may want to have more if your scene calls for it.

The scene in Figure 14–9 was created to resemble that kind of canyon. The terrains are all set up sideways to represent the canyon walls. From the

Figure 14–9 Hard rock canyon with vertical walls was created by standing a set of terrains on their side.

camera angle, you're not even able to see the canyon's rims, so no terrains are placed there.

Vertical Cliffs

Vertical cliffs are formed in rock that is generally hard but which has softer areas. As water cuts through an area where the softer rock is under some hard rock, the softer rock is worn away, undercutting the harder layer of rock above. The weight of the rock causes the overhanging rock to break off, thereby forming a sheer vertical surface.

Making Vertical Cliffs in Bryce

Form vertical cliffs using the Filtering tool. You can also create cliffs by putting in a vertical drop-off using the Filter tool. Drag the cursor so that there's a vertical drop off.

You can also exaggerate vertical cliff faces by enlarging the terrain on the *y*-axis.

Stair-Step Canyons: Mix and Match Rocks

In the formation of sedimentary rock, multiple layers of different types of rock were deposited at different times under different conditions. When water cuts through more than one layer of rock, each layer erodes in its own way. Where hard rock alternates with soft rock, the manner of erosion alternates as well. Hard rock erodes to form vertical cliff formations. Soft rock erodes in gentle sloping formations. The resulting series of straight cliffs interspersed with gentler slopes forms a "stair-step" canyon. See Figure 14–7 for a side view diagram. The most famous example of a stair-step canyon is the Grand Canyon.

To make stair-stepped terrain, use the Filtering tool in the Terrain Editor.

Figure 14–10 shows the process of creating a stair-stepped canyon. The canyon begins with a meandering river (see Figure 14–10a). The Terrain Editor coaxed it into a broader terrain by a click on the Erode button (see Figure 14–10b). After the basic shape was created, the terrain was inverted. Then the terrain was stair-stepped by an apply on the Filtering control (see Figure 14–10c) to result in the terrain map shown in Figure 14–10d. With materials and haze, Figure 14–10e is the rendered result.

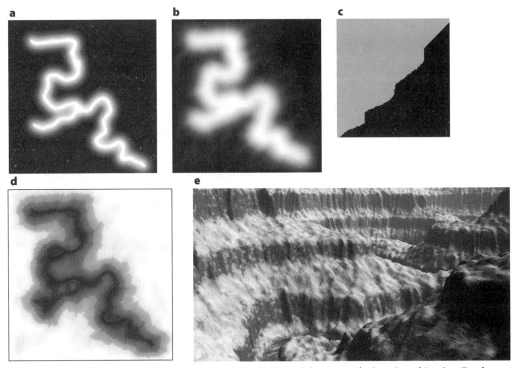

Figure 14–10 Creating a stair-step canyon: a) Beginning with a meandering river; b) using Erode to broaden the terrain in the Terrain Editor; c) stair-step filtering on the inverted terrain; d) resulting terrain map; e) final rendered canyon.

Volcanoes

Earlier, I discussed volcanoes as one way new mountains are born. A volcano can be the beginning of the mountain's life. Later, after time and erosion have worn down the volcanic combination of hard and soft rock, a different type of volcanic terrain develops. The hard and soft rock are a result of the volcanic birth. The volcano erupts, spewing material everywhere. The channel through which lava passes is called a root, or throat. Molten magma that subsided back into the throat, never erupting, is harder than the surrounding pile of volcanic debris. Over time the surrounding apron of debris from the outer volcano erodes away, leaving the now-solid core of harder rock that remained in the neck. That becomes a cylindrical high plateau or spire.

Shiprock in New Mexico and other dramatic vertical rocks of the American Southwest are ancient volcano plugs. Make your own by using the Subcontours control and the Filtering tool in the Terrain Editor. Figure 14–11a shows a volcanic plug scene and 14–11b, the subcontoured terrain that created it.

a

b
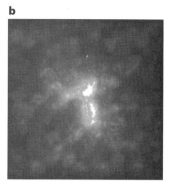

Figure 14–11 Volcanic plugs: a) The rendered scene; b) terrain map with Subcontours applied.

MULTIPLE TERRAINS

The earlier discussion of multiple terrains focused on the use of several different-sized terrains placed in different locations in order to create a sense of depth and scale in the scene. But there is also a way to use multiple terrains in close proximity with one another for a different natural effect. Portions of one terrain protrude from another to create realistic image detail. Stones scattered over a landscape; high-relief cliff faces emerging from a gradually sloping valley; rock formations that jut at an angle—all can be created by popping one terrain out of another. The element common to all is one terrain emerging from another. There are peculiarities with each, the lurid details of which I divulge in these pages.

Stones 'n Water

This first technique allows you to scatter stones across a landscape or plop them in shallow waters. The foreground of the "Fjord Mud" image was created this way. Different rock elements protrude from the water. The stones are in a separate terrain positioned under the main water plane or the main terrain. (Spain has nothing to do with it, 'enry 'iggins!) The stone terrain varies in height. It is lower in most places, except, of course, where the stones pop through the top. Figure 14–12 is a side view diagram of two terrains. The stone terrain pokes through the main one.

Figure 14–12 Side view of one terrain poking out of another.

Terrain Stone Shaping

There are two things necessary to create nice boulder-like stones: The stones should have a pleasing rounded shape, and they should be distinct from one another. To create the rounded shape, your terrain map should have diffused blotches of gray. If your G2H map has points of light, you will create pointy rocks, which won't be as convincing. So, to make stones that *are* convincing, use a few specific Terrain Editor tricks.

1. Create a terrain. In the Terrain Editor, enlarge it to at least 256.

2. To get your diffused patches of gray, try applying Mound or Subplateaus (or both). Subplateaus has a definite left-creep effect on the terrain. To put the terrain back in the center again, activate the Zoom area, position the marquee so it occupies most of the terrain canvas area—but is on the right—and then click the Fit button. Deactivate the Zoom area.

3. Follow that with an apply of Subcontours to make the stones distinct.

The areas in between stones are darker, thereby making each one "freestanding." The rendered result of this process is in Figure 14–13.

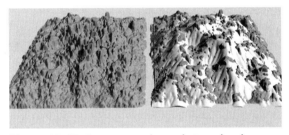

Figure 14–13 A stony terrain ready to poke above water or another terrain.

Of course, another way to create stones is to take that ol' paintbrush and put a dollop of light gray or white pixels on each place that you desire a rock to be. For the squarish boulder-like effect, pass your rocks through that subplateau control, or in Photoshop, try processing a terrain gray map with a Diffuse filter with a Lighten mode.

Obviously there is more than one way to create stone boulders. Consider this a starting point and don't ignore the little leanings that strike you along the way.

Angled Terrains

Not all rock formations are conveniently oriented vertically. Some rocks jut from the ground at an angle. If you rotate the terrain so that it is at an angle, you'll get the very unreal result of the higher edge poking out from the ground. Not cute.

Here's a method to get around that high edge: Create the elusive angled terrain *with overhangs.* The secret to making terrains with angled orientations is in the Edit Palette. For this, make sure that you have set the Edit controls to work in World Space.

Recipe for a Terrain Overhang

1. Create a terrain. (See Figure 14–14a.)

2. In the Edit Palette, rotate along the *z*-axis so that the terrain is tilted diagonally as you look at it from the front. (See Figure 14–14b.)

3. Then, shorten or heighten the terrain along the *y*-axis. (See Figure 14–14c.)

4. Rotate back on the *z*-axis so that the bottom of the terrain is level again. Notice that the peaks of your mountain are all drooping toward one side. Instant overhang! Shortening and heightening cause the terrain to lean in opposite directions. (See Figure 14–14d.)

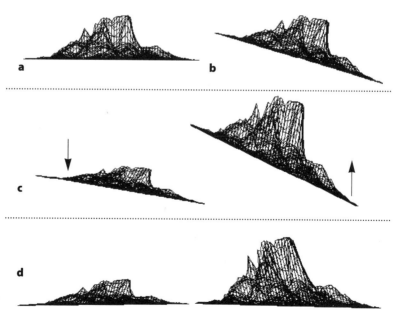

Figure 14–14 Creating an overhang: a) Beginning terrain; b) rotated; c) shortened or heightened; d) rotated back to level.

a

b

c
heighten

d
rotate

c
shorten

d
rotate

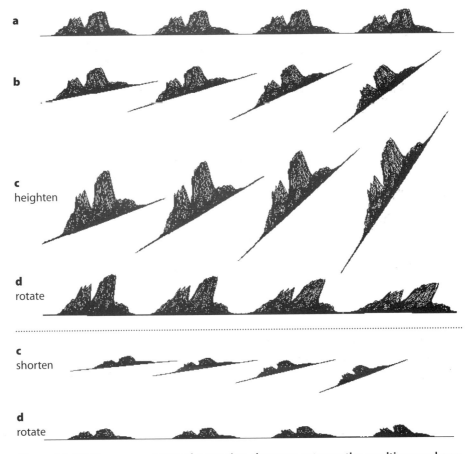

Figure 14–15 The more extreme the rotation, the more extreme the resulting overhang.

a

b

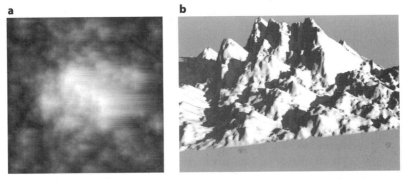

Figure 14–16 a) Photoshop's Wind filter applied to a terrain, resulting in b) an angled effect.

The more you rotate the terrain before changing it along the *y*-axis, the more extreme the terrain's angle will be (see Figure 14–15). The parts of the figure are marked a, b, c, and d to match the steps from the previous recipe.

Look at angled terrains from another angle, all you Photoshop fans. Take a terrain map into Photoshop and apply the Wind filter. The resulting terrain map is lighter on one side than another

Figure 14–17 Jutting rocks: an angled terrain placed below another terrain.

(see Figure 14–16a). This creates a leaning geological formation of another sort (see Figure 14–16b).

For the terrain's surface appearance, give the 3D Solid Texture an angled setting. Rotate the noise in the Deep Texture Editor's Set Noise... dialog box to shift the grain to an angle.

Finally, take any of these terrains and plop them under a regular terrain for those jutting rock protrusions. See Figure 14–17.

UNDERSEA WORLDS

One of the disadvantages of being creatures with lungs is that we don't have the same opportunities to observe undersea landscapes as we do basic mammal-inhabiting landscapes. But don't let this stop the Jacques Cousteau fans among you from creating undersea scenes. Here are a few things to bear in mind while you create exotic waterlogged vistas.

The undersea world has two limits: the sea floor below and the water's surface above. When creating undersea worlds using Bryce, use these two objects to provide the limits of your watery world: the ground primitive becomes the sea floor, and an infinite plane becomes the surface water above. Add terrains to taste. Terrains that go above the surface of the infinite plane are all the more convincing.

Sky & Fog settings make your sea look as realistic as possible. Set them to make your undersea world cool and murky. Besides water, there are plankton, minerals, and nutrients suspended in this liquid soup! You won't give that impression if you have a crystal-clear "sky." A high Haze setting (70 or more) will give everything its briny appearance. The Altitude setting also affects the haze. On a clear day, you can never see forever underwater. Haze Color is the predominant Sky & Fog setting that gives your sea its color. Keep your colors on the cool side: blues, greens, olives, drab browns, purples. Crank back the saturation so that they aren't so vivid, unless, of course, you're in a tropical undersea world.

Combine the haze with a complementary Fog Color. Fog will cling to the sea floor, so you can create a second localized murk color. Give fog a high amount and low height. You needn't keep the color aqua-cool. Sandy colors and drab olives as well as deep ultramarines will give you some intriguing sea effects.

Figure C14–18 (see the color section) shows the same sea scene using different colors.

Creating Underwater Plant Life

To create underwater plant life for your scene, you will have to coax Bryce to grow seaweed. Use primitives and wrap plant forms around them, whether they are picture textures or textures generated within Bryce's texture generator.

Figure 14–19 shows a series of undersea plant studies. Inverted cones, spheres, symmetrical lattices, and rocks make different types of seaweed. For each of the rock objects in the figure, there are two stone objects of the same shape and nearly identical size. The inner stone object is your normal stone. Then it is duplicated and enlarged ever-so-slightly. The outer rock is given a seaweed mossy plant material, with alpha-driven transparency so that the rock underneath shows through.

Figure 14–19 Seaweed studies.

A RIVER RUNS THROUGH IT

To make a meandering river, create a terrain that is fairly flat. Copy it to the clipboard and open up Photoshop. Using the Brush tool, paint a meandering path through the terrain. Remember, water doesn't usually travel in a straight line. It can, at times, but it usually meanders.

Figure 14–20a shows an image created from a Julia Set in the KPT Fractal Explorer. The wireframe and the Julia Set river source are shown in Figure 14–20b. A Julia Set has the right S-shapes of a river. After a bit of cleanup, it was made into a terrain, where a river ran through it!

a

b

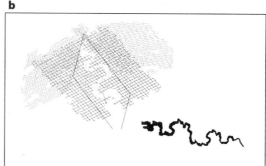

Figure 14–20 River created from Julia Set: a) Rendered image; b) top view wireframe and Julia set source.

For the riverbed terrain, the darker part is the river. Create a plane in the scene. Stretch it out to fill the same area as the riverbed. The plane becomes the river surface. Lower it into the river terrain.

If you've got a waterfall in your scene, then this method won't work. For a river that turns into a waterfall, you'll have to create the water surface from a terrain. A copy of the land terrain is a good place to start, as it will follow the contours of that particular area. Here's a very quick description of the waterfall terrain. A thorough recipe can be found in Chapter 8, "Terrains, Symmetrical Lattices, and the Terrain Editor."

Make your waterfall terrain have two flat levels. The higher level is the water surface before the fall, and the lower level is the pool or river below. To fit the waterfall or a limited body of water snugly in your terrain, you'll need to clip off the unused portions of the terrain. See Figure C14–21 in the color section.

RAINY WEATHER

To create sheets of rain that fall from your clouds, create a plane (not an infinite plane or an airplane!). Give it a material setting with a 2D Picture texture. Some of them are supplied on the CD. A nice, smudgy rain-falling image is good for that. This scene by Eric Wenger (see Figure 14–22) uses grayscale PICT images to create rain smudges.

The 2D Picture texture is used again as its own Opacity Map. With alpha-driven Transparency to cut away the excess, you have a rain smudge. This image, shown from top view (Figure 14–22a), shows the placement of the weather-smudge rain sheets amidst the clouds.

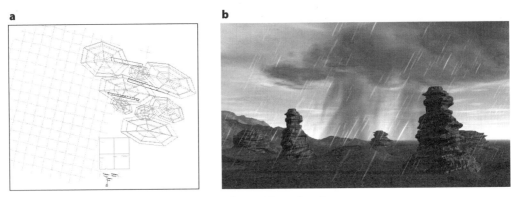

Figure 14–22 "Rainy Day": a) Top view wireframe; b) rendered scene.

If you want to create rain falling on a watery surface with puddle drops, then use the KPT Gradient designer to create concentric circles. Or, if you're feeling really adventuresome, try creating the raindrop effect in the Deep Texture Editor. Figure 14–23 shows two different solutions, using pictures and texture means to create water droplets on the water's surface.

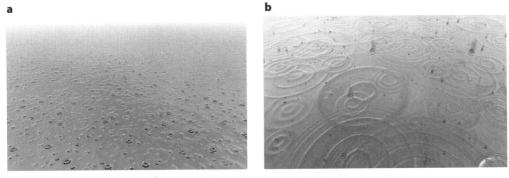

Figure 14–23 Rain on water created by a) Terrain map; b) 3D Texture.

USGS MAPS G2H INFORMATION

If you want to create superlative nature imagery, how about recreating real places? Render real terrains from real places on Earth! The USGS has created DEMs (Digital Elevation Models) for the United States. They can be converted to grayscale information in order to make terrains. See Chapter 8 (which deals with terrains), Chapter 13, and this book's CD-ROM for more information.

THE GREENING OF BRYCE

Why don't "real" trees work easily with high-quality renders? You may have noticed by now that Bryce does not have an icon for a tree in the Create Palette. Version 2.1 is an improvement, with some pre-created greenery in the Object libraries, and the ability to import 3D objects. The software Tree Pro, by Onyx (see the discussion of Tree Pro in Chapter 13, "Bryce and Other Software") creates all manner of foliage, however expensive in render time. To create trees that have as much depth and detail as the rest of Bryce requires the ability to model all of the different surfaces of foliage. For a tree with thousands of leaves, that is a lot of computation.

In addition to the expensive Tree Pro method of creating foliage, there are a series of tricks and techniques for introducing virtual chlorophyll for ray-tracing photosynthesis in Bryce. Here are a few methods:

- *Terrain Forest.* If you're looking at a faraway scene, you can create a terrain that has many pointy spires to emulate a forest of trees. Use the Terrain Editor's Sharpen feature or the Spikes control. Have the spiky terrain poke out through the surface of another terrain for large patches of forest. The terrain map in Figure 14–24a resulted in the rendered forest shown in Figure 14–24b.

- *Variation on a Terrain Forest.* Use a terrain or a symmetrical lattice to create tree shapes. In the scene "African After Dream," Eric Wenger has used both (see Figure 14–25a). For the trees in the fore-to-mid ground, a symmetrical lattice is used to provide the full shape of the foliage crown. The no-texture render of this scene shows the shape of the objects more clearly than the final textured render (see Figure 14–25b). The symmetrical lattice and the other terrains (which are more or less the same shape and clipped at the bottom) all share a material created from a 3D texture, complete with transparency for the foliage appearance.

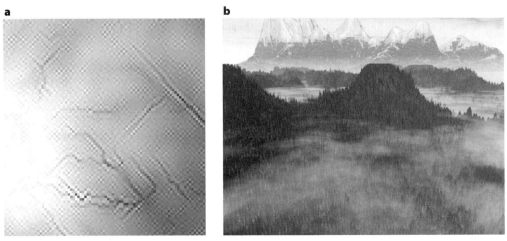

Figure 14–24 Forest: a) Terrain map for trees; b) rendered image: "Four Aest," by Kai Krause.

Figure 14–25 "African After Dream": a) Rendered scene without textures; b) rendered with textures. *Scene by Eric Wenger.*

- *Picture Trees.* You can take a picture of a tree, cut out the non-tree parts with an alpha channel mask, and assign it to a plane in your scene. Of course, you will need to be facing in the direction of the tree. Or, take the same plane and create several copies that all rotate around the common center. Figure 14–26a is a set of wireframe planes, also shown in top view (b). The Picture Library shows how the alpha mask cuts away the extraneous "nontree" area (see Figure 14–26c) to result in a final rendered tree image (see Figure 14–26d). Eric's "Abisko Pine Trees" uses this method. Some individual trees in "African After Dream" also use this method to create the trunk, with additional foliage pictures mapped to the top of spheres to create the branches and leaves of the tree.

- *Terrain Trees.* This method, similar to the Picture Tree method just described, has been around since the early days of Bryce. I first saw the solution posed by

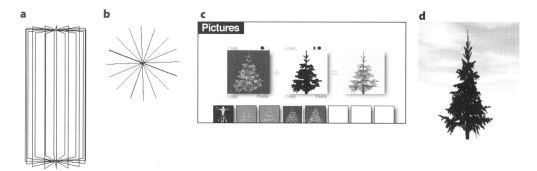

Figure 14–26 "Abisko Pine Trees": a) Wireframe from main and b) top view; c) Picture Library with trees and their masks; d) rendered tree.

Andrew Penick. A cone serves as the trunk, and small terrains make the branches on trees, with picture images. (See Figure 14–27.) Penick has focused on smaller scale horticulture in the scene, "Bushes." Very low resolution terrains (set to 16) provide the shape; the leaves are a picture texture. By the time all the terrains are assembled (see Figure 14–28), the number—and results—are quite staggering, as you can see in Figure C14–29.

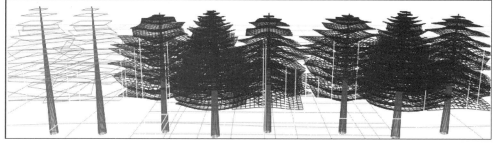

Figure 14–27 Andrew Penick's terrain tree collection.

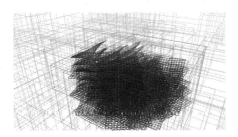 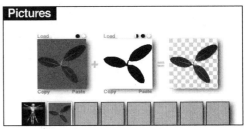

Figure 14–28 The making of "Bushes," by Andrew Penick: a) A detail view of the wireframe; b) picture texture.

- *Painting trees.* Paint your own trees, whether as an after-the-render post process, or as a before-the-render element for the scene. Dennis Berkla's The Garden Hose, distributed by Fractal Design, uses Painter's Image Hose as a means to get foliage elements onto a digital canvas. It is a good resource for creating foliage elements. For more information, see the discussion on The Garden Hose in Chapter 13, "Bryce and Other Software."

LIGHTHOUSE NARRATIVE STEP BY STEP

Although the scene, "Lighthouse at Twilight," is not exactly *the* superlative nature image (I've seen, and even created, much better), it fits well into some of the overall approaches to nature scene-making described in this chapter. Plus, it's a scene that is readily available to all Bryce users, since it's on the Bryce 2.1 application CD-ROM. I'll take you through the steps I went through to create the scene—both thoughts and techniques. Consider this a hands-on integration of topics covered elsewhere in this chapter and earlier in the book.

The "Lighthouse at Twilight" scene began with the following direction—make an exemplary Bryce scene, a nature scene that also had booleans in it, and used families and other Bryce features, and would render fairly quickly.

With that as a direction, I started out....

The Nature Scene

First I made the nature scene. I started with basic composition, and created some initial terrains.

Terrain Placement

I created a terrain and then adjusted it in the Terrain Editor. (I have a personal preference for eroded terrains.) After clicking the Eroded button, I added a bit of Mounds, using the slider for subtlety. I increased the resolution of the terrain to 256, since the terrain would be close to the camera. Figure 14–30 shows the terrain gray map.

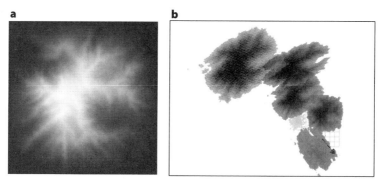

Figure 14–30 Recycling the same terrain map: a) Terrain map; b) top view of terrain placement in wireframe view (note the similar shape among terrains) for "Lighthouse at Twilight."

I placed the first terrain off to the right. To add more terrains, I simply duplicated the first one. The new one was moved to its new spot, increased in size, and rotated. The same terrain, rotated this way and that, will provide enough variety so that the mountains look random. At the same time, there's enough uniformity to suggest a common geological formation process. After another duplication, the third terrain was placed further in the distance, and enlarged somewhat (see Figure 14–31). These three hills, with their low, rolling erodedness, seem to suggest shallow, sloping, coastal hills.

Figure 14–31 The terrain placements for the scene: a) First terrain; b) more terrains beyond the first; c) filling the foreground area with a terrain.

For a coast, then, there should be water. I selected the ground and assigned one of the water presets from the Materials Preset Library.

Setting up the sky

Somewhere during the terrain setup process, I decided that a lighthouse would be a rather cool addition to the scene; it's a "man-made" building that can be constructed from primitives, will utilize a bit of simple booleanizing, and incorporate a light object or two. This idea brought me to the conclusion that I needed to have darker lighting in this scene, so that the lighthouse would actually shine and believably cast light into the night.

First, I set the sun lightsource where I wanted it. Light from low on the horizon is more dramatic. To make the sky a dark color required some experimenting. I had tried the nighttime settings, and the Sky Mode's Dark Sky setting as well as the default Soft Sky that I had started out with. But the sky dome wasn't dark or blue enough for my tastes. So I chose Custom Sky and selected my own colors— dark shades of blue for Sky Color and Solar Halo (Haze Shift was much lighter). At this point, I introduced a little cheat. Darkening the Sun Color would lend the illusion that the moon was shining onto the scene, even though it was actually the sun that was shining. To create a cool, dark feel, I set the Ambient Color to dark blue, to make all shadows dark. Since the light source was low on the horizon, a bit of additional overhead light augmented pale light from the sun-turned-moon. I chose dark green for the Sky Dome Illumination color—dark for subtle light, green for the hue. Then, for a bit of mystery, I placed fog in the scene—not a lot, but just enough to hug the ground level. The Sky & Fog Palette for the scene is in Figure C14–32 in the color section. This scene, with its dark lighting, would make an inviting place to build a lighthouse.

Foreground Composition

To add a bit of interest to the composition, something was needed in the foreground. Once again I duplicated one of the terrains, enlarged it, and then squashed it down on the *y* axis to make it lay low in the foreground.

From top view, the camera's position was adjusted while looking at the Nano Preview on the Control Palette. The pop-up menu was set to both Current Camera and Auto-Update during this stage. Once the camera and the foreground terrain were positioned just so, with water to the right and land to the left, the boundary between them lead the eye to look at the mountains in the distance.

A few stones, when added to the scene, provide a bit more shoreline realism. In this earlier stage they are merely "hanging out" in mid-air (have you ever noticed that there's no such thing as gravity in Bryce?); they will be placed more precisely later on.

To add a bit of complexity in the foreground, the foreground terrain was duplicated, then changed in the Terrain Editor by an apply of Mounds. To make distinct edges, Subcontours was applied (sound familiar?). Finally, to emphasize certain areas, the Raise/Lower Elevation effect was applied, undone, then selectively painted back by using the Brush Controls set to Paint Effect.

This resulting terrain was duplicated and placed in the distance as a nice rocky place onto which a lighthouse would be built. The result of the landscape process is shown in Figure C14–33 in the color section.

Lighthouse

The second stage was the creation of the lighthouse. It took place in a separate scene file, for later merging. For a lighthouse, what is required? The shape is cylindrical, yet slightly tapered. The base is wider than the top. A cone, stretched really tall, will have the gradual tapering required. However, the cone will stretch far above the proper top edge of the height of a lighthouse. A boolean operation to subtract the surplus from the top of the lighthouse will do the trick.

The Tower

A cone was created and elongated on the y axis, followed by duplicating the cone and converting it to a cylinder. The cylinder was shortened and aligned with the top edge of the cone by selecting both objects and clicking the Align tool (Align Y Top). The cylinder was changed to negative so that it would subtract from the positive cone, and the two were grouped.

The Platform and Railing

To create the floor for the top of the tower, I created a cylinder, placed it at the top of the tapered cone, and flattened it to appropriate platform-thickness. Next came a railing to go on the outside edge of that platform, for the giddy who need to hold onto something while looking down from the dizzying heights. What constitutes a railing? A set of thin cylinders and a small torus as the hand-rail.

Solo mode came in handy here, so that the tower boolean was hidden while focusing on the railing construction. The platform cylinder was duplicated to become the beginnings of the railing. The duplicate was resized so that it was rail-thin, but tall. Once it was at the desired size, I duplicated multiple copies in a circle.

On a Mac, the best technique for that is to use multi-replication—31 copies, rotated 11.25° on the *y* axis, and offset by 1.5 on the *x* axis. In Windows, Multi-Replicate is crippled, so only eight cylinders at a time can be rotated and then manually offset a lá the four-part multi-replication process described in Chapter 7, "Booleans and Multiple Object Construction." Another option is to duplicate the first cylinder, move the duplicate, group the two, and then duplicate the group followed by a 90° rotation around the common center. Continue duplicating and rotating until the circle is filled.

After creating the entire circle, the cylinders were grouped together and resized as a whole to match the size of the platform cylinder. For final adjustments, they were positioned from side view so that they'd rest upon the platform cylinder.

Now for that hand-railing: a torus was created and unrotated (from the pop-up menu on the Edit Palette under the Rotate control). After ensuring that the Edit controls were set to operate in World Space, I reduced the torus along the *y* axis to flatten it. Using the Torus Editor, the fatness radius was reduced to make the torus very thin. Then I aligned the torus with the circle of cylinders. Together with the cylinders they were all assigned the same family identity and grouped. Then they were positioned on the cylinder platform.

A test render showed that the railing size was too thin and the definition was lost in the anti-aliasing. In order to fatten the cylinders, they had to be changed along two axes, *x* and *z*. The only way to change the size on two axes simultaneously is to use the 3D Transformation dialog box. (It is possible to use the Object Attributes dialog box, but it doesn't display meaningful information for more than one object in different locations.) 3D Transformation adjusts the object relative to its current position. So I increased the size by a few percentage points, say 10, on the *x* and *z* axes. After a few rounds of resizing, the "fatness" of the column shaped up nicely. After one last check to make sure that all the alignment matters were okay, the platform and railing assemblies were grouped together, assigned a unique family identity, and Solo mode was switched off. See Figure 14–34.

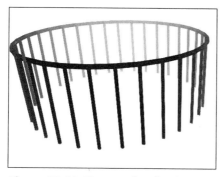

Figure 14–34 The completed railing.

The House

The next item constructed was the house atop the platform—here's where the lighthouse's light lives.

The house is made of a cylinder. To make it hollow, it was duplicated and slightly reduced on all axes. While the inner cylinder was still selected, it was assigned to be negative in the Object Attributes dialog box. Then the two cylinders were grouped together and assigned a plain glassy material—with refract index—in the Materials Composer. It was given its own family identity.

The same basic boolean process was used to create the conical roof. I created a cone and set it atop the glass assembly (Copy and Paste Matrix came in handy here to get the cone into its initial position). Then I duplicated it and moved the duplicate down slightly, then made it negative. The two were grouped together to create a hollow conical roof. The roof was assigned its own family name and color. See Figure 14–35.

a   **b**

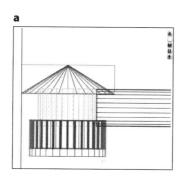
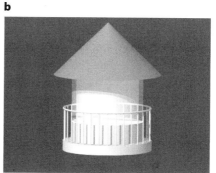

Figure 14–35 The glass house and conical roof: a) Wireframe view and b) rendered.

The lights

Now that there's a tower and a house, it's time to say, "Let there be light!" The Round Spotlight—in the shape of a cone—was chosen to be the light emanating from the lighthouse. After creating the light, I rotated it so that it faced sideways. The Shift key for constraining rotation allowed for a quick, precise rotation. Once the light was at the right angle, it was dramatically elongated using the direct manipulation handles on the object. In the Edit Lights dialog box, the Visible Light option was checked. (Had I constructed the scene initially in Windows, the elongation would not have been necessary, since the Infinite Light option would have accomplished the same thing.)

The way that the spotlight works, the light is faintest at the edge of the cone. This happens to be where the strongest point of light is, right next to the spotlight light source. To create a "cheater" light glow, I made a glowing cylinder that extends from the lighthouse. (Since the time I made this scene, I discovered the significance of the Transparency setting in the Materials Composer for visible lights. The light could have been made brighter that way. If I were starting this scene today rather than when I did, just before Bryce 2.1 for the Macintosh began shipping, I would not have included the glow but would have reduced the transparency of the light instead.) I duplicated the light and then used the Object Conversion tool to change it to a cylinder. The cylinder was then the same size and orientation as the light. I decided that two things should determine the size of the cylinder. It should not be larger than the lighthouse glass window, and it should extend out until its circumference matches the circumference of the cone. After resizing, the cylinder was assigned a Shading mode of Fuzzy Additive. Since the edge is fuzzy, the object could be enlarged slightly beyond the size of the lighthouse glass. Test renders helped to determine the final size. (The difference in the ratio of brightness to distance makes a difference across platforms. Therefore it's difficult to exactly match the Windows spotlight to the Macintosh version.)

Finally, a light was placed within the lighthouse glass. After creating a radial light, here's how it was quickly put in place: After selecting the lighthouse glass group, I copied the matrix (under Edit menu). Then I selected the radial light and pasted the matrix. That placed the radial light in the exact position as the glass group. From there, the radial light was reduced slightly. Then I edited the light, making it visible and reducing its brightness slightly (the refracting glass made it quite bright already). The light was given a pale yellow color.

At this point, I saved the lighthouse scene (see Figure 14–36). Throughout the process of creating the objects, I gave them unique identities so that they could be selected by logical grouping, and not merely by primitive type.

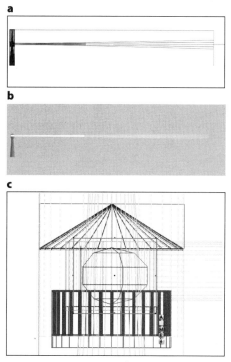

Merging the Two Scenes Together

For the next step, the completed lighthouse was brought into the nature scene. First, I opened up the nature scene. Then, in the File menu, I selected Merge... navigated to the lighthouse scene, and clicked Okay. When the lighthouse entered the nature scene, it was far too big for its surroundings! (See Figure 14–37.)

Remember, in order to get the nice tall lighthouse, elements were considerably enlarged. So they had to be adjusted to fit the scale of the rest of the scene. The lighthouse came into the scene already selected. I grouped it. Then I did a two-part resize. I reduced the lighthouse some. I enlarged the rest of the scene some (a light's size has an effect on how bright the light may be, so it is possible to make a light *too small*). This is how:

Figure 14–36 The lighthouse scene: a) Wireframe; b) rendered; c) wireframe detail of glass house and lights.

First I enlarged everything else. In order to keep the relationships among the objects, they were grouped together before enlarging. Once the lighthouse was selected, ⌘-Shift-A (Macintosh) or Ctrl+Shift+A (Windows) selected everything else. After the size was increased, there were a few details to

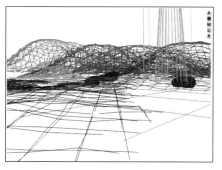

Figure 14–37 Freshly merged lighthouse, far too big for its surroundings.

attend to. The objects needed to be raised, since resizing occurs from the object's or group's center. The camera needed to be moved back. The resolutions for the terrains lying closest to the camera needed enlarging to hold detail. To roughly match the newly-sized scene with the old one, I used the rendered first scene as a guide. I did partial test renders of portions of the scene to get as close a match as I could.

Then the lighthouse was reduced slightly, as a fine-tuning measure. Once the scale of the lighthouse matched the rest of the scene, the lighthouse needed to be oriented so that the light shone on the land. It was rotated from top view. Since the center of the grouped object was not the lighthouse proper, but halfway between the lighthouse and the end of the spotlight, and since an object rotates around its center, the lighthouse had to be repositioned again after it was rotated.

Incidentally, all of the carefully named families from the lighthouse scene lost their identification when the scene was merged into the nature scene. That's because the labeling of the host scene takes precedence. Those secondary scene families still retain their unique colors, and it didn't take much effort to select each family, see what it was, and then rename the family.

Stones

The stones, which were haphazardly located in midair, were brought into the foreground of the scene and positioned in water. The Land Object command was used to position them. Even so, a few nudges down using the Page Down key was necessary, since landing objects only makes them touch the object below. For the appearance of weight, they needed to be solidly planted in the ground under the water.

Surface Materials

Now that the scene was finally taking shape, it was time to set the surface materials for the objects. In the case of this scene, the distant mountains do not have any textures other than a diffuse color of green. This saves render time. Of course, if the scene were to be rendered at a larger size, then naturally textures would go nicely. But for the Brycean default size, the distant mountains can stay as is. The foreground objects took their texture from presets in the Preset Libraries, though each was modified slightly.

Import the chairs

Finally, to reinforce the idea that there are humans inhabiting this scene, a couple of chairs were imported (oh yeah, and it also showed off another cool capability of

Bryce, too!). The chairs come from a model made available by Zygote, which is a DXF file. Using the File > Import Object... command, the DXF object was brought into the scene. Instead of importing the object twice, the imported object was duplicated after it was brought into the scene. The chairs were resized to fit the scale of the scene, and then from top view, rotated so that they'd face one another in a social conversational

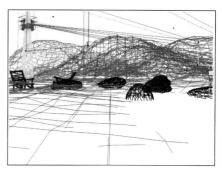

Figure 14–38 "Lighthouse at Twilight," final wireframe.

grouping. Since the chairs were resting on a terrain with a slight incline, they were tilted so that all four legs rested comfortably on the ground. Finally, they were given a slight yellow color to provide a nuance of wood grain texture. To add more texture than that might not work out as well, since the object imported as one cohesive whole and a wood grain would have been applied to the fabric portion of the chair as well. Figure 14–38 shows the final wireframe and Figure C14–39 in the color section shows the rendered image. The CD-ROM contains the two earlier scenes in the folder for this chapter. The final scene file is located on your Bryce software application CD-ROM.

CHAPTER FIFTEEN

Out of this World

A Follower of Goddard
And a rising Astrogator
Were agreed that superthermics
Was a spatial hot pertater.

They reached a Super-Nova
On a bicycle named Beta
And I'd tell you more about it
But they fused with all the data.

FREDERICK WINSOR, *THE SPACE CHILD'S MOTHER GOOSE*

IN THIS CHAPTER...

• Outer space images—planetary and ringed planets

• Lunar spheres in Brycean skies

• Abstract Brycean images

• More suggestions for using 2D Picture Textures

In this chapter, I offer a sampler of things to do in Bryce besides your basic, normal, Brycean landscape. I take you on a trip through out-of-this-world landscapes, abstract images, and other cool effects that don't fit into the "nature imagery" category.

BRYCE STAR GALACTICA

Although Bryce's original purpose was to make outdoor scenery, with a click and a drag here and there on the Sky & Fog Palette, you can have instant outer space Brycescapes.

Recipe for Space Scenes

This recipe walks you through the steps to create space scenes. You'll make a multi-sphere planet world and a planet with rings.

For space scenes to be convincing, your planets must live inside a hostile environment, maybe even one that's devoid of atmosphere. That's easy enough to arrange, as follows:

1. In the Sky & Fog Palette, under the Sky Mode pop-up menu, select the No Atmosphere option. Then use the color swatch to select the color for your Sky Backdrop. Black or extremely deep colors are good.

2. For Fog and Haze, you have a few options. Set them to zero for "deep space." Or use them judiciously to create some additional color. If you do include haze, you will need to position your objects and camera angle so that you miss the horizon. Aim the camera up somewhat. Then choose a nice dark, rich color for haze, just to add a sense of mystery. Likewise, with fog, take the *height* all the way to maximum and make the *amount* rather small. Choose a deep color for the fog and watch it mix with the haze.

Create your planets with sphere primitives. Your planet system can be as easy as *one-two-three:*

One is a solitary sphere, the planet itself, devoid of atmosphere.

Two is a planet with rings, where the second sphere is larger, yet squashed to be nearly flat.

Three is a planet with atmospheric conditions—the planet sphere, the cloud layer sphere, and the diffuse atmosphere layer sphere.

Solitary Sphere

I'll talk first about the settings for the planets and then discuss the two- and three-sphere systems.

Start with the initial sphere, your planet. Now, "make it so!" via the Materials Composer, as follows:

- *Shading mode.* Set to either Normal Shading or Additive.

- *Illumination channels.* No Ambience. Lots of Diffusion and some Specularity. Your planet is not self-illuminating; it is lit by the major stellar light source. In some cases you may want to have lots of specularity with brightly-lit Specular Coefficient (see Color, below, for more about this).

- *Optics.* Reflectivity and Transmitivity off (if your planet has water on it that is somewhat reflective and your Alpha is set for reflection, then set Reflection low for greater realism).

- *Bump Height.* By all means, put a bit of bump gain in there! Keep it subtle, though, because by the time you get into outer space, the elevation difference between Death Valley and Mount Everest appears negligible.

- *Color.* If driven by a texture source, then let the texture drive both Diffuse and Specular color. Maximize the Specular Coefficient for high contrast between lit and shaded parts of the planet.

Two-Sphere Planet—Saturn Rings

Now that you have your first sphere—your planet, duplicate it (or create another sphere) to make your rings. Enlarge it proportionally so that it extends considerably beyond the planet itself. Then reduce it along the *y* axis to flatten it. Rotate it to a jaunty angle. Next, you need to create some type of ring pattern on it. Parts will be transparent and other parts will be "ring-y." For this, you need an alpha channel arrangement of some sort in order to create transparency. There are two ways to use alpha-driven Transparency in the Materials Composer: with a 2D Picture and with a 3D Texture.

2D Picture Texture

To create an alpha channel, you need to make a mask for transparency. You can create a color layer to color the rings—or not—but you definitely need an alpha mask. Use the KPT Gradient Designer to make this.

To make a 2D Picture and mask is possible. However, you'll find that there's too much going back and forth—from the application you use to create the mask, to Bryce, to the object, back for more refinements of the image, and so on. You'll also need to set your image resolution high enough (with a sufficient number of total pixels, but always, always at 72 ppi!) so that the rings aren't affected by anti-aliasing at the curved edges.

However, I prefer using the second method—3D Texture—because you can perfect your planet rings without ever leaving Bryce.

3D Texture

In the Material Preset Library , find the preset Wild n Fun > Dali Bee Stripes. It has stripey yellow lines (Figure 15–1a). Figure 15–1b shows an example of using this preset.

This preset is a good starting place to get you where you want to go because it already has stripes and Alpha Transparency to cut out the other half of the stripes. When applied to the flattened sphere, it makes a good start for rings. With a few adjustments and some noodling, you'll have your rings. I won't go into the specifics of the noodling here because it is one of the tutorial examples for modifying

Figure 15–1 Planet rings: a) Dali Bee Preset ; b) planet rings created from that preset.

an existing preset that is presented as a tutorial, "Recipe for the Ringed Planet Material Adjustment," toward the end of Chapter 9, "Material World."

Three-Sphere Planet—Planet, Clouds, and Atmosphere

This planet and atmosphere world comprises three spheres, one set inside the other: the planet proper, a cloud layer atop the planet, and a fuzzy atmospheric layer.

1. With your basic planet selected, duplicate twice. You now have three spheres (even though it appears that you have one).

2. Using the Tab key or the smaller arrow on the Selection Palette, select only one sphere and make it slightly smaller using the Proportional Resize tool on the Edit Palette. Hold down the Option key for greater precision. This sphere will be the planet's surface. Assign this innermost sphere its own family (wireframe color) so that you can tell easily which sphere is which.

3. Select another sphere and enlarge it using Proportional Resize. Assign it to a unique family. This sphere will be your atmosphere layer.

Figure 15–2 shows (a) wireframes and (b) the resulting render of a three-sphere planet.

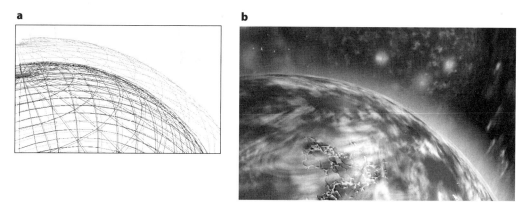

Figure 15–2 Three-sphere planet world: a) Wireframes for the planet, cloud layer, and atmosphere layer; b) rendered image. *Image by Eric Wenger.*

You now have three spheres. The first, with a color and size you did not change, is your cloud layer. Inside that is your actual planet. Outside both of those is your outer atmospheric sphere.

Now, what about the Material settings for each? All of your spheres have a planet Materials setting (assuming you created one following the previous steps). Now you need to change the settings for the outer two spheres to cloud and fuzzy atmosphere, respectively.

Clouds

The cloud layer sits just outside of the planet's edges. The 3D Texture called Atmosphere (accessed from the pop-up menu from one of the four Texture Sources) is a good one for providing clouds. So are any of the other cloudy ones (Stratus, Cumulus, Low Smog, TurboCloud).

• *Shading Mode.* Normal.

• *Illumination.* Lots of Diffusion, some Specularity, and no Ambience (well, maybe an eentsy bit, but clouds don't show up when in shadow).

- *Optics & Bump*. You'll want to see the planet underneath the cloud layer, so there will be some Transparency. In this case, Transparency is driven by the texture. Thin out the cloud layer by adding more Transparency (using the slider) to taste.

- *Color*. Global uniform color using the swatches. For clouds, they should be white (or another color if you want your clouds to be a strange alien-world color).

If your planet was set to the shading mode Additive, then the clouds you just added, though shadowed, will appear where the planet is darkest. Change the planet back to Normal Shading.

Atmosphere

This is the little extra glowing part, where the atmosphere extends beyond the planet's surface.

- *Shading Mode*. Fuzzy Additive (the edge of the atmosphere is not crisply defined and the atmosphere glows).

- *Illumination*. High Diffusion, low Ambience, Specularity to taste. (All are global illumination settings.)

- *Optics & Bump*. Some Transparency, depending on how strong an atmosphere you want.

- *Color*. Choose a color for your atmosphere.

Add some space effects in one or more infinite planes for stars and intergalactic phenomena. Then render.

"Clair De Lune"

If you don't want to be in outer space, then you can put a little "luna-tic" fringe in your scene and have partial or multiple moons. In this section, I discuss lunar (and planetary, if you desire) phenomena in Brycean skies when viewed through an atmosphere. Bryce's own moon is always directly opposite the sun. But if you put a moon or other planet somewhere else, it will reflect the sun's light, as Earth's own moon does when it's in other phases.

Materials Settings and the "Moon Lighting"

A partial moon in Bryce is made from a combination of Shading Mode and Illumination settings in the Materials Composer. Forget any notion about what revolves around what or what rotates and what doesn't. In Bryce, it doesn't matter. What does matter is the relationship between the location of the light source and the location of the lunar object, as well as the lunar object's Material settings.

- *Shading Mode*. Additive. The only part of the sphere that is visible is the part that is directly lit. (This depends, in part, on Illumination, discussed next.) If your sphere is "in front" of another object (say, a terrain), the shaded part of the sphere will cut through that other object and all you'll see is the object in the back.

- *Illumination*. The Illumination type to use is Diffusion. No Ambience, no Specularity. Any Ambient light will add a slight glow to the shadowed part of the sphere. If you use it, do so sparingly. Specularity will create a hot spot. If you adjust the Specular Coefficient to something in the high 240's, then Specularity could work. Adjust the strength of Diffuse light depending on the circumstances. The higher the setting, the stronger the appearance of the lunar surface in the sky. Stay away from Specularity, too, unless you arrange it so that the Specular Coefficient creates a large highlight on the lunar surface. Figure 15–3 shows a series of moons that have different Diffusion settings.

- *Optics & Bump*. Put a little dent in your moon using a 3D Texture to drive Bump Height. You don't need much to get the feeling for lunar dimension. Too much will make it look as though the moon is too small and too close.

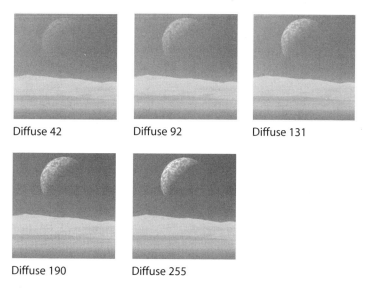

Diffuse 42   Diffuse 92   Diffuse 131

Diffuse 190   Diffuse 255

Figure 15–3 Lunar surfaces with different Diffusion settings.

- *Color.* To make your moon a uniform color, select a color from the Diffuse Color swatch. Or, if you want to see slight lunar surface details, then let the texture drive your Diffuse Color. Light and dark variations will appear. (If you decide to try Specularity, then you can also have Specular Color driven by your texture.)

Your partial moon can be in Bryce's sky during day or night (as set by the Sun control on the Sky & Fog Palette). When viewing the moon by night, keep in mind the following: If you are going to have Bryce's moon light up your sphere-moon, then remember that the moon shines from the opposite direction indicated by the Sun in the Sky & Fog Palette. You will need a higher Diffusion setting to compensate for the presence of less light at night.

When you are in "night" using the Atmosphere Off option (from the Sky Mode pop-up menu), you will not be able to light the lunar surface from Bryce's "moon" light source. You'll get a fainter projection from the sun on the opposite (lower) side of the Bryce sky dome.

Ring Around the Moon

When you look at Earth's moon through high hazy moisture, there's a ring around it. The fuzzy outer atmosphere from the three-sphere planet works to create this effect. Make the sphere significantly larger than the moon. Be careful with the Haze settings for this kind of scene. Moderate haze will show more of the shaded surface and the atmosphere, resulting in a too-artificial effect. See Figure 15–4.

Figure 15–4 A ring around the moon made with an atmosphere sphere and a slight haze.

Making a Full Moon Elsewhere at Night

To create a moon that is large, imposing, and glowing, one that dominates your scene, use a separate sphere. Do all that has been mentioned here previously but crank up Ambient to make the moon self-illuminating. You'll probably need to add a light source to cast light from that moon.

STRANGE TERRAIN-BASED IMAGES

In the terrain chapter (Chapter 8), I discussed how to set up a scene for an image-as-terrain. The possibilities here are endless.

Now I give a few examples and talk about the integrated approach to doing this. Using the alpha channel as a means for creating a bump map, you can give different looks to your terrain image.

"Necrofelinia"

The image in Figure C15–5 (see color section), by Phil Clevenger, is a prime example of how strange picture terrains can be. The original cat image was filtered with Xaos Terrazzo to get the kaleidoscope effect. It was then brought into the Terrain Editor, where it was blurred, inverted, and eroded a bit. The inverted erosion created the veiny bumps and ridges. It was then inverted back. In the Materials Composer, the color image was applied to the terrain, with Illumination settings being high Diffuse, medium Ambient, and low Specular.

The camera angle swoops down from above. There is no atmosphere and the "cloud" color is black. A generous layer of black fog is the final touch to make this the killer kitty with the macabre meow.

PICT Terrain Chrome

What can be done with the Materials Composer's alpha-driven optics using picture textures? For your run-of-the-mill "slap a 2D Picture on a square and cut out the background using alpha-driven transparency," you'll have a high-contrast alpha mask that has black and white. However, when using an alpha mask that has gray values (see Figure 15–6a), the outcome is not quite so simple. When the mask contains grays, you run the risk of generating mesh patterns and other artifacts when driving transparency (see Figure 15–6c). When your image is also in your alpha channel, alpha-driven Transparency is probably not your best bet. However, the Materials Composer's other Optic control, Reflection, can be used to powerful effect with picture terrains with picture textures. Where the alpha is black, the texture is reflective (recall from the discussion from Chapter 9 "Material World" that picture alpha information is swapped: black is white and white is black). To make this highly polished chrome, Reflection was adjusted to maximum (see Figure 15–6d). As the gray levels in the mask change from black to white, the surface texture makes a transition from a titanium-looking metal to chrome.

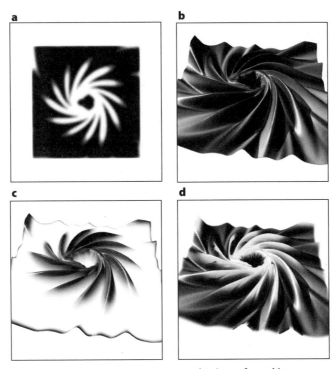

Figure 15–6 A Picture terrain created using a fractal image:
a) The alpha mask is a variation of the terrain gray map;
b) no alpha-driven effect; c) alpha-driven transparency;
d) alpha-driven reflection.

GlockenFondue

The GlockenFondue series in Figure C15–7 (see color section) demonstrates additional ways to manipulate a picture terrain using the alpha channel. There are two sets of variations at work. First, there is alpha-driven reflection, which is further modified by the Illumination and Color controls. Then there is the alpha-driven Bump Height.

Mixing and matching these two results in some new metallic looks.

The original image of the clock parts, courtesy of PhotoDisc, is the basis of the terrain, 2D Picture Texture and the alpha channel. It is a photograph of a clock's metal gears, so it begins with metallic colors. The image works well as a terrain when it is smoothed slightly. In the first set of variations, the Opacity Map uses the fine-engraved detail to emphasize the object's shape when driving Bump Height. Figure C15–7 shows two sets of the same image with and without bump.

Make sure to experiment with Bump Height for your picture-based terrains with 2D Picture Textures.

The other alpha-driven variation is Reflection. One set of images has Reflection adjusted near maximum, the other set has alpha-reflection at zero. For these two, Reflection is operating together with the Illumination and Color settings. The GlockenFondue images all have a dulled appearance although Specularity is set to maximum. Instead of the usual bright hot spot, the dulled appearance results from the texture-driven Specular Color (as well as Diffuse Color). This softens the metallic appearance of the texture. A sheen is added to the object, but it's a muted sheen. Rather than a brash chrome reflection, the result is subtle.

For an object that began with metallic coloring, these treatments result in an unusual metallic appearance. The CD-ROM has additional GlockenFondue images which explore the result of different settings in the Materials Composer.

In other picture terrain images where the image itself has no metallic elements, the same technique will make a pleasing pewtery look. Again, there is alpha-driven Reflection without any specular hot spots in this alternative treatment of the original kitty image (the same source used in Phil Clevenger's "Necrofelinia"). (See Figure C15–8 in the color section.) The kitty image is used for the terrain, as well as the 2D Picture Texture and the alpha mask. For the Optics & Bump channels, the texture drives both Bump Height and Reflection (with sliders set to generous amounts for both). The Optics & Bump settings result in surface detail indentations and a metallic sheen where the terrain is highest and brightest. In the Color channels, the texture drives Diffuse and Specular Color. So even though the terrain reflects, it's not a shiny chrome reflection. Rather, the result is a soft, pewter-like, brushed metal surface.

If you want to alter the alpha mask image, borrow the Terrain Editor for the task! (The Terrain Editor is, after all, a very specialized image editor.) See the Picture Texture section of Chapter 9, "Material World," for more about how to make adjustments to your alpha channel image mask without leaving Bryce.

ABSTRACTS

You can create abstract images with Bryce. Start from scratch to make something that is neither landscape nor object, but merely interesting shape and lighting and surface. Or you may be working with some scene and decide that you'd like to render just one area.

The Zoom to Selection command is good for this. In Render mode, drag a marquee around the area that interests you. Select Zoom to Selection from the pop-up menu next to the marquee (you need to have the Plop Render display switched on to access the menu). Begin rendering again to create that abstract image.

The presence of Multi-replicate is an aid in the abstract process, as you may have gathered from Chapter 7, "Booleans and Multiple Object Construction." Another aid in the abstract process, if you have the patience for the render time, is to use the random form of a terrain as a means to distort your view using the Refract Index. Here are a couple of different approaches to this. Figure C15–9 is my rendition of looking at a landscape through glass blocks. Here, cubes are stacked to form blocks. Then they are given a texture-driven Bump Height setting, with Transparency and Color and the all-important Refract Index set to 130-something to make the distortion. You are viewing a landscape through glass blocks. Figure 15–10a and b are two sets of Bryce scenes by Bill Ellsworth. Part a is a scene without any distortion, the "before" image. In Figure 15–10b, a terrain is placed between the scene and the camera, assigned high Transparency with the Refract Index set to 119. This is the means to generate unusual effects that you'd not normally associate with Bryce right from the get-go. (Also see more of Bill's work in the "Bill & Zox's Excellent Adventure" show in the Gallery folder on the CD-ROM.)

a

b

Figure 15–10 Abstract before and after by Bill Ellsworth: a) Before ; b) after placing a transparent refracting terrain between objects and camera.

SCI-FI

Having donned oxygen masks and outfitted ourselves for the hostile environment of space earlier in the chapter, it comes as no surprise that Bryce is an excellent tool for creating science-fiction worlds. Figure C15–11 is an image by Tony Kashinn that blends together the principles discussed earlier about space scenery with other landscape imagery to make science fiction.

There are many science fiction-type images on the CD-ROM in the gallery section; go and browse! Make your planets other worldly, and populate them with whatever forms of life or technology that you see fit. Bryce is an excellent tool for visualizing other places.

STILL LIFES: MILES OF TILES

While I'm on the topic of interesting terrain-based images, here's a twist—make ceramic tiles with terrains! Certainly, if the Terrain Editor allows you to make virtual earth in the form of mountains, then it can be put to the task of creating derivative forms of earthenware. Chris Casady—known to some as TileNut—has done just that. He uses Bryce to create virtual ceramic tiles, based on his massive backyard hoarde of buried tile molds from the old Batchelder Tile Co. in Los Angeles (heyday, circa the roaring 20's). After scanning the tile mould and creating the grayscale imagery to build the terrain, Chris uses duplicates of the terrain with glazey materials to create the ceramic glaze. His Bryce images become virtual ceramics, all without clay dust, kiln firings, glazes, or gas bills. See Figure C15–12 (and the gallery on the CD-ROM). Chris calls his Bryce/Mac combo "the most energy-efficient kiln of all time."

ABSTRACT 2D PICTURE AND 3D TEXTURES

The most obvious application of materials in Bryce is to create realistic-looking natural objects. The wealth of noises and processes for 3D Textures create natural-looking forms. 2D Pictures are good for placing picture images inside your Bryce world, so that you can be in your own scene, if you'd like! However, there are a whole other set of fascinating uses for textures—to make abstract forms.

This section draws on the inspiration of Richard Vanderlippe, whose tinkerings with Bryce 1 and 2 have resulted in some material solutions that have an "Aha!"

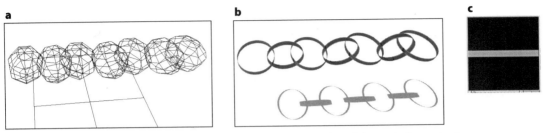

Figure 15–13 Interlocking rings: a) Overlapping spheres; b) rendered rings; c) picture texture.

feel. The most simple graphic forms and shapes, when applied with a stroke of mad genius, provide startling results. This is a different approach to what you'd get with booleans, where something cuts out a part of the object. In this case, the alpha-driven Transparency cuts away portions of the object.

In the 2D Picture category, there is a simple way to make interlocking rings using spheres. The scene in Figure 15–13, adapted from one of Vanderlippe's scenes, has interlocking rings. Spheres are placed together so that they overlap and then are alternately rotated (see Figure 15–13a). The interlocking rings (see Figure 15–13b) are created with a picture texture that's a simple horizontal bar (see Figure 15–13c).

Figure 15–14 shows an application of PICT texture that I find particularly charming. A basic spiral (the image is the same as the alpha mask, see Figure 15–14a) is applied to a sphere. In this case, Object Front was used and the object rotated, but Object Top mapping would work just as well. The spheres were elongated, then rendered. Of course, alpha-driven Transparency made it all work. With some tweaking of the Illumination channels to get high amounts of Ambience and Diffusion, the spirals were made to glow. (See Figure 15–14b.)

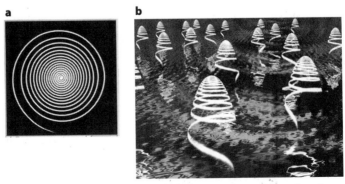

Figure 15–14 Spirals: a) The spiral picture texture; b) rendered images.

In the 3D Texture category, Vanderlippe has expanded on his quest for the basic shape material to come up with the following basic shape. Figure 15–15 shows some very basic object cutouts. These are taken from a set of material pre-

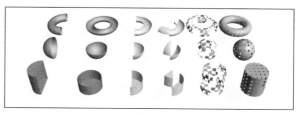

Figure 15–15 Richard Vanderlippe's 3D Texture alpha-driven Transparency masks. Each material is shown on three different object primitives.

sets that are available on the CD-ROM (Bryce Utilities > Presets > Vanderlippe). Portions of the object are cut out in certain ways. Look at the samples here, load up his presets from the CD-ROM, and after examining them for a bit, you may be inspired to try out your own variations.

2D Picture Texture Hints

When you are working with picture textures that are realistic instead of abstract, and you seek to have them blend into the surrounding area, there are a couple of things to be aware of:

- *Lighting.* The lighting in Bryce needs to match the lighting in your photograph. It adds to realism if you can take colors from the imported image and assign them to your Bryce textures used in the scene. Of course, if you are working with objects modeled and rendered in another 3D application, then you can make the lighting in the 3D application match Bryce's.

- *Shadows.* Your picture object will cast shadows, which, of course, helps to maintain the illusion that it's a three-dimensional entity. However, beware of the shadows from other elements in your scene that might fall on the object. If they do, they will betray the fact that the object is flat, thereby ruining your beautiful illusion of full, three-dimensional depth.

- *Reflection.* If you want to create realistic reflections, you may need to mix Bryce elements with Picture

Figure 15–16 Scene in which the photography's window-panes are replaced with Bryce windowpanes so that the floating pencils reflect in the window.

elements. The image in Figure 15–16, by Michael Pilla, has a picture image of French doors with Brycean "glass panes." Pilla used an alpha mask to remove the photograph's glass panes. He then created his own glass in Bryce using square primitives so that *all* objects in the scene would reflect from the glass surface.

Whether outer space or inner place, whether abstraction or strange picture terrain-based images, Bryce makes more than just a normal basic hum-drum everyday nature scene. In fact, it can be otherworldy.

CHAPTER SIXTEEN

Printing Bryce Images

Still, somehow, the thing got finished at last, without much loss of temper.

KENNETH GRAHAME, *THE WIND IN THE WILLOWS*

IN THIS CHAPTER...

- All about resolution and printing
- Different categories of printers
- A strategy for working with image resolution
- Conversion from RGB to CMYK
- Strategies for grayscale
- Strategies for color

At some point, you'll want to print your images. It's inevitable. Given the type of images Bryce creates, and the plummeting costs of desktop color printers, it's only a matter of time. How do you get that beautiful image from your computer's monitor onto paper of some sort?

Whether you want to print one copy of your Bryce image so that you can give it to your sweetheart or tack it up on your bulletin board, or whether you're going to take the image to four-color process offset printing, you'll have to wade through some issues besides the best place to position your sun, or terrain, or whatever.

If you haven't yet printed images, then this chapter is for you. Here, I introduce the basic concepts of printing, so that you get a feel for what you have just gotten yourself into once you say, "I want to print that image I just created!"

If you're an old hand at taking RGB (Red/Green/Blue) PICT images and converting them to CMYK for printed output, then you probably aren't reading this chapter anyhow. (You've got your nose stuck in the section that talks about the Deep Texture Editor, don't you?) Still, you'll find one section useful: Bryce Images and CMYK Printing.

THE BASIC SITUATION

Although MetaTools has added printing capabilities to Bryce 2, I don't think of Bryce as primarily a printing application. In fact, I've hardly even used it to print images at all. Although my old faithful laserwriter printer had no problem with printing images and wireframes, my cute sleek inkjet color printer and Bryce knocked heads during the process, and I've yet to sucessfully print a rendered image in color directly from Bryce. When it comes to desired results, which printer would you rather use—ugly old grayscale or a brilliant color inkjet? I thought so.

As a rule, wireframe views take a long time to process; they are more than a screen dump of what you see; there is a deeper vector conversion process taking place to bring the wireframe mesh to printed form. Depth cueing is included in the printed image. A rendered image print is processed much faster, though the one time I got the color printer to print *anything*, half of the image was noise soup. Bryce's excellence and uniqueness lies in its ability to create and render way cool imagery. Focus on that and leave that print command alone.

"Fine," you say. "Cute. This is a chapter on printing and you start it out by saying, 'don't use Bryce's Print command.' What is this leading to?" If you find yourself thinking that, I don't blame you. It *is* a rather strange way to begin a chapter. However, there is plenty to say about the process of printing images. Since Bryce's printing is not up to snuff, it's best to say so and dispense with it from the beginning. Having done that, we can now launch into a more fruitful discussion about how to bring your sublime image out into the tangible world of paper or film.

You create scenes and render them and save the rendered images as PICT or BMP documents. To print your images, use other software whose image printing abilities are robust. To get that image from intangible data on disk to some physical printed form, it will have to undergo a transformation or two. Photoshop is the staple application for this. Indeed, when it comes to rendering to disk or exporting images, Bryce itself makes no bones about it; after doing either of those two processes, the documents you've just created happen to have the Photoshop document icon! What greater endorsement is needed?

AN OUTPUT DEVICE PRIMER

When you print an image, you will be choosing from among a plentiful array of printers, or output devices. (I use the term "output device" because a computer monitor fits into this category—yet it does not print.) Each output device has its own optimal setup and preferred image resolution.

Every type of output device has its own setting for the degree of detail it can print. The device's own detail capacity is expressed in dots per inch (dpi), that is, how many single points of detail can the device fit into an inch? The dpi is a fixed number; it's derived from the physical specifications of the output device. Physically, any output device can do so many *somethings* in an inch. The somethings vary from device to device. A monitor projects electron beams, various printers use laser beams, and inkjet printers eject individual spurts of ink.

The physical specifications also concern the particular media involved. The output device is doing *something* to *something else*. You can shoot a higher number of individual laser beams onto a smoother, harder surface (film or resin-coated photo-sensitive paper) than you can onto a softer, more porous surface (paper). Therefore devices that output to film generally have significantly higher dpi settings than those that output to paper.

So that's dpi. There's a relation between the output's dpi and the individual image resolution, or pixels per inch (ppi). In the document itself is a header that says (more or less): "This is the total number of pixels in this document. Smoosh them in such a way that N many pixels fit into one inch." The default image setting of 72 ppi matches the old 72 dpi standard for monitors (from the days before multi-sync).

Let's look at this relation between the output device's dpi and the image's ppi. A good start is to examine the first few render passes of a Bryce scene. At first, the image has large, square, chunky pixels. Why do those large pixels seem odd to us? Because the image does not have the level of detail that the monitor (output device) is able to display. This is why for the first few render passes, clicking the Zoom tool enables you to see a more detailed version of the render. You are changing the resolution of the image in order to see as much of the image's detail as can be seen for that output device. Otherwise the image looks too chunky, or pixellated.

This works fine for the first few passes. After a point, though, the render reaches a threshold where there are more individual points of information in the image than you can see at that output device's resolution. (Remember: The monitor has a fixed dpi; it can show only 72 distinct pixels in an inch. Multisync monitors that display at different resolutions muddy this situation somewhat, but for the purposes of discussion here, I'll stick to the 72 dpi figure.)

This last example discussed the situation common to all output devices. They are capable of output at a higher resolution than 72 dpi, the default image size. Therefore they need more information going *in*. The image itself needs to be bigger. It needs more pixels so that more of them can be packed into a square inch. For any given device, you'll need to have a corresponding setting for image resolution (ppi).

If this "somethings per inch" is not confusing enough, there is yet another level of confusion for certain types of printers—lines per inch (lpi), or linescreen. (Are you *sure* you really want to print that Bryce image? After a moment of staring at it longingly, you'll probably conclude that you do in fact want to press on with these matters of your own private printing press. Take two or three deep breaths, then let's continue.)

Most printers are not capable of laying down pigment color in all shades of the rainbow. If you're using a grayscale printer, you have a choice between two colors—black and white. So to create all those shades of gray, the printer distributes little black dots of certain sizes. For dark gray, the dots are either fatter or more numerous. For light gray, the dots are either tinier and more sparsely distributed. This is referred to as a halftone, that is, there are tones generated from bits of color that are either black or white. When the eye takes in the image, the dots are blended in with the neighboring area, thereby creating the illusion of all the tones of gray that are in between black and white.

Color printing does the same thing, only it uses four primary colors: cyan, magenta, yellow, and black (CMYK). So where does linescreen come in? The number of lpi is set independently of the printer's physical dpi capability or the ppi image resolution. Linescreen is dependent on the printed paper's ability to accept ink and hold image detail. It is also dependent on the printer's overall dpi.

Newsprint is a porous paper. It can hold only a 65–80 linescreen (65–80 lines of halftone dots per inch). If the linescreen is any higher, the ink bleeds together and the image becomes dark and fuzzy. On the other hand, glossy coated paper can hold 150 or 175 linescreen, even 200. The higher the linescreen, the greater the detail you are able to display. The greater the detail you are putting *out,* the greater the amount of detail you need to have going *in.* So the higher the linescreen, the higher the image resolution.

To review the three different "somethings per inch" just discussed:

- *ppi, or pixels per inch.* The image document's resolution, or how much pixel detail is in an inch.

- *dpi, or dots per inch.* The output device's capability for detail.

- *lpi, or lines per inch, or linescreen.* In half-tone printing, the measurement of the density of the dot pattern.

The dpi of the device determines how much detail you can see. For linescreen halftone, the possible number of lpi (lines) is far below the total dpi (dot) capability of the printer. In other words, the printer can use many more dots to print a solid line than it uses halftone dots to create an illusion of continuous color tones. The image resolution, or image's ppi, is dependent on the output device's capacity. When the image will end up being printed using halftone dots, the image resolution (ppi) is determined by the number of lpi.

Here is one of the hazards of printing images. The size you make your Bryce image depends on the requirements of the output device. Different devices have different requirements. So the image that has a set number of pixels can be output to a film imagesetter to create a full color 8- × 10-inch CMYK image or output to a slide recorder to create a piece of 35mm color transparency film. The physical size of the actual printed entity is very different, but the amount of information that went into it is not, since each printing device handles information of different densities.

DIFFERENT KINDS OF PRINTERS

So far I've discussed printers as "output devices," noting that different ones have different physical capabilities and requirements. Now I take a general look at the major categories of printers. For more-detailed information about what each type of printer requires, consult the manufacturer's specifications or a service bureau.

Many of these printers are for one-off printing. The (one) print is the end, not the means to a mass-produced end. With these, you can create individual prints of your image for that sweetheart, bulletin board, or gallery show.

Laser printers and inkjet printers generally can output at 300–600 dpi. This means the printer can output 300 or 600 distinct points of information in an inch.

- *Desktop inkjets* (Apple, Canon, Hewlett-Packard, Epson, Tektronix). These printers lay down different colors of ink on your page. Individual cartridges hold the ink. The printers come in one-color (black) or multi-color (CMYK) varieties. The patterns created by each color are blended together by the human eye, thereby creating the optical illusion of continuous-tone color. Special papers receive the ink in such a way as to produce a brilliant color.

- *Large inkjets* (Iris, Laser Master, Encad). The larger inkjets come in two basic types. The first, electrostatic, lays stippled dots of color on the paper (maximum paper size is approximately 36 × 48 inches). The printer head assembly moves back and forth over the surface of the paper as the paper advances through the printer. A new type of inkjet has the same type of moving print head assembly, though it lays down color differently than the electrostatic method. The Encad Novajet color printers are able to print on a variety of media, including canvas. The second type of large ink jet, the Iris, has the paper set on a rotating drum. The ink heads stay stationary relative to the "left and right" parts of the page. They move, however, in the sense that they advance "down" the page. This type of setup results in a much higher precision. Printers range in size, with the maximum able to print on 30 × 47-inch paper. The Iris will print on a variety of papers, including watercolor paper for a "fine art" digital print. Some service bureaus specialize in fine art printing. They work with different types of inks and treatments to make the print far more stable than it would be otherwise.

- *Dye Sublimation* (3M Rainbow, Kodak XL Series, Tektronix, Shinko). These printers take ink dyes and fuse the dyes to the surface layers of a specially-prepared paper. The dye is vaporized as it is forced onto the paper's surface, resulting in an unusually smooth image that appears to be a continuous tone print. This is a CMYK color process.

- *Color Laser* (Apple, Canon, Xerox, Tektronix). This is a combination of computer and color photocopy technology, similar to the way the black-and-white laser printer is a further development on photocopy technology. In the photocopy analogy, the image is exposed to light and the rays captured. (See? More ray-tracing of a different variety! It's all over the place!) Areas that are dark create a static charge on the toner drum surface. Toner adheres to the areas that are charged. The toner then is transferred to the paper surface and fused there by heat to produce the copy. A laser print operates in the same way. Instead of using a photographic process to determine which area receives an electrostatic charge, the image is computer processed to tell a laser beam to etch the areas that will receive toner. For a color image, several passes are needed to produce the color layers. These color laser printers can print on paper of up to 11 × 17 inches.

- *Thermal Wax Printer* (Tektronix, QMS, Shinko). This type of printer does CMYK printing. A thin layer of waxy substance is on a mylar sheet. During printing, the waxy substance is transferred to the special printing paper. This type of printer can be used to make transfers for T-shirts, mugs, and other novelty-type applications.

- *Film recorder* (Solitaire, LVT). This type of printer takes the information from your image file and exposes film transparency to create a color "slide." Different sizes of film can be used, from 35mm to 2 inch, to 4- × 5-inch and 8- × 10-inch film. It's better to think of "total number of pixels" for a film recorder than to think of "image resolution." When printing to a film recorder, you aren't talking about variable sizes (say, like an image that takes up 5 × 7 inches on your 8- × 11-inch piece of paper). To generate 35mm film, your image should be no larger than the prescribed w pixels × h pixels. That's your final number. End of story.

- *Photographic Process* (FujiX Pictography). This relatively new process generates a photochemical print. The process is similar to how the color laser printer is an adaptation of a related image reproduction process, in which the light exposure is replaced by computer image processing to determine what does or does not print for the final output. It's the same general process as exposing a color negative to special photographic paper. Instead of a darkroom enlarger and negative being involved, however, the printer is fed information from an image document. It creates a "donor" plate that transfers the photochemicals to paper that is subsequently developed to result in a final print. Because this is a photographic process, it works in RGB.

- *Film Imagesetter.* This type of printer is used for reproduction more than one-off printing. It is more precise; it can produce from 1200 to 3000 dpi. It can output only one color at a time and is used to create film for offset printing, whether for one-color (black) or four-color process film. Whether one piece of film or four, the actual film can be either black (opaque) or white (transparent). Any shade in between is composed of small dots (halftone).

INTERPOLATING IMAGES

Suppose you want to create a poster-sized image (22″ × 30″ or so). It would be sheer madness (sheer "RAMdess" actually) to render at the full size at a high enough image density for that size. It's time-consuming to render images at extreme sizes in Bryce. Instead, you can render an image to a fairly large size and then use an image editing application such as Photoshop or Live Picture to enlarge the image even further. When you enlarge, you create new pixels. The means of determining which color those new pixels will be is called *interpolation*.

Bryce's anti-aliasing pass, which checks the surrounding area to determine the final color of each pixel, is a friend of image interpolation. The oversampling to determine the pixel colors also helps when resolution is increased. When those new pixels come into being, they do so based on the pixels that are there, and where anti-aliasing has taken place, it's based on an oversampling of the surrounding area of that one point. As a result, Bryce images interpolate to larger sizes rather smoothly. Photoshop's bicubic interpolation method is an excellent choice for doing this. If you have Live Picture, use it to resize the image. Live Picture's interpolation routine is even better. Don't do it all in one fell swoop, however, especially if you are using Photoshop. Interpolate to one size. Then do it again. You will probably need to do a bit of custom touch-up at the end.

When you set up your Bryce scene, figure out what your target resolution is going to be for the ultimate image size. Then set your Bryce resolution to render your image to a size that's comparable, say one-half or one-fourth. Make it the same ratio, but smaller.

COLOR MODELS

One of the fascinating and troublesome things about printing Bryce images (or any computer generated image, for that matter) is the inevitable switch from one type of color model to another. When you are creating your scenes, you are working with colors that are generated in RGB color space. This is called *additive color* because when you add the colors together, they form white. Red, green, and blue are the primary colors when you are using anything that projects light—a computer monitor, video, cinema, and transparency film.

If you are going to be printing in a four-color process, CMYK, you are working in what is called a subtractive color space. The combination of all colors results in black, not white. White is the absence of color. Most color printers and the entire established color printing industry are based on this standard, where actual pigments are placed on paper and light bounces off them, reflecting back certain colors as it reaches the eye.

There are certain problems inherent in transferring an image from one type of color space to another. The gamut of possible colors is larger in the RGB color space than it is in CMYK color space. Brilliant electric blues and hot reds, highly saturated colors, and hot purples don't make the transfer from RGB to CMYK.

It's far beyond the scope of this chapter to discuss all the whys and wherefores of color. Entire books have been written on the subject. A new system of color printing, Hi Fi color, has even been developed in response to the problem of different color gamuts. Hi Fi color takes advantage of six- and seven-color presses to add back some of the colors that are lost during the conversion to CMYK. It would be ludicrous to attempt to sum up in a paragraph or two what the entire computer, color imaging, and printing industries have come up with over the last eight or nine years' worth of hard work on the issue of color. The best that can be done here is to put up a signpost that says "caution" and to point you to resources that are more thorough. I leave you with the experts here. These include books about desktop color, color separation houses, and service bureaus, as well as user groups and various discussion groups on online services and the Internet. (An especially good one is in America Online's Photoshop SIG, under the topic "CMYK Separation." When on America Online, use keyword "Photoshop" to get there.)

Not all color output devices are CMYK, though. The photographic printer mentioned earlier works in the RGB color space, and film recorders take in RGB images and then output them the same way. One good way to create a color separation for offset print is to print your image as a color transparency (from RGB to RGB) and then have it traditionally separated.

BRYCE IMAGES AND BLACK AND WHITE PRINTING

Okay, so maybe I'm not the *only* one out there who has set out to create many Bryce images that are eventually printed in black and white. I'll pass on to you what I learned in the process of creating all of the grayscale illustrations in this book.

When you are setting up your scene for optimum color, a straight conversion to grayscale probably won't get you a desirable image with accompanying contrast. For just about every scene that was converted to black and white, I had to do some custom tweaking. I'll tell you a couple of my favorite methods. Yes, it's in Photoshop (where else?). It involves using the Hue Saturation dialog box (⌘-U for Mac, Ctrl+U for Windows), where you can choose to alter colors or alter the entire image.

I select Master, which globally affects the file, and then I pull saturation all the way to the left (or nearly all the way to the left, in case I wanted to tell what my original colors were). This drains the image of color and provides an onscreen preview of the image in grayscale, but I'm still working in the RGB color space. At this point, I can see where I need to add contrast and adjust lightness color by color. There's immediate feedback. After using Photoshop's Hue/Saturation dialog, I adjust further with curves or levels if necessary to provide overall contrast.

My other favorite method is to look individually at each of the Red, Green, and Blue channels to see how the image shapes up from there. Then I'll either use one of those channels, or copy and paste another channel over the first and try some of Photoshop's apply modes, such as Normal, Screen, Multiply, Hard Light, Soft Light, and Overlay. Usually the upper layer is applied at a reduced percentage, ranging from 30-70%.

BRYCE IMAGES AND CMYK PRINTING

Now that I've discussed the concepts of converting from RGB to CMYK in general, I'll talk about a couple of situations and Bryce.

Smooth Gradations and Banding

When you convert Bryce images from RGB to CMYK, the images tend to have marked banding, especially in the sky area. Two things are happening to cause banding. First, there's a change to a smaller color space in CMYK (especially where blues are concerned). Second, the sky area can be a gradation with a limited number of steps between the two end colors (from, say, medium blue to light-medium blue). The best solution here is to add a very slight amount of noise while the image is still in RGB color space. I like to use KPT Hue Protected Minimum and press the 1 key down for a very light application. In most cases, changing from RGB to CMYK after that either eliminates or drastically reduces the banding.

To apply a noise to only one area of the scene (the sky), do a mask render with all objects selected. The only thing that will be left over is the sky. Load that mask as a selection and then apply the noise. You will have only applied it to the one area and not necessarily globally to the image.

Another approach for good color separations is to use Live Picture. The internal space uses 16 bits per channel, not the 8 bits of Photoshop. (This doesn't mean that you have 512 shades of gray, but rather 65,536 shades.) When trying to make the best switch from one color gamut (RGB) to another (CMYK), the ability to work with as much information as possible will result in better-looking separations. Plus, Live Picture's build process will automatically add a little (or a lot of) noise. Many of the color separations for the images in this book were made using Live Picture's color separation technology.

Preparing Images for Printing: Adding Room for Bleeds

Before concluding this chapter, I offer you a technique you might find handy when preparing images for print. Suppose you are working on an illustration for a client. The client requests, "Show me several treatments of a subject in a vertical format that measures $6\frac{1}{2}$ inches high by $4\frac{1}{4}$ inches wide." You do so at screen resolution of 72 ppi (306×468 pixels), and after providing some roughs, the client settles on the image of choice. Now it's time to render for print. But before you click the 1:3 button, you review the print specifications with the client. The images will bleed off one edge by a quarter-inch, so you need to make the image larger. There's plenty of scene information that you can render. The biggest challenge here is to change the image size so that it matches what you had before and adds image only where you want it. What do you do? (Note: this is a true story.)

1. Calculate the new size in screen resolution. $4\frac{1}{2}$ inches wide is 324 pixels. That makes for a difference of 18 pixels (from 306).

2. Write down all of your current settings for the scene in the Camera dialog box. Take special notice of the Scale and the Pan Horizontal and Vertical.

3. Change the Docuement Resolution in the Document Setup dialog box to the new dimension (in this case, 324×468).

4. Go back to the Camera dialog box. Did everything stay the same? If not, change them back to what they were before.

What do you have? When you have the exact same camera settings as before, your new scene has been enlarged from the center. The 18 pixels have been evenly divided on both sides. So what do you need to do? You need to shift the offset over by *half* the difference, or by 9 to make the image flush to the left or to the right.

5. If you need to add the image area to the right side, you'll need to pan to the left. Moving left is a negative thing—that is, the numbers move in a negative direction, and you'll be subtracting to get your result. So you'll subtract 9 from whatever the current value in the Pan H (horizontal) portion of the dialog box. (Of course if that number was already negative, say, –20, then you'll have a "higher" negative number, –29.)

6. If you need to add the image area to the left side of the image, you will pan your camera to the right, and consequently add 9 to whatever is in the Pan H area of the dialog box.

If precision is absolutely vital and you don't trust the numbers, or you have a complex set of alterations to make (add image area on three sides, for instance) then you can always double-check your work with screen shots. Take a screen shot of the wireframe before, and after making one move. Open up the screen shots in Photoshop, crop away the excess area, and set them atop one another in a two-layer document. Make the top layer transparent so that you can see both, and double check your alignment. Line up the screen shots along whatever edge remains the same. You'll see what you need to do and can check your work along the way.

If you need to add image area to the top or the bottom of the image, the same principle applies. Adding to the top means a move down, or subtracting, and adding to the bottom means a move up, or adding.

CHAPTER SEVENTEEN

Professional Images and Real Bryce Projects

'Twas brillig, and the slithy toves
  Did gyre and gimble in the wabe;
All mimsy were the borogoves,
  And the mome raths outgrabe.

"It seems very pretty,' she said when she had finished [reading the poem], "but it's rather hard to understand!" (You see she didn't like to confess, even to herself, that she couldn't make it out at all.) "Somehow it seems to fill my head with ideas—only I don't exactly know what they are!"

LEWIS CARROLL, THROUGH THE LOOKING-GLASS

IN THIS CHAPTER...

- Way cool images created in Bryce

- Projects featuring work in Bryce

Not only is it fun to work in Bryce and see what you can do with the software using your imagination and a little virtual elbow-grease, but it's fun to see what others are doing with the software. Here is the eye-candy chapter of the book, where a select group of cool Bryce images resides. This chapter also discusses some Bryce-related work by a few people in various disciplines. In addition to the work that is shown in these pages, be sure to check out the rather extensive gallery collection of Bryce images on the CD-ROM for this book. There are over 80 contributors.

BRYCE TREATS

Here is a collection of excellent Bryce works by artists from around the world, a representative sample of the range of work possible in this versatile application. The artists have traveled to different times and places to "bring back" these images.

Tony Kashinn took a trip back in time, when the dinosaur lived, with a revisit just after the dinosaur's demise. See Figure C17–1 in the color section.

David Palermo, whose pursuits lean toward outer space and planetary phenomena, created these two views from other planets. See Figure C17–2.

In another space departure—literally—Terry Musgrove witnessed the discarding of a spent rocket on this trip away from the earth. See Figure C17–3.

Harald Seiwert explores human figures and their environments. In "A Ghost in the Bathroom" he takes a hygienic look at the return of an ethereal figure to very ordinary surroundings. Many's the artist who has studied the works of masters by copying their work, as this "Vermeer" attests. See Figure C17–4. (Seiwert is also responsible for the castle shown in Figure 7–15.)

Speaking of art and galleries, David Bazemore created both the art collection and the museum housing the art. He also created an illustration about smoking. See Figure C17–5.

Chris Kawalek has ventured into the land of modeling, exploring the re-percussions (get it?) of so many primitives located in close proximity, with this snare drum, in Figure C17–6.

In a fit of home improvement, Chris Casady dug up the ground next to the tower (originally shown in Figure 7–29) to install a swimming pool, and in Figure C17–7, we look up at the pool's reflection on the tower, while nearby, a kite soars in the sky.

Andrew Penick sojourned for adventure and in his travels came upon this "Abandoned Passage," in Figure C17–8.

Jacquelyn Verdun and Per Nordin have traveled to places of serene beauty, bringing back these Brycean snapshots. See Figure C17–9.

Paul Ware took a trip of fancy out to an undisclosed rural location, where he was inspired to portray the vehicle and environs in "Are We There Yet?" See Figure C17–10.

Hilary Rhodes used Bryce for a musical journey for this music CD cover (see Figure C17–11). Note the infinite hall with arches in different perspectives, reminiscent of the perspective warps used by M. C. Escher. (Speaking of Escher, Hilary created another homage to his work in the house and staircase image in Figure 7–14.)

SANCTUARY

Sanctuary is an interactive game that can be played on the World Wide Web. Navigate through different locations to solve the challenges posed by the game's plot. Bryce was used to generate the environments for the gameplay. Figure C11–39, at the end of the Bryce EnLightenment chapter, is a scene from within one of the Sanctuary environments. Figure C17–12 here is another view of the same room. Both images are by Glenn Riegel, one of the artists working on the project.

According to Riegel, the advantages to using Bryce for the project—besides the normal standard landscape, rendering and image quality that's a part of Bryce—are the object placement and camera controls. In an environment where one navigates from one position to the next, and then stands in one place and looks around at all sides, it is vital that there be continuity throughout all the views. The light source in the east needs to stay in the east, whether one is facing north, south, east, or west. The success of game play comes from being immersed in the environment; any fracturing of consistency from view to view detracts from the experience. So how did Riegel work in Bryce to maintain continuity? He built a master world, a mega-scene file that includes the basic form and shape of everything in the world. It was the central reference point for all objects in the world. Riegel would set up the camera shots for a specific location in the master scene, and create a derivative scene based on it. All positions of all objects in the world are based on their position in the master scene file.

Of course, a scene file that huge and all-inclusive is impractical to work in for individual scenes. In the individual scenes, close-up views of one or another element in the environment requires high-resolution terrains, picture textures and the abundance of supporting objects to make a place believable upon close examination. To include that amount of detail for an area, over and over again for each camera view throughout the world, would make the master scene too cumbersome. By the time all those objects are in place, the onscreen redraw of objects has slowed down to a frustrating glacial pace, or else the number of objects being juggled by Bryce has tapped out all the available memory (or both!).

So Riegel used a several stage approach to build his scenes. The master scene became the basis for the smaller scenes. Once the camera was in place for the close up area, items that did not affect the view were deleted, and this new, derivative scene was saved under a different name. The process of honing in on detailed views of a place is demonstrated in Figure 17–13a through c. The master scene in part a, shown in top view, includes the location of all major objects in the world.

Part b shows how the scene building has focused in on one part of the environment, ridding the scene of elements unnecessary to that part of the world. Part c shows what the camera is looking at, a set of double doors. Note how there are many more objects in the scene in Figure 17–13c than exist in the establishing shot scenes.

For the construction of the objects with finer detail, Riegel would build elements in separate scene files and then merge them into the host scene—the individual detailed view of a part of the environment. Theoretically, with a powerful enough computer and sufficient RAM to juggle all of the objects in each scene, all of the detailed views could be merged together into one backbreaking scene file that would contain all of the high resolution detail, and each object would occupy its respective place in the world with spatial coherency.

PLANETARY TRAVELER

"Planetary Traveler" is a feature-length animated motion picture created for television broadcast and home-video distribution using Bryce. It is the visual flight log of an exploratory journey to a star system containing eight planets. The movie is a melding of vision and sound in

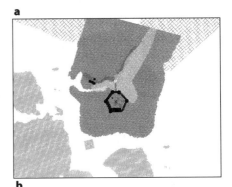

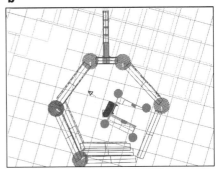

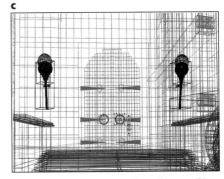

Figure 17–13 Progression of scene files used for the Sanctuary web-game project:
a) The master world scene top view;
b) derivative scene focusing only on one portion of the entire environment;
c) close-up scene looking at one portion of the world, built in detail.

an exploration of different planetary environments. A group of Brycers created and animated scenes in a production captained by Jan Nickman, who was the Producer/Director of "The Mind's Eye." Rodney L'Ongnion was the Production Supervisor and Art Director for the project.

You may wonder how a Bryce animation project could emerge at a time when no animation version of Bryce is available. The makers of "Planetary Traveler" used special "under develoment" versions of Bryce. No doubt the experience of working on a full project using software-in-progress will aid in the development of the final, shipping animation version of Bryce. In any case, "Planetary Traveler" is a watershed event for the Bryce software, to say nothing of the feat of creating a feature-length motion picture using desktop Macintosh computers.

A plethora of scenes was created as still images, using software with features that later were incorporated into Bryce 2.1. Those scenes were then animated and rendered. In motion picture animation, each frame needs to be individually rendered, and to create the movie, over 300,000 still frames were rendered. The "Planetary Traveler" renderfarm consisted of a total of 15 machines rendering full-time and 13 rendering part-time spread out over several locations throughout the United States. The PowerMac 8100 I used to work on the images for this book was originally a member in good standing of the "Planetary Traveler" renderfarm. Figure C17–14 show some still frames from the "Planetary Traveler" movie. Look on the CD-ROM for the "Planetary Traveler" trailer.

One challenge that is the same for any complex project is keeping track of all the data that becomes a part of the production. This situation is true whether you create a web-based game, a multi-media project, an animated movie (where each individual frame is rendered as a single image file!), or, for that matter, a book. Working on an extended project is different from creating a single illustration. Continuity is necessary, whether it's continuity from frame to frame as a series of fast-moving individual pictures melded together into a fluid, moving whole, or whether it's the continuity between different still views of an environment that are navigable by a game player. To pull it off, you need to keep your Bryce work well organized.

MARS IMAGES

In these images for *Scientific American*'s November 1996 issue discussing Water on Mars, shown in Figure C17–15, I sought to recreate a portion of the Martian landscape, showing it at different epochs of the planet's history—at present, and in the past when Mars has plenty of water on its surface.

The scenes use actual Martian elevation data. To create the grayscale image data, I used the Digital Elevation Maps that come on the CD-ROM for Vista Pro, a sister product to Bryce. (Vista Pro creates digital landscapes, though it lacks the ray-tracing renderer, the complex sky model, and procedural texture generator that give such photo-realism to Brycean rendered images, to say nothing of the interface and look and feel that gives Bryce its soul.) In any case, Vista Pro is great for importing Martian DEMs and converting them to grayscale PICTs to use in Bryce. I imported the Martian DEMs, sixteen at a time, and generated a grayscale map from that information. After generating four quadrants for a large terrain map (from a total of 64 individual DEMs!), I made alignment adjustments in Photoshop, and imported the resulting image to Bryce. The view is a site near the Olympus Mons (a very b-i-i-i-i-g mountain) on Mars.

Like the "one small step for man, one giant leap for mankind" statement, these images are more than dual pictures of an interesting landscape under differing climatic conditions, made with Brycean expertise. The snow and water image harks back to the time when the surface of Mars was flowing with water. The dry, red planet is the planet of today. That is the smaller step. The giant leap is the ability to make visible what has heretofore been impossible to see. These images are a demonstration of the ability to take information gleaned from a place that no human has visited—information gathered by interplanetary explorer craft, and beamed back to earth from millions of miles away. The information has made its way into a digital elevation format, which, after being converted to grayscale, becomes cloaked in a Bryean environment, where you can wander at will with the Brycean camera (or create QTVR movies to wander at will over rendered landscapes!). Using Bryce as the culmination of various technologies, you are virtually taken onto the surface of our nearest neighbor planet, far, far away from our home world. The fine details of surface are left to your imagination, but you are transporting yourself to the Martian surface—or transporting the Martian surface to your computer! Beam me up!

INTERFACE DESIGN

In this era of multimedia and the web, interface design is a growing art, complete with books dedicated to the topic of using imaging applications to create user interfaces. Bryce is an excellent candidate for interface design. Of course, the first ones to use Bryce as a tool for interface design are the ones who designed the application itself. The second revision of Bryce features an interface that was created in Bryce itself. But before that, Bryce was used to create the interface for the KPT Spheroid Designer, the hallmark of KPT 3.0. (See Figure C17–16.)

What is an interface? It is the thing you interact with to manipulate another thing. It is the collection of controls that you touch using your mouse, trackball, or stylus, to make something work. In a car, the user interface consists of the steering wheel, the gas pedal and brake, the clutch and stick shift, and dials and readouts to advise you of its status. On a computer, it is the operating system and the software design. In multimedia, it is the means to navigate around your collection of sounds, images, and movies.

There are cues to tell you about the state of the object you are working with. Sights and sounds tell you that a particular thing is selected, and you may now choose actions to perform on that object. If you want to create a sphere in Bryce, you pass your mouse over the Create Palette. When your mouse is positioned over the Create Sphere icon, the icon changes to show a wireframe as well as the sphere. If you keep the mouse pointing at the sphere, it will pulse between the normal and wireframe state. When you click the Create Sphere icon, the icon turns white for the duration of the time that the mouse is pressed, and upon releasing the mouse, a sphere wireframe shows up in your scene. You have directly manipulated the user interface—the controls—to tell Bryce to refer to the geometric formula for a sphere and place one of those in the scene, *here*. Way down deep in the computer's processor, the underlying logic is being performed in millions of on and off actions by transistors and resistors, as electrons are being shunted this way and that to build your sphere.

The philosophy of user interface is an entirely separate topic, but if you want to have a GUI, a graphical user interface, then you need to generate the graphics. Bryce excels here, since you can create objects, arrange them to your liking, and change the surface appearance at will. Test renders will allow you to see if your design is workable, and alterations are easy to make. No doubt you've been looking at the Bryce user interface as a set of controls to understand—"Which icon controls what action? How do I change the size of that sphere I just created?" But take a moment—if you haven't done so already—and look at the Bryce user interface as a product of Bryce creation itself. To aid you to do that, look at Figure C17–17, a render of the user interface elements, from a perspective you don't see when you launch Bryce.

If Brycing can be done to show Bryce spheres, cubes, cones, and terrains as a user interface, then you can do it to create elements for your web site, multimedia show, or other projects that require interface design.

THE VISION THING

Is it any wonder that the images shown here have a common theme—making something real in a way that couldn't be done otherwise? Bryce is all about envisioning something that is otherwise very difficult to see, from an interface, to the physically remote Martian planet, to a trip to a far-off solar system, to the mental places in armchair adventures on the web, or to visions that emerge from the minds of creative individuals.

Bryce's capabilities apply photo-realistic quality to anything you create. The content, the *what* that's created, is the fruit of your own thought processes. What you envision, Bryce brings into reality. The optical laws are there. Perspective is there. Haze-in-the-distance is there. Despite those givens, there *is* a learning curve to Bryce (indeed this book is dedicated to that learning curve). Once mastered, Bryce is a tool for you to manifest those visions that were otherwise elusive.

It's vogue to discuss the relevance of the computer as a tool for art and creative vision. When discussion is not focused solely on technique, but on content, too, it's a sign that the medium is beginning to mature. Bryce joins company with other imaging applications and tools, indeed, the computer itself, as well as new media—multimedia and the web—that are in various states of development and maturity. The consensus seems to be that the new media pretends to be the old familiar one (is television like radio?), until a time when the media matures enough to shape itself, rather than resemble its forbears. Bryce as a tool, as an artistic medium for visualizing, is likewise undergoing a maturation process. What strikes me as one of the most exciting things about the software is its ability to visualize the unseen, whether it's a personal vision, making elusive concepts concrete, or providing a sense of place to something that is otherwise uninhabitable.

Bryce is an envisioning tool. This book has guided you through all of its workings and quirks, and has, I hope, guided you toward the ways that the software can be used to bring your own visions to light. Pick up your own virtual brush. Express your own phantasm on a rich canvas of pixels. Let Bryce be the binder to hold the pigment of your creative vision onto a canvas for all to see.

Figure C14–32 The Sky & Fog Palette for "Lighthouse at Twilight."

Figure C14–33 The nature scene at the end of the first stage of scene building.

Figure C14–39 "Lighthouse at Twilight," final render.

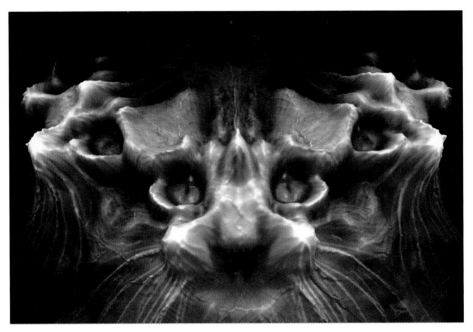

Figure C15–5 "Necrofelinia," by Phil Clevenger. *Original image courtesy Digital Stock.*

Bump Gain, Reflection

No Bump Gain, Reflection

Bump Gain, No Reflection

No Bump Gain nor Reflection

Image provided by ©1995 Photo Disc, Inc

Figure C15–7 GlockenFondue series comparing two Material channel settings, Bump Height and Reflection, on an object where terrain, picture texture and alpha mask are all derived from the same image source. *Original image courtesy PhotoDisc.*

Figure C15–8 A dull metallic surface from an image that began with no metallic look.

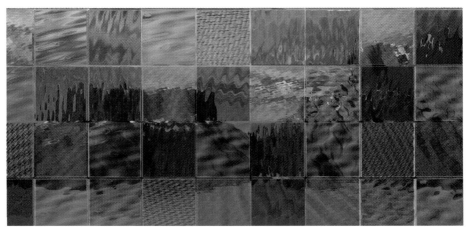

Figure C15–9 Glassblocks, a semi-abstract Bryce landscape viewed through Brycean glass blocks.

Figure C15–11 "Moons of Wenhra," by Tony Kashinn.

a

b

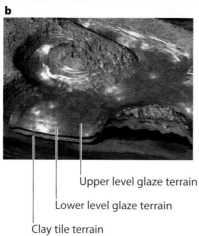

Upper level glaze terrain

Lower level glaze terrain

Clay tile terrain

Figure C15–12 Tiles from terrains: a) Chris Casady's virtual kiln created these adaptations of Ernest Batchelder tiles; b) a cross-section close up demonstrates how the glaze interacts with the clay tile.

Figure C17–1 "Prehistoric" series. *Images by Tony Kashinn.*

a

b

Figure C17–2 Space imagery:
a) "Europa"; b) "Moonrise." *Images by David Palermo.*

C56

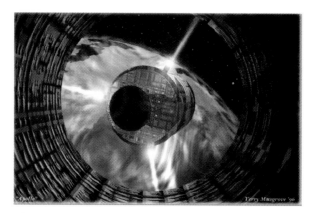

Figure C17–3 "Apollo." *Image by Terry Musgrove.*

a

b

Figure C17–4 a) "A Ghost in the Bathroom";
b) "Vermeer." *Images by Harald Seiwert.*

Figure C17–5 a) "The Gallery"; b) "Virtual Sculpture #2"; c) "Smokers." *Images by David Bazemore.*

Figure C17–6 "Snare Drum."
Image by Chris Kawalek.

Figure C17–7 "Pool Tower Fence." *Image by Chris Casady.*

Figure C17–8 "Abandoned Passage." *Image by Andrew Penick.*

a

b

Figure C17–9 a) "Canyon Mist,"
by Jacquelyn Verdun; b) "Lake 4,"
by Per Nordin.

Figure C17–10 "Are We
There Yet?" *Image by
Paul Ware.*

Figure C17–11 Pastance CD cover art, Hilary Rhodes.

Figure C17–12 An interior view of a hall for the game Sanctuary. *Image by Glenn Riegel.*

Figure C17–14 Still frames from "Planetary Traveler:" a) "Bristle Rocks"; b) "Lichen Field"; c) "Stained Glass," all by Cathy Faye Rudolph; d) "Meridien Sumoc" by Bill Ellsworth and Rodney L'Ongnion; e) "Canyon Gully" by Susan A. Kitchens; f) "Rivershore" by Susan A. Kitchens. *Planetary Traveler* ©*MCMXCVI Third Planet Productions.*

Figure C17–15 Ancient, water-covered Mars and Mars today. *Images by Susan A. Kitchens for* Scientific American.

C64

Figure C17–16 The interface for the
KPT Spheroid Designer, created using
Bryce.

Figure C17–17 The Bryce user interface elements as a
Bryce scene.

APPENDIX
A

Vendors for Bryce-Related Products

Adobe Systems Incorporated (Photoshop—the workhorse of the pixellated masses!), 345 Park Avenue, San Jose, CA 95110-2704. Phone: (408) 536-6000; Fax: (408) 536 6799. Web: http://www.adobe.com/

Equilibrium (DeBabelizer), 3 Harbor Drive, Suite 111, Sausalito, CA 94965. Phone: (415) 332-4343; Fax: (415)332-4433. Web: http://www.equilibrium.com/

Fractal Design Corporation (Poser; Garden Hose publisher), P.O. Box 66959, Scotts Valley, CA 95067-6959. Phone: (800) 846-0111, (408) 430-4000; Fax: (408) 438-9670. Web: http://www.fractal.com/

Live Picture, Inc. (Live Picture, Live Picture XT), 5617 Scotts Valley Drive, Suite 180, Scotts Valley, CA 95066. Phone: (408) 438-9610; Fax: (408) 438-9604. Web: http://www.livepicture.com/

MetaCreations, Inc. (Bryce, Kai's Power Tools, MetaPhotos), 6303 Carpinteria Avenue, Carpinteria, CA 93013. Phone: (805) 566-6200; Fax: (805) 566-6359. Email: kptsupport@aol.com; Web: http://www.metacreations.com/

Onyx Computing (Tree Professional), 10 Avon Street, Cambridge, MA 02138. Phone: (617) 876-3876; Fax: (617) 868-8033. Email: info@onyxtree.com; Web: http://www.onyxtree.com/

Photo and Art Resources

Direct Imagination (The Grammar of Ornament), P. O. Box 93018, Pasadena, CA 91109-3108. Phone: (818) 793-8387; Fax: (818) 449-6083. Email: DI@dimagin.com; Web: http://www.dimagin.com/

Digital Stock Incorporated, 400 South Sierra Avenue, Suite 100, Solana Beach, CA 92075. Phone: (619) 794-4040; Fax: (619) 794-4041. Web: http:///www.digitalstock.com/

DigArts (The Garden Hose), P. O. Box 4953, Chico, CA 95926-4953. Email: DigArts@dcsi.net; Web: http://www.dcs-chico.com/~digarts/

3D Models

Viewpoint Data Labs International, 625 S. State, Orem, UT 84058. Phone: (800) DATASET, (801) 229-3000; Fax: (801) 229-3300. Web: http://www.viewpoint.com

Zygote Media Group, 1 East Center Street, Provo, UT 84606. Phone: (800) 375-7389, (801) 375-7220; Fax: (801) 375-7389. Email: sales@zygote.com; Web: http://www.zygote.com/

Ergonomics

Prio Corporation (special glasses for painlessly staring at monitors for hours on end), 4000 Kruse Way Place, Suite 2-355, Lake Oswego, OR 97035. Phone: (800) 621-1098; (503) 636-3707. Fax: (503) 636-1747. Web: http://www.prio.com/

(Note: if you decide to get a pair, make sure to ask for non-tinted glasses if you require color fidelity!)

For up-to-date links to Bryce-relevant resources, check out my website: http://www.auntialias.com/.

Additional Reading Resources

Alton, John. *Painting With Light.* Berkeley: University of California Press, 1995.

This is one of the two books on lighting listed in this appendix. Written by the celebrated cinematographer, this discussion focuses on motion picture cinematography and equipment. Brycers who are interested in lighting can gain much from this explanation of the equipment, mechanics, and techniques of motion picture cinematography for creating mood in a film.

Nicholas, Jeff, and Jim Wilson. *Islands in the Sky: Scenes from the Colorado Plateau.* El Portal, CA: Sierra Press, 1991.

This is a smallish coffee table book (8 by 7 inches) containing wonderful color photographs from the Colorado Plateau (located in the southwestern United States, home of natural parks such as Grand Canyon, Bryce, Zion, Canyonlands, Arches National Monument, Monument Valley). The photos are broken down into four sections—Earth, Rock, Water and Sky. Islands in the Sky has been an inspiration and reference for my own Brycing, especially for making terrains and textures.

Hogarth, Burne. *Dynamic Light and Shade.* Reprint Edition. New York: Watson-Guptill Publications, 1991.

Hogarth, famous for his "Tarzan" illustrations, expounds on the nature of light and shade in a drawing. The book is filled with black-and-white and grayscale illustrations, many of the human form, with explanation throughout on different principles. His discussion of different kinds of light and their purposes in illustration is extremely valuable to the Brycer who wants to better wield the Sky & Fog controls and the light sources.

Murphy, Pat, Paul Doherty, and William Neill. *The Color of Nature.* San Francisco: Chronicle Books, 1996.

If Bryce makes you look at the world more closely and you want some analytical assistance, this beautiful book is it. The color photographs are accompanied by explanation of the natural phenomena that make colors the way they are. This book will hone your nature-observer's eye with an undergirding of easily comprehensible scientific explanation.

Lauer, David A. and Stephen Pentak. *Design Basics, Fourth Edition.* Ft. Worth, TX: Harcourt Brace College Publishers, 1995.

This is an excellent resource for basic design. Chapters are devoted to different design concepts (e.g., unity, emphasis/focal point, scale/proportion, balance, rhythm, etc.). Text is minimal, providing explanation of each concept, with plenty of illustrations. Except for the section covering color and design, the illustrations are in black and white.

Stokes, William Lee. *Scenes of the Plateau Lands and How They Came to Be.* Salt Lake City, UT: Starstone Publishing Company, 1969.

This small booklet explains the geological processes that went into creating the Colorado Plateau in the southwestern United States. The text is illustrated with pencil drawings. You may have to contact the publisher directly to obtain it (1283 E. South Temple Street, Salt Lake City, UT 84102); I purchased it at a bookstore in Bryce Canyon National Park and have not seen it anywhere else.

In addition to these books, check my web site for any additional reading resources: http://www.auntialias.com/.

INDEX

Important message to users of Bryce 2 for Windows 95/NT:

MetaTools released the Windows version of Bryce 2 late in the development of this book, and we've done everything we can to cover usage of Bryce on the Windows platform. Unfortunately there wasn't room on the CD-ROM for Windows versions of all the great material Susan Kitchens assembled, but we didn't want to drive up the cost of the book by including 2 CDs.

So here's what we've done: bound into the book is a single hybrid CD that will work on both Mac and Windows systems. It has the complete contents for Macintosh, as well as the most important Windows content (tutorial scenes, gallery images, step-by-step slide shows, sample software, etc.), so you'll be able to get up and running quickly. We've also put together a second *Windows-only CD* that contains Bryce scene files and utilities that we couldn't fit onto the first one. To get a copy, just fill out this card, tape it shut, and pop it in the mail.

It's that simple!

The friendly folks at Peachpit Press

Yes! I'm proud to be a Bryce for Windows user!
Please send me the special WINDOWS-ONLY CD-ROM.

Name _____

Address _____

City _____**State**_____**ZIP** _____

Please allow 3-4 weeks for delivery.   EC 40133